COPING WITH PSYCHIATRIC AND PSYCHOLOGICAL TESTIMONY

FIFTH EDITION

JAY ZISKIN, Ph.D., LL.B.

with chapters by

David Faust
Michael K. Gann
Mitchell Earleywine & Michael K. Gann
John C. Yuille, Judith (Cutshall) Daylen,
Stephen Porter & David Marxsen
Ralph Underwager & Hollida Wakefield
Christopher D. Webster & Natalie H. Polvi
J. Ric Gass & Samuel H. Solomon

Volume I

BASIC INFORMATION

LAW AND PSYCHOLOGY PRESS
Post Office Box 24219
Los Angeles, California 90024
(310) 475-2108 — FAX (310) 474-5938

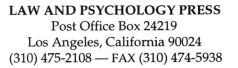

Library of Congress Catalog Card Number: 95-78594
International Standard Book Numbers:
Volumes I, II, and III: 1-879689-04-9
Volume I: 1-879689-05-7
Volume II: 1-879689-06-5
Volume III: 1-879689-07-3

PRODUCTION STAFF

Editor:	Janet Cornwell
Coordinator:	Richard D. Burns
Book Design:	Mark M. Dodge
Typesetting:	Regina Books

LAW AND PSYCHOLOGY PRESS
Post Office Box 24219
Los Angeles, California 90024
(310) 475-2108
FAX (310) 474-5938

Manufactured in the United States of America.

ACKNOWLEDGMENTS
Permission to quote from the following works is hereby gratefully acknowledged: I.G. Sarason, *Personality: An Objective Approach,* 2nd ed., © 1972, reprinted by permission of John Wiley & Sons, Inc.; N.J. Smelser & W.T. Smelser, eds., *Personality and Social Systems,* © 1970, reprinted by permission of John Wiley & Sons, Inc.; A.J. Storrow, M.D., *Introduction to Scientific Psychiatry,* © 1967, by permission of Prentice-Hall, Inc., Englewood Cliffs, New Jersey; D.L. Rosenhan, "On Being Sane in Insane Places," *Science* 1973, Vol. 179, pp. 250-258, © 1973 by the American Association for the Advancement of Science; D.F. Klein & J.M. Davis, *Diagnosis and Drug Treatment of Psychiatric Disorders,* © 1969, the Williams and Wilkins Company, Baltimore; L.S. Kubie, "Multiple Fallacies in the Concept of Schizophrenia," *Journal of Nervous and Mental Disease,* 1971, Vol. 153, pp. 331-342, the Williams and Wilkins Company, Baltimore; Paul E. Meehl, *Psycho-Diagnosis: Selected Papers,* University of Minnesota Press, Minneapolis, (c) 1973 by the University of Minnesota; chapters by R.H. Woody, Frederick C. Thorne in *Clinical Assessment in Counseling and Psychotherapy,* by R.H. Woody and J. Woody, eds., © 1972 by permission of Prentice-Hall, Inc., Englewood Cliffs, New Jersey; the *Seventh Mental Measurements Yearbook,* Oscar K. Buros, ed., © Gryphon Press, Highland Park, New Jersey, 1972; C.S. Hall & G. Lindzey, *Theories of Personality,* 2nd edition, © 1970, reprinted by permission of John Wiley & Sons, Inc.; Martin Blinder, M.D., *Psychiatry in the Everyday Practice of Law,* The Lawyer's Cooperative Publishing Co., 1973; the *Eighth Mental Measurements Yearbook,* edited by Oscar K. Buros, by permission of the University of Nebraska Press, © 1978 by the Gryphon Press; Robert Schulman, "To Be or Not to Be an Expert," *Washington University Law Quarterly,* Vol. 57, 1973; Bernard Diamond, "From Durham to Brawner, A Futile Journey," *Washington University Law Quarterly,* Vol. 57, 1973; Bernard Diamond, "Criminal Responsibility of the Mentally Ill," *Stanford Law Review,* Vol. 14, 1961; H. Fingarette, *The Meaning of Criminal Insanity,* the University of California Press, 1972; John Exner, *The Rorschach: A Comprehensive System,* Vol. I (1974) and Vol. II (1978), © John Wiley & Sons, reprinted by permission of John Wiley & Sons, Inc.; E. Miller, *Recovery and Management of Neuropsychological Impairments,* © 1984. Reprinted by permission of John Wiley & Sons, Ltd.; V. Simons & K.S. Meyer, *Child Custody and Evaluation: Issues and Trends,* © 1986 John Wiley & Sons, Inc. Reprinted by permission of John Wiley & Sons, Inc,.; R. Rogers & W. Seman, "Murder and Criminal Responsibility: An Examination of MMPI Profiles," in *Behavioral Sciences & The Law,* Vol. 1, 1983, pp. 89-95, © 1983 John Wiley & Sons, Inc. Reprinted by permission of John Wiley & Sons, Inc.; C.R. Reynolds & A.S.Kaufman, "Clinical Assessment of Children's Intelligence with the Wechsler Scales," in *Handbook of Intelligence,* B.B. Wolman, ed., © 1985 John Wiley & Sons, Inc. Reprinted by permission of John Wiley & Sons, Inc.;J. Exner, *The Rorschach: A Comprehensive System,* © 1974 John Wiley & Sons, Inc. Reprinted by permission of John Wiley & Sons, Inc.; J.E. Exner, Jr., *The Rorschach: A Comprehensive System, Vol. I: Basic Foundations* (2nd ed.), © 1986 John Wiley & Sons, Inc. Reprinted by permission of John Wiley & Sons, Inc.; J.L. Horn, "Remodeling Old Models of Intelligence," in *Handbook of Intelligence,* B.B. Wolman, ed., © 1985 John Wiley & Sons, Inc. Reprinted by permission of John Wiley & Sons, Inc.; J.I. Escobar, book review, *The Journal of Nervous and Mental Disease,* Vol. 174, pp. 251-252, © by Williams & Wilkins, 1986, by permission of Williams & Wilkins; P.M. Sinaikin, "A Clinically Relevant Guide to the Differential Diagnosis of Depression," *The Journal of Nervous and Mental Disease,* Vol. 173, pp. 199-211, © by Williams & Wilkins, 1985, by permission of Williams & Wilkins; C.E. Wells, "Pseudodementia and the Recognition of Organicity," in *Psychiatric Aspects of Neurological Disease,* Vol. 2, Benson & Blumer, eds., 1982, by permission of Grune & Stratton, Inc.; Anne Anastasi, *Psychological Testing,* 5th ed., © 1982 by Anne Anastasi. Reprinted with permission of Macmillan Publishing Company; W. Bromberg, M.D., "Psychiatric Traumatology," *Psychiatric Annals* Vol. 14-7, 1984, pp. 500-505, by permission of Slack, Inc,; Howard Gardner, *The Shattered Mind: The Person After Brain Damage,* © 1975, reprinted by permission of Alfred A.Knopf, Inc.; Herb Kutchins & Stuart A. Kirk, "The Reliability of DSM-III: A Critical Review." Copyright 1986, National Association of Social Workers, Inc. Reprinted with permission from *Social Work Research & Abstracts,* Vol.22, No. 4 (Winter 1986), p. 11; W.M. Alves, A.R.T. Colohan, T.J. O'Leary, R.W. Rimel & J.J. Jane, "Understanding Posttraumatic Symptoms After Minor Head Injury," *Journal of Head Trauma Rehabilitation,* © 1986, by permission of Aspen Publishers, Inc.; J. Platt & S. Husband, "Post-Traumatic Stress Disorder in Forensic Practice," *The American Journal of Forensic Psychology,* Vol. IV, No. 1, 1986. *The American Journal of Forensic Psychology* is a publication of the American College of Forensic Psychology, 26701 Quail Creek, Number 295, Laguna Hills, California 92656; L.G. Rorer & T.A. Widiger, "Personality Structure and Assessment." Reproduced, with permission, from the *Annual Review of Psychology,* Vol. 34, © 1983 by Annual Reviews, Inc.; Michael Rutter, "Depressive Feelings, Cognitions and Disorders: A Research Postscript," in *Depressions in Young People,* Izard, Read & Rutter, eds., © 1986, by permission of Guilford Publications; *Stanford-Binet Intelligence Scale: Fourth Edition.* Reprinted with permission of the Riverside Publishing Company from pages 16 and 30 of *Stanford-Binet Intelligence Scale Guide for Administering and Scoring the Fourth Edition,* by R.L. Thorndike, E.P. Hagen, and J.M. Sattler. The Riverside Publishing Company, 8420 W. Bryn Mawr Avenue, Chicago, IL 60631. Copyright 1986; D.C. Turk

To my parents
for the high value they placed on knowledge,
to my children Ken, Laura, Nina and Randy
for the pleasures they have given me,

and to my wife, Mae,
without whom nothing ever would have happened.

—Jay Ziskin

ABOUT THE AUTHOR

Dr. Jay Ziskin received his LL.B. from the University of Southern California in 1946 and subsequently practiced law for approximately ten years. He is still a member of the State Bar of California.

He received his Ph.D. in Clinical Psychology from the University of Southern California in 1962. He practiced as a clinical psychologist for approximately six years thereafter and appeared as an expert witness. He is currently a licensed psychologist in the state of California.

Dr. Ziskin's background also includes: Instructor in Law and Psychology, University of Southern California Law Center and Chief Research Psychologist, University of Southern California Institute of Psychiatry and Law. He has taught various courses in Psychology and in Psychology and Law at both the University of Southern California and California State University at Los Angeles. He has served as contributing editor for the *Journal of Professional Psychology* and on the Editorial Review Board of *The American Psychologist.* He was a member of the American Psychological Association Committee on Psychology and the Law and has been President of the American Psychology-Law Society (now Division 41 of the American Psychological Association).

Dr. Ziskin is co-author of *Brain Damage Claims: Coping with Neuropsychological Evidence* (with David Faust, Ph.D. and James B. Hiers, Jr., J.D.).

He is a fellow of the Divisions of Psychology and Law, Clinical Psychology, and Consulting Psychology of the American Psychological Association. He is also a Fellow of the American Psychological Society.

Dr. Ziskin serves as a consultant to attorneys in regard to psychiatric/psychological evidence in specific cases as well as an expert witness on this subject.

PREFACE TO
THE FIFTH EDITION

The first sentence of the first edition of this book, published in 1970, states: "It is the aim of this book to demonstrate that despite the ever-increasing utilization of psychiatric and psychological evidence in the legal process such evidence frequently does not meet reasonable criteria of admissibility and should not be admitted in a court of law, and if admitted, should be given little or no weight." Criteria for admission of expert evidence have changed considerably since then along with decades of acceptance by the courts, making admissibility almost, but not quite, a non-issue. However, little has happened in the more than two decades since that declaration was made which would require any alteration of the statement regarding weight.

The same paragraph in the 1970 edition states: "It seems most likely that movement toward a productive and valid law and behavioral science relationship can best be served by placing in the hands of lawyers tools by which they can aid courts and juries to distinguish science from authoritarian pronouncement and validated knowledge from conjecture." Since that original publication, and the publication of the second edition in 1975, third edition in 1981, and fourth edition in 1988 progress toward these goals has been confirmed by communications from lawyers describing their effective use of the information provided in those publications, as well as from behavioral science professionals indicating the book has been a factor in improving the quality of psychological evidence.

Citation of the prior editions in several appellate court opinions, along with citation, quotation or discussion of the book in a large number of books and journal articles, and use as a textbook or recommended reading at several universities, indicate that the book has had an impact and is recognized as an authoritative reference work in the field of psychiatric and psychological evidence.

The need for this fifth edition arises from three factors. One factor is the need to keep the text up-to-date with the new material appearing in the scientific and professional literature. This will enable the lawyer to deal with a witness who attempts to denigrate the earlier editions by claiming that the materials are outdated or that "we have learned a great deal since then."

The second factor involves changes that have taken place within the mental health professions, including the appearance of research in areas where it was previously lacking. In addition, several popular psychological tests have been published in a revised form. And the Diagnostic and Statistical Manual has been reissued in a new edition, the DSM-IV. Furthermore, eight topics, which have become more prevalent in the forensic field, have been added as new chapters, plus an additional chapter on the use of visual techniques in courtroom presentation.

The third factor is the sheer volume of material. Whereas the fourth edition contained over 1400 references, this edition contains nearly 2000 references. Much of the older material has been retained, although generally it is discussed in less detail than before. Older material has been retained where it helps to demonstrate a line of research over ten, twenty or even thirty or more years to show the continuing existence of problems, such as the low reliability and validity of evaluations, and the failure of new approaches or innovations to solve them. Among other things, this should provide ample reason to seriously doubt the ultimate success of a newly introduced procedure or approach for which it is claimed, on the basis of minimal evidence, that problems have been solved.

Volume I contains basic information that is relevant to most cases involving psychological and/or psychiatric testimony. For example, Chapter 5 of Volume I is devoted to clinical judgment, which, with its deficiencies, will be pertinent to virtually any case. Similarly, the other chapters in Volume I offer bases for challenging the underlying concepts which provide the foundation for qualifying experts in most situations. Thus, Volume I includes challenges to the scientific status of the field, the classification systems employed, the conclusions derived from clinical examinations, and the weight accorded to the factors of experience, education, training and specialty certifications. Former Chapter 17, which describes the famous Rosenhan study, is now subsumed within Chapter 7, which critically analyzes the conclusions of psychiatric and psychological evaluations. And former Chapter 21, which addresses the vulnerability of Board Certifications, is now incorporated in Chapter 9, together with challenges to the education and training of psychologists and psychiatrists.

Volume II, for the most part, addresses specific areas that may be, but are not necessarily, relevant to an ongoing case or even a lawyer's practice. For example, Chapter 21 of Volume II is devoted to challenges to experts on eye-witness evidence which may be central, or may be irrelevant, in any particular case. In addition to up-dating all the material in the prior edition, we have added six new chapters to Volume II covering the special topics of recovered memories, eye-witness testimony, treatment, child abuse, dangerousness, and child custody.

Volume III presents the procedural, or "how to do it" material. Chapters on strategies and tactics, objecting to admission of psychiatric evidence, and cross-examination, with examples of each, are included, as well as new material on the various ploys and tactics employed by the experts and how to deal with them. Volume III also provides material related to the total management of any case where a psychological issue may be anticipated. Such management begins with investigation, reading and analyzing experts' reports and taking of depositions, and concludes with objections to admission and cross-examination. These tactics are illustrated in general and in particular types of cases, such as criminal, personal injury and child custody. Three new chapters in Volume III deal with recently developed guidelines for serving as a forensic expert and general ethical principles for psychologists, responses to criticisms leveled at those who rely on this work, and the potential benefits of employing visual aids in the courtroom along with descriptions of available equipment.

The Appendices in Volume III contain materials adapted from the authors' case files. The cases include child custody, murder, personal injury and brain damage. Each case illustrates both unique materials and materials that apply to a range of cases. Appendix A illustrates a skilled cross-examination that essentially impairs the credibility of a highly credentialed expert. Appendix B shows how a highly skilled witness who is *not* cross-examined in as skilled a manner can create considerable problems for the lawyer. The author provides instructive comments and suggestions for all cases. Although no case management or cross-examination can be perfect, these materials offer a sense of the process as it occurs in actual litigation. They present models with which lawyers can sharpen their skills and effectiveness in coping with psychiatric and psychological testimony. For mental health professionals, the materials should help them anticipate challenges they may encounter in the courtroom and avoid mistakes or procedures in the course of assessment that increase their vulnerability beyond that created by the current limits in the field.

Lawyers and mental health professionals are busy people and we expect there will be few who have the time to read all three volumes cover-to-cover. We would strongly suggest that the reader first concentrate on Volume I and become familiar with these basic materials, for they are the foundation for all that follows.

For the most part, Volume II can be used selectively. The reader might pick out chapters most pertinent to his or her practice or case, or perform concentrated study of selected chapters if and when the need arises. Those who have read previous editions should be aware that a considerable amount of re-organization has taken place, much material added, and entirely new, highly pertinent topics introduced (e.g., prognosis and treatment; use of ethical principles). Also, a detailed index has been provided.

A WARNING: We have found that some lawyers skim through the book materials, perhaps pick out some questions from Volume III, and then try to proceed on this basis. This is risky. A witness who is at all skilled can place one who prepares in this manner at a considerable disadvantage. We might contrast this to a recent case in which a lawyer, although rarely forced to deal with psychiatric testimony, not only read these materials thoroughly but obtained original articles on key issues. In a very difficult case, this allowed him to negate the testimony of a psychologist with considerable courtroom experience. Evasive tactics by the expert were effectively countered and inaccurate descriptions of "supportive" studies were immediately recognized and challenged. Few may be quite this zealous, but it illustrates one end of the continuum.

It is the plan of this book to supply the attorney with a systematic and methodical basis for cross-examining psychiatrists and psychologists by using the scientific literature in the experts' fields. This information can be utilized to educate judge and jury. If used properly, it can systematically and methodically reduce the credibility of psychiatrists and clinical psychologists to the point where it could be easy for a judge or jury to disregard their testimony.

The book consists largely of peer-reviewed literature which negates the expertise of mental health professionals. There is literature not contained in this book that is supportive of forensic psychiatry and psychology, although for some topics this literature may be slim or close to nonexistent (e.g., there is considerably more empirical research showing that experience is not related to assessment accuracy than empirical research supporting experience). The exclusion of supportive literature is *not* to cause readers to believe it does not exist. As noted, it may or does exist. However, although perhaps of academic interest, such supportive evidence is viewed as largely irrelevant in a forensic context.

If, for example, there is a body of literature indicating that psychiatric diagnoses are made with a fairly high degree of validity and there is another body of literature of approximately equal quality indicating that psychiatric diagnoses are not made with a high degree of validity, the least that can be said is that the issue is in doubt and is therefore unresolved within the profession itself. Therefore, if the scientific and professional literature casts doubt on the validity of psychiatric diagnoses, the fact that a portion of that literature supports it does not remove the doubt. The jury should not be asked to resolve scientific and professional issues that the scientists and professionals have not been able to resolve. In the face of such doubts, no weight should be given to such evidence. Therefore, from a legal perspective, the recitation of some supportive literature is viewed as an exercise in futility. Further, it is *not* as if, for even some of the topics we cover, there are many supportive studies and a few non-supportive ones. With few if any exceptions, there are either a substantial number of critical or non-supportive studies or, if there are fewer overall studies available, a considerable proportion, if not the majority or nearly all, are non-supportive.

As far as possible, conclusions about the current scientific standing or status of topics and issues within psychiatry and psychology are based on the scientific and professional literature, not on the author's personal observations. When personal experiences are referenced, it is typically to illustrate some point or to describe witnesses' tactics that have been observed. Such comments do not "establish" or make a scientific point. Scientific points should be based on science. Experiences as a consultant may not provide a representative sample. Thus the reader is cautioned against drawing generalizations on this basis. Indeed, more generally, the lawyer is cautioned against accepting "authoritative" pronouncements in the fields of psychiatry and psychology unless supported by methodologically sound research evidence. The state of knowledge in these fields is so amorphous that glib pronouncements are easily made with a sound of conviction, and are hard to disprove. For this reason an effort has been made to document the support for each point raised in this book. Two types of documentation have been employed. One type consists of statements of authorities which challenge notions that less critical colleagues claim have been accepted. The second type presents research evidence which negates, or at least casts serious doubt upon, current theories, principles and assumptions, or demonstrates the inefficacy of procedures and practices on which the forensic activities of psychiatry and clinical psychology are based.

Some case materials are presented or described in all volumes of this work. These materials are discussed as an educational tool. They are not intended to be a commentary or critique of the performance or competence of any particular person or the outcome of an individual case. The comments or opinions expressed are based upon the case materials as they have been presented in this work, and do not necessarily reflect the actual performance of any particular individuals.

While this is not an edited work, several new chapters in Volumes II and III were contributed by people with many publications in their particular field. Fourth edition co-author David Faust did not participate in this edition except for the excellent revision of the neuropsychology chapter.

Most of the chapters in this book were written or re-written by Jay Ziskin. Where the terms "we" or "us" or "our" appear they are used as the editorial "we." At times the term "clinician" is used to encompass both psychiatrists and clinical psychologists. Unless otherwise indicated, chapters were written by Ziskin and he is solely responsible for their contents.

I would like to offer thanks to the editor, Janet Cornwell, for a terrific job working against the clock. Also, Richard D. Burns of Regina Books was extraordinarily conscientious in designing and typesetting this work and adhering to the schedule. As always, Mae Ziskin was everywhere all the time, resolving computer crises, seeing that there was enough paper, lending an intelligent ear—in a word being the center of everything that needed to be done except the writing itself.

JAY ZISKIN
Los Angeles, CA
May, 1995

Summary of Table of Contents

Volume III

Appendices

Contents: Volume I

CHAPTER 1

The Bases of Expert Testimony

The Dubious Status of Psychiatrists & Psychologists

INTRODUCTION

Over the last several decades there has been an ever increasing utilization of psychiatric and psychological evidence in the legal process. Often such evidence does not meet reasonable criteria of admissibility. Many experts are less than completely candid concerning weaknesses in their knowledge base and methodology. When such evidence is admitted, the opposing side should expose its weaknesses so that it will be given little or no credibility. It is the aim of this book to provide lawyers with information with which to aid courts and juries to distinguish science from authoritarian pronouncement and validated knowledge from conjecture. It is hoped that use of this information will ultimately lead to a truly useful participation by psychiatrists and psychologists in the legal arena. Meanwhile, this information may be useful in helping lawyers educate triers of fact to view mental health expert testimony with appropriate skepticism.

While most readers will be familiar with the law regarding expert evidence, a brief recapitulation is in order here. While some variations in definition occur, generally an expert is described as one who is so qualified by study or experience that he can form a definite opinion of his own respecting a division of science, branch of art, or department of trade concerning which persons having no particular training or special study are incapable of forming accurate opinions or of deducing correct conclusions (31 Am. Jur. 2d, 494).

The theory underlying expert testimony is that experts, because of their knowledge, training, and experience, are able to form better opinions on a given state of facts than opinions formed by those not so well equipped, such as ordinary jurors, and their opinions are admitted in evidence to aid the jury in understanding questions which inexperienced persons are not likely to decide correctly without such assistance. If the subject is one of common knowledge, and the facts can be intelligibly described to the jury, and they can form a reasonable opinion for themselves, the opinion of an expert will be unnecessary. Thus, expert opinion may or may not be admissible, depending upon whether or not the subject matter is within common experience or whether it is a special field where the opinion of a skilled and experienced expert will assist, and *be of greater validity* than that of the ordinary juryman.

The mere fact that a witness may have more knowledge about the subject of inquiry or may understand it better than the jury, does not necessarily justify his giving opinion instead of fact. Even though having less skill or experience, the jurors may be able to draw their own conclusions. A jury might be entirely without knowledge of a certain field, but might become sufficiently informed during the trial so as to reach accurate conclusions, in which case there is no real need for expert opinion.

Furthermore, the qualifications of the expert need to be carefully scrutinized to prevent being led astray by the pseudo-learned or charlatan who may give erroneous or overly positive opinions without sound foundation. It will be shown in later chapters that much of psychiatry and psychology involves pseudolearning, and that the opinions of psychiatrists and psychology are often given without sound foundation.

Rheingold (1968) has delineated the basis of medical expertise as follows: (1) education, training, and subsequent learning; (2) experience; (3) books and periodicals; (4) scientific principles and facts, general medical knowledge, statistical information, and methodologies of tests.

Rheingold describes the difficult problems that arise when the concepts or facts upon which the doctor relies are not commonly or wholly accepted by the medical profession. In that instance, it is not the application of set principles to individual cases that causes the dispute, but the *validity of the basic suppositions themselves.* At times the courts have refused to allow a doctor to base his testimony on scientific procedures or methods such as narco-analysis, lie detectors, or hypnosis, where there was not a commonly accepted medical belief as to their validity or at least reliability.

In *Frye vs. U.S.* (1923), a leading case re expert testimony (based on polygraph evidence) the court states:

> Just when a scientific principle or discovery crosses the line between the experimental and demonstrable stages is difficult to define. Somewhere in this twilight zone the evidential force of the principle must be recognized and while courts will go a long way in admitting expert testimony deduced from a well recognized scientific principle or discovery, the thing from which the deduction

is made must be sufficiently established to have gained general acceptance in the particular field in which it belongs.

In another case involving the lie detector, *State vs. Bohner,* the court stated:

> We are not satisfied that this instrument during the 10 years that have elapsed since the decision in the Frye case has progressed from the experimental to the demonstrable stage. In his work on Principles of Judicial Proof (2nd edition, 1931), Dean Wigmore says, "Looking back at the range of possibilities for experimental psychometric methods of ascertaining concrete data for valuing testimonial evidence it will be seen that, thus far, the only new psychometric method that has demonstrated any utility is the blood pressure method which detects lies;...the record of psychometric testimony is still meager...the conditions required for truly scientific observation and experiment are seldom practicable. Testimonial mental processes are so complex and variable that millions of instances must be studied before safe generalizations can be made." It seems to us that this statement offers little comfort to one who contends that this device is past the experimental stage. While it may have some utility, at present, and may ultimately be of great value in the administration of justice, it must not be overlooked that a too hasty acceptance of it during this stage of its development may bring complications and abuses that will overbalance whatever utility it may be assumed to have. The present necessity for elaborate exposition of its theory and demonstration of its practical working in order to convince the jury of its probative tendencies, together with the *possibility of attacks upon the soundness of its underlying theories and its practical usefulness* (italics ours) may easily result in the trial of the lie detector rather than the issues in the case. In this connection, such procedure would resolve into a swearing match and, not to overlook the human element, we can foresee conditions where to ascertain the truth it would become necessary to require the operator of the machine to submit to a test to determine the truthfulness of his interpretation.

The arguments in the *Bohner* case seem to apply with equal or greater force to psychiatric and clinical psychological evidence (henceforth in this text "psychological" shall mean clinical psychological unless otherwise indicated). It shall be shown by reference to the scientific and professional literature that in many areas, particularly those with forensic relevance, it is doubtful that psychiatry and psychology have crossed the line between the experimental and demonstrable. It seems that the burden for establishing demonstrability should lie with the profferer of such evidence.

An article titled "Astrology Thrives on the Gullibility Gene," written by Carol T. Tavris, described as a social psychologist and writer living in Los Angeles, appeared in the *Los Angeles Times* on May 5, 1988. Tavris notes that under scientific investigation, efforts to document a key tenet of astrology—that one's life and character can be assessed from one's birth chart—have consistently failed. Tavris notes that astrology continues to be popular because people are just as happy with their wrong charts that have nothing to do with them as they are with the ones that are correct, quoting the famed circus showman, P.T. Barnum, to the effect, "Always have a little something for everybody." Tavris quotes Geoffrey Dean, a scientist who wrote of a two-part investigation of astrological claims, as describing astrology as "psychological chewing gum, satisfying but ultimately without real substance." Dean concludes that there is no problem with it if it is used as entertainment or even as a form of religion. But Tavris points out if astrology is advertised as the truth, then consumers are being defrauded and possibly harmed. Tavris points out that a century ago, phrenology, a system for interpreting personality from bumps on the skull, enjoyed more popularity than astrology. Tavris states, "It wasn't true either, but it 'worked' as an effort to explain human behavior." Tavris also notes that in the investigations of the accuracy of astrological predictions, the experience of the astrologer did not improve the results. The reader may wish to keep the state of astrology in mind as an analog to the status of psychiatry and clinical psychology. Indeed, we might note that when it is argued that psychiatry has "withstood the test of time," astrology has "withstood" this test for a much longer time.

Slovenko (1988) describes the "impartial expert" concept as naive and an illusion. Slovenko notes that there are many critics who charge that mental health professionals have no useful place in the courtroom and cannot answer forensic questions with reasonable accuracy or help to reach more accurate conclusions than would otherwise occur. He then seems to state that the marketplace is a measure of value and that it is entirely reasonable to assume that one who had special training in understanding people and spends his life studying and thinking about people is in a position to bring relevant and probative testimony about behavior. Of course, the same argument could be made for astrologers. At least some of them have had special training in understanding people on the basis of astrological signs and they spend their lives studying and thinking about people. Therefore, using the Slovenko test, one would be inclined to say that testimony of astrologers should have approximately the same level of usefulness in a courtroom as that of psychiatrists and psychologists. Of course we should also once again note that it would be entirely reasonable to assume that one who has had special training in practicing medicine and spent his life studying and thinking about medicine would be perfectly justified in using bleeding in the 17th and 18th centuries to treat all sorts of diseases. The key word in Slovenko's argument is "assume." In response to this kind of contention, we would assert that in the face of the quantity of literature which negates that argument, it is not entirely reasonable to make such an assumption.

Slovenko, apparently in support of the use of psychiatric testimony, notes that criminal trials without psychiatrists are likely to be bland and that, without such testimony, jurors may go to sleep. He states, "Trials without psychiatric testimony are not very interesting or satisfying" (refer again to Tavris above on astrology). Slovenko notes further that the so-called "battle of the experts" heightens tension and increases attention, stimulates thought and enhances deliberations. Surely there must be better ways of maintaining the attention of the trier of fact than by putting on a psychiatric circus. Slovenko notes that while trials have more to do with justice than with show business, criminal cases in particular are morality plays to some degree. In dealing with the criticism concerning the difficulty in achieving reliable classification in psychiatry, Slovenko points out that diagnostic categories are of less use than they are in other medical fields. He describes psychiatrists as being like biographers or historians, noting that Freud's case histories could probably have won a Nobel Prize in literature. He explains that different biographers writing about the same individual will present variations in the story and it is the same with psychiatrists, and that while each tells a story, that is not to say any are false. However, we would note this is not to say that all, or any, are true. For example, one would not say that when Psychiatrist 1 declares under oath that the defendant lacked the capacity to distinguish right from wrong and Psychiatrist 2 declares under oath that defendant did not lack the capacity to distinguish right from wrong, that neither of those statements are false. Similarly, if one expert says that plaintiff has psychological problems caused by a certain accident and another expert says either that plaintiff does not have such problems or that the problems were not caused by the accident, one of those statements is false, i.e. not true.

The knowledge base of any discipline claiming to be scientific lies in the scientific and professional literature of the discipline. The level of expertise that can be demonstrated is limited to that which is confirmed by this body of literature. Where the reliability or validity of the principles or knowledge base on which the expertise is based is in doubt, the expertise is therefore in doubt and cannot be demonstrated. Where the knowledge base or the purported scientific methodology is in doubt, any conclusions based on it cannot be considered other than speculation. Where there is substantial conflict or controversy among respectable members of the discipline, as reflected in the literature, then as to that issue there is doubt.

In previous editions of this book, the issue of admissibility of mental health expert evidence was raised. The paradoxical position of the courts, in expressing little confidence in the expertise in these fields, but nevertheless continuing to admit it has led us to a conclusion, that showing how poor or doubtful such evidence is will not lead to its exclusion.

Therefore, it was expected that the issue of admissibility was not, in general, worth consideration in this edition.

However, because of some apparent conflicting language by the U.S. Supreme Court in *Daubert vs. Merrell, Dow Pharmaceuticals, Inc.* 113 S.Ct.2786 (1993) this issue may have been reopened.

In *Daubert*, a Federal case, the court discarded the traditional *Frye* test of "general acceptance" as the standard for admission of purportedly scientific evidence. The Court held that, at least in Federal jurisdictions, admissibility is governed by Rule 702 of the Federal Rules of Evidence, "if scientific, technical, or other specialized knowledge will assist the trier of fact to understand the evidence or to determine a fact in issue, a witness, qualified as an expert by knowledge, skill, experience, training, or education, may testify thereto in the form of an opinion or otherwise." The Court indicated that the intent of the Rule was to "liberalize" the admission of opinion testimony. Had the Court simply stated the reasoning for discarding *Frye*, that would probably have ended the matter. However, in their appropriate concern for maintaining some restraints on "scientific" evidence, they went on to point out that the trial judge must perform a role as gatekeeper to determine that the evidence is "scientific knowledge" and will assist the trier to understand or determine a fact in issue. They note this involved a determination that the reasoning underlying the testimony is scientifically valid and can be properly applied to the facts in issue. While expressing confidence in the ability of judges to perform this task, and while not presuming to set out a definitive checklist or tests, they nonetheless proceed to offer several observations (guidelines?) which are obviously intended to indicate variables which the judges should consider. These include the following:

1. A key question to be answered in determining whether a theory or technique is scientific knowledge that will assist the trier of fact will be "whether it can be (and has been) tested." The placement of "has been" in parentheses is puzzling. One would think that it would be more important that testing has been done rather than it merely be possible. Perhaps this relates to the courts' definition of "scientific" as implying a grounding in the methods and procedures of science possessing the property of falsifiability or testability and their definitions of "knowledge" as connoting more than subjective belief or unsupported speculation. Clearly, with regard to some theories of human behavior or psychology, a judge could exclude testimony because such theories have been described as unfalsifiable (e.g. psychoanalysis, see below). Also, it would seem that a theory that had not been adequately validated could not provide opinions that are other than subjective beliefs or speculation. One interesting possibility here relates to those experts who claim an eclectic orientation or practice. If the expert is eclectic in the sense of operating

on the basis of different theories depending on the particular situation or case, this may not be an issue. However, many clinicians are eclectic in the sense of combining elements from different theories (see below, Chapter 3). In this instance, the expert is concocting his or her own theory which probably will not have been tested and likely will not have had publication or peer review, in which case such testimony might be excludable.

2. Another question is whether the theory or technique has been subject to peer review and publication, although publication alone is not necessarily synonymous with peer review. The court indicates that publication (or lack thereof) in a peer-reviewed journal thus will be a relevant, but not dispositive, consideration in assessing the scientific validity of a particular technique or methodology on which an opinion is premised. This issue could be used by a judge to exclude evidence based, for example, on tests which have little or no publication or have only had publications by the author or producer of the tests.

3. Known or potential rate of error should also be considered, as well as the existence and maintenance of standards controlling the technique's operation. The court does not provide a guide as to acceptable or unacceptable rates of error, so presumably this is in the reasonable discretion of the trial judge. In those instances in which the rate or potential rate is not known, a judge could exclude the evidence. Query, what is the known or potential rate of error in diagnoses or assessments based on psychiatric interviews? What is the error rate for assessment of mental states weeks or months prior to the examination? Is there research establishing such rates for mental health experts generally? Is the rate acceptable? This would appear to be an issue of validity (see Chapter 7), regarding which this test might not be met. Could this test be applied to the individual expert? What is his rate of error? Absent a study of his individual validity, this is probably unknown.

4. "General acceptance" while not required, can be considered, along with the particular degree of acceptance in the relevant scientific community. The court does provide some guide on this issue by stating that "widespread acceptance" can be an important factor in ruling particular evidence admissible. "Widespread" is not further defined but minimal support may properly be viewed with skepticism.

The court states, "The inquiry envisioned by Rule 702 is, we emphasize, a flexible one. Its overarching subject is the scientific validity—and thus the evidentiary relevance and reliability—of the principles that underlie a proposed submission. The focus, of course, must be on principles and methodology, not on the conclusions that they generate."

Chief Justice Rehnquist and Justice Stevens, while concurring in the finding in the instant case, dissent with the general observations, expressing concern that among other things, these observations may require or authorize federal judges to become amateur scientists in order to perform their role. Perhaps the legal system would be better served if, indeed, judges did take such a stance and require more than a declaration by experts to establish the existence of expertise.

As of this writing, it is too early to predict how courts will react to *Daubert*. Will federal judges follow the implications of the observations or the declaration of the court that the Rules are interpreted to liberalize admission? And, of course, it is not known at this time whether state courts will adopt the observations.

The scientific and professional literature appearing around the close of the decade of the 1980s continues to cast serious doubt, and continues to present serious concerns, regarding the utility and validity of mental health expert opinion in legal matters.

The thrust of the remainder of this chapter will be to illustrate the dubious status of psychiatrists and psychologists as experts in relation to legal issues. This will be illustrated through judicial opinions, dissents, or dicta and opinions of writers in legal periodicals. Statements found in the scientific and professional literature of psychiatry and psychology provide another line of evidence indicating a lack of expertise regarding psychological assessment generally, and specifically in regard to legal issues.

THE LEGAL LITERATURE

In a number of appellate decisions, courts, either in the majority holding or by way of dicta or in dissenting opinions, have created an aura of doubt concerning psychiatric and psychological expertise. Some writers in legal periodicals have contributed to these doubts.

Over the last three decades, judicial decisions and legal periodicals have contained statements critical of psychiatric and psychological evidence. The bulk of these negative statements concern the difficulty of accurate diagnosis, the shaky status of knowledge, lack of predictive validity, and subjectivity and operation of bias. Numerous appellate reports and legal journal articles make reference to the lack of established validity and the uncertainty of psychiatric diagnoses and of professional judgment. (Burger, Dissent in *O'Connor vs. Donaldson*, 1975; *People vs. Burnick*, 1975; *Suggs vs. LaValle* [Kaufman concurring opinion] 1978; *Conservatorship of Mabel Roulet* [Dissent, subsequently majority opinion on rehearing] 1979; *People vs. Coleman*, 1981; *Addington vs. Texas*, 1978; *Stamper vs. Virginia* [frequent changes in classification] 1985; *Barefoot vs. Estelle*, 1983; Dix, 1971; Alexander, 1982; Shell, 1980; Morse, 1982; Ennis and Litwack, 1974; Roesch and Golding, 1985).

Some decisions have indicated a requirement of "demonstrable validity" of psychological tests (*Griggs vs. Duke Power Company*, 1971; *Albemarle Paper Company*, 1975. See Plotkin, 1972, Fincher, 1973 for discussions of these cases). Bersoff (1988) discusses the decision of the Supreme Court in *Watson vs. Fort Worth Bank*, 487 U.S., 108 S.Ct., 2777 (1988). Of interest here is Bersoff's statement, "Perhaps of most relevance to APA members, the plurality stated 'that employers are not required, even when defending standardized or objective tests, to introduce formal validation studies showing that particular criteria predict actual on-the-job performance'." (p. 1017) It may be that this decision may nevertheless dilute or diminish the holding in the case of *Griggs vs. Duke Power Company*. It remains to be seen what will happen when the court decides another case on a similar issue (see *Daubert*, supra, re known error rate).

Judge David Bazelon has criticized the use of labels or jargon by psychiatrists in *Washington vs. the United States*, 1967, and in an article, 1974. He has urged psychiatrists to avoid speculation in *Washington vs. U.S.* Similar concerns were expressed by Morse, 1982. Bazelon has also urged psychiatrists to acknowledge limitations in the knowledge base (*Washington vs. U.S.*, 1967; Bazelon, 1981).

Reference to psychiatrists' inability to predict was made in *People vs. Burnick*, 1975 and in the American Bar Association standards, 1984.

Examiner effects, such as subjectivity and bias, have also been noted by the courts (*Smith vs. Schlesinger*, 1975; *In re Roulet*, 1979; *Estelle vs. Smith*, 1980; *Rosenblitt vs. Rosenblitt*, 1985).

Courts and legal journals have taken note of what we call the "gap": the lack of established relationship between a particular disorder or set of symptoms and a legal issue, e.g. schizophrenia and inability to distinguish right from wrong (*Addington vs. Texas*, 1978; Roberti, 1980; Rubinstein, 1982).

Juries have been instructed that they can disregard psychiatric testimony (*People vs. Teague*, 1981; *People vs. Jones*, 1982; *Jones vs. State*, 1985; *Taylor vs. State*, 1982).

Bersoff (1992), a professor of law at Villanova University School of Law and professor of psychology, Hahnemann University, has described the incongruity between the Supreme Court's preference for professional rather than judicial decisionmaking in cases regarding evaluation and treatment of people allegedly mentally disabled, and the Court's long-standing skepticism about the ability of psychiatrists and psychologists to provide sound clinical judgments. He notes that critical literature and empirical studies support the Court's apprehension. He notes that a "forty year record of denigration of expertise by mental health professionals has been expressed by most members of the court regardless of political ideology and their views on constitutional jurisprudence." Bersoff calls attention to a "burgeoning literature" on judgment that negatively impacts on the reliability and validity of clinicians' decision making. He notes that, in many cases, experience is more of a hindrance than a help.

Perlin (1991) describes "identification biases" which may be unconscious (e.g., being on one side of a legal battle) or conscious due to a particular set of values or ideological leanings or just a hope of victory for his own opinion. He notes this may lead to many subtle distortions in testimony.

Judge Jorgenson (*Boynton vs. Burglass*, 590 So. 2d 446, 1991) notes the inexactness of psychiatry and issues of foreseeability and predictability of future dangerousness as gray areas of psychiatry.

As this text has been widely cited in the scientific and professional literature, as well as in appellate decisions, and has been used as a textbook in major universities, perhaps a lawyer could request a court to take judicial notice of its contents.

SCIENTIFIC AND PROFESSIONAL LITERATURE

It is not necessary to rely on the negative perceptions of the judiciary and legal scholars to establish the dubious status of psychiatric and psychological expertise in relation to legal matters. Numerous comments by members of these disciplines, found in their scientific and professional books and journals, provide ample reason to have serious doubt concerning the usefulness of evidence offered by these professionals. These comments include negative statements about the knowledge base of these disciplines, about their participation in forensic matters, the operations of bias and examiner effects, inability to accurately determine prior mental states, inability to predict, lack of sufficient evidence of validity of opinions, propensity to overdiagnose pathology, and the "gap" between diagnosis and legal issues. Of course, it should be understood that many mental health professionals are not in agreement with all of the statements contained in the citations below. Indeed, many of the writers cited, although providing such negative descriptions, also include more positive affirmative views as well. Some indicate that despite the shortcomings and doubts, psychiatric and psychological evidence is useful. Nevertheless, their statements indicate that a respectable segment of these professionals add their voices to the doubt concerning forensic psychiatric evidence that will be raised in subsequent chapters.

INADEQUACIES OF
KNOWLEDGE BASE AND PROCEDURES

A substantial body of the scientific and professional literature in the 1970's and 1980's contains statements directly or indirectly indicating that psychiatry/psychology lack a validated knowledge base or methodology sufficient to support opinions on most legal issues (Kubie, 1973; Pollack, 1971; Torrey, 1974; McNeal, 1972; Mechanic, 1978; Meehl, 1971; American Psychological Association Task Force, 1978; Saks, 1978; Garfield, 1978; Page and Yates, 1974; Klerman, 1979; Rappeport, 1976; Stein, 1979; Halleck, 1969; Havens, 1981; Fishman and Neigher, 1982; Robinson, 1980; Sarason, 1981; Kimble, 1984; Adams, 1984; Sechrest, 1985; Furlong, 1981; Goodwin, 1984; Brody, 1985; Sabshin, 1985; Rorer and Widiger, 1983; Levy, 1978; Faust, 1985; Slovenko, 1983; California Legislature Joint Committee For Revision of the Penal Code, 1979).

With the amicus briefs of the American Psychiatric Association and other groups in the *Tarasoff* case (*Tarasoff vs. The Regents of the University of California*, 1977) the facade of psychiatric expertise crumbles. This matter will be dealt with at length because, if properly understood, the declaration of the official organization of psychiatry should bring to an end the prematurely-granted status of "expert" to psychiatrists and clinical psychologists.

The facts of this case, briefly stated, are as follows: A young woman was killed by a student who had told a counselor he was seeing at the University that he intended to kill her. The counselor called campus police, who felt the student appeared rational and no further action was taken. The young woman's parents sued the University because no one had warned the victim, alleging the therapist had a duty to warn. The trial court sustained a demurrer to the complaint without leave to amend. Plaintiffs appealed.

The District Court of Appeal and ultimately the Supreme Court of the State of California held that when a therapist determines, or, pursuant to the standards of his profession, should determine that his patient presents a serious danger of violence to another, he incurs an obligation to use reasonable care to protect the intended victim against such danger. The discharge of this duty may require the therapist to take one or more various steps, depending on the nature of the case. Thus it may call for him to warn the intended victim or others likely to apprise the victim of the danger, to notify the police, or to take whatever other steps are reasonably necessary under the circumstances. This holding, at the level of the California District Court of Appeal, caused a furor among mental health professionals. They perceived the ruling as threatening their ability to carry on the practice of psychotherapy, as it impaired the principle of confidentiality, which they view as absolutely essential to the conduct of psychotherapy. On appeal to the Supreme Court of California, an amicus brief was filed by the American Psychiatric Association and joined in by numerous other mental health professional organizations, including the California State Psychological Association. It is the source and the contents of this brief, rather than the holding of the court, which is of significance here. It should be borne in mind that the quotations from this brief represent the position of the official body of American Psychiatry. The American Psychiatric Association states: "This newly established duty to warn imposes an impossible burden upon the practice of psychotherapy. It requires the psychotherapist to perform a function which study after study has shown he is ill-equipped to undertake; namely, the prediction of his patient's potential dangerousness." (p. 5)

Note this statement of lack of expertise pertains even to the treating psychotherapist. It is often asserted that the therapist knows much more about and better understands a person he is seeing as a patient in psychotherapy than he would be able to know and understand of an individual with only the more limited observations that are involved in the usual forensic diagnostic evaluation. The Brief states further:

> The Court's formulation of the duty to warn fundamentally misconceives the skills of the psychotherapist in its assumption that mental health professionals are in some way more qualified than the general public to predict future violent behavior of their patients. Unfortunately study after study has shown that this fond hope of the capability to accurately predict violence in advance is simply not fulfilled. The burden of the new duty to warn, therefore, is formulated and imposed without reference to the actual ability of the therapist to sustain it. As the very recent American Psychiatric Association Task Force on Clinical Aspects of the Violent Individual (1974) reported:

>> Neither psychiatrists nor anyone else have reliably demonstrated an ability to predict future violence or "dangerousness." Neither has any special psychiatric "expertise" in this area been established. (American Psychiatric Association Task Force Report 8, *Clinical Aspects of the Violent Individual*, July, 1974, 28)

To the same effect, Steadman and Cocozza (1975) have stated:

> Because some ex-patients are involved in murders, rapes, and other violent crimes, we call upon psychiatrists to predict which ones will become violent. Unfortunately, *the assumption that psychiatrists can accurately predict such behavior...lacks any empirical support.* Rappaport presents the problem: "There are no articles that would assist us to any great extent in determining who might be dangerous, particularly before he commits an offense." Seymour L. Halleck adds: "Research in the area of dangerous behavior...is practically non-existent. Prediction studies which have examined the probability of recidivism have no focus on the issue of dangerousness. If the psychiatrist or any other behavioral scientist were asked to show proof of his predictive skills, objective data could not be offered." (italics added.)

Other recent research reinforces the conclusion that therapists have no special expertise in the prognosis of violence. (For more detailed coverage on the prediction of dangerousness, see Chapter 24.) From an in-depth study of 256 cases of incompetent, indicted felony defendants for whom psychiatric determinations of dangerousness were necessitated by New York Law, H. J. Steadman (1973) concluded:

> A question that might be raised at this point is whether *our* data can address the issue of the abilities of psychiatrists to make these predictions as to dangerousness. This question rests on the assumption that there are bases in psychiatric training, perspective, and skills that give psychiatrists the special ability to make such predictions. In the 256 studied here, we have examined how the psychiatric prediction of dangerousness is actually being done...there seems to be little in the way of special abilities evident in these cases. It is our opinion that our data together with a lack of documentation in the literature for psychiatric abilities to accurately predict dangerousness, *seriously question any assumption that there is such special psychiatric expertise.* (emphasis added) (pp. 6-8 of the Brief)

It may be worth noting that in a footnote supporting this statement, the American Psychiatric Association refers to the Ennis and Litwak (1974) article and *authorities cited therein.* Inasmuch as one of the most extensively quoted authorities in Ennis and Litwack is the First Edition of *Coping With Psychiatric and Psychological Testimony,* one can at least argue that the American Psychiatric Association has accepted that book as authoritative.

The Tarasoff Brief continues:

> What these studies and numerous similar ones show is that absent a prior history of violence, no therapist can accurately predict whether his patient is in fact dangerous or not. This Court's newly formulated duty to warn directly conflicts with this growing body of scientific evidence. In the first place it assumes that a "reasonable" psychotherapist will under certain circumstances be able to predict violence. In fact, the above cited studies show that the reasonable therapist acting in conformity with the present standards of his profession cannot make any reliable prediction as to the possibility of his patient's future violence in the absence of a history of prior violent behavior. The newly imposed duty to warn is also inconsistent with the finding of scientific research that no special professional ability or expertise has yet been demonstrated in the prognoses of dangerousness. Instead the few studies which have been done..."strongly suggest that psychiatrists are rather inaccurate predictors"; inaccurate in an absolute sense and even less accurate when compared with other professionals...and when compared to actuarial devices, such as prediction of experience tables. (pp. 8-9)

The obvious conclusion from the APA brief is that it would be close to unconscionable for a psychiatrist to give testimony regarding the issue of dangerousness in civil commitment proceedings. If a psychiatrist is willing to do so in the face of this contrary official position of the APA, no court should allow the psychiatrist to testify in regard to this issue.

The brief states flatly, baldly, and unequivocally that psychiatrists do not possess such expertise. Given the difficulties that other areas of expertise (e.g., fingerprinting and lie detection) have encountered in inducing the courts to recognize their expertise, it would seem too paradoxical, even for the often observed intellectual gymnastics of the judiciary, for the courts to say, "Despite the fact that your official body has declared you non-experts in this particular field, we nevertheless will continue to accord you the status of expert in this area."

The more significant implications of the APA brief are less obvious and therefore require more elucidation.

Note, first of all, that in the first quotation from the brief there is reference by APA to the *fundamental misconception* of the court regarding the skills of psychotherapists in its *assumption* concerning the qualifications of mental health professionals. Further, note the quotation from Steadman and Cocozza to the effect that the assumption that psychiatrists can accurately predict such behavior lacks any empirical support and further, the quotation of Halleck to the effect that if the psychiatrist or any other behavioral scientist were asked to *show proof* of his predictive skills *objective data* could not be offered. It seems clear that the American Psychiatric Association is (at least by implication) adopting the standards which the courts have adopted with regard to experts in almost all other fields, and which the authors urge lawyers to demand and the courts to adopt with regard to psychiatric testimony. These are exactly the criteria referred to in the brief, to wit: empirical support and objective data confirming the expertise of the psychiatrist and the validity of his evaluations. The brief reveals the paramount importance of maintaining the safeguards with regard to according the status of experts by the courts. For many years, countless thousands of psychiatrists have paraded through courtrooms or submitted reports asserting that a given individual, as a result of his mental condition was, in fact, dangerous—as a result of which hundreds of thousands of people have been incarcerated for greater or lesser periods of time in mental institutions. Surely, these evaluations must have been rendered with a belief in their "reasonable medical certainty," as is required by law for such opinions, and certainly with the approval or at least without reprimand or contrary instruction from the American Psychiatric Association. To assert otherwise would be to accuse the entire profession of such chicanery or of such reprehensible conduct in terms of their performance vis-à-vis the law, perhaps even to the point of outright deception of the courts, as to render this entire body of professionals unacceptable to the courts as expert witnesses, at least until such time in the distant future as they have demonstrated their "rehabilitation" (that they are not yet "rehabilitated," see comment of Dr. Coleman, below).

The larger implications of the Tarasoff Brief may now be illuminated. Is not the admission of psychiatric opinion and evaluation as "expertise" in areas other than dangerousness *equally predicated upon the assumption by the courts that psychiatrists possess the requisite skills and that their evaluations possess the requisite validity?* Where are the empirical supports and objective data referred to in the brief to demonstrate such skills and validity? They are virtually nonexistent. Instead, what has finally come to light in this brief is that in virtually all areas, psychiatric experts have been admitted into court prematurely. Where is the empirical support and the objective data to support the assumption by the courts that psychiatrists can evaluate an individual's capacity to distinguish right from wrong at some time in the past or to substantially appreciate the wrongfulness of his behavior or conform his conduct or whatever test of criminal responsibility one may use? Where is the empirical support and the objective data which demonstrate that psychiatrists can relate any diagnosis of mental condition to any legal issue? Where is the empirical support and objective data which demonstrate that psychiatrists are able to accurately determine the cause of a so-called "psychic injury," or the course of such a condition? Where is the empirical support and objective data to demonstrate that psychiatrists can accurately distinguish a person with genuine psychological difficulty from one who is malingering for whatever motive of gain or avoidance of the consequences of his behavior? Such empirical supports or objective data are lacking, and because they are lacking, in virtually all, if not all cases where psychiatrists are permitted to testify, the courts are committing the same error they have committed according to the statement of the APA with regard to the prediction of dangerousness, to wit: *They are according a status of expertise on the basis of sheer assumption.*

In the face of this clear and unequivocal demonstration that the assumption is wrong in at least one area, it would seem incumbent upon the courts to re-evaluate the entire issue of psychiatric testimony, bar it from admission as expertise in every area, until, in each area, psychiatry has established empirical supports and objective data which would entitle it to expert status. If the courts do not do this on their own initiative, it would seem to be incumbent upon lawyers with public interests, such as prosecuting attorneys, to forcefully present such a demand to the courts. Probably those attorneys who represent institutional defendants, such as insurance companies in personal injury suits, have an equal duty to attempt to prevent the harm that may come to their clients through the admission of evidence based on such unsubstantiated "expertise."

While not directly related to the major point above, the following should be noted in connection with the Tarasoff Brief. After making the previously described elaborate demonstration of the inability of psychiatrists to predict dangerousness, the APA, in its brief, makes the following statement:

> The proper solution to this problem has already been pointed out by the California Legislature in the Lanterman-Petris-Short Act. Under the Act, instead of attempting to protect an individual and potential victim by the slender thread of a warning, the legislature has chosen to treat the source of the problem; namely, the potentially violent person. Pursuit of this course of action is the *clinically proper* [emphasis added] and the legislatively chosen method for dealing with potentially violent mental patients. It results in greater protection for society and lesser invasion of the patient's rights than does the court's formulation. (pp. 42-43)

In a letter supplied for use of the court in this matter, Dr. Lee Coleman, a San Francisco psychiatrist and author of one of the articles cited in the brief, makes the following statement:

> These are truly astounding arguments, for it now seems that the predictive *inability* of psychiatrists which was used by the Amici in support of *no warning,* is now suddenly good enough to justify incarceration of the patient. They even go so far as to claim that to incarcerate the patient would be less an invasion of the patient's rights than to warn the potential victim...it is hard for me to understand how the psychiatric community can ask to have it both ways—to be free of obligation to warn on the basis of *inability* to predict dangerousness, and yet have the authority to incarcerate patients on the basis of *ability* to predict dangerousness. It seems to me that in light of our inability to make accurate predictions that the Court was wise in finding cause of action for failure to warn but not for failure to incarcerate, because the warning involves an immeasurably lesser invasion of rights than does incarceration. A patient's confidentiality *is* invaded by a warning, but the alternative offered by Amici (incarceration) is a much bigger breach, not only of confidentiality but of personal liberty as well. The Court's way leaves the patient not only free from incarceration, but also free to terminate therapy if he feels the therapist's warning makes the therapist unacceptable. The Amici's way locks up the patient on the basis of a prediction they (Amici) have taken great pains to show is worthless. (pp. 2-4)

In case it is not clear to any reader, the reference to the Lanterman-Petris Act is to the commitment or detention of an individual for a period of time on the basis of a psychiatric prediction that he is dangerous. This is the glaring inconsistency to which Dr. Coleman refers. It is a further illustration of the Alice-in-Wonderland quality of psychiatry. Some further comments in Dr. Coleman's letter may be of interest:

> The real irony of the Amicus Brief is that all of the arguments with regard to inability to predict violence, breach of confidentiality, lessening of the availability of psychotherapy to violence-prone individuals, etc., are those arguments which indicate that their remedy (the use of involuntary treatment as a means of preventive detention) is without merit from either a social or clinical point of view. The irony is that in attempt to disagree with an obligation to warn (which might be more convincingly argued if the remedy suggested, that is, incarceration, were not far more onerous than a warning) the Amici have

suddenly embraced a position which they routinely violate in daily practice. Every day, hundreds of psychiatric patients have their confidentiality violated by being forced to enter psychiatric facilities against their will; in addition their bodies are also often violated by being forced to take psychiatric drugs against their will. (p. 5)

Coleman further states:

Thus the Amicus Brief would be an excellent document to question the whole edifice of psychiatric power and it is unfortunate that they instead seek to use their data in a misleading manner in an effort to protect *themselves*, rather than as they claim, their patients or society. They are in a poor position to raise the issue of invasion of constitutional rights to therapeutic confidentiality and the right to medical treatment without state interference, when they are engaged in a violation of these rights on a daily basis and when their recommendation is to continue with these violations. (p. 6)

Although we had made the same observations upon reading the brief as Dr. Coleman makes, it is of some importance to have the statements come from one who is, himself, a practicing psychiatrist.

In proceedings of potential significance for the future of forensic psychiatry and psychology, a joint committee on revision of the penal code of the California Legislature called hearings on April 11 and 12, 1979, on "The Role of Psychiatry in Determining Criminal Responsibility." Subsequently, on December 4 and 5, 1979, the same committee held hearings on "The Defenses of Diminished Capacity and Insanity."[1]

In the first hearing, the committee raised questions as to the proper form, basis and scope of expert psychiatric testimony as follows: "Should such testimony be limited to diagnoses, observations and test results, or should testimony relating to legal conclusions be permitted?" "Should certification be required to qualify as an expert psychiatric witness? (If so, what body should so certify?)" "What type of testimony is most useful to a jury?" In the second hearing, among questions the committee addressed to the witnesses were: "Assuming the validity of the diminished capacity defense, should psychiatric testimony be admissible to prove the defense?" "Should the psychiatrist, as expert witness, be permitted to testify to the ultimate legal conclusions of defendant's criminal responsibility, or should such testimony be limited to the psychiatrist's observation of the defendant and to general data about pathology and probability or statistical frequency of the occurrence of legally relevant behavior by persons with similar behavior traits or pathology of

---

[1] Hearings on the Defenses of Diminished Capacity and Insanity, Joint Committee on Revision of the Penal Code, Senate Committee on Judiciary, Criminal Justice Committee of the State of California, Hearings held Tuesday, December 4, 1979 and Wednesday, December 5, 1979. Transcripts of these hearings were obtainable by writing to the California Legislature Joint Committee For Revision of the Penal Code, 1116 9th Street, Room 175, Sacramento, CA 95814.

the defendant? What specific information about a defendant's mental illness is relevant to determining the question of intent?" Thus, in both hearings, the committee addressed questions as to possible limitations on the nature and scope of psychiatric evidence to be admitted. However, it seems noteworthy that after having taken considerable testimony from public defenders, prosecuting attorneys, law professors, psychiatrists and psychologists in the first hearing, the committee appears to have shifted to some extent in the direction of asking whether psychiatric evidence should be admitted at all.

The transcript of the first hearing can be summarized as revealing major disagreements among the lawyers and among the mental health professionals as to the nature and boundaries of legitimate psychiatric testimony and as to matters about which psychiatrists should and should not be allowed to testify. This was only to be expected, given the state of confusion over the state of knowledge in psychiatry and the lack of hard data. *It is the legitimacy of such a debate that ought to preclude admission of psychiatric testimony.* Given such a disparity of views stated by reputable professionals in the field, it would be impossible to state that the legitimacy of psychiatric testimony as it occurs in practice is generally accepted by a scientific community, one of the requirements for expert evidence admissibility. The testimony presented in these hearings simply highlights the proposition stated earlier to the effect that psychiatric evidence was prematurely admitted without the safeguards and scrutiny that the courts ordinarily apply before admitting evidence as expert (e.g., polygraph, voice prints). It seems likely that if psychiatrists had never before testified in court, and given the nature of the testimony before this committee and all of the documentation provided in this book, that such a committee or the courts would rule that such evidence did not meet the requirements of the law for expert evidence in most of the areas in which it is used. (This statement is qualified to the extent that there may be areas of expertise that these professionals possess, such as the effects of drugs or alcohol on behavior.)

The testimony of Stephen Morse to the committee is particularly cogent to the thesis of this chapter, which is that psychiatrists and psychologists do not meet the test for admission to the courts as experts. Dr. Morse is a professor of Law and Psychiatry at the University of Southern California Law Center and is both an attorney and a Ph.D. psychologist, suggesting that he brings to this issue a perspective that is broader than that of most of the witnesses, in view of his dual status. In opening his testimony, he states his aim of limiting mental health expert testimony in criminal cases. Toward this end he makes a number of relevant statements. (Note: He had previously provided the committee with a lengthy article on this topic titled, "Crazy Behavior, Morals and Science: An

Analysis of Mental Health Law" which appeared in the *Southern California Law Review* and also a shorter version of the same article called "Law and Mental Health Professionals" published in *Professional Psychology*, in August, 1978, pages 389 to 399. In these articles, he provides documentation for his position.) Consider the following assertions of Dr. Morse:

> Let me say right off the bat, that the point of view I take is that the time when considering "expert testimony" where people supposedly have the kinds of knowledge and skills that would allow them to draw conclusions that laypeople can't draw, it is time, when considering that, to stop saying let's rely on degrees; let's [sic] rely on our assumption about what doctors and psychologists do and do not know [Authors' Note: Given the general tenor of Dr. Morse's statements we are confident that he meant to say let's "not" rely on our assumptions]. I say it is time to start looking at some data, some evidence, what can be demonstrated, what can't be demonstrated. And so, I take a very data-oriented approach to this whole matter and I can't begin to lay out any data for you here but it is all in the paper and I refer you to it. Let me state specifically the positions I take and then I will try to convince you in 10 or 15 minutes that they're right.
>
> First, is that professionals here, I mean psychologists, psychiatrists and all those who would be qualified to testify as expert witnesses in criminal cases. But those professionals have considerably less to contribute on legal issues than is commonly supposed. I think if we just start to look at the data about how much psychiatrists really know about diagnosis, how much psychiatrists really know about the causation of behavior, how much psychiatrists really know about predicting future behavior; you will find as a matter of expertise as opposed to clinical intuition, you're just in a house of cards that would fall apart at the first close examination, it just doesn't exist and I think we have to distinguish very, very carefully here between what is useful knowledge and skills in a clinic or in a hospital and what is useful knowledge and skills in a courtroom dealing with social, ethical and legal questions. Now I think we can make those distinctions.

With these statements, Dr. Morse lends another voice to the thesis we have previously advanced, to wit: 1) that psychiatrists lack the expertise generally attributed to them in regard to legal issues, and 2) that laymen can make the kinds of judgments that psychiatrists provide. Thus, on these tests which lie at the heart of the admission of testimony as expert, psychiatrists and psychologists fail.

In other portions of his testimony, Morse asserts that neither psychiatrists nor psychologists nor anybody else can tell us with any degree of reasonable scientific certainty why anybody does anything: they just do not know. He also asserts that the issues involved in psychiatric testimony should be determined by the data and not by opinion. He provides as an example the testimony of psychiatrists to the effect that frontal lobe injury deprives one of substantial capacity to conform, while the research data indicates that criminal behavior is no more prevalent among people with frontal lobe injuries than in the general population.

To avoid misrepresenting Morse's position, it should be stated that he does not take the view that clinicians have nothing to offer or no role to play. He indicates that clinicians can provide useful evidence in terms of their behavioral observations of the litigant and that they know how to ask questions that would "bring out" whether people are crazy or have other kinds of pathology that the untrained person would not know to ask. For example, a clinician might ask whether the individual "hears voices sometimes" whereas the layman might not ask such a question. It may be noted that other witnesses before the committee expressed similar views referring to the clinicians" ability to "dig out," "sniff out," "tease out" evidence of psychopathology. However, Morse and the others completely overlooked the fact that the clinical interview is a highly unreliable data gathering process. This problem is covered more extensively below (see Chapter 6), but needs to be dealt with to some extent at this point, as there was considerably more agreement among the witnesses regarding this "contribution" by the clinicians. Morse and these other witnesses completely overlook the clear demonstration in the scientific and professional literature that the data that is gathered by clinical methods is to a considerable extent determined by the theoretical, social, philosophical and personal biases of the clinician. Further, it has been shown through research (see below) that clinicians are prone to over-emphasize indications of psychopathology. In addition, the very process of data gathering influences the data that are elicited. When a documents expert examines a document, the evidence for or against genuineness is not changed by his examination. Similarly, when a ballistics expert examines a bullet, the markings on the bullet are not altered by his examination. The following examples from cases in which the author served as a consultant illustrate how differently this process works in psychological examinations. In Case 1, the defendant shot his wife and two of his children, firing at and missing a third child. He was interviewed by psychiatrist X, who in the course of the examination asked "Did you have any thoughts of suicide after shooting the children?" and the defendant said "No." He was later examined by psychiatrist Y who also inquired concerning thoughts of suicide and defendant replied, "I'm not sure, I don't recall." A little later he was examined by psychiatrist Z who also asked this question, to which defendant responded, "Yes, if I had had another bullet in the gun, I would have killed myself." What subsequently came out in that psychiatrist's report was that defendant "undoubtedly would have killed himself if he had had another bullet." We have to ask the question "Which psychiatrist's raw data would have been correct?" Which one "dug out" or "sniffed out" the evidence of suicidal thought? One need not have clinical training to realize that in this situation it is possible either that defendant, over the course of these interviews, began to realize that it might be to his benefit to indicate that he had thoughts of suicide, or that merely the repetitive asking of this question began to plant the idea in his mind that he had had such thoughts. It is worth noting that, because only the third psychiatrist testified in court, had the reports of the other two psychiatrists not been available, it would not be possible to determine that this process had taken place and the jury would have had only the information that the defendant would have killed himself if he had another bullet.

In Case 2, the defendant had carefully planned to kidnap and rob a beauty parlor patron and had not only executed the plan but after so doing, took the victim to a lonely spot in the country, killed her and concealed her body. The defendant was a young man with a moderate record of juvenile criminal activity, including thefts, and had been in and out of juvenile hall where he had had contact with other offenders and with clinicians. When the examining psychiatrist, noting that the victim was in an age range that would be appropriate for defendant's mother, asked him, "Did she remind you of your mother?" defendant apparently had the wits to recognize a potential escape route and replied "Yes." The psychiatrist then rose to the occasion and proceeded to "dig out" the facts that defendant had had some problems with his mother during the course of growing up and did not particularly like her. This led to the opinion in his report that defendant was unable to form the required intent and that he killed this victim purely and simply because she represented his mother.

Third, in several cases involving so-called "traumatic neuroses," psychiatrists asked plaintiffs if they have any difficulty sleeping, if they have nightmares, if they feel tense and anxious and if they feel depressed, and the plaintiffs always seem to answer these questions in the affirmative. A plaintiff would have to be of quite modest intellectual endowment not to realize that there were dollar signs attached to all of those answers. In this connection, the question arises as to whether the psychiatrist can determine when he is getting the truth and when he is not. This will be dealt with much more extensively below, but for the present purpose it is sufficient to simply state that there is virtually no evidence that psychiatrists possess particular skills in this regard, or demonstrate that they are able to distinguish truth from falsification.

Furthermore, if defendant's "craziness" can only be detected or elicited by a psychiatrist, as Morse may be suggesting, what relevance could it have with regard to any legal issue? That is, if the defendant is "crazy" but does not behave in a crazy manner, it would seem clear that he is able to judge the rightness or wrongness of behavior and has sufficient self-control to keep from displaying his craziness. Surely, it must require more "craziness" than that to meet the intent of the exculpatory defense of insanity.

The following excerpts from the December 4 and 5, 1979, testimony before the joint committee are also illuminating. It should be understood that this quoted material is excerpted from more extensive testimony by the various persons quoted, and therefore does not completely represent their views regarding psychiatric or psychological evidence. However, these witnesses appeared before the committee by invitation, which at least implies considerable recognition of their stature, knowledge and "expertise" regarding the matters before the committee. Thus, their negative views on some aspects of forensic psychiatry are worth noting.

One of the witnesses was Dr. Bernard Diamond, whose name should be familiar to almost anyone who has any involvement with forensic psychiatry or psychology. His statements should be taken in the context that he is board-certified in psychiatry, board-certified in forensic psychiatry and a member of the forensic psychiatry certifying board. A discussion took place between Dr. Diamond and State Senator Bob Wilson concerning the biases of experts, and Senator Wilson's observation that a good deal of expert witness "shopping" goes on until the lawyer finds one who is going to say what he wants. Senator Wilson stated:

> Now the process by which he probably got there is that the defense attorney may have gone through several psychiatrists that said this person was sane before he came to that psychiatrist that makes the conclusion that the person is, in fact, insane.
>
> The whole process that I see all the time in personal injury cases, of doctors coming in and saying that this person cannot work for the rest of his life, that doctor got there usually after screening out many doctors that said he could go to work tomorrow. (p. 29)

Dr. Diamond responded:

> Well, I would deal with that problem by the law's insistence not to use experts or anybody else for clairvoyant predictions of the future. I don't think that psychiatrists, or anybody, sociologists, or lawyers, or judges, are very capable of predicting what's going to happen. I would insist that any opinions of experts be limited to things that have already happened, so that the idea of predicting the future dangerousness, the recovery, or lack of recovery of an individual, is a very hazardous, unobjective matter. (p. 29)

Thus, this eminent forensic psychiatrist appears to be stating that psychiatrists cannot provide valid evidence regarding the future and, therefore, should not be allowed to testify on such an issue.

Another witness was Ronald Tochterman, Judge of the Municipal Court. Judge Tochterman had been appointed to the bench just prior to his appearance before the committee, and prior to that he had been chief trial deputy in the District Attorney's Office. In his testimony, Judge

Tochterman describes the expert witness "shopping" that takes place. He also refers to two cases of local notoriety in which he made motions to bar or limit the psychiatric testimony. He states:

> The judge, in both cases that I tried, said, 'I'm impressed with your arguments. If it were up to me, I would grant your motion, but the legislature has enacted as the law and the policy of the state that psychiatrists are able to do this.' Well, they're really not. I mean, they cannot. I mean, that's obviously an enormous issue amongst forensic psychiatrists, and among lawyers. My opinion is that they cannot. In the second case the judge said frankly, "I would have granted your motion but for section 1026 of the Penal Code." (p. 146)

He notes that the very competent defense attorney in the first of two locally notorious cases, after having called five or six psychiatrists, gave up and did not once in arguing to the jury refer to the testimony of the psychiatrists. Judge Tochterman interprets that as "an abject concession that they had nothing to offer." (p. 147) In the second case he notes similar circumstances with a large number of mental health experts, including two board certified psychiatrists and one board certified psychologist, and that after the trial was over, the jurors, having all served their time, were invited back for a discussion of the psychiatric testimony. During that discussion, the defense attorney stated that he wished that Tochterman's motion to bar the psychiatric testimony had been granted. Judge Tochterman asserts, "The psychiatric testimony in both cases was an absolute embarrassment, and it consumed enormous amounts of court time, and it was enormously expensive." (p. 147) In a personal communication, Judge Tochterman related that in the discussion with the jury they described the psychiatric testimony as "useless."

Judge Tochterman also stated:

> No psychiatrist can tell you whether the defendant knew the wrongfulness of his act, or had the capacity to conform his conduct to the requirements of the law, or could harbor malice, at least none can do so better than any lay person. In fact, I think there's compelling evidence that they're not as well able because of the various biases that they bring with them to do it.

Judge Tochterman describes the problem of shopping for and steering witnesses as follows:

> I was on a panel with [an attorney] who defended [a killer], and he was being very candid, and he was a very nice, likable, unpretentious man, and he said, well I went to Dr. A., and I said, Dr. A., I think [killer] is just wacko, he's a psychotic, depressive, whatever. Dr. A. talked to [killer] and he said, well, I think, possibly he was a psychotic, and possibly he couldn't harbor malice, and deliberate, and premeditate. So, [lawyer] said, then I went to Dr. B., and said, you know, I was just talking to Dr. A., and Dr. A. thinks that [killer] is a—was psychotic, and couldn't deliberate and premeditate, and he described the process of escalation from one psychiatrist to another, and I have verified that in cases that I've tried.

I have determined precisely that to be the case, to be true. There's an awful lot
of manipulation that goes on, there's an awful lot of witness shopping. (p. 147)

The next witness was Stuart Rappaport, Deputy Public Defender,
Los Angeles County. For several years Mr. Rappaport was chief of superior court trials, which means he headed up felony trials for the public
defender's office in downtown Los Angeles. He notes that from the defense side, a psychiatric defense is a poor defense. He states:

Using a psychiatrist in a courtroom is generally detrimental to the defense. I'm
surprised to hear somebody say, as a psychiatrist, that he'd have to have five
psychiatrists for the five that the defense has called, because the best prosecu-
tors I know, do not want to have any psychiatrists on their side, because they
then can take the attitude with the jury, as though it's all nonsense. All they
have to do is get different diagnoses by each psychiatrist, tell them "Look,
c'mon, they're just a sham." (p. 152)

Mr. Rappaport points out (pp. 172-173) that jurors do not rest their
decisions on the psychiatric testimony but on other factors. For example
in the Dan White case, the fact was that the defendant was a veteran,
served his community as a fireman, policeman, elected official and was a
good family man. In response to these statements, State Senator David A.
Roberti responded:

Well, yes, but if a jury rests its decision on that, then I frankly feel that a jury's
decision should rest on that, and therefore, the camouflage of diminished capacity shouldn't be there.

I think the public has a benefit to have a decision rest upon which the decision
rests [sic], and all this talk I've heard about hidden agenda, everybody knows
there's a hidden agenda in almost every trial case then why did we go through
the subterfuge of psychiatric witnesses that I would say that the *preponderence
of testimony I've heard from the psychiatric profession itself would indicate
them being incapable of making these determinations anyway.* (italics added)
(p. 173)

In 1981, the legislature of California, the most populous state in the
union, enacted Sections 28 and 29 of its Penal Code, eliminating the defense of diminished capacity and severely curtailing the testimony of
mental health professionals in criminal proceedings. These sections read
as follows:

Section 28 [Evidence of mental diseases, mental defect or mental disorder]

(a) Evidence of mental disease, mental defect or mental disorder shall not be
admitted to negate the capacity to form any mental state, including, but not
limited to, purpose, intent, knowledge, or malice aforethought, with which the
accused committed the act. Evidence of mental disease, mental defect or mental
disorder is admissible on the issue as to whether the criminal defendant actually
formed any such mental state.

(b) As a matter of public policy there shall be no defense of diminished capacity, diminished responsibility, or irresistible impulse in a criminal action.

(c) This section shall not be applicable to an insanity hearing pursuant to section 1026 or 1429.5.

Section 29. Mental state; Restriction on expert testimony: determination by trier of fact.

In the guilt phase of a criminal action, any expert testifying about a defendant's mental illness, mental disorder or mental defect shall not testify as to whether the defendant had or did not have the required mental states, which include, but are not limited to, purpose, intent, knowledge, or malice aforethought, for the crimes charged. The question as to whether the defendant had or did not have the required mental states shall be decided by the trier of fact.

These constraints on mental health evidence were enacted by the legislature only after the very extensive hearings described above were held. While the introduction of this legislation may have been triggered by the state of high emotion which followed the successful diminished capacity defense in the Dan White case, the length of time consumed by these hearings remove the ultimate passage of the legislation quite far from the passions engendered by that notorious case.

California State Senator David A. Roberti, Chairman of the California Legislature Joint Committee for Revision of the Penal Code, summarized testimony of the many legal and mental health experts before his committee (1980):

No testimony was presented to show as a general rule that mental illness causes criminal behavior. Reference was made to a few specific mental diseases that have a probability of causing criminal behavior, but the present rules on diminished capacity and insanity extend far beyond these specific diseases.

Roberti further states:

Testimony that few mental diseases are causally related to criminal behavior raises serious questions. Are persons we now classify as insane, or diminished in capacity, simply persons who don't meet our expectation of normal? Is the "obsessive compulsive personality" a disease or a quirk? Does it make any difference? Is the percentage of obsessive-compulsive personalities committing crime any greater than the percentage of corporate heads involved in crime? Or the proposition of Justice Fleming, that 99% of any group does not commit crimes. If mental illness and criminal behavior are not as a general rule causally related shouldn't the question of reaching responsibility for "abnormal behavior" be decided by the jury?...Perhaps as New Hampshire, we should have no insanity defense; and diminished capacity should be limited to mental diseases that have been scientifically proven to prevent a person from being able to form intent as legally defined.

More recent literature has contined to raise this problem. Detre (1987) urges psychiatry to abandon false boundaries between mind and brain and to make a commitment to the scientific validation of prevailing theories of the etiology of psychiatric disorders (p. 621). He states:

> Our having come up with many new and not necessarily well-conceptualized theories about the etiology and treatment of psychiatric disorders throughout our relatively short history is not surprising. What is astounding is how little effort has been made to test the validity of our theories and how long we have remained a shelter for bankrupt ideas. Undoubtedly, what appears solely as evidence of our gullibility is also a product of complex sociopolitical interactions. (p. 622)

Levy-Leboyer (1988) indicated that the study of instances in which psychology is applied successfully or unsuccessfully shows that psychology is too easily and too loosely applied (p. 779) and further, "...whenever a psychological problem is an important issue, any theory that presents either a solution or suggestions on how to act in order to solve the problem is adopted without any reservation" (p. 780).

McHugh (1987) describes three special problems in psychiatry for all who wish to move the discipline forward as well as to practice and teach. The first is the sectarianism, which proclaims one approach authentic and abuses others as descriptive or soft-nosed or moribund. A second problem is the ambiguity concerning the special nature of psychiatry that distinguishes it from other specialties, and the third, and according to McHugh, most dismaying problem, is the "troubled discourse between psychiatry and the sciences that relate to it." McHugh's concern appears to us to deal with the problem of the "self" and the difficulties of science in dealing with such a concept, while psychiatrists must deal with some such concept in their daily work. As he notes, "Psychiatrists cannot wait for ultimate explanations." (p. 579) We would not take issue with McHugh on the need for psychiatrists in their daily practice to use whatever knowledge is available and whatever concepts serve them best in helping people deal with their mental or psychological problems. We would, however, wonder how much weight should be given to evidence coming from a discipline which is divisive almost to the point of "cultism" within itself, not clearly discriminable from other specialties, and has difficulty relating to science.

Brady (1988), responding to McHugh, asks what basic science subject matter can be taught and what are the clinical skills to be mastered in the absence of a science base, including those of behavioral and neuroscientists whom he feels appear to be the object of McHugh's plea. Brady states, "To assert that the behavioral science developments have attracted less attention than they deserve, or have exerted less influence on the field of psychiatry than they will ultimately prove capable of, is to understate the case." (p. 582)

Russakoff (1989) states, "As a medical specialty, psychiatry stands out for the disparate number of approaches that are granted credibility by the profession. Although there are other isolated examples in the rest of medicine, where diametrically opposed positions are maintained by opposing but respected camps, psychiatry appears to have raised disagreements and controversy to an art form." (p. 118) If the purpose of psychiatric expert testimony is to "inform" the judge or jury, should those fact finders then not be entitled to hear from all of the various controversial points of view within psychiatry? How many experts might it take to accomplish this purpose? Would the courts be willing to have their exceedingly scarce time taken up with presentation of how a particular situation or issue or evaluation might be viewed from the perspectives of psychoanalysis, behaviorism, and existentialism, and from Adlerian, Jungian, Sullivanian, etc., etc., points of view?

Wakefield (1992) states, "Although the concept of mental disorder is fundamental to theory and practice in the mental health field, no agreed on or adequate analysis of this concept currently exists."

Sechrest (1992), a former president of the Division of Clinical Psychology of the APA, describes the continuing "Psychiatrization" of "almost every foible imaginable" by both psychiatry and clinical psychology. He acknowledges that scientific knowledge in psychology has increased over the past five decades but that while new knowledge has been gained, there has been little if any discarding of the guesswork and half knowledge. He states that clinical psychology cannot agree on its scientific base, cannot agree on what "is" scientific, or even whether clinical psychology should "be" scientific. With regard to professional competence, he notes that a plan for peer review was destroyed before it could even be tried. He avers that clinical psychology lacks standards of practice. In an example that would be amusing if the subject were not so serious, he describes how the APA, in a statement concerning the use of anatomically detailed dolls in forensic evaluations, first states that such use of dolls has no uniform standards, and then in another section states that psychologists who use such assessments should be competent in the use of such techniques. He raises the obvious question: "How can one be competent in an activity for which there are no standards?" We should point out that Sechrest notes that the views expressed in this article are "personal," and undoubtedly not widely shared among clinical psychologists, although not altogether without support.

Kaplan and Miller (1991) express concern that the increasing "biologization" of psychiatry will cause psychiatry to lose any claim to expertise on the way individuals live in the world and respond to particular circumstances and will become experts only on treatment by trial and error with psychoactive medications.

Prochaska (1993) observes that research in psychology has little impact on practice and that the reason for this is that there is no consensus across psychologists. He states that where there is no consensus there is no science.

Wittmann (1988) notes that the reliability and validity of the mental health disciplines have been questioned because they have been described as "soft" sciences that lack the precison and "cumulative" character of many of the natural sciences. He says these difficulties are related to methodological problems and the nature of the subject matter of the psychological sciences (p. 94).

Reppucci and Crosby (1993) cite controversy over the question of when research is ready for dissemination in legal areas such as the courts as one of the major problems within the field of law and psychology.

Melton (1990), while expressing belief that public interest activity is a professional responsibility of psychology, states that the public interest is served as much by delineation of the limits of expertise.

Prochaska (1993) notes that not only does research have little impact on practice within psychology, but that it also has little impact on psychological science. He is critical of case studies, viewing them as useful for generating hypotheses but not for creating consensual validation which is needed to build a science and profession. We should point out that much of the foundation of present day psychiatry was based historically on case reports but many of those hypotheses have been reified into principles without sound research validation.

Golding (1992), writing an introduction to a special issue of *Law and Human Behavior* on expert evidence, indicates the numerous controversies involving psychologist's participation as expert witnesses. He describes these as including the lack of scientifically acceptable theories and methods, impartiality of experts, distortion of scientific expertise because of the adversarial system, and the extent to which expertise is "for hire," among others. He states, "Perhaps the most controversial aspect of psychological expertise (or, for that matter, any expertise) is the problem of knowing when the specialized knowledge is sufficiently reliable and valid to qualify, either scientifically or legally, as expertise. A corollary is the determination of when a person has such expertise." (p. 254) He also observes that mental health practitioners have generally shown great reluctance to accept an affirmative responsibility to expose the limitations of their own expertise. He notes that, among other things, the Specialty Guidelines adopted by the American Psychology-Law Society (Division 41 of the American Psychological Association) require an evaluation of whether the proffered testimony is based on an acceptable application of the underlying scientific literature. This interpretation seems consistent with our insistence that weight, if not admissibility, be based on the state of knowledge on a particular issue as evidenced by the scientific literature.

EXAMINER EFFECTS AND BIAS

"Examiner effects" refers to the ways in which characteristics or behavior of the examiner (including bias) affect psychological evaluations (see Chapter 6, below). There are numerous descriptions and expressions of concern regarding this issue in relation to forensic psychiatry/ psychology (Diamond, 1973; Halleck, 1974; Pollack, 1971; McNeal, 1972; Hardisty, 1973; Robitscher, 1977; Mechanic, 1978; Poythress, 1977; American Psychological Association Task Force, 1978; Saks, 1978; Rappeport, 1976; Robitscher and Williams, 1977; American Psychiatric Association, 1985; Nussbaum et al., 1982. See also *Smith vs. Schlesinger*, 1975; *Estelle vs. Smith*, 1980).

DETERMINATION OF PAST MENTAL CONDITION

Several writers have commented about the difficulties or lack of capability of psychiatrists/psychologists to determine psychological status vis-a-vis legal issues at a time prior to the examination (Silber, 1974; Kubie, 1973; Silber, 1976; Rappeport, 1976; Slovenko, 1983, Pollack, 1971).

PREDICTION

Given the problems and shortcomings described above, one would not expect psychiatrists/psychologists to have a high rate of accuracy in predicing future mental states or behavior. While some authorities (e.g., Pollack, 1971; American Psychological Association Task Force, 1978) describe prediction generally as the weakest area of psychiatry, a significant portion of the literature on prediction has to do with inability to predict "dangerousness" (Howard, 1974; Clanon, 1975; Stone, 1975; Monahan, 1981; Mullen and Reinehr, 1982; Rofman et al., 1980; Steadman, 1978; Monahan, 1978; American Psychiatric Association Amicus Brief in *Tarasoff vs. Regents of the University of California*, 1977).

VALIDITY

Lack of adequate validation research has been noted (Robitscher, 1977; Pollack, 1971; Garfield, 1978; Bank and Poythress, 1982). For more extended discussion on validity, see Chapter 7.

Matarazzo (1990), while criticizing our works for the exclusion of supportive literature, nevertheless in his Presidential address (to the American Psychological Association) states, "...There is no body of research that indicates that psychological assessment across the whole domain is valid or is other than clinical art" (p. 1015). He states further,

"That is, because no such body of research has been yet published, I am not discussing the clinical reliability (and thus, the potential validity) of the personal, social, medical and psychological portrait of the individual that is typically contained in the comprehensive 10-20 page psychological or neuropsychological assessment of a patient involved in the increasing number of cases being adjudicated in our nation's courtrooms" (p. 1012). Matarazzo goes on to assert his "hope" or "expectation" that research will soon be accomplished which will provide evidence for the validity of such testimony. We are quite willing to support this hope, but are not willing to accept hope as a substitute for the actual validating research, nor should any trier of fact. In science, hope is not a substitute for research evidence, and it is obviously questionable to dismiss negative literature that does exist for hypothetical evidence one hopes will be obtained when future research is conducted. (See Volume III for detailed refutation of Matarazzo's critique.)

OVERDIAGNOSIS OF PSYCHOPATHOLOGY

The well-known propensity to overdiagnose psychopathology has been noted (Torrey, 1974; Mechanic, 1978; Poythress, 1977; Sabshin, 1985).

THE GAP

The "gap" refers to the frequent absence of relationship between a diagnosis of a mental disorder and a legal issue, i.e., a diagnosis of schizophrenia does not mean the individual could not distinguish right from wrong. Several writers have noted this problem (Kubie, 1973; Schulman, 1973; Diamond, 1973; Baumrin, 1982; Nussbaum et al., 1982; Henn et al., 1974; Pollack, 1971; Bazelon, 1975; Gunn, 1977; Roesch, 1979). Diamond (1973) has provided an excellent description of the nature of this problem. Continuing discussion of the Brawner decision, Diamond (1973) makes some statements which, considering the eminence of the source, should at the very least be startling to the courts and legislatures which for decades have blithely accorded to psychiatrists qualification as experts in matters relevant to the criminal justice system. Diamond states:

> In short, Durham, as does Brawner, and every other modern rule of criminal responsibility of the mentally ill, expects that the expert can make a precise diagnostic formulation; that he can communicate the basis for that formulation to the trier of fact so that a decision can be made as to whether the defendant is "mad" or "bad"; and that for those defendants who are found to be "mad," effective treatment can be provided in some sort of non-punitive institution.
>
> I submit that today the psychiatrist is unable to perform effectively any of these tasks well; further, that he does them less well now than he did 18 years ago

when Durham was adopted; and still further, that he is not going to do any better under any variant of the American Law Institute formulation, no matter how legally sophisticated it may be presented.

Diamond gives as his principle reason for this dismal prediction the inability of psychiatrists to provide accurate diagnosis, as he states is the case in other fields of medicine. Diamond states further:

> Unless the psychiatric expert can testify as to exactly what condition the defendant suffers from and can give a particular description of the manner in which the abnormality affects those mental and emotional processes relevant to the criminal act, he will have no credibility before the jury; however, the psychiatric expert if he is scrupulously honest, can seldom so testify. His evidence should rather sound something like this:
>
> > I think, but I am not certain, that the defendant has a mental disease, or an abnormality, or what merely may be a normal variation, which has substantially affected his mental or emotional processes in ways which I find difficult to understand and explain to you and this has possibly, but maybe not, substantially affected his behavior controls in ways which could be, but are not necessarily, relevant to criminal act of which he is accused and which, as yet, I am not even sure he has committed.
>
> If this is the true expert opinion, it will have little significance to the jury no matter how it is fleshed in with clinical details (p. 114).

It may be worth noting that within forensic psychiatry, Dr. Diamond occupied a pre-eminent position and was a winner of the Isaac Ray Award for his contributions to forensic psychiatry.

Frances et al. (1990), discussing possible impact of DSM-IV on issues beyond its intended clinical, research, educational and statistical uses, note the reality that DSM diagnoses will be used in other areas, such as disability and reimbursement decisions. They state, "Perhaps the arena of greatest possible abuse is the assessment of criminal responsibility, in which the presence of a diagnosable DSM disorder should not be regarded as sufficient to confer the sick role" (p. 1442). They also note that an expanded statement on cautions in the use of the manual may be necessary (see Chapter 4). (Frances is the Chairperson of the DSM-IV Committee.) We think that if the diagnosis is not sufficient, the only alternative appears to be the psychological "portrait" discussed by Matarazzo (supra) which he says lacks validation through research. One can clearly make a strong argument that under these conditions the mental health professions have little, if anything, to offer on this issue.

STATEMENTS RE FORENSIC ACTIVITIES

Statements abound in the scientific and professional literature that are critical of the participation of psychiatrists or psychologists as expert witness generally or in regard to specific issues, (e.g., prior psychological condition, future psychological condition, etc.) (Howard, 1974; Silber, 1974; Halleck, 1974; Torrey, 1974; Pollack, 1971; Meehl, 1971; Schulman, 1973; Diamond, 1973; Robitscher and Williams, 1977; Stein, 1979; Halleck, 1969; American Medical News, 1979; Bank and Poythress, 1982; Pasewark, 1981; Wesley, 1981; Petrella and Poythress, 1983; Sabshin, 1985; Coleman 1984; Simon, 1983).

Grisso (1987), a former president of Division 41, the Division of Psychology and Law of the American Psychological Association, notes that while the involvement of many psychologists is motivated to some extent by desires to improve the quality of justice or test the application of their science to real world issues, nevertheless the legal forum is a market and that neither scientific nor economic issues can be ignored. He expresses concern about two problems in particular: one, the possibility that the legal system will reward mediocrity; and second, the schism between researchers and practitioners. He includes in the points discussed in the body of his article how forensic assessments of the past have fallen short of psychology's standards and the types of research that must be done to reach those standards. He observes there is little empirical information about the quality of forensic evaluations by psychologists and that many mental health professionals, legal scholars and courts have complained about the irrelevance, intrusiveness or insufficiencies of mental health examiners' assessments and testimony, although he notes that these observations concern mental health professionals generally and not psychologists specifically. He cites other writers to the effect that normative practice in forensic psychology is not what it ought to be. He states:

> When assessment models that have served psychologists well in clinical settings are applied without modification in response to legal questions, they guide the assessment process toward clinical concerns, for example, symptom description, etiology, and diagnoses....The problem comes, of course, when the psychologist attempts to infer from the results of these clinical evaluations answers to forensic questions about human capacities and abilities. Often such assessments are doomed from the start, because the specific legal constructs that the court must address—ranging from the various legal competencies...to dangerousness—are quite different from general clinical constructs of personality and psychopathology. (p. 834)

The reader may recognize this statement as the problem we have generally referred to as "the gap." Grisso stresses the need for research to translate psychological knowledge for forensic application; that is, research that will relate principles from basic psychology to legally relevant questions. Again, this appears to support our concept of the gap. Still further along the lines of the gap, he states:

> In some cases, what is needed is research that relates psychologists' traditional clinical instruments to specific legal questions. One example of this need was

reflected in a recent survey that showed that intelligence tests and personality and projective instruments are widely used by psychologists to evaluate parents in child custody cases (Keilin & Bloom [1986]). These results are not startling until one considers that there is almost no empirical information concerning how to use parents' Wechsler or MMPI results to make inferences about their abilities to perform specific parenting functions. (p. 835)

He states further:

The psychologist's open recognition of limits in forensic practice faces a negative incentive in the context of the legal forum. The psychologist must anticipate an increase in the number of times that he or she might have to say to the attorney who seeks testimony, 'I'm sorry, but my technology and empirical base do not allow me to testify confidently on that matter.' So saying, the psychologist may fear that the attorney will turn to other psychologists or psychiatrists whose less rigorous empirical standards do not restrict them from forming an opinion on the same issues. (p. 836)

He points out the obvious, that this then poses a threat of financial loss for more empirically-based practitioners (p. 836).

Grisso also urges psychologists to educate consumers of information in legal arenas to cause them to demand a higher standard for psychologist assessments than has been the case in the past. We are somewhat comforted to find such a statement coming from an individual of Grisso's stature, which we feel, at minimum, supports the aims of this book, whether or not Grisso would agree with our method. Grisso does indicate his belief that psychology can improve and do better.

Volpe (1989) points out that "even among psychiatrists themselves, there is no common agreement on the meanings of the terms mentally ill or mentally disordered or the criteria that designate various types of psychoses." She states, "Although differences among professionals may seem inevitable, varying interpretations may have so much latitude that any possibility of consistency and predictability is negated....In light of the complexities of both legal and medical jargon, the task of understanding such testimony and arriving at a 'sound' decision is a very difficult one." She further notes that psychiatrists' value judgments are likely to reflect various biases and attitudes concerning law and justice, which allow the psychiatrist to apply his own standard of proof in the absence of any articulated standards.

Yuille (1989) evaluates arguments for and against testimony based on clinical assessments and generalizations drawn from psychological research. He concludes that there are two fundamental problems for psychologists in the role of expert, stating, "First, the types of assessments clinicians are asked to make (e.g., concerning the accused's mental state at the time of committing the offense) may exceed the capacity of the discipline; such assessments are problematic. Second, the research foundation that psychologists employ in court does not always apply to the court situation in the way the experts imply; the application of laboratory research findings to real world context is sometimes premature" (p. 181). He admonishes psychologists to adopt a more conservative response to requests to provide expert evidence. In his article, Yuille makes reference to the controversy created by an article in *Science* (Faust and Ziskin, 1988) and the responses of Matarazzo and Fowler as presidents of the American Psychological Association. He states the report of the APA response was too brief to permit an evaluation of the counter-arguments, but "at present, the empirical foundation of Faust and Ziskin's conclusions is uncontested" (p. 193). The reader, however, should be aware that some writers have criticized the *Science* article.

Smith (1989) observes that the courts have now entered the age of the mental health expert and rely on a very broad range of "informed speculation" which is "too often more 'speculation' than 'informed.'" Utilizing as an example the now notorious case of *Barefoot vs. Estelle* (op. cit), he states:

> In what may be the most bizarre justification for permitting mental health testimony, the Court noted that such testimony was not always wrong, just usually wrong. It also argued that mental health experts had not been proved to be *less* reliable than others in predicting dangerousness. *Barefoot* hints that courts are looking to mental health experts for something other than scientific expertise, perhaps for the illusion of being able to answer questions that in fact cannot be answered. (p. 146)

We would of course add that it is irresponsible for those claiming to operate from a scientific base to contribute to such an illusion. We should note that Smith does state (p. 146) that increased use of mental health experts has served to improve the quality of justice frequently but that the courts, however, have not carefully controlled the limits of this testimony. He notes that parties to litigation do not expect or want experts to be neutral or impartial. Rather, they want evidence favorable to their side, that is, a partisan expert. He recites a statement from a noted trial attorney, "I would go into a lawsuit with an objective, uncommitted, independent expert about as willingly as I would occupy a foxhole with a couple of non-combatant soldiers" (p. 151). He notes that in child custody cases, the mental health experts may be required to give an opinion on what will be in the best interests of the child, which he describes as "a prediction of such complexity that surely most palm readers would be reluctant to make it." He makes a point that the courts do not uniformly apply rules of admissibility, but are inconsistent, using as an example the contrast between courts that reject some of the various new "syndrome" types of evidence with their willingness to admit predictions of dangerousness. He says this is inconsistent in that prediction of dangerousness may be even more unreliable than the syndrome evidence. He argues this occurs because some types of information have become so ingrained in the legal system that it would be difficult to do without them and notes, "This testimony, like cigarettes, would not be permitted if now introduced for the first time, but it is so thoroughly a part of the system that it cannot now be banned" (p. 161).

Smith discusses the heavy reliance the courts place on cross-examination as a way of assessing mental health testimony, but asserts that a high level of confidence in cross-examination is not always well placed. In this regard, he describes difficulties in presenting validity and reliability questions to juries. He also notes that very confident witnesses may simply deny the issues of reliability and validity. He also comments on the difficulties of cross-examination in trying to establish the basis of clinical judgments, let alone their validity or reliability, noting how frustrating this can be for attorneys (p. 165). He also comments on the role of hidden value judgments in testimony on ultimate issues (p. 166).

Lanyon (1986) introduces his article as follows: "It is by now no secret that widespread dissatisfaction exists with the use of traditional psychological evaluation procedures in court-related settings (e.g., Poythress, 1981). Such procedures have often been justified on the basis of the psychologist's 'experience', a justification that nowadays has diminishing credibility in the absence of empirical back-up" (p. 260). He then notes that many of the issues on which psychologists have been asked to use evaluation expertise are not personality-related questions at all, and that many psychologists have simply continued to do what they have always done in terms of administering the more or less standard personality assessment batteries. Lanyon does make the point that psychology has a technical basis for making important contributions to the court situation, but that some clarifying and sorting and a substantial amount of new development is needed. He makes some suggestions as to how to proceed along those lines.

Bloom and Rogers (1987) note further, "Negative views of forensic psychiatry are not confined to public opinion. The psychiatric profession itself is actively debating the role of forensic psychiatry and its effect on the profession as a whole" (p. 847). They further state, "The fact that statutes call for psychiatric diagnoses and determinations of dangerousness does not mean that psychiatrists must come forward to make these determinations" (p. 847). They further note, regarding prediction of dangerousness, essentially that absent proof that psychiatrists are able to make such predictions in a valid manner, they simply should not do so, as it gives a misleading air of science to what is intentionally or unwittingly the psychiatrist's own moral judgment. We would amplify this admonition. Why should a requirement for proof that psychiatrists are able to make predictions be limited to dangerousness? Why should this not be required with regard to any area in which psychiatrists make predictions in legal matters?

Showalter and Fitch (1987) state, "...the involvement of psychiatry in the criminal justice process has been the subject of significant controversy. At the heart of this controversy is the view held by many that psychiatry is too imprecise a science to be permitted the degree of influence it has on determinations of criminal responsibility—that many psychiatrists are ill-prepared to address this and related issues and too often exceed the bounds of their expertise in the opinions they render."

Rogers and Ewing (1989) argue that the proscription against experts rendering an ultimate opinion in criminal cases involving insanity defenses is only a "quick and cosmetic fix" with more apparent than real value. They note that this proscription is not only unwarranted and unnecessary but also unworkable in practice for a number of reasons. The reasons they argue are: (1) clinical judgment and clinical observations are inseparable; (2) ultimate opinions are an inevitable outcome of the forensic assessment process; and (3) no meaningful distinction can be made between ultimate opinions and ordinary expert opinions.

They go on, however, to state additionally that their observations in support of ultimate opinion testimony are not necessarily a defense of current practices. They indicate that expert testimony based on insanity evaluations requires critical examination. They point out several problems in current practice. One of these is the obvious and well known problem of "hired guns." They assert that the prevalence of hired guns is difficult to ascertain. They note that another problem worthy of investigation is the possible relationship between the attitudes of mental health experts and their conclusory opinions, indicating that the only systematic data gathered on this issue suggest there may well be a relationship between attitudinal bias and outcome in insanity assessments. They also observe, however, that the data on this issue is limited.

Rogers and Ewing describe the accuracy of mental health experts' understanding of legal standards as another problem. They also raise the issue of the validity of forensic decision-making, taking the position that clinical decision-making is best reproduced as a linear model and they state, "Simply increasing the amount of clinical information available to a psychologist does not appear to improve the reliability or validity of their judgments" (p. 370). Thus, they support the literature we have cited on this topic in Chapter 5. They suggest the consideration of strategies for reducing the experts' over-reliance on global or quasi-configural judgments. They state, for example, "Forensic conclusions can be glorified under the vague and unwieldy rubric of 'clinical judgment' or 'clinical impression'. Such judgments are not only empirically unjustified but do not allow triers-of-fact to understand either the reasoning or the evidence behind the experts' conclusions regarding the defendant's diagnosis and cognitive or volitional capacities." (p. 370)

Rogers and Ewing further note the need for research examining the usefulness of specific psychological measures in the assessment of criminal responsibility. They make some recommendations for improving the adequacy of insanity evaluations, including standardization of such evaluations. They also suggest establishing higher standards for mental health experts, citing as an example the recent legislation in Alaska requiring that psychologists who testify on criminal responsibility be diplomates in forensic psychology. They note, however, as well they should, "The relationship of such standards to the quality of insanity evaluations in expert testimony could and should be investigated." (p. 373) As we have noted, however (see Chapter 9), there are not to our knowledge any plans for such research to be conducted—at least by the respective certifying boards in psychiatry and psychology.

Phillips et al. (1988) state, "Forensic psychiatry is a field that is long on controversy but short on data." (p. 605) In their study, Phillips et al. gave as their best estimate that 1% of the "schizophrenic persons" in Alaska are arrested for violent crimes each year. This is in comparison to a rate of 0.5% of all of the entire remaining population without "schizophrenia" in Alaska. Arguably, one could say that schizophrenics are twice as likely to be arrested for a violent crime as non-schizophrenics and that, therefore, there is a relationship between schizophrenia and violent crime. On the other hand, the obvious fact is that 99% of "schizophrenic" persons are not arrested for violent crimes each year, which would seem to argue pretty strongly against "schizophrenia" as the responsible factor in the commission of violent crimes and would seem consistent with the findings of an earlier study of Henn et al. (1974). (Author's note: When we report on studies which use the term "schizophrenia" or other diagnostic labels, we are following the language of the article and not necessarily endorsing the concept.)

Melton (1990) while indicating that organized psychology should play a role in developing and providing expressions of scientific consensus where such exists to inform policy makers, states, "At the same time, I believe that the public interest is served as much by delineation of the limits of our expertise as by the sharing of what we do know about social issues." (p. 316)

Zusman (1990) states:

> The scientific foundation of mental health expert testimony is seriously deficient. It has not been possible to find any published authorities who, after reviewing the scientific bases of mental health expert testimony, report that such testimony is adequately founded (Though certainly some aspects of testimony, those primarily involving observation and classification of current behavior

involve fewer assumptions and untested hypotheses and are therefor more accepted).

Even defenders of the current approach to mental health expert testimony seem to agree that more and better research is needed to support the validity of expert opinions and they usually express the hope or belief that such research will soon be forthcoming. Presumably for want of anything better (as well as other reasons), the proponents believe the current approach should continue.

By contrast, there are a number of well known reviews (indeed just about all of the reviewers who have set out to examine the quality of scientific support seem to have come to the same conclusion) which strongly make the point that the issues on which mental health experts usually testify are lacking in empirical support." (p. 6)

Repucci and Crosby (1993) note that one of the major difficulties in the law and psychology relationship is the question of when research is ready for dissemination through expert testimony in the courtroom. They cite Faigman (1989, *Emory Law Journal*, 38, 1005-1095) to the effect that the standard for judging usefulness of social science findings should be their scientific strength, the ability of social scientists to provide valid answers to the questions posed. This issue of when the data are sufficiently valid, consistent, and generalizable to be applicable to the real world is also raised in an exchange between Elliott (1991a, 1991b) and Ellsworth (1991).

Roesch et al. (1991) discussing amicus curiae briefs, note the difficulties of obtaining accurate and unbiased summaries of scientific literature in the adversary system and the difficulties of judges and juries to deal with scientific evidence in an adversary system. They state, "Courts frequently rely on the statements of a small number of expert witnesses to assess consensus, often resulting in a situation in which two experts reach different conclusions about whether a particular finding is well established." (p. 5)

Golding (1992) takes note of the "great" reluctance of mental health experts to accept an affirmative responsibility to expose the limitations of their own expertise. This observation, along with the issues of scientific development adequate for forensic purposes may illustrate the raison d'etre of this book. Most treatises, and certainly most witnesses in our experience, emphasize claimed knowledge. It is essential that lawyers have the information with which to compel (or provide) the counterbalancing literature.

Brekke et al. (1991) take note that the appropriateness of adversarial procedures for presenting scientific evidence has been questioned. They describe the usual problems of bias, witness "shopping," and the battle of experts. They cite an earlier study (Sheppard and Vidmar, 1989) to the effect that witnesses interviewed prior to testifying by an adversarial attorney deliver more biased testimony than experts whose prior interview was done by a non-adversarial attorney. One is reminded of the term "steering a witness" sometimes used by lawyers.

Otto (1989) describes a substantial body of literature illustrating the operation of both conscious, intentional bias and unconscious, unintentional bias in mental health expert testimony and asserts that the latter may provide the greater threat of the two.

Walsh (1987) states, "Clinical training, based on a medical tradition focused on psychopathology, is skewed toward assessment of disorders, conflicts, and deficits with little attention to positive aspects of functioning and almost no contact with non-clinical families" (p. 496). Walsh notes that personal and theoretical biases strongly influence clinicians' judgments and observations with regard to family variables that may be relevant in custody determinations. Walsh also points out the need for adequate base rate data about normal families and expresses some concern that absent such data, psychopathological interpretations may occur where none are actually warranted.

Melton and Wilcox (1989) express concern that psychologists must be careful not to exceed the bounds of their expertise. With regard to the "best interest" standard, they note that these issues require judgments about the desirable outcomes for children and the characteristics of responsible parents. They state, "Although psychology may contribute to an understanding of likely outcomes, the determination of the 'best' outcome involves moral and legal judgments properly reserved to the courts. Unfortunately, even knowledge about the empirical questions often is still limited."

Wittmann (1988) notes that the assumption that clinicians think about individual and family problems in a scientific manner is an important part of the relationship between the court and the expert witness. He notes that the mental health disciplines have been described as soft sciences lacking both precision and the cumulative character of many of the natural sciences, which raises questions about the validity and reliability of mental health observations and inferences. He further notes that these difficulties are related to methodological problems and particularly the nature of the subject matter. He states, "Due to our continued struggle for a common clinical language, our concepts appear alarmingly fluid to the court system and tend to unexplainably 'fade away'." (p. 94) He also notes that because of their special influence on the lives of children in family court dispositions, it is important that clinicians be aware of the limitations of their science. He also notes that only recently have there been widespread attempts to empirically validate the effectiveness and the validity of the diverse concepts of family therapy. He notes that "family-oriented clinicians are asked to testify in an adversarial arena that demands a level of precision and empirical foundation from a field usually unable to offer these things." (p. 98) He warns the expert to be prepared to provide a summary of the research in his field that supports his conclusion.

Bolocofsky (1989) notes that there is broad support for some form of regulation of both child custody evaluators and child custody evaluations beyond that which currently exists. He states, "The present system of mental health regulation primarily relying on educational training, experience, and examinations in general psychology, social work or medicine, has not been found to bear any significant relationship to competence, particularly in forensic mental health services." (p. 210) Further:

> The over-reliance of mental health professionals on questionable sources of data and the inadequacies of clinical judgment employed in child custody evaluations strongly point to the needs for standards governing the form of evaluation and the limits of testimony. At the very least, mental health professionals should be required to identify the sources and limitations of their data and conclusions and justify the use of psychological measuring devices through presentation of their psychometric properties relative to child custody determinations. Given the current scientific status of the mental health professions, ultimate opinions should be limited to those conclusions with adequate empirical support. (p. 210)

Given the foregoing four references, one wonders how much weight courts should give to evaluations by mental health professionals in such serious matters as custody disputes.

Dawes (1994), in a book titled *House of Cards,* describes expertise of mental health professionals as "myths." He criticizes professional psychologists for ignoring existing research in their practice. Dawes is professor of social and decision sciences at Carnegie-Mellon University and a widely recognized researcher on psychological evaluation and decision making. This book has been praised by other highly regarded psychologists, including university professors, directors of law and psychology training programs, president of the American Psychological Society, and a past president of the American Psychological Association. We mention these credentials and praise to indicate that Dawes is not some off-the-wall lunatic, but is highly regarded by reputable people in psychology. We think this is useful because we think he is, if anything, more critical of professional psychology than we have been. Thus, his book and the praise it has received may serve as another counterbalance to those who assert that there is little support for our views among psychologists. Indeed, Dawes cites our book in his.

SUMMARY

Well over 100 references from the legal and scientific and professional literature provide substantial evidence that there is doubt as to the level of expertise, or even the existence of expertise, that the mental health professions can provide to aid in the determination of legal issues. The remainder of the book contains more than 1500 references which, in more detail, cast doubt on such expertise. Because the law regarding expert evidence appears to be somewhat ambiguous at the time of this writing, no position is taken regarding the admissibility of psychiatric and psychological evidence. There are some indications that it should be admitted only where it has demonstrated adequate validity. It may not be unreasonable for lawyers to challenge admission on this and other grounds provided in this book. In any event, a lawyer can use these negative views by members of both the legal and mental health professions to disabuse triers of fact of any illusions they may have (or be persuaded to have) regarding the degree of credibility to be afforded these experts.

Perhaps the most eloquent description of the status of mental health experts is provided by an attorney instructing both lawyers and mental health experts regarding direct examination: "In short, go heavy on qualifications, short on facts."

REFERENCES

Adams, H.E. (1984). The pernicious effects of theoretical orientations in clinical psychology. *The Clinical Psychologist*, Summer, 90-94.

Alexander, M.P. (1982). Traumatic brain injury. In D.F. Benson and D. Blumer (Eds.), *Psychiatric Aspects of Neurological Disease* (pp. 219-249). Vol. 2. New York: Grune and Stratton.

American Bar Association Standards For Criminal Justice, 71.1 etc. (1980) (Adopted by the ABA House of Delegates on August 7, 1984). 2d edition.

American Psychiatric Association Statement on the Insanity Defense, December, 1982.

American Psychiatric Association (1974). Task Force Report 8, *Clinical Aspects of the Violent Individual*, July, 28.

American Psychological Association (1978). Report of the task force on the role of psychology in the criminal justice system. *American Psychologist, 33*, 1099-1113.

Bank, S.C. and Poythress, N.G., Jr. (1982). The elements of persuasion in expert testimony. *The Journal of Psychiatry and Law*, Summer, 173-204.

Baumrin, B.H. (1982). A philosophers view of ethical issues in forensic psychiatry. *The Journal of Psychiatry and Law, 10*, 29-39.

Bazelon, D. (1981) *APA Monitor*, October, *10*, 5.

Bazelon, D.L. (1974). Psychiatrists and the adversary process. *Scientific American, 230*, 18-23.

Bazelon, D.L. (1975). A jurist's view of psychiatry. *The Journal of Psychiatry and Law, 3*, 175-190.

Bersoff, D.N. (1988). Should subjective employment devices be scrutinized? *American Psychologist, 43*, 1016-1018.

Bersoff, D. (1992). Judicial deference to nonlegal decisionmakers: Imposing simplistic solutions on problems of cognitive complexity in mental disability law. *SMU Law Review, 46*, 329-372.

Bloom, J.D., and Rogers, J.L. (1987). The legal basis of forensic psychiatry: Statutorily mandated psychiatric diagnoses. *American Journal of Psychiatry, 144*, 847-853.

Bolocofsky, D.N. (1989). Use and abuse of mental health experts in child custody determinations. *Behavioral Sciences & the Law, 7*, 197-213.

Brady, J.V. (1988). Editorial: Psychiatry and its poor relations: "Less than warmly embraced, more than misunderstood," a response to Paul McHugh. *The Journal of Nervous and Mental Disease, 176*, 581-584.

Brekke, N.J., Enko, P.J., Clavet, G., and Seelau, E. (1991). Of juries and court-appointed experts. *Law and Human Behavior, 15*, 451-475.

Brody, E.B. (1985). Patients rights: A cultural challenge to western psychiatry, *American Journal of Psychiatry, 142*, 58-62.

Burger, W.E. (1964). Psychiatrists, Lawyers, and the Courts, 28 Fed. Prob., 3, 7.

Clanon, T.L. (1975). *Los Angeles Times*, December.

Coleman, L. (1984). *The Reign of Error.* Boston: Beacon Press.

Dawes, R.M. (1994). *House of Cards: Psychology and Psychotherapy Built on Myth.* New York: The Free Press.

Delman, R.P. (1981) Participation by psychologists in insanity defense proceedings: An advocacy. *The Journal of Psychiatry and Law, 9*, 247-262.

Detre, T. (1987). The future of psychiatry. *American Journal of Psychiatry, 145*, 621-625.

Diamond, B.L. (1961). Criminal responsibility of the mentally ill. *Stanford Law Review, 14.*

Diamond, B.L. (1973a). From Durham to Brawner, A futile journey. *Washington University Law Quarterly, 57*, 109-125.

Diamond. B.L. (1973b). The psychiatrist as advocate. *The Journal of Psychiatry and Law, 1*, 5-21.

Diamond, B.L. (1974). The psychiatric prediction of dangerousness, *University of Pennsylvania Law Review, 123*, 439-451.

Dienstbier, R.A. (1977). Exceptions to the rule. *Law and Human Behavior, 1*, 207-216.

Dix, G.D. (1971). Psychological abnormality as a factor in grading criminal liability: Diminished capacity, diminished responsibility and the like. *The Journal of Criminal Law, Criminology and Police Science, 72,* 313-335.

Dolin, M. (1979). The trouble with psychiatric testimony in the courtroom. *San Francisco Examiner,* February 4, 1979.

Elliott, R. (1991a). Social science data and the APA: The *Lockhart* brief as a case in point. *Law and Human Behavior, 15,* 59-76.

Elliott, R. (1991b). Response to Ellsworth. *Law and Human Behavior, 15,* 91-94.

Ellsworth, P.C. (1991). To tell what we know or wait for Godot? *Law and Human Behavior, 15,* 77-90.

Ennis, B.J., and Litwack, T.R. (1974). Psychiatry and the presumption of expertise: Flipping coins in the courtroom, *California Law Review, 62,* 693-752.

Faust, D. (1985). Declarations versus investigations: The case for the special reasoning abilities and capabilities of the expert witness in psychology/psychiatry. *The Journal of Psychiatry and Law, 13,* 33-60.

Fincher, C. (1973). Personnel testing and public policy. *American Psychologist, 28,* 489-496.

Fishman, D.B., and Neigher, W.D. (1982). American psychology in the '80s: Who will buy? *American Psychologist, 37,* 533-546.

Frances, A., Pincus, H.A., Widiger, T.A., Davis, W.W., and First, M.B. (1990). DSM-IV: Work in progress. *American Journal of Psychiatry, 147,* 1439-1448.

Furlong, F.W. (1981). Determinism and free will: Review of the literature. *American Journal of Psychiatry, 38,* 435-439.

Garfield, S.L. (1978). Research problems in clinical diagnosis. *Journal of Consulting and Clinical Psychology, 46,* 596-607.

Golding, S.L. (1992). Increasing the reliability, validity, and relevance of psychological expert evidence. *Law and Human Behavior, 16,* 253-256.

Goodwin, D.W. (1984). Review of the book, *Disease and Its Control* by R.B. Hudson. *American Journal of Psychiatry, 141,* 1001-1002.

Grisso, T. (1987). The economic and scientific future of forensic psychological assessment. *American Psychologist, 42,* 831-839.

Gunn (1977). Criminal behavior and mental disorder. *British Journal of Psychiatry, 130,* 317-329.

Halleck, S.L. (1969). The psychiatrist and the legal process. *Psychology Today, 2.*

Halleck, S.L. (1974). A troubled view of current trends in forensic psychiatry. *The Journal of Psychiatry and Law, 2,* 135-58.

Hardisty, J.H. (1973). Mental illness: A legal fiction. *Washington Law Review, 48*, 735-762.

Havens, L.L. (1981). Twentieth century psychiatry: A view from the sea. *The American Journal of Psychiatry, 138*, 1279-1287.

Henn, F.A., Herjanic, M., and Vanderpearl, R.H. (1974). Forensic psychiatry: Diagnosis and responsibility. *The Journal of Nervous and Mental Disease, 162*, 423-429.

Howard, J.W., Jr. (1974). Law enforcement in an urban society. *American Psychologist, 29*, 223-232.

Joint statement of the American Medical Association and the American Psychiatric Association Regarding the Insanity Defense. (1985). *American Journal of Psychiatry, 142*, 1135-1136.

Kaplan, L.V., and Miller, R.D. (1991). On psychiatry and its disavowal of mind: Legal and cultural implications. *The Journal of Psychiatry and Law, Fall/Winter*, 237-278.

Kimble, G.A. (1984). Psychology's two cultures. *American Psychologist, 39*, 833-839.

King, R.D., and Leli, D. (1979). Teaching mental health and law: A reply to Goldenburg. *Professional Psychology, 10*, 771-772.

Klerman, G. (1979). *American Psychological Association Monitor*, November, 9.

Kubie, L.S. (1973). The Ruby case: Who or what was on trial. *Journal of Psychiatry and Law, 1*, 475-491.

Lanyon, R.I. (1986). Psychological assessment procedures in court-related settings. *Professional Psychology: Research and Practice, 17*, 260-268.

Levy, A.M. (1978). Child custody determination—A proposed psychiatric methodology and its resultant case typology. *Journal of Psychiatry and Law, 6*, 189-214.

Levy-Leboyer, C. (1988). Success and failure in applying psychology. *The American Psychologist, 43*, 779-785.

Matarazzo, J.D. (1990). Psychological assessment versus psychological testing: Validation from Binet to the school, clinic, and courtroom. *American Psychologist, 45*, 999-1017.

McHugh, P.R., (1987). Editorial: Psychiatry and its scientific relatives: "A little more than kin and a little less than kind." *The Journal of Nervous and Mental Disease, 175*, 579-583.

McNeal, H.J. (1972). The value of a psychiatrist. In C.H. Wecht (Ed.), *Legal Medicine Annual* (pp. 303-313). New York: Appleton-Century-Crofts.

Mechanic, D. (1978). Explanations of mental illness: An editorial. *The Journal of Nervous and Mental Disease, 166*, 381-386.

Meehl, P.E., (1971). Law and the fireside inductions: Some reflections of a clinical psychologist. *Journal of Social Issues, 27.*

Melton, G.B. (1990). Law, science, and humanity: The normative foundation of social science in law. *Law and Human Behavior, 14,* 315-332.

Melton, G.B., and Wilcox, B.L. (1989). Changes in family law and family life. *American Psychologist, 44,* 1213-1216.

Monahan, J. (1981a). *The clinical prediction of violent behavior, a monograph series.* U.S. Department of Health and Human Services, National Institute of Mental Health, Rockville, Maryland.

Monahan, J. (1978) *The prediction of violent criminal behavior: A methodological critique and prospectus in deterrence and incapacitation: Estimating the effects of criminal sanctions on crime rates.* National Academy of Sciences, 1978, 244-269.

Morse, S. (1978) Law and mental health professionals. *Professional Psychology, 9,* 389-399.

Morse, S.J. (1982). The morality and practicality of the insanity defense. The Law Center, University of Southern California. 27-36 (published in the December 1982 issue of *Litigation*, published by the ABA).

Mullen, J.N., and Reinehr, R.C. (1982). Predicting dangerousness of maximum security forensic mental patients. *The Journal of Psychiatry and Law, 10,* 223-231.

Nussbaum, K., Puig, J.G., and Arizaga, J.R. (1981-1982). Relevance of objective assessment to medical legal psychiatry. *The American Journal of Forensic Psychiatry, 2,* 17-20.

Otto, R.K. (1989). Bias and expert testimony of mental health professionals in adversarial proceedings: A preliminary investigation. *Behavioral Sciences and the Law, 7,* 267-273.

Page, S., and Yates, E. (1974). Fear of evaluation and reluctance to participate in research. *Professional Psychology, 3,* 400-408.

Pasewark, R.A. (1981). Insanity plea: A review of the research literature. *The Journal of Psychiatry and Law, 9,* 357-401.

Penal Code of the State of California. Section 28: Evidence of mental disease, defense of diminished capacity. Section 29: Mental state. Restriction on expert testimony, determination by triers of fact.

Perlin, M.L. (1991). Power imbalances in therapeutic and forensic relationships. *Behavioral Sciences and the Law, 9,* 111-128.

Petrella, R.C., and Poythress, N.G., Jr. (1983). The quality of forensic evaluations: An interdisciplinary study. *Journal of Consulting and Clinical Psychology, 51,* 76-85.

Plotkin, L. (1972). Coal handling, steam fitting, psychology, and law. *The American Psychologist, 129,* 202-204.

Phillips, M.R., Wolf, A.S., and Coons, D.J. (1988). Psychiatry and the criminal justice system: Testing the myths. *American Journal of Psychiatry, 145,* 605-610.

Pollack, S. (1971). Principles of forensic psychiatry for psychiatric-legal opinion-making. In C.H. Wecht (Ed.), *Legal Medicine Annual.* New York: Appleton-Century-Crofts.

Poythress, N.G., Jr. (1977). Mental health expert testimony: Current problems. *Journal of Psychiatry and Law, 5,* 201-227.

Prochaska, J.O. (1993). I think we can. *Professional Psychology: Research and Practice, 24,* 250-251.

Rappeport, J.R. (1976). The psychiatrist as expert witness. *Medical World News,* October 25.

Reppucci, N.D., and Crosby, C.A. (1993). Law, psychology and children. *Law and Human Behavior, 17,* 1-10.

Rheingold, P.D. (1968). The basis of medical testimony. *Examination of Medical Experts.* New York: Matthew Bender and Company.

Roberti, D.A. (1980). Who is criminally insane? *Prosecutor's Brief, 5,* 7-9.

Robinson, D.N. (1980). *Psychology and Law: Can Justice Survive the Social Sciences?* New York: Oxford University Press.

Robitscher, J. (1977). Isaac Ray Lecture I: Psychiatric labelling, predicting, and stigmatizing. Isaac Ray Lecture II: Psychiatric Control of Behavior. *Journal of Psychiatry and Law, 5,* 333-404.

Robitscher, J., and Williams, R. (1977). Should psychiatrists get out of the courtroom? *Psychology Today, 11,* 85.

Roesch, R. (1979). Determining competency to stand trial: An examination of evaluation procedures in an institutional setting. *Journal of Consulting and Clinical Psychology, 47,* 542-550.

Roesch, R., and Golding, S.L. (1985). Who is competent to stand trial? The lawyer's evolving role, *Trial, 21,* 40-45.

Roesch, R., Golding, S.L., Hans, V.P., and Repucci, N.D. (1991). Social science and the courts: The role of amicus curiae briefs. *Law and Human Behavior, 15,* 1-11.

Rofman, E.S., Askinazi, C., and Fant, E. (1980). The prediction of dangerous behavior in emergency civil commitment. *American Journal of Psychiatry, 137,* 1061-64.

Rogers, R., and Ewing, C.P. (1989). Ultimate opinion proscriptions: A cosmetic fix and a plea for empiricism. *Law and Human Behavior, 13,* 357-374.

Rorer, L.G., and Widiger, T.A. (1983). Personality structure and assessment. *Annual Review of Psychology, 34,* 431-63.

Rubinstein, L. S. (1982). *Mental Disability Law Reporter, 6,* 352.

Russakoff, L.M. (1989). Book review. *The Journal of Nervous and Mental Disease, 177,* 118-119.

Sabshin, M. *Napa Register*, February 25, 1985.

Saks, M.J. (1978). Social psychological contribution to a legislative subcommittee on organ and tissue transplant. *American Psychologist*, 680-689.

Sarason, S.B. (1981). An asocial psychology and a misdirected clinical psychology. *American Psychologist, 36,* 827-837.

Schulman, R.E. (1973). To be or not to be an expert. *Washington University Law Quarterly*, 57-66.

Sechrest, L.B. (1985a). Presidential address. Division Twelve, Clinical Psychology, American Psychological Association Convention.

Sechrest, L. (1992). The past future of clinical psychology: A reflection on Woodworth (1937). *Journal of Consulting and Clinical Psychology, 60,* 18-23.

Shell, R.W. (1980). Psychiatric testimony: Science or fortune telling? *Barrister, 7,* 6-8.

Sheppard, B.H., and Vidmar, N. (1989). Adversary pretrial procedures and testimonial evidence: Effects of lawyer's role and machiavellianism. *Journal of Personality and Social Psychology, 39,* 320-332.

Showalter, C.R., and Fitch, W.L. (1987). Objectivity and advocacy in forensic psychiatry after Ake v. Oklahoma. *The Journal of Psychiatry and Law, Summer,* 177-188.

Silber, D.E. (1974). Controversy concerning the criminal justice system and its implications for the role of mental health workers. *American Psychologist, 29,* 239-244.

Silber, D.E. (1976). Ethical relativity and professional psychology. *The Clinical Psychologist, 29,* 3-5.

Simon, R.J. (1983). The defense of insanity, *The Journal of Psychiatry and Law, 11,* 183-201.

Slovenko, R. (1983). Commentary: Psychiatric postdicting and the second opinion on Grigorenko. *The Journal of Psychiatry and Law, 11,* 387-412.

Slovenko, R. (1988). Commentary: The role of the expert with focus on psychiatry in the adversarial system. *The Journal of Psychiatry and Law, Summer,* 333-373.

Smith, S.R. (1989). Mental health expert witnesses: Of science and crystal balls. *Behavioral Sciences and the Law, 7,* 145-180.

Steadman, H.J. (1973b). Some evidence on the inadequacy of the concept and determination of dangerousness in law and psychology. *Journal of Psychiatry & Law, 1,* 409, 421-422.

Steadman, H.J., and Cocozza, J.J. (1975). Stimulus/response: We cannot predict who is dangerous. *Psychology Today, 8,* 32 and 35.

Steadman, H.J., Cocozza, J.J., and Melick, M.E. (1978). Explaining the increased arrest rate among mental patients: The changing clientele of state hospital. *American Journal of Psychiatry, 135,* 816-820.

Stein, D.D. (1979). Witnessing experts in forensic psychology. *The Professional Psychologist, 3,* 4-5.

Stone, A.A. (1975). Mental health and law: A system in transition. *Crime and Delinquency Issues: A Monograph Series.* Rockville, Maryland: National Institute of Mental Health Center for Studies of Crime and Delinquency.

Tavris, C.T. (1988). Astrology thrives on the gullibility gene. *Los Angeles Times,* May 5.

Torrey, E.F. (1974). *The Death of Psychiatry.* Radnor, Pennsylvania: Chilton Book Company.

Volpe, P. (1989). Psychiatric testimony in the criminal prosecution process, 10, Canadian Criminal Forum, 26.

Wakefield, J.C. (1992). The concept of mental disorder: On the boundary between biological facts and social values. *American Psychologist, 47,* 373-388.

Walsh, F.W., (1987). The clinical utility of normal family research. *Psychotherapy, 24,* 496-502.

Wesley, F. (1981). Burger's challenge. *APA Monitor,* April, 3.

Wittman, J.P. (1988). Family therapists as expert witnesses: Helping family court understand a new language. *The Journal of Psychiatry and Law, Spring,* 91-104.

Yuille, J.C. (1989). Expert evidence by psychologists: Sometimes problematic and often premature. *Behavioral Sciences & the Law, 7,* 181-196.

Zusman, J. (1990). Abolish the neutral witness: A modest proposal. *Annual Meeting of the American Psychological Association, 1990.*

CITATIONS

31 Am. Jur. 2d, 494.

Addington vs. Texas, 441 US 418 October term 1978.

Albemarle Paper Company vs. Moody, 95 S. Ct. 2362 (1975).

Barefoot vs. Estelle, U.S., 103 S.Ct. 3383 (1983).

Boynton vs. Burglas, 590 So. 2d 446 (1991).

Conservatorship of the Person and the Estate of Mabel Roulet, 23 Cal.3d, 219 (1979).

Conservatorship of the Person and the Estate of Mabel Roulet, L.A. 30730, Super. Ct. No. 105 919 (as reported in the Los Angeles *Daily Journal,* 1979).

Daubert vs. Merrell, Dow Pharmaceuticals, Inc., 113 S. Ct. 2786 (1993).

Estelle, Corrections Director vs. Smith, 451 U.S. 454 1980.

Frye vs. U.S., 293 Fed. 1013, 1014 (D.C. Cir. 1923).

Griggs vs. Duke Power Co., 401 U.S. 424 28 L ed 2d 15 8 91 S Court 849 (1971).

Jones vs. The State of Texas, 699 SW 2d 583 (Tex. App. 6 Dist. 1985) p. 583.

O'Connor vs. Donaldson, 42, U.S. Law-Week, p. 4929 (June 24, 1975).

People vs. Burnick, 14 Cal. 3d 306 (1975).

People vs. Drew, 22 Cal.3d, 333 (1979).

People vs. Jones, 440 N.E. 2nd 261 (1982).

People vs. Ralph Terry Coleman, 120 C.A., 3rd, 530 (1981).

People vs. Teague, 439 N.E. 2nd 1066 (1981).

Rosenblitt vs. Rosenblitt, 486 N.Y.S. 2d 741 (1985).

Smith vs. Schlesinger, 13 F.2d 462 (D.C.Cir. 1975).

Stamper vs. Virginia, (1985).

State vs. Bohner, 210 Wis 651, 246 N.W. 314-317, 86 ALR 611. (See also 23 ALR 2d, 1307-11 for additional cases to the same effect.)

Suggs vs. LaVallee, 570 F.2d pp. 1092-1120 (1978).

Tarasoff vs. The Regents of the University of California, 17 C.3d 425 (1977).

Taylor vs. State, 440 N.E. 2nd 1109 (1982).

United States vs. Brawner, 471 F 2d, 1969 (DC C. 1972).

Washington vs. The United States, 390 F 2nd 444 (1967).

Watson vs. Fort Worth Bank, 487 U.S., 108 S.Ct., 2777 (1988).

CHAPTER 2

Science and the Scientific Method

This chapter provides an understanding of what is or is not within the bounds of science and scientific methods, as generally understood. This subject is important because psychology and psychiatry purport to be sciences, with all the weight and prestige that is attached to that connotation. However, in many cases the "knowledge" of these disciplines is based on materials which are either "non-science" or "bad science." The attorney should be aware of differences between science, with its rigorous methods of acquiring and testing knowledge, and the interesting but deceptive appearance of knowledge such as may be contributed by the exercise of art, philosophy, or speculation. In other words, it is important for the attorney to be able to explore and expose how the expert "knows," and to be able to demonstrate that the expert does *not* know in those cases when he really does not or cannot *know*. The attorney can show the jury whether the expert's conclusions are drawn from valid and verifiable studies of empirical relationships or whether they are based on deductions from some speculative theory which has yet to be validated, or based upon the expert's own unvalidated experience or the unvalidated experience of others. In order to understand the nature of the expert's knowledge and to attach appropriate value to it, an understanding of the methods by which "knowledge" is acquired is indispensable.

The statements of a "scientific" expert witness can be assumed to be no better than the scientific basis from which they are drawn. In one sense, this is well known to attorneys by the rule of law that in order to be admissible, evidence purporting to be scientific must rest on the basis of reasonably well validated scientific procedures and principles, or at least upon general acceptance of the principle or procedure by the scientific community. In a second sense, this fundamental principle is important even where certain kinds of evidence or a certain kind of data, or certain procedures have received considerable support and acceptance within the scientific community. In many such cases it may be shown on cross-examination that the scientific basis on which that acceptance rests is, in fact, very shaky and not really scientific as the term is generally defined. The materials here will help the lawyer critique and challenge unfounded claims for the scientific basis of experts' opinions.

SCIENCE, THE SCIENTIFIC METHOD, AND SCIENTIFIC KNOWLEDGE

The term "science" is typically used in one of two interrelated ways. First, it refers to the procedures or methods used to gather scientific knowledge. Second, it refers to a body of knowledge that is *established* through these scientific methods. This chapter focuses primarily on the methods or procedures that distinguish science from other means of pursuing knowledge. Scientific method can be considered preliminary to scientific knowledge—if one does not use scientific method, then one cannot obtain scientific knowledge. However, the use of scientific method alone is not sufficient, or does not guarantee, the production of established or firm scientific knowledge. Many branches or areas of science, the biological sciences included, required many years before the use of scientific method led to the attainment of "hard" scientific knowledge. The lawyer should keep in mind, then, that the absence of scientific method precludes scientific knowledge, but that the reverse does not hold. The use of proper scientific method does not ensure established scientific knowledge, and this must be established separately along grounds or criteria we will discuss subsequently.

To return for a moment to the issue of community standard or acceptance, it should be recognized, and it often can be clearly shown, that acceptance cannot be equated with "scientifically sound" or "established," no matter what psychologists or psychiatrists declare. First, it is obvious that groups of individuals can share incorrect beliefs. For example, it was once an accepted "fact" that the world was flat or that the sun revolved around the earth. A major function of the scientific enterprise is to test belief and to uncover error, and the frequency with which science has corrected mistaken common or common-sense notions attests to its need and usefulness in this regard. Second, regardless of claims to the contrary, a field does not attain scientific status because its practitioners say they have done so or because they happen to share some common set of beliefs. Claims by themselves prove little (except that someone is willing to make them) and must be appraised for their accuracy or support. Thus, a psychologist or psychiatrist may claim that a principle is broadly accepted, and this could be true, but this does not establish the principle's scientific status. Further, it is easy to point out instances in which men of medicine generally accepted some belief that was not scientifically established, perhaps even claimed that the belief was scientifically supported, and later turned out to be just plain wrong.

At one time the medical community assumed that the practice of bleeding a patient had desirable curative effects. We now take it as obvious that bleeding was not such a medical "find," but it was not until data were gathered by appropriate investigative techniques that it became "known" that this widely accepted practice among the medical community was generally unwarranted. Point: Where scientific evidence is lacking or indicates that a principle or belief is doubtful or just plain wrong, this state of knowledge (or lack thereof) should be accorded precedent even over common professional belief.

In one case in which we consulted, a psychiatrist rejected the example of "bleeding" as an illustration of the inferiority of clinical observation in contrast to scientific study as a means of arriving at accurate knowledge. He asserted that bleeding is an effective treatment for certain conditions (mainly circulatory or respiratory), that it had its origins in clinical observation and was finally discarded due to clinical observation, not science.

His assertion that bleeding cures or relieves some disorders is correct. However, it was used to treat a wide variety of disorders for which it was ultimately shown to have little or no effect. Although observations of some practitioners may have contributed to the demise of this practice, it was only the production of scientific knowledge that brought it to an end. That is, after some 150 years, some clinicians may have noticed that some patients were not being cured and that some might be getting worse. This may have contributed to bringing the matter under more extensive scientific scrutiny with the result that eventually the practice was abandoned.

Bloodletting provides a useful courtroom example and thus some articles on its history are illuminating. Siddall (1980) states, "Due to the scientific advances in physiology and pathology and due to an increasing popular resistance to all venesection therapy, the long accepted remedy of bloodletting was finally abandoned in the twentieth century." (p. 102) Siddall notes what could be summarized in modern terminology as a "placebo" effect of the procedure which could have contributed to its longevity. (p. 102, footnote) He comments on the importance of the "laboratory" studies of Gabriel Andral in France in the nineteenth century, thus emphasizing the role of science in dealing "a death blow to one theory underlying the use of bleeding in certain problems of pregnancy." In his conclusion he states, "Scientific advances gradually revealed the false premise on which bloodletting rested." (p. 110)

Risse (1979) states, "Statistical evidence gathered by the French physician, Pierre C.A. Louis in Paris, demonstrated by 1835 that bloodletting could not arrest the natural evolution of pneumonia, one of the most frequent and specific indications for bloodletting since Hippocratic times." (p. 4) He notes, "The final blow came from the newly acquired insights into physiology and pathology." (p. 5) He also states, "Renewed scientific studies of the blood further discouraged bleeding as a therapeutic measure." (p. 5) Risse points out that negative evidence did not necessarily have an immediate impact on clinical practice. He discusses the persistence of therapy measures in the face of negating evidence (which he states in more positive terms as showing "the stability and essential conservatism" of medical practices).

Even if clinical observation contributed to the end of bloodletting as a panacea, the reader is reminded that this took centuries, even though scientific methods were available, and continued for a long time after scientific knowledge counterindicated it. Therefore, bleeding remains as a dramatic example of the inadequacies of clinical observation when compared to scientific methods.

Preston (1981) also describes the role of science in detecting and correcting mistaken beliefs. He quotes Aldous Huxley to the effect that "The tragedy of science is that frequently a beautiful hypothesis is slain by an ugly fact." Preston notes that "in medicine, most opinions have historically been incorrect." (p. 97) Preston indicates that the scientific method provides a check against inaccurate beliefs or impressions. He notes that "the heart of the scientific method is to take ideas as hypotheses only, subject to verification by rigorous testing." (p. 97) He observes that an essential function of science is to eliminate erroneous conclusions. He states: "In the end, science is a method of checking the belief systems that are rational creations of man. It is not intended as a replacement for beliefs, but as a means of assessing them against the facts of the natural world." (p. 98)

As noted, throughout history, many such observations or beliefs have been shown to be questionable, or simply wrong, on a basis of scientific testing. Kety (1969) indicates that at the beginning of the current century, there was "uncritical enthusiasm" for the belief that "schizophrenia" was the product of brain damage. Kety notes:

> This was followed by a period of questioning which led to the design and execution of more critically controlled studies and, eventually, to the present consensus that a pathological lesion characteristic of schizophrenia or any of its subgroups remains to be demonstrated. (p. 142)

Campbell (1985) notes that observation of treatment outcome may create misleading impressions. He reviews various therapies that appeared promising but whose efficacy was not subsequently supported through formal scientific research. These treatments include stimulating the brain with electric current during periods of sleep, castration, blood transfusions, the injection of malaria and other infective agents, and the use of hallucinogenics, such as LSD. He states as regards the latter that initial reports were "enthusiastic," but that "when control and comparison groups were introduced into studies, little evidence could be found to substantiate prior claims." (p. 1572)

Mora (1985) reviews historical developments in psychiatry which clearly illustrate how often assumptions founded on the basis of clinical observation or nonscientific methods can lead to error. Mora describes numerous historical views of disorder and treatment in psychiatry. Although some of these views may seem almost amusing, they probably did not seem so at the time and illustrate the need to subject "clinical observations" to scientific test. Mora indicates that Galen, whom he describes as "undoubtedly the greatest physician of Roman times," believed that imbalance among four bodily "humors" (including blood, phlegm, yellow bile and black bile) often accounted for medical illness. According to Mora, Galen provided many clinical descriptions of the interrelationships between these four humors, illness, and treatment responses. Mora discusses earlier treatments of "mental disorders," which included such things as skull trepanation, or literally drilling holes in the skull. A seventh century treatment ("rediscovered" in the eighteenth century) was to swing the "disordered" from a wicker basket attached to the ceiling.

Mora provides further examples of treatment approaches and mistaken concepts from the eighteenth to the twentieth century. In the eighteenth and nineteenth centuries, many individuals believed that mental abilities could be measured by assessing bumps on the skull (the practice of phrenology). Benjamin Rush, often considered the father of American psychiatry, relied extensively on bloodletting. Further, Rush included as predisposing factors to psychiatric disorder "intellectual occupations, excesses of climate, certain forms of government, revolutions, and particularly religious tenets." (p. 47) Treatments in the nineteenth and twentieth centuries included malaria "therapy." Mora also notes that Carl Jung, a personality theorist whose ideas remain influential among some psychiatrists, formulated certain of his beliefs after direct involvement in spiritual seances and was influenced by the work of alchemists. Alchemists, among other things, worked on methods for combining base metals into gold and for extending life indefinitely.

The scientific method thus serves to safeguard against the mistaken beliefs that often stem from clinically based observations. In this regard, it is worth noting that the diagnostic manual of the American Psychiatric Association, DSM-III-R, states as regards revisions in the prior manual:

In attempting to evaluate proposals for revisions in classification and criteria, or for adding new categories, *the greatest weight was given to the presence of empirical support from well-conducted research studies,* though, for most proposals, data from empirical studies were lacking. (p. xxi) (italics added)

It thus seems clear that at least this important branch of the psychiatric "establishment" recognizes the superiority of scientific data over other informational sources (e.g., clinical observation), a point that may be quite useful should an expert attempt to brush away non-supportive research or argue for the superiority of his clinical observations.

Psychologists or psychiatrists may claim that the theory they use is a "good" one. Again, these claims, by themselves, do not establish the scientific status of the theories they use. The theories employed may be "good" in the sense that the psychiatrist thinks the theory helps him understand, or the psychiatrist believes the theory "works" with his or her patients. Thus, psychoanalytic theory is embraced by a broad range of practitioners, and they may describe the theory as a good one, but as we will show, the theory does not bear up under the weight of scientific testing and certainly cannot be considered validated. Defining a theory as "good" in a clinical sense should not be confused with "good" along criteria formally used to evaluate scientific theory, such as established validity, predictive power, or other such features we will discuss. In fact, one would not be far off the mark claiming, as some psychologists do, that no theory in clinical psychology even approaches the strict tests of scientific quality or "goodness" that theories in other branches of science would pass.

SOME DISTINGUISHING FEATURES OF SCIENTIFIC METHOD

Scientific method, reduced to its basic meaning, is really nothing more nor less than a certain way of going about knowing something. There are other ways individuals attempt to know or learn about things. One may "know" about things through religious experience, or one may "know" about things as a matter of intuition. How these other ways of knowing compare to scientific method need not be debated here. Our purpose is served by stating clearly that these are not scientific methods and that such knowledge is not admitted into the court as evidence. What, then, are science's distinguishing features?

EMPIRICAL TESTING

An essential feature of science is that it tests its conjectures. Ordinarily, testing of knowledge, principles, or hypotheses involves prediction of one kind or another. Prediction is the process whereby one states that given the occurrence of events A, B, and C, one will then be able to observe event X. If under conditions A, B, and C, X is observed consistently, the hypothesis or the assumption is supported. If X does not appear, the hypothesis or knowledge is not confirmed and it is left in doubt. If after repeated attempts to produce X from A, B, and C, it appears that X cannot be produced consistently in that manner, the hypothesis may be considered incorrect. Similarly, if with A, B, and C, X is sometimes observed, but sometimes Y or Z is observed, no principle has been scientifically established (unless the conditions under which each will appear have been verified).

MANNER OF DEFINING TERMS

The manner in which terms are defined is another feature that sets science apart from other intellectual endeavors. In science the attempt is made to anchor definitions of terms or concepts to concrete observables, as contrasted to the literary type of definition. Literary definitions almost always lead to some degree of ambiguity or uncertainty as to exactly what is meant by the given term. For example, the psychoanalytic term "libido" has been given the following four meanings (English and English, 1958):

> *Libido:* (Psychoan.) 1. sexual craving; 2. Any erotic desire or pleasure; 3. any instinctual manifestation that tends toward life rather than death, integration rather than disintegration, synonym, eros, life instinct; 4. Any psychic energy constructive or destructive, synonym, horme. (p. 294)

Thus when the term "libido" is used, the listener or reader is really left without any meaning except the meaning he places on it, because the term has multiple meanings. Also, the defining words are themselves often as vague and ambiguous. Most concepts in clinical psychology and psychiatry are of the literary type, leading to ambiguity and uncertainty and, therefore, to a large degree, to untestability.

The process of operational definition, for example, stands in contrast to literary definition. In this type of definition a concept or term is known by the operations which make it or its functioning observable. Thus, for example, hunger may be defined in terms of so many hours without food. This, of course, says nothing about the feeling of hunger, but it does allow a researcher to postulate a certain state defined by the hours of food deprivation and then to predict certain behaviors as a result. If the predicted behaviors occur, it can be said that the definition of the concept of hunger is then anchored at both ends in observables—at the antecedent end in the observable number of hours of food deprivation, and at the terminal end by the production of a certain kind of behavior associated with a state of hunger, for example, eating.

It is not contended here that literary definitions are of no value. They are useful in stating the general nature of a concept, and in the early development of a science or of a particular theory they are quite useful in providing some representation of the various processes to be studied. In the final analysis, however, unless there is a way to reduce the definition to operational definitions or more precise terms, there is almost no way to be sure that two people are talking about the same thing when they use a particular term or concept. This is an important matter, especially in view of the fact that so much of clinical psychology and psychiatry rests on psychoanalytic formulations which are almost exclusively of a literary type, and thus are difficult, if not impossible, to state as operational concepts, or with clarity and precision. For example, many hours are spent in hospitals, clinics, universities, and training seminars in arguments over what Freud really meant by terms such as "libido," "sexual," "Id," "instinct," etc. The complaints of lawyers regarding psychiatric "jargon" are well known.

In a way, it may be said that the distinction between literary and operational definition is the same as or parallel to the distinction between philosophy and science. The function of the philosopher is served when he has engaged in speculation about certain events or phenomena and has organized his speculations into a coherent and interrelated form, and perhaps has cited anecdotal evidence to support his speculations. The scientist, on the other hand, generally picks up where the philosopher leaves off, although he may also engage in a certain amount of speculation and organization of his speculations. However, he then translates these into hypotheses which he submits to scientific tests, that is, he specifies the operations whereby the phenomena and concepts he speculated about can be observed and evaluated. Thus, for example, psychology in its early days dwelled entirely within the province of philosophy, and at such institutions where it was taught, it was taught within the department of philosophy. It was only with the development of methodologies, tools by which psychological phenomena could be evaluated and measured and defined, that psychology began to emerge as a science. It is true that even today many "humanistic" psychologists speak with some contempt of the "brass instrument psychology" initiated by Wilhelm Wundt in 1879 in Leipzig, Germany. It is equally true that in the minds of most people it is precisely this kind of brass instrument approach, involving as it does techniques of quantification, measurement, and prediction, that constitutes the meaning of science. It is for this reason that it is important for the attorney to be able to educate a jury or judge regarding the essentially nonscientific status of psychiatry and much of clinical psychology.

SCIENTIFIC METHODS:
NONEXPERIMENTAL & EXPERIMENTAL

NONEXPERIMENTAL METHODS

The primary defining feature of the nonexperimental method is that one does not manipulate (alter) or control the phenomena or variables under study but more or less studies or observes them as they occur. These nonexperimental methods vary greatly in their rigor and precision, and some fall at what may be considered the outer fringes of scientific method. For example, some may or may not consider the "clinical method" a "scientific" and legitimate variant of nonexperimental method. Freud's work provides a classic example of the clinical method, which often involves many observations on one or a few individuals, although it may involve larger numbers of people and less intensive observation. Freud observed a relatively small number of patients, intensively and frequently, looking for consistencies in their behavior that could be classified and related to other aspects of their behavior or mental life, in order to try to understand causal relationships between such things as early childhood experience and personality development.

A good deal of the research in clinical psychology and psychiatry fits under some category of nonexperimental method. Those employing these methods attempt to classify, explain, and predict events on the basis of their observations. Obviously, everyone is a psychologist in this sense. However, the scientific psychologist seeks to organize his observational data systematically, usually with the aim of reducing them to some quantified form and then systematically testing or checking on the hypotheses derived from such methods. Further, various measurement instruments or tools may be used in an attempt to increase the rigor of data collection.

Nonexperimental methods, and the clinical method in particular, have various inherent weaknesses. This is one reason why hard sciences often rely primarily on experimental techniques. One weakness of the clinical method in particular is the lack of control over events and conditions, and perhaps lack of preparation to observe. In the clinical method one has to take the data that come along and do the best one can with it, although, one can bring some degree of pressure to bear to elicit additional information. Other shortcomings concern the conditions of observation, what facts will be attended to and remembered, and problems of interpretation. These shortcomings will be dealt with in more detail in the chapter on the clinical examination. Research has delineated a dozen or so different factors in the observing situation which can influence the data that are obtained. The facts that will be attended to are inevitably subject to a certain bias of observation. One tends to see or hear what he is tuned in for. Thus, for example, the Freudian psychologist or psychiatrist is likely to be particularly attentive to communications of the patient with regard to sexual material or "Oedipal" conflicts, whereas an Adlerian psychologist or psychiatrist would be particularly attentive to those communications dealing with inferiority, power struggle, or other concepts that are more relevant to an Adlerian approach. This selectivity or bias in what one attends to in itself constitutes one of the error-producing conditions of observation. Many studies have shown that by the nature of the manner in which a clinician or observer responds to certain kinds of material (often material that seems to support his views), he can inadvertently encourage the patient or person being observed to produce more of that kind of material. Thus, whether intentionally or not, the patient becomes a participant in the production of tainted or biased information. Subsequently, when the examiner concludes that the patient has exhibited material pointing, for instance, to sexual conflicts or power struggles, he may be overlooking the effect of his theoretical bias on the subject's productions.

The bias of the observer can also create major problems, or even distortions, in the interpretation of the data obtained. The problems of interpretation often may be the most serious, because in this method you often do not know if the observed relationships are meaningful or fortuitous (e.g., the fact that you see a patient who is now having some mental or emotional "disorder" and subsequently find that he had a childhood sexual trauma simply does not prove that there is an actual or causal relationship between the two). That is, an investigator picks up a clue or gets a notion from an observation that is made, and then proceeds to look for evidence that will support that notion. Further examples of the erroneous conclusions that may stem from the clinical method appear in Chapter 5.

EXPERIMENTAL METHOD

In the experimental method one manipulates (varies) and/or controls the events to be studied. By holding background factors constant or controlling or minimizing their influence, and by then varying the factor of interest (e.g., the intensity of electrical shocks), one can study the factor of interest in the "cleanest" or most exacting manner. In some cases it is possible to measure the degree to which a given variable affects the outcome of a certain event or to measure the degree of relationship between the two variables. The scientist can vary the conditions of observation and check his hypothesis against alternative hypotheses. The aim of the experimental method is to reduce subjectivity, ambiguity, and uncertainty as much as possible. Publication of research requires that the scientist state the procedures and methods employed in observing a particular event so that another researcher may reproduce those conditions in an effort to determine if the results hold up. In some cases it permits other researchers to point to methodological flaws which may bar the drawing of the conclusion that has been made. It also permits the same researcher or another researcher to vary the conditions to show that conclusions based on the original study do not hold up when conditions are thus varied, and cannot therefore be generalized to other conditions.

The following example may be used to illustrate the experimental method. Suppose you wish to find out which of two fertilizers, A or B, is the better. There are several ways you might try to answer this question. You might locate some farmers, each of whom used one or the other kind of fertilizer and ask them what kind of yield they got, or you might measure their yield yourself. This would be a simple form of nonexperimental method. However, the information obtained in this manner would be limited and ambiguous, and it would not allow one to eliminate a series of alternate explanations. After you got the information in this manner, you would have knowledge of a very poor quality. You would not know whether the difference in yield was truly attributable to fertilizer differences, because there would be many other possible sources of the differences of yield. For example, there might be differences in fertility of the soil on Farm A as against Farm B, Farmer A might be a more skillful farmer than Farmer B, Farm A may have received more rainfall than Farm B, or Farmer A may have used different seeds than Farmer B. Thus, not just one thing (i.e., the fertilizer) but a number of other things would all be varying at the same time, and it would not be possible to determine what caused the eventual result.

In the experimental method you could try to arrange conditions so that any difference in yield that occurred would be attributable to the difference in the fertilizer. You could do it in the following manner. You could select a plot of ground and divide that plot into an equal number of equal-sized sub-plots. Half of the sub-plots would be treated with fertilizer A and half with fertilizer B. To ensure so far as possible that there would be equivalence of soil, you would determine which treatment a given plot would get, for example, either by assigning A or B treatments on a random basis and assuming that given a reasonable number of sub-plots, inequalities, if any, would be equalized. Alternatively, you might use a safer procedure which would be to set up a system such as a checkerboard arrangement so that for each A plot there would be an adjoining B plot. You could have the same farmer plant the seeds and tend the plots for both the A and B treatment. Thus, any difference due to farming skill would be eliminated, as both treatments would have the same farmer. You could give instructions as to the amount of water to be given each plot ensuring that each plot received the same amount of water as the other plots. In the same manner you could try to control the operation of any other variables that you thought might affect the outcome so that when the crop was finally grown, harvested, weighed and measured, and it turned out that the crop from plots given fertilizer A was significantly greater than the crop harvested from plots given fertilizer B, you have obtained some initial supporting evidence that fertilizer A is superior to fertilizer B. As a scientist, could you be *sure* that this was the case, or claim that you have established a hard and fast scientific fact? No. One supportive experiment is not enough, although some expert witnesses may support their opinions by citing one or another supporting study. Therefore, the lawyer should be aware of what else has to be shown or accomplished before one can legitimately claim a fact or hypothesis has been scientifically "established." Some of these necessary steps or hurdles will be discussed under the next heading.

GETTING FROM DATA TO ESTABLISHED SCIENTIFIC KNOWLEDGE: HURDLES

THE NEED FOR STATISTICAL TESTS

The following quotation may illustrate the relevance of statistics in research (Guilford, 1950):

1. *They permit the most exact kind of description.* When all is said and done, the goal of science is description of phenomena, description so complete and so accurate that it is useful to anyone who can understand it when he reads the symbols in terms of which those phenomena are described. Mathematics and statistics are a part of our descriptive language, an outgrowth of our verbal symbols peculiarly adapted to the efficient kind of description that the scientist demands.

2. *They force us to be definite and exact in our procedures and in our thinking.* The writer once heard a prominent psychologist defend his rather vague conclusions by saying that he would rather be vague and right than to be definite and wrong. But the alternatives are not to be either "vague and right" or "definite and wrong." One can also be definite and right, and it is the writer's contention that the odds for being right are overwhelming on the "definite" side of the matter.

3. *Statistics enable us to summarize our results in meaningful and convenient form.* Masses of observations taken by themselves are bewildering and almost meaningless. Before we can see the forest as well as the trees, order must be given to the data. Statistics provide an unrivaled device for bringing order out of chaos; of seeing the general picture of one's results.

4. *They enable us to draw general conclusions,* and the process of extracting conclusions is carried out according to accepted rules. Furthermore, by means of statistical steps, we can say about how much faith should be placed in any conclusion and about how far we may extend our generalization.

5. *They enable us to make predictions* of "how much" of a thing will happen under conditions we know and have measured. For example, we can predict the probable mark a freshman will earn in college algebra if we know his score in a general scholastic-ability test, his score in a special algebra-aptitude test, his average mark in high school mathematics, and perhaps the number of hours per week that he devotes to studying algebra. Our prediction may be somewhat in error because of other factors that we have not accounted for, but our statistical methods will also tell us about how much margin of error to allow in our predictions. Thus not only can we make predictions but we know how much faith to place in them.

6. *They enable us to analyze some of the causal factors out of complex and otherwise bewildering events.* It is generally true in the social sciences, and in psychology and education in common with them, that any event or outcome is a result of numerous causal factors. The reasons why a man fails in his business or in his profession, for example, are varied and many. Causal factors are usually best uncovered and proved by means of experimental method. If it could be shown that, all other factors being held constant, certain businessmen fail to the extent that they possess some defect of personality X, then it is probable that X is a cause of failure in this type of business. Unfortunately for the social scientist, he cannot manage men and their affairs sufficiently to set up a good experiment of this type. The next best thing is to make a statistical study, taking businessmen as we find them, working under conditions as they normally do. The life insurance expert does the same kind of thing when he follows the trail of all possible factors that influence the length of life and determines how important they are. On the basis of these statistical findings, he can predict about how long an individual of a certain type will probably live, and his insurance company can plan an insurance policy accordingly. Statistical methods are therefore often a necessary substitute for experiments. Even where experiments are possible, the experimental data must ordinarily receive appropriate statistical treatment. Statistical methods are hence the constant companions of experiments. (p. 3)

Returning to our fertilizer example, one application of statistical techniques would be to determine if, in the first place, the differences in yield across the two fertilizers was an actual or real one or merely the product of chance. This is what is known as testing for the significance of the differences, or as significance testing. The aim is to determine how likely it is that the observed differences represent actual differences or chance occurrences.

This distinction between chance and actual differences can be illustrated with an example. Suppose two crooks want to mint some coins for their gambling operation. For our purposes, we will define a "fair" coin as one that comes up heads 50% of the time and tails 50% of the time. Our crooks do not want to create fair coins, but rather coins that come up tails more often than heads, based on their assumption that the majority of individuals betting on the outcome of coin tosses say heads rather than tails. If they can create coins that tend to come up tails, but not with such frequency that gamblers become suspicious, they figure to clean up.

Our sophisticated criminals test the first coin by flipping it 100 times. If it comes up 51 heads and 49 tails, there is no need to conduct a statistical test. It will not show that the coin favors tails. Suppose, however, the result they obtain is 49 heads and 51 tails. What they want to determine is if the result provides evidence that their coin design has succeeded or if the result is merely the product of chance. Obviously, this small difference could represent a chance or nonrepeating occurrence. This is the point of significance testing—to determine whether obtained findings are likely due to actual differences or chance.

Through significance testing, the researcher obtains a probability figure which indicates the likelihood that the result was a chance finding. The probability is expressed as a percentage, e.g., .43, which represents a 43% likelihood of obtaining the result by chance. In the social sciences, a probability at or below 5%, or .05, is frequently set as the standard to be met before accepting that the obtained results represent a true difference and not a fortuitous one. A .05 level indicates that the difference that was obtained would be produced by chance in only 1 of 20 cases. More conservative researchers may use the .01 level as the standard. This stricter level might also be used when a number of related comparisons are being made and the odds would not actually be 1 in 20, but rather considerably higher, that at least one of these comparisons will meet the .05 standard. One can see that in either case the probability of chance findings must be fairly low before a researcher should conclude that the obtained difference is an actual one. This is because most scientists consider it a serious error to accept into the scientific knowledge base an erroneous belief about a relationship. If in doubt, one should assume the relationship is unproven and attempt to obtain more definitive data. This is not unlike standards of evidence in criminal cases, in which one assumes innocence (the absence of a relationship) unless proven otherwise by evidence that establishes the case beyond a reasonable doubt.

The Problem of Large Samples

Samples can be so large that the researcher, under most circumstances, is virtually ensured of obtaining at least some "significant" findings, merely because no two groups are ever exactly alike. For example, if one conducts a study of 1,000 males and females and examines their food selection, many statistically significant differences are likely to emerge. However, many of these statistically "significant" differences are likely to be essentially trivial. In the above example, a difference of even a single percentage point (e.g., 78% of females and 77% of males liking French fries) may achieve statistical "significance" but would obviously help little in distinguishing between females and males. This also leads us to the important distinction between statistically significant and practically or clinically significant.

Even If It Is Statistically Significant, Is It Practically Meaningful?

Research results may be statistically significant, but this does not mean that they are of practical use. Suppose, for example, that we administer a test to a group of murderers and a group of pacifists and they obtain statistically significant differences on a few of the scales, although the actual size of the differences is not particularly great. The expert may claim that these results establish the validity of the scale and its potential use in formulating opinions. However, statistical significance does not establish the practical usefulness of the measure, much less its usefulness in aiding the trier of fact. It might actually turn out that the use of the test leads to far more erroneous than correct predictions.

Experts may fail to draw the distinction between the statistically significant and the practically useful or significant and rather use the two interchangeably. What is statistically significant may or may not be practically useful, and the lawyer can ask in what sense the term "significant" is being applied. Does the expert mean statistically significant or practically useful? When the former meaning is implied (but not stated) it may seem overly impressive, but the impact is likely to be reduced if it can be made clear that the expert is referring to a statistical result and not a finding that necessarily has practical utility. In fact, it is not uncommon for opinions to be based on statistically significant research results that are actually of little practical meaning.

Statistical significance and forensic utility are in large part independent matters, and one can mount a strong challenge when support for statistical significance is misrepresented as support for forensic utility (see Chapter 10 for the guidelines for determining practical significance or usefulness).

DOES IT REPLICATE?

It is a fundamental canon of scientific method that one study by itself does not produce secure knowledge, even if statistically significant differences are uncovered, and that one has to repeat the study to determine if the same findings will again be obtained, or if the results can be replicated. The need for replication is a very basic methodological concern. For example, almost all scientific journals in psychology specifically instruct authors to describe the methods they use in sufficient detail so that another researcher can repeat their study. One reason for replication is that statistical tests that reach significance show only that the results obtained probably are not a product of chance, but do not ensure that this is the case. Recall, for example, that if the .05 level of probability is used, there is a one in twenty chance that differences of such a magnitude could be a chance finding. This simply leaves too much room for error, particularly if a number of researchers are involved in the same topic and it becomes fairly likely that at least one of them will obtain "significant" findings by chance alone. It may be this one significant finding that appears in the literature, and under such circumstances it is not trustworthy. Another reason for replication is that the particular circumstances under which a study is conducted may favor or bias outcome such that, although no true relationship exists, a statistically significant result is still obtained. This may occur even though the researcher makes a scrupulous effort to eliminate biasing effects. There is a saying in medicine that one should use newly discovered and promising treatments early, before their effects are lost. This saying reflects an awareness of the frequency with which research findings are ephemeral and do not necessarily hold up when further investigation is conducted.

The need for replication is not an "ivory tower" concern. Rather, it is a practical necessity. There are innumerable instances, particularly in the social sciences, in which what seems to be an important or impressive finding cannot be replicated. The simple truth of the matter is that, regardless of how well a single experiment is conducted, that it may come out differently when repeated. As Franzen and Golden (1985) state, "Despite rigorous attempts to maintain impartiality, there may be some overlooked variables which have influenced data collection which would not be present when an independent replication is attempted. Alternatively, the results of the first analysis and its dependent replication may be influenced by variables which are idiosyncratic to that particular laboratory." These authors, then, argue that replication by the original researchers in the original research setting is not sufficient, but that results should be replicated by an independent group of researchers working in an independent research setting.

Although the need to replicate research results is broadly recognized and endorsed, and it would indeed be the very unusual scientist who said he did not share these views, a major problem exists. Replication is rare in the social sciences, as discussed by Frankel and Kaul (1978). Thus, it is also the rare instance in which the lawyer cannot score points by bringing out the need for replication. Have the expert explain why it is necessary. Then one simply has to ask whether the study or studies upon which the expert relied were replicated, and whether they were replicated in an independent research center. If the expert then insists that replication is not necessary in this case, one can show that inconsistent standards are being applied, with the expert using more "liberal" standards with studies that support his point of view and harsher standards with studies that do not. We would note in this regard that replication need not always involve an exact reproduction of a prior study, but may involve closely aligned or similar elements. If a consistent outcome is obtained, the initial results or findings may be strengthened or considered more trustworthy.

MULTIVARIATE TECHNIQUES

Multivariate techniques are a special set of statistical procedures used when an investigator wishes to study a series of variables simultaneously. For example, an investigator may administer a set of 15 scales to two groups of individuals. Rather than examining each scale one at a time, one may wish to determine which one of the scales, or which scales in which combination, best distinguish between members of the two groups. Discriminant analysis and factor analysis are among the more widely used multivariate techniques.

The use of multivariate techniques involves a host of technical considerations, but there are two points that are relatively nontechnical and often quite relevant. First, multivariate techniques are frequently misused by researchers. Second, a common result of this misuse is to produce inflated results, or results that may look very impressive but are actually not trustworthy. For example, a researcher may claim that the "discriminant analysis shows that 90% of individuals can be correctly classified." However, more proper or further analysis may instead reveal that the procedure results in little better than chance accuracy.

To produce trustworthy results, at least two things are generally required. First, there must be an adequate subject-to-variable ratio. All this refers to is the number of variables or measures used in relation to the number of subjects. For example, if there are 10 subjects and 10 variables, the subject to variable ratio is 1:1. If there are 100 subjects and 10 variables, the ratio is 10:1. Second, cross-validation usually needs to be performed. This refers to repeating the analysis with a new set of subjects. On replication or cross-validation, multivariate procedures often look much worse or less effective, which is why cross-validation is needed.

At times, experts will partially or even mainly rely on studies that have employed multivariate procedures improperly or without cross-validation. Thus, although the supportive research may sound impressive, its foundations may be extremely shaky. The lawyer need not master the technicalities of multivariate procedures, but can ask a series of questions (particularly on deposition) to determine whether the issue is worth pursuing. First, one can ask whether any of the studies (or which of the studies) the expert cites relied on multivariate procedures. Second, one can ask, "What was the subject-to-variable ratio?" Third, one can ask whether cross-validation was performed. If the expert does not know the answer to any of these questions, it may well be worth obtaining consultation from a statistical expert. In any case, lacking knowledge of the answers, the expert is in no position to determine whether these studies are trustworthy, given the frequency with which studies using multivariate techniques are questionable. If the expert indicates a subject-to-variable ratio of less than 5:1, and/or indicates that cross-validation has not been performed, again, a consultant might be obtained. The studies cited by the expert may actually provide little or no support for his claims, and thus with a consultant's help one can effectively undermine the expert's evidentiary basis.

THE NEED FOR CONTROL GROUPS

We have been discussing hurdles or steps that must be overcome to move from research results to the establishment of secure scientific knowledge. To illustrate the need for control groups, let us return to our fertilizer example. Suppose we have shown that the differences obtained between fertilizer A and B reach statistical significance. Suppose, in addition, we have been able to replicate these findings. We have thus tentatively concluded that fertilizer A is the superior one. Can we now form the scientific conclusion that fertilizer A is useful or that it has a positive effect on yield? Again, we must say no. There are additional obstacles to overcome.

The fact that fertilizer A may be better than fertilizer B does not prove that fertilizer A is any good but only shows that it is better than fertilizer B. This may seem to be stretching the point or splitting hairs, but it is not. For example, perhaps both fertilizers A and B have detrimental effects on crop growth, and A comes out better than B only because its detrimental effects are less serious. To clarify matters, for one wishes to minimize supposition or guessing in science, one needs a control group.

To conduct our fertilizer experiment with a control group, one would still use fertilizers A and B on separate plots that are as similar as possible, and then add another similar plot and use, say, no fertilizer at all. One could then determine not only if fertilizer A was better than B, but also if the results achieved with fertilizer A were better than those achieved without it. One might find that fertilizer A was better than B but no better than using no fertilizer at all, or one might find that the fertilizer did yield superior results to no fertilizer at all. The point is that one does not typically *know* the result ahead of time, and this is why a control group, or a group in which the treatment is not applied, is needed.

One might not use a control group and instead guess or assume that fertilizer A provides an advantage. For example, one might use past figures on crop yield without the use of the fertilizer, but these past observations are uncontrolled and hence do not eliminate alternate explanations. Lower past yields may have been a product of less fertile soil or less favorable weather conditions. A control group is used so that one can reduce or eliminate these alternate explanations instead of relying on guesswork. This is the essential notion behind the use of control groups. One adds a group that gets no exposure to the variable of interest, or no treatment at all, but in all other ways possible keeps the group similar to those receiving the treatment. In this way, one can determine not only which treatment is more effective, but whether the treatment is effective at all or compares favorably to no treatment.

The principle is the same in different types of studies. For example, let us return to our "study" on the scores of murderers and pacifists on a personality test. The murderers did in fact obtain some different scores, but without a control group it is difficult to know what these differences represent. Thus, one probably should add a control group. In this case, one might obtain a group of normal individuals who are as similar as possible to the two groups except for the presence of marked aggressive or pacifist tendencies. For example, one might seek a group with a similar distribution of age, education, socioeconomic status, etc. It might be that on the scales on which the murderers obtained higher scores than the pacifists, their scores are no higher than those of the normal individuals, and thus their test performance is not specific to murderers and does not set them apart from anyone but pacifists. This example might seem ludicrous, but it is not at all uncommon that differences found between two clinical groups (e.g., two groups with different forms of brain damage) separate these two groups from each other but not from controls or normals, and thus have limited clinical utility.

The need for control groups in social sciences research is well illustrated by the history of studies on psychotherapy outcome. In the early days, research in this area consisted of treating people psychotherapeutically and observing whether or not a cure, or, at least, an improvement in their condition occurred. If it did, it was then concluded that the particular method of psychotherapy was effective in treating the particular condition. Eventually, someone asked the question, "How do we know these people would not have shown improvement without psychotherapy?" The next step was to establish an experimental situation in which half of the people coming to a certain clinic for psychological treatment were given the treatment, while the other half were placed on a waiting list and told they would not receive treatment for, say, a period of six months. The untreated half then constituted the control group for this particular study. Group A got psychotherapy, Group B did not get psychotherapy. At the end of six months a second evaluation was made to see if there was significantly more improvement in Group A, the treated group than there was in Group B, the untreated group. If there was more difference in Group A (and one had controlled for other variables which need not be gone into here), one could then state with relative confidence that it was the difference in treatment—receiving it or not receiving it—that caused the difference in outcome. Therefore, one could conclude that the particular form of psychotherapy was effective. On the other hand, if the results showed that the untreated group improved approximately the same as the treated group, then even though the treated group had improved, it could not be said that the improvement was due to psychotherapy because it is equally likely that some other variable was operating, for example, just the passage of time.

This concept of the use of controls in research is a handy one for the attorney, as a great deal of research on which behavioral scientists base their opinions—particularly research in the earlier days—was done without any kind of adequate control. For example, in the early development of psychoanalysis, Freud and his colleagues were getting no free associations from "normal" people, so there was no way to know if the material being provided by the patients they were seeing was, in fact, any different from that which normals would provide. Thus, it is not justified to conclude that certain events, X, Y, and Z, in childhood caused an adult "neurosis" simply by finding that many neurotics had X, Y, and Z in their childhood. You would have to know the incidence of X, Y, and Z in the "normal" population to see if it were less than in "neurotics." If not, then apparently X, Y, and Z do not cause neurosis. Something else is necessary. This failure to use control groups can be brought out with considerable effect in cross-examinations, both in terms of theoretical knowledge and in terms of the specific expert. For example, it might be embarrassing for an expert to have to answer the question as to how many normal people he has examined and if, as it usually would be, the answer is "none or very few," the question arises as to how he then knows that he is dealing with abnormal responses (unless base rates have been established: see Chapter 5).

DOES IT GENERALIZE?

Generalization refers to the practice of extending a principle established on the basis of one set of data to another set of data, or applying a principle shown to be applicable to one event to another event. In psychology, for example, the question is often raised as follows: To what extent can one generalize to human beings, in general, findings established in research using the most common and convenient human subjects, members of freshman psychology classes. The answer is that, lacking scientific support, one usually cannot safely generalize from a principle established with one population or under one certain set of conditions to another population, or to another set of conditions. For example, one ought not to generalize principles observed in working with the usual run-of-the-mill, middle-class, "neurotic" patients who are seen in private practice to hardened criminals, or for that matter, to individuals from different cultures or extremely different socioeconomic backgrounds. One can use the original conclusions to set up a study with the new population and *find out* if the principle applies. If it does, of course, then it can be applied. In the fertilizer case, to be sure that fertilizer A will be better than fertilizer B in the state of Arizona, for example, we would have to do a study similar to the one outlined above in Arizona. Would we, then, in order to apply the principle in each of the 50 states, have to carry out a similar study in each state? Probably not. If we were, for example, to carry out the additional study in Arizona and perhaps one in Oregon, one in Maine, and one in Alabama, and if we found in each of these studies that fertilizer A was better than fertilizer B, we could legitimately conclude that the difference existed regardless of soil and climate conditions and we would then be fairly safe in concluding that fertilizer A will be better than fertilizer B in Nevada, in Washington, in Michigan, and in Massachusetts, even though we had not conducted the study in these places. There would still be the possibility that we could be wrong. However, having checked the generalization to that extent, we would have considerable safety in relying on it.

RELIABILITY AND VALIDITY

The terms reliability and validity are most commonly used in relation to the area of tests and measurements. However, the concepts involved are equally applicable to almost any type of assessment and in a more general way to almost any form of data collection and interpretation. As these concepts will be frequently mentioned throughout the remainder of the book, some acquaintance with them is necessary.

Reliability refers to the probability of the existence of a fact. More specifically, it refers to the consistency or stability that is possible in terms of observing a particular fact. Reliability means that given the same circumstances the observer who perceives the fact will perceive it again, and given the same set of circumstances other observers will perceive the same fact. In behavioral science this often involves repeated observation of the same response or phenomenon under the same or highly similar circumstances. To illustrate: If an intelligence test is administered to a 10-year-old boy at 9 o'clock in the morning on Monday, and he achieves an IQ of 118, and if he is given the same IQ test at 10 o'clock in the morning on Tuesday, if the test is reliable, then he should receive an IQ of 118 or thereabouts in the second testing. He should achieve similar scores for all subsequent testings. However, if he achieves an IQ of 118 on Monday, then on Tuesday with the same test, he achieves an IQ of 72 and on Wednesday he achieves an IQ of 150 and on Thursday an IQ of 133, no trustworthy statement can be made about his IQ level. The data are simply not consistent enough to warrant the statement that his IQ is 118, or 72, or any other level. This does not mean that he does not have an IQ. There is the possibility that IQ does not represent a sufficiently stable entity or process to permit measurement or evaluation. The more probable explanation is that the method employed to appraise his intelligence level is in some way faulty. It fails to consistently measure that which it purports to measure. Where the method of appraisal leads to such inconsistency or instability, obviously, no prediction can be made. This is the meaning of low reliability.

The lawyer may appreciate some analogy between the concept of reliability and the evidentiary concept "probability of trustworthiness." Circumstantial probability of trustworthiness in the law generally refers to some set of conventions by which a conclusion is drawn as to whether or not evidentiary material is or is not likely to accurately portray a fact. These conventions in the law usually have to do with, first, the opportunity of the observer to have accurately observed and accurately reported the fact and, second, his capacity or willingness to report the fact accurately. If a witness were to tell quite a different story each time he was interviewed, he would be considered to have a low probability of trustworthiness, or in the terminology of behavioral science, he would have a low reliability, just as in the case of the intelligence test which gave a different report each time. If the 10-year-old boy had been given a different intelligence test upon each occasion of retesting and the scores once again came out at great variance with each other, we would be inclined to think that our modes of assessing the intelligence level were quite unreliable (or at least all but one of them would be unreliable, and we would not know which one). Similarly, if five different witnesses each gave a different description of a hold-up man in a robbery, we would have considerable difficulty in knowing which was the correct description, if any were, and consequently, we would not know which description described the existent fact. The probability that any one of the descriptions is correct would be quite low where such variance existed.

When psychiatrists cannot agree as to the existence of a certain condition, for example, a personality disorder, which is the "fact" in question, the method of determining the existence of the fact would be said to be unreliable or to have low reliability. Of course, it is possible that the "fact" is not a fact at all, that is, it is not itself a reliable phenomenon, because it depends on who is doing the observing. However, if the fact does have a basis in a valid concept, then the method of psychiatric examination would be said to be of low reliability as an indicator of that condition. As will be shown in the chapter on clinical method, the manifold opportunities for biased observation and report in the psychiatric interview make it very unlikely that there should be high inter-observer reliability. Empirical studies will show that even with a single observer the reliability is still quite low.

Validity is a term which refers to the relationship of one fact or one variable to another. It is a term for determining what a fact means, what conclusions can be drawn from it. If X can be established, can one, then, assume the presence of Y with at least a fair degree of accuracy? Stated differently, validity refers to the correctness or truth value of a statement or proposition. Is the statement or assumption correct, and if it is correct, what else can it tell us or help us to predict or understand? For example, it may be "true" that Joe wears blue socks often, but so what? In contrast, $E = mc^2$ can potentially help us to learn about or predict many important phenomena. Thus, questions about validity are usually broad ones, in that one asks not only whether or to what extent an assumption is true; but also whether, and to what extent, it relates to or helps us to predict other important phenomena. It is possible for there to be a highly reliable phenomenon which, however, is not related to anything else of importance. It would, then, be reliable but would have no validity. Although reliability may exist without validity, it is generally accepted that reliability is a prerequisite or necessary condition for validity. Thus, an observation or test lacking in reliability is almost certainly an observation or test lacking in validity. This will become apparent if one recalls that an unreliable phenomenon means a phenomenon for which observation fluctuates a great deal in relation to itself. Thus, its relationship to other phenomena could be no more stable than to itself and, therefore, would likely be low.

The example of the boy with the 118 IQ may be used to illustrate validity. In his case, because his IQ is somewhat above average, we would expect that his intellectual achievements would also be somewhat above average. We could then study his intellectual level in relation to his achievements in school. If it is found with relative consistency that boys with an IQ of around 118 achieve better than average in their school performance, then we would feel that we have established a form of validity for the IQ in relationship to academic achievement. A statement concerning the validity of a psychological test or diagnostic procedure always carries with it a requirement that it be specific, i.e., that there is a specification that it is valid for some specific purpose. Thus, in this case, we might say that the XYZ intelligence test is a valid indicator of academic potential. Of course, one could also state that the XYZ intelligence test score is a valid indicator of anything else with regard to which its validity has been empirically established, but only for those things for which its validity has been established. It would not, for example, be established as a valid indicator of the color of people's eyes. This is important to keep in mind with psychological tests, diagnostic procedures, and deductions from theories. It is an all too frequent occurrence that a test or principle, whose validity in relation to conclusion A has been supported, is expanded to make statements concerning fact B, although its validity in relation to B has never been established, and there is only some assumed similarity or relationship between A and B. This is an example of inappropriate generalization, previously discussed.

The analogue in the law of evidence to the concept of validity is that of relevance or probative value. What is the tendency of A to prove B? A string of witnesses, no matter how high a number, testifying with perfect consistency that Mr. X has blue eyes (high reliability) may have no relevance or probative value in relationship to a fact in issue, for example, whether or not he was cruel to his wife. In other words, no valid relationship has been established between blue eyes and mental cruelty. There are few, if any, relationships psychiatrists testify about where adequate validity has been established.

FIGURE 1

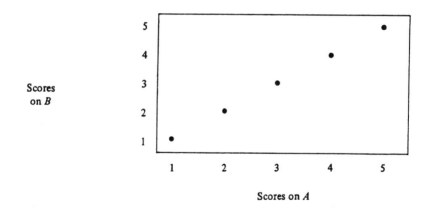

Scores on *B*

Scores on *A*

Most commonly in evaluating reliability and validity, the statistical concept of correlation is employed. Correlation refers to the degree of correspondence or co-relationship or co-varying between two variables. Correlation figures range from +1.0 to -1.0, with these two extremes representing "perfect" or complete correlations. Figure 1 shows a positive correlation of 1.0. As you can see, scores on variable B change exactly in proportion to change of scores on variable A. Thus, any time you know the score on A, you can tell what the score on B will be. Figure 2 is also a correlation of 1.0, but it is a negative correlation, that is, the scores on

B vary inversely with the scores on A. As the scores on A go up, the scores on B go down. The relationship between the two variables is just as strong as the relationship in the positive correlation of 1.0. Any time you know the score on A, you can tell what the score on B will be.

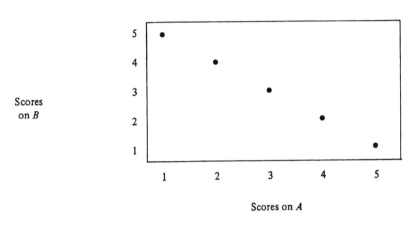

Scores on *A*

In behavioral sciences we seldom, if ever, find correlations of 1.0 or perfect correspondence between variables. Figure 3 shows a more typical situation where there is a positive relationship between A and B but the scores on B do not vary directly or exactly with the scores on A. In some cases a relatively higher score on A is accompanied by a relatively lower score on B. Through the use of mathematical formulas it is possible to compute a correlation coefficient expressed as a number something less than 1.0. For example, in Figure 3 the correlation coefficient is 0.70, indicating a moderate degree of co-varying between A and B such that you could make predictions with a moderate amount of accuracy, but in many cases you would undoubtedly be wrong predicting from A to B.

There are different approaches and meanings given to the term validity. A common meaning of validity that is arguably most relevant within the forensic arena is in terms of predictive validity. What this means is that given certain knowledge concerning variable A, one can state with a known degree of probability the likelihood of the occurrence or coexistence of event B, which may be a score on some other type of measure or a certain kind of behavior, or the degree to which certain characteristics are present. In other words, the statement refers to the correlation coefficient between A and B. Referring again to Figure 3, it can be seen that as the scores increase on form A, they increase also on form B, but as previously pointed out, there are several cases in which the reverse is true. That is why the correlation coefficient is 0.70 rather than

1.0. However, it is also clear that the scores on form A are somewhat valid predictors of the scores on form B, although not to a very high degree. That is because the correlation coefficient of 0.70 indicates that measurements on form A account for about half of the variability or variance on form B. (Through mathematical procedures it can be demonstrated that the amount of variance accounted for by the particular correlation coefficient is the square of that correlation. Thus, 0.70 squared is 0.49, or approximately half of the variance. This means that other variables not measured by form A are of about equal influence upon the performance on form B.)

FIGURE 3

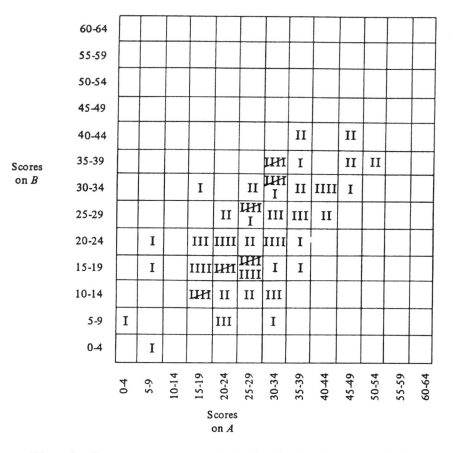

There is disagreement among behavioral scientists as to the lower limits to which a correlation coefficient may fall and still be considered within a range of acceptable validity. Many argue for a minimum of 0.60

to 0.70, but others will argue for limits as low as 0.45. To a large extent
the solution of this disagreement depends upon the purpose for which the
measurement or assessment is being made. For example, in a situation
where one is trying to locate the largest possible number of people who
might meet a certain minimum criterion of performance and one is not
overly concerned with the number of people who might fail, a relatively
lower minimum validity might be acceptable. On the other hand, where
one had to identify a fairly small percentage of qualified individuals from
a large number of applicants for a particular task, one would then want a
much higher validity coefficient to ensure making the best possible
choices. It seems quite likely that for legal purposes relatively high limits
should be set. For example, one might set as a minimal standard correct
prediction in 72% of cases, and this might require a validity coefficient
of approximately 0.85 before one would wish to accord a prediction
much weight in the legal situation. Recall that the square of 0.85 is 0.72
so that one, then, would have a measure which would account for a substantial portion of the variation in the thing to be predicted, or would
likely achieve a very modest level of accuracy. In any event, using a coefficient of correlation as the index of validity, one is at least able to state
mathematically and quantitatively the degree of relationship between A
and B. The importance of this is that the degree of relationship is known
and the court can thus make its own evaluation of the weight to be accorded to it.

It should be noted that in terms of reliability, there is general agreement that the correlation coefficient between different observations of
the same variable should be at least 0.90 to be acceptable, although there
is some argument presented for a lower limit of 0.80.

In terms of predictive validity it is sometimes possible to disregard
the coefficient of correlation and simply use the data as laid out in Figure
3, which is called a scatter diagram, to make a determination of a certain
score Y from the score X by establishing a cut-off point. For example, in
Figure 3 it can be seen that no one with a score of 40 or more on form A
received a score below 25 on form B. Only 2 out of 23, or less than 10%
scoring 35 or above on A got a score below 25 on B. Thus, if a score of
25 is established as "passing" or meeting a certain criterion, one can predict with about 90% probability of being correct that a person scoring 35
or better on A will meet the criterion. Conversely, because only 3 out of
33 who scored below 25 on A scored 25 or better on B, one can predict
with about 90% accuracy that people scoring below 25 on A will "fail"
or will not meet the criterion. Unfortunately, quantitative relationships of
this type are rare in clinical psychology and psychiatry.

Concurrent validity is actually the same as predictive validity except
that instead of predicting some future event or outcome, the test scores

are compared to some presently available measure or data. One can compare a score on an intelligence test, for example, to a student's current grade point average. This method has been widely used for personality tests, in which one can check a present personality test score or configuration of scores against such things as peer ratings or psychiatric diagnoses. Concurrent and predictive validity are actually so closely related that they are often both referred to under the general term *criterion-based validity.*

Another kind of validity is "content" or "face" validity. Validity in this sense rests upon the obvious resemblance of the material of the test to the kind of ability or the characteristic that it is supposed to measure. For example, if the test consisted of a series of problems in multiplication, it would seem obvious that it measured the ability to multiply. Even with this obvious resemblance to the variable being measured, the test still might not provide an accurate assessment. It might be contaminated by factors which might affect the score, such as complex instructions which require a high verbal ability, or too much emphasis on speed, or some other unknown factor. Face validity, by itself, is usually of limited value. It has the deficiency that one does not come out with a numerical index of validity, as in the case of predictive validity. Thus, one is still dealing with an assumption as to how valid the test is, no matter how reasonable the assumption may seem. Most importantly, it does not by itself demonstrate that the test accurately measures what it purports to measure. For these reasons, evidence for face validity can almost never substitute for the other, more rigorous forms of validity testing. Saying a test is face valid is essentially the same as saying, "I think the test is valid."

An additional word of caution is suggested here. Many tests carry particular names, or have subtests given particular names such as Test of Neuroticism or Anxiety Test. One should not be misled by the name of the test, as quite often research data will fail to support the belief that the test measures the named characteristic. Thus, one should not assume that just because a test is named "X Anxiety Scale" it necessarily measures anxiety.

Finally, there is "construct" validity. This is a comprehensive concept which includes one or more of the other types of validity. It refers to the extent to which the test may be said to measure a theoretical concept, such as intelligence or mechanical comprehension or anxiety. It entails a broader, more enduring, and more abstract kind of behavioral description. The Taylor Manifest Anxiety scale may be cited as an example of construct validity. From the title, it obviously purports to be a measure of anxiety. Anxiety, however, is a theoretical construct which cannot be directly observed, and thus, one cannot directly measure the predictive capacity of the test. In the case of an anxiety scale, a gradual accumulation of information from a variety of sources is generally required to establish construct validity. The Taylor scale has been shown, for example, to relate to other test measures of anxiety, and the test has been shown to relate to clinical diagnosis of anxiety and to behavioral measures believed to involve anxiety. On the other hand, studies attempting to relate the Taylor score to physiological measures thought to be associated with anxiety have not been successful. Nevertheless, because 5 out of 6 lines of evidence, encompassing a considerable number of different studies, have shown that the Taylor scale does predict some phenomena associated with anxiety, it may be concluded that construct validity has been demonstrated and that the Taylor Manifest Anxiety Scale does measure anxiety. However, it would still be risky to use a score on the scale to predict certain behaviors based on support for construct validity which suggests that the behaviors are theoretically related to anxiety. One could only be safe in making the prediction following a test of the relationship between the Taylor score and the occurrence of that particular behavior. In that instance, of course, one would then be dealing with predictive validity. It is only in predictive and concurrent validity that one can know the degree of probability of being right or wrong in the prediction that is made.

One way to increase the reliability of a test is to extend it or to add more items. Stating this in more familiar terms, one does not conduct a political poll with just a few individuals but obtains a larger sample in order to increase reliability or reduce measurement error. The specific reasons why reliability usually increases as the sample size or length of a test increases need not be specified; it can be taken as a basic measurement principle.

By extension, it has been argued that by increasing the number of tests that are given or by extending examination procedures, one can increase both the reliability and validity of psychological or psychiatric evaluations. This is one reason why many psychologists conducting forensic examinations administer a battery or group of tests, rather than a single test; the use of batteries are frequently justified by the claim that they are more reliable and valid than one or a few tests. These arguments can sound compelling to a jury, and they are indeed plausible.

As it so often turns out, however, claims or plausible assumptions are not supported by scientific testing. A number of studies show that obtaining greater amounts of information leads to little or no gain in judgment accuracy (see Chapter 5). This is why we need science—because what appears likely to be true or obvious often turns out to be otherwise once assumptions are put to test.

An important question can now be raised. What would happen if we would attempt to apply the concepts of reliability and validity outside the field of testing? For example, what if we attempt to apply them to the clinical evaluation by a psychologist or a psychiatrist? What would happen if on a cross-examination we would ask the psychologist or psychiatrist for his reliability coefficient or for his validity coefficient? In other words, what would happen if we ask him in what percentage of cases his predictions or evaluations have been established as correct? It would be a rare individual who could honestly say that he has kept some kind of formal record. Therefore, he could probably not truthfully answer the question other than to speculate. This is the real heart of the problem in the testimony of psychologists and psychiatrists. A professional license or certification is no guarantee of either reliability or validity. The author has had the experience of hearing a highly respected psychologist on the staff of a well-known institution raise the complaint that she estimated that she had done more than a thousand diagnostic examinations in that particular institution and did not know in a single case whether or not any of the predictions or statements she had made were, in fact, correct because there was no follow-up. Goldberg (1968b) stated it thus:

> If "clinical wisdom" results in linearly reproducible judgments of rather low validity, it becomes sensible to ask whether these judgments could not be improved through training. Leonard G. Rorer and I reasoned that the major cause of the low validity coefficients reported for the judgments of practicing clinicians is the fact that in most, if not all, clinical settings there is no realistic opportunity for the clinician to improve his predictive accuracy. For learning to occur some systematic feedback regarding the accuracy of judgmental response must be linked to the particular cue-configuration which led the clinician to make that judgment, but in clinical practice feedback is virtually non-existent and in relatively rare cases when feedback does occur the long interval of time which elapses between the prediction and the feedback serves to ensure that the initial cue-configuration leading to the prediction has disappeared from the clinician's memory.

In other words, what Goldberg is saying is that there is virtually no reliability or validity information available concerning the data upon which clinical judgments are made (other than that available for certain psychological tests). Thus, the process of clinical judgment appears to rest upon some process that may be mystical or perhaps art, but clearly is not science.

Haynes et al. (1993) note that there can be many possible causes for a single behavior problem and that people may differ regarding the importance of various causes for the same behavior problem. They state, "Many clinicians base treatment decisions on their subjective judgments of causality. Such judgments can be based on their reading, training, clinical experience, and other idiosyncratic factors." (p. 281)

They acknowledge that such judgments may be unavoidable and can be a powerful source of causal hypotheses, but that they are subject to numerous sources of bias. Because so many forensic situations involve "cause," it would seem that the legal decision makers would not want to rely on "hypotheses" derived from such an unscientific method. Similarly, Goldfried (1993) notes there has been acknowledgment of the importance in scientific inquiry of distinguishing between the context of discovery and the context of verification. He states, "The discovery of many important phenomena occurs in clinical practice. Because of the uncontrolled and potentially biased nature of such insights, however, they ultimately need to be looked at under more controlled conditions." (p. 2) These declarations support the point made above in the example of the "clinical" observation as to which brand of fertilizer was better.

TIME AND SCIENCE

Scientific validation takes time. This is very important in evolving areas such as the mental health/behavioral science field. It takes time for research to be done, written up, submitted for publication, reviewed, often rewritten, resubmitted, and finally gotten into the flow of publication to be published at some later time. Then, this process has to be repeated, probably several times, as other researchers take up the issue, replicating, expanding on or challenging the material. As an illustration, the Millon Clinical Multiaxial Inventory was first published in 1983 and was revised in 1987 (MCMI-2). Still, in 1993, two articles (Chick et al., 1993, and Inch and Crossley, 1993) were published on research with the MCMI-1. This is 10 years since the test first appeared. This is not at all uncommon in this field. Note that a revision of one of the most widely used psychological tests, the MMPI, was published in 1989 and the current revision of the diagnostic manual, DSM-IV, was published in 1994. Legal decision makers should be informed that at least 10 years from those dates will be needed to scientifically evaluate these revisions. Until then, they should be viewed as experimental and their admission into evidence and the weight to be given them should be determined accordingly.

REFERENCES

Campbell, R.J. (1985). Miscellaneous organic therapies. In H.I. Kaplan and B.J. Sadock (Eds.), *Comprehensive Handbook of Psychiatry* (4th ed.). Baltimore: Williams and Wilkens.

Chick, D., Sheaffer, C.T., Goggin, W.C., and Sison, G.F. (1993). The relationship between MCMI personality scales and clinician generated DSM-III-R personality disorder diagnoses. *Journal of Personality Assessment, 61,* 264-276.

Diagnostic and Statistical Manual of Mental Disorders (3rd ed., revised) (1987). The American Psychiatric Association.

English, H.B., and English, A.C. (1958). *A Comprehensive Dictionary of Psychological and Psychoanalytical Terms*. New York: Longmans, Green and Company.

Frankel, R.H., and Kaul, J.D. (1978). The Hawthorne experiments: First statistical interpretation. *American Sociological Review, 43*, 623-643.

Franzen, M.D., and Golden, C.J. (1985). Multivariate techniques in neuropsychology: III. Discriminant function analysis. *International Journal of Clinical Psychology, 7(2)*, 80-87.

Goldberg, L.R. (1968b). Simple models or simple processes? Some research on clinical judgments. *American Psychologist, 23*, 483-496.

Goldfried, M. (1993). Implications of research for the practicing therapist: An unfulfilled promise? *Clinician's Research Digest, Supplemental Bulletin #10, November 1993.*

Guilford, J.P. (1950). *Fundamental Statistics in Psychology and Education* (2nd edition). New York: McGraw Hill.

Haynes, S.N., Spain, E.H., and Oliveira, J. (1993). Identifying causal relationships in clinical assessment. *Psychological Assessment, 5,* 281-291.

Inch, R. and Crossley, M. (1993). Diagnostic utility of the MCMI-I and MCMI-II with psychiatric outpatients. *Journal of Clinical Psychology, 49,* 358-366.

Kety, S.S. (1969). Biochemical theories of schizophrenia: Part I. In D. Rosenbaum and P. London (Eds.), *Theory and Research in Abnormal Psychology.* N.Y.: Holt, Rinehart and Winston.

Mora, G. (1985). Historical and theoretical trends in psychiatry. In H.I. Kaplan and B.J. Sadock (Eds.), *Comprehensive Handbook of Psychiatry* (4th ed.). Baltimore: Williams and Wilkins.

Preston, T.P. (1981). *The Clay Pedestal.* Seattle: Madrona.

Risse, G.B. (1979). The renaissance of bloodletting. A chapter in modern therapeutics. *Journal of the History of Medicine*, 3-22.

Siddall, A.C. (1980). Bloodletting in American obstetric practice. *Bulletin of the History of Medicine, 54*, 101-110.

CHAPTER 3

Challenging the Scientific Status of Psychology & Psychiatry

INTRODUCTION

The distinction is often made between the "hard" and the "soft" sciences or between the advanced sciences and the less advanced or fledgling sciences. As discussed in the chapter on scientific method, the term "science" can be used to refer to one or both essential features of science—the methods that are employed to gather knowledge, and the knowledge or the status of knowledge gathered through scientific method. Either or both of these features can be used to help demarcate the differences between the more and less advanced fields of science and to evaluate the standing of a scientific field. Our purpose in this chapter is to utilize such criteria to analyze and critique the scientific status of psychiatry and psychology. We will indicate that, within the areas of psychology and psychiatry most pertinent to the typical domains in which the expert witness operates, scientific status is seriously deficient.

In the prior chapter we emphasized scientific methods. Awareness of this area is most relevant for critically examining knowledge claimed by the expert to be "scientific," but which was actually not derived from scientific methods, or which utilized beginning or less rigorous forms of scientific method that allow for conjecture but rarely produce trustworthy scientific knowledge. In this chapter, we will emphasize the status or scientific standing of knowledge in psychology and psychiatry. We choose this emphasis for one essential reason. Although one cannot produce scientific knowledge in the absence of scientific method, the use of the scientific method does not ensure advanced scientific knowledge. As we described previously, branches of what are now considered the "hard sciences" typically required many years before "hard" or powerful knowledge was produced. Thus, if proper scientific methods were not used, or particularly if scientific methods were not used at all, it is quite unlikely that the end product will be reliable or trustworthy scientific knowledge.

However, what of the expert who cites or relies on studies that utilize perfectly acceptable scientific method? The lawyer will gain little by trying to show that the derived knowledge was not produced by proper scientific method and thus cannot be relied upon. Rather, when method cannot be criticized, or when this line of questioning is relatively unproductive, the lawyer should know how to challenge the scientific status of the information, assumptions, or theory upon which the expert relies. In any case, the lawyer is in the most advantageous position if both method and knowledge can be effectively challenged. Thus, we will start by briefly discussing some bases for evaluating the scientific status of knowledge, and then we will see where psychology and psychiatry fit against these standards. These bases or standards can serve as a sort of checklist for the lawyer, or topics that one might wish to cover in cross-examining experts.

BASES FOR EVALUATING SCIENTIFIC KNOWLEDGE

ESTABLISHED OR STABLE BODY OF FACTS AND LAWS

The harder sciences, such as physics and chemistry, are characterized by "hard" facts and laws, or a stable and reliable body of facts and laws upon which further achievements are built. Laws of planetary motion, or combinations of chemical elements that form more complex substances, are examples of important observations and laws that have served for long periods of time as part of the fundamental knowledge base of astronomy and chemistry, respectively.

There is considerable debate within the philosophy of science about the precise nature of scientific advance or progress and whether, strictly speaking, new ideas and theories utilize previously established facts and laws as building blocks or actually serve to alter or reorganize these prior facts and laws to some degree. Thus, historians and philosophers of science debate whether Einstein really built his theory upon Newton's, or whether Einstein's theory represents a break with and recasting of previously established ideas. We need not enter into the fine points of this debate, but a few points are pertinent, especially because some experts may try to establish parallels between "problems" in the hard sciences and problems in psychology and psychiatry. In turn, they may try to argue that the lawyer has overblown problems in the soft sciences or has suggested an invalid or artificial distinction between the hard and the soft sciences.

Whether Einstein recast Newton's theory or not, it is still the case that a range of highly accurate predictions was, and is, possible with Newtonian theory. Additionally, scientists did not give up Newtonian theory because they grew tired of it or because they decided it was not any good. Rather, an even better alternative was *shown* to be available. What we mean by "shown" is that, with few exceptions, scientists did not convert to Einstein's theory until a very impressive and remarkable investigation provided validating evidence for the theory. Additionally, although Einstein's theory covers a wider range of phenomena than does Newton's and is more exact, in many cases one must carry out calculations to the *n*th degree to show the superiority of Einstein's theory over Newton's. Finally, few physicists would debate whether Einstein's theory represented a step forward. It simply became obvious over time that it was a forward step. Thus, although there is room to debate the *type* of advance that has occurred, it seems quite clear that physics, like other hard sciences, does indeed show progressive advance and that, in this sense, new theories build upon old ones.

Contrast these changes in the hard sciences to those more typically found in psychology and psychiatry. Sets of ideas, or what one can refer to loosely as theories (see below), are commonly abandoned simply because individuals grow tired of them or just plain give up on them. Many current non-Freudians did not give up Freudian theory because, although it allowed for highly accurate predictions, another theory received validating evidence that demonstrated it was even better. Rather, they considered Freudian theory rather hopeless from a scientific standpoint and decided to try something different. It is important to recognize that this set of circumstances is not at all unusual in the social sciences—new ideas or theories are developed because one gives up on the old ones, and one then tries to obtain validating evidence for these new theories. It is *not* the case that powerful validating data are first obtained, or that an alternative theory first receives strong evidence in its support and is then accepted. New theories may be ventured on the mere hope of future promise, because the available alternatives are viewed so negatively. Thus, one is actually starting almost anew, or from "square one." One may have learned something from past failures (as opposed to successes), and thus one may be less likely to repeat the same mistakes again, but this is not truly *building* on anything. Rather, it is simply starting over again and virtually revamping things entirely. One must start almost from the beginning, testing the new theory and carrying out the usually lengthy work of developing, refining, and changing the theory as new evidence is gathered.

As we will show in subsequent chapters, these statements characterize many "innovations" or "advances" in psychology and psychiatry, including repeated revisions of the diagnostic manual and the proliferation of new approaches to psychotherapy. Philosophical debate will continue regarding fine distinctions about scientific advances, but one does not need to make fine distinctions to realize that there are very fundamental differences between the status of facts and laws, and the nature of scientific advance across the soft and hard sciences. *In the soft sciences, facts typically are soft or unstable, and change usually does not bring one forward so much as back to the beginning stages of theory development and validation, and to a point at which most prior work is rendered largely, if not entirely, irrelevant.*

POWERS OF EXPLANATION AND PREDICTION

Hard or advanced scientific knowledge is characterized by the range of phenomena that can be predicted and the precision with which they can be predicted. For example, it is possible to predict eclipses of the sun or the moon years in advance, often down to the minute or second they will begin and end. These predictions are made possible by established scientific knowledge. Although not so precise, the effects and courses of many disease agents can also be predicted with a fair degree of accuracy.

What of explanation? What does it prove or establish if the scientist can explain phenomena in a compelling manner? By itself, this proves almost nothing—explanation in lieu of the power to predict is a weak test of scientific knowledge. All that the power to explain shows is that somebody is convinced by the explanation. Great novelists, for example, are wonderful at explaining human behavior, or at helping us seem to understand the underlying motivations and actions of individuals. However, Shakespeare was not a scientist, and although a reading of *Hamlet* may seem to reveal great insights into human nature, the play by itself does not constitute scientifically validated knowledge. As we will see, the parallel can often be applied to psychologists or psychiatrists, who, even when almost completely lacking in well validated scientific knowledge, can paint a compelling explanation of an individual's behavior. Thus, it is important to be able to distinguish the power of explanation or persuasion from scientifically validated claims. Prediction, and prediction alone, is ultimately what separates mere conjecture from scientifically validated knowledge. *If tests of prediction have not been performed and passed, then no matter how persuasive an explanation may seem, it cannot be considered scientifically established, proven or trustworthy.* Time and again, explanations that seem compelling have been shown to be wrong when put to scientific test.

It is also important to distinguish scientific forms of explanation from everyday forms of explanation. A scientifically adequate explanation is one that is consistent with some scientific theory. For example, when an object falls to the earth, a scientist may "explain" this as a product of gravitation, gravitation being a force postulated by theory. Note that such an explanation would also provide predictive powers, as one would be able to predict the speed with which the object will fall toward the earth. This situation is not unusual—when it is possible to provide a theoretically-based explanation of a phenomenon, one can also use the same theoretical constructs that provided the explanation to make predictions. A scientifically adequate explanation is *not* provided when, in principle, a set of opposing facts can be equally well explained by a theory. Stated differently, if virtually everything that could occur can be "explained" by the theory, the explanation must be inadequate, or the theory must be lacking in some essential manner. Good theories specify not only what can occur, but also what cannot occur, or what is not possible. That is, what they preclude is as important as what they permit. Let us explain why this is the case.

Suppose we invent a theory as follows: "All human behavior is caused by the actions or decisions of three alien beings who monitor our planet." Probably all would agree that this is not a very good theory, or at least one that is not scientifically established. However, our "theory" is capable of explaining all human action, albeit not in a scientific manner. If defendant Jones stole all the money from the bank and then placed it in a Swiss bank account, we can explain his behavior as caused by our alien beings. If Jones stole the money and then gave it to charity, we have our alien beings to thank. If Jones changed his mind and did not steal the money at all, our explanation might be that one of these alien beings liked Jones and convinced the other two to look out for Jones's interests (and those with accounts in the bank). So we have explained all of these possibilities with Jones, and indeed we can explain the actions of anyone else as well.

What are the problems with our theory? One problem is that it can easily explain inconsistent or conflicting forms of evidence. If Jones does one thing, the theory can explain it; however, if Jones does the opposite thing, the theory can explain it equally well. An advanced scientific theory cannot explain a set of facts that conflict with each other; rather, it can only explain facts consistent with the theory. Note further that if a theory can explain everything, then there is nothing that it cannot explain, or nothing that can occur that would provide evidence that our theory is in error. It is the unusual scientist who starts out by assuming that his or her theory renders "truth" in absolute form. Rather, the scientist assumes the theory will need to be modified, refined, and perhaps expanded as new data are gathered. A theory that can explain everything cannot be shown to be in error—or rather, one cannot find out how it is in error, and thus one cannot correct it as needed.

Additionally, and perhaps most importantly, although our theory of alien beings may be capable of explaining everything, it can do so only after the fact—that is, it cannot predict events before they actually occur. We may be able to "explain" why Jones did what he did, but our theory would have been of no use in predicting what Jones was actually going to do. Thus, a theory that can explain everything can explain nothing scientifically, is not capable of being tested, and has no predictive power. And a theory that can explain nothing scientifically, that cannot be tested or improved as needed, and that cannot predict has hardly achieved advanced scientific status. In fact, in the eyes of many or most scientists, such a theory would not be considered scientific at all. These are some of the reasons why, ultimately, the test of a theory's scientific power is not its explanatory power alone, but rather its predictive power.

These points are important to consider when an expert justifies a theory by its explanatory power. When this occurs, one can always ask the expert to discuss the limits of explanation as a means of gauging scientific status (a rebuttal witness may be needed if the expert witness is not versed or candid on these rudimentary points). Once it is shown that explanation alone is of little or no power in the absence of predictive power, one can ask the expert about the predictive power, as tested scientifically, of the theory he employs. Virtually all theories relied upon by mental health experts have, at best, very meager predictive powers. Thus, it can be established that the theory upon which the expert relies has very limited scientific status, if it can be claimed to be scientific at all, as regards established knowledge.

LEVEL OF AGREEMENT

Branches of the hard sciences are characterized by uniform or near uniform agreement on a range of matters, such as certain definitions, measurement procedures, or laboratory techniques. Stated in a different way, one can say that some basics are pretty well settled. For example, in physics, it is well established that light travels at a specific speed. Additionally, with well established observations or procedures, one can typically assume that if the correct or proper technique or steps are repeated, one will obtain the same results or outcome, and that this will hold true regardless of which scientist performs the procedures or in which laboratory the work is done. For example, almost any introductory chemistry text or training manual describes a range of experiments that students can perform, including the results they can expect when they perform the experiments correctly. When a student fails to achieve the expected results, one does not assume that a new discovery has occurred, but rather that the student did something wrong, and that if these errors are uncovered and corrected the right result will be obtained.

Agreed upon, relied upon, and broadly repeatable procedures and observations, in contrast, are rare in the soft sciences. For example, as we will describe, most psychiatrists have their own particular variations in the interview procedures they use. Further, it is the rare instance in which one can know, with any degree of certainty, whether the right result has been obtained. It is also rare to find widespread agreement across practitioners or settings on the results of psychiatric evaluations, and equally rare to find widespread agreement on even very basic "facts," "laws," or theoretical principles (see Havens' [1981] comment below). In fact, such agreement is virtually nonexistent, as even the most basic notions are widely disputed, such as the existence of "the unconscious" or the relative contributions of genetic and environmental factors in shaping or determining human behavior.

CLASSIFICATION

We will have much to say about the state of classification in psychiatry and psychology in the next chapter, and thus will cover this topic only briefly here. It should suffice to say that in the advanced sciences, classification is often taken for granted, because a system has already been devised which can handle many or most existent cases. Rather, it is the unusual case in which classification becomes a problem, either because a new phenomenon has been observed that does not fit neatly into any of the current categories or because certain phenomena show features common to more than one category. In most cases, it is clear into what category an entity or fact falls, practitioners in the field show uniform or near uniform agreement about categorization, and there are few outliers (i.e., entities that resist clear classification). The table of elements in chemistry provides a good example. One will not find chemists arguing about whether a sample of oxygen is or is not a sample of oxygen or how it should be classified. Most elements can be identified and appropriately classified and there are set, standardized, long-standing procedures for doing so. Some new elements have been discovered in recent years, and there is debate about how they should be classified, but these are certainly the exception rather than the rule. Old elements have not been eliminated as new ones have been discovered. Given the severe difficulties in classification in psychology and psychiatry, many practitioners envy a system as strong as the one developed by chemists, and they recognize that the current system they use has not even begun to approach this level of agreement, reliability or precision.

STRUCTURAL AND PROCEDURAL FEATURES
OF THEORIES

A theory is a conceptual system used to organize observations and data into categories and classes which, in turn, are often organized into more basic or fundamental classes. The theory attempts to state the nature of the relationships between data and classes, and between one class and another, and then further attempts to use these statements or principles to explain what is found in nature and to predict what will be found when new observations or experiments are conducted.

A theory may be restricted to a relatively narrow range of phenomena, in which case it is usually referred to as a "single domain" theory. Thus, for example, theories about human color vision are single domain theories. Other theories do not restrict themselves to a narrow range of phenomena but instead might be quite general, attempting to explain or predict a wide range of phenomena. Psychoanalytic theory is a general theory in this sense. It attempts to explain, or is purportedly capable of potentially explaining, all or most of human behavior.

Evaluative statements about theories, such as calling a theory a "good" one, can be employed in very different ways by scientists and can mean very different things. One scientist may call a theory good, meaning that the theory seems useful in providing a direction for research efforts. However, good can also be used to mean that the theory shares the characteristics of other theories that are scientifically advanced. Thus, a theory may be good in the first sense, but it may be no good, or even downright awful in the second sense. It is important to know the difference between theories that are deemed "helpful" in the sense of organizing observations and guiding research, and theories that have achieved the features characterizing reliable or advanced scientific knowledge. Many theories in psychology or psychiatry might be called good in the first sense, but few if any of the theories pertinent to expert testimony can be considered good in the second sense. What is needed—but lacking—is a theory that is good in the second sense, that could provide the accuracy in diagnosis and prediction that would aid a trier of fact.

Scientifically advanced theories are characterized, for one thing, by their precision; that is, terms and postulates are stated precisely. It is common, in fact, for postulates to be expressed in mathematical terms. In contrast, most postulates in psychology, particularly those contained in personality theory, are expressed verbally, often in a rather vague manner (e.g., "paranoia results from fear of latent homosexuality"). Along these lines, the reader might recall our statements in the previous chapter about definitions in the hard and soft sciences.

Theories in the advanced sciences also help to create the conditions necessary for precise measurement and observation. For example, theories in astronomy and physics allow for very exacting measures of the distance and size of heavenly bodies. To a large extent, advanced measurement techniques reduce the role of subjective judgment through the use of precise measurement techniques, prespecified and set procedures, and set rules of interpretation. Thus, it is possible to achieve very high levels of consistency across scientists. To provide what may seem like a banal example, two scientists do not feel an object to judge its heat, but rather use a standardized instrument for doing so, and merely take the readings off the instrument. If the two had to rely instead on actual physical touch to gauge heat (which was once the only method available), they might well reach different conclusions, their likelihood of being precisely correct would be poor, and—even worse—there would be no way of knowing who was the more accurate. Thus, for example, a highly accurate instrument for gauging heat bypasses almost entirely the need for subjective judgment, allows for data that can be scrutinized by other scientists (unlike subjective judgments that take place only in the scientist's head), provides exact figures, and produces results easily agreed upon by scientists.

There is obviously a very sharp contrast between this public and essentially objective form of measurement and the assessment performed by a psychiatrist of, for example, internal conflicts. The measurement procedures of the psychiatrist are neither standardized nor objective, but rather quite subjective. They are not based on advanced scientific theories or formally proven postulates but rather on what is essentially a loose set of vague conjectures.

The "readings" that one psychiatrist obtains are often quite different from the "readings" that are obtained by another practitioner, and there is often considerable dispute about the "figures" and what they might mean. These are some of the reasons why an expert's report that he or she relied on his or her own (subjective) judgment processes in reaching a conclusion, even when stated with great conviction, and as if a positive factor, can be taken merely as a confession that there was nothing better to rely upon (this "something better" being the type of scientific theory or measurement procedure that allows for reasonable certainty). A physicist who told his colleagues that he should be accorded greater credibility because he decided to discard his precise measurement instruments and instead relied on his subjective "feel" for the data would probably be met by disbelief and scorn. We would add here that there is one way in which psychologists and psychiatrists could make the data on which they rely more public and open to scientific scrutiny—that is by videotaping their assessments (see below).

Theories, whether advanced or not, should also maintain logical consistency, or avoid statements or postulates that conflict with one another.

For example, a theory that can be used to simultaneously explain and predict conflicting facts may well contain postulates that, in fact, conflict with one another or that are not logically consistent. Many critics of Freudian theory point out its lack of logical consistency as one of its fatal weaknesses.

Finally, although all do not agree on this matter, probably the majority of scientists, in particular those in the hard sciences, would argue that a theory must be testable if it is to be considered useful, because without testing, the theory is nothing more than speculation. Conclusions drawn from the theory, therefore, are nothing more than speculation as well, and the courts generally do not accept speculation.

THE MASK OF OBJECTIVITY OR
ADEQUATE SCIENTIFIC STATUS

According to the standards we have described above, the theories commonly relied upon by clinician-experts have not yet even approached advanced scientific status. Rather, when placed under careful scrutiny, they are found to contain very serious deficiencies. This is not, however, what many experts claim; instead, they may use any one of the following arguments to create what, in the final analysis, is really only a mask of objectivity or scientific status.

Some experts will defend the scientific *methods* underlying the studies, or some of the studies, they cite. In the cases in which these claims can be defended, one should keep in mind that method alone does not make an advanced science. Rather, adequate method is a means to an eventual end—scientific knowledge. Just because method has been adequate, it does not provide assurance that an advanced theory has been developed. For example, the fact that there have been some methodologically sound studies of certain personality assessment techniques does not establish these assessment techniques scientifically. Golding's (1992) comment (supra, Chapter 1) concerning the controversy over lack of scientifically acceptable theories and methods is salient here. In actuality, many of the studies have revealed glaring weaknesses and inadequacies in the techniques. Thus, for one thing, methodologically sound studies may produce counterevidence for certain theories and postulates, as opposed to supportive evidence. Second, it frequently takes years of very intensive study and testing before rudimentary scientific knowledge is derived, much less advanced knowledge. An expert who claims that this or that study "establishes" the validity of a test instrument or a theory has either used the term "established" in a very narrow or limited sense, or perhaps has not recognized, or is not telling, the full story.

Another important point to bear in mind, because it is very much the rule rather than the exception in psychology and psychiatry, is that if one can cite a number of well conducted supportive studies, there also exist well conducted, nonsupportive studies. There are *very few* areas in the social sciences in which a considerable body of research is consistent. The lawyer should be aware that the existence of conflicting studies often does not deter the expert from citing the one or a few studies, perhaps well conducted ones, which support the position he or she is trying to defend. Thus, it is often necessary to ask the expert to discuss the studies that do not support his position, and if he can cite and discuss none of these, a consultant-expert can be used to discuss the pertinent literature. Alternatively, the expert may claim that the disconfirming studies are methodologically unsound or inferior to the supportive studies. This could be true, but more likely the expert has used one standard to critique the supportive studies and another, much harsher standard to critique the nonsupportive studies. We will subsequently refer to this practice as using a double standard of evidence—more relaxed standards for the evidence that supports one's opinion and much tougher standards for studies that do not.

Suppose there is a set of studies, some supporting a position and others conflicting with it, and further suppose that, overall, there is no clear superiority in the methods employed across the supportive and nonsupportive studies. Can one justifiably claim that the position has been "partially" supported? Probably the best answer is no, and that if one were forced to take sides the best conclusion is that the position, at least for now, should be assumed to be *invalid*. This is because in scientific work, disconfirmation is generally considered a stronger form of evidence than confirmation. Let us explain why.

Suppose one postulates that *all* individuals with red hair have hot tempers. Suppose further that the first 35 redheads we study indeed have hot tempers, a result that supports our postulate. However, beyond question, red-haired individual Number 36 is calm and relaxed, and by no stretch of the imagination is hotheaded. This one single case of disconfirmation totally undoes our postulate that *all* red-haired individuals are hotheaded. It does not matter how many further supportive cases we obtain, our postulate is wrong. We might modify the postulate to state that most redheads are hot-headed, or that the majority are, or whatever, but if we are to be scientifically responsible we will have to change it in some fashion.

Although we have simplified some rather complex issues within the philosophy of science, we have correctly represented mainstream thought among many leading philosophers of science and probably also among psychologists who are informed in the area—that disconfirming evidence is more powerful than confirming evidence and that the two should not be considered equal (e.g., Greenwald, 1975; Mahoney, 1977; Meehl,

1978; Weimer, 1979). Thus, one probably should not conclude that if two-thirds of the studies support a position and one-third do not, the position is in pretty good shape. This point is important because of the considerations we have mentioned above—that even should the expert be able to cite some well conducted, supportive studies, there are quite likely to be some, if not a substantial number of nonsupportive studies. The existence of such studies creates considerable doubt, if not actual disconfirmation. Doubt erodes credibility. One might add that if there exists mixed evidence and the scientific community has yet to solve the issue, of what help could it be to the trier of fact? The courtroom is not the place to try to solve scientific controversies.

As we have discussed above, an expert witness may also refer to a theory as a good one, and thereby imply acceptable scientific status. The lawyer should be aware, however, of the actual meanings the term "good" is likely to have when used in this context. First, the actual meaning of "good" may be that the clinician believes the theory helps him to understand or explain behavior—that it helps him make some type of sense out of an individual's thoughts or actions. Here we must again reiterate that understanding or explanation, in lieu of demonstrated predictive power, is a limited scientific achievement. Second, the practitioner may also mean that the theory is good or useful for directing or generating research. Obviously, such a function is largely independent of whether the theory consists of scientifically well validated hypotheses or laws; a theory can indeed be useful for directing research, even if very limited scientific support for the theory is available. Third, the term good may be used to mean or imply that the theory is embraced by many practitioners. However, this proves little or nothing as regards its scientific status. It is fair to say that within psychology and psychiatry, no matter the theory one uses, one is likely not in the majority: there are more practitioners who embrace differing theories, or at best there are a considerable number of practitioners who embrace some other theory. There are many instances in which broadly accepted facts or "laws" were clearly in error, as in the previously discussed examples of bleeding or the belief that the world was flat. "Broadly accepted," in the absence of validated scientific evidence, establishes only that it is broadly accepted.

As another strategy, the expert may try to point out that speculation is common in all fields of science, and therefore argue that the existence of speculation in the social sciences makes it like, rather than unlike, the hard sciences. This is actually a very weak defense and open to challenge on a number of fronts. First, speculation is common in almost all areas of intellectual endeavor, such as economics, politics and fortune-telling. That one engages in speculation provides no support for any contention that this strengthens one's underlying scientific status or that it provides an important point of similarity across the soft and hard sciences. Nevertheless, authors like Delman (1981) point out that experts in other fields, such as physics, also show disagreement, as if this proved something about psychology or psychiatry. A second and related point is that speculation and disagreement among those in the soft and hard sciences have a very different quality. In the soft sciences, researchers debate almost everything, and almost nothing is agreed upon. In the hard sciences, a corpus of knowledge is taken as a given, and speculation mainly involves subject matters at the growing edge of scientific activity, or work that attempts to expand what is already known. Thus, two psychologists may argue about the most rudimentary issues in psychological testing, whereas two physicists do not argue about the speed of light.

A previously described article by Green (1981) makes a similar point. Green states, "No one argues over the physical concepts of length, volume, mass and momentum, nor is there serious disagreement over how these concepts should be measured." But in the social sciences, he states, "There is controversy not only about how concepts should be measured and the precision of those measurements, but there is also considerable controversy over the meaning of the constructs themselves."

Any branch of science that has any hope of moving forward from what is already known will evidence speculation and disagreement at the growing edge of knowledge. The important question is where this growing edge starts, or how much is already known or well established. One thing that separates a hard science from a soft science is that, in the former case, a great deal is already known and generally accepted. Disagreement and speculation jump off from a sturdy and considerable platform of knowledge, whereas in the soft sciences the practitioners are commonly arguing about whether there is a platform at all, or how they should best go about starting to build one.

With these points of distinction in mind, we can briefly discuss two occurrences or phenomena in psychology and psychiatry that are "symptoms" of "illness" as regards scientific status. First, a number of authors either allude to or provide direct evidence for the assumption that practitioners place only secondary emphasis on scientific status when selecting evaluative procedures. One such reference comes from Reynolds et al. (1985). They describe research suggesting that practitioners in clinical psychology ranked scientific support quite low in comparison to other factors when selecting among automated services for the interpretation of psychological test results. Rather, for example, the price of the services was ranked above the amount or quality of the research backing up the programs or services. It is hard to know what to make of these findings, although Reynolds et al. labeled them as "disheartening." One will find numerous instances in which the practices of psychologists and psychiatrists cannot be backed up scientifically, and one must question how often this occurs, regardless of claims to the contrary, because there are no clear scientific winners but rather a large and diverse collection of scientific "losers," or, more kindly stated, hypotheses and speculations which have yet to be proven.

A second symptom of scientific "illness" may be the preference of many researchers for adopting what they refer to as an "atheoretical stance." What this means is that they do not explicitly assume that any theory is best or correct, but rather plan to collect data that will form the starting point for the construction of an adequate theory. The prominent behaviorist, B.F. Skinner, is a strong proponent of this approach; the task force responsible for developing psychiatry's new diagnostic manual(s) has seemingly also tried to avoid theory as much as possible, and Exner (1986) describes his approach to the Rorschach as atheoretical. There is an issue in this emphasis on "atheoretical" approaches. It is a clear statement on the part of the researcher that he believes that the theories to date are inadequate or not worth using.

Sales (1986) also notes a rift between the science and the profession of psychology. He states, "The conflict between scientists and professionals within APA has a longstanding history and continues to this very day." (p. 1)

Phillips (1989) points out that despite the need for the science and practice of psychology to be joined, they have not become joined in the most meaningful and significant sense. He notes that it has been suggested that scientists and practitioners are so different as to require a split. (p. 3) He also notes that professional practice needs to be extensively altered and that psychological science is a tool for this purpose, but that there is a difficulty because technological advances can become subversive to professional practice. That is, as psychological science uncovers or refines lawful relations and behavior, it "tends to subvert established views in the nature of professional practice." (p. 4)

MacKay (1988) cites Royce (1984) to the effect that in general, "Psychological theories do not mesh well with the relevant data....Psychology's history in this regard reveals a pattern of extreme pendulum swings between observation and theory—that is between the empirical and rational epistemologies, with only the occasional investigator attempting to bring the two together." (p. 559)

Finally, some experts will point to their success in psychotherapy as evidence for the accuracy of their diagnoses or underlying theoretical orientation. There are *many* problems with such an argument, only one of which we will mention here (for further discussion, see Chapters 8 and 22). A considerable and consistent body of research shows that paraprofessionals (i.e., those lacking in professional training) achieve, on average, at least equal psychotherapy outcome to professional therapists. This evidence has been derived from studies, which we will discuss later, in which patients or subjects for psychotherapy were treated either by professionals or those without professional training, and the success of the treatment was then compared. Across these studies, the professionals and non-professionals usually performed about equally well, although in some studies the *paraprofessionals did somewhat better* and in some studies the professionals did somewhat better. In any case, the literature does not show that professional therapists, on average, obtain significantly better treatment results.

Experts may respond to these studies, if they are aware of them, by claiming that better trained therapists or professionals were not used, but such a claim is simply inaccurate, because a number of studies included highly trained professionals. The expert may also claim that no matter what these studies show, in his experience he has achieved very good outcomes and is sure that his results are better than those that nonprofessionals would have achieved. One would assume that many of the professionals included in the actual studies believed the same thing, but when these beliefs were put to actual scientific test they were not supported. Thus, in reality, the weight of the evidence is against the expert, and his claim to exemption, no matter how sincere it might be, is merely guesswork (unless the therapist's outcomes have been scientifically compared to those achieved by a paraprofessional with comparable patients). We might also note that the paraprofessionals in many of these studies had received little in the way of preparation before attempting treatment, and their background training or knowledge of the field, perhaps with rare exception, could not be considered anywhere near equal to that of the professionals.

Thus, what happens if one gives credence to the claim that treatment outcome is a reasonable means for determining scientific status? The obvious conclusion to be drawn from the study of para- or nonprofessionals is that a clinician's spouse (whether they are or are not professional therapists), or at least any nonprofessional who engaged in these studies, should be allowed to testify in court as an expert witness if the expert's claim is to be taken seriously. In fact, why should nonprofessionals be required to establish their treatment effectiveness at all? In most cases, the expert has not either. Perhaps all that should be required is a belief on their part that they are effective. After all, these individuals are likely to achieve equal treatment effects, and thus we must conclude that (because treatment effects are allegedly a proper way to gauge scientific status) these nonprofessionals' beliefs about human behavior are of equal scientific status to those of the professional. On the other hand, we could draw what are arguably more rational conclusions, namely, that an individual clinician's impressions about his treatment effects are a poor means for gauging scientific status, prove little or nothing in the fields of psychiatry and psychology, and are not a sufficient basis for granting expert status.

Further, even if treatment outcome were better for experienced professionals it would not mean that diagnoses were correct, because there is evidence diagnosis is not related to treatment outcome (see Chapter 22).

Preston (1981) puts the matter this way when discussing physicians' evaluations of their own treatments:

> Most of the "knowledge" on which therapy has been based has been incorrect, but, at every stage in the history of medicine, the knowledge of contemporary doctors was considered authoritative....Current practices always have been believed to be true and accurate. (p. 158)

Further,

> In no aspect of clinical medicine is the use of scientific method more needed or less in evidence than in the assessment of therapies. Historically, doctors have enthusiastically embraced therapies which ultimately turned out to be of no benefit to their patients, and there is evidence of the same today. (p. 105)

APPLICATION OF THE STANDARDS
TO ASSESS SCIENTIFIC STATUS

With these bases for gauging scientific status in mind, we can consider how, in the eyes of some rather prominent psychologists and psychiatrists, psychology and psychiatry measure up. In our coverage we will emphasize the status of personality theory, simply because it is personality theory that is typically most relevant to the forensic assessment performed by psychologists and psychiatrists.[1] We will start with a general overview, and then proceed to detailed coverage of perhaps what still may be the dominant personality theory, at least among psychiatrists—psychoanalytic theory.

In the original edition of a textbook widely used for courses in personality theory, Hall and Lindzey (1957) describe several dimensions for evaluating psychological theory. Under the heading of formal characteristics, they mention three: 1) Clarity and explicitness. They indicate this may range from the literary descriptive to the mathematical, with literary descriptive being the least clear and mathematical the most clear. 2) The relation to empirical phenomena. This refers to processes from simple naming to operational definitions. 3) Empirical research generated. This refers to the capacity of the theory to stimulate research and generate new data.

---

[1] In the text, "personality" is used in a broader psychological sense than in common parlance, such as "he has a nice personality." For example, one might refer to Freud's theory as a theory of personality.

Hall and Lindzey discuss more than a dozen substantive issues as bases for comparing one theory to another. All of these are issues on which current theories disagree among themselves to some extent. They represent unresolved issues in psychology and psychiatry, and the list is impressive. In the most recent edition of this text (Hall et al., 1985), this list has been compressed into nine categories, which include conscious vs. unconscious, heredity vs. environment, past vs. present, person vs. situation, purposive vs. mechanistic, and normal vs. abnormal. When an expert has revealed his stand on any of these issues, his credibility can be lowered by showing that he has committed himself to one side of an unresolved controversy.

Hall and Lindzey (1957) describe more than a dozen major theories of personality, all possessing some degree of current acceptance, and show how they differ from each other in terms of these numerous criteria. In a second edition of their outstanding book, Hall and Lindzey (1970) find no significant advances which require them to alter their fundamentally negative conclusions concerning the state of personality theory over the period of thirteen years which elapsed since the publication of the first edition. Thus, the negative conclusions they drew in 1957 as regards the overall status and validation of personality theories are repeated in their 1970 edition:

> The fact of the matter is that all theories of behavior are pretty poor theories and all of them leave much to be desired in the way of scientific proof. Psychology has a long way to go before it can be called an exact science. Consequently the psychologist must select a theory he intends to follow for reasons other than those of formal adequacy and factual evidence. (p. 71)

After pointing out that no current theories meet all the requirements of a good theory, they note certain deficiencies. Specifically, most theories "lack explicitness," making it difficult to identify the basic assumptions that underlie the theory. Relying on "vivid word images," many theories "seem more oriented toward persuasion than exposition." Furthermore, there is "frequent confusion between that which is given or assumed and that which is stated empirically and open to test." Consequently, serious confusion exists in the process of deriving empirical statements from the theory. (p. 15)

Hall and Lindzey further state:

> In comparing the theories we shall focus on the differences in form. Our principal reason for overlooking formal differences derives from our conclusion that at this stage of development, there is little basis for choice among these theories on such grounds. All are in need of considerable improvement before they can be considered even *minimally* [italics ours] adequate in terms of formal criteria such as explicitness of statement and adequacy of definition. (p. 584)

They then go on to delineate the multitude of differences amongst the various theories on a wide variety of critical issues. In fact, should the lawyer wish to make use of it, they provide an excellent tabular representation of the differences among 17 current personality theories along the dimensions of 22 issues of critical importance which are still unresolved in personality theory. In the 1985 edition (Hall et al.), they provide a similar summary table (pp. 574-575) covering 20 theories and nine dimensions.

In the current edition of the text, Hall et al. (1985) indicate that some advances have been made but reiterate many of the limits discussed above. For example, they note that "the diversities and disagreements" across personality theories are "more striking" than points of similarity (p. 587), and that "We are still a long way from a single, comprehensive theory." (p. 587) They again note that different elements of theories often conflict with one another or are in "flat disagreement" (p. 587), and they discuss limited predictive power, lack of explicit meaning and organization, and other shortcomings (see Chapter 1 of their text).

Sarason (1972), discussing the study of personality, asserts that both data gathering and data integration are needed in the development of personality theory, but that if forced to be arbitrary, he would see data gathering as the more immediate need in an objective study of the behavior of persons. Sarason states:

> Most psychologists agree that owing to the newness of their field and the complexity of its subject matter the development of theories of behavior is still rudimentary. This certainly applies to the psychological approach to personality. As we have mentioned, a major characteristic of workers in the area of personality is their preoccupation with internal processes and the effects of these on individual overt behavior. Some of these processes are susceptible to reliable measure. These include such bodily phenomena as blood pressure and brain waves. However, much less is known about mental and intangible processes such as thinking and intellectual and personality functioning. (p. 9)

As do Hall and Lindzey, Sarason elucidates a number of crucial but unresolved issues in the field of personality theory. Other authors (Buss, 1984; Pervin, 1985; Smelser and Smelser, 1970) emphasize the relative immaturity in the fields of personality theory, sociology and anthropology, leaving most reviewers "critical and pessimistic" about the status of personality psychology.

Moving to more specific statements, a number of writers have addressed the lack of validated or established scientific facts within the field. Coleman (1984) notes that despite the extensive utilization of psychiatrists in legal matters, they have *no* valid scientific tools or expertise. Matarazzo (1986a), a former president of the American Psychological Association, who has written a broadly used text on intellectual assessment, states that the *"professional psychologist is first and last an artisan."* (p. 20) He states further, "Clinical psychology today is still an art based on some scientific background and not a mature science." (p. 20) Matarazzo goes on to argue that this lack of scientific maturity can be expected to continue for an indefinite period of time. He further argues that, "Psychological assessment is currently almost exclusively a still-to-be-well-validated work of a legislatively sanctioned, clinician-artisan." (p. 20) Robinson (1980) states, "Psychiatry is a 'social science,' which is to say that it is not a science at all. And the same is true of psychology and sociology. The experts drawn from these disciplines do not bring to the trial a body of durable knowledge, a set of scientific laws, or even an assortment of reliable measures or procedures." (p. 61)

While the problems attending specific areas of research are too numerous to list, Kahn (1982) offers a sample in his evaluation of the research evidence for the male sex role identity (MSRI). Despite the virtual absence of support for such an entity, the research reveals a refusal by psychologists to abandon these theories. They survive, according to Kahn, "for lack of an alternative, better perspective."

Whether the topic is personality theory, theory in general, or specific areas of clinical concern, the scientific status of psychology and psychiatry leave much to be desired. Along these lines, Fishman and Neigher (1982) state that current knowledge in psychology may be "living on borrowed time." Goodwin (1984) argues that no one has the slightest idea what they mean by disease and that nobody can define it. He contends that psychiatry tends to run about 200 years behind the rest of medicine.

Paul Meehl (1973), another former president of the American Psychological Association, states: "I consider it unnecessary to persuade you that most so-called theories in the soft areas of psychology (clinical, counselling, social, personality, community, and school psychology) are scientifically unimpressive and technologically worthless." In examining the literature of the previous thirty years he observes that theories in psychology seem never to die, they just slowly fade away; this is in contrast to developed sciences where theories either become widely accepted and built into a larger body of well tested knowledge or suffer destruction in the face of recalcitrant facts, and then are abandoned. Growing bafflement about inconsistent or unreplicable empirical results finally produces a loss of interest as psychologists turn their attention elsewhere.

In another article that touches on both the lack of validated scientific principles and additional criteria for evaluating scientific status—the power to explain and particularly to predict—Meehl (1979) points out that in the other sciences two conditions are necessary before powerful predictions can be mediated on the basis of theoretical constructs. These conditions require that the theory be well worked out and well corroborated, possessing high "verisimilitude," and also that there be a powerful technology of measurement. Meehl states, "since we meet neither of those conditions in clinical psychology, we should not be surprised to find out that our predictive powers are limited."

McFall (1991) in his presidential address to the Society for a Science of Clinical Psychology, a section of the clinical division of the American Psychological Association, states that the only legitimate and acceptable form of clinical psychology is scientific psychology. He argues that where there are lots of unknowns, such as in clinical psychology, it is imperative to adhere as strictly as possible to the scientific approach and not to rely on intuitive and non-scientific approaches. He states, "It is time to declare publicly that much of what goes on under the banner of clinical psychology today simply is not scientifically valid, appropriate or acceptable." (p. 79) He urges members of the organization to blow the whistle whenever they encounter invalid practices, announce that "the emperor is not wearing any clothes" and insist on discriminating between scientific and pseudoscientific practices.

Many authors describe the extreme diversity and intensive disagreement that characterize theory and practice in psychology and psychiatry. Lesse (1977) describes the appearance over the previous seventeen years in the *American Journal of Psychotherapy* of numerous editorials indicating "the frailties, inadequacies, and anachronistic concepts" that have characterized the traditional schools of psychotherapy.

Freedman and Kaplan (1972) declare in their introduction that one might assume that a book about interpreting personality offers within its pages a single definition of personality and, perhaps, of psychoanalysis, but such is not the case. No single theory of personality adequately explains or predicts normal or abnormal functioning.

Fiske (1979) asks whether psychology is a science and answers in the negative. He states, "It does not have a single paradigm. It does not have a theory to which most psychologists subscribe. There are few beliefs or values accepted by most of the field."

Cattell (1975) observes that diversity in viewpoint and frequent "innovation" are characteristic of less well developed sciences. He asks, "What is the status, as a science, of psychiatry today?" and answers by noting the lack of stability of concept and maturity, characteristic of a developed science; instead, there is an "illusion of progress" created by rapidly changing from one emphasis to another—for example, from psychoanalytic therapy to behavior therapy. (p. 669) However, Cattell does observe that more recently, an increasing emphasis on quantitative methods is a more promising sign.

There is also very considerable diversity across the theories and approaches underlying treatment, or psychotherapy. Appelbaum (1985) indicates that a survey of the field of psychotherapy would indicate a situation that is, "to put it as politely as possible, uneven." He states:

> We have an ever-increasing glut of procedures—around four hundred at last count—each one stemming from different technical beliefs and different social, political, and philosophical conceptions of persons practiced and promoted by people of wildly different training and talent. Competition is carried on mainly at the level of debate with formal research, often even disciplined thought, honored more in the breach than in the observance. Patients or clients are subjected to one or another procedure by the accident of which therapist's office they enter.

Havens (1981) states that "Psychiatry as an agreed-on body of knowledge hardly exists. Instead, we have a variety of psychiatries—psychoanalytic psychiatry, biological and behavioristic psychiatry, social and interpersonal psychiatry, existential analysis—the list can be made even longer." Sechrest (1985) describes clinical practice as chaotic, lacking in standardized or agreed upon assessment procedures, and possessing virtually no set rules.

Sadler and Hulgus (1992) observe that medical/psychiatric practice poses problems both within and outside the scientific realm and that the biopsychosocial model is not able to account for clinical problems to which the methods of science do not apply. They note that concerns are voiced about this model's lack of utility in everyday clinical decision making and its inability to differentiate between important and unimportant data.

Reiss et al. (1991) declare that psychiatry has always been a "precarious" discipline and that it has been forced into a chronically uncomfortable position of straddling biomedicine and the social sciences.

Omer and London (1988) note the dramatic proliferation of schools of psychotherapy within the decade, 1976-1986, rising from 130, according to one author, to 250 to 300 to over 460 reported in 1986. They observe that the previously orderly state of separate and almost isolated systems has been subverted by new therapies, and by new research and skeptical challenges to the major systems from within, ultimately producing "today's turmoil." (p. 171)

Beitman et al. (1989) similarly note, "Psychotherapy systems appear and vanish with bewildering rapidity on the diffuse, heterodox scene in the United States," (p. 138) and similarly point out the rise from 36 systems in 1959 to more than 400 reported in 1986. They state that this proliferation "has been variously characterized as confusion, fragmentation and discontent." (p. 138) They note that no single theory has been able to demonstrate superiority in terms of validity or utility and that there is a growing consensus that no one approach is clinically adequate for all problems, patients and situations.

Johnson and Brems (1991) refer to studies showing that both clinical and counseling psychologists most frequently identify themselves as eclectic. They cite Zook and Walton (1989) as apparently indicating 14 theoretical orientations as important enough to be included in their study of preferred approaches.

Lane and Schwartz (1987) note that emotion is a quite complex phenomenon only incompletely understood and that a coherent framework for understanding the nature of normal as well as psychopathological emotional states does not yet exist. They state, "The conceptual framework we have at present for understanding individual differences in the emotional lives of patients and the changes that occur in the experience of emotion during the course of treatment is quite limited." (p. 133)

A number of authors also describe problems subjecting theories to scientific test. We said earlier that theories that cannot be tested must be considered mere speculation, and that the courts should not allow mere speculation. Along these lines, Cooper (1985) argues that there is a paucity of validating strategies for testing psychoanalytic theories. As one partial solution or aid, he suggests that information from other disciplines be used to provide a check on the findings and theories of psychoanalysis. Bartol (1983) points out that vague and imprecise theories cannot be tested scientifically, and therefore, even should they be false, this cannot be demonstrated. We might also add that even if they happen to be true, or at least correct in some respects, in the absence of scientific testability one cannot gather any firm evidence on the correctness of assumptions, either. Thus, the theories remain supposition only. Bartol argues that, given this resistance to scientific testing, the use of these theories can be extended indefinitely, regardless of their validity or deficiencies. He uses Freudian theory and neo-Freudian theory (i.e., variants of Freudian theory) as illustrations of vague and imprecise theories that resist scientific testing and, therefore, verification. He notes that proponents of these theories can assert their validity while remaining immune from counterevidence or scientific test. If the reader finds himself drawing parallels with our "theory" of the three alien beings who control human behavior, a theory that could "explain" everything and predict nothing, we would not necessarily attempt to counter any such perceptions.

Lomranz (1986) states, "The various personality theories differ widely in their overt and covert conception of people and accordingly in their content and methodology." (p. 551) He states further, "Such diversion seems to represent not only personality theory per se, but psychology as a whole; this raises the question as to the position of personality theory in the field of psychology." (p. 551) He notes that almost all reviewers of the field in the last decade or so have been rather critical or even pessimistic, viewing the field as being in a state of crisis, lacking advancement, fragmented among conceptualizations, research and clinical relevance, and perhaps impossible altogether.

Levy-Leboyer (1988) states:

> The discrepancy between what psychologists can bring to bear on a problem and what they are expected to provide has a double impact on the extent and the nature of application in psychology. On one hand, tools, techniques, and general rules of behavior are too often taken for granted and applied without further scrutiny. On the other, psychological application that upsets deeply rooted representations or social habits meets strong resistance. (p. 779)

He goes on to point out that new ideas are too easily accepted and applied in psychology, even if they are based on poor evidence.

The lawyer can bring out in cross-examination that there are well over a dozen theories of personality or behavior possessing sufficient status and acceptance as to require their inclusion in a textbook on theories of personality. Nobody really knows which theory (if any) is correct, nor which is best. Woodmansey (1967) states that there is a "glut of conjectural systems of psychopathology, but generally without much root in factual evidence." Woodmansey also states: "There can be no more urgent or conspicuous problem in psychiatry as a scientific discipline than that it lacks a generally agreed theoretical framework on which to base practice and teaching." Therefore on cross-examination, to the extent that the expert admits he relies principally on one theory or another, he can be challenged to demonstrate the superiority of proof of that theory over others. Thus, if the witness testifies from a basis of Freudian psychoanalytic theory, he can be asked whether other clinicians use other theories, and how his theory has been shown to predict better than Adlerian theory, Jungian theory, behavioristic theory, Levin's field theory or any other theory. Such a demonstration cannot be made.

PSYCHOANALYTIC THEORIES

Two theories or approaches frequently encountered in the courtroom are the "psychoanalytic" and the "eclectic" (i.e., combining elements from different theories). For coverage of other theories, the lawyer can consult any of a variety of texts that describe personality and related theories, such as Hall et al. (1985).

The terms "psychoanalysis" and "psychoanalytic" are used in many different ways by diverse people. It is perhaps symbolic of one of the severe defects of this approach that the nature of the approach itself lacks clear definition.

One difficulty is encountered due to three divergent uses of the term "psychoanalysis." In one use, psychoanalysis refers to a conceptual theoretical system for understanding human development, personality, and behavior. In a second use, psychoanalysis refers to a specific method of investigation. Ordinarily that method is used in conjunction with psychoanalytic theory. The third use of psychoanalysis refers to a specific method of psychotherapy. For the most part, in this book, the term "psychoanalysis" or "psychoanalytic" is used in the sense of a theory (except in Chapter 22 which deals with treatment).

Even in the use of the term "psychoanalysis" as a theory, disagreements rage between groups who regard themselves as "orthodox," because they continue to adhere to the system and methods developed by Sigmund Freud, and other groups who have elaborated or modified the theory as presented by Freud. The latter groups are generally called "neo-Freudian."

Although strict Freudians disagree vehemently, and there is no genuine consensus among others, generally the term "psychoanalysis" is applied to any system which gives great emphasis to unconscious motivation, psychic determinism, and the genesis of present behavior in early childhood experience. English and English (1958) define psychoanalysis as:

> (1) A body of doctrines set forth by Freud with modifications by his close disciples. The doctrine is based on the concepts of unconscious motivation, conflict and symbolism. The boundaries of psychoanalysis are not sharply defined. In America, it is applied to positions that deviate in many ways from Freud's (but where the deviation is considerable, Neo-psychoanalysis is preferable). (p. 417)

THE MAJOR BASES OF ATTACK ON PSYCHOANALYTIC SYSTEMS

Bearing in mind the confusion and lack of clarity that exist in the term "psychoanalysis," there are six major bases of attack upon the psychoanalytic systems. These bases, which will be discussed at length below, are: 1) disagreements among the Freudians, 2) disagreements among psychoanalytic schools, 3) disagreements between psychoanalysis and other approaches, 4) basic defects in the psychoanalytic system, 5) some common criticisms of specific aspects of psychoanalytic theory, and 6) evidence contrary to the validity of psychoanalytic theory.

A substantial group of authorities, including past presidents of the Academy of Psychoanalysis and the American Psychopathological Association, is in general agreement to the effect that psychoanalysis has failed to meet the test of appropriate scientific rigor and that Freudian psychoanalytic theory is in danger of soon passing from the scene, although some express the hope that by modifying itself in the future and adopting a more scientific approach, psychoanalysis may survive and come to earn its place in the sciences.

Disagreement among the Freudians

Even among those who espouse the Freudian system, there is disagreement on many points; for example Freud's intended meaning in the use of terms such as "sex" or "sexual," or the status of concepts such as "id," "ego" and "super-ego." Thus, if it cannot be established what the system specifies, how can it be used to explain human behavior? Furthermore, the fact that nearly all of Freud's early followers, virtually disciples, broke with his doctrine within a relatively short period of time, and formed independent schools of thought, underscores the point that even loyal and devoted adherents found it impossible to accept the Freudian system.

Disagreements among Psychoanalytic Schools

The development of a number of schools of thought within the psychoanalytic movement, usually called Neo-Freudian, illustrates the divergences of thought among various psychoanalytic approaches. Thus, for example, the Adlerian school emphasizes the drive to superiority and power, in contrast to Freud's emphasis on sexuality as the wellspring of human behavior. Jung, meanwhile, differed from both Freud and Adler in that he placed even less significance on conscious determinants of behavior. While his approach is generally regarded as too "mystical," Jungian institutes remain quite active. Rank, another early follower, broke with Freud in almost all respects, and emphasized "separation anxiety" as the basis for all personality development. Inherent in all of this is the important fact that even within the psychoanalytic approach (which is itself only one of many existing approaches to understanding human beings and human behavior), there is no consensus and there is widespread disagreement at the present time.

With such extensive disagreement, and in the absence of a convincing demonstration by any one school of the superiority of its position over that of the other schools concerning the nature and causes of human behavior, what legal value can any evidence have which is based on any one of these theories—or for that matter, upon several of them employed together (i.e., eclectically)? Although none of the schools can claim as many adherents as the Freudian, there are, nevertheless, substantial numbers of psychiatrists and psychologists who follow the schools of Adler, Jung, or the Neo-Freudians even today, and thus, there is no consensus.

Disagreements between Psychoanalytic and Other Approaches

Even within psychiatry itself there are practitioners who espouse the so-called organic or descriptive point of view as distinguished from the psychoanalytic or psychodynamic point of view. This point of view is much more "sickness" oriented, seeking the cause of deviant behavior or personality development in some form of physiological, biochemical, or anatomical dysfunction, and is less given to theorizing about development than to attempting to describe various psychopathological states. Although this view may not be accepted by the majority of American psychiatrists (there is a trend in this direction), it has numerous adherents and contributes to the further dilution of the possibility of any particular approach being able to meet the admissibility requirement of general acceptance. That these organic and descriptive approaches have been no more successful than the psychodynamic is illustrated by the many quotes that can be found in the literature to the effect that there has been no demonstration of organic basis for most of the common forms of psychopathology, nor has any adequate or satisfactory system been developed even for describing various syndromes (see Chapter 7 under the heading, "Not Medicine Either").

In addition to the foregoing divergent approaches, there are a large number of theories of sufficient current importance to be described in a book such as Hall and Lindzey's *Theories of Personality* (Hall et al., 1985), and which are of sufficient importance to be taught in courses in personality or systems of psychology. This may best be illustrated by looking, for example, at the table of contents in the Hall et al. book which, in addition to the psychoanalytic theories, discusses such theories as Murray's Personology; Lewin's Field Theory; Allport's Psychology of the Individual; Sheldon's Constitutional Psychology; Factor Theories; Stimulus-Response or Learning Theories; Rogers' Self Theory; Skinner's Operant Reinforcement Theory; Existential Psychology; and theories that emphasize social learning. All of these approaches differ from the psychoanalytic approach, from the organic approaches and from each other, and several have substantial bodies of followers.

The import of all of the foregoing is that there is simply no agreement as to the theoretical bases of human behavior and thus no approach can be considered to be "generally accepted." As Hall and Lindzey (1970) put it in the second edition of their book:

> If one concedes that psychoanalytic theory is guilty of at least two serious faults—first, that it is a "bad" theory and, second, that it has not been substantiated by scientifically respectable research (and also mindful of the fact that many other criticisms might have been cited), the question then arises as to why psychoanalytic theory is taken seriously by anybody and why it was not relegated to oblivion long ago? How are we to account for its dominant and influential status in the world today?

> The fact of the matter is that all theories of behavior are pretty poor theories and all of them leave much to be desired in the way of scientific proof. Psychology has a long way to go before it can be called an exact science. Consequently, the psychologist must select the theory he intends to follow for reasons other than those of formal adequacy and factual evidence.

A moment's thought will reveal the startling implications of this statement. What Hall and Lindzey are saying, in effect, is that the only reason psychoanalytic theory continues to occupy its place in psychiatry and psychology is not because it is any good or has been demonstrated to be any good, but simply because there is nothing better—or as they put it, there are not any good theories. Thus in one succinct paragraph they damn both psychoanalysis and all other extant theories of personality.

Hammet (1965) pointed out that psychoanalytic theory has been accepted mainly on the basis that there is nothing else that is any better. This certainly does not justify its acceptance by courts as a basis for expertise. Obviously, the same argument could be made for the polygraph, or for that matter, astrology or crystal-ball gazing.

Basic Defects in the Psychoanalytic System— the Non-Scientific Status of the Psychoanalytic Approach

An overriding defect in the psychoanalytic system from a legal point of view is that it is not scientific in the commonly understood meaning of that term, although it pretends or claims to be so. Thus, the psychoanalytic system has been described as subjective, vague in its concepts, non-predictive, non-quantitative, circular, tautological, unvalidated, untestable, and subject to the *maximum* probability of bias and distortion in its gathering, reporting, and interpretation of data. This contrasts sharply to the general understanding that a science is objective, quantifiable, has reasonably clear terminology, has testable hypotheses, rests upon a body of established and validated principles, and employs methodology designed to *minimize* the probability of bias and error in the collection and interpretation of data.

Probably from a courtroom point of view, the most significant deficiency has to do with the investigative methods of psychoanalysis. The claim of psychoanalysis for credibility and validity rests primarily on an extensive accumulation of clinical and case study reports, yet it has been abundantly stated, and demonstrated beyond dispute that the analyst, who is the investigator, exercises considerable influence over the kind of data that patients will produce. There are strong grounds for maintaining that the many case studies in which psychoanalytic concepts have presumably been "confirmed" by the productions of patients constitute little but some sort of compliance with the wishes, conscious or unconscious, of the analysts. This, of course, is in addition to the deficiencies of the clinical method, which involves the selective perception, memory, and interpretation of the analyst. This point simply cannot be stressed too much (see Chapter 6). It again must be emphasized that, to a large extent, the kinds of data and the verbalizations produced by the patient in analysis or in any diagnostic situation are heavily influenced by either conscious or unconscious needs or wishes of the analyst. In addition, what is reported in the literature is often not even the raw data produced by the patient, but rather the analyst's interpretation of those productions which, whether truly supportive or not, will "conform" to the preconceptions he holds. It must be further understood that research has shown that there is a marked tendency to ignore those productions of the patient which do not fit in with the theory (see confirmatory bias, Chapter 5). Exposure of the deficiencies of the clinical examination can effectively counter statements by psychiatrists that certain principles have been "verified" by clinical experience.

The significance of the foregoing is that there is *no substantial body of reliable scientific data* supporting the claim of psychoanalysis to validity or to scientific status. This statement may be shocking to some, but it is nevertheless true. Hall et al. (1985) note that although studies at two universities have produced results that have been viewed as supportive of Freud's work, other research efforts have "failed to confirm psychoanalytic theory." They also note that widely differing views have been taken on existent research. They indicate that much of the basis for psychoanalytic theory has lacked scientific rigor and that considerable additional research is needed.

As Davidman (in Hoch and Zubin, 1964) has stated: "Massive clinical reports of psychoanalysis have filled files in analytic institutes with material that is unreliable and totally inadequate for meaningful research." Because of this defect in its primary mode of "investigation," psychoanalysis must at present be considered not science but conjecture.

Another feature upon which the psychoanalytic approach clearly lacks adequate scientific "credentials" is the ambiguity and lack of clarity in the definitions of terms and concepts it employs. Psychoanalysis employs literary definitions, frequently compounded and confused by esoteric and dramatic terminology such as that employed by Freud and some of the other psychoanalytic theorists. Such terms, for example, as "libido," "instinct," "catharsis," "id," "sexuality," "orality," "anality," and "narcissism," among others, lack both specific external referents and specific meaning. Therefore, they are highly susceptible to different usage and interpretation by different people. Thus, in many instances, it is not possible to be sure of the meaning of any given term or concept in the psychoanalytic system.

Another defect of psychoanalysis as science is that it is unable to predict. For example, many psychoanalysts will glibly state after the fact that an individual performed a given act because of his "unresolved Oedipal conflict." But there are few, if any, instances in which the psychoanalyst can tell you in advance that this individual has an "unresolved Oedipal conflict" and therefore will perform the given act. The assumed causal relationships of psychodynamic processes to present mental conditions fail to appear when subjected to objective investigation.

Difficulties or near impossibilities in quantifying many concepts is another area of deficiency in the psychoanalytic approach. Thus, for example, while Freud speaks of quantities of libido invested in various erotogenic zones of the body, there is virtually no way to attach the "correct" number to those quantities. It is highly problematic to identify that quantity of "Oedipal conflict" which may be considered pathological. Thus, in an approach which states that the pathological is only a matter of differing in degree from that which is normal, how does one state those quantities which fall within the normal or within the pathological range?

Kupfersmid (1992) concludes that the Oedipus complex is an elusive hypothetical construct, it has never been satisfactorily measured, and its explanation as a causal factor in psychopathology is questionable.

The indefiniteness of the psychoanalytic approach's definitions and its virtual inability to predict or quantify give rise to another serious deficiency we have previously discussed—they make core aspects of the theory untestable, or incapable of proof or disproof. In the ordinary procedures of science, it is possible to clearly specify a given variable, state a hypothesis predicting a certain outcome based on what is known or believed about that variable, and submit it to a test under controlled experimental conditions. As a result of the experiment, one might either confirm the prediction or admit that under objective and controlled conditions it is not possible to confirm the hypothesis. This type of research is commonly difficult or almost impossible in the psychoanalytic approach. Rather, the psychoanalytic tenets, assumptions, hypotheses, fantasies, and speculations frequently have to be, or are taken on faith. Many psychoanalysts defend against the criticism on the grounds that psychoanalysis is yet a young science. It is, of course, legitimate for a young science to develop new concepts and hypotheses in its endeavor to become a mature science. The legitimacy of speculation in the effort to make progress is not a matter for criticism. However, conclusions based on such speculative and unconfirmed hypotheses have no place in a courtroom. They should not be allowed into evidence and, if erroneously allowed, should be given no weight. In no event should they be given the status of science.

Because essential elements are virtually incapable of external scientific verification, the psychoanalytic approach attempts to prove itself by itself, thus giving rise to the criticism that it is circular or a "tautology" (Ovesey, 1960; Sarason, 1972).

Strupp (1971), in our view a proponent of psychoanalysis, expresses serious concern about the current state of psychoanalysis, although in this article he generally takes the position of a supporter. However, he clearly reveals that it can by no means be considered an accepted theory of human behavior. He states that psychoanalysis is described as antiquated, passé, obsolete and even defunct. He also states that it is based on formulations and working assumptions which are in dire need of a massive overhaul and its status as a branch of the behavioral sciences appears to be approaching a nadir. He also indicates that psychoanalysis has failed.

Strupp goes on to comment critically on the use of the clinical method for the purpose of acquiring knowledge, stating that more or less uncontrolled observations made by a therapist in the course of psychotherapy as it is typically practiced are not very likely to lead to significant discoveries. And, finally, Strupp concludes that psychoanalysis has lost its scientific respectability in 1970.

Further criticism may be found in the *International Journal of Psychoanalysis* (Volume 52, 1971, pp. 11-47) in a discussion of issues in research on the psychoanalytic process where they describe the informal clinical case study as having formidable scientific limitations in spite of its compelling power. Slater (1975) provides additional evidence of the shortcomings of psychoanalysis, noting that the tremendous work of orchestration employed by Freud freed his theory from any compulsory ties to objective standards, thus making it possible for his theories to explain all phenomena. Since nothing could prove the theory wrong, therefore it must be true. Slater continues by noting that psychoanalytic theory and method form a closed system in which the method is validated by the facts that are revealed and the truth of the revelations is proved by the infallibility of the method.

Slater points out that psychoanalytic theory and method form a closed system in which the method is "validated by the 'truths' revealed and the truth of the revelations is proved by the infallibility of the method." He states: "It is only over the lapse of decades that we have become aware that Freudian causation is nonempirical and that his causative entities are not hypotheses, but fictions." (p. 217) Slater concludes that psychoanalysis is not a science and is not one of the medical arts (and he incidentally points out that to the extent that psychiatry is identified with psychoanalysis it follows that medicine has no place in psychiatry).

Meehl's point (1979) that psychology lacks both a well worked out and well corroborated theory and one that provides a powerful technology of measurement is of course applicable to psychoanalytic as well as any other psychological theory. He notes the attack by Fleiss on Freud as far back as 1900, when Fleiss told Freud that "the thought reader merely reads his own thoughts into other people." Meehl describes this as the fundamental problem concerning psychoanalytic concepts (that is, determining whether the thought reader's thoughts concerning other people's thoughts are correct). Meehl points out that this problem, along with the rise of two powerful therapeutic competitors, behavior therapy and rational-emotive therapy, has diminished the interest of psychoanalytic therapists in pursuing this problem.

Bilmes (1990) notes a diminishing interest among psychiatric residents for psychoanalysis. He also describes the inability of psychoanalysts to agree on "what psychoanalysis is." (p. 17)

Frank (1979) provides an extensive discussion of the current status of psychoanalysis, as well as reviews of the divergent thinking of many of the spokesmen from the psychoanalytic field regarding its status and future. Frank points out that as a general theory psychoanalysis is undergoing a number of crises and that, while psychoanalysis has been accustomed to challenges from outside, the impetus for the current revolution comes from within, thus indicating the extensive disagreement among adherents of this school of thought. He notes that some of the disputes involve demands for elimination or alteration of the influence of Freud's orientations, philosophy, epistemology, and vocabulary. He notes that many of the critics assert that the established views in psychoanalysis are encumbering rather than helping and may form a major obstacle to needed revisions and advances.

Brody (1988), when reviewing a book by D.P. Spence (*The Freudian Metaphor: Toward Paradigm Change in Psycho-analysis,* New York: Norton, 1987), states, "Spence, a psychoanalytically trained psychologist, is an effective writer that pulls no punches. The heart of his message, couched in frequently biting language, is that the (Freudian) 'emperor has no clothes'." (p. 576) He cites a number of pungent quotes from this book dealing with various aspects of psychoanalytic propositions. For example, "little more than sophisticated demonology," "a literature of anecdotes," "a dumping ground of observations which have little more evidential value than a thirty-year-old collection of flying saucer reports." Brody also points out that while it is not clear at the end, Spence does not appear ready to abandon psychoanalytic theory and method altogether, but suggests that new approaches to it are needed.

Time Magazine (Gray, November 1993) carries an article describing the serious doubts and challenges that have arisen concerning the status of psychoanalysis. Gray notes a number of new books attacking Freud and psychoanalysis for numerous "errors, duplicities, fudged evidence and scientific howlers." (p. 47) He cites, among others, *Validation in the Clinical Theory of Psychoanalysis* by Adolf Grünbaum (International Universities Press) as providing a "devastation" of psychoanalysis as a science. Grunbaum is a noted philosopher of science and professor at the University of Pittsburgh.

Chertok and Stengers (1988) make reference to Freud's view of his theory as analogous to chemistry. They note that under inquiry about the power of psychoanalytic "truth" to explain its processes, it would be found to stand up to the criteria of scientific method no better than does Mesmer's fluid, a now discarded concept. They state, "Imagination is still with us as a problem, not a scientifically controllable factor." (p. 647)

Dumont (1994) points out that there is little support of "Freudism" as a science among philosophers of science. He observes that the constructs that "are essential and specific to the Freudian system are still without scientific warrant" (p. 197) With regard to the Freudian and Neo-Freudian labels, he states "The labels lead us to think that we are anchored in historically validated principles. The anchoring in fact is too often in antiquated myths." (p. 197)

Dujovne (1991) notes that a major issue of controversy in Freudian theory has been the masculine theory of female development, pointing out that resistance to new ideas has been particularly true of Freud's psychology of women. She describes a heterogeneity of current views ranging from orthodox to questioning to radical departures and notes that some psychologists may ask whether psychoanalytic theory of early female development is worth keeping in view of the disagreements between classical and revisionistic views. (She thinks it is.)

The foregoing material is highly significant in relation to forensic psychiatry. It helps to explain how rational judges and juries have been persuaded to buy the psychoanalytic formulation of a litigant's mental condition as a fact, when in truth, it is fiction. For example, the judge in *People vs. Gorshen* (one of the trilogy of cases in California establishing the "diminished capacity" defense), stated that the formulation (what we term a work of fiction) presented by one of the nation's leading forensic psychiatrists provided the only evidence in the case which would make the defendant's behavior understandable. Of course, as pointed out above, the psychoanalyst can always provide an explanation; he can always explain the behavior psychoanalytically. The misfortune, as indicated above, is that there is almost no way of knowing whether the explanation presented has any relationship whatsoever to reality. It is for this reason that lawyers can be vigorous in their efforts to bar any testimony based on this fictional, religious or art form as evidence in a court of law and, if unsuccessful in this effort, can expose to the trier of fact the fictional nature of such evidence.

SOME COMMON CRITICISMS OF SPECIFIC
ASPECTS OF PSYCHOANALYTIC THEORY

In addition to the foregoing deficiencies of psychoanalysis as a theory in general, many, if not all, of the psychoanalytic concepts have come under heavy criticism and are highly controversial. In particular dispute are the instinct theory, libido theory, the stages of psychosexual development, penis envy, Oedipal conflict, castration anxiety, the over-emphasis on biological factors in some psychoanalytic theories and the over-emphasis on social-cultural factors in other psychoanalytic theories, the difficulty of applying the theory outside of the field of the "neuroses," Thanatos or the death wish (the notion that the organism seeks a tensionless state, which is contrary to modern scientific evidence), and psychic determinism.

It is not argued that these concepts are bad simply because they are esoteric or even seem fantastic. It is quite possible that when it was first proposed that the world was round instead of flat, the notion seemed fantastic. However, if one advances notions which seem fantastic, it is incumbent upon one to supply adequate proof or be subject to disbelief and ridicule. Psychoanalysis has failed to provide substantial proof of the validity of most, if not all of the above concepts. Ridicule, in fact, is one effective means of dealing with many of these concepts in cross-examination.

The lawyer may also make use of the fact that many psychiatrists themselves reject one or more of the above concepts. In particular, the concept of Thanatos (the notion that all organisms seek death, or have a wish for death) is widely rejected except among the most rigid orthodox analysts. If the witness has testified that he relies in part on psychoanalytic theory, it is proper to ask him if he accepts the Thanatos concept. If he says he does not, it is then appropriate to ask him how he has determined to reject that concept while accepting other concepts of the theory. If he replies that there is not adequate evidence to support that notion, he can be asked to affirm the evidence that he finds inadequate to support this particular notion is the same kind of evidence often used to support other psychoanalytic notions. In fact, Freud produces exactly the same kind of logical deductions from anecdotal data in support of the death wish as he does in support of all the other psychoanalytic concepts. Unless the expert selectively relies on aspects of the theory for which mixed, but perhaps some supportive, formal, scientific research has been conducted, he will almost have to concede the point.

EVIDENCE CONTRARY TO THE VALIDITY
OF PSYCHOANALYTIC THEORY

In addition to the foregoing, there is some research evidence which is specifically contradictory to the validity of psychoanalytic theory. It goes without saying that it is almost impossible to disprove a theory in an absolutely final manner, particularly a theory in which the definitions and concepts are as vague and elastic as those in psychoanalytic theory. Usually, the closest one can come is to point to the efforts to test or validate the theory and their failure to produce supportive evidence. In the case of psychoanalysis, one line of evidence comes from the failure to validate psychoanalytic treatment. There is virtually no evidence to indicate that the psychoanalytic approach is superior to any other approach, or that the psychoanalytic treatment itself was responsible for the results obtained.

Statements by several eminent authorities within psychoanalytic and psychiatric circles attest to the fact that it has not been possible to produce any appreciable amount of respectable scientific evidence supporting the validity of psychoanalytic theory (Boignon, 1966; Chodoff, 1966; Davidman, 1964; Eisenberg, 1962; Eysenck, 1964; Grinker, 1964; Marmor, 1966; Millet, 1966; Rothman, 1962; Ruesch, 1966b). For example, Marmor (1966) states:

> On the other hand, the unhappy fact is that classical psychoanalysis as a *body of theory* [italics ours] has failed to meet the challenge of modern scientific scrutiny in recent years...Clearly, passionate personal conviction in this area is not a substitute for controlled scientific experimentation. Unfortunately, psychoanalysts who were first to make the world aware of the significance of the phenomena of resistance have themselves in large measure become its most striking exemplars....
>
> It will no longer suffice in today's scientific world to argue that psychoanalytic inferences need only be confirmed in the framework of the psychoanalytic method. If the inferences are correct they must, like any other scientific inferences, lend themselves to validation by alternative techniques and by independent observers. Otherwise, they simply do not qualify as scientific hypotheses. (p. 4)

He states in conclusion:

> If we wish to be taken seriously by our colleagues, however, the inferences that we draw from our data will have to be subjected to the same kind of rigorous evaluation and testing that is implied in any other field of scientific endeavor. In science, nothing is sacred except the *method* of science and, to modify John Dewey's paraphrase from the Book of Job, "although this method challenge our most cherished beliefs, yet we must be prepared to trust it." (p. 9)

Hammet (1965) elaborately argues that the continued existence of psychoanalysis is due largely to its efficacy in satisfying the emotional needs of psychiatric residents in training, rather than upon any merited scientific status. He states:

The emphasis upon psychoanalytic theory which has prevailed in psychiatric residency and post-residency training during the past twenty years is largely due to two factors: The residents' great need that is born of the urgent emotional determinants described above for an orderly method of approach to the problem of therapy in psychiatry and the absence of any other reasonably complete body of knowledge or convincing theory about the psyche in health and in disease. The unvarnished truth is that we are beset by great ignorance regarding the factors which determine human behavior. Psycho-dynamics has attempted to remedy this uncomfortable situation by elaborating an explanatory theory. In so doing, it has responded to the emotional needs of psychiatrists in training and thereby has won much favor.

Hammet also states:

Is all this training necessary or even desirable in the face of much evidence that psychoanalysis has never been proven any more effective for the cure of the manifestations of psychopathology than various other methods of treatment? (p. 47)

Miller and Alexander (1972) point out evidence that behavior modification as a treatment appears to be superior to therapeutic techniques using psychoanalytic principles.

Stoller (1973) describes five concepts of sexuality that run through Freud's writings—bisexuality, infantile sexuality and the Oedipus complex, libido theory, the primacy of the penis and conflict—and tests each against recent advances in sex research. He indicates that current research strongly suggests that Freud's theory of sexual development is wrong. Regarding the primacy of the penis, Stoller indicates that Freud accepted as a given belief that the superior sex is male, and points out that Freud, coming from a culture in which male authority still manifestly resided in fathers, did not have to question his principle that "anatomy is destiny." Stoller, however, says that any theory in which this idea is an essential building block is weakened if the principle is incorrect. He then cites evidence in conflict with the evidence Freud offered as support for his theoretical position, concluding that Freud's argument seems disproved. Recall Stoller's position that if this position is wrong, and it is an essential building block of Freudian theory, then the theory is weakened. Stoller also cites research and argument which is contradictory to libido theory, another building block of psychoanalytical theory.

Hall and Lindzey (1970) state, in reference to psychoanalytic theory:

The theory stands silent on the knotty problem of how the interplay of cathexes and anticathexes are to be measured quantitatively. In fact, there is no specification of how one must go about estimating, even in the roughest terms, differences in quantity. How intense does an experience have to be before it is traumatic? How weak must the ego be before it can be overridden by an instinctual impulse? In what ways do the various quantities interact with one another to produce a given result? And yet everything depends in the final analysis upon just such specifications. Lacking them no laws can be derived. (p. 71)

One might think that these often scathing criticisms of psychoanalytic theory over a period of many years would have eventually signaled the end of its reign. However, although its popularity has perhaps diminished, psychoanalytic theory and its newer variants remain broadly embraced, and continue to be criticized severely as well, as we will show through a sampling of more recent references. This perpetuation of psychoanalytic theory brings to mind Bartol's (1983) earlier point, that theories that are vague and imprecise resist scientific testing and thus can continue on and on, no matter their accuracy or lack thereof. No matter how negative an outcome may be, a proponent of psychoanalytic theory will always be able to come up with some way to explain the finding away, and thus, claim that it does not conflict with the theory. Therefore, even when incorrect, there is no final way to falsify the theory or to prove it is incorrect (or correct, for that matter, since one cannot have it both ways with a theory that can explain everything and predict nothing).

Pardes (1980) notes that, although there are some training programs with an exclusively psychoanalytic orientation and some with mixed orientations, other training programs exclude psychoanalytic concepts entirely. Thus, there is obviously disagreement within the field itself regarding the status of psychoanalytic theory. Research, such as that by Natale (1979), which examined psychoanalytic assumptions about the relationship between anger and depression, may be among the reasons why some training programs are now excluding psychoanalytic training. Natale stated that his findings "blatantly" contradicted psychoanalytic formulations regarding these relationships.

In an issue of the *Clinical Psychology Review* (Vol. 5, 1985) devoted to the status of psychoanalytic theory Eagle and Wolitzky (1985) provide an overview and critique of the articles that were presented. Their basic view is that, although there are some encouraging developments, psychoanalytic theory remains largely untested scientifically and that proponents have placed too much reliance on the case study method. Thus, more rigorous scientific testing is needed and one cannot consider the theories to be substantiated at present. Their critique is particularly important because it covers newer and popular variants of psychoanalytic theory, such as what is called "self-theory" or "object-relations" theories. Many experts who embrace psychoanalytic theories may respond to criticisms of Freudian theory or more traditional theory by claiming that they do not embrace such theories but rather newer, more modern, and better variants. Such responses can create the impression that the theory or theories they rely upon are better proven or supported, or worthy of greater trust, when actually these newer variants have not been subject to any more scientific testing. Thus, one could conjecture or guess that they may be better, but there has not yet been sufficient opportunity to place them under intense scientific scrutiny. At best, one can say that they are seemingly promising but unproven; at worst, one can maintain that they have simply not yet had the opportunity to be as thoroughly criticized or disconfirmed as have more traditional psychoanalytic theories.

Detre (1987), noting the ready acceptance of psychoanalysis in the United States in military psychiatry during World War II, states, "What is astounding is how little effort has been made to test the validity of our theories and how long we have remained a shelter for bankrupt ideas."

The foregoing deficiencies and negative authoritative opinion could be brought out in cross-examination of the psychologist or psychiatrist if he bases his opinion and testimony to any extent upon psychoanalytic theory. In the event the witness should refuse to concede any of the foregoing points, one should be prepared with this reference material and, additionally, be prepared to call rebuttal witnesses who have familiarized themselves with the reference material. Such rebuttal witnesses may be found in the psychiatric community or, if not, can easily be found in the psychology department of a nearby university, as a large number of academic psychologists take a dim view of psychoanalytic theory. Those who teach courses in Contemporary Psychology, Systems of Psychology, or Theories of Personality should be particularly well versed in all of this material and be able to present a lucid and convincing critique of psychoanalytic theory based upon the above deficiencies.

The foregoing description of the non-scientific and non-accepted status of psychoanalytic theory gives rise to some intriguing possibilities. First, there is the possibility of objecting successfully to the admission of any testimony based in whole or in part upon psychoanalytic theory. It would appear, based upon the foregoing exposition, that psychoanalytic theory has not achieved scientific status, nor has it even achieved that degree of acceptance among the scientific community that would justify its recognition as a science by the court. It is difficult to close the door once it has been opened, as it has been in the case of such testimony. Nevertheless, it appears that psychoanalytic theory is a highly controversial and speculative system, and that some courts would be willing to take the point of view that testimony based on it is simply too lacking in trustworthiness and probative value to be admitted. It cannot justifiably be stated, for example, that psychoanalysis is in any higher state of scientific respectability than the polygraph, which at the present writing is not admitted as evidence. Perhaps this attack could be made on voir dire or by objecting to the first substantive question put to the psychiatrist on the grounds that it is irrelevant and incompetent.

A further intriguing possibility follows from this approach. At least in some cases, the exclusion of testimony based on psychoanalysis might effectively bar some psychiatrists from testifying at all, in view of the fact that they could not in all honesty state that they were not relying, at least in part, on psychoanalytic theory. This is true because for many psychiatrists the major conceptual approach, sometimes the only conceptual approach, that they have learned is that of psychoanalysis and without it they have little or no basis for formulating their opinions.

There is one more intriguing possibility. If one can successfully exclude testimony based on psychoanalytic theory, but the psychiatrist states he is nonetheless able to base his opinion on some other theory, one can immediately object on the ground that there is no other theory in psychiatry that has received even as much acceptance as psychoanalytic theory. That is, if the psychiatrist says that he is not basing his testimony on psychoanalysis, he could be asked on what he is basing it. If he states that he is basing it on any other theory, it is immediately subject to the challenge, regardless of what that theory may be, that it has not gained any kind of widespread acceptance among the scientific community in psychiatry. That is, none of the other theories—Adler, Jung, Horney, Fromm, Sullivan, or whatever—has achieved as much acceptance as has Freudian psychoanalytic theory; therefore, none of them can be said to have achieved acceptance among the scientific community. Further, it cannot be claimed that any of them has been scientifically or experimentally validated.

If the psychiatrist indicates that he is not basing his testimony on theory of any kind, but upon his own experience and observations, one has made a major gain, because it should be possible to effectively rob psychiatric testimony of any aura of science or any claim that it is based on scientific principles. Also, experience in psychiatry is a very tenuous and vulnerable basis upon which to form opinions (see Chapter 8).

THE ECLECTIC POSITION

Recognizing the inadequacies of any particular school of thought, many contemporary clinicians, perhaps the majority, would avoid or deny adherence to any one school of thought. They will indicate that rather than narrowly following the dictates of a particular theory, they take selectively from some number of the existing theories such material as they feel is most useful. Whether they use the term or not, this is the position described as "eclectic." At first glance, this looks good. It suggests that the clinician has wisely avoided premature commitment to unvalidated theory. This illusion disintegrates upon closer scrutiny, however. It does not mean the clinician functions in the absence of a theory or free of the constraints of theory. When a clinician combines what he feels are the "best" or "most useful" elements of various theories, what he is doing, in fact, is creating his own theory. Thus, for example, if Dr. X combines elements of Freudian theory, of Adlerian theory, of existentialist theory, and behaviorist theory, what he has actually done is developed his own theory of human behavior. The name of this theory is "Dr. X's Idiosyncratic Theory of Human Behavior and Personality." Inasmuch as it likely has never been published anywhere, nor subjected to the scrutiny and criticism of his colleagues, nor to any formal scientific tests, it is simply a far-out, highly conjectural, unsubstantiated theory, accepted by no one but him. Therefore, no testimony based on such a theory should be admitted into a court of law. The completely idiosyncratic nature of eclecticism can be made clear either on objection to the testimony or in cross-examination.

It should be noted that frequently psychiatric testimony appears in the form of a so-called "psychodynamic" formulation. This formulation can only be derived from theory. Obviously, in the absence of an adequately validated or generally accepted theory, such a formulation is merely speculation and as limited in value as the theory upon which it is based.

In a survey of theoretical orientations among a sample of clinical psychologists, Garfield and Kurtz (1977) found that a majority of the sample labelled themselves as eclectic. However, in their survey they found that the term "eclectic" meant different things to different participants in their survey. For some, it simply meant flexibility in the choice of therapeutic techniques, attempting to adopt or utilize the particular technique that seemed best suited to the patients' needs. For others, it did not represent a wide-ranging combination of different theoretical positions, but merely utilization of two or three of the many existing theories. For yet another group, the process represented an attempt at amalgamation of theories or aspects of theories, or a combination of many orientations of facts. Similar findings were reported in a subsequent survey by Norcross and Prochaska (1982), which also showed that many psychologists view themselves as eclectic and embrace some synthesis of diverse theories.

Yager (1977) observes that eclecticism has become fashionable in some psychiatric circles and a cause for concern in others. He also notes that the term has been used with different meanings, being regarded as any psychiatric ideology including more than just psychoanalytic psychiatry, interest in anything except psychoanalytic psychiatry, and a practice of eclecticism in selecting treatment procedures. Yager notes that the theoretical perspective is important because no one perspective is able to supply a full appreciation of all the data, and observers oriented to different approaches tend to focus on different data and draw different conclusions. He indicates that little is known about the reasons a given clinician selects a specific theoretical orientation, but notes, among the possibilities, the influence of teachers, the age of the clinician, the modes of thought to which he has been exposed, and personality differences and attitudinal variables. Notably absent from Yager's postulations of the possible reasons for selection is perhaps the only really important one—scientific validation.

More recently, Held (1984) noted that the controversy over eclecticism has received increased attention. She argues that those who combine a variety of approaches in their treatment may indeed achieve greater effectiveness. However, those who attempt to combine elements of different theories, or eclectic theorists, may face contradiction and confusion. We might state this a little differently. If one recalls that theories consist of *interrelated* postulates, then it is hard to see how one can select out isolated elements. In some sense, one brings other parts of the theory with these elements, as well. Further, because theories differ or disagree on many fundamental issues, it is exceedingly likely that combining these will create contradictions, unless one modifies them at one's own choosing. This, as pointed out earlier, is really not selecting out parts of theories, but essentially creating one's own new theory. How could the courts possibly allow original and completely untested theories to be used?

Given the exceptional proliferation of theories or schools of thought described above, the recent past has seen increasing numbers of mental health professionals taking an eclectic position rather than following a single school.

Beitman et al. (1989) declare, "*Eclecticism.* This is a vague and nebulous term with connotations ranging from 'a worn out synonym for theoretical laziness' to the 'only means to a comprehensive psychotherapy.' In some corners eclecticism is prized as complex, relativistic thinking by people united in their respect for the evidence. In other corners, it connotes undisciplined subjectivity and muddle-headedness." (p. 139) They also note that eclecticism is only one component of an emerging integration of positions in psychotherapy.

Norcross and Prochaska (1988) echo the ambivalent views of eclecticism stated by Beitman et al. They state, "In definition, the connotation of *eclecticism* is emotionally ambivalent, if not negative, for many clinicians." (p. 173)

Norcross (1990) makes reference to nine different eclectic approaches to psychotherapy. He also notes that according to his count, there are currently more than fifty separate, published models of psychotherapy ostensibly integrative or eclectic in nature. He declares there is a dearth of controlled outcome studies on "these nascent eclectic approaches," (p. 298) but that this same criticism can be made of the "nonintegrative" therapies.

Johnson and Brems (1991) refer to studies showing that both clinical and counseling psychologists most frequently identify themselves as eclectic. They cite Zook and Walton (1989) as apparently indicating there are fourteen theoretical orientations important enough to be included in their study of preferred approaches.

Lazarus et al. (1992) describe the shift over the past three decades of psychotherapists who were members of a "school" to an eclectic orientation. They note that eclecticism can mean selecting what appears to be best in different doctrines or can mean a blending of concepts from the more than "400" separate "schools" of psychotherapy in often arbitrary, capricious, subjective ways. (p. 11)

Conway (1988) found that less than half of young scientist-practitioners and senior scientist-practitioners adopt an eclectic theoretical orientation, in contrast to 61% of young practitioners and 55% of clinical psychologists in general taking such a position. Obviously, eclecticism is at best controversial, and one can question whether the eclectic position has been "accepted" by the "scientific" community in view of the less than majority of scientists or scientist-practitioners who endorse that position. Having so said, it should also be stated that in comparison to any other theories, far more, even among the scientists, favor the eclectic position than any other particular theoretical school. However, it should further be noted that practitioners who endorse an eclectic view may differ somewhat, or entirely, on the elements and combination of elements they incorporate into their theoretical scheme. As such, much like a wastebasket category in a diagnostic system, the category of eclecticism lumps together those with heterogenous, and often contrasting, theoretical views. It is a paradoxical community of individuals, not an unified entity.

There is one other point that we will cover in much greater detail in Chapter 5 on judgment. There is considerable evidence, which we will review, which shows that individuals have extraordinary difficulty in properly combining or integrating even very limited amounts of information—certainly far less information than the amount contained in a diverse set of theories. Thus, one flaw with the eclectic approach to theory construction, and quite possibly a fatal one, is that although it may sound attractive, there is virtually no evidence at this time that psychologists and psychiatrists are able to effectively combine such large amounts of information. Rather, the results are likely to be highly problematic. Therefore, when a clinician says he is eclectic, he also reveals that he is attempting what may well be nearly impossible—effectively integrating large amounts of information. One would hardly wish to take a clinician's word that the result has been successful, without subjecting the product to any formal test of scientific validity.

In light of the above findings and comments, it is important to determine from a testifying clinician who describes himself as eclectic whether he uses the term in reference to selection of therapies or in reference to his understanding and assessment of human behavior. In the latter case, it will be necessary to determine which theories he alternates between or among and whether he attempts to amalgamate or integrate the different theories. If he alternates among theories, then one can inquire which theory he is relying on in the particular case, and proceed with the attack on lack of validity of that particular theory. If he claims to amalgamate several theories, it can be brought out that he is then simply operating on his own idiosyncratic theory, produced by combining elements of other theories, thus relying on an unvalidated and, in this instance, probably an idiosyncratic theory, of which he is probably both the "leader" and only follower.

REFERENCES

Appelbaum, S.A. (1985). The state of the art in psychotherapy. *Psychotherapy, 22,* 696-701.

Bartol, C.R. (1983). *Psychology and American Law.* Belmont, California: Wadsworth Publishing Company.

Beitman, B.D., Goldfried, M.R., and Norcross, J.D. (1989). The movement toward integrating the psychotherapies: An overview. *American Journal of Psychiatry, 146,* 138-147.

Bilmes, M. (1990). Psychoanalysis in psychology; prospects: Dawn or twilight. *The California Psychologist, January, 1990,* 16-17.

Boignon, M. (1966). Commentary on Dr. Chodoff's paper. In Masserman, J. (Ed.), *Science and Psychoanalysis,* Vol. 10. New York: Grune and Stratton.

Brody, E.B. (1988). Review of the book, *The Freudian Metaphor: Toward Paradigm Change in Psychoanalysis* by D.P. Spence. *The Journal of Nervous and Mental Disease, 176,* 575-576.

Buss, D.M. (1984). Evolutionary biology and personality psychology. *American Psychologist, 39,* 1135-1147.

Cattell, R.B. (1975). Personality theory derived from qualitative experiments. In A.M. Freedman, H. I. Kaplan, and B.J. Sadock. (Eds.) *Comprehensive Textbook of Psychiatry,* Vol. 1, 2nd edition, pp. 669-687. Baltimore: Williams and Wilkins.

Chertok, L., and Stengers, I. (1988). Editorial: From Lavoisier to Freud. A historical epistemological note with contemporary significance. *The Journal of Nervous and Mental Disease, 176,* 645-647.

Chodoff, M. D., (1966). Feminine psychology and infantile sexuality. In J. Masserman (Ed.), *Science and Psychoanalysis*, Vol. 10. New York: Grune and Stratton.

Coleman, L. (1984). *The Reign of Error*. Boston: Beacon Press.

Conway, J.B. (1988). Differences among clinical psychologists: Scientists, practitioners, and scientist-practitioners. *Professional Psychology: Research and Practice, 19,* 642-655.

Cooper, A.M. (1985). Will neurobiology influence psychoanalysis? *The American Journal of Psychiatry, 142,* 1395-1402.

Coryell, W., and Wetzel, R.D. (1978). Attitudes toward issues in psychiatry among third-year residents: A brief survey. *American Journal of Psychiatry, 135,* 732-735.

Davidman, H. (1964). Evaluation of psychoanalysis; a clinician's view. In Hoch, P., and Zubin, J. (Eds.), *The Evaluation of Psychiatric Treatment.* (Proceedings of the 52nd Annual meeting of the American Psychopathological Association.) New York: Grune and Stratton.

Delman, R.P. (1981). Participation by psychologists in insanity defense proceedings: An advocacy. *The Journal of Psychiatry and Law, 9,* 247-262.

Detre, T. (1987). The future of psychiatry. *American Journal of Psychiatry, 144,* 621-625.

Dujovne, B.E. (1991). Contemporary revisions of classical psychoanalytic theory of early female development. *Psychotherapy, 28,* 317-326.

Dumont, F. (1994). Ritualistic evocation of antiquated paradigms. *Professional Psychology: Research and Practice, 25,* 195-197.

Eagle, M.N., and Wolitzky, D.L. (1985). The current status of psychoanalysis. *Clinical Psychology Review, 5,* 259-269.

Eisenberg, I. (1962). In Hoch, P., and Zubin, J. (Eds.), *The Future of Psychiatry*, p. 252. New York: Grune and Stratton.

English, H.B., and English, A.C. (1958). *A Comprehensive Dictionary of Psychological and Psychoanalytical Terms.* New York: Longmans, Green and Company.

Exner, J.E., Jr. (1986). *The Rorschach: A Comprehensive System, Volume I: Basic Foundations* (2nd. Ed.). New York: John Wiley and Sons Inc.

Eysenck, H.J. (1964). The outcome problem in psychotherapy: A reply. *Psychotherapy, 1,* 97-100.

Fishman, D.B., and Neigher, W.D. (1982). American psychology in the '80's: Who will buy? *American Psychologist, 37,* 533-546.

Fiske, D.W. (1979). Two worlds of psychological phenomena. *American Psychologist, 34,* 733-739.

Frank, A. (1979). Two theories or one? Or None? *Journal of the Psychoanalytic Association*, *27*, 169-206.

Freedman, A.M., and Kaplan, H.I. (Eds.) (1972). *Interpreting Personality*. New York: Atheneum.

Garfield, S.L., and Kurtz, R.A. (1977). A study of eclectic views. *Journal of Consulting and Clinical Psychology*, *45*, 78-83.

Glover, E., (1955) *A Technique of Psychoanalysis*. London: Baillere, Tindall, and Cox.

Golding, S.L. (1992). Increasing the reliability, validity, and relevance of psychological expert evidence. *Law and Human Behavior, 16,* 253-256.

Goodwin, D.W. (1984). Review of the book, *Disease and Its Control* by R.B. Hudson. *American Journal of Psychiatry*, *141*, 1001-1002.

Gray, P. (1993). The assault on Freud. *Time,* November 29, 47-51.

Green, B.F. (1981). A primer of testing. *American Psychologist*, *36*, 1001-1011.

Greenwald, A.G. (1975). Consequences of prejudice against the null hypothesis. *Psychological Bulletin*, *82*, 1-20.

Grinker, R.R., Sr. (1964). Psychiatry rides madly in all directions. *Archives of General Psychiatry*, 10.

Hall, C.S., and Lindzey, G. (1957). *Theories of Personality*. New York: John Wiley and Sons.

Hall, C.S., and Lindzey, G. (1970). *Theories of Personality* (2nd ed.). New York: John Wiley and Sons.

Hall, C.S., Lindzey, G., Loehlin, J.C., and Manosevitz, M. (1985). *Theories of Personality* (3rd ed). New York: John Wiley and Sons.

Hammet, V.O. (1965). A consideration of psychoanalysis in relation to psychiatry generally. *American Journal of Psychiatry*, *122*, 42-54.

Havens, L.L. (1981). Twentieth Century Psychiatry: A view from the sea. *The American Journal of Psychiatry*, *138*, 1279-1287.

Held, B.S. (1984). Toward a strategic eclecticism: A proposal. *Psychotherapy*, *21*, 232-241.

Johnson, M.E., and Brems, C. (1991). Comparing theoretical orientations of counseling and clinical psychologists: An objective approach. *Professional Psychology: Research and Practice, 22,* 133-137.

Kahn, A.S. (1982). Shedding an inadequate theory of maleness. *Contemporary Psychology, 27,* 606-607 (A review of *The Myths of Masculinity* by Joseph H. Pleck).

Kimble, G.A. (1984). Psychology's two cultures. *American Psychologist*, *39*, 833-839.

Kupfersmid, J. (1992). The "defense" of Sigmund Freud. *Psychotherapy, 29,* 297-309.

Lane, R.D., and Schwartz, G.E. (1987). Levels of emotional awareness: A cognitive-developmental theory and its application to psychopathology. *American Journal of Psychiatry, 144,* 133-143.

Lazarus, A.A., Beutler, L.E., and Norcross, J.C. (1992). The future of technical eclecticism. *Psychotherapy, 29,* 11-20.

Lesse, S. (1977). Editorial: What price confusion—the status of psychiatric education. *American Journal of Psychotherapy, 3,* 181-184.

Levy-Leboyer, C. (1988). Success and failure in applying psychology. *The American Psychologist, 43,* 779-785.

Lomranz, J. (1986). Personality theory: Position and derived teaching implications in clinical psychology. *Professional Psychology: Research and Practice, 17,* 551-559.

MacKay, D.G. (1988). Under what conditions can theoretical psychology survive and prosper? Integrating the rational and empirical epistemologies. *Psychological Review, 95,* 559-565.

Mahoney, M.J. (1977). Publication prejudices: An experimental study of confirmatory bias in the peer review system. *Cognitive Therapy and Research, 1,* 161-175.

Marmor, J. (1966). Psychoanalysis at the crossroads. In J. Masserman (Ed.) *Science and Psychoanalysis*, Vol. 10. New York: Grune and Stratton.

Matarazzo, J.D. (1986a). Computerized clinical psychological test interpretations: Unvalidated plus all mean and no sigma. *American Psychologist, 41,* 14-24.

McFall, R.M. (1991). Manifesto for a science of clinical psychology. *The Clinical Psychologist, 44,* 75-88.

Medewar, P.B. (1972). *The Hope of Progress.* London: Methuen.

Meehl, P.E. (1973). *Psychodiagnosis: Selected Papers.* Minneapolis: University of Minnesota Press.

Meehl, P.E. (1978). Theoretical risks and tabular asterisks, Sir Karl, Sir Ronald and the slow progress of soft psychology. *Journal of Consulting and Clinical Psychology, 46,* 806-834.

Meehl, P.E. (1979). A funny thing happened to us on the way to latent entities. *Journal of Personality Assessment, 43,* 564-581.

Miller, M.H., and Alexander, A.A. (1972). In E.A. Spiegel (Ed.), *Clinical Psychiatry In Progress in Neurology and Psychiatry, An Annual Review*, Vol. 27. New York: Grune and Stratton.

Millet, J.A.P. (1966). The academy of perspective past, present and future. In J. Masserman (Ed.), *Science and Psychoanalysis.* New York: Grune and Stratton.

Natale, M. (1979). The relationship of imipramine plasma levels and verbalized hostility in non-delusional endogenous depressives. *The Journal of Nervous and Mental Disease, 167,* 620-625.

Norcross, J.C. (1990). Commentary: Eclecticism misrepresented and integration misunderstood. *Psychotherapy, 27,* 297-300.

Norcross, J.C., and Prochaska, J.O. (1982). A national survey of clinical psychologists: Affiliations and organizations. *Clinical Psychologist, 35,* 1-6.

Norcross, J.C., and Prochaska, J.O. (1988). A study of eclectic and integrated views revisited. *Professional Psychology: Research and Practice, 19,* 170-175.

Omer, H., and London, P. (1988). Metamorphosis in psychotherapy: End of the system's era. *Psychotherapy, 25,* 171-184.

Ovesey, L. (1960). In P. Hoch and J. Zubin (Eds.), *Current Approaches to Psychoanalysis.* New York, London: Grune and Stratton.

Pardes, H. (1980). Psychoanalytic concepts in psychiatric training. *American Journal of Psychiatry, 137,* 613-616.

Pervin, L.A. (1985). Personality: Current controversies, issues and directions. *Annual Review of Psychology, 36,* 83-144.

Phillips. B.N. (1989). Role of the practitioner in applying science to practice. *Professional Psychology: Research and Practice, 20,* 3-8.

Preston, T.P. (1981). *The Clay Pedestal.* Seattle: Madrona.

Reiss, D., Plomin, R., and Hetherington, E.M. (1991). Genetics and psychiatry: An unheralded window on the environment. *American Journal of Psychiatry, 148,* 283-291.

Reynolds, R.V.C., McNamara, J.R., Marion, R.J., and Tobin, D.L. (1985). Computerized service delivery in clinical psychology. *Professional Psychology: Research and Practice, 16,* 339-353.

Robinson, D.N. (1980). *Psychology and Law. Can justice survive the social sciences?* New York/Oxford: Oxford University Press.

Rothman, T. (1962) In Hoch, P., and Zubin, J. (Eds.) (1962). *The Future of Psychiatry.* New York: Grune and Stratton.

Ruesch, J. (1966b) The future of psychoanalytically oriented psychiatry. In J. Masserman (Ed.) *Science and Psychoanalysis, 10.* New York: Grune and Stratton.

Sadler, J.Z., and Hulgus, Y.F. (1992). Clinical problem solving and the biopsychosocial model. *American Journal of Psychiatry, 149,* 1315-1323.

Sales, B. (1986). President's column: Important issues ahead. *American Psychology-Law Society Newsletter, Summer, 6,* 1.

Sarason, I.G. (1972). *Personality: An Objective Approach* (2nd ed.). New York: John Wiley and Sons.

Sechrest, L.B. (1985b). President's message: Specialization? Who needs it? *The Clinical Psychologist, 38,* 1-3.

Slater, E. (1975). The psychiatrist in search of science: The depth psychologies. *British Journal of Psychiatry, 126,* 205-244.

Smelser, N.J., and Smelser, W.T. (Eds.) (1970). *Personality and Social Systems* (2nd ed.). New York: John Wiley and Sons.

Stoller, R.J. (1973). Overview: The impact of new advances in sex research on psychoanalytic theory. *American Journal of Psychiatry, 130,* 241-251.

Strupp, H.H. (1971). Some comments on the future of psychoanalysis. *Journal of Contemporary Psychotherapy, 3,* 117-120.

Weimer, W.B. (1979). *Notes on the methodology of scientific research.* Hillsdale, N.J.: Erlbaum.

Whitman, R.M. (1972). In E.A. Spiegel (Ed.), *Psychoanalysis in Progress in Neurology and Psychiatry*, Vol. 27, Chapter 21. New York: Grune and Stratton.

Wolpe, J. (1970). In R.B. Stuart, *Trick or Treatment.* Champaign, IL: Research Press.

Woodmansey, A.C. (1967). Science and the training of psychiatrists. *British Journal of Psychiatry, 113,* 1035-1037.

Yager, J. (1977). Psychiatric eclecticism: A cognitive view. *American Journal of Psychiatry, 134,* 736-741.

CITATION

People vs. Gorshen 336, p.2nd 492.

CHAPTER 4

Challenging Principles & Systems of Classification

Classification may seem like a straightforward matter in science. One decides upon the categories one will use, decides how objects or observations will be classified, and goes on from there to gather information about the categories. However, this is hardly the case in practice, and an adequate classification system cannot be developed out of thin air. Rather, it may require fairly advanced scientific knowledge. For example, think about how far medical science had to come before viral diseases could be classified in even a rudimentary way. It was many years before these postulated entities were scientifically established as real things, and still more years before procedures began to emerge that would permit reliable classification or subdivision for even some of these entities. Adequate classification develops as scientific knowledge develops. Thus, it is not surprising to find, given the serious deficiencies and limits in scientific knowledge within psychology and psychiatry, that nothing approaching an adequate classification system has yet emerged.

CRITERIA FOR JUDGING THE STATUS OF CLASSIFICATION SYSTEMS

The lawyer should be aware of some basic criteria for judging the status of classification systems in order to be able to challenge unfounded claims for the adequacy of classification in psychiatry. The two most important criteria are reliability and validity.

Reliability, as pertains to classification systems, has essentially the same meaning as the one we discussed in the chapter on scientific method. Thus, a reliable system of classification is one in which different practitioners will evidence a high level of agreement in the diagnoses they make, and, assuming that the actual disorder does not change over time, they will render the same diagnosis that they had made previously when the same condition or individual is assessed a second or third time. There is no final or absolute standard for reliability, and perhaps the simple term, "high level of agreement," is a precise enough definition. Some might require that this agreement be present in nearly 100% of the cases, others in at least 90% of the cases, and still others may be more lenient. However, it becomes obvious that if we dip much lower than this 90% level, calling such a figure "a high level of agreement" is dubious.

It is important to recognize that the establishment of reliable diagnosis, by itself, is a very limited achievement. By itself, all it proves is that diagnosticians can agree; it does not prove that the classification system or diagnoses are correct or valid. As stated in a prior article (Faust and Miner, 1986):

> Reliability is actually quite easy to achieve. The decision rule "Classify all people as normal" would attain this end. The achievement, however, would be vacuous, and the example shows how vacuous reliability is when it is a primary goal and not combined with other concerns or requirements. The most important requirement is some idea about the things that are worth measuring reliably. (p. 965)

In another context, Cancro (1973) states:

> The need to improve diagnostic reliability in schizophrenia is so obvious as to not require additional confirmation....Improved diagnosis will almost certainly not increase our understanding of what schizophrenia is and an increase in reliability does not affect validity. We can standardize our misconceptions in such a way that the same person will be identically mislabeled by an even larger number of colleagues. (pp. 146-147)

Thus, Cancro's statement also shows that, by itself, an improvement in reliability makes no true inroads into the problem of validity.

The major importance of reliability is that, ultimately, it is a precondition for valid diagnoses, at least as regards practical use. It should be obvious that if a group of practitioners all render different diagnoses, then all of them cannot be right. Rather, at most, only one of them can be right. Thus, in some sense, if one can establish that a diagnostic system has serious deficiencies in reliability, one should be able to stop there, because there is almost no point in inquiring about validity. One essentially knows that a system which is not reliable will not be valid, either.

A diagnostic system's validity ultimately comes down to its power to relate diagnoses to other sets of facts or occurrences. Stated differently, one can ask if knowing what the diagnosis is tells us anything important about the individual, other than that he has been assigned the diagnostic label. These other things might relate to the individual's current status, past status, or future status. For example, if an individual is assigned a diagnosis of organic brain syndrome, will this tell us something about his current level of functioning or his capacity to return to his prior level of employment?

It is sometimes argued that the value of diagnosis is to help us "understand" an individual. This is well and fine, to a point, but one should recall the comments we made in the prior chapter regarding understanding or explanation alone. As is the case with a theory or hypothesis, unless testing has been conducted of the power of the category to "predict" other past, current, or future occurrences, it cannot be considered scientifically established; it must instead be considered mere speculation. We would also note that in the case of postdiction, one must be able to postdict events or occurrences that are independent of the facts or the things already known that contributed to the diagnosis. For example, if a diagnosis of schizophrenia is partially rendered on the basis of repeated psychiatric hospitalizations, "postdicting" these already-known occurrences which contributed to the diagnosis proves little or nothing. In contrast, if one can postdict "new" things, such as specific types of behavior this individual engaged in with others, and then goes ahead and obtains unbiased and independent information about past interpersonal relationships which demonstrates one to be correct, then at least one piece of validating evidence has been obtained.

Another critical limitation of explanation and understanding by themselves, is that they almost never help to answer the most pertinent questions in the forensic arena. Rather, what is typically required is the capacity to relate the current "understanding" or diagnostic label to some other past, present, or current condition or occurrence. For example, if an individual who committed a violent act is diagnosed as schizophrenic, a critical question is likely to be whether, previously—at the time of the crime—he was capable of comprehending the nature of his actions or of distinguishing right from wrong. If one is considering compensation for personal injury, a critical question will likely be, regardless of the diagnostic label, whether this individual is currently able to return to work or will be able to do so in the future. If one is considering the more suitable parent in a disputed child custody case, regardless of any diagnostic label that is rendered, one will want to be able to predict how the child will fare with either parent. Thus, with almost all questions relevant to the court in which the psychologist or the psychiatrist becomes involved, understanding per se, or the diagnostic label per se, is of limited or no value; rather, the question is what this understanding or label can help us to know about past, current, or future conditions or occurrences. This is of particular pertinence for the diagnostic labels in psychiatry because, by themselves, they can rarely tell us any of these things. We will return to this point momentarily.

Some of the things one wants an adequate classification system in psychiatry to tell us are: (1) the cause or etiology of the disorder, (2) the preferred type of treatment, and (3) the expected course of the disorder, or prognosis. It is rather obvious that even if the system could answer these questions, it might still remain sorely deficient for pertinent forensic questions (e.g., Could the individual plan and premeditate? Was the individual capable of harboring malice? Will this individual perform adequately as a parent? What is the extent and nature of impairment?). The point here is that the rudiments or basics of classification remain highly problematic in psychiatry, and thus it is rather unrealistic to expect that current diagnostic systems might help us with these much more advanced or complicated questions. As things currently stand, and we will cite many articles to support this statement, psychiatrists and psychologists still often have very considerable difficulty even agreeing on what diagnostic label is appropriate—in fact, there is considerable debate about whether mental illness even exists at all or what it might represent.

Two other desirable features of diagnostic systems are worth mentioning. First, one wishes to have categories with minimal overlap, such that a single individual will clearly fit into one or another category, as opposed to showing some features from various categories. This is not to say that there is necessarily a problem if an individual clearly fits into more than one category, for individuals may have more than one disorder simultaneously. Rather, we are referring to cases in which it is not clear into what category someone falls, for they do not fit cleanly into any one; they meet some of the requirements, but not all of them, for a series of different categories. Second, the greater the number of important commonalities among individuals who fit into the same category, the better. The more ways in which the categories encompass important points of similarity, the greater their potential usefulness in telling us something important about those so diagnosed. For example, if those within the same category sometimes do and sometimes do not share some features, they will represent a "mixed bag" and it is unlikely that we will be able to formulate accurate predictions by knowing their diagnostic category alone. In contrast, suppose we know that everyone who truly falls within the category will evidence a rapid worsening of their condition, or conversely that they are almost certain to recover. Obviously, the category then has far more utility for purposes of prediction. When one is referring to the first of these desirable qualities (that is, clean fits into diagnostic categories), one often speaks of minimal overlap across categories. The term "homogeneity" is often used to refer to this second desirable quality—or consistency within categories—as opposed to heterogeneity, or inconsistency within categories.

THE GAP REVISITED:
DIAGNOSTIC CATEGORIES

The above discussion of criteria for diagnostic categories leads ulti-mately to a more refined question about diagnosis and the law. Rather than simply asking whether diagnostic categories are valid, which is a rather global question, one must ask whether they are valid for purposes of the law. Suppose, for example, that a certain diagnostic category does eventually attain a satisfactory scientific status. The diagnosis can be made reliably, there is minimal overlap with other diagnostic categories, those who fall within the category evidence substantial homogeneity, and we can make accurate statements about the cause of the malady, the pre-ferred method of treatment, and its probable course. Even were this hoped-for scientific status eventually attained, the diagnostic labels might still be of very limited utility from a forensic standpoint, for they may have little demonstrable relationship to the relevant questions. Thus, it is very important to distinguish clinical utility or scientific status from forensic utility. One can have the former, even in abundance, but be nearly or completely lacking in the latter. This separation between clini-cal utility or status and forensic utility is a variant of the "gap" to which we referred earlier. The problem is a serious one because the great ma-jority of applied scientific work in psychology and psychiatry addresses clinical utility, while only a small minority addresses forensic utility. Thus, although research is expanding (see Chapter 7), there is still lim-ited scientific work directed at attempts to develop or test the forensic utility of procedures for classification, description, or prediction of hu-man behavior. One must always ask, therefore, what utility a diagnostic label may have for forensic purposes, regardless of the level of support for clinical use or validity. Indeed, DSM-III-R and DSM-IV contain spe-cific cautionary statements regarding the use of the manual for forensic purposes (see below).

A number of writers have addressed this problem of the gap as re-gards various diagnostic labels. Livermore et al. (1968) state:

> All this suggests that the concept of mental illness must be limited in the field of civil commitment to a necessary rather than a sufficient condition for com-mitment. While the term has its uses, it is devoid of that purposive content that a touchstone in the law ought to have. Its relative meaning makes for such dif-ficulty of analysis that it answers no questions that the law might wish to ask. (p. 80)

Along the same lines, Nussbaum et al. (1981-82) state that, "There is increasing evidence that diagnostic formulations are of limited relevance to objective assessment of psychiatric impairment."

Rubinstein (1982) states, "Mental illness—even the existence of psy-chosis—does not, of itself, determine whether, at a particular moment, a person is incapable of obeying the law. Indeed, many studies have shown, that as a group, those diagnosed as mentally ill commit fewer crimes than the population as a whole." He states further that, "The more sophisticated psychiatric knowledge becomes, the less psychiatrists are able to say (and the less they should be allowed to say), that certain impairments *caused* certain criminal acts." Morse (1983), when asked about the relationship between psychiatric diagnosis and insanity as defined legally, stated that, "Applying DSM-III correctly is a proper issue for the psychiatric classroom or consulting room, but not for the courtroom." Baumrin (1982) states:

> If psychiatrists really were clear about what their ethics were and why they did what they did, they would have no timidity about saying that a determination of legal insanity does not follow from a determination of mental illness. One can testify about the latter (mental illness) and have no scientific opinion about the former—namely legal insanity. Psychiatric opinions about legal insanity are *irrelevant,* for as yet we have no satisfactory way of determining which mental defect, and of what magnitude, *invariably* leads to lack of criminal responsibility.

There is also considerable research (see Chapter 1 above, Chapter 7 below) indicating that diagnostic labels are not useful in the prediction of assaultive or violent behavior. Thus, by themselves, diagnostic labels are of little use in predicting violent behavior.

The gap pertains not only to general diagnostic categories but to more specific ones, and to psychiatric symptoms as well. For example, some psychiatrists will assert that command hallucinations can create irresistible impulses. To say that someone has command hallucinations is a fancy way of saying that someone hears voices which tell him what to do (e.g., touch his feet three times or assault a particular individual). Therefore, it would seem that a specific psychiatric symptom has a direct bearing on the commission of violent behavior, and that in this case the gap is closed. Or is it?

In the case of *Colorado vs. Francis Connelly* (1986), a man purportedly experienced command hallucinations that instructed him to confess to murder. A psychiatrist testified that the man made this confession because schizophrenics are compelled to obey command hallucinations. The psychiatrist then postulated a direct relationship between the disorder or symptoms and the performance of an action. However, the American Psychological Association filed a brief which asserted that most individuals who experience command hallucinations do not follow them, particularly if this involves action that leads to physical harm. Further, when the hallucinations are followed, the individual is generally able to comprehend the nature of the act and its consequences. Resnick (1984) also states that most individuals who experience command hallucinations do not obey them. In fact, Resnick asserts that to obey these hallucinations is so unusual that an individual who reports such hallucinations and indicates that he cannot help but obey them should be suspected of feigning illness. In any case, if most individuals who experience command hallucinations do not obey them, then the presence of such hallucinations, by themselves, does not explain an individual's actions, and the gap remains.

The gap also exists for a variety of other psychiatric diagnoses the lawyer may encounter in the courtroom. For example, the diagnosis of Post-Traumatic Stress Disorder (PTSD) is being applied with increasing regularity to individuals who purportedly have been psychologically damaged by stress or traumatic occurrences. As regards PTSD, Packer (1983) argues that the diagnostic label does not help to determine impairment in everyday functioning. According to Packer, some individuals who are assigned the diagnosis do have significant problems in adaptation, but others have minimal problems only. Further, although PTSD has been used as a defense in criminal cases either to show that the defendant meets legal tests of insanity and/or was not responsible for his behavior, Packer argues that diminished capacity or impaired reality testing is rare in PTSD. Further, Packer asserts that there is often no direct relationship between PTSD and the commission of a crime. He concludes by stating, "An analysis of the cases presented here reveals that diagnosing an individual as experiencing PTSD is neither a necessary or sufficient condition for determining that individual's sanity at the time of a commission of an offense." (p. 133) Similar assertions can be made about the limited forensic utility of other diagnoses (e.g., see Chapters 15, 19 and 20).

In recent years there have been increasing, although still limited, attempts to close the gap. Some researchers have conducted direct scientific tests of the usefulness of evaluative procedures and psychological instruments in addressing forensic issues or questions. Other work has been directed toward developing useful procedures (see Chapter 7). This work has often yielded poor or discouraging results. Problems in predicting violent behavior are best known, but there are other examples. It has become obvious that the gap represents a large scale problem that will resist any easy solutions.

There are various factors underlying the difficulty in closing the gap, but perhaps the primary one is that the interests and concerns that have occupied the attention of those involved in applied clinical research and diagnosis are typically very different from the issues and concerns of greatest relevance in the courtroom. Thus, one is required to draw broad generalizations from currently existing, and often limited knowledge, to situations, individuals, and questions that may show only limited resemblance, and many points of discontinuity with typical populations and questions of interest. Even small steps in the expansion of procedures or knowledge are often quite problematic, for example, the difficulties in applying testing procedures developed for middle-aged adults to elderly individuals (see Chapter 16). Thus, one can anticipate that years of intensive, difficult, and painstaking work will be needed to begin to resolve the types of challenges the gap creates.

The point to be recognized here is that there is good reason to assume that attempts to close the gap will require years of effort. This assumption is supported by the actual attempts that have been made to date on the generalization of clinical procedures and diagnoses to forensic questions and issues. As such, the clinician who asserts that a diagnostic label can be usefully applied to a legal question can be challenged on this point. If any actual scientific testing of this assertion has been conducted, the results that have been obtained are quite likely to have been largely negative, or at best mixed. If the assertion has not been tested, one cannot safely assume that it is correct.

THE STATUS OF PAST AND CURRENT DIAGNOSTIC SYSTEMS

This section deals with the history and analyses of Diagnostic and Statistical Manuals prior to the current DSM-IV. We think it is important background for dealing with the DSMs. A reader who wishes information more directly on DSM-IV can proceed to the last section of this chapter.

Lack of a reliable and valid diagnostic or classification system has been a major stumbling block within the mental health professions. The principal focus in attempting to alleviate these problems has been on the issue of reliability. Many practitioners or researchers view the attainment of reliability as a precondition for validity and argue that these problems have to be solved first, before one can move on to the more important work of validation. As such, one can draw one's own inferences about this continuing focus on issues of reliability.

Psychologists and psychiatrists should know that usually the best predictor of future behavior is past behavior. Extending this tenet to classification, it is worthwhile to provide at least a brief overview of the problems with reliability and validity that have plagued earlier attempts to create an adequate diagnostic manual before providing more detailed coverage of problems with the current diagnostic manual. Before we do so, however, it is worthwhile to describe some unresolved, general problems with classification in psychiatry. These difficulties in defining abnormality and separating it from normality, and tendencies to identify things as abnormal that arguably are not abnormal (i.e., overpathologizing), are not isolated to any one of the past diagnostic manuals or to the current one. Rather, they cut across the past and current attempts to derive an adequate system of classification, and they will likely hinder future efforts. Stated differently, these might be called fundamental and perpetual problems that in part underlie and explain the inordinate difficulties of achieving a reliable and valid system of classification.

FREQUENT "INNOVATION" OR EXPERIMENTATION

The first official *Diagnostic and Statistical Manual of Mental Disorders,* or DSM-I, was published by the American Psychiatric Association in 1952. Its revision, DSM-II, was published in 1968. The next revision, DSM-III, was published in 1980. The next revision, DSM-III-R, was published in 1987. The current revision, DSM-IV, was published in May of 1994. We know of no current projections for DSM-IV-R, DSM-V, DSM-V-R, etc., but judging from this past track record it may not be many years before their appearance, although the chair of the DSM-IV committee has suggested that no "fully" revised DSM-V appear before 2005 (Frances et al., 1991). Obviously, the rate of revision cannot continue to accelerate much longer, but the frequent and quickening changes do show the unstable, tentative, and experimental nature of the diagnostic manuals and diagnostic categories. The law, as it relates to expert evidence, has long had a repugnance for those areas of expertise that must be viewed as no more than experimental. To date, it is equally clear, as evidenced by these continual changes in systems, that psychiatric diagnosis and diagnostic manuals are experimental documents. Judging from the very substantial changes between DSM-II and DSM-III, for example, and the more than 200 minor and major changes in DSM-III-R and more than 225 changes from DSM-III-R to DSM-IV (see below), one can anticipate not only future revisions, but large-scale revisions that entail the creation of entirely new diagnostic categories, the elimination of entire categories, and substantial changes in many categories that remain.

DSM-I and DSM-II consisted almost entirely of literary or narrative descriptions of disorders which led to severe lack of reliability among diagnosticians. In an effort to increase reliability, DSM-III was a radical departure, employing specified sets of criteria for each diagnostic category. It was a success in that it did improve reliability, but a failure in that it did not achieve a satisfactory degree of reliability for a large number of diagnoses. However, because of the radical change in approach, it could only be considered an experimental system, a problem which continues to haunt its successors. Further, because of the substantial changes, it was tantamount to sweeping clean the library shelves of research, because one could not believe, let alone be certain, that populations researched under prior manual diagnoses were the same as populations with that diagnosis under the new system (Vincent et al., 1983; Robins and Helzer, 1986; Silverstein et al., 1982; Keisling, 1981). For example, in the study of Silverstein et al. (1982), almost one half of patients diagnosed with schizophrenia under DSM-II did not receive this diagnosis under DSM-III. This, also, is a problem which haunts it successors. Finally, even with improved reliability, establishment of validity remained a task unaccomplished. Again, because of the frequent changes, this remains a problem with the successive manuals.

Given the widely acknowledged enormous difficulty of the task and given the historical failure of DSM-I and DSM-II to provide an adequate remedy, the safest prediction that one could make was that DSM-III would also fail. One reason for predicting such failure is that the method of producing the manual has not materially changed. It is still produced by a committee through a process of consensus and compromise, rather than by scientific research. Such a process is inevitably subject to pressures from groups with political, occupational, and economic interests. For example, the classification of "neurosis" was originally excluded by the committee, then put back in, based on concerns of psychoanalytic psychiatrists, then taken out again.

The well-publicized dispute among psychiatrists concerning the issue of homosexuality as a mental disorder was dealt with in DSM-III. A referendum submitted to all psychiatrists in 1974 had determined by a vote of roughly 4,000 to 3,000 that homosexuality per se was not a mental disorder. This view was adopted in DSM-III, which has only a classification 302.00, "ego-dystonic homosexuality." The essential features are a desire to become heterosexual accompanied by distress over homosexual arousal. Homosexuals who did not wish to change did not have a mental disorder. Only homosexuals who wished to be heterosexual had a mental disorder. Homosexuality disappeared as a named disorder in DSM-III-R. In DSM-III-R and DSM-IV the closest diagnosis became 302.9, "Sexual disorder not otherwise specified," with persistent and marked distress about one's sexual orientation given as an example. This is just one demonstration of the instability of DSM diagnoses such that one cannot put any faith in them.

From a forensic viewpoint, the most significant aspect of DSM-III was that for several years following its official publication in 1980 it could not be considered other than experimental. Following its publication, there was a need for some period of time for practitioners to become familiar with the manual's use, and then more time for researchers to assess the degree of reliability obtainable for the numerous categories contained in the manual. Additionally, there is the time lag between research accomplished and publication of the results of research. Therefore, it normally takes a minimum of five years from the date the manual is published before its adequacy can be assessed. It should be noted that the DSM-III committee did perform some field testing with the categories involved and had made some revisions on the basis of such testing. However, only the utilization of the manual by the tens of thousands of practitioners, along with research, could provide data for final evaluation of this manual. One would hope that the courts would not permit the use of any of the diagnostic labels contained in the manual absent proper research to demonstrate their adequacy. Failing that, the lawyer confronted with such "jargon" should make sure that the trier of fact is informed of its experimental nature. (Unlike DSM-III, in which reliability figures from field trials assessing new diagnostic categories were reported, DSM-III-R reports essentially no reliability data on new diagnostic categories or altered diagnostic criteria.)

DSM-III was likely an improvement over DSM-II. Its more extensive specification of criteria for many listed disorders seemed likely to result in some increase of reliability (agreement) concerning diagnoses. Whether such improvements led to reliability sufficiently high for purposes of the legal system was not demonstrated. Subsequent research has been negative in this regard (see below). Obviously, until the issues of reliability are determined, research on validity is severely hampered. Even if these issues could have been favorably resolved from a clinical and scientific point of view, there still remains the further problem of bridging the gap between diagnosis and any relevant legal issue which can only be accomplished by scientific demonstration of a relationship between a given diagnosis and such legal issues. From a forensic point of view, DSM-III should be viewed as, at best, a beginning step of a long journey before psychiatrists and psychologists can be considered to have developed the knowledge and skills which would justify granting them the status of experts in legal issues.

Implementation of DSM-III in practice was tantamount to virtually sweeping clean the library shelves containing the past hundred years of publications concerning the various diagnostic categories. This is because only rarely will previously published literature have employed the same descriptions and criteria for the various diagnostic categories employed in DSM-III. Consequently, this revised manual just about placed the mental health professions back at the starting line so far as any accumulated data base was concerned (Vincent et al., 1983, effect of changes on MMPI; Robins and Helzer, 1986, "the existing body of literature based on the former nomenclature is called into question"; Silverstein et al., 1982, DSM-II diagnoses of a significant number of patients changed by DSM-III). Any use of or reliance on research done with diagnoses using a manual other than the current one can be challenged because there can be no assurance that the populations given the diagnosis are the same. From the viewpoint of the mental health professions this is not necessarily bad—it probably represents a necessary step in beginning to accumulate a reasonably reliable and valid data base. From a forensic point of view, however, it means that knowledge of diagnoses and their implications is just beginning and therefore is remote from even a grey area between the experimental and the demonstrable, as the test is stated in the *Frye* case. It also means that so far as the education and training of clinicians in diagnosis is concerned, that training has been rendered virtually irrelevant, as the classification system has been radically changed. For several years, everyone will have to be viewed as "inexperienced" in making these new diagnoses, although this may be less true regarding assessment of symptoms. Obviously, DSM-IV now stands where DSM-III was in 1980. History instructs that the above statements should apply to it as well.

Triers of fact who hear the testimony of experts which involves psychiatric diagnosis can be informed about the instability and changing nature of these diagnostic systems. How can any legal decisions be made on the basis of such an ephemeral classification system? It can be made abundantly clear to any judge or juror that the psychiatric establishment does not have an established diagnostic system, but rather is trying to develop one. It is trying to find out what it ought to be doing, and certainly there is no criticism of that, but the fact remains that a system has not yet been developed that assures classification that would justify legal decision making.

THE ELUSIVE DEFINITION OF ABNORMALITY

Imagine if one had a classification for animals but could not define what an animal was, or had frequent difficulties telling the difference between an animal and a plant and/or was not at all sure about the defining features of "animalness." Obviously, such a classification system would have some very fundamental problems and could hardly be considered satisfactory.

Fortunately, biology has overcome such problems for the most part, and it is the unusual case in which a living thing does not clearly fall into the category of animal or plant. Psychiatry, however, has not overcome even these most rudimentary or basic problems in classification. There is no agreement or understanding as to what constitutes the "healthy" or "normal" personality. What does seem likely is that when an acceptable definition emerges, it will encompass a much greater appreciation of individual differences, and therefore a much wider range of behaviors or personality configurations than has been the case in the past. For lack of consensus as to the dimensions of normality, the logical starting point for the determination of abnormality appears to be lacking. For lack of such a baseline, it seems highly likely that any classification of mental disorders will be a poor one.

Different writers have addressed various aspects of this problem, defining abnormality or separating the normal from the abnormal. Some discuss the general problems in this area. For example, Strupp and Hadley (1977) point out the lack of a consensus on what constitutes mental health despite extensive literature on conceptions of mental health. They note that a multiplicity of meanings are attached to the term "mental health" and ask, "If conceptions of mental health are fuzzier than ever how can we determine whether a particular intervention has led to improvement, deterioration, or no change?" They note that most mental health professionals view the person's functioning within the framework of some theory of personality structure and define mental health largely in reference to some theoretical model of a "healthy" personality structure. Given the diversity in theory discussed in the previous chapter, the obvious implication is that views of health and disorder also vary greatly across clinicians. Along the same lines, Coles (1967) indicates that there is considerable doubt that what are called psychiatric disorders should be so called. Shubow and Bergstresser (1977) argue that the concept of normality is culturally dependent. This argument implies that such definitions are quite unstable or elastic, and that what is called abnormal in one cultural setting might well be called normal in another. Imagine if the use of, say, X rays was so flexible that what was viewed as a clean break in someone's leg by a physician in France was considered perfectly normal by a physician in Germany.

Other critics have emphasized not only the vagueness or inconsistency in definitions of abnormality, but also that the definition is tied to personal values, as opposed, for example, to any kind of conclusive scientific evidence. Schacht and Nathan (1977) quote Spitzer and Endicott as describing the World Health Organization's definition of health as "virtually worthless...as a guide toward the development of a classification of mental disorders," but Schacht and Nathan point out that the mental health professions "already employ unstated, inchoate definitions of healthy process at the roots of the value judgments which determine what is to be labelled as a disorder."

A whole issue of a reputable psychological journal *(The Counseling Psychologist,* Volume 4, No. 2, 1973) was devoted to a collection of contributions by professionals and academicians in both psychiatry and psychology on the definition of "the healthy personality." Space does not permit discussion of each of these articles. It is sufficient to say that a number of different points of view were present which illustrate the lack of consensus or understanding regarding what traits or behaviors or personality structure represent the healthy or "normal" personality, which would obviously appear to be the prerequisite base rate information for determining that certain traits, behaviors, etc., are abnormal or unhealthy. The thrust of a number of the articles was to the effect that most conceptions among "mental health" professionals of the so-called healthy personality consist primarily of value judgments arrived at either idiosyncratically or on the basis of membership in some unvalidated school of thought on the subject.

Halleck (1967), a leading authority in forensic psychiatry, indicates that there is no definition of mental illness that is not dependent on the value judgments of psychiatry and society. He further indicates that it has not been possible to develop definitions of mental illness upon which psychiatrists can agree. In another article, Halleck (1969) reiterates the role of value judgments in defining mental health and further indicates that any such criteria are thus vague and equivocal. He further asserts that there is minimal chance that agreement will be reached in the future on definitions of such terms as "mental illness." More recently, Spitzer (1981) stated that, "The concept of 'disorder' *always* involves a value judgment." (p. 214) (italics added)

It is important to realize that this infusion of values into the definition or identification of mental disorder represents a very serious problem. First, as noted above by Halleck, one result is that any such definitions or criteria will be vague. How can values be applied to carving out precise definitions of mental disorder? Second, if judgments of abnormality are value laden, there is almost certain to be considerable variation across practitioners by mere virtue of the fact that our individual values often differ considerably. For example, a psychiatrist with a liberal bent might label some things as normal (e.g., long hair) that a practitioner with a conservative bent might well label abnormal, and vice versa; indeed, research that we will later review shows such variance to be the case when values differ across clinicians. Third, basing such judgments on values is not basing judgments on scientific criteria. Thus, an expert witness in the courtroom, if being absolutely candid, perhaps should say something like the following: "I have labeled defendant Jones as having condition X because he does not share my values or way of thinking, or on the basis of the value system I use as a psychiatrist (or person), and not really on the basis of any agreed upon scientific definition of abnormality."

The introduction to DSM-IV (p. xxi) acknowledges the inadequacy of the definition of mental disorder. There is not only disagreement about the definition of mental disorder, but *there is disagreement about whether mental disorder exists at all.* To return to our original illustration, this is akin to biologists disagreeing not over whether something is an animal or a plant, but over whether animals even exist. Bauer (1962-

63) argues that such terms as "neurosis" and "psychosis" will never be satisfactorily defined "for the simple reason that they do not exist." (p. 14) Dr. Phillip Q. Roche (1958a, 1958b), winner of the Isaac Ray Award of the American Psychiatric Association, argues that there is no such thing as insanity or such a thing as mental disease. Perhaps the most famous critic is Dr. Thomas Szasz (1961, 1963). We will describe his views in greater detail below; for now, merely listing the title of his widely read book should suffice in representing his overall view on the issue. The book is called *The Myth of Mental Illness* (1961).

It follows logically that if one does not know what mental disorder represents or how to define it, there will also be trouble on the other side of the coin, that is, in defining what it is not, or what psychological health represents. Stiles (1983) states:

> Whereas physiological normality is universally the same and universally desirable, psychological normality is heterogeneous. Body temperature, blood pressure, pituitary hormone levels and a host of other physiological indexes has precisely quantified normal values from which any substantial deviation signifies disease. By contrast, even a casual consideration of one's friends and relatives will show that there are enormously many *different* modes of psychological health (even if one's friends and relatives are not all psychologically healthy). Study of different groups and cultures reveals a still greater diversity of successful patterns of living.

> We all recognize that the old popular stereotype of a standard, certifiable, "well-adjusted" person is false—a picture of rigid conformity rather than psychological health...are models of personality...describe a healthy individual as having a wide range of options. That is, freedom from psychopathology opens up many paths...rather than converging on a single pattern of good adjustment.

Havens (1981) states:

> Contemporary psychiatry seeks symptoms and signs and the collection of these into syndromes or disease states. Health is considered to be an absence of these disease states, a preponderance of what are called negative findings. The foundation of the psychiatric disease concept is therefore a largely negative description of health.

Havens notes that although it might appear that the same points apply to the physical disease concept, they do not, because physical disease is always defined against a literally palpable awareness of health. He then states:

> It is true that the mental status or psychological examination, the chief diagnostic tool of the disease school, includes some tests of mental health. The strongest of these concern memory, grasp, orientation, and calculation. It is no accident that these are the parts of the psychological examination closest to neurology, which is replete with other tests of neurohealth. However, the psychological examination is weakest where it is most needed by the psychiatrist: in tests of normal affect, sociability, self-image, capacity for self protection, and coping, among others.

Given the general problem of distinguishing or defining normality and abnormality, it also follows that there will be considerable difficulties making these separations for specific forms of thinking or behavior. For example, it is often uncertain whether a specific behavior represents a "psychiatric symptom" as opposed to normal behavior, or behavior seen among normal individuals. In many cases, there is little or no information about the frequency with which certain behaviors occur across normal individuals (see the discussion of these frequencies, or "base rates," in Chapter 5). As such, one does not even know if a behavior labeled abnormal is really unusual at all, or at all specific to individuals with supposed psychiatric disorders. A number of writers address this problem, and research shows that behaviors often thought to be nearly exclusive to individuals with disorders are not really so exclusive at all.

Robins (1985), in reporting on a study that explored the prevalence rates of various psychiatric disorders, states that: "The presence or absence of disorder is decided on the basis of the degree of resemblance of a particular patient's self-report and the physician's observations of the patient's ideal type of diagnosis. *Symptoms used to diagnose most psychiatric disorders are found with some frequency in those persons deemed not to have the disorder.*" (p. 921) (italics added)

Research that was reported on in the *California State Psychologist* (Volume 19, 1984), conducted by Kay Jamison at the U.C.L.A. Neuropsychiatric Institute, found that periods of intense creativity in artists and writers is characterized by increased enthusiasm and energy. This suggests that such features may be normal, at times, for artistically creative people and may not reflect the abnormalities they are often assumed to represent, such as a variant of manic depression. Mellinger et al. (1985) found in a survey conducted in 1979 that insomnia afflicts 35% of all adults during the course of a year and that half of these adults experience the problem as a serious one. Thus, such a problem, which is considered a symptom of a wide variety of mental disorders, may indeed be relatively common among normal individuals. An issue of *Clinicians Research Digest* (1985) presented a special feature on a classic study by George Vaillant (from the *Archives of General Psychiatry*, Vol. 42, pp. 107-118). In describing the findings, one of the statements was as follows: "Neurotic defensive styles or mechanisms like repression, isolation, or displacement were frequently used by all of the men in Vaillant's study, regardless of adjustment and populations." Stated differently, for those forms of thinking and behavior supposedly characterizing individuals with psychiatric disturbance, Vaillant did not find that they were never, or rarely, or sometimes also present among normal individuals, but that they were *frequently* present among normal individuals.

Many other prominent writers and researchers (see Chapter 7) have addressed these problems in defining mental illness, determining the boundaries between the normal and the abnormal, or the considerable overlap in thinking and behavior evidenced across normal individuals or individuals without psychiatric disorders, and individuals purported to have psychiatric problems. Discussing one such problematic separation, Wooten (1972) states, "It is time to admit that the sick and the wicked are not scientifically distinguishable."

OVERPATHOLOGIZING

Some of the implications of the above problem are worth noting, starting with the following facts or assumptions. As described, there exists no clear, broadly accepted definition of mental disorder, or criteria for its identification; further, there is substantial overlap in the thinking and behavior of those who are and are not normal. In many cases one does not know the frequency with which behaviors that supposedly characterize abnormality appear among normal individuals, or even if these supposedly abnormal behaviors occur with substantial frequency among normal individuals. Next, put yourself in the place of the psychiatrist. You have been entrusted with the care of others who come to you to relieve their suffering. Although there is nothing particularly good about calling something abnormal that is not, you have had drummed into you throughout your training that the much more serious error is to miss abnormality when it is present. Question: What is likely to result from this set of conditions?

The answer is that you are likely to overdiagnose abnormality. The jargon that is used to describe this widespread and pervasive tendency is called "overpathologizing." As regards this tendency, Livermore et al. (1968) state:

> Probably the most pernicious error is committed by those who classify as "sick," behavior that is *aberrant neither in a statistical sense* nor in terms of any defensible biological or medical criteria but rather on the basis of the clinician's personal ideology of mental health and interpersonal relationships. Examples might be the current psychiatric stereotype of what a good mother or a healthy family must be like or the rejection as "perverse" of forms of sexual behavior that are not biologically harmful, are found in many infra-human animals, in diverse cultures and have a high statistical frequency in our own society. (p. 79)

Numerous other psychiatrists and psychologists also describe this problem of overpathologizing, and there are a number of research studies demonstrating its existence. This work is described in detail in Chapter 7, and only one illustrative study of the phenomenon is presented here. Sattin (1980) introduces his study on the topic by providing some background information. Sattin states, "Laymen usually assume that the mental health professional is an unbiased expert on the classification of the mentally ill. Congruently, the mental health professional assumes that his diagnostic decisions are based upon a scientific examination of the available data. However, several sociological observers of the diagnostic process have questioned whether these assumptions are legitimate." Sattin cites Mechanic (1967) to the effect that the diagnostic conclusions of professionals presume that mental disorder is present. In his study, Sattin created situations of high and low expectancy of psychopathology. Four interviewees were described to psychiatric residents as being either undergraduates taking psychology courses who volunteered to participate in an experiment or undergraduates who were recently evaluated for psychiatric hospitalization. Sattin found that the degree of psychopathology attributed to the interviewees in the high expectancy context was greater than the degree of psychopathology attributed to the same interviewees when heard within the low expectancy context.

Consider that in many clinical evaluations, one starts with the expectancy that pathology or difficulties will be found, for why else would someone be bringing themselves to the psychiatrist or psychologist? This expectancy may be heightened considerably when evaluation is conducted for purposes of litigation. Frequently, the lawyer directly states or implies that the individual is being referred because they are strongly suspected of having some malady that bears upon their legal situation, e.g., that the individual is suspected to have met the legal definition of insanity at the time of the offense, or that the individual suffered brain damage or impairment as a result of a personal injury. Should one object that Sattin's study involved psychiatrists in training, the material in Chapter 7 should prove helpful because it demonstrates similar results among professionals, including highly experienced ones.

OVERLAP ACROSS CATEGORIES
AND LIMITED SPECIFICITY

Considerable difficulties are created not only by the substantial overlap in behavior and thinking across normal and abnormal individuals, but also by the overlap in symptoms across various disorders. For example, anxiety or tension is supposed to accompany various forms of disturbance, and thus by itself this symptom does little to help one identify what specific condition may be present. In other cases, the entire set of symptoms accompanying different diagnostic categories are actually quite similar. In theory, there are distinguishing symptoms, or at least some areas of uniqueness, that should help in the differential diagnosis of disorders with shared features. However, in practice, it appears that this overlap creates considerable difficulty distinguishing one "disorder" from another.

For example, in discussing what is described as an adult form of attention deficit disorder, Wender et al. (1985) cover a range of defining features. These features include difficulty sustaining attention, impulsivity, and moodiness and irritability. Such problems as impulsivity and moodiness, however, are also defining features of various other disorders, and thus the authors warn that one must be careful to determine when such characteristics are actually symptomatic of those other disorders, such as major depression or what are called borderline disorders (the latter being an extremely nebulous category itself; see Chapter 19).

Symptoms purportedly associated with depression, because they are so common and are associated with such a wide variety of diagnostic categories, further illustrate the problems that overlap and lack of specificity create. First, as various writers have noted, it is often difficult to distinguish a depressive disorder from other types of disorders. For example, Wamboldt et al. (1986) point out that various medications can produce symptoms that mimic or can be confused with depressive disorders. Schuckit (1986) indicates that alcohol abuse can also produce symptoms that can be confused with depressive disorders, and he lists various factors that contribute to this confusion. Second, other writers describe the difficulties separating true depressive disorder from normal feelings of sadness, and distinguishing different types of depression. Michael Rutter (1986), an eminent psychiatrist, describes the problem as follows:

> It might be thought that the criteria of multiple depressive phenomena, persisting over time and associated with substantial social impairment, should be sufficient to differentiate depressive disorders from normality, but this has been disputed. The controversies center around three main issues: (1) depression versus "demoralization," (2) depression versus normal grief (or other stress) reactions, and (3) depression versus "distress" reactions to physical illness. (p. 494)

Rutter states further:

> The differentiation between depression and "normal" grief or stress reactions raises rather difficult issues. It is accepted that many grief reactions fulfill the diagnostic criteria for major depressive disorders, but it is argued that they should be regarded as "normal" phenomena rather than illnesses because they are both common and understandable. (p. 495)

Rutter goes on to critique this latter notion and points out that it is quite uncertain, at this time, what the correct answer might be and that the issue can only be resolved through research efforts. Rutter then points out difficulties in distinguishing different types of depression, stating:

It has proved clinically useful to make various distinctions within a broad group of depressive disorders...however, it remains quite uncertain whether these types refer to different conditions or rather variations within the same condition. Also, there is continuing doubt on where to draw the boundaries of depression—especially with respect to schizoaffective disorders, conditions with prominent anxiety, and chronic mood disturbances." (p. 499)

Many writers have commented on the difficulties of distinguishing between depression and brain damage. The tendency to mistake depression for brain damage or true intellectual impairment is so widely acknowledged (particularly among elderly individuals) that there is even a term for patients who present as if they were brain damaged but are actually depressed. This term is "depressive pseudodementia." For example, a study by Plotkin et al. (1985) suggests that subjective memory complaints, which are often considered a possible indicator of brain damage or dysfunction, actually show a close association with depression and may, in fact, reveal more about depressive status than memory functioning. Sweet (1983) points out that emotional conditions, depression in particular, may partially explain lowered performance on tests of intellectual or neuropsychological functioning. Thus, by implication, such states may be confused with brain damage, which these measures are designed to detect. In another article (Fisher et al., 1986) in which Sweet was the second author, it is pointed out that repeated evaluations can help in making "the often difficult distinction of neurological disorder from depression." (p. 17) Fogel and Sparadeo (1985) state:

Adverse effects of depression on cognitive function have been well documented in the psychiatric and psychological literature. Depressed patients have been shown to have reversible impairment of memory, of abstract reasoning, and of performance on cognitive and motor tasks requiring sustained effort. (p. 120)

So there things stand. One often does not know what type of disorder "depressive" symptoms might indicate. One often does not know whether such symptoms point to any disorder at all. One may not even know whether the symptoms reflect depression per se or brain damage. How is a field that labors under such a state of affairs supposed to help the trier of fact?

THE PROBLEM OF OUTLIERS

Although some individuals may seem to fit cleanly into some diagnostic categories, other individuals are not so easy to classify and do not fit cleanly into any category. We will call individuals who resist clear classification "outliers." The existence of outliers is one reason that many of the general categories in DSM-III contained a subdivision that starts with "atypical," as in "atypical affective disorders" under the more general heading, "Affective Disorders;" or "atypical anxiety disorder" under the more general heading, "Anxiety Disorders." Also listed were atypical conduct disorders, atypical eating disorders, atypical tic disorders, atypical specific developmental disorders, atypical or mixed organic mental disorders, atypical or mixed organic brain syndromes, atypical paranoid disorders, atypical psychotic disorders, atypical impulse control disorders, and other atypical disorders as well. Obviously, categories for atypical disorders are not themselves atypical and rather are included under many general headings. Thus, it is not unlikely that the lawyer will be involved in cases in which an individual is assigned one or another "atypical" diagnosis. The reader should be aware that DSM-III-R and DSM-IV have dropped the term "atypical" and seem to have substituted the phrase "not otherwise specified" (NOS). Thus, where "atypical depression" appears in DSM-III, "depressive disorder NOS" appears in DSM-III-R and DSM-IV. Whatever the exact wording, the meaning appears the same: NOS is used when a "disorder does not fit criteria for any of the specific disorders listed within a category."

Virtually any classification of an individual into one of the NOS categories can be challenged. One should realize that these NOS categories are, in almost all cases, what are commonly referred to as "wastebasket" terms. By this one means that a category is used for individuals who do not fit into one of the currently defined specific categories, and rather they are lumped or thrown together into what is essentially a miscellaneous category.

These NOS or wastebasket categories are by no means specific (otherwise they would not be named NOS but would be given specific names for the disorder or subtype of disorder they represent). Those who fall within an NOS category often represent a very mixed or heterogeneous group, and thus the label, by itself, is minimally informative. The use of an NOS category is typically an admission that one does not really know, specifically, what disorder the individual might have. Rather, the individual falls within one of a possible series of yet-to-be defined disorders, or perhaps within some disorder that has not yet attained sufficient support to be "honored" by a place within the current diagnostic manual. An article by Beeber and Pyes (1983) illustrates some of these difficulties as pertains to depressions that do not fit cleanly into any existing category in DSM-III but are rather considered atypical. They indicate that opinion is highly divided as regards depressive or depressive-like entities that do not fit within the range of currently defined "typical" disorders. Where these atypical depressions fit is quite uncertain. Further, various forms of atypical disorders could conceivably fit DSM criteria for adjustment disorder with depressed mood, dysthymic disorder, atypical affective disorder, and other categories as well. Note that adjustment disorder, for example, is not even a subcategory of depression, and thus one does not even know if some of these atypical "depressions" should be considered depressions at all.

How common are outliers, or individuals who resist clear classification? Perhaps extremely common. Strauss et al. (1979) note that psychiatric diagnostic systems have been criticized for limitations of reliability, validity and applicability. They note that while syndromes exist that fit traditional diagnostic categories, the large majority of patients do not fit neatly into these syndromes and that forcing the diagnostician to choose among the categories requires arbitrary decisions that are disturbing to diagnosticians who recognize how misleading the diagnosis can be. The lawyer should be aware that DSM-III, DSM-III-R and DSM-IV allow for more than one diagnosis, thus alleviating this problem to some extent. However, these DSMs call for designation of a "principal" diagnosis, leaving room for disagreement on this issue.

Perhaps some, or even the majority of adolescents should be considered outliers also. Ehrenworth and Archer (1985) state, "The psychological assessment and diagnosis of adolescent patients is a markedly complex task due to the lack of clear demarcations between normal and abnormal behavior for this development period." (p. 413) Weiner (1983) states, "Current reviewers are now able to acknowledge that adolescents have problems that go beyond normative adjustment issues, face the task of knowing what to call these problems. Adolescents remain difficult to diagnose. Several factors, methodological and conceptual, contribute to this difficulty." (pp. 741-774)

Problems with the classifications of elderly individuals, women in general, the socially disadvantaged, and minority group members have also been broadly acknowledged (see Chapter 16). In fact, considering all of these characteristics together, one has encompassed well over half of the population. Thus, perhaps the large majority of individuals assessed for legal purposes could be considered outliers, or individuals for whom there have been serious questions raised about the applicability and appropriateness of past and present diagnostic systems.

THE PROBLEM OF DOUBLE STANDARDS

There are some reports which indicate that diagnostic practices may differ considerably depending upon the context in which evaluation is being performed. Schurman et al. (1985) report that in typical practice, the only diagnostic service that psychiatrists may be likely to perform is a mental status exam, and that in the clinical practices under investigation, mental status exams were provided in only 30% of visits. They indicate that in about 66% of visits to psychiatrists, no diagnostic procedures were performed at all. This would suggest that although psychiatrists perform diagnostic services in the forensic arena, they apparently often feel that they are not very significant in their practices.

Sharfstein et al. (1980) found a high rate of disagreement between diagnoses listed on insurance forms and diagnoses rendered separately and confidentially on the same patients by the same practitioners. As the authors discuss, these differences were likely due to therapists' concerns about patient confidentiality and the potential impact of diagnostic labels on the individuals with whom they are involved. What this does apparently show, however, is that therapists may willingly and knowingly alter, or arguably falsify, diagnoses in order to serve the interests of those they treat or assess. If a psychiatrist is willing to do this with insurance companies, who is to say that he will not also alter information in forensic cases, in which certain labels may be to the benefit or detriment of an individual. Our point here is not to pass judgment, nor are we indicating that such actions are conducted with anything other than a positive intention in mind. However, this article may be of great value to the lawyer, as further discussed in Chapter 7.

BRIEF OVERVIEW OF DSM-I AND DSM-II

The past lack of success in attempting to develop a satisfactory system of classification helps to put current, ongoing work in some perspective. Past occurrences may be the best predictors of current or future occurrences. That DSM-I and DSM-II failed to meet requirements for an adequate diagnostic system certainly should not lead to rosy predictions for other or upcoming versions of the diagnostic manual. It is also worthwhile to show that many problems are not new ones, but have plagued attempts at classification from the start and will likely continue to do so. Consequently, newer versions of the diagnostic manual, in many respects, are not necessarily better but simply newer, that is, they have not resolved or overcome longstanding difficulties. One is again reminded of Paul Meehl's (1978) previously mentioned lament that the soft sciences often fail to show a truly progressive nature, and that instead, new work replaces old work rather than building upon it.

The negative literature on DSM-I and DSM-II has been extensive, with the overall tone being that these attempts at creating adequate diagnostic systems were failures (Menninger, 1968; Halleck, 1967; Agnew and Bannister, 1973; Roche, 1958a, 1958b; Mosher and Feinsilver, 1973; Spitzer et al., 1975; Strauss, 1975; Hine and Williams, 1975; Bachrach, 1974).

OVERVIEW OF DSM-III

DSM-III was published in 1980. While it became obsolete after only 7 years, some exposition of it is necessary because it constitutes the format for subsequent Manuals.

DSM-III represented a radical departure from the previous diagnostic manuals. The major differences include the use of a multi-axial framework; greater specification of the symptoms comprising a particular disorder; and the inclusion of over a hundred new diagnostic categories. The inclusion of categories of "conditions not attributable to a mental disorder," such as malingering, may be of particular interest to the lawyer.

For multi-axial classification, five axes were selected and the manual recommends that each individual receive an evaluation on each axis. The five axes are:

Axis I   Clinical psychiatric syndrome(s) and other conditions

Axis II   Personality disorders and specific developmental disorders (In DSM-III-R, certain Axis I disorders have been moved to Axis II, thus expanding Axis II to cover a broader range of "developmental disorders," e.g., mental retardation.)

Axis III   Physical disorders and conditions

Axis IV   Severity of psychosocial stressors

Axis V   Highest level of adaptive functioning past year

The manual notes that Axes I and II comprise the entire classification of mental disorders, conditions not attributable to a mental disorder and administrative categories. The manual provides for multiple diagnoses within both Axes I and II, so that there could be several disorders stated under each axis.

Regarding Axis IV, psychosocial stressors, the manual directs the clinician to indicate the specific psychosocial stressors that are judged to be significant contributors to the development or exacerbation of the current disorder and a rating of the overall severity of stress that an "average" person with similar socio-economic and cultural circumstances would experience. This rating of severity of stressors appears to call upon the clinician to make a judgment for which, in almost all cases, he would have no adequate data base.

For example, among possible psychosocial stressors the manual lists: "*Legal:* e.g., being arrested, jailed, lawsuit or trial." What do psychiatrists know about the amount of stress experienced by average people, let alone average people in various socioeconomic and cultural groups, who are involved in lawsuits? Although the manual provides examples for various ratings on a 7-point scale of severity, it is clear that ratings on this axis call for highly subjective judgments by the clinician.

The same problem is true for Axis V, the highest level of adaptive functioning, which also calls for highly subjective judgments, or, in other words, speculations on the part of the clinician. (DSM-III-R does provide somewhat greater specification to guide clinical ratings of Axis V, although subjective judgment is still required, particularly because prior status must be assessed. In DSM-III-R, the clinician now provides a rating not only for the past year, as in DSM-III, but also for functioning at the time of evaluation.) Fernando et al. (1986) have independently outlined some of the shortcomings of this Axis, indicating that it requires crude and subjective inferences and fails to take into account duration of the present illness. They further note that the *assumption* is made that this Axis is useful prognostically but then offer, "We can find no research evidence in support of this contention." Thus, according to these authors, there are not only likely to be problems making reliable evaluations, but even if reliable evaluations can be achieved, it remains to determine whether the ratings will be of any real use.

DSM-III, particularly in its introduction, provides a number of statements that are relevant in the forensic arena. The introduction provides a statement of the mixed reaction with which successive drafts of the document met, including alarm, despair, excitement and joy. These mixed reactions suggest much disagreement over its structure and contents (p. 1). As further evidence of continuing disagreements, the Manual notes (p. 3) that while they attempted to resolve various diagnostic issues by reliance on research evidence as much as possible, even when data were available from research studies, interpretations of task force members often differed. The Manual also notes that in connection with conferences with other professional organizations, there were different points of view which often were resolved to the satisfaction of all concerned, but that in some cases this was not possible and differences were left unresolved (p. 4). The Manual notes that no assumption should be made that each mental disorder is a discrete entity with sharp boundaries between it and other mental disorders, or between it and the absence of mental disorder. They note continuing controversies concerning the diagnoses of depressive disorders (p. 6) and elimination of the class of "neuroses" (p. 9). From a general reading of the introduction it should be clear that the classifications which were finally sanctioned are the result of committee procedure which included many compromises. In other words, the Manual is not the product of the scientific discovery and verification of these separate categories, but was arrived at through a process that was essentially political in nature. (Many of the above points are also made in the introduction to DSM-III-R [see below].)

The introduction notes that there has been growing recognition of the importance of diagnosis for both clinical practice and research over the last decade. It notes the need to have a common language with which clinicians and research investigators can communicate about the disorders with which they deal. Thus, the Manual would appear to confirm the statement above that for lack of this common (reliable) language in the past, nearly all of the research and education in the field has been, for all practical purposes, of little value.

The introduction describes the purpose of the Manual as the provision of clear descriptions of diagnostic categories so that clinicians and investigators will be able to diagnose, communicate about, study and treat various mental disorders. The introduction, under the heading "CAUTIONS" (p. 12) states that the use of the Manual for other than clinical purposes would have to be examined in each case within an appropriate institutional context, giving as examples the determination of legal responsibility, competency, insanity, or third party claims. Although the import of this statement is not entirely clear, the existence of special caution seems to suggest that the Manual was not designed for forensic use, and that its use in forensic matters is beyond the purposes for which it was developed and may be questionable. Clearly, there are reservations concerning the use of the Manual in forensic matters.

Of considerable importance is the introduction's warning (p. 6) against the misconception that all individuals described as having the same mental disorder are alike in all important ways, noting that although they show at least the defining features of the disorder, they may differ in other important ways. This is relevant to our prior discussion of "the gap" because it means that even if one were certain of the particular diagnosis to attach to the individual, this would not really tell one anything in terms of most legal issues.

The Manual also states that while DSM-III provides more specific diagnostic criteria than previous manuals, for most of the categories, the diagnostic criteria are based on "clinical judgment and have not yet been fully validated by data about such important correlates as clinical course, outcome, family history and treatment response." (Given what we will describe about the limits of clinical judgment in Chapter 5, especially when a well validated scientific foundation is lacking, such a statement should be cause for considerable concern, if not alarm.) They also appear to state that the criteria provided are simply a preliminary step and that many of these criteria will need revision as more data are acquired. The research we will cite below certainly shows that, in this instance at least, a group of psychiatrists achieved predictive accuracy. The numerous revisions incorporated in DSM-III-R also confirm the prediction.

Prior to the publication of DSM-III, field studies were conducted to determine inter-rater reliability for the various classifications to be included. The results are given in the Manual (Appendix F) and represented by the Manual to show "good" reliability. The reader is reminded that establishing "good" reliability does not necessarily indicate validity, but is merely a prerequisite to a determination of validity. Thus, the assertion that the new system provides good reliability may be questioned.

To assess reliability in these field trials, or agreement across diagnosticians, a statistic was utilized that is called the "Kappa Coefficient." One derives a kappa using a statistical procedure that corrects for chance agreement, thus providing a more rigorous test than some other correlation statistics.

The use of chance-corrected procedures for assessing diagnostic agreement seems to be a step forward over more traditional methods, and they are likely to become standard tools. The reader should be aware, however, that a number of writers have expressed reservations about kappa (Janes, 1979; Kutchins and Kirk, 1986; Robins, 1985). For example, Robins points out that this statistic may prove misleading when the frequency of a condition is low, and Janes discourages the use of kappa for assessing diagnostic agreement. McCall indicates that confidence intervals are wide and thus the obtained kappa may significantly over- or underestimate actual level of agreement. (Personal communication. Dr. Chet McCall holds a Ph.D. in Mathematical Statistics and has published several articles in the field of statistics. He has been Professor of research methods within the Graduate School of Education and Psychology at Pepperdine University.)

The field studies of reliability were conducted in two phases, with Phase II involving modifications based on the results in Phase I. Therefore, this discussion will deal only with the results found in Phase II. As the Manual asserts that a kappa 0.70 or better represents good agreement, that figure will be used as the dividing line between good and not good agreement. The reader should be aware that because of the correction for chance agreement, a kappa of 0.70 indicates agreement of something above 70%. However, the caveat described above still applies. Given the wide band of confidence limits, the degree of agreement might actually be more or less than 70%. In any event, utilizing 0.70 as the boundary, most of the broad classifications exceed that level—for example, organic mental disorders, schizophrenic disorders, and the like. The range is from a kappa of -0.005 for factitious disorders to a high of 0.83 for the gross category of affective disorders. The overall kappa for Axis I classifications is 0.72. However, several of the gross categories have subdivisions many of which fall below the 0.70 boundary.

Even the above figures are subject to some question in light of the methodology of the field trials.

Kutchins and Kirk (1986) cover a number of these points in their detailed review of the DSM-III field trials. They point out that reliance on the kappa statistic poses a number of potential problems and that the field trials actually seem to violate certain assumptions necessary for the proper use of this statistic. Kutchins and Kirk then review the field trial data, including both diagnoses rendered by pairs of clinicians conducting joint or separate interviews, and diagnoses rendered on the basis of relatively detailed case summaries. They note that if one accepts the standard of reliability previously suggested by Spitzer himself, the majority of figures for the field trials fall below this established level, and that for the case summaries (another basis on which reliability was tested), not a single one of the kappas for the major diagnostic categories, much less the specific diagnostic categories, surpass this 0.70 standard. The results from the field trials for children and adolescents are even worse; among the few kappas surpassing the 0.70 standard, half were based on the assessment of one patient only. The above results were obtained for Axis I, and Kutchins and Kirk indicate that the results are still worse for Axis II (personality disorder) diagnosis. They observe that reliability figures for the field trials are based on agreement about general categories of disorder, and not on specific diagnoses. They indicate that consensus on broad categories was considered "perfect" agreement. Kutchins and Kirk note, however, that in such cases of "perfect agreement," the specific diagnoses may not have agreed and indeed might describe very different disorders. They note that figures showing agreement across general categories can thus be quite misleading and of little practical meaning.

As regards the field trials, Kutchins and Kirk state:

> The developers of DSM-III have repeatedly asserted that careful, systematic field trials established the improved scientific reliability of DSM-III. However, important information about the methods and findings of the field trials has never been reported. Some of the reports are inconsistent. The field trials themselves could more accurately be described as uncontrolled, nonrandom surveys in which several hundred self-selected and unsupervised pairs of clinicians throughout the country attempted to diagnose non-randomly selected patients and, after some sharing of information, made "independent" assessments of these patients. The possibility for contamination between clinicians obviously was great, although it has been claimed that this was a minor problem based on self-reports of the participants. Other than the researchers' through-the-mail admonitions that participants should avoid conferring about their diagnoses, the researchers had no way to control contamination that would bias the data in the direction of higher reliability scores. Furthermore, nowhere is it reported how many clinicians *initially* agreed to participate in the reliability studies versus how many eventually submitted usable data. Were those who had more difficulty with the diagnostic system or those pairs who found that their diagnostic judgments were in disagreement less likely to submit their results than were

others? If this happened, it would bias the data in the direction of greater agreement. (p. 10)

Despite the fact that aspects of the methodology of the field trials may have inflated diagnostic agreement, the reliability for major classes of disorders was questionable even if the researchers' own standards were applied. On no axis are the reliability data (as expressed in kappa) consistently good. And in some important areas, such as personality disorders and diagnoses for children and adolescents, the reliability data often are poor. (p. 11)

LIMITS, WEAKNESSES & CRITICISMS OF DSM-III

Nussbaum et al. (1981-82) observed that at a symposium someone from the floor pointed out that "Ziskin would have no difficulty in publishing an antidote to DSM-III." That unknown commentator may find his or her opinion supported in the material that follows. However, in accomplishing this task, one need not rely on the critical skills of only one or a few individuals, as many thoughtful individuals, and by now a fair amount of research make considerable contributions in this regard.

Politics and Not Science

In theory at least, a diagnostic manual should be constructed on the basis of scientific evidence and not on the basis of what can be viewed as political considerations. Imagine a scientist at a convention saying, "Today I will discuss a new diagnostic category for which I do not have clear scientific evidence but which I think will delight practitioners because it opens up new avenues for reimbursement from insurance companies." Or, "Although I really believe condition 'X' represents a psychiatric disorder based on the available evidence, let us not label it as such or include it in the new diagnostic manual because it is likely to get some people upset." Or, "You have your views and I have mine, so let's compromise and satisfy everybody a little bit—you vote for one of the disorders I prefer for inclusion in the Manual and I will vote for one of the disorders you prefer." Is this any way to run a scientific program aimed at deriving a sound classification system? Of course not. And yet, according to a number of authorities, such types of thinking and behavior, to an uncertain extent, shaped DSM-III.

McReynolds (1979) states:

The process whereby new categories of disturbance are introduced into psychiatric nosology is clearly not a scientific one. No recognizable process of scientific discovery is evident with regard to the scores of new disorders in DSM-III. (p. 123)

He further states:

These are not new human problems. The processes whereby they have come to occupy a new place in psychiatric nosology are social and political, not scientific, in nature. (p. 123)

Goleman (1978) describes the humorous reaction of one psychiatrist to some of the new categories in DSM-III. The psychiatrist expresses the hope that his hospital insurance will cover hospitalization and treatment should he decide to stop his use of both tobacco and coffee, and that if the treatment is not successful he will be eligible for disability benefits and early social security benefits, since the use of tobacco and caffeine are to be listed as official illnesses. The same psychiatrist expresses the further hope that when DSM-IV is compiled, missing a three-foot putt on the 18th hole will also be classified as a psychiatric disorder.

Other prominent figures in psychiatry note the operation of social, political, economic, and practical factors in diagnostic practices as well as the presence of value judgements and compromise (Zubin, 1977-78; Robins and Helzer, 1986; Spitzer, 1981, 1985).

All of these above reports are mild compared to an article that appeared in *Time Magazine* (December 2, 1985). Although *Time* is obviously not a scientific journal and the report must be interpreted in this light, it is also the case that such an outlet potentially permits a wider latitude for statements that are not constrained by the niceties that most scientific journals respect. The article describes the negotiations of the DSM Committee with representatives of women's organizations (e.g., the chair of the Women's Caucus of the American Psychological Association) on the inclusion of a new disorder to be known as "Masochistic Personality Disorder." APA caucus chairperson Lenore Walker is quoted in the article as saying, "At one point, they offered us a deal....If we backed off on Masochism, they would create a sadistic disorder to cover wifebeaters." The article states that as compromise clauses hummed through the air, Walker said, "We sat there horrified." The article goes on to quote psychologist Renee Garfunkle, a staff member of the American Psychological Association, to the effect that the low level of intellectual effort was shocking with diagnoses developed by a majority vote on the level we would use to choose a restaurant: you feel like Italian, I feel like Chinese, so let's go to a cafeteria. The *Time* article notes the similarity of the process to the well-known battle royal that took place previously when the committee attempted to determine whether homosexuality is or is not a mental disorder, finally deciding by a referendum on a roughly 4,000 to 3,000 vote, that homosexuality is not a mental disorder, though in DSM-III it became a mental disorder if the homosexual person was unhappy with being homosexual. (Changed in DSM-III-R to the category "Sexual Disorders Not Otherwise Specified," with the following example: "persistent and marked distress about one's sexual orientation." [p. 296])

DSM-III: PSYCHIATRY, NOT PSYCHOLOGY

Many psychologists, including some in the governance of the American Psychological Association, had consistently voiced objections to DSM-III, and such objections were already being heard *for* DSM-III-R even before its official publication. These objections included conceptual obscurity/confusion, questionable broadening of range and scope of categories, use of a categorical rather than dimensional system, and scientific flaws. It is thus abundantly clear that leaders within the psychological community have grave misgivings about DSM-III and about DSM-III-R. This raises an interesting dilemma when a psychologist serves as an expert witness and uses any of the diagnostic categories from DSM-III (or DSM-III-R or DSM-IV). The psychologist is then employing a document that some of his very eminent colleagues consider seriously deficient, and such a practice seems discordant with the views or attitudes of important individuals within his own profession.

Actually, in a survey, Jampala et al. (1986) found that only about half of practicing psychiatrists in their study liked DSM-III and would use it if they did not have to and about half did not believe the criteria were valid.

DSM-III: NOT (GOOD) SCIENCE EITHER

In this section we present some overviews and critical commentary on DSM-III, and in the next section we discuss direct research on reliability and validity. McLemore and Benjamin (1979) state:

> Let us survey some of the shortcomings of DSM-III. As in the past, diagnosis still rests partly on impressionistic clinical judgment, including, for example, global ratings of the "severity" of psychosocial stresses and of the patient's highest level of adaptive functioning during the past year. (p. 17)

Other writers expressed various criticisms of DSM-III. McReynolds (1979) notes that it will take years to determine the validity of new categories and that the rationale and guiding principles of DSM-III can be seen as inadequate social science hypotheses from the beginning.

Schacht and Nathan (1977) state that many of the new features were created as reactions to criticisms of DSM-II rather than as positive expressions.

At the 1982 annual meeting of the American Psychiatric Association, a debate was held under the title, "Do the Advantages of DSM-III Outweigh the Disadvantages?" The moderator was Dr. John C. Nemiah. Speaking for the affirmative were Doctors Gerald L. Klerman and Robert L. Spitzer. Taking the negative were Doctors Robert Michels and George E. Vaillant. All of the above are psychiatrists of some eminence. What is most striking about this debate is the absence of a strong assertion by speakers on either side to the effect that DSM-III is really a good diagnostic system. Similarly, one is struck by the unanimity with which all of the participants referred to the coming of DSM-IV.

Frances and Cooper (1981) note that "the DSM-III criteria are only as valid as the current research evidence in psychiatry which means that they are quite tentative and future research will validate and discard them."

Other writers have challenged the fundamentals of the approach used in DSM-III or its theoretical underpinnings. Faust and Miner (1986) state: "We will argue that DSM-III's appearance of objectivity is largely illusory. Theory and inference have perhaps been reduced somewhat but eliminated nowhere—the document is replete with presuppositions and theoretical assumptions." (p. 963) Further, they conclude:

> The methodological program of DSM-III emphasizes description and the reduction of inference and theory. Regardless of appearances to the contrary, these goals have not been approached, cannot be attained, and should not be pursued at least in their extreme form. They are throwbacks to earlier and now revised views of science. These goals give the highest priority to things that either should not receive it or that are secondary outgrowths of other accomplishments, and they have the potential to discourage the conceptual and theoretical developments that are the prime movers of scientific progress. (p. 962)

Eysenck et al. (1983) provide an extensive review of DSM-III and not only reach some very negative conclusions but also attack a very fundamental aspect of the document, that is, its reliance on categories or types. They state: "This new scheme is based on foundations so insecure, so lacking in scientific support, and so contrary to well established facts that its use can only be justified in terms of social need." They warn psychologists to be aware of the weaknesses of any scheme based on democratic voting rather than scientific research. They assert that the reliabilities are unacceptably low and that there is an absence of any indication of validity. These authors also add themselves to the list of those who object to a categorical approach as exemplified in DSM-III, in opposition to a "dimensional" approach which allows for more gradation. These authors also note that it usually takes a long time, perhaps as much as fifty years, for material to find its way from scientific finding to professional application.

Millon (1984), a member of the DSM-III Task Force, touches on both the scientific limitations of DSM-III and its political underpinnings. He states as regards DSM-III criteria that, "The specific criteria themselves are but crude approximations, speculative proposals that lack diagnostic comparability, syndromal comprehensiveness, and empirical foundations. Those of us working to upgrade the auspicious beginning in

DSM-III have recommended numerous proposals for criteria modification and elaboration." (p. 455)

RESEARCH ON RELIABILITY

Uebersax (1983) notes that disagreements among diagnosticians are common and argues that more attention should be paid to methods for uncovering sources of disagreement in order to improve agreement.

Some investigators have limited their focus to specific DSM-III axes. As previously mentioned, Fernando et al. (1986) have raised questions about the potential for achieving reliable ratings on Axis V (highest level of adaptive functioning). A number of studies have found poor reliabilities for Axis II (personality disorders) (Mellsop et al., 1982; Drake and Vaillant, 1985; Frances, 1980).

Robins (1985) provides a methodological critique of a large-scale project that tried to establish the prevalence rates of various DSM-III diagnoses. The project was conducted at two sites, and as regards agreement rates, Robins states:

> While the DSM-III's specific criteria should increase the likelihood that psychiatrists will agree, these results show that agreement is not automatic. Clearly, psychiatrists in the two sites did not apply DSM-III criteria in identical ways, although each study reported *intrasite* consistency for its psychiatrists. (p. 920)

Robins' statement is significant because it supports a point we made above, that is, that when reliability is established among a limited set of practitioners or among those at a common site or with similar backgrounds or training, the generalizability of the results is questionable. It is well known that those with similar background or training (e.g., trained at the same university) often achieve higher agreement rates than those trained in different settings. However, a document like DSM-III is not intended for use at only one or a few settings or only for those with similar training, rather, it is designed for general use. Perhaps the most relevant question, then, is not whether a restricted group of practitioners can achieve agreement, but whether a representative group of clinicians—a group similar in overall composition to the range of practitioners that use DSM-III in practice or forensic settings—can achieve satisfactory agreement.

Robins adds, as regards the results obtained across sites, "This instability is implicit in the fact that psychiatric disorders lack definitive tests for their existence." (p. 921)

Issues of reliability extend beyond agreement across diagnosticians. One also needs to demonstrate consistency or stability over time. Thus, presuming an individual's condition does not change, he or she should receive the same diagnosis when evaluated a second or third time.

Instead, if the results keep changing, it would appear that the diagnosis rendered is not so much a product of any disorder an individual may have but of the time or setting of the evaluation. Alternatively, it may be that "disorders" are so unstable themselves that they resist reliable measurement. Whatever the reason, if stability over time cannot be demonstrated, a diagnosis is typically of little use for legal purposes. Should we hold a different trial after every evaluation because we may deal with a different diagnosis each time? What can be the possible usefulness of a diagnosis if it is so likely to change according to time and place? How could we possibly, for example, formulate any predictions when one of the supposed bases for reaching such formulations, the diagnosis, is not a constant?

The article by Robins also addresses this problem of changes in diagnosis over interviews conducted at different points in time. He indicates that on a second interview, interviewees often failed to report symptoms they had previously reported, and that this may have been one factor underlying diagnostic instability. Robins notes that this finding cannot be explained by changes in individuals' symptoms over time, for in these interviews (separated by a relatively short period of time) a number of questions pertained to lifetime occurrence—whether certain symptoms had been experienced at any time in the past. Even the results obtained on the previous occurrence of symptoms changed across the interviews.

A study by Boxer and Garvey (1985) also demonstrates the instability of diagnosis rendered at different points in time, particularly when assessment is conducted by different practitioners.

The previously mentioned article by Kutchins and Kirk (1986) also overviews studies on reliability separate from the field trials. These studies on reliability show that level of agreement on DSM-III categories is often quite low. For example, in a study by Lieberman and Baker (1985), only the kappa for alcohol abuse surpassed 0.70, and kappas for other major classes of disorder ranged from 0.29 to 0.62. Kappa was 0.41 for schizophrenia and 0.37 for organic brain syndrome. Kutchins and Kirk discuss a study with children and adolescents which suggests that the reliability of DSM-III Axis I diagnoses may be slightly *lower* than reliabilities obtained for DSM-II categories. Overall, this article by Kutchins and Kirk is broadly useful in countering assertions that DSM-III has "solved" the problem of reliable diagnosis. These authors state:

> Moreover, the same standards that were used to criticize DSM-II would make the claims of reliability for DSM-III even more questionable. For DSM-II, "high reliability" seemed to refer to kappas above .80; "only satisfactory," to kappas from .70 to .79; "no better than fair," for kappas of .55 to .69; and

"poor," for kappas less than .55. Using these standards one would interpret only a few classes of DSM-III as having high reliability, a few more as only satisfactory, and the rest as no better than fair or poor.

Few have bothered to conduct the kind of additional, independent, rigorous reliability studies that are needed and long overdue; and few have asked why only partial reliability data were published prior to, with, or subsequent to the publication of DSM-III. So successful that no one seems to have noticed that many diagnostic categories were retained in DSM-III *regardless* of their reliability! High, only satisfactory, or poor reliability appears to have had little effect on the decisions about what was included in the diagnostic system.

Finally, the frequent claim that the reliability of DSM-III is "better" than DSM-II serves the function of warding off potential critics and obscuring the serious weaknesses in the methodology, analysis, and results of the field trials. It also clouds the use of a troubling double standard of interpretation. (p. 11)

RESEARCH ON VALIDITY

The research on the validity of DSM-III diagnostic categories is relatively restricted. In a number of cases, investigators have attempted to determine whether the diagnostic criteria allow clinicians to identify certain forms of disorder when they are actually (or supposedly) present. Alternatively, investigators may present cases of known or strongly suspected disorders and determine whether clinicians can identify them. Merely testing whether conditions can be identified is a very rudimentary test of validity. One would hope that, at minimum, a diagnostic system would allow one to recognize what it describes, and it could be maintained that these are studies of reliability as much as validity. As we have noted before, reliability is a preliminary but not sufficient condition for validity. To "establish" the validity of a diagnostic system, we need to do a great deal more. For example, one needs to determine whether the Manual provides a valid description of the disorders, or conceptualizes or divides the disorders correctly. To make these determinations, one ultimately needs to look at the predictive power of categories. For example, do they allow us to identify the cause of a disorder, its likely course, or the types of behaviors (e.g., aggressiveness) that an individual so diagnosed is likely to evidence in the future? It is these types of studies that will be necessary to close "the gap" when diagnosis is conducted for legal purposes, but such studies are sorely lacking. However, even studies with more modest aspirations have often yielded discouraging results.

Some authors have attacked the validity of the concepts or approaches DSM-III uses to identify disorders. Beaber et al. (1985) state that, "While DSM-III acknowledges and briefly describes malingering and fictitious disorders, it gives only limited information on their differentiation from 'true' psychiatric entities. Given that most mental disorders are diagnosed on the basis of subjective symptoms, the possibility for diagnostic error is substantial." (p. 1478)

DSM-III-R

Although the revised diagnostic manual, DSM-III-R, was published in 1987, it was essentially "dead" at the time of its birth, in view of plans to publish DSM-IV about 1992. DSM-III-R notes: "The DSM-III, published in 1980, stated '...DSM-III is only one still frame in the ongoing process of attempting to better understand mental disorders.' DSM-III-R represents another still frame." (p. xvii)

This statement well expresses the continual changes in, and experimental nature of, diagnostic practices. As DSM-IV was published in May, 1994, DSM-III-R has become obsolete at the time of this writing. However, because of delays in litigation, cases using DSM-III-R diagnoses are likely to continue to appear as late as 1996 or 1997. Therefore, a discussion of this version still has relevance. Obviously, in any case where diagnosis was based on DSM-III-R the criteria or even presence of the diagnosis in DSM-IV should be compared as the litigant may no longer meet the new criteria for the disorder. We recommend that lawyers who have copies of DSM-III and DSM-III-R retain them so that comparisons can be made.

The Introduction to DSM-III-R reiterates many of the points raised in the Introduction to DSM-III, discussed above. Included are difficulties determining "precise" boundaries in defining mental disorder or in distinguishing between different types of mental disorders, and the fact that people assigned to the same diagnostic category may differ "in important respects." It is also stated that the Work Group to Revise DSM-III tried to rely on scientific evidence in reaching decisions, but that information in this regard was often lacking. A reading of the introduction also makes it quite apparent that, like its predecessor, DSM-III-R is the product of committee deliberations and frequent compromise.

DSM-III-R also indicates that the etiology for many diagnostic categories is unknown. It is further stated that:

> The major justification for the generally atheoretical approach taken in DSM-III and DSM-III-R with regard to etiology is that the inclusion of etiologic theories would be an obstacle to use of the manual by clinicians of varying theoretical orientations, since it would not be possible to present all reasonable etiologic theories for each disorder. (p. xxiii)

It is also noted that many theories have been presented to explain various DSM-III-R disorders. These statements say something about the diversity and fragmentation of psychiatry. The lawyer might well question how an expert can draw trustworthy inferences about the cause of any DSM-III-R category for which etiology is too uncertain to include in the Manual and for which such diversity in orientation exists. An expert with a different orientation could take a very different view.

DSM-III-R makes numerous statements about limits or problems in DSM-III, which reveal the tentative nature of psychiatric diagnoses. In this regard, the lawyer may find Appendix D of DSM-III-R quite useful. This appendix not only details, point-by-point, differences between DSM-III and DSM-III-R, but also includes the rationale or reasons for revisions and often notes continuing doubts about current diagnostic categories. Perhaps the most powerful statement in this regard appears in the Introduction, where it is noted:

> Despite extensive field testing of the DSM-III diagnostic criteria before their official adoption, experience with them since their publication had revealed, as expected, many instances in which the criteria were not entirely clear, were inconsistent across categories, or were even contradictory. Therefore, all of the diagnostic criteria, plus the systematic descriptions of the various disorders, needed to be reviewed for consistency, clarity, and conceptual accuracy, and revised when necessary. (p. xvii)

Although the Introduction to the Manual clearly indicates that data from "well-conducted research studies" were given "the greatest weight" when proposals for revisions were evaluated, it is further stated that, "for most proposals, data from empirical studies were lacking." (p. xxi) It is noted that in such cases "primary importance was usually given to some other consideration." Other considerations mentioned include clinical experience and "a judgment as to whether the proposal was likely to increase the reliability and validity of the diagnosis...." (p. xxi) This seems to mean, in essence, that scientific data in this regard were lacking, and thus, the committee members speculated or guessed about whether proposals would increase reliability and validity. It is also mentioned that if proposals involved dropping or adding diagnostic categories, then two additional considerations were taken into account, one of these being, "How compelling is the research or clinical *need* for the category?" (p. xxi) (italics added) Note here that research or clinical *need* is discussed, and not scientific support for the category. One might also question what it means to say that a category might be included because there is a clinical need for it. One would think that diagnostic categories might arise out of systematic observation and study, not clinical need.

This admission that data from scientific studies were frequently lacking in evaluating proposed revisions creates a series of problems, particularly given the endorsement in the Manual for the importance of scientific information. First, as noted in the Manual, given this lack of scientific data, "primary importance" often had to be given to such factors as clinical experience or judgments about whether proposals were likely to improve reliability and validity. However, there is considerable research to suggest that clinical judgment is often faulty (see Chapter 5) and that experience does not lead to greater diagnostic or predictive skills (see Chapter 8). Indeed, DSM-III-R states, *"for most of the categories the diagnostic criteria are based on clinical judgment,* and have not yet been fully validated by data about such important correlates as clinical course, outcome, family history, and treatment response." (p. xxiv) (italics added) Thus, the lawyer may wish to make judge and jury aware that many of the changes in DSM-III-R are not based on research evidence but rather what is essentially unvalidated guesswork or conjecture. Further, when an expert uses a DSM-III-R diagnostic category, one should be able to establish that clinical judgment was a basis upon which the category was formed. This may provide another entry for introducing the clinical judgment research described in Chapter 5.

Second, and related to the above, in certain respects the revised diagnostic categories in DSM-III-R are even more speculative than those that appeared in DSM-III. Unlike DSM-III, for which reliability data were reported on the basis of field trials, no such reliability data are reported in DSM-III-R. DSM-III-R indicates that field trials were conducted to aid in the development of diagnostic criteria for disruptive behavior disorder, pervasive developmental disorders, and for agoraphobia without history of panic disorders, and generalized anxiety disorder. It is further stated, as regards two of these three field trials, that they used "clinicians' diagnoses as the criterion." This may mean that clinicians diagnosed individuals as having one or another of these disorders, and study was made of the individuals in order to learn more about these supposed disorders. In any case, many changes that appear in DSM-III-R (see below) include diagnostic categories that were *not* examined in these reported field trials. Thus, although members of the Work Group may have believed, or guessed, or hoped that modifications would increase diagnostic reliability or validity, it appears that in many cases data were not available from field trials by which one could determine whether these goals were actually achieved. It would also seem that clinicians using such diagnostic categories in which revisions have been made, lacking data on reliability, would also be guessing or hoping that better reliability has been achieved.

Third, whatever considerations were used in evaluating proposed revisions, the Work Group apparently encountered a number of instances in which consensus could not be achieved. For example, it is stated, "several controversies, particularly in the areas of childhood, psychotic, anxiety, and sleep disorders, could be resolved only by actually polling committee members." (p. xx) This statement is of interest in a number of respects. Although the advisory committees which participated in the revision of DSM-III-R were "selected on the basis of their expertise in particular areas," consensus still could not be reached for a number of categories. If acknowledged experts cannot agree even on criteria for diagnostic disorders, it is no wonder that professionals often disagree in the courtroom. Further, although it is stated that several controversies were "resolved" by conducting a poll of committee members, this would seem to mean that a poll (or vote) put an end to the discussion but did not resolve matters in the sense of reaching consensus. Additionally, the areas in which it is specifically stated that consensus could not be achieved are potentially relevant to a range of forensic cases. "Psychotic" diagnoses often come up in criminal cases, and diagnoses involving anxiety or sleep disorders often appear in personal injury cases. Finally, only examples are given of areas in which consensus could not be achieved, rather than a comprehensive listing. Thus, a clinician using the DSM-III-R would not necessarily know if he is employing one of the categories in which controversies could be resolved only through a poll. The lawyer may wish to ask a series of questions like the following: "Doesn't the DSM-III-R state that consensus could not be achieved in certain cases and had to be settled by polling committee members?" "The DSM-III-R does not indicate specifically all of the controversies that had to be resolved in this fashion?" "So you don't know if the diagnosis you used was one of those for which agreement could not be reached, even by these recognized experts, but had to be 'resolved' by a poll, much like the debate about whether homosexuality was a mental disorder had to be resolved by a vote?"

In the Introduction, the Manual contains a section (pp. xxvi to xxvii) with the heading, "Cautions in the Use of DSM-III-R." In particular, cautions are advised in the use of DSM-III-R with individuals from different cultures. The manual states: "When the DSM-III-R classification and diagnostic criteria are used to evaluate a person from an ethnic or cultural group different from that of the clinician's, and especially when diagnoses are made in a non-Western culture, caution should be exercised in the application of DSM-III-R diagnostic criteria to assure that their use is culturally valid." (p. xxvi) The Manual, however, provides minimal guidance regarding how one is to assure culturally valid application, and given the disputes, conflicting research, and lack of scientific knowledge regarding assessment of minority groups (see Chapter 16), one is left wondering how such a feat could possibly be accomplished. Indeed, the Manual states, "...the DSM-III-R categories are not based on extensive research with non-Western populations." (p. xxvii) The Manual also indicates that an experience or behavior (e.g., certain types of hallucination) "should not be regarded as pathological" if they are "entirely normative for a particular culture." This seems to be a warning for a clinician to avoid overpathologizing when applying the DSM-III-R to individuals from different cultures. It is further noted that:

> It is important that the clinician not employ DSM-III-R in a mechanical fashion, insensitive to differences in language, values, behavioral norms, and idiomatic expression of distress. When applied in a non-Western-language community, DSM-III-R should be translated to provide equivalent meaning, not necessarily dictionary equivalence. The clinician working in such settings should apply DSM-III-R with open-mindedness to the presence of distinctive cultural patterns and sensitivity to the possibility of unintended bias because of such differences. (p. xxvi)

This and another section also contain cautionary statements regarding forensic use. One statement reads, "…the clinical and scientific considerations that were the basis of the DSM-III-R classification and diagnostic criteria may not be relevant to considerations in which DSM-III-R is used outside of clinical or research settings, e.g., in legal determinations." (p. xxvi)

On a separate page that appears immediately prior to the DSM-III-R diagnostic categories, with a heading in bold type, "CAUTIONARY STATEMENT," it is noted:

> The purpose of DSM-III-R is to provide clear descriptions of diagnostic categories in order to enable clinicians and investigators to diagnose, communicate about, study, and treat the various mental disorders. It is to be understood that inclusion here, for clinical and research purposes, of a diagnostic category such as Pathological Gambling or Pedophilia does not imply that the condition meets legal or other nonmedical criteria for what constitutes mental disease, mental disorder, or mental disability. The clinical and scientific considerations involved in categorization of these conditions as mental disorders may not be wholly relevant to legal judgments, for example, that take into account such issues as individual responsibility, disability determination, and competency. (p. xxix)

This statement touches upon issues we have discussed in our coverage of "the gap," but it leaves certain ambiguities. It is not clear if the last sentence refers to the two disorders that appear before it (pathological gambling and pedophilia) or rather uses these two categories as examples illustrating a point that applies to diagnostic categories broadly. We will leave the reader to draw his own conclusions about the meaning of this statement, although we would note that it is *not* clear that the statement *does not* refer to "the various mental disorders." (see below, "Use of DSM-IV in Forensic Settings," DSM-IV, p. xxiii)

DSM-III-R retains the five axes used in DSM-III. Some of the disorders that appear under Axis I in DSM-III have been shifted to Axis II in DSM-III-R (i.e., mental retardation, specific developmental disorders, and pervasive developmental disorders). This change is likely to have little bearing on actual cases seen by the lawyer. Axis I includes clinical syndromes and also V codes, i.e., "conditions not attributable to a mental disorder that are a focus of attention or treatment." Axis II includes developmental disorders and personality disorders. Axis III consists of physical disorders and conditions, Axis IV is "severity of psychosocial stressors," and Axis V is "global assessment of functioning." DSM-III-R indicates that "Axes IV and V are available for use in special clinical and research settings; they provide information that supplements the official DSM-III-R diagnoses (on Axes I, II, and III)...." (p. 16). Judgments for Axis IV still appear to involve considerable subjectivity. DSM-III-R states, "the rating of the severity of the stressor should be based on the clinician's assessment of the stress an 'average' person in similar circumstances and with similar sociocultural values would experience from the particular psychosocial stressor(s)." (p. 19) DSM-III-R lists, as does DSM-III, "*Legal:* e.g., arrest, imprisonment, law suit or trial" (p. 20), as an example of a psychosocial stressor that may be of etiological significance. For Axis V, ratings are now made for level of functioning at the time the evaluation is conducted and also, as in DSM-III, for highest level of functioning over the past year.

We cannot begin to detail all the many changes made in DSM-III-R. As noted above, Appendix D of the DSM-III-R is exceedingly helpful in this regard. By our own count, *more than 200 changes appear across DSM-III and DSM-III-R.* Some of these changes are relatively minor and involve alterations in wording; other changes are not so minor. For example, there are numerous changes in diagnostic criteria and classification rules, and a number of diagnoses have been either dropped or added. Changes relevant to diagnostic categories which are discussed at some length in this text, such as PTSD, depression, and organic mental disorders are covered where this topic appears in the text. Given the number of changes, individuals who received a certain diagnosis under DSM-III might not "qualify" for this diagnosis under DSM-III-R. Thus, as the need arises, the lawyer might consult Appendix D of DSM-III-R to determine what changes may have occurred in diagnostic criteria and the effect this might have on diagnostic conclusions.

The DSM-III-R also contains a Symptom Index (pp. 517-552) that may be useful. A list is provided of numerous symptoms (e.g., impaired judgment) and the various disorders for which these symptoms appear, either exactly or generally, within the diagnostic criteria. For example, "decreased energy" appears among criteria for 21 different disorders; "psychomotor agitation" appears across 27 disorders; "inability to maintain attention or poor concentration" across 33 disorders; "hallucinations" across 27 disorders; and "insomnia" across 33 different disorders. It is noted in general that the importance of a particular symptom may differ across disorders. Nevertheless, the Symptom Index certainly illustrates something about the extent of symptom overlap across diagnostic categories. Further, although each of the diagnostic categories contains a combination of symptoms or criteria that are unique as a whole, many of the specific symptoms are not unique to any single disorder but rather common to many disorders. In some cases, a clinician may indicate that he is more certain about the presence of some of the symptoms or diagnostic criteria for a disorder as opposed to others. In other cases, the evidentiary basis may be considerably weaker for some symptoms versus others, and the clinician may "stretch" to meet all of the diagnostic criteria. The lawyer can often use this symptom index to determine if those symptoms for which the evidence is less compelling are critical distinguishing features for the diagnosis made, or are the features that set it apart from one or more other categories. If this is the case, then the only criteria about which the clinician may be relatively "certain" are those that, even when combined, are common to other diagnostic categories, some of which may be considerably more "benign" than the diagnosis made by the clinician. For example, if a diagnosis of "generalized anxiety disorder" is made, but if there is doubt about whether certain of the criteria are met, the criteria that remain may overlap entirely with "adjustment disorder with anxious mood," a less "serious" diagnosis.

Subsequent to publication of DSM-III-R publications continued to appear supporting the criticisms which had followed or immediately preceded the publication of DSM-III and indicating the continuation of controversy and doubt concerning these manuals.

Fenton et al. (1988) argue that frequent changes in diagnostic schemes in the absence of evidence of improved validity are likely to impede ongoing research. They state, "We question whether it is desirable for the American Psychiatric Association to change its 'standard' definition too often because to do so will again reduce the extent to which we can generalize from current and past research." They conclude, "Research progress will be impeded if we are forced to rediscover the wheel every seven to ten years." (p. 1448)

Gift (1988), commenting on the Fenton et al. article, addresses a number of issues concerning the process for deciding on altering diagnostic criteria. He notes, "The appropriate standard of proof with respect to altering diagnostic criteria is not immediately evident." (p. 1414)

Coryell and Zimmerman (1987) note that the three most widely used diagnostic systems in American psychiatry, the Feighner criteria, the Research Diagnostic Criteria (RDC), and the DSM-III appeared at four-year intervals. They observe that while each succeeding system incorporated changes in most diagnostic categories, implying progress toward greater validity, that assumption has rarely been directly tested and in their study, they found that the three systems did not show increments in validity with successively developed criteria sets. They note that as a result of the changes, many patients were given changed diagnoses. They are not declaring that diagnostic revisions are never warranted, but rather that the rate of revisions has outpaced the rate at which investigators in the field have generated and replicated the data on which changes should be based. They suspect that many changes are based on nothing more than committee members' clinical intuition. They state, "By this process, changes in criteria are likely to reflect new committee membership rather than new, empirically-based knowledge." (p. 1473) They state further, "Regrettably, unwarranted changes cost the field a great deal. Not only does diagnosis in psychiatry begin to appear whimsical to the public and to the rest of medicine, but the accumulation of knowledge regarding a given condition becomes slower and more difficult; investigators using different criteria will describe groups that only partially overlap despite identical labels." (p. 1473) They go on to recommend a far more circumspect approach to revision of criteria and propose a requirement of empirical and independently replicated evidence that the suggested change will increase diagnostic reliability or validity. They suggest very few proposals would meet such criteria within short periods of time. We might mention that for a number of disorders, the committees or subcommittees for DSM-III-R contained few, and in some cases no, members of the DSM-III committees other than Dr. Spitzer, who was the chair who served on virtually all committees, and Janet B.W. Williams, who served as the text editor. For example, the DSM-III-R committee on mood disorders had 27 members, of which, excluding Spitzer and Williams, only two had been on the DSM-III committee, which had ten members. With regard to any particular class of disorders, the attorney may find it worth his while to check the committee memberships in DSM-III-R against those in DSM-III, as one will often be able to point out the possibility that change in criteria represents nothing more than change in committee members, as asserted by Coryell and Zimmerman.

The following comparison of post-traumatic stress disorder under DSM-III and DSM-III-R illustrates the problem created by changes in the diagnostic criteria:

TABLE 1

Case 1, Alice Adams

PTSD under DSM-III	PTSD under DSM-III-R
A. (Assume adequate stressor)	A. (Assume adequate stressor)
B. None	B. Intense psychological distress at exposure to events that symbolize or resemble an aspect of the traumatic event.

PTSD under DSM-III	PTSD under DSM-III-R (cont'd)
C. Markedly diminished interest in one or more significant activities. Feelings of detachment or estrangement from others. Constricted affect.	C. Markedly diminished interest in significant activities. Feelings of detachment or estrangement from others. Restricted range of affect.
D. Sleep disturbance. Hyperalertness. Trouble concentrating. Intensification of symptoms by exposureto events that symbolize or resemble the traumatic event.	D. Difficulty falling or staying asleep. Hypervigilance. Difficulty concentrating.

Observe that in December 1986, Alice cannot be diagnosed with PTSD because she has no symptoms under category B under DSM-III but she can be diagnosed with PTSD in August 1987 under DSM-III-R although her symptoms are the same. Alice is unchanged, but she now has PTSD because intensification upon exposure to resembling events has been moved in the DSM from a D category symptom to a B category symptom. From a research standpoint, the problem is that it is not known whether any or how many Alice Adams's were in the populations of people who composed the research samples. Therefore, one cannot generalize from research done on samples that may not represent the populations of people with the disorder; you cannot apply research done on apples to oranges.

Case 2, Bill Brown

PTSD under DSM-III	PTSD under DSM-III-R
A. (Assume adequate stressor)	A. (Assume adequate stressor)
B. Recurrent dreams of the event.	B. Recurrent distressing dreams of the event.
C. Constricted affect.	C. Restricted range of affect.
D. Hyperalertness. Sleep disturbance.	D. Hyperalertness. Difficulty falling or staying asleep.

Bill can be diagnosed with PTSD in December 1986 under DSM-III but cannot be diagnosed with PTSD in August 1987 although he still has the same symptoms, because while only one Category C symptom was required in DSM-III, DSM-III-R requires three Category C symptoms. This is the reverse of the research dilemma posed by Alice Adams. Now there is a body of research on PTSD performed with an unknown number of people who did not have PTSD according to the (1987) current DSM. You cannot apply research findings on such non-PTSD people to people with PTSD. Bear in mind that when research on PTSD is reported, it is rare if ever, that the reports would indicate what proportions of the sample had which symptoms, only that the sample was diagnosed with PTSD. In the absurd extreme, all of the research prior to 1987 could have been done on samples made up entirely of Bill Browns. While this is absurd, it would be virtually impossible for anyone now to know what proportion of the supposed PTSD patients were Bill Browns.

Winokur et al. (1988) express concern over the existence of different sets of diagnostic criteria for research. They note that research often contains such statements as "diagnoses were made using the Feighner criteria with the agreement of two raters," or "the patients were reviewed and met all DSM-III criteria for bipolar illness; the controls met criteria for other psychiatric illnesses." Their concern is that:

> Presumably having read these statements, we are supposed to accept the reliability of the diagnosis as well as the validity. The latter is a complex problem that we need not go into here, except to say there is little reason or evidence to believe that any one of these three sets of criteria is really better than the others. The more basic question, the one psychiatry has set its sights on during the past two decades, is the question of diagnostic reliability. (p. 683)

They note that there are research publications in which an investigator's unconventional diagnostic practices seem apparent but note concerns about undetectable misinterpretations of criteria. They state, "Moreover, just because investigators report that they were reliable does not mean that they correctly interpreted the criteria." (p. 684) They concede there has been some improvement in the criteria, but they are still a long way from perfect. It should be noted that these statements refer to other diagnostic criteria sets as well as those of DSM-III.

Widiger et al. (1988) discuss many concerns and issues regarding DSM-III classifications of personality disorders. They note that while they considered establishing dimensional classification, there were at that time insufficient data to justify making such a change. They discuss difficulties with the polythetic approach to criteria (multiple sets of criteria), but state:

> Because most diagnoses are based on limited empirical data and the boundary between the presence and absence of a personality disorder is inherently arbitrary, the optimal cut-off points for establishing personality disorder diagnoses remain unclear. Setting the threshold higher or lower can dramatically influence the base rates of given disorders and the overlap among them. Moreover, polythetic criteria sets may allow for more heterogeneity than is acceptable. For example, there are 93 different ways to meet the DSM-III-R Borderline Personality Disorder criteria and it is possible to meet the criteria without possessing unstable-intense relations, identity disturbance, or affective instability, even though most clinicians would agree that these are the hallmark of the disorder. (p. 787)

We would add that the problem of meeting the criteria in a large number of different ways is true of disorders other than just the personality disorders. This reinforces the point that two individuals with the same diagnosis may differ considerably. The following example of Mr. X and Mr. O provide an illustration of the way two people with no symptoms in common can be diagnosed with the same disorder (PTSD). The example assumes that criterion A, a severe stressor, has been met for both X and O.

B. The traumatic event is persistently reexperienced in at least one of the following ways:

   1.   Recurrent and intrusive distressing recollections of the event.

   2.(O) Recurrent distressing dreams of the event.

   3.   Sudden acting or feeling as if the traumatic event were recurring.

   4.(X) Intense psychological distress at exposure to event that symbolize or resemble an aspect of the traumatic event.

C. Persistent avoidance of stimuli associated with the trauma or numbing of general responsiveness (not present before the trauma) as indicated by at least three of the following:

   1.(O) Efforts to avoid thoughts or feelings associated with the trauma.

   2.(O) Efforts to avoid activities or situations that arouse recollections of the trauma.

   3.(O) Inability to recall an important aspect of the trauma.

   4.   Markedly diminished in significant activities.

   5.(X) Feelings of detachment or estrangement from others.

   6.(X) Restricted range of affect.

   7.(X) Sense of a foreshortened future.

D. Persistent symptoms of increased arousal (not present before the trauma), as indicated by at least two of the following:

   1.(O) Difficulty falling or staying asleep.

   2.   Irritability or outbursts of anger.

   3.(O) Difficulty concentrating.

   4.(X) Hypervigilance.

   5.(X) Exaggerated startle response.

   6.   Physiological reactivity upon exposure to events that symbolize or resemble an aspect of the traumatic event.

Graphic displays showing the Alice Adams/Bill Brown and X and O phenomena might be useful in persuading a judge or jury to give little credence to conclusions based an DSM diagnoses. (We note that similar situations are found in DSM-IV).

Kutchins and Kirk (1988) offered several criticisms of DSM-III-R, many of which Williams and Spitzer (1988) respond to in the succeeding issue of the *Harvard Medical School Mental Health Letter*. However, Williams and Spitzer concede that Kutchins and Kirk correctly point out that, "Independent researchers have often obtained lower reliability scores than those reported in the field trials" (p. 14). They note the issue is important and some of their own studies were disappointing, but on the other hand, there were studies reporting comparable or even better reliability values. This, of course, leaves the situation in its usual state of "doubt." As some studies report good reliability and some report poorer reliability, what *is* the reliability of any particular DSM disorder? They conclude by stating, "Kutchins and Kirk convey the impression that the developers of DSM-III and DSM-III-R consider the problems of diagnostic reliability almost completely solved. We do not. We are devoting the major part of our professional careers to solving the tremendous problems that remain. The issue is whether the diagnostic glass represented by DSM-III and DSM-III-R is half empty or half full. We think it is best described as half full" (p. 5). From a forensic point of view, we would ask what difference would a decision on that issue make? Do we want to decide legal matters on the basis of an issue that is half resolved (or half unresolved)?

Zimmerman and Spitzer (1989) describe the procedures one subcommittee followed in writing the DSM-III-R criteria that may be devastating to the credibility of any diagnosis based on the DSM-III-R. Zimmerman and Spitzer relate the proceedings of a meeting of an Ad Hoc Committee appointed to review research on the validity of the DSM-III criteria for Melancholia, to provide alternative proposals for the DSM-III-R, and to develop new criteria for this category. There have not been many publications describing the operations of the DSM-III-R committees in considerable detail, and thus we will devote substantial space to this one. Following the group's discussion of various material provided by a literature review as well as some unpublished research by some committee members, the committee turned to formulating alternative proposals for defining Melancholia in DSM-III-R. Without detailing the nature of these proposals, we would simply inform the reader that four suggestions were made. After the four proposals were listed, there was a discussion of reasons for and against them. Finally, the issue came down to a vote on the alternatives. There were twelve committee members in the discussion and the votes went as follows: One vote for proposal 1; zero votes for proposal 2; six votes for proposal 3; and four votes for proposal 4. The reader will note that this totals only eleven votes, as one of the committee members left the meeting early and did not vote. Proposal 3 then apparently carried on the basis of six votes of an original twelve members, or 50% of the subcommittee. The remainder of the meeting was devoted to developing the new Melancholia criteria and deciding on a minimum number of features that would be required for a positive diagnosis. Zimmerman and Spitzer state, with regard to some questions that they had, "Before deciding on the minimum number of symptoms required for a diagnosis of Melancholia, the group asked, 'What percentage of depressed inpatients should meet the Melancholia criteria?' Two assumptions influenced this estimate." (p. 25) The authors then describe the two assumptions and they go on to state, "The committee believed that approximately two-thirds of depressed inpatients should be diagnosed as melancholic and guessed that a cut-off score of five criteria would produce this prevalence." (p. 25) The reader will note that the procedure for this diagnosis involved a "guess," a "belief," and two "assumptions." We think it may be appropriate for an attorney to ask any expert who is giving a DSM-III or DSM-III-R diagnosis to make a declaration as to whether he does or does not know whether similar procedures were followed in whatever diagnosis is involved in the case.

(We do not yet know whether and to what extent similar procedures were involved in the production of DSM-IV.)

Frances et al. (1990) provide a picture of some of the directions that were being taken by the current DSM-IV work groups. They note that regardless of its important contributions, DSM-III was not universally popular or without disadvantages. They think the most serious problem may not have been in the manual itself, but from the way it was viewed and used, making the point that many practitioners "reified" the criteria, despite the fact that most were based on expert opinion rather than systematic evidence and were meant to guide clinical practice rather than subject it to rigid rules. They note that it also stirred numerous controversies, some concerning definitions of particular diagnoses, while others related more generally to professional, forensic, economic or social consequences of the system (p. 1439). We would remind the reader that one of the original purposes of DSM-III was to get psychiatrists and psychologists to mean the same thing when they used diagnostic nomenclature. In order for that purpose to be accomplished, it would be essential for the criteria to be subject to rigid rules, rather than to be used as a "guide," which leaves the clinician free to deviate from the rules. Given this freedom, it cannot be known how many clinicians will exercise this option on frequent occasions, leading to the same state of diagnostic chaos that existed prior to the formulation of DSM-III which, with all of its faults, appears to at least have produced some degree of improvement in reliability.

Frances et al. elaborate on the origins of DSM-III-R, undertaken to correct inconsistencies found after publication of DSM-III and to include new evidence. They state, "The revision of DSM-III was probably more substantial than had originally been anticipated. Although DSM-III-R was useful in demonstrating that the system is self-correcting, it may have been too big a change too soon, with consequent disruption to clinical research and educational endeavors." (p. 1439) Of particular importance, these authors note concern about the possible impact on a wide variety of issues beyond its clinical and research uses and state, "Perhaps the arena of greatest possible abuse is the assessment of criminal responsibility, in which the presence of a diagnosable DSM disorder should not be regarded as sufficient to confer the sick role." (p. 1442) They display concern as to effects DSM-IV task force decisions might have beyond immediate clinical domains and note that it would be irresponsible to ignore obvious detrimental effects, but they indicate that if the system is to have credibility in its clinical uses and research uses, these uses must have priority. They state, "It may also be necessary to expand the statement on 'cautions in the use of DSM-III-R.'" (p. 1442) The authors discuss the importance of a precise definition establishing what a mental disorder is for clinical practice, forensic proceedings and decisions about what conditions are on the border between normality and pathology. They state such a definition should be included in DSM-IV, but "unfortunately no previous definition of illness, disease or disorder has ever been particularly successful and we have no illusions that we can provide a better solution." (p. 1442) Finally, they declare the intention that DSM-IV will try to move toward greater emphasis on the objective accumulation of empirical evidence.

Sprock et al. (1990) note the controversy in the classification of personality disorders, such as appear in the DSM-III and DSM-III-R. They note that there has been advocacy for alternative models such as dimensional systems. They are more concerned with another major area of controversy—the possibility of sex bias in the symptoms that constitute each category, with certain diagnoses being given more frequently to women and others more frequently to men. In their study, they found that there does appear to be such differential use of diagnoses based on gender. However, they consider the findings suggestive only and feel that other research is needed to determine whether the differential frequencies are inappropriate.

Heumann and Morey (1990) note that categorical models, which characterize DSM-III and DSM-III-R, have not achieved high levels of interrater reliability for personality disorders. They note that a number of authors have suggested that such low reliability is inevitable with categorical models of personality disorder and that greater reliability could be achieved by use of a dimensional model. They note, however, that there is a lack of empirical evidence to directly support that conclusion. They conducted a study of five clinicians, three psychologists and two psychiatrists, with a mean of 11 years of clinical experience. They had the five clinicians make various judgments for each of ten case vignettes, utilizing both categorical and dimensional approaches. They found that their reliability estimates support previously unconfirmed statements that dimensional judgments are substantially more reliable than categorical diagnoses.

Several authors specifically criticize the personality disorders in DSM-III. These include Widiger et al. (1988), Morey (1988), Livesley et al. (1987), Reich (1987), Widiger and Frances (1987), and Cloninger (1987).

Dingemans (1990) found that interrater agreement on the International Classification of Disease (ICD-9-CM) was too low to provide for any kind of current mental health statistics. He states that statistics based on the ICD-9-CM coding system are without scientific value. While the ICD system does not come up very often in American legal matters, it is worthwhile for the attorney to have this information available for the cases in which it appears. Also, the Introduction to DSM-IV states its attempts to be compatible with the ICD.

DSM-IV

Prior to the publication of DSM-IV in May of 1994, several articles were written by people associated with the DSM process or knowledgeable about it.

Zimmerman (1988), a member of one of the DSM-III-R subcommittees, (melancholia) declares his skepticism that changes in DSM-IV will not be primarily data-based, citing his DSM-III-R experience (See Zimmerman and Spitzer, 1989, supra). He states that accumulated data suggested that the DSM-III criteria for melancholia were not valid, but that the changes that were made in the criteria were not data based, but rather based on group consensus. He notes that changes "of an ofttimes unscientific nature" occurred on other sections as well. He points out that even seemingly minor changes can have unforeseen effects. He cites a study of criteria for major Depressive disorder between DSM-III and DSM-III-R where a seemingly minor change resulted in only about one half of the patients who met the broader criteria for loss of interest or pleasure in DSM-III, meeting the narrower criteria in DSM-III-R.

Strakowski (1994) based on a review of existing literature, concludes that the literature does not provide support for schizophreniform disorder as defined in DSM-III-R. He concludes these criteria identify a very heterogenous group of psychotic illnesses and recommends it not be used and that the diagnosis "psychotic disorder, not otherwise specified" be used instead for such patients. Thus, he provides another instance in which DSM-III-R is not science based.

Spitzer (1991), chairperson of the DSM-III and III-R committees, predicts that final decisions about DSM-IV will be based primarily on expert consensus rather than data, as was the case with its two predecessors. He notes that the DSM-IV literature reviews in most cases simply document the absence of critical data for decisions about diagnostic criteria. He states that most of the major proposed innovations were prompted by conceptual concerns rather than new data from empirical studies. He also indicates that, because of their design, most of the data from the field studies will shed little light on the comparative validity of criteria sets being studied. He notes that by using videotapes for reliability studies, they eliminate the variability in data gathering that more accurately reflects what happens in the real world of clinical assessment. He also notes that the number of patients per diagnosis (5) is too small for generalization to different diagnoses.

Carson (1991) asserts that the format for developing DSM-IV is constrained in several ways that seriously impair its quality. Among these ways are inappropriate assumptions of a categorical model, ensured persistence of traditional categories of disorder, excessive concern with agreement between diagnosticians, insufficient attention to validity, and excessive concern with acceptance by clinicians. He expresses doubt that anyone can really believe that DSM-IV criteria for schizophrenia will be a significant improvement. He notes that despite an extensive body of research, this area lacks anything "even vaguely resembling" an invariance among any independently defined set of persons who exhibit classical schizophrenia. He declares that the possibility must now be considered that such invariance is just not there to be found and that somehow psychiatry has carved out a category that has no counterpart in nature. He further asserts that other parts of the taxonomy may suffer from this same problem.

Frances et al. (1991) (Frances is Chair of the DSM-IV Committee) declares that Work on DSM-IV abounds in conundrums wherein issues have multiple plausible solutions, none of which are completely satisfying. In an article titled "An A to Z Guide to DSM-IV Conundrums" they note the DSM-IV Task Force has not and does not expect to resolve fully any of these issues. The following are among 26 issues they describe.

1. *The relation of Axis I to Axis II.* They note that clear definitions that differentiate between these disorders are lacking resulting in inconsistencies in the way relations between Axis I and Axis II are

handled in DSM-III-R. They indicate four options for dealing with these problems and conclude that given current available knowledge there are no clear grounds for selecting one of these alternatives as decidedly superior. We conclude that this means that whatever was done regarding this issue, it was on other than scientific grounds.

2. *Categorical vs. dimensional.* They simply point out the existence of controversy in this area and state the lack of compelling evidence for the "too radically innovative" dimensional approach.

3. *Field trials.* They note that the more a field trial strives for internal consistency and research rigor, the less likely it will achieve external validity and generalizability to clinical practice.

4. *Mental disorder.* They state there could not be a more unfortunate term, but acknowledge they have been unsuccessful in finding an alternative.

5. *Validation.* They express concern over the fact that "so little validation is available for many of the most crucial decisions."

6. *When.* They observe there is never a good time to introduce a new diagnostic system. It is always too soon and too late. Too soon disrupts research, clinical discourse and training (they note this was undoubtedly the case with DSM-III-R). Too late and the system is superseded by more recent data. In any event, we note, the good news is that they declare that any fully revised DSM-V before 2005 will be premature. We also note that in their concluding thoughts they describe their current classification decisions as "temporary." If we understand correctly, the two statements taken in conjunction mean that there will be nothing but a temporary diagnostic system until 2005. Probably, any trier of fact should be so informed.

7. *Xenophilia vs. Xenophobia.* Here they describe requirements to use the ICD-10 codes and terms. They note however, that the ICD-10 research criteria did not have the extensive empirical review and support expected in DSM-IV.

DSM-IV was published in May, 1994, about 7 years after the appearance of DSM-III-R. Some authorities felt this was an insufficient period of time for this project and some indicated that questions had been raised concerning possible financial motivation as this publication apparently produces a great deal of income to the American Psychiatric Association (Zimmerman, 1988). The most significant concern was, as before, the detrimental effect on existing research. To the extent that criteria for diagnoses are changed, research done with populations diagnosed with prior criteria, cannot be applied to people diagnosed under the changed criteria because it is uncertain that they are properly represented by the research population (see post-traumatic stress disorder and somatization disorder examples below). For this reason, we recommend that copies of DSM-III and DSM-III-R be retained for comparison purposes.

As with the two previous DSMs, the introductory material and appendices contain much material that is very useful to lawyers who must contend with the diagnostic basis it represents.

Foremost among the introductory material is a specific section titled "Use of DSM-IV in Forensic Settings," which while waffling at the end, goes further than previous cautions in this regard. The Manual states, "When DSM-IV categories, criteria, and textual descriptions are employed for forensic purposes, there are significant risks that diagnostic information will be misused or misunderstood." (p. xxiii) They note these risks exist because of an imperfect fit between legal issues and the information contained in diagnoses. They note that in most situations the diagnosis is not sufficient to establish the existence of a mental disorder, mental disability, mental disease or mental defect for legal purposes. This seems to be a statement similar to our descriptions of the "gap" between diagnosis and legal issues, described in Chapter 1. This statement in the manual also cautions that nonclinical decision makers should be aware that an individual's diagnosis does not necessarily carry implications about the causes of a disorder or its associated impairments. They point out, as in the past, that the manual represents a "consensus" at the time of its publication and that new knowledge from research or clinical experience will "undoubtedly" lead to identification of new disorders and "removal" of some disorders in future classifications and as well, reconsideration of text and criteria in the light of evolving information. We respect the producers of the manual for their candor in this area. However, we wonder about the degree to which the legal system should make use of evidence of such indeterminate status. Perhaps this is the issue that the manual writers intended to raise.

We also would wonder how well validated the diagnoses are if they indeed are this evanescent. That is, if they are based on sound scientific research one would expect them to last more than a few years. If they are not durable, one would then think they were not well-validated. In any event, we would be remiss if we did not mention that the same section of the manual declares that if the legal setting is informed of the limitations, the diagnoses when used appropriately can assist decision makers in their determinations; e.g., when the presence of a mental disorder is the predicate for a legal determination, as in civil commitment or in facilitating understanding of relevant characteristic of mental disorders. However, if the criteria are as fluid and flexible as the manual states elsewhere, we have trouble seeing how the diagnosis will facilitate understanding of the characteristics. We understand the manual to say that while there are criteria, clinical judgment should be employed. Further, for the most part, the characteristics of any disorder may vary a great deal among people who have the disorder so that no particular characteristic can be said to exist in an individual by virtue of the diagnoses given him. (See PTSD example, Mr. X and Mr. O, supra.) However, while the language is not absolutely clear, the phrase "should be informed" and "non-clinical decision makers should be cautioned," sound like the manual directs any expert using a DSM-IV diagnosis in a forensic setting to make clear on direct examination the limitations and risks described in the manual. An expert who does not follow this direction would seem subject to damaging cross-examination as to candor and possibly to a motion to bar or *in limine*.

There is a further, separate "Cautionary Statement" (p. xxvii) which defines the purposes of the manual to provide clear descriptions of diagnostic categories to enable clinicians and researchers to diagnose, communicate about, study and treat people with mental disorders. They state that inclusion in the manual does not indicate that the condition meets legal criteria for mental disease, disorder, or disability. They state, "The clinical and scientific considerations involved in the categorization of these conditions as mental disorder may not be wholly relevant to legal judgments, for example that take into account such issues as individual responsibility, disability determination, and competency." Is there some particular significance to this statement in light of the statement of the Supreme Court in *Daubert vs. Merrell, Dow* assigning to the judge the task of ensuring that, among other things, the expert's testimony "is relevant to the task at hand"? Should a motion *in limine* be granted as to any DSM-IV diagnosis in view of this and other statements in the manual? What is the status of the physician (psychiatrist) as an expert in medicine which is generally described as the "diagnosis" and treatment of disease or disorder if she cannot present a diagnosis and base her testimony on it? Given the similarity of the field of clinical psychology, the same questions seem applicable.

We think most people will understand that the presence of these cautions and statements about risk and misuse indicates that the DSM committee has serious doubts about the uses of DSM-IV in forensic situations other than in a very limited way.

The introduction also includes a section on ethnic and cultural considerations (p. xiv) which describes types of information included in the manual which are specifically related to cultural variations in the clinical presentation of various disorders (see Chapter 16).

DSM-IV continues to be produced by committees—now called work groups—consisting of 5 or more members. The largest work group had 16 members, while 6 or 7 seemed to be the most common number. In addition, the groups had input and critiques from anywhere from 50 to

100 "advisers" representing diverse clinical and research expertise, disciplines, backgrounds and settings. While this input seems valuable, it is difficult to imagine that there were not differing, even opposing views expressed. Thus while the manual makes repeated reference to consensus, it is not clear how this was obtained. The determining process must have been that of the work groups of relatively small numbers. How were differing inputs resolved? Was there voting, formally or informally? Was opposition ultimately relinquished in order to bring the task to a conclusion? We would note that the work groups for DSM-IV were as a rule very much smaller than the committees or subcommittees for DSM-III-R. Thus, for example, the Advisory Committee for Anxiety Disorders in DSM-III-R had 31 members, plus 30 (with some overlap) on the sub-committee for Post-Traumatic Stress Disorder, which is included among the anxiety disorders. The DSM-IV Work Group for Anxiety Disorders had only six members (there was no subcommittee on PTSD) of whom 5 had been on the III-R committee. Of the advisers, 6 of the original 31 were included (plus the 5 in the Work Group). Of the 30 on PTSD, 9 were included in the advisers. For Mood Disorders, 3 of the 29 III-R committee were included in the 6 members of the IV work group. An obvious question arises—to what extent do changes reflect scientific advances vs. changes in personnel makeup? That issues existed is made clear by the publication in 1991 of the DSM-IV Options Book which described different approaches in many disorders and requested input to help resolve these issues. Also, the Introduction to the Manual at p. viii indicates that even after reviews of the literature, different options were available and a selection had to be made.

The Manual has a section delineating the limitations of the categorical approach it uses. They note that use of a dimensional system has been suggested which conveys more information and which might work better than categories that do not have clear boundaries. Many of the criteria for various disorders are found to some degree in people who do not have mental disorders. In a dimensional approach measurement would be required to determine quantities sufficient to be considered symptoms. However, they note limitations of this approach also, and while not ruling it out in the future, they feel further research is needed.

From the foregoing, it seems clear that they not only have the problem of determining the existence of the various mental disorders and what the criteria for such diagnoses should be, but the preliminary problem of how to go about this task given the limitations of existing sound research. We do not say this as criticism of those attempting to establish a diagnostic system, but only to emphasize the enormous difficulty of the task to highlight with regard to courtroom presentations the experimental nature not only of the conclusions, but of the process itself.

In a section on clinical judgment, they declare that the diagnostic criteria are meant to be guidelines informed by clinical judgment and not to be used in a cookbook fashion, giving the example that clinical judgment may justify giving the diagnosis even though the clinical presentation falls just short of meeting the full criteria as long as the symptoms that are present are persistent and severe. On the other hand, they state, excessively flexible and idiosyncratic application of criteria or conventions substantially reduces the Manual's utility as a common language. We think this is matter of considerable concern in forensic situations. There is already a certain amount of looseness (clinical judgment) in determining whether a given criterion is present, e.g. how long is "persistent" and what intensity is required to be "severe"? How little emotional display warrants the description "lack of affect"? These are precisely where a dimensional system is clearly superior. To say, in addition, that where the criteria for the disorder call for two out of five symptoms in subset A of the criteria and 3 in subset B, but it is okay to make the diagnosis even if there are only 2 in B, makes a mockery of the use of criteria and can lead to miscommunication rather than improved communication. The cafeteria menu of criteria for many disorders is bad enough, without making them still more elastic. It is already the case, that two people with no symptoms in common can be given the same diagnosis. The example of Mr. X and Mr. O (supra) illustrate this point.

The Manual provides an Annotated Listing of Changes in DSM-IV (Appendix D, p. 773). One change not noted is that DSM-IV contains 686 pages in smaller type size in contrast to 363 pages in DSM-III-R. Also, in many instances the appendix fails to completely express the extent of changes. For example, the changes in Somatization Disorder are described: "Based on the literature review, data reanalysis, and field-trial results, the DSM-III-R list of 35 items has been condensed, simplified, and divided into four symptom groupings (pain, gastrointestinal, sexual and pseudoneurological)." (p. 783) This does not begin to portray the dramatic change that has taken place in this diagnosis (see example of Abe Allen, below).

There are more than 225 changes from DSM-III-R to DSM-IV involving more than 100 disorders. Some of these changes are minor, involving moving items from one place to another or clarifying wording or conforming to the ICD. Many are substantive in nature such that people who might have been diagnosed with the disorder previously cannot be so diagnosed now and contrariwise, people who could not have been diagnosed with the disorder before, now can be. This is why prior research on such disorders cannot be utilized under the new Manual. This means that once again, there is only a diagnostic manual which is still in an experimental stage. In addition, 13 new disorders have been added. Eight disorders have been deleted or subsumed under other DSM-IV categories. Several DSM-III criteria that were discarded in DSM-III-R were *restored* in DSM-IV. Can the legal system afford to allow judgments to be made based on disorders which may not exist or be recognizable in a few years?

Post Traumatic Stress Disorder (PTSD) is a diagnosis that appears frequently in litigation, particularly personal injury litigation, but occasionally in criminal matters as well. We provide the following fictitious examples to illustrate the problems of using an experimental, impermanent, ever-changing diagnostic system in the resolution of legal matters. Earlier in this chapter we provided examples of this problem in DSM-III-R in the cases of Alice Adams and Bill Brown.

A similar situation now exists between DSM-III-R and DSM-IV PTSD where 15 changes have taken place. For sake of this discussion, we will assume that Ann Atkins has met the criteria of each manual respectively for the Stressor (Criterion A) although these are markedly different in the two manuals.

TABLE 2
Case 1, Ann Atkins

PTSD under DSM-III-R, Dec. 1993	PTSD under DSM-IV, May 1994
A. (Assume adequate stressor)	A. (Assume adequate stressor)
B. None	B. Physiological reactivity on exposure to internal or external cues (i.e., events), that symbolize or resemble an aspect of the traumatic event.
C. 3. Inability to recall an important aspect of the trauma. 6. Restricted range of affect 7. Sense of foreshortened future.	C. 3. Same 6. Same 7. Same
D. 1. Difficulty in staying asleep. 2. Irritability. 6. Physiological reactivity upon exposure to events that symbolize or resemble an aspect of the traumatic event.	D. 1. Difficulty in staying asleep 2. Irritability

Thus in December 1993, Ann does not meet the criteria for PTSD because she has no symptoms in category B, but in May 1994 she does although her symptoms are identical on both occasions.

Another example, in reverse, is provided by Somatization disorder when comparing DSM-III-R to DSM-IV.

Somatization Disorder
Abe Allen

DSM-III-R, Dec. 1993	DSM-IV, May 1994
A. (Assume met)	A. (Assume met)
B. Symptoms	B. Symptoms
Gastrointestinal	Gastrointestinal
1. Vomiting	1. Vomiting
2. Abdominal pain	2. Abdominal pain
3. Nausea	3. Nausea
4. Bloating	4. Bloating
5. Diarrhea	5. Diarrhea
6. Intolerance of several foods	6. Intolerance of several foods
Pain:	Pain:
7. Pain in extremities	7. Pain in extremities
8. Back pain	8. Back pain
9. Joint pain	9. Joint pain
10. Pain during urination	10. Pain during urination
11. Other pain	11. Other pain
Cardiopulmonary:	Cardiopulmonary:
12. Shortness of breath when not exerting oneself	12. Shortness of breath when not exerting oneself
13. Palpitations	13. Palpitations
Sexual: None	Sexual: None
Pseudoneurological: None	Pseudoneurological: None

DSM-III-R requires 13 symptoms out of a list of 31 (for males) from 5 categories, but without specification of any particular number from any particular categories, so that in December 1993 Abe meets the criteria for this disorder. However, DSM-IV, in section B, requires only 8 symptoms of which 4 must be in the pain category, 2 in the gastrointestinal, one in the sexual and one in the pseudoneurological. Therefore, Abe does not come close to meeting the criteria for this disorder in May 1994 although his symptoms are exactly the same. Conversely, a person who had 8 symptoms distributed among the categories as required by DSM-IV, would meet the criteria in May 1994, but with the same symptoms would not have met the criteria of 13 symptoms required by DSM-III-R in December 1993.

PTSD will be discussed in more detail in Chapter 20 below. The point to be noted here is the ephemeral character of the diagnoses such that within a matter of months the same person with the same symptoms can or cannot meet the criteria for the diagnosis. What were the symptoms of the subjects in research conducted on people with these diagnoses over the past 14 years? Would they have PTSD or Somatization Disorder under DSM-IV? Does anyone know? If we do not know or cannot be sure, clearly we cannot apply research from one population to a population which may differ in critical aspects such as having or not having the disorder. Do the safeguards that constitute the *raison d'etre* for the laws of evidence mean so little that courts will allow legal matters to be decided on the basis of such flimsy foundations as this? In any event, the trier of fact should be made aware of this state of affairs regarding the diagnostic system.

Given the length of time it takes to perform research, get it published, have replications, critiques, and research by others done and published, it will be at least several years before the reliability and validity of any of the diagnoses can be established. Meanwhile, there is the certainty described in the manual that changes will be necessary, what changes no one knows.

We had hoped to provide more analysis of the data base which was used by the DSM-IV people. They are producing books on this called DSM-IV Source Books which will appear in 5 volumes. Unfortunately, at the time of this writing, only Volume 1 has appeared, and we are informed that it is likely to be at least a year before the others will be available. In particular, the volumes dealing with data reanalyses and dealing with field studies may contain important material. At such time as all 5 volumes become available, we will provide an update to this chapter should the material in those volumes warrant it.

SUMMARY

The foregoing should be sufficient to make clear that the assessment and diagnostic systems utilized in psychiatry and clinical psychology do not rest upon any basis of soundly established scientific principles. This is well known to many lawyers who have had the frustrating experience of hearing different psychiatrists employ different diagnostic categories for an individual, although their diagnoses are based on the same clinical data. In other words, the data concerning the patient or subject do not dictate the conclusion as they must in any scientifically established discipline, but rather it is the manner in which the individual psychiatrist *chooses* to define the category and interpret the data that dictates the diagnosis. If the diagnostic categories are as unstable as this, then assessment of current state, and even more so the postdiction of prior state or the prediction of future state from such unstable categories, is not to be trusted.

Given such a non-scientific and preliminary status, a judge should seriously consider a motion to bar the use of these diagnostic terms as being, at present, too experimental in nature to meet the requirements of the laws of evidence. Some attorneys might prefer to allow the expert to use this diagnostic jargon and then demonstrate on cross-examination that the expert is using an experimental and unvalidated diagnostic system. The attorney can often elicit from the expert the admission that the diagnostic labels are used in different ways by different diagnosticians, that no stable meaning can be attached to them, that available diagnostic criteria are still evolving and changing, and there is generally no established body of knowledge tying these diagnostic categories directly to legal questions or issues.

REFERENCES

Agnew, J., and Bannister, D. (1973). Psychiatric diagnosis and a pseudo specialist language. *British Journal of Medical Psychology, 46,* 69-73.

American Psychiatric Association (1952, 1968, 1980, 1987, 1994). *Diagnostic and Statistical Manual of Mental Disorders.* Washington, DC: American Psychiatric Association.

Bachrach, H. (1974). Diagnosis as strategic understanding. *Bulletin of the Meninger Clinic, 38,* 390-405.

Barsky, A.J., and Klerman, G.L. (1983). Overview: Hypochondriasis, bodily complaints, and somatic styles. *The American Journal of Psychiatry, 140,* 273-283.

Bauer, A.K. (1962-1963). Legal responsibility and mental illness. *Northwestern University Law Review, 57,* 12-18.

Baumrin, B.H. (1982). A philosophers view of ethical issues in forensic psychiatry. *The Journal of Psychiatry and Law, 10,* 29-39.

Beaber, R.J., Marston, A., Michelli, J., and Mills, M.J. (1985). A brief test for measuring malingering in schizophrenic individuals. *American Journal of Psychiatry, 142,* 1478-1481.

Beeber, A.R., and Pyes, R.W. (1983). The nonmelancholic depressive syndromes: An alternate approach to classification. *The Journal of Nervous and Mental Disease, 171,* 3-9.

Boxer, P.A., and Garvey, J.T. (1985). Psychiatric diagnoses of Cuban refugees in the United States: Findings of medical review boards. *American Journal of Psychiatry, 142,* 86-89.

California State Psychologist (1984), *19,* 1.

Cancro, R. (1973). Increased diagnostic reliability in schizophrenia: Some values and limitations. *International Journal of Psychiatry, 2,* 54.

Carson, R.C. (1991). Dilemmas in the pathway of the DSM-IV. *Journal of Abnormal Psychology, 100,* 302-307.

Clinicians Research Digest (1985).

Cloninger, R.C. (1987). A systematic method for clinical description and classification of personality variants. *Archives of General Psychiatry, 44,* 573-588.

Coles, R. (1967). *The Progressive, 31,* 5.

Coryell, W., and Zimmerman, M. (1987). Progress in the classification of functional psychoses. *American Journal of Psychiatry, 144,* 1471-1473.

Dingemans, P.M. (1990). ICD-9-CM classification coding in psychiatry. *Journal of Clinical Psychology, 46,* 161-168.

Drake, R.E., and Vaillant, G.E. (1985). A validity study of Axis II of DSM-III. *American Journal of Psychiatry, 142,* 553-558.

Ehrenworth, N.V. and Archer, R.P. (1985) A comparison of clinical accuracy ratings of interpretive approaches for adolescent MMPI responses. *Journal of Personality Assessment, 49,* 413-421.

Eysenck, H.J., Wakefield, J.A., Jr., and Friedman, A.F. (1983). Diagnosis and clinical assessment: The DSM-III. In M.R. Rosenzweig and L.W. Porter (Eds.) *Annual Review of Psychology, 34,* 167-193.

Faust, D., and Miner, R.A. (1986). The empiricist and his new clothes: DSM-III in perspective. *American Journal of Psychiatry, 143,* 962-967.

Fenton, W.S., McGlashan, T.H., and Heinssen, R.K. (1988). A comparison of DSM-III and DSM-III-R schizophrenia. *The American Journal of Psychiatry, 145,* 1446-1449.

Fernando, T., Mellsop, J., Nelson, K., Peace, K., and Wilson, J. (1986). The reliability of Axis V of DSM-III. *American Journal of Psychiatry, 143,* 752-755.

Fisher, D.G., Sweet, J.J., and Pfaelzer-Smith, E.A. (1986). Influence of depression on repeated neuropsychological testing. *The International Journal of Clinical Neuropsychology, 8,* 14-18.

Fogel, B.S., and Sparadeo, F.R. (1985). Single case study: Focal cognitive deficits accentuated by depression. *The Journal of Nervous and Mental Disease, 173,* 120-124.

Frances, A. (1980). DSM-III personality disorders section; a commentary. *American Journal of Psychiatry, 137,* 1050-1054.

Frances, A., and Cooper, A.M. (1981). Descriptive and dynamic psychiatry: A perspective on DSM-III. *American Journal of Psychiatry, 138,* 1198-1202.

Frances, A., Pincus, H.A., Widiger, T.A., Davis, W.W., and First, M.B. (1990). DSM-IV: Work in progress. *American Journal of Psychiatry, 147,* 1439-1448.

Frances, A.J., First, M.B., Widiger, T.A., Miele, G.M., Tilly, S.M., Davis, W.W. and Pincus, H.A. (1991). An A to Z guide to DSM-IV conundrums. *Journal of Abnormal Psychology, 100,* 407-412.

Gift, T.E. (1988). Editorial: Changing diagnostic criteria. *American Journal of Psychiatry, 145,* 1414-1415.

Goleman, D. (1978). Who's mentally ill. *Psychology Today, 4,* 34.

Halleck, S.L. (1967). *Psychiatry and The Dilemma of Crime.* New York: Harper and Row.

Halleck, S.L. (1969). The psychiatrist and the legal process. *Psychology Today,* 2.

Havens, L.L. (1981). Twentieth Century Psychiatry: A view from the sea. *The American Journal of Psychiatry, 138,* 1279-1287.

Heumann, K.A., and Morey, L.C. (1990). Reliability of categorical and dimensional judgments of personality disorder. *American Journal of Psychiatry, 147,* 498-500.

Hine, F.R., and Williams, R.B. (1975). Dimensional diagnosis and the medical students' group of psychiatry. *Archives of General Psychiatry, 32,* 523-528.

Jampala, V.C., Sierles, F.S., and Taylor, M.A. (1986). Consumer views of DSM-III: Attitudes and practices of U.S. psychiatrists and 1984 graduating psychiatric residents. *American Journal of Psychiatry, 143,* 148-153.

Janes, C.L. (1979). Agreement measurement and the judgment process. *The Journal of Nervous and Mental Disease, 167,* 343-347.

Keisling, R. (1981). Underdiagnosis of manic-depressive illness in a hospital unit. *American Journal of Psychiatry, 135,* 672-673.

Kutchins, H., and Kirk, S.A. (1986). The reliability of DSM-III: A critical review. *Social Work Research & Abstracts, Winter,* 3-12.

Kutchins, H., and Kirk, S.A. (1988). The future of DSM: Scientific and professional issues. *Harvard Medical School Mental Health Letter, September,* 4-6.

Lieberman, P., and Baker, F. (1985). The reliability of psychiatric diagnosis in the emergency room. *Hospital and Community Psychiatry, 36,* 291-293.

Livermore, J.M., Malmquist, C.P., and Meehl, P.E. (1968). On the justification for civil commitment. *University of Pennsylvania Law Review, 117.*

Livesley, W.J., Reiffer, L.I., Sheldon, A.E.R., and West, M. (1987). Prototypicality ratings of DSM-III criteria for personality disorders. *The Journal of Nervous and Mental Disease, 175,* 395-400.

McLemore, C.W., Benjamin, L.S. (1979). Whatever happened to interpersonal diagnosis: A psychosocial alternative to DSM-III. *American Psychologist, 34,* 17-34.

McReynolds, W. (1979). DSM-III and the future of applied social science. *Professional Psychology*, 123-132.

Mechanic, D. (1967). Some factors in identifying and defining mental illness. In T.J. Scheff (Ed.), *Mental Illness and Social Process*. New York: Harper and Row.

Meehl, P.E. (1978). Theoretical risks and tabular asterisks, Sir Karl, Sir Ronald and the slow progress of soft psychology. *Journal of Consulting and Clinical Psychology*, *46*, 806-834.

Mellinger, G.D., Balter, M.B., and Uhlenhuth, E.H. (1985). Insomnia and its treatment. *Archives of General Psychiatry*, *42*, 225-232.

Mellsop, G., Varghese, F., Joshua S., and Hicks, A. (1982). The reliability of Axis II of DSM-III. *American Journal of Psychiatry*, *139*, 1360-1361.

Menninger, K. (1968). *The Crime of Punishment*. New York: The Viking Press.

Millon, T. (1984). On the renaissance of personality assessment and personality theory. *Journal of Personality Assessment*, *48*, 450-466.

Morey, L.C. (1988). Personality disorders in DSM-III and DSM-III-R: Convergence, coverage, and internal consistency. *American Journal of Psychiatry*, *145*, 573-577.

Morse, S.J. (1983). Predicting future dangerousness. *California Lawyer*, *3*, 16-18.

Mosher, L.R., and Feinsilver, D. (1973). *International Journal of Psychiatry*, *2*, 7-55.

Nussbaum, K., Puig, J.G., and Arizaga, J.R. (1981-82). Relevance of objective assessment to medical-legal psychiatry. *American Journal of Forensic Psychiatry*, *2*, 17-20.

Packer, I.K. (1983). Post-traumatic stress disorder and the insanity defense: A critical analysis. *The Journal of Psychiatry & Law*, *11*, 125-134.

Plotkin, D.A., Mintz, J., and Jarvik, L.F. (1985). Subjective memory complaints in geriatric depression. *American Journal of Psychiatry*, *142*, 1103-1105.

Reich, J. (1987). Prevalence of DSM-III-R self-defeating (masochistic) personality disorder in normal and outpatient populations. *The Journal of Nervous and Mental Disease*, *175*, 52-53.

Resnick, P.J. (1984). The detection of malingered mental illness. *Behavioral Sciences & The Law*, *2*, 21-38.

Robins, L.N. (1985). Epidemiology: Reflections on testing the validity of psychiatric interviews. *Archives of General Psychiatry*, *42*, 918-924.

Robins, L.N., and Helzer, J.E. (1986). Diagnosis and clinical assessment: The current state of psychiatric diagnosis. *Annual Review of Psychology*, *37*, 409-432.

Roche, P.Q. (1958a). Symposium on Criminal Responsibility and Mental Disease. 19th Annual Law Institute, University of Tennessee (1958), and 26 Law Review (1959), 221, 240-241.

Roche, P.Q. (1958b). *The Criminal Mind.* New York: Farrar, Straus, and Cudahy.

Rubinstein, L.S. (1982). *Mental Disability Law Reporter, 6* (November/ December, 1982), p. 352.

Rutter, M. (1986). Depressive feelings, cognitions, and disorders: A research postscript. In M. Rutter, C.E. Izard, and P.B. Read (Eds.) *Depression in Young People. Developmental and Clinical Perspectives* (pp. 491-519). New York: Guilford Press.

Sattin, D.B. (1980). Possible sources of error in the evaluation of psychopathology. *Journal of Clinical Psychology, 36,* 99-105.

Schacht, T., and Nathan, P.E. (1977). But is it good for the psychologist? Appraisal and status of DSM-III. *American Psychologist, 32,* 1017-1025.

Schuckit, M.A. (1986). Genetic and clinical implications of alcoholism and affective disorder. *American Journal of Psychiatry, 143,* 140.

Schurman, R.A., Kramer, P.D., and Mitchell, J.B. (1985). The hidden mental health network. *Archives of General Psychiatry, 42,* 89-94.

Sharfstein, S.S., Towery, O.B., and Milowe, I.D. (1980). Accuracy of diagnostic information submitted to an insurance company. *American Journal of Psychiatry, 137,* 70-75.

Shubow, L.D., and Bergstresser, C.D. (1977). Handling the psychiatric witness. *Trial, 13,* 32-35.

Silverstein, M.L., Warren, R.A., Harrow, M., Grinker, R.R., and Pawelski, T. (1982). Changes in diagnosis from DSM-II to the research diagnostic criteria and DSM-III. *American Journal of Psychiatry, 139,* 366-367.

Spitzer, R.L. (1981). The diagnostic status of homosexuality in DSM-III: A reformulation of the issues. *American Journal of Psychiatry, 138,* 210-215.

Spitzer, R.L. (1985). DSM-III and the politics-science dichotomy syndrome. *American Psychologist, 40,* 522-526.

Spitzer, R.L. (1991) An outsider-insider's views about revising the DSMs. *Journal of Abnormal Psychology, 100,* 294-296

Spitzer, R.L., Endicott, J., and Robins, E. (1975). Clinical criteria for psychiatric diagnosis and DSM-III. *American Journal of Psychiatry, 132,* 1187-1192.

Sprock, J., Blashfield, R.K., and Smith, B. (1990). Gender weighting of DSM-III personality disorder criteria. *American Journal of Psychiatry, 147,* 586-590.

Stiles, W.B. (1983). Normality diversity and psychotherapy. *Psychotherapy: Theory, Research and Practice, 20,* 183-189.

Strakowski, S.M. (1994). Diagnostic validity of schizophreniform disorder. *American Journal of Psychiatry, 151,* 815-823.

Strauss, J.S. (1975). A comprehensive approach to psychiatric diagnosis. *American Journal of Psychiatry, 132,* 1193-1196.

Strauss, J.S., Gabriel, K.R., Kokes, R.F., Tizler, B.A., Van Ord, A., and Tarana, E. (1979). Do psychiatric patients fit their diagnoses? *The Journal of Nervous and Mental Disease, 167,* 105-113.

Strupp, H.H., and Hadley, S.W. (1977). A tri-partite model of mental health and therapeutic outcomes. *American Psychologist, 32,* 187-196.

Sweet, J.J. (1983). Confounding effects of depression on neuropsychological testing: Five illustrative cases. *Clinical Neuropsychology, 5,* 103-106.

Szasz, T.S. (1961). *The Myth of Mental Illness, Formulation of a Theory of Normal Conduct.* New York: Hoerber-Harper.

Szasz, T.S. (1963). *Law, Liberty & Psychiatry.* New York: The Macmillan Co.

The Counseling Psychologist (1973). *4(2).*

Time Magazine (December 2, 1985), p. 76.

Uebersax, J.S. (1983). Structural analysis of diagnostic disagreements. *The Journal of Nervous and Mental Disease, 171,* 199-206.

Vaillant, G.E. (1985). *Archives of General Psychiatry, 42,* 107-118.

Vincent, K.R., Castillo, I., Hauser, R.I., Stuart, H.J., Zapata, J.A., Cohn, C.K., and O'Shanick, G.J. (1983). MMPI code types and DSM-III diagnoses. *Journal of Clinical Psychology, 39,* 829-842.

Wamboldt, F.S., Jefferson, J.W., and Wamboldt, M.Z. (1986). Digitalis intoxication misdiagnosed as depression by primary care physicians. *American Journal of Psychiatry, 143,* 219.

Weiner, A.S. (1983). Emotional problems of adolescence: A review of affective disorders and schizophrenia. In C.E. Walker, and M.C. Roberts (Eds.), *Handbook of Clinical Child Psychology.* New York: John Wiley and Sons.

Wender, P.H., Reimherr, F.W., Wood, D., and Ward, M. (1985). A controlled study of methylphenidate in the treatment of attention deficit disorder, residual type, in adults. *American Journal of Psychiatry, 142,* 547-552.

Widiger, T.A., and Frances, A. (1987). Covariation of criteria sets for avoidant, schizoid and dependent personality disorders. *American Journal of Psychiatry, 144,* 767-771.

Widiger, T.A., Frances, A., Spitzer, R.L., and Williams, J.B.W. (1988). The DSM-III-R personality disorders: An overview. *American Journal of Psychiatry, 145,* 786-795.

Williams, J.B.W., and Spitzer, R.L. (1988). DSM-III and DSM-III-R: A response. *The Harvard Medical School Mental Health Letter, October,* 3-5.

Winokur, G., Zimmerman, M., and Cadoret, R. (1988). 'Cause the Bible tells me so. *Archives of General Psychiatry, 45,* 683-684.

Wooten, B. (1972). The place of psychiatry and medical concepts in the treatment of offenders. *Canadian Psychiatric Association Journal, 17,* 365-375.

Zimmerman, M. (1988). Why are we rushing to publish DSM-IV? *Archives of General Psychiatry, 45,* 1135-1138.

Zimmerman, M., and Spitzer, R.L. (1989). Melancholia: From DSM-III to DSM-III-R. *American Journal of Psychiatry, 146,* 20-28.

Zubin, J. (1977-1978). But is it good for science? *The Clinical Psychologist, 37,* 286-190.

CITATION

Colorado vs. Francis Connelly, 107S.Ct 115, 55L.W4043 (1986)

CHAPTER 5

Challenging Clinical Judgment

INTRODUCTION

Given the paucity of established scientific knowledge and the serious deficiencies that we will discuss in the methods by which psychiatric evaluations are conducted (see Chapter 6), an expert that is effectively challenged on these matters will often defend his opinions by falling back on his clinical judgment capabilities or powers. In fact, once the mask of established scientific knowledge or method is removed, there is little other basis on which the expert can retreat to make his stand. Not infrequently, experts will even admit that their work is not solely or even predominantly science, but rather an art, implying or claiming that their "artistic" powers are sufficiently great to produce reliable opinions. Claims for these artistic powers, whether explicitly stated or not, almost always come down to the clinician's purported judgment capacities.

Thus, clinical judgment is ultimately the fulcrum on which the whole matter of credibility may swing. Indeed, experts often act so as to cultivate faith in their judgment powers or capability. For example, any time an expert begins a sentence with a phrase like, "Based on my experience...," or, "Based on my training...," or, "In my professional judgment," he implies that his qualifications, or training, or experience have produced refined and trustworthy judgment skills. These types of statements often strike a responsive chord because, on the surface, they seem so plausible. Most of us believe that individuals get better with practice, so certainly one would expect this to apply to experts as well (but see Chapter 8). Further, many laypersons assume that doctors have special knowledge or reasoning abilities that allow them to make judgments beyond the capability of other individuals. As a result, a lawyer may go to great lengths to undermine the scientific basis of expert testimony only to be confronted by the expert who says, in essence, that all the things pointed out by the lawyer may be true but that "In this case I am extremely confident of my opinion." The jury may find these claims difficult to resist, and their views may be swayed considerably.

However, the lawyer need not be stymied by these tactics. We need not rely on an expert's statements or beliefs about the veracity of his own opinions. There is a vast body of research on human judgment, a good deal of which has been conducted with mental health practitioners. This research allows us to scientifically examine claims about reasoning power and accuracy, and about factors purporting to produce greater accuracy, such as experience or training. It also allows us to evaluate the accuracy of experts' subjective beliefs about their own judgment practices or powers. Do experts really know what data shaped their opinions? Are experts who are more confident in their opinions actually more likely to be correct? [1]

A 1989 edition of the journal, *Behavioral Sciences and The Law* (Volume 7, Number 4), was devoted to judgment and decision processes in the legal context. Included are articles by Arkes (1989), which surveys judgment literature relevant to legal proceedings; by Dawes (1989), which summarizes research demonstrating the lack of relation between experience and accuracy of clinical judgment; by Faust (1989), which reviews research examining clinicians' capacity to integrate information; and by Meehl (1989), which reprints and updates his article, "Law and The Fireside Inductions: Some Reflections of a Clinical Psychologist."

Arkes's article reviews such issues as base rates, co-variation analysis, overconfidence, judgmental biases, and strategies for decreasing judgment error. In Dawes's article, he states, "Mental health experts often justify diagnostic and predictive judgments on the basis of 'years of experience' with a particular type of person....However, research shows that the validity of clinical judgment and amount of clinical experience are unrelated." (p. 457) Dawes goes on to describe factors that impede experiential learning. In Meehl's article, he indicates that there is little need to modify the statements contained in his original publication. He further indicates that numerous licensed practitioners are not able to evaluate data scientifically, and states further, "A judge, in admitting expert testimony and instructing the trier of fact about it, naturally assumes that while experts may disagree, any expert knows the basic facts and tools of the trade, and knows how to reason about them properly....In the 'soft' areas of psychology (clinical, counseling, community, social, personality, developmental) this cannot be safely presumed." (p. 547)

---

[1] In this chapter we will overview research findings but discuss only a few studies in detail given the voluminous literature on the subject. A lengthy list of citations will be provided and a number of these studies will be further discussed in subsequent chapters.

Rock et al. (1987) note that various reviews of clinical judgment indicate that biases exert a negative influence on judgmental accuracy and that judgment errors are common. They discuss, for example, research pertaining to illusory correlation, overconfidence, and the lack of relation between experience and accuracy. They do question whether this judgment research accurately portrays the performance of clinicians in actual practice, and they discuss an approach that might be used to address this issue. However, they do not cite research which supports the possibility they raise, or which indicates that the accuracy of clinical judgment in everyday practice exceeds the level of accuracy demonstrated in judgment studies. We would further note that there are numerous judgment studies that do address Rock et al.'s concerns. Dawes et al. (1989) address this matter of application to everyday practice in the context of research on clinical versus actuarial judgment. They indicate that multiple studies have involved judgments that are commonly made in the course of clinical practice and which experts claim to perform with a high degree of accuracy. Along these lines, Dawes et al. cite studies involving the distinction between major and less severe psychiatric disorder, the identification of brain damage, the separation of medical and psychiatric disorder, and the prediction of treatment outcome. They note further that various naturalistic studies have been conducted, or studies in everyday practice settings in which judges were allowed to collect the data that they wanted in their preferred manner. They also note that even as of 1966, Sawyer was able to identify over 15 studies comparing clinical and actuarial judgments that were based on both psychological interviews and testing. Dawes et al. indicate that these types of studies have yielded findings comparable to other investigations on clinical versus actuarial judgment. Thus, although it is conceivable that additional studies examining everyday practice might yield different results, a claim to the effect that "clinical judgment is better (or more accurate) in everyday practice" must be considered an assumption or unsupported belief. Such a claim disregards considerable evidence that does exist on clinical judgment in favor of evidence one hopes would be forthcoming were additional or different studies conducted.

Rock et al. further indicate that practitioners have neglected research on clinical judgment, and they suggest that one reason might involve defensiveness. They state, "After four, five, or six years of graduate education, what professional would appreciate hearing that their secretary is as accurate as they are in diagnosing 'brain damage' using the Bender-Gestalt, or that graduate student trainees are as accurate as MMPI experts in using the MMPI to diagnose psychiatric patients?" (p. 651)

Responding to Rock et al.'s article, Garb (1988) indicates that not all studies demonstrate poor performance on clinical judgment tasks.

However, Garb then points out that one of the studies that Rock et al. reanalyzed, which they claimed showed that the MMPI interpretations of experienced clinicians were more accurate than less experienced clinicians when difficult cases were involved, in fact showed only about a 2% to 3% advantage for psychologists over graduate students, and only about a 6% advantage over undergraduates. Rock et al. (1988) respond to Garb by indicating that some of the materials Garb cited to support his contention that clinical judgment is not as consistently bad as Rock et al. portrayed, according to Garb's own description, more strongly favors the proposition that clinical judgments are inaccurate as opposed to accurate. More specifically, they cite a review of evidence on incremental validity, that is, studies examining whether judgmental accuracy improves as clinicians gain access to additional information. They note the finding that providing direct access to interview data does not increase judgmental accuracy. This finding clearly aligns with that of Sawyer (1966), who found that clinical judgments based on the combination of test data and interviews were generally less accurate than judgments based on tests alone. This point is important, as witnesses may claim that particular studies on clinical judgment or on diagnostic reliability or validity did not allow clinicians direct access to interviews. Rock et al. further note that the majority of evidence does not support the contention that additional information leads to an increase in judgmental accuracy.

Otto et al. (1993) analyzed judgments of expert panelists with regard to reconstructive psychological evaluations (psychological autopsies) arising out of the explosion and allegations of intentional suicidal acts on the USS *Iowa* in 1989. They found that while there were some broad areas of agreement, in many areas it was difficult to discern even a broad consensus. They note there is no widely accepted systematic procedure for evaluating data of third parties in a psychological reconstruction. They state, "Existing guidelines for psychological autopsy go little beyond menus of content to be considered (Ebert, 1987; Shneidman, 1981) leaving considerable room for idiosyncratic data reduction by the clinician. Nor is there an explicit calculus for integrating that which emerges from the filtering and selection process. This lack of procedural rigor and control maximizes the potential for variation in judgments and conclusions (Selkin and Loya, 1979)." (p. 440) (See also Chapter 6 re examiner effects in interpretation.) They urge caution in the use of postmortem psychological reconstructions.

Rubenzer (1991), concerned with recommendations that computer-based test interpretations (CBTI) be validated against "sound clinical judgment," declares that advocates of traditional assessment are ignoring the preponderance of research on clinical judgment which indicates significant limitations in reliability and validity. He states, "Many will assume that even if the individual data or tests have deficiencies, the artful combination of data will overcome the individual weaknesses. Research on human judgment gives little support to such an argument. Increasing the amount of information available often does not increase judgment accuracy." (p. 64)

Spielberger and Piotrowski (1991), responding to Rubenzer (it was their article that triggered his), maintain their position regarding CBTI (actually they were reporting on a survey of clinicians), but state that they agree with his concerns that there may be "equal cause for reserve regarding clinical judgment." (Spielberger is a former president of APA.)

Garb (1992) also responds to Rubenzer. He asserts that while the research results on clinical judgment are mixed, Rubenzer cites only the negative evidence. Of course, for the lawyer's purpose, mixed research is sufficient as it would leave the validity of clinical judgment in doubt. However, Garb goes further and states, "Rubenzer is correct in saying that, in empirical studies, (a) judgments made by psychologists have not been more valid than judgments made by graduate students, and (b) more experienced clinicians have not been more accurate than less experienced clinicians (see Garb, 1989)." (p. 96) He then goes on to point out that in some tasks with some kinds of information, clinical judges were more accurate than *lay* judges. We can live with that.

Kleinmuntz (1991) in an article on "Decision Making for Professional Decision Makers," does not limit his discussion to mental health professionals, but clearly includes them. He states, "Another reason for professionals to be concerned with the nature and quality of their decisions is the research showing that individuals are often unaware of the frequency and severity of decision errors. Blithe overconfidence in judgmental abilities leaves decision makers (and those who depend on them) open to a variety of nasty and unpleasant surprises and undermines attempts to aid and improve decision making." (p. 138)

Dahlstrom (1993) reiterates the fallibility of human judgment. He seems to be arguing in favor of more use of objective data such as tests. He states, "Dawes, Faust, and Meehl (1989) have summarized the research bearing on the various elements that enter into the complex set of processes that comprise human judgment and have pointed out the central role that objective data such as test findings can play in the substitution of predictive formulae for much more fallible human integration of information about individuals under study." (p. 395) He notes that specific formulae are more likely to generate more accurate decisions than human judges using the same information sources. (This article was originally presented as part of a Distinguished Professional Contributions award address at the 100th Annual Convention of the APA, indicating the considerable stature of Dahlstrom in the psychological community.)

Kazdin (1993) states, "In fact, the accumulating verdict regarding judgmental biases in decision making in general and, more specifically, within the context of clinical work has not been kind. Research on causal attributions and expectations of clinicians, illusory correlation, clinical prediction, overconfidence in inferences and biases in information processing have emphasized the limits of perceptions...." (p. 13)

The lawyer should be aware of a study by Rock and Bransford (1992) in which, using a different model for evaluating judgment, they concluded that accuracy was not uniformly poor but was varied. They state that clinicians, rather than being either good or poor at clinical judgment as a whole, can be very good at some tasks and poor at others. They state that this should motivate clinicians to search for weaknesses and try to find methods to improve. We mention this study in case some expert should try to cite it as evidence that clinical judgment is good. That is not the finding. In addition, the number of subjects was small (N=16), consisted of graduate students, and the criterion was clinical judgments by four "expert" clinicians. It cannot serve to tip the scales of the substantial body of literature indicating serious problems with clinical judgment.

The following two articles provide what we believe are useful discussions of processes by which clinicians, and perhaps clients or other consumers of their services, may develop false or inflated beliefs in their powers of diagnosis and prediction. These articles are relevant to the topic of overconfidence, and also the topic of experience, as clinicians may view client endorsement of their interpretations as a useful source of information for testing or validating their judgment accuracy or theories of behavior.

Goldberg (1986) reviews some background research on graphologists (handwriting analysts) that fails to show a difference between the accuracy of graphologists and non-graphologists, and he also describes a study involving a presumed expert in this area. This study did not support the presumption of expertise. Goldberg suggests that while certain aspects of graphology may have some degree of accuracy, belief in the method far exceeds the accuracy of judgments based on handwriting analysis. Goldberg then explores the reasons why graphologists (experts) and consumers of their services believe so strongly in the method. He suggests that one reason is the general belief that extensive experience leads to the improvement of skills, or expertise. He notes that seeing many cases, by itself, does not ensure expertise, and rather that this depends on receiving useful feedback about the accuracy of one's judgments. As discussed below in Chapter 8, experts often receive little or no feedback about their judgmental accuracy, and the feedback they do receive may be of poor quality or prone to misinterpretation due to a variety of factors. Goldberg suggests further:

> Our gullibility comes also from another major myth, namely that called personal validation: "If it works for me, it must work equally well for others." The problem here is what we want to work may actually seem to do so (just like the placebo effect in medicine) even when it doesn't. There have now been many dozens of studies that demonstrate that the information in a false "test report" (often the same report is given to all subjects) comes to be believed as highly personalistic and incredibly accurate by a large majority of the individuals exposed to it. (p. 291)

Hyman (1977) describes the same type of phenomenon, that is, how various individuals convince others, and sometimes themselves, that they have special insight into another person. We highly recommend this article, as it provides a compelling and informative discussion of the mechanisms by which individuals come to falsely believe in methods or procedures, and of the need to verify impressions through scientific methods. Hyman refers to the human tendency to "make sense out of nonsense" as powerful and pervasive. He cites as an example psychologists' belief in personality instruments. He notes that some widely used personality tests have not fared well when tested scientifically, but that the lack of scientific validation has not stopped many psychologists from placing reliance upon these methods. He states that in the practice of using personality tests, psychologists and their clients become convinced that the procedures are effective. He goes on to explain how this happens.

Hyman discusses features that are common to a variety of individuals, such as fortune-tellers, who attempt to "read" the characteristics of others. He discusses various factors which lead to a high rate of acceptance of personality interpretations, and he notes that even if the reader starts with little faith in his own method, that the frequency of client agreement is likely to bolster his confidence in his method and himself. He notes that one of the factors that leads to ready acceptance is that the reader provides the client with what seems to be an individually tailored assessment. In the case of charlatans, he notes that those who are particularly effective with readings keep three basic points in mind: that individuals are more alike than unalike; that problems in life tend to come from the same general set of life events, such as work, marriage, and old age; and that people come to have these readings because they wish to have someone listen to their concerns involving either health, money, or interpersonal relations. This set of assumptions provides the reader with a basis from which it is possible to generate plausible-sounding statements about the individual. Hyman further notes that even should a reader not be particularly skilled, or able to discern features of the individual, that a high rate of agreement may still be obtained. He indicates that given the proper circumstances, individuals will "make sense" out of almost any statements from a reader and find a way to suit the material to their own lives. He notes that the reader need only make out a plausible argument for why the generated material ought to fit the individual, and the individual will then find a way to make it "fit." Hyman discusses additional characteristics of successful reading, including the presentation of material with confidence, the use of gimmicks, such as a crystal ball or tarot cards (he does not specifically mention pages with ink blots on them), and the creation of the impression that one knows more than he is actually revealing.

Hyman goes on to describe studies which show that individuals are, in fact, highly accepting of personality sketches. He describes a study in which individuals received a sketch of their personality based on the MMPI, which was constructed to be as accurate as possible, and a fake sketch. He notes that more than half of the subjects selected the fake sketches as being more accurate. We do not know to what extent this is more a comment on the MMPI than it is on individuals' tendency to endorse false information, but in any case, it would seem to clearly illustrate flaws relying on client feedback in order to discern one's accuracy or to "validate" one's theory of personality or behavior. This is also why a statement such as, "Based on my experience…" may be meaningless, as the type of feedback the clinician receives in the context of clinical practice, such as acceptance of erroneous judgments, is unlikely to improve judgmental accuracy. Hyman concludes that readings work so effectively because they tap into necessary and basic human processes. He notes that in order to understand ongoing events, one must apply one's knowledge and expectations and that in typical situations, accurate interpretations often result. He observes, however, that the use of memory and context, which allows us to draw the inferences needed to interpret the statements of others, can go awry when no actual meaning is being expressed. He states that:

> Instead of picking up random noise we still manage to find meaning in a situation. So the same system that enables us to creatively find meanings and to make new discoveries also makes us extremely vulnerable to exploitation by all sorts of manipulators. In the case of the…reading the manipulator may be conscious of his deception; but often he, too, is a victim of personal validation. (pp. 36-37)

It is critical to recognize that forensic assessments almost never rely solely on set or prespecified methods of data collection and interpretation, but rather depend on the expert's reasoning or clinical judgment. Although some components of the assessment may be prespecified (e.g., some standard psychological tests are administered in a set manner), other components are not. For example, the clinician decides what data collection procedures to use (e.g., what tests to administer, often what interview questions to ask). Combining or interpreting the obtained data again typically depends on clinical judgment processes. Although there may be automatic (actuarial) procedures for interpreting single tests, there are virtually no scientifically established procedures for combining information from different tests. Similarly, there are few established procedures for the selection of interview questions or tests. Thus, ultimately, the clinician often has little choice but to rely on his judgment in deciding such matters.

Almost any expert will admit that data combination ultimately depends on judgment processes. In fact, most experts will insist on this point. When a lawyer presses them as to how they arrived at their opinions, or asks about the influence of one or another piece of information, they will state something to the effect that they relied on most or all of the data together rather than any individual item, and, further, that this is the correct and proper way to reach conclusions. Experts sometimes use such statements to be evasive, but they often believe that this type of data integration is required, is within their capabilities, and is the preferred or best means by which to reach accurate conclusions. This usually requires use of clinical judgment. Therefore, it is important to be able to acquaint judge or jury with the literature indicating that opinions based on clinical judgment are exceedingly unreliable and often wrong.

LEVEL OF PERFORMANCE ON CLINICAL JUDGMENT TASKS

Throughout the book, we provide hundreds of references showing deficiencies in the reliability or accuracy of diagnostic conclusions or predictions, and thus we can cover the topic briefly here. There are a number of studies showing levels of performance no better than, or even worse than could be attained if one flipped coins to make decisions.

In one such study, Oskamp (1965) provided judges,[2] including clinical psychologists, with a very detailed description of an individual. The level of detail, in fact, was quite comparable to, if not more extensive than, the amount of information that might be gathered in a typical psychiatric interview or series of interviews. The judges were then presented with a series of multiple-choice items. Each item described a situation and various possible responses to the situation (e.g., "When Bill finally made a decision about his work, he: a) decided to continue in the current situation, b) demanded a raise from his boss, c) decided to seek employment elsewhere," etc.). The judges were asked to select the alternative or

---

[2] The use of "judge" here and in descriptions of other such studies obviously does not refer to a courtroom judge. Rather, the term is commonly used to describe subjects in judgment studies, because they are making judgments.

response that they thought had occurred. All of these situations had actually taken place, and thus the individual's responses were known to the experimenter, providing a means for clearly assessing the accuracy of the psychologists' choices. Not only was the psychologists' overall accuracy low, it was so low that it did not surpass the level one could have obtained through random guessing or chance.

Other studies, some with psychologists and some with psychiatrists, show similar or lower levels of performance. For example, a number of studies (see Chapters 7 and 24) demonstrate poor performance in the prediction of violence. In a study by Farber et al. (1986), temporal lobe epilepsy was identified at about a 5% level of accuracy. The Rosenhan study (see Chapter 7) and the Faust et al. study (see Chapter 18) showed 0% accuracy in the detection of malingering; in the Temerlin and Trousdale study (see below), psychiatrists uniformly diagnosed abnormality when no abnormality was present.

CLINICAL VERSUS ACTUARIAL OR STATISTICAL JUDGMENT METHODS[3]

The terms "clinical judgment" and "actuarial judgment" refer to contrasting ways of combining or interpreting information, such as scores from a psychological test or data from interviews. In the first method, the judge combines and processes the available information in his head. In the second method, the judge is eliminated and information is combined on the basis of prespecified or automatic, empirically established decision rules. The difference can be illustrated by contrasting approaches used by two hypothetical life insurance agents. Agent Jones uses the clinical approach. He obtains background information about such things as health and age, and then he uses his judgment to formulate an estimation of risk. This estimation may be based on his background experience or knowledge. In any case, Jones works on the information in his head in order to reach a conclusion. Agent Smith obtains exactly the same information, but rather than combining and interpreting the information in his head, he depends entirely on tables and charts to look up the obtained figures, and he follows a set formula to calculate risk. These tables and charts contain established knowledge about the relationship between these variables and life expectancy. Note that Smith could have been eliminated from this interpretive process entirely. Instead, his secretary could have looked up the figures or he might have a computer

---

3 For a more detailed review of clinical versus actuarial methods and the pivotal study of Sawyer discussed below, see Appendix 5A. This and other appendices are provided for this chapter in order to aid the reader who wishes to gain a more in-depth understanding of certain issues.

program available that could do the work.[4] Thus, in the clinical method data are combined or interpreted in the head, and in the actuarial or statistical method data are combined or interpreted on the basis of established empirical relationships. Stated differently, in the clinical method the clinician decides and in the actuarial method the method decides based on the facts.

Clinical judgment does not refer specifically to clinical psychologists or psychiatrists, but rather refers to a judgment method. Thus, a clinical psychologist or psychiatrist may or may not use the clinical method, and individuals in various walks of life (like our insurance agents) may use the clinical or actuarial judgment method. Further, within psychiatry and psychology, the endpoint or product of the clinical or actuarial method may be of various types, such as a description of an individual's personality or a prediction of future behavior. Virtually any type of formulation or prediction that a clinician can make can also be made, in theory, with the actuarial method, although this is not to say that the accuracy of such judgments will be equal, as we will see. Finally, we have described pure forms of the clinical and actuarial methods, but there are shades in between. For example, when combining information in his head, a clinician might consider, or try to take into account, actuarial findings. Some individuals refer to this combination of methods as "clinical-actuarial." Subtle distinctions are often of little practical relevance because whether they are made or not, research generally comes out the same (see below).

There have now been over 100 studies comparing the accuracy achieved by actuarial versus clinical methods. Many of these studies involve mental health practitioners and encompass a wide range of diagnostic and predictive tasks. Paul Meehl (1984), whose classic book (1954) on this topic stimulated much of this research, summarized research findings as follows:

> This controversy [actuarial vs. clinical judgment]...has suffered the fate of so many controversies in psychology and other social sciences, to wit, that one group of persons considers it to have been settled, a second group continues to resist the massive empirical evidence and think it still controversial, and a sizable number of people don't even seem to know that an issue exists, or that it is of any practical importance. It is safe to say...that the mass and qualitative variety of investigations of the predictive accuracy of subjective impressionistic human judgment, such as that exercised by the individual clinician or case

---

[4] On the other hand, just because data might be combined by computer does not mean that the actuarial method has been used. If the computer program combines or interprets the data based on established empirical relationships, the method is actuarial. However, one might program the computer to model the reasoning used by Agent Jones, or to copy what Jones normally does in his head. The computer is thus copying a procedure that is not based upon empirically established relationships or decision rules, and thus it is not employing the actuarial method.

conference or psychiatric team, versus that of even a crude non-optimized mechanical prediction function (equation, monograph, actuarial table) is about as
clearly decided in favor of the latter predictive mode as we can ever expect to
get in the social sciences. *I am unaware of any other controversial matter in
psychology for which the evidence is now so massive and almost 100% consistent in pointing in the same direction....* That this body of data has had so little
effect on clinical practice reflects on the scientific mental habits of practitioners
and the defects of training programs. It is, alas, not unique because it can be
paralleled with other examples, such as the continued reliance on costly skill-
demanding projective tests which have been repeatedly shown to have low *absolute* validity and negligible *incremental* validity for purposes of making
practical decisions that matter to the welfare of the patient and use of the taxpayer's dollar. (p. xii)

Similar conclusions have been reached by Einhorn (1986), Goldberg
(1968a), Thorne (1972), Wiggins (1981), and Pitz and Sachs (1984).

As the studies of such researchers as Dawes (1971) and Goldberg
(1965) show, even very simple actuarial formulae equal or exceed the
level of accuracy achieved through clinical judgment. For example,
Goldberg found that a simple actuarial compilation of MMPI scales was
more accurate in predicting discharge diagnosis than every one of 13
psychologists using the clinical method. Dawes found that actuarial predictions based on even a single variable allowed for more accurate prediction of success in graduate school than the clinically-based predictions
of an admissions committee working with a considerably greater range of
data. The study by Dawes also suggests that actuarial methods can produce superior results even when they are placed at an informational disadvantage, such as when they have less data with which to work than do
clinicians using clinical judgment methods.

Sawyer (1966) conducted a thorough re-analysis of nearly 50 available studies on clinical versus actuarial methods and reached a series of
conclusions that have been supported by considerable subsequent research. Sawyer distinguished methods of data collection and methods of
data interpretation. He divided methods of data collection into *set* or prespecified procedures (e.g., standard psychological tests) versus *variable*
procedures, or what might be considered procedures tailored to the examinee and the examination (e.g., interviews). He divided methods of
data interpretation into *clinical* versus *actuarial* procedures. These distinctions allowed for four possible variations in data collection and interpretive procedures, as summarized below.

(1) set data collection-actuarial data interpretation (e.g., tests
    interpreted actuarially)

    (2) variable data collection-actuarial data interpretation (e.g., interview interpreted actuarially)[5]

    (3) set data collection-clinical interpretation (e.g., tests interpreted clinically)

    (4) variable data collection-clinical interpretation (e.g., interview interpreted clinically)

Working from 75 comparisons of the four variations described above, Sawyer found that no comparisons across the various studies contradicted one another. For example, if one study showed that variation (1) above was equal to or better than variation (2) above, any other study making the same comparison found the same thing. This permitted Sawyer to rank the four variations above from best (most accurate) to worst (least accurate). The order of accuracy followed the listing above: variation (1) was the most accurate, variation (2) the next most accurate, and so on. Stated differently, actuarial interpretation always equaled or exceeded clinical interpretation, no matter how data were collected (although this is *not* to say that *any* of these approaches achieved a high level of accuracy).

Sawyer's findings are of great importance, because order of accuracy seems to show a negative relationship with the frequency with which different methods are used in forensic assessment. For example, in cases on which we have consulted, the majority of psychiatrists have used variable methods of data collection (e.g., interview and review of background data) and clinical methods of data interpretation, which Sawyer found to be the *least* accurate approach. Some psychiatrists and psychologists will rely on interview and test results (the latter being a fixed method) and combine these results clinically, which Sawyer found the next worst approach.[6] Thus, clinicians seem to rely the most often on the least, or less, accurate approaches, a point worth raising in cross-examination.

Of interest, Sawyer also found that when data are interpreted clinically, less accurate conclusions are reached when one adds interview data to test data. That is, clinicians on average reach more accurate conclusions if they disregard interview results entirely and base their interpretations on test results alone. This finding may provide a powerful counter to the clinician who claims that by interviewing an examinee he

---

    [5] Interviews can be interpreted actuarially if observations are coded into a format that permits mathematical analysis.

    [6] We have not listed all of the variations Sawyer analyzed, one of these being fixed *and* variable methods of data collection together with clinical interpretation. We have also altered Sawyer's terminology somewhat. For further discussion of both matters see Appendix 5A.

is able to reach more accurate conclusions. The finding can also be raised any time a clinician indicates that one or another interview "finding" provided a basis for his opinion. One can ask, for example, "Aren't there large numbers of studies showing that when test results are available, more accurate conclusions are reached on average when clinicians completely disregard interview results?"

When a clinician who violates these preferred methods is confronted with Sawyer's findings or the results of the other studies on clinical versus actuarial judgment, whether this takes place in a case conference or in a courtroom, perhaps the most typical defense is something like the following. Assuming the clinician has any familiarity with this research (and actually many are not thoroughly versed), he will argue that all of this research may be fine and good, but that it doesn't apply to the particular case under consideration. Although an actuarial analysis may show this or that, in this case the clinician believes the actuarial analysis is wrong and that a different conclusion (his, of course) is correct. In essence, the clinician is claiming that he knows best when to use or disregard the actuarial analysis, and that by exercising such discretion he can improve on the accuracy one would achieve using the actuarial method alone. The clinician is thus arguing that in this particular case, and by implication in other cases as well, he can rely on his own judgment about when to rely on his own judgment.

Fortunately, we need not rely on subjective assertions in order to assess the veracity of such claims. Sawyer did uncover a few studies in which clinicians were given the outcome of actuarial analysis and were allowed to use or disregard the analysis at their own discretion. In other words, they could rely on the actuarial analysis or on their own clinical judgment when the two conflicted. The clinicians' accuracy was compared to that achieved when the actuarial results were used uniformly, or without exception. The studies all showed the same thing—that the clinicians' attempts failed and that they would have achieved a higher level of accuracy had they adhered to the actuarial method uniformly.

Since the time of Sawyer's review there have been few additional studies on this topic. One such study was performed by Leli and Filskov (1981). The judgment of interest was the identification of brain damage and associated features based on test results and background information. The accuracy achieved using an actuarial procedure was compared to that achieved by clinicians who were given the results of the actuarial analysis and could use it or disregard it, and to clinicians who relied on the clinical judgment method. Across various analyses, the actuarial method came out the clear overall winner, followed by the results obtained by the clinicians who were given the actuarial results but were free to disregard them, followed by the clinical judgment method. Thus, in this study, as in those reported by Sawyer, clinicians would have done better overall by adhering uniformly to the actuarial method.

Dawes et al. (1989) review research on clinical versus actuarial judgment. They note that in virtually every one of the nearly 100 studies in the social sciences comparing the two methods, the accuracy of the actuarial method has equalled or exceeded that of the clinical method. They discuss factors underlying the superiority of actuarial methods. They note, for example, that actuarial methods are consistent (that is, the same data always lead to the same conclusion), unlike human judges, who show random fluctuations in judgment. They indicate that random fluctuations decrease the reliability of judgment, which in turn decreases the validity or accuracy of judgment. They also note that properly developed actuarial methods ensure that variables will be included or used based on the extent to which they show predictive power. They note that in contrast, clinicians may have considerable difficulties distinguishing valid and invalid variables. They further discuss factors that make it difficult for clinicians to appraise their own level of judgmental accuracy objectively, and which promote a sense of overconfidence. They note, for example, that individuals tend to recall their past predictions as more consistent with outcomes than is actually the case. They further note that various studies show that clinical judgments based on interviews tend to be of low, or negligible, accuracy. When discussing clinicians' resistance to research on clinical versus actuarial judgment, Dawes et al. state:

> Clinicians must chose between their own observations or impressions and the scientific evidence on the relative efficacy of the clinical and actuarial methods. The factors that create difficulty in self-appraisal of judgmental accuracy are exactly those that scientific procedures, such as unbiased sampling, experimental manipulation of variables, and blind assessment of outcome, are designed to counter. Failure to accept a large and consistent body of scientific evidence over unvalidated personal observation may be described as a normal human failing or, in the case of professionals who identify themselves as scientific, plainly irrational. (p. 1673)

Hall (1988) compared the accuracy with which clinical versus actuarial judgment predicted recidivism among released sexual offenders. The actuarial method outperformed the clinical method across all analyses. Further, across most judgments, clinical prediction was only slightly better than chance. Hall describes the clinicians' inability to predict repeat sexual offenses as discouraging given the fact that they worked in a program designed to treat sexual offenders.

Walters et al. (1988) compared the effectiveness with which three groups of clinical judges—graduate students in psychology, professional psychologists, and MMPI experts—identified malingering on the basis of the MMPI. MMPI experts were identified through review of MMPI textbooks and the authors' professional contacts. The third author of this article, Roger L. Greene, has written a widely read text on the MMPI. Some caution is called for in interpreting the results of this study as the methods for sorting subjects into malingering versus non-malingering groups were not definitive, or were not ultimately verified. In any case, actuarial procedures based on the MMPI equaled or exceeded the accuracy of the clinical judges, and the best actuarial procedure outperformed all 60 judges in the study. Further, only about one-third of the judges achieved a rate of accuracy that surpassed chance level. Additionally, the judges' accuracy was unrelated to their clinical training or experience. In fact, the students performed as successfully (or unsuccessfully) as the MMPI experts. Nor was a statistically significant relation obtained between the judges' confidence in their diagnoses and the accuracy of these diagnoses. Finally, according to the authors, many of the clinical judges did not seem to make proper use of the base rate information that was provided to them.

Kareken and Williams (1994) state that in estimating IQ clinicians are best advised to use an actuarial formula. They state that actuarial formulas anchor clinicians to one estimate and control idiosyncratic bias.

Given the limited number of studies on the topic, the issue cannot be considered decided. However, the bulk of the evidence clearly suggests that clinicians will achieve a higher overall level of accuracy if they adhere uniformly to the results of actuarial analysis and rarely, if ever, decide to supersede the actuarial results based on their clinical impressions. Therefore, the clinician claiming that this or that particular case is an exception can be confronted with these findings. At best, one could say that although there is a possibility that the clinician could be right, to date the research suggests that clinicians do not know how to identify when these exceptions occur and that there is certainly no strong support for any such contention on the clinician's part. Rather, *the research suggests that clinicians cannot rely on their own judgment about when to rely on their own judgment.*

THE QUEST TO IDENTIFY THE EXPERT JUDGE & PSYCHIATRISTS VERSUS PSYCHOLOGISTS

Sawyer's work and studies on clinical versus actuarial interpretation would suggest that the expert "judge," or at least the most accurate one, can be located quite easily: the actuarial method is the expert, as opposed to a particular clinician or group of clinicians. Yet one might ask whether some clinicians show particular or outstanding judgment powers, powers that permit them not only to outdo the actuarial method but also to achieve a high level of accuracy overall. We still seem to be searching for experimental verification that such an individual exists. Researchers have had extraordinary difficulty finding judges who stand out from the more common psychologist or psychiatrist. The reason for this may be simple. Clinical prediction is an exceedingly complicated and difficult task, and in the absence of an adequate scientific knowledge base, it may be that the demands for accurate prediction outstrip the resources of even the most capable. Einstein is reported to have said once, when asked why great advances had not recently been made in physics, that maybe physics was too hard for the physicists. Given the contrast in the state of science across physics and psychology, one would imagine that Einstein might say that accurate prediction is much too hard for even the brightest clinicians.

Based on a review of available research in the early seventies, Wiggins (1973) made a statement that applies equally today: "Surprisingly, there is little empirical evidence that justifies the granting of 'expert' status to the clinician on the basis of his training, experience, or information-processing ability." (p. 131) An overview of the research that led Wiggins to reach this conclusion, and the research conducted since that time, creates no need to modify it (see Chapter 8).

There are different ways in which one might try to locate the extraordinary judge. One is by identifying the particularly experienced individual. However, a considerable body of research suggests that level of experience is minimally related to judgment accuracy (e.g., Goldberg, 1959; Oskamp, 1965; Goldsmith & Mandell, 1969; Stuart, 1970). Goldberg (1968b) sums up this matter thusly: "One surprising finding—that the amount of professional training and experience of the judge does not relate to his judgment accuracy—has appeared in a number of studies." (For extended discussion of this topic, see Chapter 8.)

Another approach is to separate individuals by discipline. However, the research has shown that judgment accuracy does not seem to vary systematically by discipline, e.g., that psychiatrists are not systematically more (or less) accurate than psychologists, who are not more accurate than social workers. For example, Stuart (1970) reviewed a series of studies and found no meaningful differences in the judgment accuracy of psychologists and psychiatrists. Such work is extremely important because testifying psychiatrists may claim that judgment studies do not apply to members of their discipline.

Various studies show poor judgment performance among psychiatrists. For example, the studies of Rosenhan (1973) and of Temerlin and Trousdale (1969) show 0% accuracy among psychiatrists. Fisch et al. (1982) found that experienced psychiatrists often disagreed among themselves in the analysis and use of cues or symptoms for evaluating depression. Further, as in the study by Gillis and Moran (see below), the psychiatrists' belief about their use of clinical data or "cues" and objective analysis of actual cue use showed marked differences. As with related studies with psychologists, the psychiatrists believed they "integrated" or combined many cues, whereas analysis showed that a few variables, often just one or two, predominantly influenced their conclusions.

Gillis and Moran's study (1981) involved 16 psychiatrists, a number of whom had been in practice ten to twenty years. Gillis and Moran analyzed reliability in the prescription of medication by presenting identical clinical cases to the various psychiatrists. Agreement levels for basic class of medication (e.g., an "antidepressant") fell at 62%, for specific class of medication at 20%, and for specific medication and dosage at 12%. These authors also performed objective analysis of cue utilization and found that different psychiatrists often placed very different weights on different cues in deciding what, if any drug to give which patient. In some cases judges used cues in an opposite fashion! For example, one psychiatrist might consider the presence of a specific symptom an indication that a certain drug was needed, whereas another psychiatrist might consider this symptom an indication that the drug was not needed.[7]

Various studies show frequent error in the prediction of violence. Many of these involve psychiatrists and some of them involve interdisciplinary comparisons. For example, a study by Werner et al. (1983) shows equal difficulty in predicting violence across psychologists and psychiatrists. A study by Montandon and Harding (1984) showed low reliability among psychiatrists in the prediction of dangerousness, no greater agreement in these predictions across psychiatrists and non-psychiatrists, and a tendency on the part of psychiatrists to predict dangerousness more often than non-psychiatrists. These results are in accord with various studies with psychiatrists (see Chapter 7) on the prediction of violence, a number of which demonstrate a tendency to make false-positive predictions of future violent behavior.

A study by Holland and Holt (1978) on pre-sentence evaluations revealed greater biases on the part of two psychiatrists and a psychologist, as opposed to a case worker with an M.A. degree. According to Holland and Holt, their results suggest that the psychologist and psychiatrists were less likely to rely on standardized methods of case appraisal, and that this may have been an important factor in the greater level of bias

---

[7] In responding to questions about this study, a psychiatrist may claim that various medications that fall within the same class are essentially similar. Thus, the lawyer may wish first to ask about the clinician's medication decisions. Many experts will claim that the specific medication used within a general class makes a difference. Further, most will concede that dosage can make a substantial difference. One can then ask the clinician whether he is aware that the psychiatrists in the study by Gillis and Moran agreed on specific medication and dosage in only 12% of the cases. At a minimum, one can point out that the psychiatrists disagreed even on broad classes of medication in more than one out of every three cases and on broad class and dosage in an even higher percentage of cases.

evidenced. The results are similar to other studies with psychologists suggesting that failure to follow standardized procedures hinders accurate judgment.

A study by Stack et al. (1983) showed a low level of accuracy in the prediction of re-hospitalization. Further, "...clinicians' prognostic judgments were biased in regard to patients' ethnicity: black patients were considered more likely to be re-hospitalized than whites, although the opposite occurred." (p. 99) In formulating judgments, clinicians seemed to rely predominantly on less useful or invalid variables (see the discussion of illusory correlation below). Although the clinical judges in the study came from various disciplines, including psychiatry, psychology, and social work, there was essentially zero correlation between discipline and judgment accuracy.

Faust and Nurcombe (1989) review research on clinical judgment. Of some significance, this article was published in a psychiatry journal, the second author is a psychiatrist, and reference is made to judgment findings cutting across disciplines. More research has been conducted on clinical judgment in psychology than psychiatry, and thus a psychiatrist may claim that such findings do not apply to him or his discipline. Faust and Nurcombe state, "Diagnostic reasoning in psychiatry is as intricate as it is risky," (p. 197) and they note that studies examining the accuracy of clinical judgment have often yielded "sobering" results. They note that studies on judgment accuracy do not show a systematic relation with the discipline of clinicians or clinicians' level of training or experience. The authors suggest that clinicians who are highly motivated to achieve accurate results may be more prone to discard, or tamper with, validated decision rules in order to achieve more accurate conclusions, but they suggest that intuitive tinkering with such validated methods is rarely successful. They observe that little work has been conducted on educational methods for improving clinical reasoning, and they discuss the need to develop such programs. They assert, however, that "before that can happen...the profession must shake off complacency and embrace the need for change." (p. 207)

Neuropsychologists (that is, psychologists who specialize in the study of brain-behavior relations or brain damage assessment) may also claim exemption from the judgment literature. However, based on a review of literature on clinical judgment in neuropsychology, Wedding and Faust (1989) state, "To the extent studied, the general findings of the judgment literature apply to the special case of neuropsychology." (p. 253) They indicate that individuals who claim exemption bear the burden of proof, and state further that research on judgment in neuropsychology "suggests that there is little relation between experience and judgmental accuracy and surprising limitations to our ability to process clinical data, particularly data which form patterned or configural relations. Finally, it appears that neuropsychologists are subject to the same judgment errors that characterize other specialists." (p. 253) They note the need for further research on clinical judgment in neuropsychology, and also provide various suggestions for improving clinical judgment accuracy. Lending credibility to this article is the fact that it was accorded the first Annual Award for Excellence in Research in 1990 from the National Academy of Neuropsychology. The award was given for the best contribution to the journal, *Archives of Clinical Neuropsychology.*

Thus, the psychiatrist who claims that judgment studies are irrelevant to his profession may not know that a number of studies demonstrating poor performance and problematic judgment practices have been conducted with psychiatrists (further studies are cited below). One might wish to make such gaps in knowledge apparent. The psychiatrist might be correct if he asserts that there are fewer studies demonstrating judgment difficulties with psychiatrists, but it should be made clear that there are fewer judgment studies with psychiatrists overall. This does not mean there are studies showing the superiority of psychiatrists. In fact, we performed a comprehensive computer-based search of the judgment literature over the last ten years that uncovered hundreds of studies, but close to none suggesting that psychiatrists were any more accurate than psychologists. In the face of the studies that do exist showing poor judgment performance and a lack of disciplinary differences, the plausible conclusion should be obvious. Many of the problematic judgment practices of physicians are laid bare in a work by Preston (1981) that is discussed below.

COMMON JUDGMENT ERRORS AND PRACTICES UNDERLYING LOW ACCURACY AND PERFORMANCE

An important factor underlying low level of accuracy on many judgment tasks is that clinicians fail to use preferred approaches and/or employ problematic judgment approaches or habits. Familiarity with these poor judgment practices can be useful to the lawyer, especially should an expert claim that he is an exception to the poor performances shown in the judgment literature. The flawed judgment practices and strategies we will discuss are so common that one will almost always be able to identify some, if not many instances of their occurrence in particular cases. Thus, one can counter the clinician's claims to exemption with concrete and clear instances of poor judgment practices committed by this expert in this case. In turn, one can create considerable doubt that conclusions based on such faulty habits and practices could be trusted or useful to the courts. We will first cover failures to utilize proper reasoning strategies, and then describe bad judgment habits.

VIOLATIONS OF PROPER JUDGMENT PRACTICES

Failure to Analyze Co-Variation and Illusory Correlation

Suppose you are trying to determine whether two things are related, such as a certain symptom and a disorder, or a form of medical treatment and the remission of a disease, or performance on a psychological test and the likelihood of future violence. To make this more concrete, we will invent a disease, called psychophobia (fear of psychologists and psychiatrists), and a symptom, episodes in which one feels tense. If most individuals, say 15 of 20, who have psychophobia show the symptom, it might seem that tension is a sign or symptom of the disorder.

In truth, based on the information we have given, there is no way to determine whether tension is actually related to psychophobia. One must know another set of facts, that is, how often those without psychophobia have the same symptom. For example, suppose we obtain a sample of 20 people without psychophobia, and it turns out that 15 of them also show episodes of tension. Thus, the frequency of the symptom is no greater among those who do and do not have psychophobia, and we cannot conclude that the symptom is truly associated with the disorder. This might be even more obvious if all 20 of our normals showed the symptom. In contrast, suppose none of our normals had the symptom. Then we would have obtained initial evidence that the symptoms are more common among those with the disorder than those without it, and thus that a true relationship might exist. The essential point is that to establish the existence of a relationship, one must show that the symptom occurs more frequently when the disorder is present than it occurs when the disorder is absent. If one does not have this full set of facts—frequency of the symptom when the disorder is *and* is not present—the determination cannot be made. Analyzing the frequency with which a symptom co-occurs with a disorder and occurs in the absence of a disorder is referred to as "analysis of co-variation."

Individuals have considerable difficulty analyzing co-variation and thus commonly draw false conclusions about relationships between two variables (e.g., Smedslund, 1963; Ward & Jenkins, 1965; Arkes & Harkness, 1980). In particular, they tend to consider only the frequency with which the sign of interest co-occurs with the condition of interest. To aid in comprehension, the reader can refer to Figure 1. Here the diagnostic "sign" is an elevated score on Scale 8 of the MMPI, and the condition of interest is "schizophrenia." Cell A refers to the "sign-present" (high score on Scale 8)-"condition-present" situation. Thus, when we say that individuals often attend exclusively to the frequency with which a sign of interest co-occurs with the condition of interest, this is the "sign-present"-"condition-present" cell in Figure 1. Some individuals also consider Cell B (sign absent-condition present), but individuals often fail to consider *all* the cells (A-D). However, short of considering all the cells, or lacking information about all the cells, one cannot determine whether an actual relationship exists between the sign and the condition.

FIGURE 1

Four Cells Needed for Analysis of Relationships

Sign

(high score MMPI Scale 8)

		Present	Absent
Condition "schizophrenia"	Present	(A) sign present- condition present	(B) sign absent condition present
	Absent	(C) sign present- condition absent	(D) sign absent condition absent

Clinicians typically confine their practices to individuals with apparent abnormalities, and thus they often cannot form adequate estimates of how often the "symptoms" they observe among abnormal individuals actually occur among normals. A common result is to assume that relationships exist between the symptoms they observe and abnormality when no such relationship actually exists. Recall, for example, a report on the work of George Vaillant discussed in Chapter 4, in which it was found that certain behaviors or defensive styles supposedly exclusive to those with psychiatric disorders were actually very common among normal individuals. This was not apparent until effort was directed towards studying such behaviors not only among those considered abnormal, but among normal individuals as well. Chapman and Chapman (1967, 1969) refer to these mistaken assumptions about relationships as belief in "illusory correlations," or beliefs about relationships that appear to exist but actually do not exist.

To further clarify these ideas, and to show how deceptive, compelling, and commonplace beliefs in illusory correlations can be, let us provide a few additional examples. Dawes (1986) quotes from a magazine article in which it is reported that a high percentage of CEOs had pets as youngsters. In the article, it is assumed that their success was partially attributed to the responsible habits and self-discipline developed through pet ownership. Dawes points out, however, that an equal or higher percentage of managers who did not become CEOs may have had pets. Thus, one cannot draw a causal connection between pet ownership and a high level of achievement. Stated within the context we have outlined, Dawes is saying that just because the thing or sign of interest (exemplary achievement or becoming a CEO) often co-occurs with pet ownership (Cell A of Figure 1), one cannot assume the two are associated. Perhaps an equal or greater number of individuals who had pets did not become CEOs (Cell C). As Dawes states, "It would make more sense to maintain that all CEOs developed self-discipline by brushing their teeth as children." (p. 432)

As another example, suppose a clinician concludes that a stressful event caused a psychological disorder. This conclusion is reached because of an assumed relationship between stress and disorder. However, the majority of persons the clinician sees are disordered, or assumed to be disordered, in the first place. Thus, the clinician's observations are almost exclusively limited to cases in which the thing of interest (disorder) is present and the assumed causative agent is present (Cell A). In truth, the clinician rarely knows how often this assumed causative agent occurs but does *not* produce the disorder (Cell C). Thus, the clinician does not really know whether there is a relationship between the stress and the disorder, and indeed may have formed an illusory correlation. Who does not experience stress? How many individuals in, say, car accidents do *not* develop what is purportedly a post-traumatic stress disorder? Based on his observations, the clinician really does not know, because people who have been in car accidents and do not report symptoms are unlikely to show up in his office. As such, the observational base is so skewed that illusory beliefs may well develop.

Dawes (1986) illustrates this problem. He states:

> Consider...the oft-repeated assertion that "one thing that we know about child abusers is that they never stop on their own without therapy." Rationally, it is impossible for a clinician or agency to reach that conclusion, because people who stop on their own may never come to the attention of that clinician or agency—hence, their number must remain a mystery. Only a researcher who has conducted prospective studies could present evidence for such an assertion. (I know of none.) Yet, that assertion is quite common. (p. 439)

Anastasi (1982) notes that any one clinician's contacts are likely to have been limited to persons who are atypical in one or more ways. At least in this respect, the clinician's experience is almost certain to produce a misleading picture, since clinicians deal almost entirely with disturbed or pathological cases, and thus may lack much in the way of first-hand familiarity with reactions of normal people.

Examples aside, there is a considerable body of evidence demonstrating illusory correlations that are likely to develop due to failure to analyze co-variation. The Chapmans (1967) conducted early work in this area. In an initial study, they used the Draw-A-Person test (DAP). On this popular test, the patient draws pictures, typically of a man and/or of a woman. The clinician then attempts to link characteristics of the drawings to the patient's personality characteristics. For example, one common interpretation is that a drawing which accents the eyes is associated with suspiciousness or paranoid tendencies on the part of the one who did the drawing. There is, in fact, a great deal of clinical lore regarding such relationships, although the empirical evidence on the validity of these assumptions has been almost uniformly negative (see Chapter 13). The Chapmans attempted to find out why clinicians might continue to utilize such measures in the face of these very negative research findings.

The Chapmans collected a series of drawings produced by patients at a state hospital, and then randomly paired symptom statements with the different drawings. For example, among drawings containing accented eyes, half might be paired with a symptom statement about suspiciousness and the other drawings paired with an entirely different statement. Thus, there were no systematic relationships between the features of the drawings and the symptom statements. Nevertheless, subjects who examined the drawings falsely believed that systematic relationships were present in the data, these relationships being those that they assumed existed in the first place. Thus, not only were illusory beliefs maintained in the face of nonsupportive data, but individuals actually believed that these nonsupportive data were supportive.

The Chapmans (1969, 1971) provide further support of the illusory correlation that goes on among clinicians. They added to their demonstration of the phenomenon in connection with the DAP by demonstrating that the same phenomenon occurs on the Rorschach. In this work the Chapmans found that clinicians continue to utilize certain signs of homosexuality on the Rorschach as indicators of homosexuality although the signs have repeatedly failed to be validated, and neglect, on the other hand, signs that have been demonstrated to hold some validity. They describe how the illusory correlations that a clinician observes are reinforced by reports of fellow clinicians who themselves are subject to the same illusions, thus providing a consensus that would "make everyone's illusions stronger." The Chapmans state they do not mean to imply that clinical psychologists are incompetent or unresponsive to the facts but that the judgment tasks they face are extremely difficult.

As the Chapmans point out, however, *sometimes* people with paranoid tendencies do emphasize eyes in their drawings just as *sometimes* other people do. We would point out that clinicians who believe in the validity of this sign are thus reinforced in their belief and are even able to point to such instances as "proof" of validity. When they talk to other clinicians, especially those of similar orientation, they reinforce each other's belief. Such beliefs are taught in courses in psychodiagnosis. The fallacy takes on the aura of truth because it is widespread (see references herein to "bleeding" as a "therapeutic" medical technique for over 200 years). Seeing this "sign," the clinician is alerted to look for other indications of paranoia or suspiciousness and, of course, if he looks for them he will "find" them, as clinicians can almost always find evidence in anybody's record to support almost any clinical hypothesis (see base rates and confirmatory bias, below).

Golding and Rorer (1972) provide further evidence concerning the phenomenon of illusory correlation as originally defined by Chapman and Chapman. They point out the interaction between a psychologist's expectations, biased or not, and the degree to which contradictory observations influence his subsequent behavior. They point out that a psychologist who *believes* he frequently notices a certain response in patients of a certain type may in the first instance be predisposed to be sensitive to that characteristic as a function of his *a priori* biases about the "response and type" relationship. They state that these biases may stem from theoretical preconceptions or from more widely shared implicit personality theories. Thus, the first of a series of errors may occur because the psychologist is not equally predisposed to noticing the same characteristics in alternative populations. They point out that many clinical formulations based on the possibly erroneous observation that a certain response is frequent among a certain type of individual end up in textbooks and clinical supervision as the statement, "the response implies the type." They also point out that human judges are usually sensitive only to positive instances of their hypotheses. They further point out that a psychologist who reads the literature with strong preconceptions about a particular "sign" will have his preconceptions reinforced by a *lean,* partial re-enforcement schedule, that is, a small number of confirmatory instances. Moreover, since negative results from experiments are hard to publish and, if published, are easily rationalized as being due to deficiencies in the experiment, the impact of research evidence on the psychologists' preconceptions is further diminished. The significance of the Golding and Rorer material is to demonstrate how it is that invalid or unvalidated assumptions are perpetuated despite available negative research literature.

Kurtz and Garfield (1978) state:

> Although the phenomenon of illusory correlation has been demonstrated in a variety of studies...relatively little has been done to show that this bias cannot be reduced or eliminated by proper training.

In their study Kurtz and Garfield found that illusory correlation was *not* reduced by simulated training sessions. They state: "This study supports the Chapman and Chapman (1969) position that the illusory correlation is a robust phenomenon."

Werner et al. (1984) found that psychiatrists attempting to predict violent behavior relied mainly on variables that, objectively, showed little or no relationship to violent behavior. These researchers conducted separate analyses to determine which of the variables they measured showed an actual relationship to violent behavior. Of the three variables uncovered, only one was related to the psychiatrists' judgments. Werner et al. interpret their results as showing substantial differences in the actual factors predictive of violence in comparison to psychiatrists' beliefs about factors predictive of violent behavior or the variables they use to formulate such predictions. Thus, the assumed relationships upon which these judgments rely are illusory. Hamilton et al. (1985) have also conducted research on the topic of illusory correlation.

A number of researchers provide general statements. Shweder (1977) states:

> Illusory correlation refers to consensually judged correlations among classes of events that are not warranted by actual experience. A major determinant of such reliably invalid inferences are pre-existing conceptual linkages among event classes. Items resembling one another in concept are judged to empirically go together or co-occur in spite of contradictory observational evidence.

Waller and Keeley (1978) state:

> Even though it seems clear that clinical psychologists have considerable room for improvement in making judgments, only recently have researchers begun to isolate factors contributing to the non-optimality of judgment and to the frequent misplaced faith in such judgments. One such factor is the presence of "illusory correlations." This tendency to maintain a belief in illusory correlates when the evidence does not support such a belief presents a major obstacle to making valid clinical judgments.

Luger and Petzel (1979) state:

> The illusory correlation phenomenon in clinical judgment has been defined as an error of judgment in which a relationship between two events is reported when in fact no such relationship exists or in which there is exaggerated reporting of a true relationship.

Nor is this recognition limited to psychologists. As reported by Slovenko (1984), in the case of *State vs. Saldana,* expert testimony was not allowed which purported to draw a link between specific symptoms and the occurrence of a specific stressor. Justice Scott wrote, "Rape trauma syndrome is not the type of scientific test that accurately and viably determines whether a rape has occurred. The characteristic symptoms may follow *any* psychologically traumatic event." If we might be allowed to paraphrase Justice Scott, this sounds much like saying that the conclusions drawn about the symptoms and their link to a specific occurrence may well be illusory. Such symptoms may occur often with other types of circumstances or conditions, and thus one cannot safely draw causal connections.

The illusory correlation problem is important in challenging clinical testimony. Often, in attempting to supply a basis for conclusions, clinicians use statements of the "We find...," or "It is commonly accepted...," or "...has withstood the test of time" variety. It is, therefore, important to adduce testimony from this witness or another to the effect that many of the notions that can only be supported by statements of this kind have been demonstrated to be false and that, despite their demonstrable falsity, clinicians continue to apply such notions on the basis of what is "commonly found" or "commonly accepted." Without demonstration by hard data, one does not know whether the particular notion being supported by common practice is valid or whether it simply represents another case of illusory correlation. It would, therefore, seem appropriate in virtually all instances in which a testifying clinician makes an assertion that begins with the words "we find" or some such thing to initiate a line of questioning designed to ascertain whether or not the words "we find," in fact, refer to a demonstrated relationship or to an unfounded belief, i.e., an illusory correlation, as these appear to abound in psychiatric and psychological assessments.

Underutilization of Base Rate Data

The term "base rates" simply refers to the frequency with which something occurs. For example, if a disorder occurs in one of one hundred individuals, we would say that the base rate is 1%. Base rates are critically important in diagnosis and prediction, although many clinicians either do not know this or fail to utilize base rate information properly. Lacking knowledge of base rates, one almost never knows the value of diagnostic signs. Recall from our discussion of co-variation and illusory correlation that in order to judge whether a true relationship exists between such things as a "symptom" and a disorder, one must know the frequency (or base rates) with which this symptom occurs among those both with and without the disorder. Aside from the fact that clinicians often fail to perform this analysis, it is evident that if the information is not available, or if one does not know the base rates, then the analysis cannot be performed. Thus, in the absence of adequate base rate information, there is really no way to know if a true relationship exists and whether the symptom is actually indicative of, or associated with, the disorder.

Indeed, base rate information is often lacking, and the skewed sample of individuals most clinicians see—those with problems in adjustment—easily lead to false assumptions about the clinical significance of behaviors or "signs" of disorder. Such behaviors or signs may seem to be nearly exclusive to those with disorder when in truth, if one knew the base rates among normal individuals, it would be apparent that there is substantial overlap across groups. This lack of base rate information, or lack of awareness about the base rate problem, may often lead to the formation of illusory correlations.

We can use an actual example to illustrate this point. A supervisor was observed pointing to a group of patients in a mental hospital who were assembled at the cafeteria one-half hour before lunch time. The supervisor used this bit of behavior to point out to a group of psychiatric residents the "oral acquisitive" nature of schizophrenics, a trait some psychiatrists believe is a central element in the "dynamics" of schizophrenia. But we may ask whether this behavior really signifies anything about the patients other than a very common propensity of human beings. What percentage of people in general, not mental, hospitals eagerly await mealtime as a high spot of a day, a break in the monotony of hospital life, one of few satisfactions available? It may well be that it is a high percentage, possibly an overwhelming majority.

Unfortunately, we do not have a count or percentage figure available on this issue so we do not really *know*. Thus we do not have a base rate. In the absence of a base rate, statements such as the supervisor's can be made and their invalidity is apparent only in such obvious examples as the one given.

Are there any among us who have never been guilty of poor judgment (which often includes distortions or misperceptions of reality or inability to reason well under stress, etc.) or of impulsive behavior (translated—inability to control one's behavior) based on a strong desire coupled with an *unwillingness* to exercise restraint in the given matter? Of course there are few, if any. If these behaviors are true of most of us, how often are they true, under what circumstances, for what populations, and so on, and so on and on. No one knows, i.e., there are no known base rates. Without base rates we have no way of knowing what the behavior signifies, if it signifies anything, and certainly we cannot know whether it signifies mental illness, or even less, a specific mental illness. What would *your* mental status appear to be if a psychiatrist interviewed you and presented a collection of your poor judgments, impulsive acts, interpersonal relationships that do not measure up to the psychiatrist's ideal, unreasonable anger outbursts and so on?

Lack of knowledge of base rates or the normality or abnormality of many behaviors in the population at large frequently leads to absurdities in clinical assessments. In our role as consultants to lawyers seeking to nullify opposing clinical evidence we have had occasion to review a large number of such assessments. We have rarely encountered one which did not base conclusions at least in part on behavior which is not demonstrably abnormal in terms of any known rate of occurrence in the general population or which would not appear to be within the normal range given a particular situational set of stimuli. For example, some reports point to an individual's emotional reaction upon being involuntarily placed in a hospital as supporting a diagnosis of severe psychopathology. In one case a highly successful man interrupted a business trip to rush home in response to a family ruse that his wife was very ill. Upon arrival he was greeted by his family and obviously healthy wife and several deputy sheriffs who, upon his refusal to accompany them to the hospital, placed him in restraints and delivered him to the hospital. The psychiatric report states, as an illustration of psychopathology, "Upon admission, party was hostile and belligerent." Who would not be hostile and belligerent under those circumstances? Another example of violation of what one would think to be a fairly high base rate phenomenon is found in cases involving so-called "post-traumatic stress disorder." Nearly all psychiatric reports in such matters we have seen contain an assertion that plaintiff has difficulty sleeping. It is appropriate to ask what percentage of the normal population has difficulty sleeping when involved in an important and tension provoking project such as an attempt to obtain a large sum of money for injuries. This is similar to the well-known phenomenon sometimes called "pre-game tension."

Base rates are thus essential for determining whether true associations exist between "symptoms" and disorders. Additionally, in the absence of base rate information about the frequency of disorders, the clinician is almost never able to determine whether a symptom or sign that does show a true association with a disorder has diagnostic or predictive utility. Even valid signs can lead to predominantly erroneous identification of a disorder.

Let us return to the imaginary disorder of psychophobia. Suppose that frequent pacing is a valid diagnostic sign of the disorder, and that 90% of psychophobics have the symptom. Further, suppose only 10% of normals pace frequently. It might appear that this sign is a fairly reliable indicator of the disorder. However, one cannot tell unless one knows the base rates for psychophobia.

Suppose the base rate for psychophobia is one per 100 individuals. If one takes a representative sample of 100 individuals, one person will have the disorder and he is likely to have the diagnostic sign. However, among our 99 normals, about 10% of them, or 10 individuals, will have the sign. Thus, if this sign is used to identify the disorder, in 10 out of 11 cases the identification will be incorrect, or a false-positive error will be made. Had the base rates for the disorder been different, the result would have been different. If the base rate for the disorder was higher, less frequent errors would result, but if the base rate was lower, more frequent errors would result.

Arkes (1981) illustrates this point using multiple personality, which he assumes for his example occurs in about one per 100,000 cases. Working from this figure, suppose one depends on a diagnostic sign always seen with multiple personality, but which occurs in only one of 100 normals. Across 100,000 cases, the one case of multiple personality may be detected, but 1 per 100 normals, or a total of 1,000 individuals, will be falsely identified as having multiple personality. Thus, when a positive identification of the disorder is made based on the sign, the identification will be wrong about 1,000 times for every time it is correct.

Thus, the diagnostic utility of a sign used for identifying a disorder is not a fixed matter, but varies depending on the base rate for the disorder. The less frequent the disorder, the more accurate the sign must be if it is to produce more correct than false identifications of a disorder. With infrequent disorders, it is generally the case that unless the sign is highly accurate (e.g., right 99 out of 100 times), identifications of a disorder based on the sign will be more often wrong than right.

Many of the conditions with which clinicians deal are infrequent, and thus it is not uncommon for the use of diagnostic signs to actually result in many more false identifications of a disorder than correct identifications. For example, the DSM-IV indicates that usual prevalence estimates for "schizophrenia" are between 0.5% and 1.0%. The Manual states that prevalence of Delusional Disorder (formerly Paranoid Disorder) is estimated at 0.3%.

Many experts are unlikely to be aware that the value of diagnostic signs varies with the base rates. Even should clinicians be aware of the issue, the base rates for many supposed psychiatric disorders are not established. *Whether the expert lacks awareness of the base rate problem or the base rates are unavailable, the result is the same. The clinician generally will not know whether the signs or symptoms he used to identify the disorder are actually useful,* or whether they result in more, or even many more, incorrect than correct identifications of the disorder— *he will not know the true value of the data upon which he relied.* Consequently, the lawyer may wish to go through the "supportive" data on which the clinician based his opinion piece-by-piece, establishing that in each instance, for lack of the needed base rate data (or awareness of the problem), the clinician does not really know if use of the "supportive" evidence results in erroneous identifications more often than correct identifications.

Psychologists and psychiatrists, if they have any awareness of the base rate problem, may agree that the use of certain signs or symptoms can lead to frequent false-positive identifications, but that it is critical not to miss disorders that are present. This may be reasonable from a clinical standpoint, but within the forensic setting it would hardly seem to justify the use of a sign that results in frequent errors, or a sign that decreases accuracy relative to the level one would achieve by discarding the sign entirely.

There are two sides to this base rate coin. First, clinicians may believe symptoms or signs are relatively exclusive to persons with a given disorder, when in fact the frequency may be high among those without the disorder, or among people in general. The likely result is over-pathologizing, that is, misinterpreting thinking or behavior that is actually normal as abnormal. This is a variation of the *Barnum effect,* in which things that are common to people in general are taken as valuable, descriptive statements or identifying features of individuals with the disorder. Rather, the statements are "correct" because they apply to almost everyone, not only to those with a specific disorder. Meehl (1973) describes the problem as such:

> The second kind of fact about the person is not true of him by virtue of his being a "patient," but is true of him simply because he is a human being—namely, he has conflicts and frustrations; there are areas of life in which he is less than optimally satisfied, aspects of reality he tends to distort, and performance domains in which he is less than maximally effective....If you examine the contents of a mental patient's mind, he will, by and large, have pretty much the same things on his mind as the rest of us do. If asked whether there is something that bothers him a lot, he will not emphasize his dissatisfaction with the weather. The seductive fallacy consists in *assuming,* in the absence of a respectable showing of causal connection, that this first set of facts, i.e., the medical, psychological, or social aberrations that define him as a patient, *flows from* the second set, i.e., his conflicts, failures, frustrations, dissatisfactions, and other facts which characterize him as a fallible human being subject like the rest of us to the human condition. (p. 246)

Adinolfi (1971) describes criticism of clinicians for their failure to understand the nature of their impressions and for their reliance on "Barnum" statements in their conceptualizations of clinical cases. He points out the difficulty this creates in situations where differential accuracy is called for in the clinical situations where base rate statements are meaningless because of the ubiquity of the stated characteristic. In other words, clinicians frequently seize upon data which would be found to be widely distributed in the normal population and use it as a basis for "establishing" psychopathology in the individual case. Mendelsohn et al. (1978) point out the wide variation in reported rates of psychiatric disorders, with estimates for certain "disorders" exceeding 50%. Can behavioral "symptoms" found in over 50% of the population be considered abnormal or pathological?

Various studies demonstrate underutilization of base rate information. For example, Kahneman and Tversky (1973) presented almost completely worthless, or ambiguous personality descriptions, and then asked experimental subjects to guess, from between two choices, the occupation of the described individuals. In addition, Kahneman and Tversky varied the base rates provided to subjects in the study. For example, in one condition, subjects were told that 70% of the described individuals were engineers and 30% were lawyers. Thus, if subjects played the base rates, they could have achieved a 70% level of accuracy. Nevertheless, the base rates were virtually ignored and these essentially useless descriptions were relied upon in formulating guesses. Many additional demonstrations of disregard for base rates are reported in this paper by Kahneman and Tversky, and by other authors as well (Arkes et al., 1986; Nisbett et al., 1976; Tversky and Kahneman, 1978). In fact, a number of researchers describe the extreme steps that must be taken before they can get individuals to use base rate information. For example, Kahneman and Tversky report that the only approach that proved satisfactory was to give individuals nothing but the base rate information, so that in essence they really had nothing else on which to rely.

The above studies on underutilization of base rates mainly involved college students, but the same failures have been described or demonstrated with clinicians. As early as 1955, Meehl and Rosen wrote an extensive article describing these destructive practices among clinicians and suggesting corrective procedures (apparently with little effect). Others have discussed the problem as well. Garfield (1978) describes the need to obtain and consider base rate information when conducting research on clinical diagnosis. Carroll (1977) describes research showing that experts tend to rely on case specific information, or the information obtained in a specific case, and to disregard base rate information that applies to that case. He points out that this occurs even when base rate information is available and has been demonstrated to produce greater accuracy.

Exner (1986), in the second edition of his classic work on the Rorschach, provides a startling demonstration of the base rate problem. He describes six "Critical Special Scores" which identify difficulty in cognitive processing, which appears to be his terminology for what in other places is referred to as cognitive dysfunction or "thought disorder." However, Exner notes that in his study of 449 nonpatients (i.e., "normals"), 75% of these normals gave at least one of these responses and that the mean number of such responses per normal subject was closer to two than one.

Of those "normals" who gave any critical responses, 23% gave deviant verbalizations (DV), 58% gave incongruous combinations (INCOM),

46% gave deviant responses (DR), 16% gave fabulized combinations (FABCOM), 10% gave autistic logic responses (ALOG), and only three people in the nonpatient sample gave contamination responses (CONTAM). Exner hypothesizes that these represent a crude continuum of cognitive dysfunction, with DV representing the least dysfunction and CONTAM the most.

DV involves distorted language use or idiosyncratic modes of expression. INCOM, according to Exner, indicates a form of discrimination failure and a kind of concrete reasoning. DR indicates a peculiarity in verbiage that may be the product of poor judgment or poor control over ideational impulses. Exner states that most DRs are "detachments from the task and often consist of circumstantial-like ramblings." He says DRs are more serious forms of dysfunction than DVs or INCOMs. FAB-COMs involve an irrational synthesizing action and reflect the very loose associations that often occur in thinking which is inconsistent, disorganized, and primitive. Exner indicates that these are most common in records of "schizophrenics" and that even one instance of DR or FABCOM should "be weighed very carefully." We would call the reader's attention to the fact, however, that DRs appear in the records of about one-third of the "normals" and FABCOMs in the records of 12% of the "normals." In a group of "schizophrenics" the percentages for these critical responses was considerably higher, except for DR, where 49% of the "schizophrenics" gave such responses in contrast to the one-third of the normals.

Exner notes that three and perhaps even four of the less serious forms of slippage are not uncommon among nonpatient adults. Where there are more than four, presumably five or more, some thinking disorder is present, according to Exner.

The main point to be noted here is that behaviors commonly classified as indicating cognitive dysfunction or thought disorder occur with considerable frequency among normal adults. If these occur almost twice in the 17-27 responses typical for the Exner Rorschach for normals, how often can they be expected to occur in one or two hours of psychiatric interviewing, i.e., what is the base rate? How many instances are needed before one can conclude there is thought disorder that is diagnostic? In fact, are these behaviors abnormal or diagnostic at all, if they are found to this degree in such a large percentage of individuals?

If base rate data are not used properly, or if such data are unavailable, a clinician cannot determine the value of diagnostic signs or indicators. In fact, the clinician may rely on signs that *decrease* the accuracy with which a particular disorder is identified. Further, and along related lines, behaviors that are common within the general population may be viewed as specific to, or indicative of, psychopathology.

Ruback and Hopper (1986) examined whether interview evaluations of potential parolees predicted behavioral infractions in prison and successful completion of parole. They found that judgments or evaluations made prior to interviews were more accurate than judgments made subsequent to interviews. That is, interview data not only failed to increase judgmental accuracy, but actually lowered it. As the authors note, the results suggest that interview impressions do not predict future behavior. Although Ruback and Hopper also found that interview impressions did not predict behavior upon parole, they note that a longer follow-up period was necessary and thus consider their results non-definitive. In summary, this study not only demonstrates low predictive accuracy, but it also demonstrates, as have other studies, that more can be less—that additional data can lower predictive accuracy. This latter result seemingly occurs when clinicians' judgments are swayed by invalid variables, or what might be labeled illusory correlations.

Schuldberg et al. (1988) found that traits that had been linked with psychopathology, such as a tendency to believe unusual or "magical" ideas, were also associated with creativity among a presumably normal population. Bernstein and Putnam (1986) state, "The overall incidence of transient feelings of depersonalization in normal subjects ranges from 8.5 to 70% depending on the definitions, methodology, and age of the sample population." (p. 727) According to the DSM-III-R (p. 397), depersonalization is "an alteration in the perception or experience of the self so that the feeling of one's own reality is temporarily lost. This is manifested in a sense of self-estrangement or unreality, which may include the feeling that one's extremities have changed in size, or a sense of seeming to perceive oneself from a distance (usually from above)." The lawyer should be aware that clinicians may attach a great deal of significance to a symptom of this type, and thus its base rate among those who do not suffer from psychiatric disorders is of significance.

Gouvier et al. (1988) conducted a study highly relevant to the topic of base rates. They note that various types of intellectual and psychological dysfunction have been reported as common consequences of head injury, but that such reports are ambiguous in the absence of base rate information on the frequency of these "symptoms" in the general population. Gouvier et al. compared self-reports and relatives' reports of various problems or symptoms among a group of college undergraduates to the problems or symptoms reported in prior studies of patients with mild to moderate head injuries. In comparing the self-reports of these presumably normal college students and those of the head-injured subjects, no significant differences in frequency were obtained on items addressing memory problems, problems becoming interested in things, loss of temper, irritability, fatigue, or impatience. The only significant differences were obtained on items addressing concentration, difficulties with reading, and restlessness. In comparing relatives' reports on these college students versus the head-injured, no significant differences were obtained on items assessing loss of temper, visual problems, irritability, restlessness, fatigue, and impatience. In fact, only one significant difference was obtained, this on an item addressing difficulty remembering things. Of further interest, although the differences did not achieve statistical significance, relatives' reports for the college students versus the head-injured indicated higher frequencies among the former for a number of "symptoms." For example, for the item, "often impatient," relatives' reports for the college students showed a 49% endorsement rate as opposed to a 35% endorsement rate for the relatives of the head-injured subjects. (These and other percentages reported below are rounded off to the nearest whole number.) The item, "often irritable," was endorsed at a 43% rate for the college students versus a 31% rate for the head-injured.

This sheer frequency with which a number of these "symptoms" were reported for presumably normal college students is also impressive. According to the relatives' reports, as noted above, frequencies for "often impatient" and "often irritable" were 49% and 43%, respectively; endorsement rates for other items included: "often loses temper"—38%, "often restless"—33%, and "tires easily"—35%. On self-reports, about one-third of the college students endorsed the items, "difficulty becoming interested" and "often loses temper." Almost 28% indicated that they tire easily and 42% indicated that they are often impatient. Clearly, then, such complaints were not at all infrequent among these college students, and certainly were not exclusive to head-injured individuals. Stated differently, these data suggest that the base rates for a number of these complaints were considerable among both the head-injured and non-head-injured, and of similar frequency across the two groups. Note also that the frequencies reported above indicate endorsement rates for single items, and obviously many of the students endorsed a number of these items. In cases in which we have consulted, clinicians have often interpreted reports of even one or a few of these types of "symptoms" as strong evidence that a head injury "caused" brain damage and exerted negative effects on the individuals' functioning. Gouvier et al. note that a determination of base rates for other groups of non-injured individuals awaits study and that further research is also needed to determine the base rates or frequency of complaints associated with brain dysfunction.

As this discussion suggests, there are many instances in which the lawyer can profitably raise questions about base rates. In our practice as consultants, we have noticed that it is the rare case in which experts show adequate awareness of this problem. Thus, it is possible to effectively challenge much of the "supportive" data upon which the expert relies as being of doubtful value, if not likely useless and misleading.

BAD JUDGMENT HABITS/BIASES

In this section we will discuss a number of problematic judgment practices, and/or biases, that pervade the collection and interpretation of clinical data and that lead to frequent judgment error.

Hindsight Bias

People who are asked to judge the predictability of an event after it has occurred, or in hindsight, often believe the event could easily have been predicted. However, when one asks other individuals to try to actually predict these outcomes, or to do so in foresight, they often find the prediction considerably more difficult than it was thought to be in hindsight. Stated differently, once individuals know the outcome of an event, they often think the outcome could have been predicted much more easily than is objectively the case. This is known as the hindsight bias, and it has been demonstrated across a range of studies with experimental subjects (e.g., Arkes et al., 1981; Fischhoff, 1975, 1980; Dawson et al., 1986; Mitchell & Kalb, 1981; Leary, 1982).

To explain the hindsight bias in more common terms, the Monday morning quarterback often thinks the Sunday quarterback was mentally feeble and should have known beforehand that this or the other play would never work. However, the Sunday quarterback might be glad to point out that, although this may have appeared obvious after the play failed, it seemed like a good idea at the time and likely to succeed. Alternatively, one of the authors has frequently been impressed by the operation of the hindsight bias in individuals' conversations about lottery numbers. Time and again, *after* numbers have been drawn, individuals will describe mental anguish because they guessed *that* number would come up but did not bother to bet on it. Obviously, if lottery numbers were that easy to guess ahead of time, these players would be considerably richer. That they are not richer shows that, once one knows the outcome, the numbers seem to be easier to predict than they actually are.

The tendency to believe that things are more predictable than is actually the case leads to certain characteristic judgment errors. In discussing some of these errors, it is important to keep in mind that individuals do not seem to recognize the operation of the hindsight bias—that is, they do not recognize how the knowledge of the outcome affects their judgments. In the case of clinicians, one result can be that almost any new piece of information about the actions or behavior of an individual they have assessed will seem expectable or consistent with what they already "know" about the individual. If a clinician is told that an individual, whom he has diagnosed as highly anxious, has handled some nerve-racking experience without difficulty, he is nevertheless likely to view this as explainable or consistent with his impressions. The clinician might state something to the effect that this particular situation was one "we would expect the individual to be able to handle" for one reason or another, this reason probably relating to something like the individual's unique personality features. If, instead, this individual became angered by the situation, or saddened, or whatever, all these things might well seem predictable or "consistent" with the individual's personality, as well. It is easy to see, then, how false impressions can become frozen when virtually *any* new data can quickly be interpreted as predictable or consistent with the impressions.

Due to hindsight bias, clinicians' knowledge about the outcome of prior evaluations exerts an unknown effect on the impressions they form. For example, in a study by Arkes et al. (1981), an identical medical case history was presented to four different groups of physicians. Four possible diagnoses were listed, and the physicians were asked to indicate what likelihood or probability they would have assigned to each of the four had they been making the initial diagnosis. Each of the four groups, however, were told something different about the actual diagnosis. For example, one group was told that this was actually a case of condition X, and another that this was a case of condition Y, etc. What they were told had a significant impact on their beliefs about the diagnoses or probabilities they would have initially assigned. For example, those told that this was a case of condition X tended to believe, had they been making the original diagnosis, that this is the diagnosis they most likely would have made. Those told it was condition Y believed this was the initial diagnosis they most likely would have made, and so on. These same effects were replicated in a separate study with neuropsychologists by Arkes et al. (1988). Arkes et al. provide a demonstration of the hindsight bias in the field of neuropsychology. They found that neuropsychologists, or clinical psychologists engaged in the practice of neuropsychology, exhibited hindsight bias when appraising case materials. Clinicians were given identical case materials, except for a statement at the beginning of the case noting that different diagnoses had been established (either brain damage secondary to alcohol abuse, Alzheimer's disease, or alcohol withdrawal). They were then asked to indicate the probability they would have assigned to each of the diagnoses, had they been performing the initial case appraisal. The practitioners tended to assign the highest probability to whatever diagnosis was stated at the beginning of the case. Arkes et al. also found that instructing clinicians, in advance of judgments, to generate possible sources of support for all three of the diagnostic possibilities effectively countered the hindsight bias.

Thus, knowledge of a prior outcome can have a significant effect on individuals' appraisals of cases, apparently without their being aware that this effect occurs. As Arkes et al. (1981) indicate, knowledge of initial opinions may have a far greater impact, or biasing effect, than is recognized. Apparently, then, a psychologist or psychiatrist who has access to prior evaluations or opinions really does not know what impact this prior information has on the opinions he forms. This opens up some potentially useful lines of questioning (see Volume III, Chapter 8).

The hindsight bias may also partly explain the limited benefits of experience on judgment accuracy. One way in which experience can be helpful is by showing us what we are doing right and should continue doing, and what we are doing wrong and should alter. However, if one can find an explanation for almost any outcome, or if it seems as if the outcome could have easily been predicted on the basis of what one knows, then error and the need for correction may be overlooked. Thus, the clinician who makes an initial diagnosis of depression but obtains subsequent data showing adequate functioning, rather than concluding that the initial diagnosis may have been wrong, concludes that the individual has recovered or that this good functioning is an expression of the personality strengths uncovered in the evaluation. Einhorn (1986) states the matter succinctly: "Given the fluency of causal reasoning, it is not difficult to construct reasons for why discrepancies in prediction occur. Indeed, in hindsight, it seems as if the outcomes could not have been otherwise." (p. 388)

Confirmatory Bias

Confirmatory bias is the tendency to maintain beliefs, even in the face of counterevidence. Put differently, people tend to get stuck on an idea or belief, and even when they should change their minds on the basis of subsequent information, they often do not. Rather, they pay particular attention to the evidence that supports their beliefs, they misinterpret ambiguous or even nonsupportive evidence as supportive of their beliefs, and/or they tend to disregard or dismiss counterevidence. As a result, even when they are wrong, they believe they are right, and even when they are confronted with what should be convincing counterevidence, they still continue to believe they are right. When patients do this it may be called a delusion.

Confirmatory bias is pervasive and has been demonstrated across a wide range of studies that involve both laypersons and professionals, mental health workers included. Even a partial listing of some of the studies and commentary on confirmatory bias forms an impressive compilation (e.g., Abramowitz et al., 1975; Adams, 1984; Anderson, 1983; Bruner and Potter, 1964; Chapman and Chapman, 1967, 1969; Cohen,

1979a; Giller and Strauss, 1984; Goodstein and Brazis, 1970; Greenwald et al., 1986; Hamilton, 1976; Luchins, 1942; Mahoney, 1977; Mischel et al., 1976; Mynart et al., 1977; Nisbett and Ross, 1980; Polanyi, 1963; Pratkanis, 1984; Revusky, 1977; Ross et al., 1975; Ross et al., 1981; Snyder & Uranowitz, 1978; Swann & Read, 1981; Tversky, 1977; Wason, 1960; Wason and Johnson-Laird, 1972; Wyatt and Campbell, 1951). Again, the above list of over 25 references is only a partial one.

We cannot review all of the studies in detail, and so will focus on five aspects of confirmatory bias: (1) "favoritism" towards one's initial hypotheses, (2) double standards of evidence, (3) premature closure, or the tendency to form initial hypotheses quickly and on the basis of very limited information, (4) the effects of confirmatory bias on data collection, and (5) manifestation (and magnification) within the forensic arena.

1. Favoring initial hypotheses. A number of investigators provide overviews of research showing that initial beliefs are often maintained, even in the face of counterevidence. Greenwald et al. (1986) discuss a number of studies documenting confirmatory bias and its potentially negative effects on judgment accuracy. They describe the work of Wyatt and Campbell (1951) and of Bruner and Potter (1964). These studies with laypersons serve to illustrate phenomena also demonstrated with professionals—how preliminary hypotheses that are founded on the basis of inadequate data hinder the interpretation of subsequent, and potentially more informative, data. In the work by Bruner and Potter, one group of subjects was exposed to slightly blurred slides; they were able to identify the pictured objects with a relatively high degree of accuracy. Another group of subjects was shown the same slides, but the initial projections were quite blurry. The focus was then sharpened until it reached a level of clarity equal to that of the slides shown to the first group of subjects. The individuals in the second group made a significantly greater number of errors than those in the first group, apparently because they formed initial conclusions about the nature of the pictured objects while the slides were quite fuzzy and did not necessarily modify these conclusions as focus was sharpened. This study demonstrated, then, how the formation of initial conclusions can interfere with the subsequent analysis of information.

Greenwald et al. (1986) state: "The Wyatt-Campbell and Bruner-Potter findings provide striking illustrations of the pervasive phenomenon of confirmation bias—the tendency for judgments based on new data to be overly consistent with preliminary hypotheses....Confirmation bias is a very general phenomenon: One's preliminary hypotheses have a decided advantage in the judgment process." (p. 216) We might add here a seemingly obvious point—that conclusions formed early and based on inadequate data have a good chance of being wrong (see the discussion of premature closure below), and thus this "decided advantage" of preliminary hypotheses is likely to have pernicious effects.

Greenwald et al. describe the variety of circumstances in which confirmatory bias has been uncovered and its negative effects demonstrated. For example, confirmatory bias has been shown in the impressions individuals form about others. Among the negative effects of confirmatory bias, the following are described:

> ...delayed discovery of simple problem solutions (Luchins, 1942; Mynart, Doherty, & Tweney, 1977; Wason, 1960)...perseverance of belief in discredited hypotheses (Anderson, 1983; Nisbett & Ross, 1980; Ross, Lepper, & Hubbard, 1975); and selective retrieval of information that confirms one's hypotheses (Snyder & Uranowitz, 1978), one's opinions (Pratkanis, 1984; Ross, McFarland, & Fletcher, 1981), or one's self-concept (Mischel, Ebbesen, & Zeiss, 1976; Swann & Read, 1981). (p. 216)

The last two points regarding self-opinions and self-concept merit attention. Work on this topic indicates that the same problems and bad habits that impede accurate judgment of others often are similarly manifest in judgments about ourselves. Thus, for example, one's own impressions about one's judgment accuracy are certainly open to judgment error. Further, as regards the difficulties of benefiting from experience, feedback that is received about one's judgments can be distorted by confirmation bias such that counterevidence is instead viewed as supporting one's initial impressions or beliefs. Thus, feedback may seem to support one's beliefs in one's judgment ability or accuracy when, objectively, it may provide little or no actual support.

Other writers discuss similar concerns. Giller and Strauss (1984) state: "The medical model based on the scientific method involves generating a hypothesis and then collecting data to decide whether the hypothesis is true or false....This hypothesis testing process, however, is often short-circuited in clinical practice. Hypotheses are frequently stated as facts rather than statements that need to be tested." Margulies and Havens (1981), discussing different approaches to the initial interview with patients, state, "How do we escape the circularity of our preconscious theories directing our perceptions, which then prove our theories?"

Fitzgibbons and Shearn (1972) base their study on the belief that schizophrenia is a function not only of the person being labelled schizophrenic but also of the mental health professional responsible for the labelling. They delineate differences based on differences in training, professional orientation and place of employment as the factors given emphasis in diagnosing schizophrenia. They state:

> Surely it makes some sense, for example, that the nature of one's training and professional identification might influence his ideas about the etiology of schizophrenia. These differences in viewpoint associated with professional

training seem to us, however, to amount to a bias which tends to hinder rather than facilitate the advancement of knowledge about schizophrenia. Each of the mental health professions in its own way seems to have been *locked into a system of beliefs that is relatively impervious to new information whether in the form of reports in the literature or even personal experience with schizophrenic patients.* (italics ours)

Bootzin and Ruggill (1988) note that research on judgment shows that clinicians' decision-making processes are vulnerable to numerous biases. They indicate that therapists' conceptualizations may be influenced to a greater degree by expectations and judgment practices than by information about the client. Arnoult and Anderson (1988) state that "recent research provides evidence that biased thinking is prevalent among both novices and experienced practitioners." (p. 209) They note that numerous factors may bias clinicians' judgment, including the treatment setting, demographic characteristics of the client (e.g., his race, gender, age, occupation, education, economic status, and marital status), and the clinician's personal experiences. They note that biases resting within the therapist may be quite difficult to recognize. They further note that if errors stemming from biases were corrected easily by exposure to cases, there would not be much cause for concern. They state, however, that "a large body of work from a variety of areas of psychology demonstrates that such expectation-based errors are extremely difficult to correct." (p. 220) The authors go on to present a number of suggestions for reducing bias in judgment, although they note that their suggestions have not been scientifically evaluated in clinical settings.

2. Double standards of evidence. This work on confirmatory bias suggests that clinicians often use different, or double, standards of evidence when assessing information—they are substantially more lenient with, or accepting of, information that supports their beliefs, and stricter or less accepting of information that runs counter to their beliefs. These tendencies may well apply not only to their use of clinical data, but also to their interpretation of research that supports their practices, beliefs, and opinions, as opposed to research that is nonsupportive or conflicting. Meehl (1973) describes these practices as follows:

I have no objection if professionals choose to be extremely rigorous about their standards of evidence, but they should recognize that if they adopt that policy, many of the assertions made in a case conference ought not to be uttered because they cannot meet such a tough standard. Neither do I have any objection to freewheeling speculation....You can play it tight, or you can play it loose. What I find objectionable in staff conferences is a tendency to shift the criterion of tightness so that the evidence offered is upgraded or downgraded in the service of polemical interests. Example: A psychologist tells me that he is perfectly confident that psychotherapy benefits psychotic depressions (a question open on available data), his reason being that his personal experience shows this. But this same psychologist tells me that he has never seen a single patient helped by shock therapy. (Such a statement, that he has never seen a *single patient* helped by shock therapy, can only be attributed to some sort of perceptual or memory defect on his part.) When challenged with the published evidence indicating that shock is a near specific for classical depression, he says that those experiments are not perfect, and further adds, "You can prove anything by experiments." (Believe it or not, these are quotations!) I confess I am at a loss to know how I can profitably pursue a conversation conducted on these ground rules. He is willing (1) to rely upon *his* casual impressions that psychotherapy helps patients, (2) to deny *my* casual impression that shock treatment helps patients, but (3) to reject the controlled research on the subject of electroshock—which meets considerably tighter standards evidentially than *either* his clinical impressions or mine—on the grounds that it is not perfectly trustworthy. It is not intellectually honest or, I would argue, clinically responsible thus to vary your tightness-looseness parameter when evaluating conflicting evidence on the same issue. (pp. 265-266)

Adams (1984) criticizes clinical psychologists' disregard of scientific evidence that disconfirms their theoretical orientation. He states, "A rather strange reaction to logical or scientific evidence which tends to disconfirm the particular theoretical position, is that the scientific method is not adequate to evaluate their theory." Meehl and Adams are not merely speculating on these matters. Many proponents of projective personality instruments attempt to explain away negative evidence by claiming that the measures are ill-suited to scientific testing, or at least testing of the type that was conducted (see Chapter 13). Additionally, various studies document the double standards of evidence among professionals that Meehl and Adams describe (e.g., Abramowitz et al., 1975; Cohen, 1979a; Goodstein and Brazis, 1970; Mahoney, 1977).

When experts engage in these practices on the witness stand, the lawyer can turn it to his advantage. For example, if the expert is confronted with the research on confirmatory bias or on other problematical judgment practices, he may counter by asserting that the research in these areas is flawed for one or another reason. To begin with, the expert has offered a Barnum statement, for the perfect piece of research has yet to be conducted in psychology, or in physics for that matter, and there is no single study that does not have some limitation or restrictions on generalization. However, the lawyer should not fear this line of defense, for it leaves the expert highly vulnerable in two ways. One approach is to establish that while each study may have some flaws and limits, the existence of several studies, as is the case with confirmatory bias, base rates and illusory correlation, for example (and most of the other points made in this book), strongly suggest that there is an issue which is in serious doubt. The expert will not be able to provide *better* research counterindicative of these findings. This leads to the second approach. If the expert takes the above tack it may be useful to draw him out, have him explain why one cannot base conclusions on these studies. Let him point out, if he can, the deficiencies—such as small numbers, uncontrolled variables, failure to report certain aspects of the study, biasing of the outcome, local conditions and so on. Let him explain that no firm conclusions can be drawn from these studies. If he does this, you will then be able to show how compromised a position he is in because he has committed himself to the argument that one should not base conclusions upon infirmly established principles or findings. He can be asked (if he has not already given them) to give the knowledge bases on which *he* has relied. Then he can be asked if his bases (research, theory, literature, experience) have been demonstrated to be free of the flaws he has described which would preclude drawing any of the conclusions he has drawn. His answer (unless he is an arrant liar or totally ignorant of the literature in his field) must be in the negative. He can be asked if he does not apply a double standard of evidence—accepting flawed evidence for what he believes but rejecting at least equally good evidence which runs contrary to what he believes. Of course, strategy may indicate that this point should be made in argument rather than in cross-examination. If the groundwork has been carefully laid, a jury will grasp the point.

We should add that, overall, much of the research on clinical judgment, from the standpoint of scientific method, is considerably superior to most of the knowledge bases from which clinical inferences are drawn. Further, some of the principles of proper judgment are based on logical, self-evident principles, in essence as ironclad as $1 + 1 = 2$. For example, one does not need experimental proof for the logical principles underlying analysis of co-variation and proper utilization of base rates.

3. Premature closure. "Premature closure" refers to the tendency to jump to conclusions. Premature closure increases the chances of starting off on the wrong track, and thus is likely to make an already serious problem—confirmatory bias—substantially worse. Resistance to correction is obviously the opposite of what is needed when correction is what is needed. The term, in fact, connotes that once these initial impressions are formed, they tend to be maintained—one's mind becomes "closed" to new evidence.

Again, contrary to psychologists' and psychiatrists' claims about using all or most of the data in formulating conclusions, research suggests that quite the opposite is true. In fact, the contrast between these claims and a number of research findings is not a matter of subtle shades but almost the difference between day and night. In an earlier study, Dailey (1952) found that diagnosticians often form impressions early in the information-gathering process and that these impressions often remain unaltered when subsequent data are collected. Meehl (1960) reports on a study which shows that psychologists often reach conclusions very early in their contact with patients and that these conclusions may change minimally over time, even after extensive psychotherapy contact. The level of contact reported on is far greater than that which is typical in forensic evaluations.

Thorne (1972) states:

> Throughout the helping professions it is unfortunately true that diagnoses are often made and therapy prescribed on the basis of inadequate case study. That is, inadequate even in the light of our limited knowledge. The major reason for this premature closure is the unwarranted belief that an arbitrary stereotyped formulation implies dynamic understanding. Such formulations served as ritualistic guardians of ignorance for those who cannot stand the anxiety engendered by the ambiguity inherent in our present ignorance. (p. 12)

Robins and Helzer (1986) observe that when diagnosticians use a free form investigative technique, they usually choose a diagnosis within the first few minutes and then spend the remainder of the time trying to confirm it. They also note that the literature provides evidence that clinicians omit collecting data even on topics they themselves believe to be essential in making a diagnosis. They compare the free form interview with the use of a checklist and cite literature to the effect that much more relevant data, that is, a much greater amount of relevant data, is obtained when a checklist is used than when a free form narrative type of interview is used. Yager (1977) notes that psychiatrists frequently form diagnostic impressions of patients within the first *two or three minutes* of contact, and sometimes in as little as *30 seconds*. One could ask at what point in data collection the first diagnostic impression was formed to determine if premature closure took place. If very early it might be premature. If late, it might indicate that a substantial amount of data was not sufficient to create even a diagnostic impression.

4. The effects of confirmatory bias on data collection. Confirmatory bias can also affect data gathering such that information supporting one's hypothesis is more likely, or much more likely, to be collected than information disconfirming one's hypothesis, even if the latter is equally (or more) plentiful and available. Considering that confirmatory bias can lead to disregard of the nonsupportive evidence of which one is aware, this problem is obviously confounded if nonsupportive data are less likely to be gathered in the first place. Supportive data have an improper advantage in the interpretive process to begin with, and thus anything that lessens the chances that nonsupportive data will be gathered at all can only make this problem worse.

How difficult is it to succeed in a supportive fact-finding mission, even if one is seeking support for an invalid belief? Not very hard at all. For one, human behavior is sufficiently variable, or inconsistent, that it is rarely difficult to find support for nearly any belief. For example, suppose the clinician forms an initial impression as regards an individual's passivity, or tendency to avoid action as a way of dealing with problems. The clinician might start firing away with questions that attempt to find support for this possibility, e.g., "Do you ever sit back and let others deal with things for you?" "Are there ever times when you feel you should be more assertive but can't get yourself to be so?" If answering these questions honestly, almost all of us would have to respond by saying yes. Virtually everyone is passive at times. The same holds for questions regarding many other matters of clinical interest, such as experiencing sad moods or being sensitive to criticism.

Further, the behavior and thinking of individuals deemed to be abnormal often shows considerable overlap with the behavior and thinking of those considered to be normal. Along the same lines, behavior and thinking that might be viewed as relatively exclusive to individuals with a specific type of disorder may also be seen across individuals who fit within other diagnostic categories. We provided an illustration of this point when discussing material from Exner's (1986) second edition, in which it was found that indices of thought disorder on the Rorschach are not at all exclusive to those diagnosed as schizophrenic. As that illustration showed, one who sought out evidence of thought disorder to support a diagnosis of schizophrenia would stand a reasonable chance of succeeding, whether the individual was "schizophrenic" or not.

Due to behavioral variability and overlap across different diagnostic groups and across abnormal and normal individuals, one is likely to find support for nearly any hypothesis, including an invalid one, and thus false beliefs will seem to have been supported. This provides another basis on which illusory correlations are formed. One starts with a rich foundation of clinical lore regarding such things as the behaviors, or symptoms, or diagnostic signs that are associated with different disorders or that are useful in formulating predictions. Whatever these beliefs, one usually should have little difficulty finding at least some supportive evidence, even if the beliefs contain only a small element of truth. These biases in data collection procedures and their effects on judgment accuracy are lucidly illustrated in a series of studies by Snyder (1981) with college students. In one of these studies, one group of subjects were told that an individual might be introverted. They tried to find support for this possibility by asking questions of the type, "Are you ever shy at parties?" Another group of subjects were told that this same individual might be extroverted. This group tried to find support for this possibility with questions of the type, "Have you ever been the life of the party?" Across the conditions, the individual answering the questions had been previously instructed by the experimenter to respond consistently. Nevertheless, those attempting to find support for introversion obtained it and concluded that this individual was introverted, and those seeking support for extroversion obtained it, as well, and concluded that this same individual was extroverted. Snyder describes the extreme difficulty he encountered in getting individuals to do anything other than seek confirmatory evidence.

As regards this problem of the search for confirming data, Wolpe (1970) states:

> Psychoanalytic theory which has dominated psychiatric thinking for half a century attributes the symptoms of "functional" psychiatric illness to hidden internal sources. The existence of these hidden processes has never been demonstrated. Nevertheless, the psychoanalytically oriented therapist assumes their presence in every case and then purports to derive a detailed image of them from the patient's verbalizations. This is not difficult to do and, rewarded by the approval of colleagues, soon becomes a confident habit.

And yet the problem does not stop here. Not only do clinicians show a bias towards seeking evidence that supports their hypotheses, they in fact may bias or affect the behaviors of the individuals they are examining such that they elicit, or in some sense artificially create, the very evidence they seek. This is sometimes referred to as "channeling effects," meaning that the one collecting the data inadvertently modifies or molds the behavior of the person he is examining such that this person's reactions conform with preconceived notions. To illustrate, suppose a therapist assumes a patient has latent, or hidden, underlying hostility. In an attempt to "examine" for this possibility, the therapist may frustrate the patient, perhaps by failing to answer what are actually reasonable questions. The therapist has only positive intentions, for one cannot work on this problem until one discovers whether it actually exists and gets it out in the open. In any case, the patient cannot stand it any more; after all, he is spending substantial dollars to obtain help that apparently is not forthcoming, and finally he makes some caustic remarks. The therapist assumes that this behavior proves that his assumption was correct, whereas quite possibly such behavior would have led many individuals to act likewise, regardless of whether or not they had a problem with "latent hostility."

As regards this problem of channeling effects, Cooper (1985) points out that our theories lead us to collaborate with patients in creating a new personal myth and life narrative more acceptable to both the analyst and patient. Cooper argues that theory will determine how the analyst shapes the patient's material. Gill and Brennan (1948) recognized such effects years earlier, stating:

> If the therapist's conceptions about psychodynamics—whether he holds them consciously or unconsciously, whether they are systematized or chaotic—influences behavior in the therapeutic situation, if his behavior influences the patient's production, it must be clear that the raw data in psychotherapeutic research are inevitably influenced by the therapist's views. If a therapist believes

dreams are important in helping a patient, he will show interest in the patient's dreams. Merely asking if the patient has any may result in including many more dreams in the raw data than are gathered by a therapist who is not especially interested in dreams. This is on the grossest level. The subtleties of showing interest in certain kinds of material, often not consciously detected either by the therapist or patient, are manifold. They may include a questioning glance, a shift of visual focus, a well-timed "aha," a scarcely perceptible nod, or even a clearing of the throat. The therapist's conception of what his interpersonal relation with the patient should be, will also seriously influence the kind of material he obtains. If one therapist believes he should be "friendly" and another that he should be "distant," the raw data obtained by each will obviously differ.

Another aspect of channeling effects is that our beliefs or impressions about others affect the way we act towards them, or the decisions a clinician makes on their behalf. These decisions, in turn, may influence how a person is treated or reacts, which can create misleading "support" for an incorrect hypotheses. For example, suppose the clinician thinks that someone he evaluates is not the kind of person that he could work with effectively. Thus, he does not offer services but may refer the person to someone else. How could this clinician possibly find out if this assumption was incorrect? There is no subsequent opportunity to review it, as the therapy is not provided and one cannot find out if the individual would have benefitted. Alternatively, he may take the case, but his pessimism inadvertently shows through and affects the patient negatively. Einhorn (1986) states:

> When decisions are based on predictions, the determination of forecast accuracy is problematic because outcomes are a function of predictions and actions (Einhorn & Hogarth, 1978). For example, if the president takes strong antirecession measures based on predictions of an economic slowdown, how is one to evaluate the accuracy of the forecast? Consider the outcome of no recession. This could result from an incorrect forecast and a useless action or from an accurate forecast and a highly effective action. Similarly, a recession could indicate an accurate forecast with an ineffective action or an inaccurate forecast with an action that causes the malady it is intended to prevent. Some actions are taken to counteract the prediction of undesirable events, but other actions cause the very outcomes that are predicted. For example:
>
> > People in a small town hear a rumor that the banks are about to fail. They think that if this forecast is accurate, they had better withdraw their money as soon as possible. Accordingly, they go to the banks to close their accounts (those skeptical of the forecast see many people withdrawing money and either take this as a sign that the rumor is true or foresee the consequences of waiting too long, thus joining the crowd in either case). By the end of the day the banks have failed, thereby confirming the rumor. (Einhorn & Hogarth, 1982, p. 24)
>
> Note that awareness of such self-fulfilling prophecies is often low and can lead to overconfidence in predictions that are of low or even zero accuracy (see Einhorn, 1980; Einhorn & Hogarth, 1978). (pp. 389-390)

In a satirical paper by Faust (1986a) that parodies common clinical practices intended to increase accuracy, often with the opposite effect, "Rule 5" describes problems created by channeling effects.

> Should one fail to find sufficient supportive evidence on an initial data sweep, follow-up procedures can be employed. One procedure is to alter data collection so as to obtain the needed supportive evidence. For example, if you believe a client is introverted, ask repeated questions about the possible occurrence of introverted behavior. You're likely to hit on at least a few of these, especially if you can develop a set of questions that almost anyone will answer in the desired direction....If this method fails, engage the client's cooperation. After all, clinicians usually have some control over behavior, and one can usually elicit hypothesis-confirming responses. For example, if you believe a client has underlying hostility, be subtly provocative to elicit angry behavior (this may occur quite naturally or even unconsciously with such withholding clients).
>
> Some patients are stubbornly oppositional and will not cooperate in ventures for obtaining hypothesis-confirming behavior. When this occurs, PATHOS [Author: Psychologist Against Tough-Hearted and Offensive Scientists] advises that the clinician postulate the presence of things not found and invent plausible reasons for their nonappearance. Viable candidates include the client's forgetting, repressing, or altering the information.
>
> Overall, the modus operandi needed to realize Rule 5 is to formulate hypotheses for which it is almost always possible to obtain supportive data and to utilize circular hypotheses-testing strategies so that you will, under no circumstances, be unable to prove your point. (pp. 595-596)

5. Confirmatory bias in the forensic arena. Confirmatory bias leads to the maintenance of false beliefs. The nature of the judgment error depends on the type of beliefs or conclusions one is likely to reach. Stated differently, what one expects to see often determines what one thinks they have seen and have found. Given the overwhelming propensity of psychologists and psychiatrists to search for and see abnormality, a false belief in the presence of abnormality is most likely to result, a false belief that may well be resistant, if not invulnerable, to counterevidence.

Temerlin and Trousdale (1969) graphically demonstrate the overwhelming propensity of clinicians to find psychopathology where, in fact, none exists, and the effects of preconception on their observation and perception of data. (Note: Referrals for forensic evaluations almost always contain the element of suggestion that someone thinks there is psychopathology present or the referral would almost never have been made.) Temerlin and Trousdale employed five groups: 156 students in an undergraduate course in personality; 40 advanced law students; 45 graduate students in clinical psychology; 25 practicing clinical psychologists selected randomly from a population of 32 cities, with an average of six years of practice; and 25 psychiatrists, including ten staff members of state mental hospitals, six residents, one university psychiatrist, four Veterans' Administration Hospital psychiatrists, and four in private practice.

They all heard a script of an actor portraying a relaxed, confident and productive man, who is enjoying life, free from psychological problems, but who is intellectually curious about psychotherapy. The script portrayed an interview in which the person interviewed quickly established a warm, interpersonal relationship with the interviewer, cordially verbalizing his inner experience in a coherent and organized fashion, without evasion, defensiveness, withdrawal or guilt.

He was not obsequious, he had no preoccupation with dirt and he was not tortured by sexual or hostile thoughts; nor was he driven to repetitive actions. He remembered his childhood clearly, articulated memories without labile affect, and freely discussed early sexual experience, without embarrassment, shame or guilt.

Specifically excluded from the script were such "pathological characteristics as anxiety, somatic preoccupation, hallucinations, delusions, conceptual disorganization, emotional withdrawal, grandiosity, hostility, suspiciousness, guilt, depressive or blunted affect, delinquency and any unusual thought content."

All but the psychiatrists were told, prior to hearing the tape, that the interviewee "looked neurotic, but was actually quite psychotic." The students and psychologists heard this from a prominent psychologist, while the law students heard it from one of their law instructors. The psychiatrists were told, "It's very difficult to get psychiatrists to help on research projects because they are very busy people. We were only able to get two, so far, both Board Members, one also a psychoanalyst, to listen to this tape. Although they agreed that the man looks neurotic but is actually psychotic, two opinions are not enough for a criterion group in a research project."

Following the interview, all subjects were instructed to "write a brief description of the patient. Be sure that your report is actually a description of behaviors which indicate personality characteristics, rather than inferential. Avoid clinical inferences, highly abstract concepts or technical terms. Simply state what you actually heard—actually observed—this person say and do." Almost all the experimental subjects found the interviewee to be suffering from neurosis, psychosis, or character disorder. The lowest group were the undergraduates, 84% of whom said the man was mentally ill. One hundred percent of the psychiatrists said he was mentally ill. In comparison, among control groups to whom the hint of psychosis was not given, the diagnosis of "healthy" ranged from 57% to 100%. The authors found that, in spite of the explicit instructions, all of the experimental subjects wrote inferential, rather than descriptive, reports. One psychiatrist, who diagnosed ambulatory schizophrenia, wrote, "This individual appears like a boastful, self-reassured [sic], outspoken person, striving to conceal a deep concern for shortcomings which he seems to be partially aware of." The authors state that, while prestige suggestion might account for inaccuracy in the initial diagnosis, it could not explain the fact that only one out of 291 experimental subjects changed the incorrect diagnosis to one of health after writing the clinical report. They point out that the subjects often leaped to a conclusion which was then defended, rather than re-evaluated in the light of subsequent observation. Note that in contrast to the Rosenhan study (Chapter 7), the Temerlin and Trousdale "patient" feigned no symptoms whatsoever, yet there was once again 100% diagnostic error by the psychiatrists. The unanimity of the finding of mental illness reveals the bankruptcy of psychiatric evaluation.

We feel it is important to comment on the psychiatric description given above, to the effect that the "individual appears like a boastful, self-reassured, outspoken person, striving to conceal a deep concern for shortcomings, etc." Forensic psychiatric and psychological reports submitted to the authors for evaluation abound in statements of this kind—"Patient has an underlying depression which he strives to conceal by appearing hopeful and optimistic"—"Patient strives to behave in a normal manner in order to cover up his underlying psychosis." If a psychiatrist sees a person who shows no pathology, but the psychiatrist decides he is "sick," then the person must be "concealing" his pathology. Given the lack of a sound knowledge base in psychiatry, this seems like unjustified arrogance.

As we mentioned before, the tendency to see psychopathology, whether disorder exists or not, is likely to be even more exaggerated when assessment is conducted for legal purposes. The lawyer who seeks out the expert may well believe, and convey, that his client was legally insane at the time of the offense, or has suffered serious impairments in his intellectual functioning as a result of a head injury. The lawyer may even state something to the effect that he usually does not rely on, say, the insanity plea, but in this case the action was so unusual or bizarre that it would seem irresponsible not to consider this defense. We are not saying that such statements are underhanded or dishonest, only that they are not necessarily uncommon and potentially create a very powerful expectation that abnormality will be found. In fact, given the operation of confirmatory bias, such a powerful expectancy may sometimes be enough by itself to preordain the "detection" of abnormality, no matter who consequently walks through the psychologist's door.

Anchoring Effects and Over-Reliance on Salient Data

Appendix B discusses anchoring effects and over-reliance on salient data, two additional bad judgment habits. "Anchoring effects" refers to the tendency for initial estimates or impressions to be insufficiently adjusted on the basis of subsequent information. For example, an initial impression of "serious" disorder may be insufficiently adjusted on the basis of additional information suggesting less severe disorder. Interestingly, at least one pair of studies suggests that this bias may be more pronounced among professionals than laypersons (see Appendix B).

Over-reliance on salient data describes the very substantial impact that a few observations, or even a single "dramatic" observation may have on conclusions, even when these observations are of limited diagnostic or predictive power. The tendency to accord inordinate weight to a very limited amount of information, which in itself may not be particularly informative, and to disregard large amounts of information, stands in sharp contrast to clinicians' claims that they integrate all of the data. This research suggests that impressions or conclusions may often be mainly determined by just a few pieces of information.

Making the Complicated More Complicated: Strategies That Increase Uncertainty and Error

Even when proceeding in the best way possible, clinical judgment error is almost inevitable and often common. However, clinicians often do not collect or interpret data in a manner that maximizes the chances of success; rather, they employ strategies that even further increase the uncertainty of clinical decision making and the likelihood of error. In Appendix C, we discuss four such strategies that, although common and intended to increase accuracy, are likely to have the opposite effects. These include: (1) failure to use standardized or set methods of data collection and interpretation; (2) abandoning established decision rules; (3) focusing on unique versus common features of cases; and (4) depending on indirect data sources when direct or concrete data are available.

Clinicians also often confuse chance differences and true differences. For example, differences among test scores that likely reflect measurement error or chance occurrences may be misinterpreted as true or meaningful differences. Misinterpretations of these chance differences can form an important but erroneous basis for experts' opinions. The second part of Appendix C thus covers common circumstances in which chance and true differences are confused and can help the reader recognize instances in which clinicians make such errors.

LACK OF INSIGHT INTO ACTUAL JUDGMENT PRACTICES AND THE DOUBTFUL SUCCESS OF APPROACHES CLAIMED TO COUNTER BIAS

Clinicians may concede that judgment can be clouded by biases but may go on to explain why their judgments in the case under consideration were not biased, or which steps they took to avoid or correct potential biases. When these claims are made, it can obviously be helpful to show that some of the biases we have discussed indeed seemed to be operating, regardless of what the expert claims. For example, if repeated instances of confirmatory bias can be brought out, one should be able to cast doubt on the expert's assertion. One need not establish that the expert is intentionally trying to make false statements as regards biases. In fact, there may be no reason to assume that the expert was anything less than sincere in his statements. Rather, one wishes to show that biases can operate beyond our awareness or even when the most sincere efforts are made to correct them, and that this apparently occurred with the present expert. Obviously, it would be an extremely rare person, if any, who could be unbiased in evaluating his own biases.

It is possible to raise considerable doubt about the effectiveness of almost any procedures, or background training, the expert claims are effective in countering bias. Research suggests that the most commonly used approaches for countering biases are of questionable value, if not completely ineffective for countering certain types of problematic judgment practices (see below).

Common views of the factors producing judgment error or bias are likely incomplete. Bias is typically viewed as distorted reasoning caused by feelings, emotions, or preferences. The following example is typical of this view. A therapist comes from an impoverished background, and, while growing up, was extremely resentful of people who were well off. As such, the feelings that now remain may result in overly negative views or interpretations of well-off clients. Stated differently, these lingering resentments impede accurate thinking. Most models or views of bias assume that some type of emotional influence clouds thinking.

Many clinicians use the term "countertransference" to refer to irrational beliefs or feelings about a patient that therapists can develop due to their own emotions, or conflicts, or past experiences. Countertransference thus refers to biased thinking on the part of the therapist stemming from emotional or experiential factors. Countertransference is often stressed in the training of clinicians, because its potential for distorting judgment is considered a danger to valid assessment or effective therapy work. In order to correct for these biases, many supervisors believe it is critical to become aware of them, or to gain insight into their occurrence. Some supervisors will see insight alone as a sufficient safeguard, and others will advise further steps. For example, a student may be encouraged to understand or resolve his underlying feelings or conflicts that lead to these biased interpretations, or may be "taught" to be aware of them as they occur and to consider alternate possibilities. In any case, insight into, or recognition of biases is usually considered essential to correction, and many approaches stress awareness of biased thinking as a major component in correction.

Research suggests, however, that many judgment errors do not stem from emotional biases, or emotional biases alone, but rather rest in just plain incorrect or insufficient reasoning habits. Further, there is evidence that individuals, even highly experienced ones, have limited insight into their actual reasoning processes, even when they believe they are very aware of the factors that can lead to judgment error. Third, a growing body of research suggests that insight, by itself, does little to correct problematic reasoning practices, even if individuals think they have corrected them.

Judgment Errors of the Heart and/or Mind?

We would not deny that emotional factors may lead to biased or distorted judgment. However, research suggests that even were one to somehow reduce or eliminate emotional biases, many problematic judgment practices and errors would not be eliminated. Problems like the hindsight bias and confirmatory bias do not seem to be based on emotional factors, or at least emotional factors alone. This is demonstrated by experiments in which researchers minimize the chances that individuals will have an emotional investment in one or another judgment or conclusion, and then study their performance on judgment tasks. For example, Edwards (1956) and Estes (1962) conducted experiments with laypersons which examined what was essentially the use of base rate information. Individuals attempted to guess which of two lights, a red and a green one, would come on next. They made these guesses over a series of trials. In one condition, the red light went on 60% of the time and the green light 40% of the time. Thus, by playing the base rates and always guessing "red," the subjects would have been correct 60% of the time. Nevertheless, individuals varied their guesses trial-by-trial, or disregarded the base rates, and achieved a lower overall level of accuracy.

We use these older experiments only for purposes of illustration. More recent studies show that even when one reduces or minimizes emotional factors in decision making, problematic judgment practices, such as disregard of base rates, and confirmatory bias nevertheless continue to occur. Thus, research suggests that *problematic judgment practices do not stem from emotional biases alone but also from faulty approaches to judgment tasks that would not be eliminated even were emotional factors corrected.* Thus, even if one believes an expert has controlled his emotional biases, it is doubtful that it solves the problem of assessment error stemming from faulty judgment practices. (Dawes, 1976; and Nisbett and Ross, 1980, provide detailed overviews of nonemotional factors in judgment error.)

The Illusion of Insight

To what extent are clinicians really aware of the underlying factors that shape their judgments or the intellectual processes they utilize in reaching conclusions? There is considerable evidence to suggest that clinicians who believe they really know these things are victims of illusory correlation. The problematic judgment practices that lead the clinician to reach erroneous conclusions about those he assesses can apparently produce comparable errors when the clinician assesses himself, or attempts to analyze his own reasoning processes.

Lack of relationship between confidence and accuracy. Research shows that subjective beliefs about one's judgment accuracy and objective measures of accuracy often disagree. We might expect, for example, a strong relationship between the strength of one's belief in one's accuracy, or subjective confidence, and actual judgment accuracy, but research has shown otherwise. For example, Slovic (1976) and Slovic et al. (1977) uncovered instances in which individuals who were absolutely certain they were correct in their judgments turned out to be flat-out wrong in a considerable percentage of cases. Apparently, then, knowing that someone is absolutely sure that they are correct provides no strong reason to assume that they are in fact correct. Other studies demonstrate no relationship between clinicians' confidence and judgment accuracy, or suggest a *negative* relationship between confidence and accuracy—the more confident judges tended to be the less accurate ones (e.g., Wedding, 1983). In several studies, the pervasive finding is overconfidence—that individuals are more confident in their judgments than is warranted by their actual performance. (For further reviews and reports, see Dawes, 1986; Fischhoff, 1982; Kelly and Fiske, 1950; Lichtenstein et al., 1982.) Fischhoff, for example, reviews a series of studies in which physicians who felt 90% sure their diagnoses were correct were actually *wrong* about 80% of the time. Hart et al. (1987) found that clinicians who actually performed at no better than chance level were nevertheless quite confident in their ability to detect adolescents feigning abnormality on tests assessing for brain damage.

This work on overconfidence has some rather interesting implications for forensic work. In order for an expert to venture an opinion, in theory, he should feel relatively confident about his conclusions. However, given that confidence and accuracy may show an inverse relationship, those who believe they are in a position to make pronouncements with reasonable certainty may actually be those less likely to be correct. In contrast, those who believe they should not venture an opinion may actually be correct more often than those who are much more confident (although their low level of confidence may properly reflect actual accuracy levels). Thus, those most willing to testify in court may often be those less likely to be actually correct. These findings on confidence and accuracy may be especially important to get to the jury in certain cases. It often happens that the responsible clinician appears unsure of his findings (as he should be) while charlatans and the ignorant often impress a jury with the sureness and confidence they display.

Subjective impressions versus objective measures of data use. Studies indicate substantial differences between the way individuals think they utilize data and the way they actually utilize data. For one, studies have shown that the factors individuals believe impact considerably on their conclusions or appraisals may actually exert little true effect, and that factors individuals believe exert little or no effect may exert considerable effect. For example, in a series of studies with experimental subjects (not clinicians), Nisbett and Wilson (1977a, 1977b; Wilson and Nisbett, 1978) obtained objective evidence about the factors influencing individuals' judgments. They also obtained individuals' subjective reports of the factors they believed influenced their judgments. They found remarkable and consistent discrepancies between these objective measures and subjective reports. For example, factors that individuals indicated they had disregarded or ignored were sometimes found to have exerted the greatest effects on their conclusions. It was not that individuals attempted to be misleading, but rather that they apparently were unaware of the influential factors.

Other researchers have performed similar studies, in which they compared individuals' subjective impressions of the factors influencing their judgment and objective measures of the influential factors (Hoepfl and Huber, 1970; Hoffman, 1960; Oskamp, 1962; Rorer et al., 1967; Slovic, 1966). For example, the Rorer et al. (1967) study of mental health professionals involved subjective impressions versus objective measures of factors influencing decisions about whether to allow psychiatric patients to leave the hospital grounds temporarily. The study by Fisch et al. (1982) (supra) involved psychiatrists' evaluations of depression, and the study by Gillis and Moran (1981) (supra) dealt with psychiatrists' medication or treatment choices. This research shows that individuals consistently overestimate the weight they attach to much of the data. They believe they have taken a great deal of information into consideration in reaching their conclusions, whereas the objective analysis shows that their conclusions can be explained, in large part, by reliance on just a few factors or pieces of information. Thus, researchers have obtained large discrepancies when they ask clinicians how they think they think, the factors they think they consider in reaching judgments, and the manner in which they reach their conclusions, and compare these reports to objective assessment of these processes. (For a brief discussion of factors underlying lack of insight, see Appendix D.)

Given all this, it seems that clinicians who claim they can rely on *their* subjective reports may well be exhibiting a double standard of evidence. The self-reports of others are questionable, but their own self-reports or beliefs in their own judgment practices are to be taken at face value. If the clinician responds by indicating that his training or experience allows him to accurately assess his own judgment processes, the lawyer can challenge this assertion with the literature we have described above. If he continues to insist that his insight is to be trusted, one can ask him if his behavior provides an example of what some members of his field describe as a double standard of evidence.

The Limited Corrective Power of Insight

The foregoing would suggest at least one critical flaw with the most commonly touted recipe for the correction of biases. If insight is indeed necessary to correct biases, numerous demonstrations that clinicians often lack insight into their internal judgment processes obviously suggests that biases will not be corrected. However, for the clinician who insists that he has achieved insight into his biases, it is important to be able to show that any such insight, by itself, is of questionable value for correcting biases or problematic judgment practices and may even be completely worthless.

A number of studies show that alerting individuals to problematic judgment practices and warning them against their effects exert little, if any, corrective influence. In a study by Feher et al. (1983), highly experienced clinicians analyzed human figure drawings. As Feher et al. explain, clinicians' assessments are often substantially influenced by the artistic quality of the drawings. For example, individuals who produce drawings of lower artistic quality are more likely to be diagnosed as having some pathological condition. However, a body of research indicates that art quality is not valid for these purposes and should be ignored. Feher et al. explained this to the clinicians in the study and specifically instructed them to disregard art quality. Nevertheless, their judgments were still substantially influenced by this factor.

Kitamura et al. (1984) report that although two clinicians attempted to disregard speech in order to appraise blunted affect as instructed, actual appraisals were still biased by this factor. Other researchers have obtained similar results when subjects were informed of, and warned about, some of the other erroneous judgment practices we have described above, such as the hindsight bias, overconfidence, and confirmatory bias (e.g., Fischhoff and Slovic, 1980; Kurtz and Garfield, 1978; Slovic and Fischhoff, 1977; Wood, 1978). For a more extended discussion of the ineffectiveness of warnings, see Fischhoff (1982), who discusses research with laypersons and various professional groups.

Thus, the research indicates that not only do individuals often lack insight into the factors that shape their judgments and into their actual underlying judgment processes, but that even if they can gain insight into some of these practices, this insight, by itself, seemingly has little corrective power. Eliminating biases and/or problematic judgment habits, then, does not appear to be just a matter of awareness or will—one cannot will them away by telling oneself not to be influenced. To put this in more common terms, one may be aware, for example, that one prefers the color blue without being aware of the intellectual mechanisms underlying this preference or how to change the preference in the specific manner desired. We suspect that many clinicians will not know of this literature showing lack of insight into problematic judgment practices and the limited corrective power of insight. The lawyer can obviously use this to his advantage, in particular when the expert claims to have neutralized his own biases in one or another way (e.g., through awareness of the "potential" problem). Kubie (1971) states in this regard: "In spite of every effort to correct for such biases, the psychiatrist and psychologist is no more immune to self-deception than is the layman."

INTEGRATING ALL OF THE DATA:
CAN IT BE DONE?

Many prominent clinicians emphasize over and over again that one should not consider data in isolation, but should look at all of the data together. Further, one must analyze interrelationships among the data, or what are often called "configural relationships." What they mean by this is one should not simply "add" pieces of data to each other. For example, if one were attempting to predict future violence, one would not take any findings suggesting the individual will act violently and tally them together, and then subtract from this total any findings suggesting the individual will not act violently. Thus, to simply say that four variables point in the direction of violence but six do not, and therefore to predict that violent behavior probably will not occur, is viewed by many clinicians as much too gross and inferior a procedure. Rather, one is supposed to look at the relationships between the various pieces of data. For example, although a certain variable may point towards violence, this variable may take on a different meaning if it appears by itself as opposed to co-appearing with other variables. To use an example from medicine, a cough may have a different meaning if it is the only presenting symptom than it may have if it co-presents with other symptoms, such as fever and/or a sore throat. Thus, one is supposed to look at the patterns or configurations formed by the data, or at interrelationships among the data.

Many prominent psychologists and psychiatrists state, unequivocally, that examining most or all of the data together, and/or analyzing configural relationships, is an absolute necessity for achieving optimal assessment results. Further, many clinicians, perhaps the great majority, endorse or accept this view and in fact claim to follow these dictates in their interpretation of data. On cross-examination to ascertain what data formed the basis for conclusions, many clinicians will assert that no single datum was important by itself but that they took all of the data together. It is important to debunk the myth that they use all of the data, so that cross-examination can pin them down to specifics or show they cannot explain what data they used.

We cannot emphasize these points enough. This is an area in which many clinicians agree on what is essential for achieving accurate judgments and claim that they can and do in fact perform these essential acts. However, a large and consistent body of research shows a massive gap between claims regarding the capacity to perform data integration and actual abilities in this regard. If clinicians cannot really do what they themselves claim must be done to achieve accurate results, then according to their own initial premises, they cannot achieve accurate results.

A few representative statements about data integration follow. Exner, for example, who is arguably the world's most recognized authority on the Rorschach, has consistently argued for a configural approach in interpreting Rorschach data. He states (Exner et al., 1984):

> All of the formally developed approaches to the Rorschach test have included recommendations for a configural approach to the interpretation of the scoring of structural data....The bulk of research concerning Rorschach variables indicates that while most can be demonstrated to correlate with relatively discrete facets of personality and/or behavior, *any accurate assessment* of a subject depends on interpreting the idiographic mixture of variables that appear in the record correctly. In other words, while the broader interpretive meaning of a variable does not change, its specific interpretive importance will vary considerably depending on the configuration of other variables. (p. 65) (italics added)

In the first edition of Exner's classic book (1974) on the Rorschach, he states:

> The meaningfulness of a particular class of responses is not simply determined by its presence or absence in a protocol but by its presence or absence *in relation* to the presence or absence of other classes of responses. For example, two protocols, one from a normal and one from a schizophrenic, might both contain the same number of color responses, and these responses could even be of the same general characteristic. The Rorschach novice might be tempted to postulate that both subjects have similar emotions....This conclusion would be premature and probably very erroneous. Any interpretation of those responses requires a careful weighing of many other elements of the protocol such as its length, location factors, form quality, scored content, organizational features, and the occurrence of other classes of response such as movement, form, and shading before even the most tentative interpretive hypothesis can be formulated. (pp. 6-7)

Further,

> There is no simple checklist of Rorschach signs which automatically may be translated as representative of "dynamics" or behaviors. All together too often, the novice interpreter seeks out these simple equations from which his task will supposedly be made easier....This supposition is "pure nonsense," and the unwitting interpreter who binds himself to that concept would do much better to select instruments other than the Rorschach for his work. (p. 230)

Apparently, then, Exner is arguing that configural analysis of Rorschach variables is an absolute necessity, and he is advising that those who think or practice otherwise not use the Rorschach at all.

Muriel Lezak (1983) is a well known neuropsychologist, whose book on the topic of neuropsychological assessment is possibly the single most popular work in the field. Lezak is another strong proponent of data integration. In the second edition of her book, she states:

> For the examination to supply answers to many of the diagnostic questions and most of the treatment and planning questions requires integration of all the data—from tests, observations made in the course of the examination, and the history of the problem. (p. 162)

In other sections of the book, Lezak describes the range of information that must be obtained and integrated. For example, one needs to gather detailed information about the patient's current circumstances and background history. We need not report the specific areas she mentions, but it should be noted that the sheer amount of information the clinician is advised to collect, and integrate, is quite considerable. (For additional statements of this type by neuropsychologists, see Chapter 15.)

Matarazzo (1986b), a former president of the American Psychological Association, has written a popular book on intellectual testing. He is a well-known advocate of data integration. In a separate work (1986a) critical of computerized interpretations of psychological tests, he states:

> As I have repeatedly stated, even if today's computerized interpretations (or Meehl's cookbook interpretations) were valid, the given product of a psychological test takes on *differential* meaning based on the unique characteristics and relevant context of the individual being assessed. This is an idea that most practicing psychologists take as a given. (p. 22)

Yes indeed. This *is* an idea that most practicing psychologists take as a given. There would be no difficulty locating many more statements by clinicians that reiterate the same sentiments and assumptions. We can now cover studies examining actual capacities in this regard.

STUDIES ON THE CAPACITY TO ANALYZE COMPLEX DATA

An enlarging research base shows that the low overall levels of performance found on many clinical judgment tasks are not rooted in biases or problematic judgment practices alone, but rather can also be explained by the limited capacity of individuals to manage or grasp complex information. This work suggests that even when clinicians are functioning optimally, they are far less capable of handling complex information than has usually been assumed. Psychiatric and psychological evaluations may well create requirements for "data processing" that are *much* too hard for clinicians or human beings in general, and well exceed their capacity to analyze or utilize information.

The evidence for these restrictions in the ability to manage complex data comes from two basic sources. One line of research examines clinicians' judgment accuracy when they are provided with varying amounts of information. A second line of research either examines the procedures that are needed to model or duplicate clinicians' actual judgments, or directly assesses individuals' capacities to grasp configural relationships.

Amount of Information and Judgment Accuracy

A series of studies compares judgment accuracy when clinicians are provided with varying amounts of information. For example, Oskamp (1965) studied predictions of behavior based on a detailed case history. The case history was presented in steps, and the psychologists made predictions after each step, or starting from a limited data base and proceeding to a much more complete data base. Accuracy did not increase as more information was made available.

Similar results have been obtained by other investigators (Golden, 1964; Kostlan, 1954; Sines, 1959; Wedding, 1983; Winch and More, 1956). This work suggests that once clinicians are provided with a limited amount of valid information, providing additional information does not lead to a significant increase in judgment accuracy. *In the study by Sines, for example, demographic information alone, such as data pertaining to marital status and age, resulted in equal or higher levels of diagnostic accuracy than that achieved when clinicians were given extensive additional information, such as the results of certain psychological tests.*

Sawyer's (1966) earlier mentioned review of studies pertaining to the clinical-actuarial debate also shows that when data are combined clinically, overall judgment accuracy is better when clinicians rely on testing results alone. Adding interview data to test data produced an overall *decline* in judgment accuracy. As we mentioned, it appears that the conclusions reached by Sawyer remain plausible today. There is a dearth of studies conducted with psychologists or psychiatrists which show—once they are given access to a limited amount of valid information—that the additional data leads to a substantial increase in judgment accuracy.

The underlying explanation for lack of gain, or even loss of accuracy, with the provision of additional information may be fairly simple. As innumerable studies show, no matter the amount of data and how well it is used, absolute levels of predictive validity in psychology and psychiatry usually remain low. Therefore, adding a great deal more data is unlikely to help matters much, if at all. Further, as more and more data are obtained, there will be more and more potentially "bad" data, or data that are not useful in formulating predictions. If one adds these bad data to the better data, the results should be negative. For example, suppose one starts off with two good predictors of adult stature (e.g., parental height and stature at 2 years of age). If one then adds in another predictor (e.g., intelligence) that is not valid, one certainly will not do better, and may even do worse, if one adjusts one's predictions somewhat on the basis of this invalid predictor. Why don't clinicians just ignore the bad data? Apparently, they often cannot tell the difference between the good and bad data, as work on such matters as illusory correlation suggests. Perhaps because they feel they must "integrate everything," they cannot leave bad data alone (apparently, unless it is contrary to their conclusions). Also, the more data gathered, the greater the opportunity to find data to support confirmatory or other biases. Undoubtedly, there are times when the additional data that are obtained do contain components that have predictive value, and the essential problem seems to lie in the difficulty clinicians have holding in mind, weighting, organizing, and integrating the data effectively (see below).

We question whether most clinicians who are willing to serve as expert witnesses recognize the implications of this research (assuming they know it exists). Clinicians are often guided by the belief that an expanded data base permits more accurate conclusions. Thus, when one takes a detailed or exhaustive history, or administers more than one personality test, these practices are guided by the belief that a more complete data base leads to more accurate conclusions. However, research shows that these assumptions are doubtful and, therefore, can be actively challenged.

Studies on Configural Analysis

A number of investigators have used mathematical procedures to construct models, or decision-making procedures, that can copy or duplicate clinicians' actual decisions. We will not discuss the more technical aspects of this work, but some explanation is necessary. In developing these models, one presents clinicians with a set of, say, clinical cases and asks them to formulate conclusions or predictions. For example, one might ask them to decide whether they would diagnose someone as neurotic or psychotic. One then subjects their decisions to mathematical analysis and tries to develop formulae that will copy their judgments when the case data are plugged into them (the formulae). It is easy to find out whether these models work. For example, one might have the clinicians judge a fresh set of cases and also plug the data from the cases into the formulae and examine the rate of agreement. One might find, for example, that the decisions of a particular judge, and the model developed for this judge, agree in a very high percentage of the cases. Such a result obviously suggests that the effort to model or duplicate this judge's decisions has been successful.

In attempting to construct these models, one has a range of mathematical procedures available. For our purposes, we need only draw the contrast between what are called "linear" models and "nonlinear" models. A linear model is one that simply adds the data together. It can be as simple as adding (variables) 1 + 2 + 3. A nonlinear model is one that does more than add variables. It also takes into account interrelationships among the data, or something quite similar to what the clinician means when he speaks of configural relationships. Thus, in essence, linear models simply add and nonlinear models consider configural relationships. In studies of modeling, researchers are particularly interested in the extent to which clinicians' judgments can be duplicated by linear models alone—or essentially by just adding up variables—or whether these models must become more complex (i.e., nonlinear) and also take configural relationships into consideration.

Rorer et al. (1967) examined the decisions about whether or not to allow psychiatric inpatients out of the hospital on a temporary pass. Judges included psychologists and psychiatrists. Rorer et al. obtained judgments on a series of cases and found that for almost all the judges, their decisions could be duplicated almost perfectly by linear models alone, or by merely adding variables together. Nonlinear models usually made a very negligible difference, such as changing the accuracy of the models by 1%.

Wiggins and Hoffman (1968) examined MMPI interpretation. The clinician-judges claimed that configural analysis was a necessary part of MMPI interpretation and further asserted that their interpretations relied heavily on configural cues. However, once again, it was possible to duplicate their judgments quite accurately using linear methods alone—one needed only to use models that added test scores together. Other studies on this topic have yielded similar results (e.g., Hoffman et al., 1968; Huber et al., 1969; Kort, 1968; Slovic and Lichtenstein, 1968; Summers and Stewart, 1968; Yntema and Torgerson, 1961). Overviews of this work are provided by Slovic and Lichtenstein (1971), and Dawes (1979).

These studies do not indicate that clinicians are unable to perform any type of configural analysis. The models that have been developed are designed to copy clinicians' decisions, and not necessarily their underlying reasoning processes. What the findings do suggest, however, is that the clinicians' decisions, which they insist depend on configural analysis, can be largely duplicated by procedures that ignore configural relationships completely. Further, if judges actually perform configural analysis that makes an essential contribution to judgment accuracy, how is it that nonconfigural models have been consistently able to reproduce their judgments with minimal difference? Although some of the issues do become quite technical here, the findings raise serious doubts as to whether any configural analysis that clinicians might perform contributes anything of importance to judgment accuracy beyond that which can be accomplished by simply adding data together. These studies thus create serious doubt about clinicians' ability to perform sophisticated configural analysis.

Goldberg (1968b), after reviewing the earlier studies on this topic, states:

> If one's sole purpose is to reproduce the responses of most clinical judges, then a simple linear model will normally permit the reproduction of 90%-100% of their reliable judgment variance, probably in most—if not all—clinical judgment tasks. While Meehl (1954) has suggested that one potential superiority of the clinician over the actuary lies in the human's ability to process cues in a configural fashion, it is important to realize that this is neither an inherent advantage of the human judge (i.e., the actuary can include nonlinear terms in his equations), nor is this attribute—in any case—likely to be the clinician's "ace in the hole." If the clinician does have a long suit—and the numerous clinical versus statistical studies have not yet demonstrated that he has—it is extremely unlikely that it will stem from his alleged ability to process information in a complex configural manner.[8]

Other studies, which mainly involve research subjects, examine the capacity of individuals to solve problems requiring configural analysis, or to decipher configural cues. This work suggests that individuals often have extreme difficulty recognizing and comprehending even relatively simple configural relationships, such as those involving fairly straightforward interrelationships between just three (or even two) variables. Some of the studies demonstrating these difficulties have been conducted by Brehmer (1969), Earle (1970), Hammond and Summers (1965),

---

[8] Meehl (1986) has altered his earlier views on this matter and now concedes that areas in which he once thought the clinician could have a potential advantage over the actuary have not panned out. In other words, based on subsequent research, Meehl has become an even more ardent proponent of actuarial approaches.

Summers (1967), Summers and Hammond (1966), and Summers et al. (1969).

Related studies suggest that judges do perform some rather rudimentary forms of configural analysis, but that these analyses do not improve upon the judgment accuracy achieved by simply adding variables together (e.g., Einhorn, 1971; Tversky, 1969). In fact, when such forms of configural analyses are used, accuracy may even decline. Further, these configural analyses do not integrate large sets of information. For example, they may "integrate" only two or three cues or variables, as opposed to many variables. In this context, one might recall the statements of such individuals as Exner and Lezak, which call for the integration of far, far larger data sets.

This research also suggests that when individuals do use these configural strategies, they *resort* to them because even the demands for linear processing, or for simply adding the variables together, outstrip their ability or willingness to handle the data. In other words, even adding the variables prove to be too much. Instead, individuals have employed configural strategies that disregarded a good deal of the relevant data, or simplified the decision-making task. The results of these and other studies (e.g., Payne and Braunstein, 1971; Slovic and Lichtenstein, 1968; Slovic and MacPhillamy, 1974; Tversky, 1969), some with laypersons and some with professionals, suggest that the configural strategies that individuals employ, far from being sophisticated and integrating large amounts of data, are actually simplifying strategies that are used when data become more complicated.[9] What this means, in essence, is that individuals seem to employ configural analysis when they cannot even manage the demands for adding variables together, or use them when they are simpler to use than other strategies. In turn, this simplicity extracts a large toll—it comes at the cost of ignoring a good deal of the available data. It appears, then, that *regardless of beliefs to the contrary, individuals typically "manage" complex data sets by essentially disregarding most of the data.* After an exhaustive review of studies on the human capacity to manage information, Slovic and Lichtenstein (1971) state: "We find that judges have a very difficult time weighting and combining information.... To reduce cognitive strain, they resort to simplified decision strategies, many of which lead them to ignore or misuse relevant information." (p. 724)

It thus appears that individuals, clinicians included, have restricted capacities to manage or utilize complex data. *Although many studies have now been conducted, virtually none of them have demonstrated or uncovered clinical capacities for complex data integration or configural*

---

[9] For additional discussion of simplifying strategies, see Appendix 5E.

analysis that even begin to approach the levels of complexity described and demanded by the many clinicians advocating such approaches. Individuals often have difficulty properly integrating even two or three variables, much less the dozens and dozens of variables produced, for example, by the Rorschach or a series of psychological tests.

Data Integration: The Obstacles

Suppose we accept clinicians' claims that the integration of large data sets and complex configural analysis are necessary to achieve accurate conclusions (which is not to suppose clinicians can actually do this). This claim could be correct. Even the relatively strongest procedures for interpreting clinical data—actuarial methods—achieve levels of accuracy that are often modest at best. Perhaps the only way the field will ultimately achieve highly accurate conclusions and predictions is through the development of methods that permit very complex data analysis. Thus, there are plausible grounds to argue that what many clinicians say is *required* (as opposed to possible) is indeed required.

If one accepts these claims for the necessity of complex data analysis, the implications seem to be devastating for clinical psychology and psychiatry. First, there are few studies examining clinicians' accuracy when they attempt to manage the exceedingly complex data sets they describe as necessary for purposes of clinical interpretation. For example, the great majority of studies on the Rorschach, as even Exner (1984) concedes, have involved one or a few variables and not the whole host of variables and their numerous interrelationships that are supposedly essential for proper Rorschach interpretation. Similarly, we know of no studies that examine the accuracy achieved when neuropsychologists attempt to sort through the rather exhaustive list of information that Lezak argues must be considered. Apparently, the closest researchers have come has been in examining the accuracy levels clinicians achieve when they are given the results of tests and interviews. We have described the results of such research, and it certainly has not been flattering to clinicians. Apparently, then, there is little research available that provides scientific testing of, or support for, these preferred methods. Further, many available studies that have examined the capacity to perform much more modest judgment tasks are overwhelmingly negative. Thus, it would seem rather unlikely that judgment tasks that are much more complex can be successfully performed.

Further, if a clinician asserts that configural analysis is the only proper way to do assessment, he would apparently have to disregard most of the existing research on tests and assessment methods because these studies are obviously inappropriate in most cases. The studies merely look at one or a few variables and almost never the very large series of variables that "must" be considered in interrelationship. Apparently, because the research examines inferior approaches, or does not attempt to employ the interpretive procedures that are often considered "musts," of what use could it possibly be? This does create a clean slate from which to work. One could disregard the negative studies, alleviating a huge burden from clinicians' shoulders, but of course one would have to disregard almost any available positive studies as well. Not only are they inappropriate, but they must be wrong, for how could positive results have possibly been achieved if assessment procedures were used that, according to the argument, did not employ methods said to be essential in order to reach accurate conclusions? Thus, we have virtually no scientific knowledge and we will have to begin anew to develop a science of psychological assessment.

Beyond all this, one should raise questions about the enormous obstacles that must be overcome if these complex forms of data integration are to be accomplished. First, one apparently needs a much more completely advanced scientific knowledge base and theory than is available in even the most fully developed areas of the hard sciences. Such advanced theory has never been approached in psychology, and many observations and forms of data will fall outside existent theory or knowledge. They cannot be "integrated" because one does not know what they mean or may represent. Much, if not most, of the data exceed current comprehension.

One must also ask how anyone could possibly consider all of the potentially available data. Take Rorschach scores, for example, which conceivably could be combined in an almost endless variety of ways. In fact, if one performs the actual calculations, the number of variables or scores one obtains when using the Exner system allows, potentially, for *billions* of possible combinations. And yet, lacking even the most rudimentary theories, the clinician is supposedly able to deal with all of the data. As we will detail, Exner himself has described his own approach to work with the Rorschach as "atheoretical" (see Chapter 13). Further, if the existent research shows that we often attend selectively to a very restricted set of data in formulating conclusions—that sometimes a single variable alone will largely account for the conclusions reached—how can we attend to even a very small proportion of the potentially available data? This would require not only a completely comprehensive and totally finished theory. It would also require superhuman mental abilities.

One must also consider what "all of the data" might involve. Presumably, the clinician must attend to not only such things as test scores, but also to every movement the patient makes, and every utterance and every word expressed. For this, too, must be part of "all of the data." How are these things possible? One cannot pay attention to everything at once when one sees a patient. So apparently some, if not a good deal of "all of the data" will never have been noticed in the first place. How can one possibly keep all the information stored in memory? Obviously, we forget considerable amounts of information over time. Further, if one assumes that all the data are needed, how can a clinician possibly justify failing to do such things as videotaping assessment sessions so that, for example, things forgotten or not noticed in the first place can be retrieved (see Chapter 6 regarding selective attention to and recall of clinical data). Therefore, it can be established that the clinician used less than "all" the data. Once that is established he can be asked to specify which of the data he did use, and can be pinned down. Often, it will be a small number of items which cannot be demonstrated to be a sufficient basis for the conclusion.

What about all of the data that could have been collected or compiled but that were not? For example, the MMPI has a series of commonly used scales, but one can also calculate scores for about 100 research scales. The data for doing so are usually available when a patient completes the MMPI in the standard fashion. If one needs to consider all of the available data, one would assume that scores on these available research scales should also be calculated. We could give many other examples, but the point is that, virtually without exception, the clinician has in his hands information or opportunity through which he could obtain many more test scores, or comparisons, or "data" than he has actually derived. Apparently, some or even most of the potential data are being disregarded.

Are all the data that have been gathered consistent? Do all lead to the same conclusions? Presumably, if the data have been integrated successfully, it has all been rendered completely orderly, with every piece fit into its proper place and shown to be consistent with the conclusions formed. But how could this be possible? Even the best psychological tests, for example, do not approach perfect reliability, and thus some of the data are merely a product of erroneous measurement or chance. And yet there are often no infallible means for separating results accounted for by fact as opposed to artifact. Further, is it really conceivable that all of the data will fit together perfectly like some gigantic jigsaw puzzle that has no missing or ill-fitted part? Will none of the data conflict and point towards opposing conclusions?

We could go on, but the matter should be obvious. Even if there were not a massive body of research strongly suggesting that clinicians actually have limited capacity to manage complex information and often stumble over just a few variables, it should be clear that the obstacles facing the clinician who hopes to integrate all of the data are not merely difficult hurdles, but impossible ones. It is hard to imagine a larger possible discrepancy between what is claimed to have been done and what actually is done and can be done, no matter how sincere these claims might be. A psychologist or psychiatrist, witnessing such a huge difference between self-belief and actual capability, a self-belief that is so implausible when carefully examined and so contrary to the available evidence, might have no hesitancy labeling the believing person delusional. Perhaps it would not be entirely unfair to say that a large percentage of clinicians do in fact evidence a shared myth about their own judgment capacities. As far as we can tell, there seems to be no plausible way one can legitimately support these beliefs on the basis of scientific evidence.

Many clinicians, when confronted with the research on judgment capacity, will argue that their reasoning processes are as much an art as a science and are not really amenable to fair scientific testing. We think the lawyer can live quite well with this answer. First of all, it is obvious that if reasoning processes cannot be invalidated by scientific testing, neither can they be validated by it. Indeed, if this is not volunteered, we recommend questioning the expert as to whether psychiatry or clinical psychology is an art or a science. The closer to art and the further from science, the less the credibility.

COMMON COUNTERARGUMENTS TO THE JUDGMENT FINDINGS

Clinicians may attempt to counter the judgment literature with various arguments. In Appendix F, we cover a number of the more common ploys and discuss further research that can be used to undermine the credibility of such defenses. Included are clinicians' arguments that the studies misrepresent actual judgment capacities, that they themselves are exceptions to the limits demonstrated with other psychologists and psychiatrists, that their reasoning is an art and thus not subject to scientific scrutiny, and that the entire clinical-actuarial debate is an artificial issue. The lawyer who plans to challenge experts on the judgment research might well wish to review this appendix.

Another common expert tactic is to claim that their success in treating patients "proves" the validity of their theories and judgments. These claims may make a very favorable impression, unless effectively challenged. There are indeed various approaches for doing so, because the argument is actually quite weak and vulnerable. The topic is covered in Chapter 8 (Experience) in the section explaining the limited benefits of experience and the problems of using feedback in general, including "feedback" about treatment effectiveness, to evaluate or improve one's judgment accuracy.

TYING THINGS TOGETHER

To help the reader tie together the considerable material in this chapter, we will provide a "classics" section on research and commentary, and end with an example which demonstrates that even the mightiest of clinicians are susceptible to problematic judgment practices.

THE CONTRAST BETWEEN
DECLARATIONS & INVESTIGATIONS

Most experts show little hesitancy in discussing the powers of clinical judgment. In fact, as previously described, if the exceedingly shaky scientific foundations for his assessment procedures and theories are exposed, the expert often feels he has nowhere else to turn in order to defend his credibility. And yet, where he does turn—to the powers of clinical judgment—seems in truth to be the weakest link in an already feeble chain. Let us contrast the declarations experts commonly make about their judgment capacities and powers and what the research shows about these matters.

I. Performance Level on Clinical Judgment Tasks

Declaration: By relying on clinical judgment skills, it is often possible (or possible in this case) to diagnose and predict with reasonable certainty.

Investigations: Clinical judgment often leads to low, if not abysmal levels of judgment accuracy. In a number of studies, accuracy has not exceeded chance levels. Other investigations involving psychologists and psychiatrists have produced 0% accuracy levels.

II. Procedures for Increasing Accuracy

Declarations: The clinician has at his disposal a number of procedures and approaches that enhance accuracy. These include gathering a more extensive data base, and using clinical judgment to decide when actuarial or other such results are likely to be misleading.

Investigations: The approaches that clinicians typically count on to increase accuracy often do not work, or actually backfire. Beyond limited amounts of valid information, even a much more extensive data base or set of tests does not seem to increase accuracy significantly, and may even lower accuracy levels. Further, clinicians would probably achieve a higher level of overall accuracy if they usually, or uniformly, relied on actuarial procedures where available. In fact, once the data have been gathered, better results could probably be achieved by eliminating the clinician from data interpretation entirely.

III. Trusty Guidelines and Judgment Processes

Declarations: By reflecting on one's own judgment practices it is possible to recognize, and thus avoid or counter, biases and erroneous judgment practices.

Investigations: Research to date suggests that clinicians actually have limited insight into, or awareness of, their own judgment practices and the factors that actually shape their conclusions and predictions. Subjective impressions and objective measures often contrast sharply. Apparently, confidence and accuracy often show little relationship, or even a negative one. Other research shows that factors believed to have a considerable impact on conclusions may have little actual impact, and vice-versa. Even should insight be accomplished somehow, this by itself seems to have minimal impact on problematic judgment practices, such as hindsight bias and confirmatory bias. Actually, the belief that such problems have been controlled may simply make matters worse, for highly confident clinicians may be the less accurate ones.

IV. Capacity to Manage Complex Data

Declarations: In order to reach accurate conclusions, it is essential that one consider most or all of the data together and analyze configural relationships. This is what we do in drawing conclusions.

Investigations: Claims for the capacity to perform complex data integration seem almost completely unfounded. Research shows that just a few variables, or even a single variable, often account in large part for diagnostic and predictive conclusions. Further, individuals often seem to have exceptional difficulties deciphering even relatively simple configural relationships, much less the exceedingly complex ones to which clinicians refer. It also appears that when individuals use configural strategies, these strategies are relatively simple, in fact even simpler than the mental operations needed to merely add the variables together. These configural strategies also seem to disregard much of the available data and do not appear to improve accuracy above the level achieved by merely adding variables together. In fact, the results of such configural analysis can be inferior. Further, simple linear models that only add variables together have successfully duplicated judgments that clinicians claim depend on configural analysis. Finally, a careful analysis of the obstacles that must be overcome in order to "integrate all of the data" suggests that its achievement must await the type of extremely advanced scientific knowledge and theory, and the type of superhuman intellectual abilities, that we can only dream about.

Given all of the negative evidence for such common declarations about reasoning powers and capacities, we recommend that many of the self-referential declarations that experts use to enhance their credibility be judged inadmissible. An example would be statements to the effect that the expert's opinion is likely to be accurate because he has integrated all of the data or because he feels particularly confident. The evidence on these matters is so negative that, at best, such statements should be considered quite doubtful. Thus, they would seem to bias the assessment of the testimony, because, while of doubtful accuracy, they can create an aura of credibility. No matter how sincere these declarations might be, they potentially lead the trier of fact to believe in what is at best unproven, and at worst wrong or false.

SOME CLASSIC WORK

It is important to illustrate that the points raised in this chapter are not the unique or idiosyncratic views of Ziskin. Further, because there has been so much material to cover, we often have provided only skeletal details. Finally, the lawyer might wish to have available a section with some particularly notable comments and quotes on the matter of clinical judgment. Thus, we will present several "classic" judgment studies in some detail, and then offer statements by authorities that touch upon many of the points we have raised.

Werner et al. (1983) review the typically low levels of accuracy in the prediction of violent behavior. They note that there has been virtually no evidence published on the reliability (inter-rater consistency) of forecasts of violence. In their study, judges included 15 clinical psychologists and 15 psychiatrists with an average of over 15 years of experience. Both groups were also experienced in the inpatient setting. The judges evaluated psychological test results for 40 male patients on a psychiatric intensive care unit. They were also informed whether a violent act had been a factor in hospitalization. Overall, they had 19 variables with which to work. Actual patient behavior on the unit was assessed by chart notes, and the base rate for violent behavior was 30% among the patients.

The judges often disagreed among themselves in their predictions, or showed low cross-judge reliability. The psychologists showed a slightly higher rate of agreement with each other than did the psychiatrists. No significant differences in accuracy were uncovered across the psychologists' and psychiatrists' predictions. Of the 30 judges, only two achieved a level of accuracy that significantly exceeded chance (Note: one would expect one or two out of thirty judges to exceed the .05 chance level by chance alone, anyway.) Even the most accurate judge achieved a low absolute level of accuracy. *All* of the judges would have done better using the base rates.

The authors were able to construct simple linear models—models that simply added variables together—that could duplicate the judges' predictions almost perfectly. The authors also found that the information with which the judges had to work had significantly more predictive value than the judges were able to utilize. In other words, the information was available to make better predictions than were made. The problem is that the judges seemed to place emphasis on the variables that were actually poor predictors (i.e., relied on illusory correlations), and tended to underutilize or disregard the variables that were better predictors. As the authors state:

> ...judges' beliefs about the relationship of the cues to imminent violence did not parallel the actual relationship of these cues to the criterion of imminent violence on the acute ward. In other words, *judges tended to give inordinate weight to cues that were in fact unrelated to imminent violence in this sample and to give lesser weight to cues that were more strongly related to the criterion.* (p. 820)

The data did suggest that a few judges relied on configural relationships, although the configural relationships that were used varied considerably across the judges (in some sense, they represented each judge's personal or idiosyncratic invention). Finally, accuracy and total years of clinical experience did not show a significant relationship. Experience in acute inpatient settings was also unrelated to accuracy.

The authors discuss some limitations of the study but note that the prediction task, which involved only relatively short time spans in a controlled setting, is probably considerably easier than is often the case in actual practice. For example, predictions may need to cover longer time spans and pertain to outside settings in which partially unknown or circumstantial factors, which are difficult to foresee, can exert a substantial impact upon behavior. The authors recommend that psychologists and psychiatrists attend more carefully to variables demonstrated to show a valid relationship to violence.

Wedding (1983) studied the accuracy of judgments about presence and type of brain damage. Most of the 15 judges were Ph.D. psychologists with fairly extensive experience with the psychological tests used in the study. The psychologists were given background information and testing results on 30 cases or subjects, which included scores from the Halstead-Reitan, one of the more frequently used batteries of neuropsychological tests. Among these 30 cases were an equal number of individuals with left-sided brain damage, right-sided brain damage, diffuse brain damage, "schizophrenia," and normal functioning. The clinicians tried to determine the group from which each case was drawn (e.g., whether it was from the normal group or the group of individuals with diffuse brain damage). The amount of information given the clinicians varied. In the high information condition, the clinicians were given all of the pertinent test scores, as well as certain demographic variables; in the low information condition they were given significantly less data, which the author argued could be collected in about one hour. The clinicians were informed of the population from which the sample was drawn and given sample base rates.

Tallying the results for all clinicians, accuracy level across the 30 cases ranged from 0% (for 3 of the cases) to 100% (for 3 cases). Obviously, it appears that different types of cases create different levels of difficulty. An actuarial formula achieved 64% accuracy in assigning individuals to their actual groups, which surpassed the clinicians' overall level of accuracy. The clinicians' accuracy did not correlate positively with the time they spent on the cases, prior clinical experience, or level of past experience with the Halstead-Reitan. No positive relationships were obtained between confidence and judgment accuracy, although there was a trend for the more confident clinicians to be the less accurate ones. The second most confident of the clinicians was the least accurate, and two of the less confident clinicians tied for highest level of accuracy. Further, although the clinicians felt more confident when more information was made available, they actually performed at a *lower* level in the high information condition. In contrast, the actuarial method became more accurate as more information was available. In short, for these clinicians, accuracy *decreased* as the data base increased; for the actuarial method accuracy increased as the data base increased. Wedding concludes: "However, the present study does address the situation in which the neuropsychologist is required to use a given set of observations to predict, categorize or classify; these findings strongly suggest that accuracy is maximized when data are combined in a mechanical manner...." (p. 54)

Anne Anastasi (1982) is widely recognized as one of the foremost authorities on psychological testing in the United States. In the fifth edition of her book on psychological testing, she observes that the clinical process is one of hypothesis formation and confirmation or disconfirmation. She notes, however, that clinicians may be unduly influenced by their early hypotheses, so that they look only for data that support those hypotheses. She asserts that they can influence what the client reports by the type of questions they ask, by the way they formulate the questions, and by subtle expressions of agreement or disagreement, and notes that this process has been termed "soliciting" as contrasted to "probing." She declares that biased data gathering techniques may account for the uniform etiologies found among the clients of some psychoanalysts. (p. 489)

In connection with the projective instruments, Anastasi notes that where adequate objective norms are lacking, the clinician is likely to rely on his general clinical experience to interpret test performance. She indicates that such a frame of reference is subject to all the distortions of memory that are themselves reflections of "theoretical bias, preconceptions, and other idiosyncrasies of the clinician." She notes that any one clinician's contacts are likely to have been limited to persons who are atypical in one or more ways, which is almost certain to produce misleading normative impressions.

She also discusses the clinicians's data synthesis function or interpretive function, and the belief of some in "clinical intuition," asserting that such a process arises partly because clinicians are unable to report the cues they employ in reaching a conclusion. She notes that, being unaware of cues that mediate his inferences, the clinician may be unaware of the probabilistic nature of the inference, and may feel more confident in it than is justified.

Other sources of error that Anastasi describes include the sharp differences that may occur in the clinicians' reports of the relative weight they assign to different data, and ways in which they combine data, as opposed to what they actually do. She also notes the influence of cultural stereotypes, and the reliance on fallacious prediction principles, including failure to consider base rates or regression effect, and the assumption that more highly intercorrelated predictors yield higher validity. (p. 490)

Arkes is an active researcher in the area of clinical judgment. In one of his articles (1981) he describes several impediments to accurate clinical judgment. Among these are the influence of preconceived notions, the lack of awareness of one's judgmental processes, overconfidence and the hindsight bias. Arkes notes there is always enough evidence in a rich source of data to nurture all but the most outlandish diagnoses. He notes that people will selectively seek evidence to confirm the hypothesis they already hold and thus will gather information in such a way as to support the hypothesis. He also notes evidence that people disregard data that contradicts their current judgment. He states, "Given selective seeking of confirmatory evidence and selective censoring of disconfirmatory evidence, a hypothesis simply cannot fail to be well substantiated. Such a hypothesis is very unlikely to be modified or discarded." He also notes that it is absolutely worthless to tell people what their bias is, and then to instruct them not to be influenced by it. Arkes suggests that lengthy consideration of alternative hypotheses might be useful in reducing biases. He also suggests that decreased reliance on memory may increase judgmental accuracy. In a previous study, he and Harkness had found that unpresented symptoms consistent with the diagnosis tended to be remembered as having been presented, while under some circumstances, previously presented symptoms inconsistent with the diagnosis were not remembered as having been presented. He notes that both types of memory errors would lead to overconfidence in the diagnosis. Thus, any diagnosis based on an insufficient recording of the events of the examination should be subject to challenge.

Thorne (1972) provides a wide ranging discussion of clinical judgment. He states:

> Many clinicians have been making unreliable and invalid judgments based on invalid premises, illogical assumptions, unproven relationships, inappropriate applications of unproven theories and other types of error. (p. 44)

> A major source of clinical error is in attempting to make clinical judgments for which no logical basis exists. The clinician must know what is and what is not possible in terms of the status of clinical judgment knowledge available at time and place. (p. 33)

> At this time the consensus is that serious gaps, inconsistencies, inadequacies, errors, and misconceptions in the field of psychopathology must be resolved before valid criteria of diagnostic entities can be established and defined exactly enough operationally to permit reliable clinical judgments. Thus the criterion issue becomes the central problem, of psychodiagnosis, clinical inference and clinical assessment. *Nothing should be taken for granted in accepting clinical judgments as to their validity.* (p. 33)

> The key to reliable and valid psychodiagnosis is to discover the cues or relationships leading to correct clinical inferences. Too often in the early history of all clinical specialties, diagnosis rests upon myths, superstition, guesses and empiric observations which have never been validated. (p. 47)

> The conclusion to be drawn from this evidence is that valid clinical judgment is not possible without detailed information concerning *base rates of conditions and sign rates of diagnostic indicators,* particularly with reference to local situations which may involve specific psychological considerations.

And referring to several previous research studies:

> The significance of these studies (also that of Potkay 1968) is that clinical judges tend to handle information differently and that many are purely idiosyncratic in their decisions as to weighting and assessing cues. The general research finding is that there will be almost as many judgments as there are clinicians. This is a deplorable state of affairs from the standpoint of establishing clinical practice as "being scientific." Until higher reliabilities may be demonstrated on clinical judges interpreting the same data it must be concluded that most clinicians are in a prescientific state of professional competency. (p. 61)

> In young sciences such as clinical psychology and psychiatry where there are almost as many theoretical orientations as there are clinicians, it is inevitable that theoretical disagreements must result in great inferential bias and judgmental unreliability. (p. 66)

> Literally, it is necessary to know what clinician made a judgment in order to evaluate its significance properly. Many institutions and clinicians manifest all kinds of biases and prejudices which must be understood in terms of their local judgment significance. Classification practices vary widely among institutions and areas and involve such specialized purposes and orientations as age, sex, location and socio-economic levels, political affiliation, religions, social class, etc. The biases and orientations of any judge must be well known if one is to

understand the reference of his judgments. This is the reason why expert testimony on any side of any issue can be obtained. It cannot be taken for granted that any clinical judge is unbiased and thoroughly objective until his referents of judgment become established. Psychoanalytic doctrine holds that the clinician must be analyzed before attempting clinical practice, so that he will understand his own unconscious biases. At best, psychoanalysis deals with only limited causes of bias and a much wider range of referents is required. (p. 78)

In general, many clinical psychologists and psychiatrists are still not facing up to the implications of what is known about clinical judgment. This is evidenced by the many different orientations with which clinicians identify (all cannot be valid), by the universally repeated research finding that many clinicians are unable to make better than chance judgments, and by the general lack of self-criticism evidenced by many clinicians in blithely making various types of judgments without substantial experimental evidence. Let us not forget the basic axiom of clinical judgment: uncritical self-confidence in the correctness of judgments inevitably results in clinical error. *At a time when accepted experimental statistical methods are available for the objective assessment of clinical judgments we can no longer take for granted the validity of any clinician's judgments. Every clinician periodically should submit his judgmental processes to objective evaluation to determine their validity.* (p. 30) (italics ours)

Turk and Salovey (1985) provide a broad overview of judgment research. They note that relatively little attention has been given to this work in textbooks or psychology training and that documented judgment problems are often treated with "benign neglect." They argue, however, that this research is particularly important to clinicians. They state that, "Unlike their medical colleagues, who at times rely on objective information, the hallmark of the practice of clinical psychology is reliance on judgment based largely on inferences derived from subjective information." (p. 20)

Turk and Salovey then discuss confirmatory bias and the susceptibility of clinicians to these and other problematic judgment practices. They state:

The theoretical orientation held by the clinician, moreover, provides preconceptions that will guide the nature of the information regarded as relevant and that is sought. The potential bias posed by preconceptions of clinicians is not an especially new idea...but one that receives little attention in clinical training and practice. Meehl (1954) cautioned that "psychologists should be sophisticated about errors of observing, recording, retaining, and recalling to which the human brain is subject. We, of all people, ought to be *highly suspicious of ourselves. We have no right to assume that entering the clinic has resulted in some miraculous mutation and has made us singularly free from ordinary errors* (pp. 27-28, italics added)." (p. 21)

The authors also discuss the problem of premature closure. They state that, "In general, initial conceptualizations and categorizations of clients are developed rapidly and often with minimal information. Once a judgment of a person has been made, this judgment is subsequently used as a basis for later inferences about the person, independent of the information upon which the judgment was originally based." (p. 22) They cite research showing that once clinicians form diagnostic impressions, they often adhere to these impressions stubbornly and largely ignore subsequent information. They further note that: "After the clinician has categorized the client, he or she tends to employ new data to confirm hypotheses rather than to generate new impressions and formulations....Thus, the clinician's schemata and cognitive processes may confirm hypotheses by guiding perception, information search (e.g., the selection of assessment procedures), and the clinician's behavior vis-à-vis clients." (p. 22)

Pertinent to channeling effects and overlap across those identified as normal and abnormal (one aspect of the co-variation problem we have described), Turk and Salovey state:

> Moreover, the client may fabricate or overemphasize conflictual material to comply with perceived demands of the situation. Most of us probably could recall some conflicts with our mothers if we were specifically asked. Renaud and Estess (1961) found some support for this contention when they interviewed "normal" individuals about their childhood. The information obtained was filled with material that is frequently encountered in the histories of psychiatric clients (e.g., conflicts with parents, psychophysiological symptoms, anxiety, phobias). The authors acknowledge that the material obtained was *sufficient to be of etiological significance for the entire range of problems enumerated in the American Psychiatric Association's Diagnostic and Statistical Manual—despite the fact that none of the individuals interviewed reported any current dysfunctional symptoms.* (p. 23)

In a point relevant to the limited benefits of feedback, Turk and Salovey discuss how preconceived notions can interfere with learning from experience. For example, if one asks clients, whom one assumes have a certain set of problems, certain types of questions, mistaken notions about relationships (i.e., illusory correlations) and about base rates usually will not be corrected or discovered to be in error. For example, if one asks only apparently depressed patients about childhood loss, such as the death of a parent, one may receive some "supportive" evidence. However, perhaps patients without depression have suffered childhood loss with equal frequency. If only the depressed patients are asked these questions, one will receive "confirming" information that will tend to perpetuate any illusory correlations. The authors cite additional research suggesting that therapists may modify clients' behavior such that they match the therapists' conceptual framework and "thereby confirm the therapist's theoretical biases." (p. 24)

The authors further note:

> Studies illustrate that clinicians' impressions of clients may be guided, to some extent, by what they expect to observe. Moreover, *what they expect to observe*

is likely to be what they will observe. In the clinical context, what the clinicians expect to observe is pathology. This expectancy may reduce judgmental accuracy, or at least introduce systematic biases in the direction of overestimating psychopathology and underestimating more positive features. (p. 24)

The authors cite a study by Kadushin (1979) in which, over time, clients' presenting problems came to match the theoretical orientation of the clinics in which they were seen. Thus, if they went to a psychoanalytic clinic, they ended up describing psychoanalytic problems, and if they went to a religio-psychiatric clinic, they ended up with religio-psychiatric problems. Kadushin noted, for example, that those seen in psychoanalytic settings often added sexual problems to their list of original complaints and dropped physical symptoms, whereas the opposite happened among those seen in hospital settings.

The authors also discuss Barnum effects, stating:

One point, however, is frequently understated by Barnum researchers: the effects that acceptance of personality descriptions by clients have on the clinician. The clinician can tell his or her client nearly any reasonable, highly probable personality assessment or therapeutic interpretation, and in many cases it will be accepted by the client. The client's acceptance of this information, moreover, reinforces the clinician's faith in this interpretation (and in his or her own clinical skills). (p. 26)

One can see, therefore, how misleading this feedback can be and why it can "teach" the wrong things, rather than having a corrective influence. Finally, the authors reiterate a point made by others, that is, that simply identifying a form of bias on the part of the decision-maker does not eliminate the bias.

Dawes (1986) describes a number of the factors that account for the limited benefits of experience, and for judgment error. Dawes indicates that we often form more accurate assessments about the chances that our predictions will be correct if we break down each component of the prediction, and then assess these components one at a time. For example, rather than thinking about the chances of Jones succeeding at college, one might think about the various "pieces" that will need to fall into place, e.g., Can Jones get the money? Does Jones have the brains? Does Jones have the grades to be accepted in the first place? Dawes argues that by breaking things down into isolated units this way, rather than by considering the "whole" or the data in integration, one is likely to reach more accurate appraisals and avoid unwarranted confidence in predictions that are actually unlikely to come out as assumed. This is an important point, given the frequency with which prominent clinicians argue for the superiority of considering all of the information together. Further, clinicians often do paint imaginary scenarios in formulating or defending their predictions, and Dawes's statements show how faulty a strategy this can be.

Dawes discusses how individuals often mistake statistical artifact for fact, for example, finding order (fact) when data are actually unordered or random (artifactual). He notes that many people believe that airplane accidents happen "in bunches." Dawes and a colleague obtained data on all commercial airline crashes between 1950 and 1970 and discovered that the crashes were essentially random, but he notes that random sequences may contain "bunches," which cause people to think that truly random sequences are not random.

Thus, Dawes describes another basis on which fact and artifact, or chance occurrences, are confused. Individuals picture chance events as almost completely disorderly. As a result, when events truly are random but do not *seem* as disorderly as people expect (and they rarely are), individuals are likely to assume that these events are patterned or reflect systematic causes or relationships. This is a partial basis for illusory correlation, and it suggests that even when clinicians obtain data that are really random or show no systematic relationships, they are prone to conclude that systematic relationships exist. In applying these notions to clinical psychology, Dawes notes that four good weeks in a row do not indicate therapeutic success nor do four bad weeks indicate failure. Nevertheless, Dawes points out the great temptation to impute causal factors to such strings. This problem that Dawes points out also helps to explain the limited usefulness of feedback and why treatment "effectiveness" does not provide an accurate guide to the validity of theoretical notions or judgment.

Finally, Dawes describes potential corrective procedures for problems in clinical judgment. He draws an analogy to Ulysses, who chained himself to the mast before hearing the sirens as a form of self-protection, indicating that the clinician needs to do something of the sort. He states, "Making judgments on the basis of experience unexamined for bias in generation or interpretation is likely to lead the judge—clinical or otherwise—astray, in a predictable direction. Precautions must be taken against the pitfalls of such unexamined judgment." (p. 440) This reiterates the point we have made above: that insight is of limited value by itself and that correction depends on the use of active strategies or decision aids. As regards these possibilities, Dawes suggests some rather simple external aids, such as keeping track of specific occurrences (such as suicide threats), and tallying results over time in order to more accurately estimate frequency. He further observes that literally writing down base rates can prevent irrational judgments. He argues that the typical case report is a substantial obstacle to the use of such external aids. For example, such reports are retrospective and subject to after-the-fact interpretations in which, regardless of validity, one can explain whatever happens subsequently (i.e., hindsight bias hinders accurate appraisal of validity). He indicates that a greater obstacle still is the difficulty of becoming convinced that one needs to take precautions against oneself, as Ulysses did.

In a discussion titled, "Why I Do Not Attend Case Conferences," Paul Meehl (1973) attacks the clinical case conference, discussing a multitude of typical procedures and approaches which render such conferences worthless. Professor Meehl is not merely a critical "academician" but has been a practicing psychotherapist for over thirty years. Although many of Professor Meehl's criticisms are directed at the case conference, they are in fact, in many instances, equally applicable as criticisms of the clinical method. Meehl's criticisms include: the practice of treating all evidence as equally good; tolerance of feeble inferences; failure to distinguish between an inclusion test and an exclusion test; failure to distinguish between mere consistency of a sign and differential weight of a sign; shift in the evidential standard, depending upon whether one is for or against a particular view; ignorance or repression of statistical logic; forgetting about base rates; forgetting about unreliability when interpreting score changes or difference scores; reliance upon inadequate behavior samples for trait attribution (Professor Meehl points out that over a period of several hours or days of unsystematic observation practically any human being is likely to emit at least a few behaviors which can be subsumed under almost any trait in the phenotypic or genotypic lexicon); and failing to understand probability logic as applied to the single case (which Professor Meehl asserts is a disability apparently endemic to the psychiatric profession, and is even found among clinical psychologists in spite of their academic training in statistical reasoning).

In a more recent article, Meehl (1986) discusses his original work, in 1954, on the clinical-actuarial debate. In this work, he took pains to point out potential circumstances in which the clinician might exceed the actuary. He states:

> I find...that I need to retract at most 5% of what I wrote in the first edition. Further, to the extent that I have to retract, I am afraid that I have to be more actuarial than the book was because my main proclinical considerations partly relied on mathematical patterning effects (which turn out to be rare, unstable, hard to detect, and of low incremental validity when present) and—what I emphasized most—the kind of complicated psychodynamic inference, with heavy idiographic component, that occurs in psychoanalysis, which seems less important today. (p. 371)

Meehl then lists a series of reasons that might explain why the majority of clinicians seem to ignore the massive evidence that favors the actuarial method. Included in this list are "sheer ignorance" and "computer phobia." Some of the other items include:

> 2. The threat of technological unemployment: If Ph.D. psychologists spend half their time giving Rorschachs and talking about them in team meetings, they do not like to think that a person with an M.A. in biometry could do a better job at many of the predictive tasks.

> 3. Self-concept: "This is what I do; this is the kind of professional I am." Denting this self-image is something that would trouble any of us, quite apart from the pocketbook nerve.

> 4. Theoretical identifications: "I'm a Freudian, although I have to admit Freudian theory doesn't enable me to predict anything of practical importance about the patients." Although not self-contradictory, such a cognitive position would make most of us uncomfortable. (p. 375)

Meehl explains much of the above as a reflection of irrationality on the part of clinicians. He states:

> I do not view human irrationality as confined to mentally ill patients or even to the milder maladjustments we see in outpatient psychotherapy, but rather as par for the course, as fairly standard for the human condition....I have learned to develop a certain Buddhistic detachment about the matter. Suppose a social worker confidently tells me that of course we can predict how this delinquent will do on probation by reflecting on psychodynamic inferences and subjective impressions, recorded in a 10-page presentence investigation, despite the malignant rap sheet record and acting-out psychometrics, and the officer's comment that "he's a real mean, tough street kid." Well, I remind myself that Omniscient Jones has not put me in charge of reforming the world. (p. 375)

Meehl further argues that the demonstrated superiority of actuarial methods, as first described in the summary chapter of his book (1954), should be readily understandable. He states:

> Why should people have been so surprised by the empirical results in my summary chapter? Surely we all know that the human brain is poor at weighting and computing. When you check out at a supermarket, you don't eyeball the heap of purchases and say to the clerk, "Well it looks to me as if it's about $17.00 worth; what do you think?" The clerk adds it up. There are no strong arguments, from the armchair or from empirical studies of cognitive psychology, for believing that human beings can assign optimal weights in equations subjectively or that they apply their own weights consistently, the query from which Lew Goldberg derived such fascinating and fundamental results. (p. 372)

Preston (1981) offers general discussion of the judgment habits and practices of physicians. Although not a judgment researcher per se and addressing medical practitioners in general, Preston touches upon a number of the points discussed in this chapter. The material should be useful in challenging claims that the psychiatrist's medical training or practice provides special advantages. Preston notes that many physicians are very overconfident, and states:

A consequence of certitude is denial of the true complexity of medicine. Decisions and answers tend to be "yes" or "no," when realistically they should be "maybe," or "probably, but we really don't know." By denying uncertainty the clinician hides the true facts of the case. (p. 86)

Preston indicates that overconfidence can lead to error, or the use of treatments that only much later are discovered to be counterproductive. He states, "The trouble with the myth of omnipotence is that it inevitably leads the physician to act as if he had powers he does not have." (p. 87)

Preston details limits and uncertainties of clinical observation. He notes that physicians often attribute the patient's recovery to the treatments they employ, but that:

Physicians do not have a systematic method for classifying facts of illness and treatment so as to be able to say a specific treatment was definitely responsible for a particular recovery. As a rule, they believe the benefits of medical practices are self-evident, and therefore do not require testing. (p. 99)

Preston further observes that many physicians allow biases to affect case appraisals, and that their conclusions commonly rest on "unsubstantiated assumptions. They rely not on science but on intuition and clinical experience." (p. 100) Although he does not refer to it as such, Preston implies that "confirmation bias" is one factor that underlies such errors. He states:

Scientific evidence bearing on a case becomes subordinated to the physician's interpretation of that evidence. He regards scientific evidence as too general to apply to individual patients—as incomplete if not incompatible with his own evaluation—and he disregards it if it does not confirm his own experience. He will even reject statements and policies of medical societies and institutions if they do not conform to his personal experience. (p. 100)

Preston is particularly critical of testimonials, noting that physicians often rely on testimonials in the same way that "quacks do." He states:

The real problem with testimonials is that they are a source of error in medical practices when they are used selectively to promote a favored therapy. In this way, they are like testimonials in television advertisements and faith healer meetings. The natural tendency of physicians is to select and to believe those testimonials supportive of their opinions. (p. 102)

This is a useful quote to have handy when a psychiatrist cites patients' positive statements as evidence for his validity. Preston further notes:

We can judge the new therapy only by comparison to what would have happened without it. Always a comparison is necessary for a scientific conclusion. And comparisons in medicine are very difficult and complicated. (p. 107)

Preston thus is essentially raising the issue of co-variation, pointing out that one must know the frequency with which a certain outcome occurs both with and without a treatment in order to accurately assess its efficacy. In the case of clinicians who rely on their treatment experience to gauge effectiveness, they would not necessarily have these points of comparison, that is, they do not know how their patients would have done had they not received the treatment. Thus, their conclusions can be mistaken.

Preston notes that individually-based clinical judgment is "incompatible with the scientific method which relies on universal, not individual, rules." (p. 102) He asserts that "to be truly scientific the physician would have to subordinate clinical judgment to an impartial and impersonal body of knowledge." (p. 102) He further notes, "The good clinician should recognize the limitations of his experience and use science to test his observations and validate his practices." (p. 113) These statements are consistent with our recommendation that the accuracy of experts' clinical judgments be directly tested and not merely assumed.

Preston indicates that clinical experience and observation can lead to erroneous and harmful conclusions, and that years or decades may be required before these errors are uncovered. He observes that in clinical decision making, physicians typically favor personal opinion over scientific information. He states:

> *This is almost a universal attitude among physicians, and is based on the common myth that the physician is somehow imbued with a mysterious sense derived from training and experience. In reality, the methods used by clinicians in problem solving are no more mysterious or difficult than those used by other people. There is no such thing as a special intuition given to the physician but denied to other ordinary persons.* (p. 101) (italics added)

EVEN THE MIGHTY FALTER

To whom do the judgment findings apply? Probably to all clinicians. Let us provide an example.

John Exner seems to have resurrected the Rorschach almost single-handedly. The system he developed and the empirical research it launched revitalized interest in the test. In the second edition of his major work on the Rorschach, Exner (1986) discusses the potential for interpreter bias in Rorschach assessment. He cautions against focusing on the test-taker's problems and dysfunctions to the neglect of assets or more complete and accurate description of the individual.

However, in an analysis of a Rorschach protocol that Exner presents in his book (p. 434 et. seq.), he inadvertently demonstrates, in our opinion, how difficult it is even for someone at his level of skill to avoid allowing biases or preconceptions to influence the interpretation of the data. He provides an analysis of the protocol of a twenty-six-year-old man, based on what is called the structural data. By the time this analysis comes to consideration of the content—the verbal responses indicating what the person saw in the blots—some hypotheses have already been formed which suggest that the individual has some passivity and is somewhat remote or overcontrolled emotionally, although it should be mentioned that all of these are couched in tentative terms. We wish to deal only with a few of the response analyses, in the interest of space and only by way of illustrating how subjective the process is and how little immunity from prejudicial interpretation exists.

The first response is given to Card I: "Looks like a bat gliding along." The analysis notes that the "passive movement" reflected in the word *gliding* has a particular interest coinciding "in an almost predictable way with previously developed hypotheses about him." It is at least arguable that, while gliding does not represent the strenuous effort of flapping the wings, neither is it an entirely passive kind of movement. In fact, in the process of gliding, the flying creature is required to make numerous adjustments to take advantage of the changes in currents. In other words, it is certainly not as passive as sitting in an airplane. Further, even accepting the analyzer's scoring of this response as passive movement, the remainder of the movement or activity responses of humans or other creatures comprise only two that are scored passive, while six are scored active. Thus, there is a total of three passive movement or activity responses and six active movement or activity responses. If passive movement coincides in a predictable way with previous hypotheses, what becomes of those hypotheses in the face of a two-to-one majority of responses that show active movement? It should be noted that Exner ascribes particular importance to the first response that is made. We feel in this instance he is providing a pretty clear illustration of preconception and confirmatory bias in operation.

Response number ten on Card V is, "It could be a bat or a butterfly. I think more a butterfly, now that I look at it because I said bat before." Here the analyzer indicates that the specific content does not add much because it is so common, but that the vacillation in the response may be important, as it ties together well with the previously developed hypothesis. It seems clear that the analyzer finds some confirmation of a previously formed hypothesis in this "vacillation." We would, first of all, question whether this response actually qualifies as vacillation. In *Webster's New Twentieth Century Dictionary,* (unabridged, second edition, Collins World, 1977), *vacillate* is defined as follows: "To sway to and fro, waver. (1) To sway to and fro; to waver; to totter; to stagger. (2) To fluctuate. (3) To waver in mind; to show indecision; to be irresolute." It does not seem to us reasonable to describe this response as vacillation according to that definition. One would think it would require at least one more shift in order to be considered a swaying to and fro. The subject here, clearly, only swayed once, only "to," not "fro." He did not sway to and fro, back and forth. He considered two possibilities and then selected one without any apparent further moving back and forth between the two options. He did not fluctuate, nor was he irresolute; he apparently resolved the issue rather readily. The reader is reminded that this presumed "vacillation" occurred in response to a stimulus which is by definition ambiguous; this, at the very minimum, justifies a certain amount of indecision, or at least perception of alternatives, on the part of a normal human being. In fact, *either* response—a bat or a butterfly—is scored as a "popular" response because they appear with considerable frequency. Finally, and perhaps most importantly, if vacillation is seen as significantly supporting a previously formed hypothesis, we would think that the fact that, out of a total of twenty-five responses, this is the only one which showed any "vacillation" would indicate just the opposite conclusion. That is, the largest number of responses suggests that this is an individual who does not characteristically vacillate. That is an equally reasonable conclusion that can be drawn about vacillation when, in twenty-four out of twenty-five instances, there is no vacillation, and there is some (possible) vacillation in only one out of twenty-five instances.[10] Again, at the risk of being repetitive, the Rorschach involves quite ambiguous stimuli, which one might expect to call forth a certain amount of vacillation. This seems to be another instance of the operation of preconception or confirmatory bias.

Finally, on Card X, response 24 (which is the second response on Card X) is, "This brown could be a deer jumping." The analyst describes this response as "more revealing" and states, "The movement is more avoidant, which is not inconsistent with many of his previous answers." We appropriately note that this is quite a cautious statement. We believe the "previous answers" referred to are a rocket ship taking off and a crab going away from you. The latter of these, certainly, is explicitly avoidant. We might note that the "bat gliding" is non-directional, with no indication whether it is coming or going, so that it was not movement away or "avoidant." However, in our opinion, what is most revealing is the way "a deer jumping," by itself and without further clarifying material, is interpreted by the analyst as "more avoidant" although there is nothing whatsoever to indicate the direction in which the deer is

---

[10] There is one other response that conceivably could be considered vacillation. This is response number 22 on card IX: "You know, this way it looks like a person on a motorcycle or a bike." However, Exner does not refer to this as vacillation and we think correctly so. Therefore, we are not dealing with it as an additional vacillation response. However, even two out of twenty-five responses to ambiguous stimuli, if indeed they involved vacillation, would not seem to us sufficient to consider this an attribute of the individual.

jumping. It could indeed be jumping away from a hungry lion, or even a startling noise, but it could also be jumping eagerly toward a friendly farmer who has been feeding it at sunset every evening. There simply is no information which indicates that this is "avoidant" movement. This appears to us, if we may use the term, as a clear example of the analyst's "projection" on an ambiguous response of the test taker. We would argue this response seems to be determined by conclusions that the analyst has already reached, which causes him to ignore the absolute neutrality of direction in this response. As we assume the analyst in this instance is Professor Exner himself, it illustrates that the most experienced and masterful of clinicians are unable to free their judgmental processes from the problems of the various biases, even though they are aware of the problem and warn others to avoid it.

REFERENCES

Abramowitz, S.I., Gomes, B., and Abramowitz, C. (1975). Publish or politic: Referee bias in manuscript review. *Journal of Applied Social Psychology, 5,* 187-200.

Adams, K.M. (1984). Luria left in the lurch: Unfulfilled promises are not valid tests. *Journal of Clinical Neuropsychology, 6,* 455-458.

Adinolfi, A.A. (1971). Relevance of person perception research to clinical psychology. *Journal of Consulting and Clinical Psychology, 37,* 167-176.

Anastasi, A. (1982). *Psychological Testing* (5th ed.). New York: The Macmillan Company.

Anderson, C.A. (1983). Abstract and concrete data in the perseverance of social theories: When weak data lead to unshakable beliefs. *Journal of Experimental Social Psychology, 19,* 93-108.

Arkes, H.R. (1981). Impediments to accurate clinical judgment and possible ways to minimize their impact. *Journal of Consulting and Clinical Psychology, 49,* 323-330.

Arkes, H.R. (1989). Principles in judgment/decision making research pertinent to legal proceedings. *Behavioral Sciences & the Law, 7,* 429-456.

Arkes, H.R., and Harkness, A.R. (1980). Effect of making a diagnosis on subsequent recognition of symptoms. *Journal of Experimental Psychology, 6,* 568-575.

Arkes, H.R., Wortmann, R.L., Saville, P., and Harkness, A.R. (1981). The hindsight bias among physicians weighing the likelihood of diagnoses. *Journal of Applied Psychology, 66,* 252-254.

Arkes, H., Dawes, R.M., and Christensen, C. (1986). Factors influencing the use of a decision rule in a probabilistic task. *Behavior and Human Decision Processes, 37,* 93-110.

Arkes, H.R., Faust, D., Guilmette, T.J., and Hart, K. (1988). Eliminating the hindsight bias. *Journal of Applied Psychology, 73,* 305-307.

Arnoult, L.H., and Anderson, C.A. (1988). Identifying and reducing causal reasoning biases in clinical practice. In D.C. Turk and P. Salovey (Eds.), *Reasoning, Inference, & Judgment in Clinical Psychology* (pp. 209-232). New York: The Free Press.

Bernstein, E.M., and Putnam, F.W. (1986). Development, reliability, and validity of a dissociation school. *The Journal of Nervous and Mental Disease, 174,* 727-735.

Bootzin, R.R., and Ruggill, J.S. (1988). Training issues in behavior therapy. *Journal of Consulting and Clinical Psychology, 56,* 703-709.

Brehmer, B. (1969). Cognitive dependence on additive and configural cue-criterion relations. *American Journal of Psychology, 82,* 490-503.

Bruner, J.S., and Potter, M.C. (1964). Interference in visual recognition. *Science, 144,* 424-425.

Carroll, J.S. (1977). Judgments of recidivism risk. *Law and Human Behavior, 1,* 191-198.

Chapman, L.J., and Chapman, J.P. (1967). Genesis of popular but erroneous psychodiagnostic observations. *Journal of Abnormal Psychology, 72,* 193-204.

Chapman, L.J., and Chapman, J.P. (1969). Illusory correlation as an obstacle to the use of valid psychodiagnostic signs. *Journal of Abnormal Psychology, 74,* 271-280.

Chapman, L.J., and Chapman, J.P. (1971). Test results are what you think they are. *Psychology Today*, November, 1971, p. 5.

Cohen, L.H. (1979a). Clinical psychologists' judgments of the scientific merit and clinical relevance of psychotherapy outcome research. *Journal of Consulting and Clinical Psychology, 47,* 421-423.

Cooper, A.M. (1985). Will neurobiology influence psychoanalyses? *The American Journal of Psychiatry, 142,* 1395-1402.

Dahlstrom, W.G. (1993). Tests: Small samples, large consequences. *American Psychologist, 48,* 393-399.

Dailey, C.A. (1952). The effects of premature conclusions upon the acquisition of understanding of a person. *Journal of Psychology, 33,* 133-152.

Dawes, R.M. (1971). A case study of graduate admissions: Application of three principles of human decision making. *American Psychologist, 26,* 180-188.

Dawes, R.M. (1976). Shallow psychology. In J.S. Carroll and J.W. Payne (Eds.), *Cognition and Social Behavior* (pp. 3-11). Hillsdale, NJ: Erlbaum.

Dawes, R.M. (1979). The robust beauty of improper linear models in decision making. *American Psychologist, 34,* 571-582.

Dawes, R.M. (1986). Representative thinking in clinical judgment. *Clinical Psychology Review*, 6, 425-441.

Dawes, R.M. (1989a). Experience and validity of clinical judgment: The illusory correlation. *Behavioral Sciences & the Law, 7,* 457-467.

Dawes, R.M., Faust, D., and Meehl, P.E. (1989). Clinical versus actuarial judgment. *Science, 243,* 1668-1674.

Dawson, N.V., Arkes, H.R., Blinkhorn, R., Lakshmanan, M., and Petrelli, M. (1986). Hindsight bias: An impediment to accurate probability estimation in clinicopathologic conferences. Society of Medical Decision Making convention, Chicago.

Earle, T.C. (1970). Task learning, interpersonal learning, and cognitive complexity. *Oregon Research Institute Research Bulletin, 10,* 2.

Edwards, W.C. (1956). Reward probability, amount, and information as determiners of sequential two-alternative decisions. *Journal of Experimental Psychology, 52,* 177-188.

Einhorn, H.J. (1971). Use of nonlinear, noncompensatory models as a function of task and amount of information. *Organizational Behavior and Human Performance, 6,* 1-27.

Einhorn, H.J. (1980). Learning from experience and suboptimal rules in decision making. In T.S. Wallsten (Ed.), *Cognitive Processes in Choice and Decision Behavior.* Hillsdale, N.J.: Erlbaum Associates.

Einhorn, H.J. (1986). Accepting error to make less error. *Journal of Personality Assessment, 50(3),* 387-395.

Einhorn, H.J., and Hogarth, R.M. (1978). Confidence in judgment: Persistence of the illusion of validity. *Psychological Review, 85,* 395-416.

Einhorn, H.J., and Hogarth, R.M. (1982). Prediction, diagnosis, and causal thinking in forecasting. *Journal of Forecasting, 1,* 23-36.

Estes, W.K. (1962). Learning theory. *Annual Review of Psychology, 13,* 107-144.

Exner, J.E., Jr. (1974). *The Rorschach: A Comprehensive System.* New York: John Wiley and Sons.

Exner, J.E., Jr. (1986). *The Rorschach: A Comprehensive System, Volume I: Basic Foundations* (2nd. Ed.). New York: John Wiley and Sons, Inc.

Exner, J.E., Jr., Viglione, D.J., and Gillespie, R. (1984). Relationships between Rorschach variables and relevant to the interpretation of structural data. *Journal of Personality Assessment, 48,* 65-70.

Farber, L.G., Schmaltz, L.W., Volle, F.O., and Hecht, P. (1986). Temporal lobe epilepsy: Diagnostic accuracy. *The International Journal of Clinical Neuropsychology, 8,* 76-79.

Faust, D. (1986a). Learning and maintaining rules for decreasing judgment accuracy. *Journal of Personality Assessment, 50*, 585-600.

Faust, D. (1989). Data integration in legal evaluations: Can clinicians deliver on their premises? *Behavioral Sciences & the Law, 7*, 469-483.

Faust, D., and Nurcombe, B. (1989). Improving the accuracy of clinical judgment. *Psychiatry, 52*, 197-208.

Faust, D., Hart, K., and Guilmette, T.J. (1988a). Pediatric malingering: The capacity of children to fake believable deficits on neuropsychological testing. *Journal of Consulting and Clinical Psychology, 56*, 578-582.

Feher, E., Vandecreek, L., and Teglasi, H. (1983). The problem of art quality in the use of human figure drawing tests. *Journal of Clinical Psychology, 39*, 268-275.

Fisch, H.U., Hammond, K.R., and Joyce, C.R.B. (1982). On evaluating the severity of depression: An experimental study of psychiatrists. *British Journal of Psychiatry, 140*, 378-383.

Fischhoff, B. (1975). Hindsight = foresight: The effect of outcome knowledge on judgment under uncertainty. *Journal of Experimental Psychology: Human Perception and Performance, 1*, 288-299.

Fischhoff, B. (1980). For those condemned to study the past: Reflections on historical judgment. In R.A. Shweder and D.W. Fiske (Eds.). *New Directions for Methodology of Behavioral Science: Fallible Judgment in Behavioral Research.* San Francisco: Jossey-Bass.

Fischhoff, B. (1982). Debiasing (pp. 422-444). In D. Kahneman, P. Slovic, and A. Tversky (Eds.). *Judgment Under Uncertainty: Heuristics and Biases.* Cambridge: Cambridge University Press.

Fischhoff, B., and Slovic, P. (1980). A little learning...: Confidence in multicue judgment. In R. Nickerson (Ed.), *Attention and Performance VIII.* Hillsdale, NJ: Erlbaum.

Fitzgibbons, D.J., and Shearn, C.R. (1972). Concepts of schizophrenic among mental health professionals: A factor analytic study. *Journal of Consulting and Clinical Psychology, 38*, 228-295.

Garb, H.N. (1988). Comment on "The study of clinical judgment: An ecological approach." *Clinical Psychology Review, 8*, 441-444.

Garb, H.N. (1992). The debate over the use of computer-based test reports. *The Clinical Psychologist, 45*, 95-100.

Garfield, S.L. (1978). Research Problems in Clinical Diagnosis, *Journal of Consulting and Clinical Psychology, 46*, 596-607.

Gill, M., and Brennan, M. (1948). Research and psychotherapy, roundtable. *American Journal of Ortho-Psychiatry, 19*, 100-110.

Giller, E., and Strauss, J. (1984). Clinical research: A key to clinical training. *American Journal of Psychiatry, 141*, 1075-1077.

Gillis, J.S., and Moran, T.J. (1981). An analysis of drug decisions in a state psychiatric hospital. *Journal of Clinical Psychology*, *37*, 32-42.

Goldberg, L.R. (1959). The effectiveness of clinicians' judgments: The diagnosis of organic brain damage from the Bender-Gestalt Test. *Journal of Consulting Psychology*, *23*, 25-33.

Goldberg, L.R. (1965). Diagnosticians vs. diagnostic signs: The diagnosis of psychosis vs. neurosis from the MMPI. *Psychological Monographs*, *79*, 28.

Goldberg, L.R. (1968a). Seer over sign: The first "good" example? *Journal of Experimental Research in Personality*, *3*, 168-171.

Goldberg, L.R. (1968b). Simple models or simple processes? Some research on clinical judgments. *American Psychologist*, *23*, 483-496.

Goldberg, L.R. (1986). Some informal explorations and ruminations about graphology. In B. Nevo (Ed.), *Scientific Aspects of Graphology* (pp. 281-293). Springfield, IL: Charles C. Thomas.

Golden, M. (1964). Some effects of combining psychological tests on clinical inferences. *Journal of Consulting Psychology*, *28*, 440-446.

Golding, S.L., and Rorer, L.G. (1972). Illusory correlation and subjective judgment. *Journal of Abnormal Psychology*, *80*, 249-260.

Goldsmith, S.R., and Mandell, A.J. (1969). The psychodynamic formulation: A critique of a psychiatric ritual. *American Journal of Psychiatry*, *125*, 1738-1743.

Goodstein, L.D., and Brazis, K.L. (1970). Credibility of psychologists: An empirical study. *Psychological Reports*, *27*, 835-838.

Gouvier, W.D., Uddo-Crane, M., and Brown, L.M. (1988). Base rates for postconcussional symptoms. *Archives of Clinical Neuropsychology, 3,* 273-278.

Greenwald, A.G., Pratkanis, A.R., Leippe, M.R., and Baumgardner, M.H. (1986). Under what conditions does theory obstruct research progress? *Psychological Review*, *93*, 216-229.

Hall, G.C.N. (1988). Criminal behavior as a function of clinical and actuarial variables in the sexual offender population. *Journal of Consulting and Clinical Psychology, 56,* 773-775.

Hamilton, D.L. (1976). Cognitive biases in the perception of social groups. In J.F. Carroll and J.W. Payne (Eds.), *Cognition and Social Behavior*. Hillsdale, NJ: Erlbaum.

Hamilton, D.L., Dugan, P.M., and Trolier, T.K. (1985). The formation of stereotypic beliefs: Further evidence for distinctiveness-based illusory correlations. *Journal of Personality and Social Psychology*, *48*, 5-17.

Hammond, K.R., and Summers, D.A. (1965). Cognitive dependence on linear and nonlinear cues. *Psychological Review*, *72*, 215-224.

Hart, K., Faust, D., and Guilmette, T.J. (1987). Pediatric malingering: The capacity of children to fake believable deficits on neuropsychological testing. In D. Faust (Chair), *Clinical Judgment in Neuropsychology: How Good Are We?* Symposium conducted at the Annual Convention of the American Psychological Association, New York.

Hoepfl, R.T., and Huber, G.P. (1970). A study of self-explicated utility models. *Behavioral Science, 15,* 408-414.

Hoffman, P.J. (1960). The paramorphic representation of clinical judgment. *Psychological Bulletin, 57,* 116-131.

Hoffman, P.J., Slovic, P., and Rorer, L.G. (1968). An analysis-of-variance model for the assessment of configural cue utilization in clinical judgment. *Psychological Bulletin, 69,* 338-349.

Holland, T.R., and Holt, N. (1978). Utilization of offender case information by "lenient" vs. "punitive" clinicians. *Journal of Clinical Psychology, 34,* 798-808.

Huber, G.P., Sahney, V.K. and Ford, D.L. (1969). A study of subjective evaluation models. *Behavioral Science, 14,* 483-489.

Hyman, R. (1977). "Cold reading": How to convince strangers that you know all about them. *The Zetetic, 1,* 18-37.

Kadushin, C. (1969). *Why People Go to Psychiatrists.* New York: Atherton.

Kahneman, D., and Tversky, A. (1973). On the psychology of prediction. *Psychological Review, 80,* 237-251.

Kareken, D.A. and Williams, J.M. (1994). Human judgment and estimation of premorbid intellectual function. *Psychological Assessment, 6,* 83-91.

Kazdin, A.E. (1993). Evaluation in clinical practice: Clinically sensitive and systematic methods of treatment delivery. *Behavior Therapy, 24,* 11-45.

Kelly, E.L., and Fiske, D.W. (1950). Prediction of success in veterans administration program in clinical psychology. *American Psychologist, 5,* 365-406.

Kitamura, T., Kahn, A. and Kumer, R. (1984). Reliability of clinical assessment of blunted affect. *Acta Psychiatr. Scandavia., 69,* 242-249.

Kleinmuntz, D.N. (1991). Decision making for professional decision makers. *Psychological Science, 2,* 135-141.

Kort, F. (1968). A nonlinear model for the analysis of judicial decisions. *American Political Science Review, 62,* 546-555.

Kostlan, A. (1954). A method for the empirical study of psychodiagnosis. *Journal of Consulting Psychology, 18,* 83-88.

Kubie, L.S. (1971). Multiple fallacies in the concept of schizophrenia. *The Journal of Nervous and Mental Disease, 159,* 331-342.

Kurtz, R.M., and Garfield, S.L. (1978). Illusory correlation: Further exploration of Chapman's paradigm. *Journal of Consulting and Clinical Psychology*, *46*, 1009-1015.

Leary, M.R. (1982). Hindsight distortion and the 1980 presidential election. *Personality and Social Psychology Bulletin*, *8*, 257-263.

Leli, D.A., and Filskov, S.B. (1981). Clinical-actuarial detection and description of brain impairment with the W-B form 1. *Journal of Clinical Psychology*, *37*, 623-629.

Lezak, M. (1983). *Neuropsychological Assessment* (2nd ed.). New York: Oxford University Press.

Lichtenstein, S., Fischhoff, B., and Phillips, L.D. (1982). Calibration of probabilities: The state of the art to 1980. In D. Kahneman, P. Slovic, and A. Tversky (Eds.), *Judgment Under Uncertainty: Heuristics and Biases*, New York: Cambridge University Press.

Luchins, A.S. (1942). Mechanization in problem solving: The effect of Einstellung. *Psychological Monographs*, *54*, 1-95.

Luger, R.J., and Petzel, T.P. (1979). Illusory correlation in clinical judgment: Effects of amount of information to be processed. *Journal of Consulting and Clinical Psychology*, *47*, 1120-1121.

Mahoney, M.J. (1977). Publication prejudices: An experimental study of confirmatory bias in the peer review system. *Cognitive Therapy and Research*, *1*, 161-175.

Margulies, A., and Havens, L.L. (1981). The initial encounter: What to do first? *American Journal of Psychiatry*, *138*, 421-428.

Matarazzo, J.D. (1986a). Computerized clinical psychological test interpretations: Unvalidated plus all mean and no sigma. *American Psychologist, 41*, 14-24.

Matarazzo, J.D. (1986b). Response to Fowler and Butcher on Matarazzo. *American Psychologist*, *41*, 96.

Meehl, P.E. (1954). *Clinical versus Statistical Prediction: A Theoretical Analysis and a Review of the Evidence.* Minneapolis: University of Minnesota Press.

Meehl, P.E. (1960). The cognitive activity of the clinicians. *American Psychologist, 15*, 19-27.

Meehl, P.E. (1973). *Psychodiagnosis: Selected papers.* Minneapolis: University of Minnesota Press.

Meehl, P.E. (1984). Foreword to Faust, D., *The Limits of Scientific Reasoning.* Minneapolis: University of Minnesota Press.

Meehl, P.E. (1986) Causes and effects of my disturbing little book. *Journal of Personality Assessment, 50*, 370-375.

Meehl, P.E. (1989). Law and the fireside inductions (with postscript): Some reflections of a clinical psychologist. *Behavioral Sciences & the Law, 7,* 521-550.

Meehl, P.E., and Rosen, A. (1955). Antecedent probability and the efficiency of psychometric signs, patterns, or cutting scores. *Psychological Bulletin, 52,* 194-216.

Mendelsohn, F.S., Egri, G., and Dohrenwend, B.P. (1978). Diagnosis of nonpatients in the general community. *American Journal of Psychiatry, 135,* 1163-1167.

Mischel, W., Ebbesen, E.B., and Zeiss, A.M. (1976). Determinants of selective memory about the self. *Journal of Consulting and Clinical Psychology, 44,* 92-103.

Mitchell, T.R., and Kalb, L.S. (1981). Effects of outcome knowledge and outcome valence on supervisors' evaluations. *Journal of Applied Psychology, 66,* 604-612.

Montandon, C., and Harding, T. (1984). The reliability of dangerousness assessments. *British Journal of Psychiatry, 144,* 149-155.

Mynart, C.R., Doherty, M.E., and Tweney, R.D. (1977). Confirmation bias in a simulated research environment: An experimental study of scientific inference. *Quarterly Journal of Experimental Psychology, 29,* 85-95.

Nisbett, R.E., and Ross, L. (1980). *Human Inference: Strategies and Shortcomings of Social Judgments.* Englewood Cliifs, N.J.: Prentice-Hall, Inc.

Nisbett, R.E., and Wilson, T.D. (1977a). The halo effect: Evidence for unconscious alteration of judgments. *Journal of Personality and Social Psychology, 35,* 250-256.

Nisbett, R.E., and Wilson, T.D. (1977b). Telling more than we can know: Verbal reports on mental processes. *Psychological Review, 84,* 231-259.

Nisbett, R.E., Borgida, E., and Crandall, R. (1976). Popular induction: Information is not necessarily informative. In Caroll, J.S., and Payne, J.W. (Eds.), *Cognition and Social Behavior.* Hillsdale, N.J.: Erlbaum.

Oskamp, S. (1962). Clinical experience and training and clinical prediction. *Psychological Monographs, 76.*

Oskamp. S. (1965). Overconfidence in case-study judgments. *Journal of Consulting Psychology, 29,* 261-265.

Otto, R.K., Poythress, N., Starr, L. and Darkes, J. (1993). An empirical study of the reports of APA's peer review panel in the Congressional review of the U.S.S. IOWA incident. *Journal of Personality Adjustment, 61,* 425-442.

Payne, J.W., and Braunstein, M.L. (1971). Preferences among gambles with equal underlying distributions. *Journal of Experimental Psychology, 87,* 13-18.

Pitz, G.F., and Sachs, N.J. (1984). Judgment and decision: Theory and application. *Annual Review of Psychology, 35,* 139-163.

Polanyi, M. (1963). The potential theory of adsorption. *Science, 141,* 1010-1013.

Pratkanis, A.R. (1984). Attitudes and memory: The heuristic and schematic functions of attitudes. Unpublished doctoral dissertation, Ohio State University.

Preston, T.P. (1981). *The Clay Pedestal.* Seattle: Madrona.

Renaud, H., and Estess, F. (1961). Life history interview with one hundred normal American males: "Pathogenicity" of childhood. *American Journal of Orthopsychiatry, 31,* 786-802.

Revusky, S. (1977). Interference with progress by the scientific establishment: Examples from flavor aversion learning. In W. Milgram, L. Knames, and T.M. Alloway (Eds.), *Food Aversion Learning,* 53-71. London: Plenum.

Robins, L.N., and Helzer, J.E. (1986). Diagnosis and clinical assessment: The current state of psychiatric diagnosis. *Annual Review of Psychology, 37,* 409-432.

Rock, D.L. and Bransford, J.D. (1992). An empirical evaluation of three components of the tetrahedron model of clinical judgment. *The Journal of Nervous and Mental Disease, 180,* 560-565.

Rock, D.L., Bransford, J.D., Maisto, S.A., and Morey, L.C. (1987). The study of clinical judgment: An ecological approach. *Clinical Psychology Review, 7,* 645-661.

Rock, D.L., Bransford, J.D., Morey, L.C., and Maisto, S.A. (1988). The study of clinical judgment: Some clarifications. *Clinical Psychology Review, 8,* 411-416.

Rorer, L.G., Hoffman, H.D., Dickman, H.D. and Slovic, P. (1967). Configural judgments revealed (summary). *Proceedings of the 75th Annual Convention of the American Psychological Association, 2,* 195-196.

Rosenhan, D.L. (1973). On being sane in insane places. *Science, 179,* 250-258.

Ross, L., Lepper, M.R., and Hubbard, M. (1975). Perseverance in self-perception and social perception: Biased attributional processes in the debriefing paradigm. *Journal of Personality and Social Psychology, 32,* 880-892.

Ross, M., McFarland, C., and Fletcher, G.J.Q. (1981). The effect of attitude on the recall of personal history. *Journal of Personality and Social Psychology, 40,* 627-634.

Ruback, R.B., and Hopper, C.H. (1986). Decision making of parole interviewers: The effect of case and interview factors. *Law and Human Behavior, 10,* 203-214.

Rubenzer, S. (1991). Computerized testing and clinical judgment: Cause for concern. *The Clinical Psychologist, 44,* 63-66.

Sawyer, J. (1966). Measurement *and* prediction, clinical *and* statistical. *Psychological Bulletin, 66,* 178-200.

Schuldberg, D., French, C., Stone, B.L., and Heberle, J. (1988). Creativity and schizotypal traits. Creativity test scores and perceptual aberration, magical ideation, and impulsive nonconformity. *The Journal of Nervous and Mental Disease, 176,* 648-657.

Shweder, R.A. (1977). Illusory correlation and the MMPI controversy. *Journal of Consulting and Clinical Psychology, 45,* 917-924.

Sines, L.K. (1959). The relative contribution of four kinds of data to accuracy in personality assessment. *Journal of Consulting Psychology, 23,* 483-492.

Slovenko, R. (1984). Commentary: Syndrome evidence in establishing a stressor. *The Journal of Psychiatry and Law, 12,* 443-467.

Slovic, G. (1966). Cue-consistency and cue-utilization in judgment. *American Journal of Psychology, 79,* 427-434.

Slovic, P. (1976). Toward understanding and improving decisions. In W.C. Howell and E.A. Fleishman (Eds.), *Human Performance and Productivity: Vol. 2, Information Processing and Decision Making,* 157-182. Hillsdale, N.J.: Erlbaum.

Slovic, P., and Fischhoff, B. (1977). On the psychology of experimental surprises. *Journal of Experimental Psychology: Human Perception and Performance, 3,* 544-551.

Slovic, P., and Lichtenstein, S.C. (1968). The relative importance of probabilities and payoffs in risk taking. *Journal of Experimental Psychology Monograph Supplement, 72,* No. 3, part 2.

Slovic, P., and Lichtenstein, S.C. (1971). Comparison of Bayesian and regression approaches to the study of information processing in judgment. *Organizational Behavior and Human Performance, 6,* 649-744.

Slovic, P., and MacPhillamy, D. (1974). Dimensional commensurability and cue utilization in comparative judgment. *Organizational Behavior and Human Performance, 11,* 172-194.

Smedslund, J. (1963). The concept of correlation in adults. *Scandinavian Journal of Psychology, 4,* 165-173.

Snyder, C.R. (1977). A patient by any other name revisited: Maladjustment or attributional locus of problems? *Journal of Consulting and Clinical Psychology, 45,* 101-103.

Snyder, M. (1981). Seek and ye shall find: Testing hypotheses about other people. In E.T. Higgins, C.P. Herman, and M.P. Zanna (Eds.), *Social Cognition: The Ontario Symposium on Personality and Social Cognition.* Hillsdale, NJ: Erlbaum.

Snyder, M., and Urbanowitz, S.W. (1978). Reconstructing the past: Some cognitive consequences of person perception. *Journal of Personality and Social Psychology, 36,* 941-950.

Spielberger, C.D. and Piotrowski, C. (1991). Clinician or technician? A reply to Rubenzer. *The Clinical Psychologist, 44,* 67-68.

Stack, L.C., Lannon, P.B., and Miley, A.D. (1983). Accuracy of clinicians' expectancies of psychiatric rehospitalization. *American Journal of Community Psychiatry, 11,* 99-113.

Stuart, R.B. (1970). *Trick or Treatment.* Champaign, IL: Research Press.

Summers, D.A. (1967). Rule versus cue learning in multiple probability tasks. *Proceedings of the 75th Annual Convention of the American Psychological Association, 2,* 43-44.

Summers, D.A., and Hammond, K.R. (1966). Inference behavior in multiple-cue tasks involving both linear and nonlinear relations. *Journal of Experimental Psychology, 71,* 751-757.

Summers, D.A., and Stewart, T.R. (1968). Regression models of foreign policy judgments. *Proceedings of the 76th Annual Convention of the American Psychological Association, 3,* 195-196.

Summers, S.A., Summers, R.C., and Karkau, V.T. (1969). Judgments based on different functional relationships between interacting cues and a criterion. *American Journal of Psychology, 82,* 203-211.

Swann, W.B., and Read, S.J. (1981). Self-verification processes: How we sustain our self-conceptions. *Journal of Experimental Social Psychology, 17,* 351-372.

Temerlin, M.K., and Trousdale, W.W. (1969). The social psychology of clinical diagnosis. *Psychotherapy: Theory, Research and Practice, 6,* 24-29.

Thorne, F.C. (1972). Clinical judgment. In R.H. Woody and J.D. Woody (Eds.), *Clinical Assessment in Counseling and Psychotherapy.* Englewood Cliffs, NJ: Prentice-Hall.

Turk, D.C., and Salovey, P. (1985). Cognitive structures, cognitive processes, and cognitive-behavior modification: II. Judgments and inferences of the clinician. *Cognitive Therapy and Research, 9,* 19-33.

Tversky, A. (1969). Intransitivity of preferences. *Psychological Review, 76,* 31-48.

Tversky, A. (1977). Features of similarity. *Psychological Review, 84,* 327-352.

Tversky, A., and Kahneman, D. (1978). Causal schemata in judgments under uncertainty. In M. Fishbein (Ed.), *Progress in Social Psychology,* 49-72. Hillsdale, N.J.: Erlbaum.

Waller, R.W., and Keeley, S.M. (1978). Effects of explanation and information feedback on the illusory correlation phenomenon. *Journal of Consulting and Clinical Psychology, 46,* 342-343.

Walters, G.D., White, T.W., and Greene, R.L. (1988). Use of the MMPI to identify malingering and exaggeration of psychiatric symptomatology in male prison inmates. *Journal of Consulting and Clinical Psychology, 56,* 111-117.

Ward, W.D., and Jenkins, H.M. (1965). The display of information and the judgment of contingency. *Canadian Journal of Psychology, 19,* 231-241.

Wason, P.C. (1960). On the failure to eliminate hypotheses in a conceptual task. *Quarterly Journal of Experimental Psychology, 11,* 92-107.

Wason, P., and Johnson-Laird, P.N. (1972). *Psychology of Reasoning: Structure and Content.* Cambridge, MA: Harvard University Press.

Wedding, D. (1983). Clinical and statistical prediction in neuropsychology. *Clinical Neuropsychology, 5,* 49-55.

Wedding, D. and Faust, D. (1989). Clinical judgment and decision making in neuropsychology. *Archives of Clinical Neuropsychology, 4,* 233-265.

Werner, P.D., Rose, T.L., and Yesavage, J.A. (1983). Reliability, accuracy, and decision-making strategy in clinical predictions of imminent dangerousness. *Journal of Consulting and Clinical Psychology, 51,* 815-825.

Werner, P.D., Rose, T.L., Yesavage, J.A., and Seeman, K. (1984). Psychiatrists judgments of dangerousness in patients on an acute care unit. *American Journal of Psychiatry, 141,* 263-266.

Wiggins, J.S. (1973). *Personality and Prediction: Principles of Personality Assessment.* Reading, MA: Addison-Wesley.

Wiggins, J.S. (1981). Clinical and statistical prediction: Where are we and where do we go from here? *Clinical Psychology Review, 1,* 3-18.

Wiggins, N., and Hoffman, P.J. (1968). Three models of clinical judgment. *Journal of Abnormal Psychology, 73,* 70-77.

Wilson, T.D., and Nisbett, R.E. (1978). The accuracy of verbal reports about the effects of stimuli on evaluations and behavior. *Social Psychology, 41,* 118-131.

Winch, R.F., and More, D.M. (1956). Does TAT add information to interview? Statistical analysis of the increment. *Journal of Clinical Psychology, 12,* 316-321.

Wolpe, J. (1970). In R.B. Stuart, *Trick or Treatment.* Champaign, Illinois: Research Press.

Wood, G. (1978). The knew-it-all-along effect. *Journal of Experimental Psychology: Human Perception and Performance, 4,* 345-353.

Wyatt, D.F., and Campbell, D.T. (1951). On the liability of stereotype or hypothesis. *Journal of Abnormal and Social Psychology*, *46*, 496-500.

Yager, J. (1977). Psychiatric eclecticism: A cognitive view. *American Journal of Psychiatry*, *134*, 736-741.

Yntema, D.B., and Torgerson, W.S. (1961). Man-computer cooperation in decisions requiring common sense. *IRE Transactions of the Professional Group on Human Factors in Electronics*, *2(1)*, 20-26.

APPENDICES FOR CHAPTER 5

5A. Further Details on Clinical Versus Actuarial Judgment and Sawyer's Analysis of the Literature

5B. Other Problematic Judgment Habits: Anchoring Effects and Over-Reliance on Salient Data

5C. Common Judgment Strategies that Do Not Decrease, but Increase Uncertainty and Error

5D. Factors Underlying Lack of Insight

5E. Simplifying Strategies

5F. Preparing for Common Counterarguments to the Judgment Findings

FURTHER DETAILS ON CLINICAL VERSUS ACTUARIAL JUDGMENT AND SAWYER'S ANALYSIS OF THE LITERATURE

Much of the credit for clarifying issues and stimulating research on the accuracy of clinical versus actuarial judgment goes to Paul Meehl (1954). Meehl's book on the topic raised a furor and a flurry of investigations. There have now been over 100 studies comparing the clinical and actuarial methods. Many of these comparisons have involved mental health practitioners, although even those that have not are of relevance because they provide broad-based knowledge about whether judges who depend on their heads or their "gut" can surpass the accuracy levels achieved by actuarial methods.[1] Within psychology, these studies have addressed such matters as diagnostic accuracy, e.g., the differentiation of "neurosis" and "psychosis;" and prediction as well, e.g., the future occurrence of violent behavior. Overall, these studies cover a wide range and involve not only a variety of judgment tasks, but also judgments made on the basis of limited versus comprehensive information, and judgments made by beginners versus highly experienced practitioners. Many of the judgment tasks that have been studied are quite typical of those performed by psychologists and psychiatrists, such as differential diagnosis.

As discussed in Chapter 5, virtually all of the studies on the topic show the same thing. With exceedingly few exceptions (and see Goldberg, 1968a for a scorching methodological critique of one of these rare exceptions), actuarial judgment methods equal or exceed clinical judgment methods, and clinical judgment methods do not produce significantly greater accuracy than actuarial judgment methods. The reader might wish to know that Paul Meehl is currently working on an updated version of his classic book, which will most likely be published by the University of Minnesota Press.

A few studies on clinical versus actuarial study can be presented in some detail. Goldberg (1965) examined the capacity of clinicians to separate or identify patients as "neurotic" or "psychotic" (as defined by discharge diagnosis) based on their results on the Minnesota Multiphasic Personality Inventory (MMPI). The MMPI is one of the most widely used psychological tests. The psychologists in the study attempted to sort the protocols. Their accuracy was compared to the result achieved with a

---

[1] The reader should be aware that while the research strongly favors the actuarial approach, there are not a large number of such actuarial formulae available in the clinical area. The point that can be made is that in their absence an inferior method is being used.

very simple actuarial formula that specified how to combine scores from a few of the MMPI scales and then how to sort the summary score either into the "neurotic" or "psychotic" category. We need not detail how this or other actuarial judgment procedures are developed. In essence, the process involves the use of statistical procedures that examine for relationships between test scores and the thing one wishes to identify or predict, and based on these results produces steps or a formula that a professional (or layperson) can follow for "interpreting" these or new test scores. The actuarial formula outperformed every one of the 13 psychologists.

Although Goldberg thus found that a simple actuarial formula could outperform judges who relied upon the clinical method, Dawes (1971) found that even simpler actuarial techniques could do the trick as well. Dawes looked at the ability of an admissions committee to predict the future success or performance of candidates for a graduate program in clinical psychology. One should note that this committee consisted of psychologists. Based on measures of actual success obtained after accepted students had completed their initial years of training, Dawes compared the accuracy of the initial ratings made by the admission committee to the accuracy achieved with an actuarial formula. Judgments based on the actuarial method outperformed this admissions committee, which relied on the clinical method.

The superiority of the actuarial method is not surprising; however, there are two remarkable aspects to Dawes's findings. First, this superiority was maintained even when the simplest imaginable actuarial formula was used—the actuarial method founded predictions on one variable alone (prior grade point average). A second and related finding was that the actuarial formula outperformed the admissions committee even when the actuarial method was placed at a distinct informational disadvantage. Specifically, the information with which the admissions committee had to work included grade point average, Graduate Record Examination scores, knowledge of the undergraduate institution attended, and the results of personal interviews. In contrast, when the information provided for actuarial analysis was much more restricted, or limited to a single variable, the actuarial method still outperformed the admissions committee. In general, when one provides more valid information for the development of actuarial formulae, accuracy improves, although it may level off by the time the third or fourth valid variable is provided. Nonetheless, even one variable, and thus the use of a suboptimal actuarial procedure, was still sufficient to establish the superiority of the actuarial method over the committee.

There are a few essential points to be taken from studies such as those conducted by Goldberg and Dawes. First, it is the rule, not the exception, that even simple, suboptimal actuarial procedures equal and often surpass the judgment accuracy achieved with the clinical method. Second, Dawes's study involved clinical judgments that were not made independently, but by a group. There is some evidence that by pooling clinical judgments, it is sometimes possible to achieve somewhat greater accuracy than that obtained when clinicians work in isolation (e.g. Wedding, 1983). Whatever the gain that might be achieved, however, the resultant product is still equaled or surpassed by actuarial methods, even simple ones. An expert may claim greater certainty about his judgment because it is in agreement with other professionals or because he consulted with colleagues. There may be some justification for such an argument in select circumstances, but it can by no means be used to justify claims that such a process produces results that surpass the accuracy achieved by actuarial methods. Finally, in Goldberg's study, the actuarial method beat every single clinician—there were no exceptions.

In Meehl's work on the clinical and actuarial method, he was mainly interested in the comparative accuracy achieved by each method in the interpretation of information or in the formulation of predictions. Thus, to provide a fair or true comparison of the two methods, each should start with the same initial information. For example, suppose one provided only restricted information to the clinician using the clinical method and much more detailed information for the actuarial method. If the actuarial method then attained better results, it would be unclear if this was because the actuarial method was better or because it was given an informational advantage. (Note that the opposite is not true: when the actuarial method, as has been shown, does better when it has less information with which to work than the clinical method, the superiority of the actuarial method is clearly established.) One of the problems with earlier investigations is that they did not provide equal amounts of information for both methods, and thus it was somewhat difficult to interpret the meaning of the findings.

However, there was another complication that seemed to justify doubts expressed by some clinicians about the superiority of actuarial methods. Many of the earlier studies involved the interpretation of psychological test scores alone. Critics argued that by denying clinicians access to interview results, which purportedly were critical to accurate interpretations and predictions, one kept clinicians from demonstrating their full skills or their potential superiority.

Sawyer (1966) sought to clarify these issues and controversies. Although his work is now nearly thirty years old, it remains contemporary, because subsequent research has remained quite consistent with Sawyer's earlier conclusions and findings. Sawyer started by making an essential distinction. On the one hand there are different methods for combining or interpreting information, such as the clinical and actuarial methods that we have discussed. In addition, however, one can also distinguish different ways of collecting information. Of the two basic types, we will call one "fixed" and the other "variable." Fixed methods are those in which one follows prespecified procedures that are *not* changed or altered based on the judgment of the examiner. For example, for many psychological tests there is a set procedure and sequence one follows in administering the items, and so long as this specified procedure is followed one can consider this a fixed form of data gathering. In variable methods, one alters the procedure based on one's judgment. For example, if an interviewer decides on what questions to ask as he goes along, this is a variable method of data gathering. In general, although there are exceptions, most psychological tests (if used as designed) are fixed methods of data gathering, and most forms of interviewing are variable forms. There can be exceptions. Some tests allow for considerable latitude in administrative procedures (or lack fully prespecified procedures), or a clinician using a test may decide to administer it in his own way, thus changing a fixed procedure to a variable one. The person performing an interview might employ a specified and predetermined set of questions. However, we will assume for now that in the studies conducted, psychological tests represented fixed procedures and interviews represented variable procedures.

FIGURE 1

Variation in Methods for Collecting and Combining Information

		Method of Combining Information	
		Clinical	Actuarial
Method of Collecting Information	Variable	(A) variable-clinical	(D) variable-actuarial
	Fixed	(B) fixed-clinical	(E) fixed-actuarial
	Both (variable & fixed)	(C) both-clinical	(F) both-actuarial

Sawyer, then, distinguished two methods of collecting information, which we have called fixed and variable, and two methods of combining information, clinical and actuarial.[2] Figure 1 represents the possible combinations of these methods graphically, and adds two more. Let us explain each of the cells in Figure 1. In Cells A, B, and C, the *clinical method* of data *combination* is always used; what is *different* across the cells is the *method of collecting information.* In Cell A, the variable method of data gathering is used, and the clinical method is used to combine these data. In Cell B, the fixed method of data gathering is used, and again these data are combined clinically. In Cell C, data gathering involves both the fixed and variable method, as would be the case if one collected both test data and interview data. In Cells D, E, and F, the actuarial method of data combination is always used. In Cell D, the variable method is used to gather data and the actuarial method is used to combine the data. (For example, one might conduct an interview, code one's clinical impressions, then subject this coded data to actuarial analysis.) In Cell E, the fixed method is used to gather data that are subsequently combined using the actuarial method. In Cell F, data are gathered using both fixed and variable methods, and then subjected to actuarial analysis.

In order to aid in the interpretation of the material that follows, we list an example for each of these cells:

Cell A	(variable-clinical): interview results combined clinically
Cell B	(fixed-clinical): test results combined clinically
Cell C	(both-clinical): interview and test results combined clinically
Cell D	(variable-actuarial): interview results combined actuarially
Cell E	(fixed-actuarial): test results combined actuarially
Cell F	(both-actuarial): interview and test results combined actuarially

Using the various possibilities described above, Sawyer was able to re-examine and organize the prior studies and comparisons that had been made across methods for gathering data and combining it. Sawyer was able to locate 45 usable studies. The methods used in each of these studies could then be grouped into their appropriate categories and the types of comparisons could then be classified. For example, a study might compare the results attained with fixed data collection and clinical interpretation to those obtained with fixed data collection and actuarial interpretation, or Cell B (fixed-clinical) and Cell E (fixed-actuarial). All told,

---

2 The reader should know that for the sake of clarity, we have altered Sawyer's terminology for describing methods of data collection and interpretation. Those interested in the original wording can obtain Sawyer's article.

the 45 studies provided 75 comparisons (some studies included more than one comparison).

Viewing the results across these 75 comparisons, not one conflicted with any other. Whenever one method was shown to be equal to or better than another in one comparison, the same results were obtained across any other studies that made the same comparison. Thus, the evidence was not mixed but entirely consistent. As Meehl (1984) notes, this is an extreme rarity in the social sciences, especially when dealing with this number of studies. Here is what Sawyer found.

Across the comparisons, the actuarial method of combining information always equaled or exceeded the clinical method of combining information, no matter what method of data gathering was used. Even when the clinical method was provided with a decided informational advantage, in no case did its accuracy significantly exceed that of the actuarial method. Indeed, even when those using the clinical method had access to both interview and test results, and the actuarial method had access only to interview or only to test results, the actuarial method always equaled or significantly exceeded the clinical method. Therefore, the results provided absolutely no support, and considerable countersupport, for the argument that clinicians have some special powers by which they can use interview data in their preferred manner (i.e., clinically) to exceed the level of accuracy achieved using actuarial methods.

Of equal interest, Sawyer was able to rank order the accuracy of the six different approaches to data collection and interpretation. The order, from best to worst, was as follows:

(1) Interview and test results combined actuarially
    (Cell F: both-actuarial)
(2) Test results combined actuarially
    (Cell E: fixed-actuarial)
(3) Interview results combined actuarially
    (Cell D: variable-actuarial)
(4) Test results combined clinically
    (Cell B: fixed-clinical)
(5) Test and interview results combined clinically
    (Cell C: both-clinical)
(6) Interview results combined clinically
    (Cell A: variable-clinical)

Of interest and great potential relevance, this ranking of methods in order of accuracy, and the actual methods used by psychologists and psychiatrists conducting forensic evaluation, quite likely show a strong negative correlation. Stated differently, clinicians typically disregard the methods that produce the highest level of overall accuracy and instead use methods that produce the lower, or lowest level of accuracy.

In cases we have consulted on, many psychiatrists rely on the results of history gathering and interview alone, and combine this information using the clinical method. Sawyer's findings show that among the range of methods he compared, this is absolutely the worst, or least accurate approach overall.[3] Some psychiatrists, and many psychologists, will rely on interview and test results and combine this information clinically. According to Sawyer, this is not the worst possible approach, but close to it. Sawyer's analysis also shows that when one uses the clinical method of interpretation, better results are achieved, on average, if one uses test scores alone and completely disregards interview findings. In other words, adding the information obtained by interview to information obtained from tests generally decreases judgment accuracy. Thus, by implication, it would be better to eliminate a psychiatrist from the assessment process entirely, for psychiatrists do not perform psychological testing. The psychologist who administers tests might be better off stopping there, because conducting interviews as well is more likely to decrease, rather than increase, the accuracy of conclusions. We have rarely encountered testing without interview in our consulting practice, and in most instances in which tests were given, interviews were conducted as well.[4] (It may be that the psychiatrist does the interviewing and requests independent testing from a psychologist, but the psychiatrist will use these testing results, together with the interview results, in reaching conclusions. If this is somehow not the case and the psychiatrist relies on interview alone, then he will have used the least accurate procedure.)

Based on Sawyer's results, the lawyer is in a position to ask some rather important questions. For the psychologist or psychiatrist who relies on interview alone, one can ask, "Is there not a considerable body of evidence which shows that interview and clinical interpretation produces the lowest overall level of accuracy in comparison to various other procedures, such as actuarial methods?" If the expert does not acknowledge that this is so, the lawyer can call a rebuttal witness. Further, anytime claims are made for the superior accuracy achieved when one not only

---

[3] When confronted with these findings, some experts may indicate that Sawyer did not analyze the results (accuracy) achieved for the type of forensic evaluations they conduct. They can be asked to recite the scientific evidence which shows that Sawyer's findings do not apply. Given the range of studies Sawyer analyzed and the consistency of his results, claims that the findings do not generalize to the experts' type of work, short of positive scientific evidence to this effect, are certainly subject to considerable doubt.

[4] We would again remind the reader that our practices are quite possibly not representative. We are not implying that what we have observed is true in general.

uses test results but combines them with interview results, one can certainly ask, "Isn't there research to show that clinicians achieve greater overall accuracy when they use tests alone and disregard interview results entirely?" Or, "Doctor, are you aware of the research which suggests that adding interview results to test results actually decreases the overall level of accuracy achieved when interpreting data in the clinical manner you described?"

There are a number of other important points to be gained from Sawyer's work. One is that more (information) can be less (judgment accuracy). As noted above, when the results from interview and tests are combined using the clinical method, the overall level of accuracy is lower than that achieved using tests alone. Thus, adding additional information (interview results) to test results does not enhance, but actually decreases overall accuracy. These findings are consistent with research cited in Chapter 5 which suggests a limited capacity of clinicians to benefit from enlarged sets of data. Therefore, clinicians' assumptions or statements that greater accuracy is to be expected by expanding the data base or by collecting extensive information can be challenged and should not be allowed to be presented as a given, or a self-evident truth.

Sawyer did find that when the actuarial method was used, the best overall results were attained when interview data were added to test data. Apparently, then, interviews can produce information of some predictive value. However, on average, any such value is lost or even reversed when the clinical method is used, and it is only the actuarial method that capitalizes on the added informational value.

Sawyer's work, and the results of other studies on clinical versus actuarial methods of data interpretation, clearly suggest that greater accuracy would be achieved if so-called experts were entirely eliminated from the data interpretation process when actuarial methods are available. A computer, or clerk, or reasonably intelligent adult is all that is required to perform actuarial data analysis. Once an actuarial formula has been developed, all one need do is take the information and plug it into the formula, and many of these formulae are quite simple (such that a child could perform the calculations). We would note that although actuarial methods are superior to clinical methods, even actuarial methods rarely produce more than modest levels of accuracy (see below).

Sawyer's work also has implications for the management of "data clashes." It is the rare case indeed when all data point toward the same conclusion or are entirely consistent, especially if anything more than a meager set of information is collected. Based on the rank ordering that Sawyer obtained, if a test points toward one conclusion and interview results toward another, one will achieve a higher level of overall accuracy by deferring to the test results. This is simply because, overall, conclusions based on tests, whether produced through the clinical or actuarial method, have higher overall accuracy than conclusions based on interview results. Further, anytime the results of an actuarial method of data interpretation clash with the results of the clinical method, even if the clinical method is based on both interview and test data and the actuarial method is based on only interview results or only test data, one should defer to the actuarial method.

These findings should not be surprising. The main point of the scientific method and the development of scientific knowledge is to decrease reliance on subjective judgment processes and to develop instead prespecified or set procedures for collecting and interpreting data. Are we surprised, for example, that an X-ray is a more reliable means for identifying a break in a bone or for determining its exact features than is clinical examination, especially if the bone lies under the surface and is difficult for the physician to assess by touch? Why do we measure things or use mathematics at all? Thus, should we be surprised that a standard IQ test provides a better measure of intelligence than clinical impression, or that the results of the test will be more accurately determined if one adds up the numbers and compares results to established information on a wide range of individuals rather than guesses about the total?

The fact that the research is so consistent in pointing to the superiority of the actuarial method and that the use of this method would free up considerable amounts of the clinician's time might lead one to expect that the actuarial method is strongly preferred. However, there is virtually no evidence to suggest that actuarial methods are used frequently, and indeed it may well be the rare psychologist, and even the rarer psychiatrist, who relies predominantly on actuarial methods. It is uncertain why this might be the case, although certain reasons seem apparent. First, as Meehl (1984) indicates, many individuals do not even know the issue exists, and others "continue to resist" the massive evidence. Meehl obviously feels that this reflects less than optimal scholarly attitudes. Whatever the case, two additional reasons may be pertinent.

Although the actuarial method is superior to the clinical method, even the accuracy attained with the former approach is generally quite modest. For example, certain actuarial interpretive procedures for the MMPI might achieve a 50% accuracy rate for a certain type of test result. How these procedures might perform for tasks other than those involved in clinical practice, or specifically for purposes of legal decision making, remains largely untested and thus unanswered, although the research to date has hardly been encouraging (see the discussion of "the gap" in Chapter 4). In any case, clinicians hope to exceed the accuracy produced by actuarial interpretation. Thus, they may disregard actuarial information entirely, thinking they can do better, or may decide selectively when to follow and not follow the actuarial results. As we have shown above, these attempts seem to backfire and produce a lower level of accuracy than would be achieved using the actuarial method alone. However, as discussed in Chapter 5, clinicians are very prone to forming illusory beliefs about their own judgment accuracy, and they may believe they are outperforming the results that would be achieved using an actuarial approach, even though they really are not. Put simply, subjective beliefs about judgment accuracy are often highly misleading and produce a false sense of confidence.

Finally, perhaps because most clinicians have simply not taken the problem seriously, there is a limited range of available actuarial methods. For example, there are very few methods for combining results across tests, and almost none for combining results across tests and interviews. Thus, although there seem to be few, if any, grounds for failing to use actuarial methods in the interpretation of single tests to the extent that they are available, when combining results across tests or across tests and interviews there is generally little option but to perform such interpretation using the clinical method. We might add that, given the research on the capacity of clinicians to combine data or to benefit as the data base expands, in many cases clinicians would almost surely be better off by restricting assessment to the much smaller range of tests that permit actuarial interpretation.

REFERENCES

Dawes, R.M. (1971). A case study of graduate admissions: Application of three principles of human decision making. *American Psychologist, 26*, 180-188.

Goldberg, L.R. (1965). Diagnosticians vs. diagnostic signs: The diagnosis of psychosis vs. neurosis from the MMPI. *Psychological Monographs, 79*, 28.

Goldberg, L.R. (1968a). Seer over sign: The first "good" example? *Journal of Experimental Research in Personality, 3*, 168-171.

Meehl, P.E. (1954). *Clinical versus Statistical Prediction: A Theoretical Analysis and a Review of the Evidence.* Minneapolis: University of Minnesota Press.

Meehl, P.E. (1984). Foreword to Faust, D., *The Limits of Scientific Reasoning.* Minneapolis: University of Minnesota Press.

Sawyer, J. (1966). Measurement *and* prediction, clinical *and* statistical. *Psychological Bulletin, 66*, 178-200.

Wedding, D. (1983). Clinical and statistical prediction in neuropsychology. *Clinical Neuropsychology, 5*, 49-55.

APPENDIX 5B

OTHER PROBLEMATIC JUDGMENT HABITS: ANCHORING EFFECTS AND OVER-RELIANCE ON SALIENT DATA

ANCHORING EFFECTS

The term "anchoring effects" refers to the tendency for initial estimates or impressions to be insufficiently adjusted on the basis of subsequent data, or for subsequent estimates to be overly influenced by the initial estimate. For example, suppose individuals are asked to guess the population of New York; some make guesses that are significantly too high and make some guesses that are significantly too low. The overestimators are informed that their guesses are too high and the underestimators that their guesses are too low, and both groups are told to make a second guess. What one typically finds is that the initial overestimators make insufficient adjustments and that their guesses remain too high, or too close to their initial estimates. Similarly, the underestimators make a parallel error and thus remain too low, or too close to their initial estimates. The relevance of such effects is that initial impressions or estimates are not adjusted sufficiently, and thus information obtained early tends to have greater impact than information obtained later. These anchoring effects have been demonstrated by a number of researchers, including Bieri et al. (1966), Tversky and Kahneman (1973), and Friedlander and Stockman (1983).

For example, in the Friedlander and Stockman study, the authors discuss how anchoring effects can lead clinicians to attach more importance to information derived early in the assessment process than information obtained later. As a result, erroneous initial impressions may fail to be sufficiently corrected. Their study primarily involved psychologists and psychiatrists, who on average had over 10 years of experience. They found that these clinicians demonstrated significant anchoring effects in their final estimates of pathology and prognosis in the case of a "moderately disturbed" client. Significant effects were not found in another more seriously disturbed case.

Friedlander and Phillips (1984) attempted to repeat these anchoring effects with college students using the same procedures as those employed in the Friedlander and Stockman study. However, no significant effects were evidenced and the replication was unsuccessful. Thus, under an identical set of circumstances across the two studies, only the professionals showed anchoring effects. As regards these effects, Friedlander and Stockman state:

The evidence that clinical judgments differ significantly as a function of time contradicts the principles of scientific interviewing in which observations provide a basis for tentative judgments that in turn suggest alternative hypotheses....If one's judgment is biased towards the first impression, foreclosure on an initial diagnosis can act as a self-fulfilling prophecy, with significant effects on later inferences.... (p. 67)

Obviously, the statement is not intended for the students but for the professionals.

OVERRELIANCE ON SALIENT DATA

Clinicians often purport to consider all of the data and not to rely too heavily on any one or a few pieces of information. However, there is evidence that, in sharp contrast to these claims, even single pieces of information can have a dramatic effect on conclusions. Further, rather than relying most heavily on the data that are most informative, or most useful from the standpoint of reaching correct conclusions, clinicians rather often (over)attend to particularly salient or dramatic data, even if these data actually have limited information value.

Faust et al. (1988c) summarize the problem as follows:

Clinicians are drawn to the dramatic and exotic. A complaint of demonic possession, for example, intuitively conveys more weight than an employment history. Unfortunately, impressionistic salience does not necessarily coincide with clinical value, wherein lies the crux of the matter. Research suggests that dramatic information tends to be accorded undue weight, and preferred to blander (but more valuable) data.

This same paper discusses a promising education course developed by Drs. Barry Nurcombe and Ina Fitzhenry-Coor (see Nurcombe and Gallagher, 1986, Chapter 27), and employed on an experimental basis at the University of Vermont with medical students on their psychiatry rotations. In this course, a systematic attempt is made to discourage these and other bad judgment habits and to encourage more effective habits. The authors note that, to their knowledge, there are no other such courses of this type within psychiatry.

Research described or conducted by Nisbett et al. (1976), Nisbett and Ross (1980), Sattin (1980), and Snyder (1977) all show the potentially powerful effects of salient and/or very limited amounts of information. For example, in the work described by Snyder, psychodynamic clinicians examined identical information about an individual, with one exception. One group of clinicians was told the individual was a patient and the other group was told that he was a job applicant. This one piece of information, even though all other information was identical, nevertheless led the two groups of clinicians to reach significantly different conclusions. (As might be expected, the "patient" was viewed as significantly more abnormal.) Further, the Rosenhan study demonstrates that even one salient symptom can have not only dramatic effects on initial impressions, but longlasting effects even in the face of considerable counterevidence for these initial impressions.

Actually, this is one area in which it is hardly necessary to depend on experimental studies to show us that bland data are often undervalued in comparison to more salient data. One need simply look at the frequency with which clinicians ignore the "bland" data produced by actuarial formulae. Surveys (e.g., Wade and Baker, 1977) show that the great majority of clinical psychologists pay little heed to actuarial methods or the data they could obtain through such methods. Mischel (1979) summarizes the problem in this way: "Not only do we naturally favor vivid but unreliable data over more complete but pallid information in our drive to confirm our causal models, we easily twist data to make them fit poor models and are reluctant and slow to revise the models themselves."

REFERENCES

Bieri, J., Atkins, A.L., Briar, S., Leaman, R.L., Miller, H., and Tripodi, T. (1966). *Clinical and social judgment*. New York: John Wiley and Sons.

Faust, D., Nurcome, B., and Fitzhenry-Coor, I. (1988c). Toward the refinement of psychiatric reasoning. I: Educational approaches. Manuscript submitted for publication.

Freidlander, M.L., and Phillips, S.D. (1984). Preventing anchoring errors in clinical judgment. *Journal of Consulting and Clinical Psychology, 52,* 366-371.

Friedlander, M.L., and Stockman, S.J. (1983). Anchoring and publicity effect in clinical judgment. *Journal of Clinical Psychology, 39,* 637-643.

Mischel, W. (1979). On the interface of cognition and personality. *American Psychologist, 34,* 740-754.

Nisbett, R.E., Borgida, E., and Crandall, R. (1976). Popular induction: Information is not necessarily informative. In Caroll, J.S., and Payne, J.W. (Eds.), *Cognition and Social Behavior*. Hillsdale, N.J.: Erlbaum.

Nisbett, R.E., and Ross, L. (1980). *Human inference: Strategies and shortcomings of social judgments*. Englewood Cliffs, N.J.: Prentice-Hall, Inc.

Nurcombe, B., and Gallagher, R.M. (1986). *The Clinical Process in Psychiatry*. New York: Cambridge University Press.

Sattin, D.B. (1980). Possible sources of error in the evaluation of psychopathology. *Journal of Clinical Psychology, 36,* 99-105.

Snyder, C.R. (1977). A patient by any other name revisited: Maladjustment or attributional locus of problems? *Journal of Consulting and Clinical Psychology, 45,* 101-103.

Tversky, A., and Kahneman, D. (1973). Availability: A heuristic for judging frequency probability. *Cognitive Psychology*, *5*, 207-232.

Wade, T.C., and Baker, T.B. (1977). Opinions and use of psychological tests: A survey of clinical psychologists. *American Psychologist*, *32*, 874-882.

APPENDIX 5C

COMMON JUDGMENT STRATEGIES THAT DO NOT DECREASE, BUT INCREASE UNCERTAINTY AND ERROR MAKING

MAKING THE COMPLICATED MORE COMPLICATED

The material in Chapter 5 should make a few things fairly clear, or at least provide considerable evidence in support of the statements that follow. To achieve the highest possible overall level of judgment accuracy, clinicians should be as systematic as possible in their methods of data collection and interpretation. As regards the latter, where available, one should base interpretations on actuarial decision rules. To the extent that clinicians stray from these dictates, their overall level of accuracy declines. For example, selective disregard of actuarial analysis is associated with reduced overall accuracy. Complete disregard of actuarial decision rules produces even worse overall results. The bottom line is that to minimize uncertainty in clinical decision making, one should rely to the greatest extent possible on previously established and scientifically supported data collection and interpretation techniques that have the highest demonstrated levels of reliability and validity.

The above is certainly not to say that proceeding as described ensures accurate judgment: only that it maximizes the chances of success. Clinical judgment is almost always a risky business, even under the best of circumstances, and even the best available procedures may still produce a high percentage of errors. Clinicians want to do better than this.

In the quest to do better, or as well as possible, clinicians often depend on decision-making strategies that are almost sure to have the opposite effect. We will call these approaches "strategies for increasing uncertainty," or for making the decidedly difficult task of accurate clinical judgment more difficult still. These strategies that increase uncertainty are sometimes used because clinicians are not aware of their actual effects, or because they do not know there are potential means for doing better (e.g., they may know nothing about the clinical-actuarial debate). Alternatively, they may choose to disregard the literature on decision making. For example, they may refuse to believe that it might apply to them. Other clinicians have what are arguably better reasons. They are dissatisfied with the level of accuracy achieved through the use of pre-specified procedures. Further, the more astute may recognize that the accuracy achieved through formal procedures or decision rules does not really satisfy the requirements of the court. Imagine an expert going into court and stating something like the following, "In truth, I am only 50%

(or 30% or 10%) certain of my 'expert' opinion, although this level is really the best we can do using established procedures." Thus, even those aware of clinical and actuarial approaches and the higher overall accuracy achieved by the latter, realize that they often cannot settle for, or justify to the courts, the level of accuracy that actuarial methods achieve. Whatever their rationale, the following procedures that clinicians use to do as well as possible are more likely to backfire and have the opposite effect.

FAILURE TO USE STANDARDIZED METHODS OF DATA COLLECTION AND INTERPRETATION

Many clinicians increase uncertainty by disregarding available methods for standardized data collection. For example, for the great majority of psychological tests, there are set ways of administering and scoring items. Most test manuals will instruct clinicians in no uncertain terms to follow these procedures closely, for a failure to do so can result in misleading scores or results that cannot be interpreted in the context of previously established data or norms collected for the test. Nevertheless, clinicians apparently often fail to conform to these guidelines. *For example, less than 20% of the clinicians surveyed by Wade and Baker (1977) indicated that they use standardized assessment procedures. Rather, the great majority use their own personalized or creative procedures.*

In other cases, there may be no standardized methods to follow, even if one wished to do so. Ramzy (1975) points out that although it may sound unbelievable, the vast literature on psychoanalysis contains hardly any references outlining the guidelines or methodological rules which the analyst follows to understand his patient. He states:

> It is thus that, however meticulously the works on psychoanalytic method are scanned, the fact remains that, no sooner is it realized how essential a knowledge of the nature of psychoanalytic inference is, and how lacking it is in understanding of the process of clinical judgment, than this basic issue is glossed over or given up as if it were an onerous or redundant task.

He points out that, as others have indicated, "Absence of any explicitly defined rules of psychoanalytic reasoning still remains the 'Achilles' heel' of psychoanalysis."

ABANDONING ESTABLISHED DECISION RULES

Many clinicians may start off by closely following standard procedures of data collection and interpretation but, in an effort to do better, abandon them over time. According to the research of Arkes et al. (1986) with lay subjects, as incentive to do well increases, the greater the tendency to disregard established procedures that achieve the highest, but still only modest, levels of overall accuracy. In the case of the expert, there is an obvious problem if established procedures or rules are abandoned. They are almost inevitably replaced by much riskier approaches—those that may seem to be worthwhile or necessary gambles, but that are inferior overall—and not replaced with something better. If there are nothing but inferior alternatives available but one pursues them anyway, it is unreasonable to expect a positive outcome.

Einhorn (1986) discusses how, in order to maximize overall predictive accuracy, one has to accept that decision rules are not perfect and live with the errors that result, rather than abandoning these rules in the false hope that one will do better without them. The latter is seen as a very risky strategy. It may have substantial payoff, but only rarely. For legal purposes, abandoning a sounder strategy for a riskier one that produces more errors but occasionally pays off seems very difficult to justify. The title of Einhorn's paper, "Accepting Error to Make Less Error," well describes the point he is trying to make. Einhorn states:

> The clinical versus statistical controversy represents a basic conflict about the predictability of behavior. The evidence is clear and convincing that the statistical approach does a better job of forecasting, but the clinical approach is not without its virtues. Indeed, I tend to think of the clinical approach as a high risk strategy; that is, the chance of being able to predict all the variance of behavior (or even a substantial amount) is very low, but the payoff is correspondingly high. On the other hand, the acceptance of error to make less error is likely to be a safer and more accurate strategy over a wide range of practical situations. Thus, the statistical approach leads to better performance on the average. In my view, this is a compelling argument for its use. (p. 394)

UNIQUE VERSUS COMMON FEATURES

Many clinicians like to point out that all individuals are unique. In fact, it seems that clinicians are often drawn to unique features of cases and tend to disregard common features, which is likely to decrease judgment accuracy. Although all individuals may indeed be unique in some ways, there are almost always points of similarity with other individuals as well. However, focusing on an individual's unique features encourages the view that the particular case is so unique or different from what is known that prior knowledge or decision rules are of little use. Thus, one is essentially taking the position, whether he realizes it or not, that he is dealing with something that is quite new and for which little, if anything, is currently known. It is difficult to think of a situation that could produce a greater level of uncertainty. In essence, the clinician is exploring territory where no one has explored before, and for which no maps (prior knowledge) are available to offer guidance. Even so, there is an apparent tendency to believe that these unique features are extremely informative, or that they provide the basis for accurate prediction.

Most any clinician with a little imagination can find unique features in any individual he sees. Further, the more active the search for these unique features, the greater the chance that the not-unique features will be overlooked. Thus, one bypasses opportunities to utilize previously established knowledge. Consequently, familiar features tend to be ignored and diagnosis, description, or prediction is overinfluenced by the assumed rarity. For a review of the research demonstrating overreliance on unique features, its mismanagement, and its detrimental effects on judgment accuracy, see Kahneman and Tversky (1982).

Any time a clinician goes out of his way to discuss the unique features of some case, and particularly when the discussion is aimed at showing that negative research does not apply to the individual under consideration, the lawyer might raise a question like the following: "Do you mean to say that you have never seen anybody just like this before or have no experience with individuals *just* like this?" The expert may respond that theoretical principles or some such thing allow him to gain a proper understanding, but theories apply to commonalities, not unique features, and the mere asking of the question should have impact.

THE SORRY WEATHERMAN, OR, WHY OBTAIN DIRECT DATA WHEN ONE CAN ENGAGE IN SPECULATION?

The sorry weatherman is the one who tells his audience, from his closed studio, "There is only a 10% chance of rain today, so get out your beach gear," at the very moment when the rain is pouring down outside. Had he stuck his head outside and obtained the "data" directly, he might have avoided this embarrassing error. Psychologists and psychiatrists may act likewise. When direct evidence, or relatively direct evidence is available, they may disregard it and instead chase after indirect data. When matters are seemingly straightforward, they complicate them and look for more complex, hidden meanings. Stated differently, when they see bicycle tracks, they infer the passing of an elephant with footwear designed to mimic bicycle tracks. One would think that achieving even modest accuracy was already difficult enough, without adding such unnecessary complexity.

There are a number of ways in which these tendencies are manifested. One is in using psychological tests to make judgments about matters that the tests are not directly designed to address, and bypassing the use of tests that are directly designed to make these judgments. For example, on many occasions, we have seen psychologists draw conclusions about intellectual abilities based on the Rorschach, a test designed to measure personality functioning and not intelligence, and then to administer only part of the intelligence test or even skip this test completely. Alternatively, they may draw conclusions about personality functioning based on intellectual testing results. These practices only complicate matters. In fact, even adjusting impressions on such a basis seems unwarranted (e.g., one concludes a low IQ score underestimates intelligence based on the results on the Rorschach).

For example, in a study by Nobo and Evans (1986), no support was provided for beliefs about the relationship between performance on certain subtests of the Wechsler Adult Intelligence Scale-Revised and certain personality traits. The authors suggest caution in drawing personality inferences on the basis of performance on the IQ test. A number of prominent psychologists have warned about this backwards way of doing things—using personality tests to draw inferences about intellectual functioning and vice-versa (see Chapter 10). If one wishes to assess intelligence, for example, use the best available means.

A second variant of these practices is to use psychological tests to "predict" what one could find out about directly by just asking, or by just studying background history. For example, one might use a personality test to draw inferences about "aggressive tendencies," never bothering to check the criminal record indicating a long list of violent crimes. Why do this if there is no reason or need to guess? As Meehl (1973) states: "A psychometric instrument is not a parlor trick in which, for some strange (union-card?) reason, you keep yourself from having access to easily available information about a patient for the fun of seeing whether you can guess it instead of getting it directly. The psychologist who doesn't understand this point is not even in the ball park of clinical sophistication." (p. 243) As an example, Meehl discusses how certain studies examine whether the diagnostic conclusions achieved through testing match with those of a separate diagnostician, such as a psychiatrist who has seen the patient. In essence, he sees such work as fruitless, stating, "Giving a Rorschach or MMPI in order to predict the verbal behavior of the psychiatrist (dynamically or diagnostically) is pointless. It's a waste of the patient's time and the taxpayer's money. If all I want to do is forecast what the psychiatrist will say about the patient's diagnosis or dynamics, it is obvious that the easiest way to do that is to walk down the hall and ask him." (p. 243)

Along similar lines, rather than asking patients directly about one or another matter, many psychologists and psychiatrists will go about this indirectly, never asking these direct questions but instead attempting to draw inferences on the basis of other behavior. For example, if one wishes to determine whether the patient has conflicts with his spouse, the clinician might not ask, "How do you and your wife get along?" Rather, the clinician asks about the patient's dreams involving women and through the response provided attempts to draw inferences about marital status. Mischel (1972) provides an extensive overview of work on this matter of direct versus indirect assessment techniques. He states:

> The most obvious and direct way to inquire about another individual's characteristics and beliefs is to ask him what they are. But in accord with the pervasive psychological assumption that people are unwilling or unable to reveal themselves directly many assessors prefer more indirect assessment strategies. Guided by Freudian theory and its newer variations psychologists have widely assumed both in clinical practice and research that what a person says about himself in response to direct questions is likely to be either superficial or defensively distorted and misleading. Therefore, seemingly irrelevant behavior (casual comments, jokes, slips of the tongue) may be construed by the clinician as important clues of the individual's "underlying" dispositions while the client's own reports about his beliefs, interests and personality attributes may be suspect. For example, the client's "explanation" of his behavior, his self reports of motives and traits may be construed as defenses and resistances that must be circumvented rather than as potentially accurate descriptions in their own right.

Mischel points out the preference of clinicians to infer underlying dispositions which cannot be observed from patients' behavior. Mischel refers to a number of studies that have been done comparing direct versus indirect methods of assessment and states:

> The foregoing studies are merely illustrations from a larger literature...they demonstrate that the relative utility of direct versus indirect measures found by Scott and Johnson (1972) for attitudes hold equally when deeper hypothesized personality dispositions are the objectives of assessment and when the comparisons are based on well established personality tests.

> Taken collectively rather than piecemeal or singly the studies on the comparative utility of direct and indirect personality assessment are consistent: the predictions possible from the subjects' own simple, direct self-ratings and self-reports generally have not been exceeded by those obtained from more indirect, costly and sophisticated personality tests, from combined test batteries and from expert clinical judges...these conclusions appear to hold for such diverse content areas as college achievement, job and professional success, treatment outcomes in psychotherapy, re-hospitalization for psychiatric patients, and parole violations for delinquent children.

Further,

> Given the overall findings regarding the limitations of the indirect-sign paradigm, assessors may want to look more at what people do and say, not as these events serve as indirect signs of underlying dispositions but rather as direct samples of their behavior. Such a focus on behavior as sample rather than as sign...leads one to a measurement strategy entirely different from the traditional personality assessment approach and in turn requires a different theoretical paradigm for studying behavior in relation to the conditions in which it occurs.

We should note that Mischel is discussing clinical assessment, and in forensic assessment, motives for self-disclosure may be quite different.

Finally, there seems to be a decided tendency on the part of many psychologists and psychiatrists to read deeper meanings into things, with the result that the plain and obvious may be missed entirely. Berry (1973) introduces a study that examines this tendency to search for deeper or more complex explanations by indicating:

> In a general study of the etiology of learning disabilities, Ames noted that "mysterious" and dynamic explanations are often given for a specific child's failure to learn, whereas further exploration frequently reveals that the child's difficulty is primarily a result of lower than average intelligence. Observation indicates that daily in the professional communication of information about child behavior complex interpretations or explanations are used when less complex and more readily testable forms may better serve the purpose.

In an attempt to test this proposition, Berry presented limited information to 16 members of a child psychiatry service, including child psychiatrists, social workers and psychiatric nurses with child care experience. Given the limited information, the professionals were then given four choices which had been categorized as simple or complex. An example of the items is the following:

> Before you examine a 4-year-old you are given the information that she does not talk. Your first thought is: (a) deafness (b) low intelligence (c) infantile autism (d) childhood schizophrenia.

After reading each item, the subjects were to select the choice most like their first impression. The first two options above would represent simple explanations and the latter two complex explanations. Berry found that among respondents' actual first choices, 72% represented complex explanations and 28% simple explanations. Berry concludes:

> It appears that, at least for this sample, professional persons engaged in work that calls for interpretation of deviant child behavior are inclined to the more complex explanation and labels when they interpret behavior....The findings supported the hypothesis that these mental health workers do tend to be more attracted to the complex labels or explanations of deviant child behavior and tend to ignore the law of parsimony.

In a classic paper, Miller (1961) discusses a subgroup of individuals who pursue personal injury suits even when they have sustained very minor physical damage. Miller indicates that some of these cases represent very obvious attempts to feign or exaggerate injury in order to gain financial compensation. He criticizes psychiatrists as unable to see what is in front of their eyes, or to recognize the obvious. He states:

> Some psychiatric conjectures about accident neurosis seem indeed to signify little more than a refusal to concede a connection between the nervous disorder and the prospect of compensation which is implicit in the facts of the case. Such an attitude may owe something to that addiction to the liquidity of thought which is an occupational risk for the psychiatrist's calling, but probably

more a natural reluctance of the mind trained in recognizing deeper motives to the acceptance of psychopathology so superficial and banal....Indeed, in these cases, where the patient is engaged in making out a case for proportionate financial redress, some degree of exaggeration of disability might be regarded as no more than an anticipated human failing. (p. 99)

CONFUSING STATISTICAL ARTIFACT WITH FACT

Most things vary over time. For example, we have our good days and our bad days. Professional athletes have their good games and their bad games. Professional pilots make their good landings and their not-so-good landings. Although there may be systematic causes for some of these changes, to a certain extent we really do not know the factors that explain inconsistency over time; often it may just be a matter of chance. For example, if we toss a coin ten times it might come out 6 heads and 4 tails, and if we flip it ten more times it may come out 4 heads and 6 tails. We would not conclude that the coin has changed. Rather, this seems to represent unexplained, or chance variation.

For the purposes of the following discussion, we will use the word "fact" to refer to changes or differences that are due to systematic causes, and "artifact" to refer to changes or differences best explained by chance. The difference is illustrated by a baseball player who has a bad week at the plate because of a troublesome injury and one who has a bad week because of bad luck (e.g., hitting the ball right at the fielders). Individuals commonly confuse fact and artifact. In the case of clinicians, this leads to misinterpretation or erroneous judgment. We will describe a number of circumstances under which such errors are common.

Mistaking Chance Differences on Tests with True Differences

First, in interpreting psychological test scores, psychologists will often analyze what is referred to as scatter, or different levels of performance across different tests. For example, patient Jones might achieve a high average score on a measure of memory and a low average score on a measure of reasoning ability. Such scatter is often used to reach conclusions about an individual's strengths and weaknesses. For example, it might be concluded that our patient Jones is relatively strong in the area of memory and relatively weak in the area of reasoning. Perhaps more importantly, scatter, especially if it seems extreme on tests of intellectual functions, is often interpreted as a sign of brain damage or intellectual impairment. Thus, if Jones had obtained considerably higher scores on measures of language abilities than on measures of nonlanguage abilities, Psychologist Smith might well conclude that Jones is brain-damaged.

The problem with this approach is that differences across tests which are interpreted as factual or true differences, may actually be nothing other than artifactual or chance differences. No test or scale has perfect stability or reliability, and thus the score that is obtained, to some extent, not only reflects one's ability but also a component of chance, as well. In the extreme case, when a test is very unreliable, the attained score may be largely a product of chance. As a result of this element of chance, consider what happens if one gives a series of ability tests, as is common in certain types of forensic evaluations (e.g., those assessing for brain damage). Even were an individual's abilities absolutely consistent across all areas (which of course would be a highly atypical situation), scores across these tests will not be perfectly consistent. They will vary to some extent, with some scores being higher or lower than others. These differences, however, will reflect the operation of chance, or artifact, rather than true differences in ability level.

Some psychologists, nevertheless, will interpret relatively small differences in scores across tests, differences that are most likely a product of chance, as reflecting true differences in ability level. This seems common with intelligence tests, in which an individual receives scores on a series of subtests. A psychologist may interpret a small difference on, say, a subtest measuring vocabulary and one measuring factual knowledge as a meaningful difference, when it is most likely a chance finding. Thus, the psychologist is likely confusing artifact with fact, and the conclusions can be challenged on this basis.

Other psychologists assume that differences in test scores are meaningful only if these differences exceed a certain level. If tests have the needed normative data, there are techniques available to determine the likelihood that differences in scores between any two tests reflect true versus chance differences. These techniques are similar to methods described in Chapter 2 for assessing the statistical significance of differences between two groups. In essence, one can derive a probability statement indicating the chances that the observed difference is a true one versus a product of chance. Unless this level is .05 or lower—unless the odds are less than 1 in 20 that the result is merely a product of chance—a psychologist may assume the difference is *not* a meaningful one.

This strategy seems sufficient for distinguishing chance and true findings, until it is examined more closely. Imagine you are blindly reaching into a jar with thousands of little balls, in which 19 of 20 are red and 1 of 20 is black. Thus, the chances of pulling out a black ball is only 1 of 20 each time you make a selection. These odds are comparable to those the psychologist may use in attempting to distinguish whether differences in test scores are artifact or fact. In each case, the odds are 1 in 20 that a chance difference will be mistaken for a true difference. However, suppose you made 100 selections. Given the 1 in 20 chance for each selection, on average, you would pull out 5 black balls. Now extend this to 1,000 selections, or 10,000, or even more. By the time you were done, you would have a pretty substantial collection of these black balls, or low chance occurrences.

When a psychologist gives a series of tests, and when a number of these tests produce a series of subtest scores, the possible comparisons that can be made across test scores multiply quickly. To give the reader some feel for this, if one scores the Rorschach according to the system developed by Exner, there are literally thousands of possible comparisons that can be made. In fact, computer programs have been developed to help with the task of scanning what can be a huge number of potential comparisons. What happens to the 1 in 20 "safeguard" under such circumstances? By the mere operation of chance, a large number of comparisons will exceed the .05 level. Thus, this standard no longer offers the needed protection against false acceptance of chance differences as real ones. If this standard, or an even stricter one is used, one is still left with numerous possible comparisons that will exceed the standard but, in truth, will simply reflect the operation of chance. The psychologist, then, is potentially left with a large number of "significant" differences, some of which may be fact and some, or even the majority of which may be artifact, usually without any trustworthy means for distinguishing the two.

Thus, whenever a large number of potential comparisons can be made, quite a number should reach "significance" through the operation of chance. Indeed, one can reach "a large number" with as few as ten test scores if they can be combined in different ways (i.e., not only score 1 versus score 2 but also score 1 + 2 versus 3, etc.). It will be difficult to determine which differences are real and which are not. This creates considerable potential for confusing fact with artifact. Nevertheless, under these circumstances, psychologists may well interpret at least some of the differences as real ones, tending to overlook the fact that these differences can be equally, or better explained by the operation of chance, and that considerable caution in interpretation is called for. Thus, the lawyer can ask a question like the following: "Given the number of possible comparisons between tests scores, shouldn't some of them have differed just by chance alone?" One can follow up with something like the following: "Don't some prominent psychologists indicate that when so many comparisons can be made, there is often no reliable way to know which differences are real and which are just a matter of chance?" (Some of these prominent psychologists include Anastasi, 1982; and Meehl, 1973.) One then follows with something like, "Doctor, isn't that what most people call guessing?"

Regression Towards the Mean

There are other circumstances in which fact and artifact are likely to be confused. There is a well known tendency for extreme occurrences to be followed by less extreme occurrences merely because of the operation of chance. This is called regression towards the mean. The phenomenon is well captured by a sports saying: You're never as good as you look when you're winning and never as bad as you look when you're losing. Extreme occurrences tend to be followed by less extreme occurrences. The student who achieves 100% on a test one time is likely to do less well the next time. One who wins the lottery one day is unlikely to do so the next day. A batter in a slump, or at a low point, will almost surely come out of it or do better subsequently. The greater the element of chance in occurrences, the greater is this tendency for extreme occurrences to be followed by less extreme occurrences. Thus, for example, if one administers an extremely unreliable test and someone achieves an extremely high or low score, chances are great that the score obtained on a retest will be much less extreme.

Regression towards the mean, indeed, is often a likely explanation for changes in test scores over time. For example, suppose we give a large battery of neuropsychological tests, and that some of these tests are not particularly reliable—chance plays an important role in the scores that are obtained. Suppose further that the clinician pays particular attention to the lower scores, tends to later retest individuals who achieved lower scores, and focuses this reassessment on "areas of weakness" as supposedly demonstrated by these lower test scores. By chance alone, even if the individual's functioning did not change at all, the lower scores should be higher on retesting, or regress towards the mean. The same, of course, would hold for someone who initially attained high scores and was retested—it is likely that the higher scores would not remain as high. Keep in mind that these changes are predictable and can easily be explained by regression towards the mean, or the operation of chance.

In the case of initially lower scores followed by higher scores, suppose a psychologist is seeing an individual following a minor head injury and examining for brain damage. Based on the initially low scores, and given the decided tendency to overdiagnose abnormality, the psychologist might form the impression that brain damage is present. The individual is scheduled for a follow-up appointment 6 months later. Now, as is well known, following head injury individuals often show improvement in their problems over time. This person is retested and indeed his scores improve, especially the lowest or most extreme ones, which seems to clinch the diagnosis. In truth, however, by the mere operation of chance, the lowest scores are most likely to show the greatest improvement, and these changes may reflect little more than regression towards the mean. The change, then, is quite possibly artifact and does not necessarily provide support for the diagnosis.

In the case of high scores followed by lower scores, it is easy to see how this can be misinterpreted as reflecting a patient's "deteriorating" condition. For example, an individual is suspected of having some kind of organic brain syndrome, perhaps due to exposure to toxic chemicals. On initial testing, the individual achieves very high scores and the testing results are considered "clean." However, in order to be thorough, one sees this individual again on follow-up. A number of the scores have now dropped, and it may seem that one may be witnessing a delayed effect of the toxins, or mental functioning that is deteriorating over time. Again, however, the changes are expectable and can potentially be accounted for by regression towards the mean, rather than by the effects of the toxic agent.

The basic point to keep in mind is that when one obtains data or results that are extreme, they are likely to be less extreme upon re-testing, due to the operation of chance. Further, these changes may well be (mis)interpreted as real ones as opposed to artifact. Along these lines, it is worth noting that a psychologist or psychiatrist will often see people when they are at their worst. For example, it is probably atypical for someone who feels a little bad to seek out the help of a psychologist, and probably much more frequent for people to wait until things have become really bad before doing so. Extremes tend to become less extreme, and thus once someone has reached their low point there is a reasonable likelihood they will improve over time, whether they receive treatment or not. Although an individual in treatment may have shown similar improvement with or without the psychologist's help, it may be assumed that it was the treatment that produced the improvement. This is just one other potential instance in which changes are assumed to be the result of specific causes, when they may merely be explained by the operation of chance.

REFERENCES

Anastasi, A. (1982). *Psychological Testing* (5th ed.). New York: The Macmillan Company.

Arkes, H.E., Dawes, R.M., and Christensen, C. (1986). Factors influencing the use of a decision rule in a probabilistic task. *Behavior and Human Decision Processes, 37*, 93-110.

Berry, K.B. (1973). Parsimony and complexity as related to the diagnostic process with children. *Journal of Clinical Psychology, 29*, 39-41.

Einhorn, H.J. (1986). Accepting error to make less error. *Journal of Personality Assessment, 50(3)*, 387-395.

Kahneman, D., and Tversky, A. (1982). Intuitive prediction: Biases and corrective procedures. In D. Kahneman, P. Slovic, and A. Tversky (Eds.). *Judgment Under Uncertainty: Heuristics and Biases*. Cambridge: Cambridge University Press.

Meehl, P.E. (1973). *Psychodiagnosis: Selected papers*. Minneapolis: University of Minnesota Press.

Miller, H. (1961). Accident neurosis. *British Medical Journal*, 992.

Mischel, W. (1972). Direct versus indirect personality assessment: Evidence and implications. *Journal of Consulting and Clinical Psychology, 38*, 319-324.

Nobo, J., and Evans, R.G. (1986). The WAIS-R picture arrangement and comprehension sub-tests as measures of social behavior characteristics. *Journal of Personality Assessment, 50*, 90-92.

Ramzy, I. (1975). How the mind of the psychoanalyst works: An essay on psychoanalytic inference. *International Journal of Psychoanalysis, 55*, 543-544.

Wade, T.C., and Baker, T.B. (1977). Opinions and use of psychological tests: A survey of clinical psychologists. *American Psychologist, 32*, 874-882.

APPENDIX 5D
FACTORS UNDERLYING LACK OF INSIGHT

How can it be that we are so lacking in insight into our internal reasoning processes? The issues here are too involved to detail fully, but two points merit consideration. First, to say we are not aware of our internal reasoning processes does not mean that some mysterious, Freudian, unconscious process is at work. Actually, a good deal of "data processing" goes on outside of our awareness. For example, while reading this material, one is recognizing the words without being aware of, or having to think about how this awareness comes about. Rather, it is automatic. Similarly, we often recognize human faces automatically without having to stop and think about what we see. In a like manner, apparently, many of our underlying reasoning processes go on automatically or outside of conscious awareness. In fact, there may be no way we can really gain access to or awareness of some of these underlying processes. For example, visual recognition of objects is exceedingly complicated and occurs at various levels of the nervous system, some of which are almost surely inaccessible to conscious awareness.

Second, many clinicians assume or recognize that introspection, or subjective beliefs about ourselves, can be highly misleading. In fact, many clinicians believe that their major therapeutic task is to correct patients' misconceptions about themselves. Further, voluminous evidence has been gathered, starting right from the very beginnings of experimental psychology, which shows that introspective reports about one's own perceptions or experiences can be quite misleading (for a review of some of this work, see Marx and Hillix, 1973). Additionally, research projects are often criticized because they rely on the subjective reports of the individuals studied, this method being seen as quite unreliable when compared to objective measures. There is a dearth of scientific evidence to suggest that clinicians are any less subject to limits in awareness or access to internal judgment processes than other persons.

REFERENCE

Marx, M.H., and Hillix, W.A. (1973). *Systems and Theories in Psychology.* New York: McGraw-Hill.

APPENDIX 5E
SIMPLIFYING STRATEGIES

Some additional details can be provided about what are termed "simplifying strategies." A number of researchers have argued that because the human capacity to manage complex data is so limited, we often must resort to problem-solving approaches that reduce mental "strain." In fact, a number of the problematic judgment habits and practices described in Chapter 5 have been explained, by some investigators, as a product of our limited abilities to manage complex information and the simplifying strategies that we must resort to as a result. For example, confirmatory bias may reduce demands for handling complex information because one attends mainly to supportive evidence and less so, if at all, to non-supportive evidence. Thus, there is less to which the reasoner attends. This clearly makes matters easier from the standpoint of the reasoner, although the use of these strategies often comes at great cost— accurate judgment. Newell and Simon (1972), and Simon (1981) have described these simplifying strategies at length, essentially viewing them as reflections of restricted capacities to process complex information. Tversky and Kahneman (1974) provide a review of many of these strategies and of the research demonstrating their existence. These researchers are not lightweights. For example, Simon has won a Nobel prize for his work on cognitive limitations. Tversky and Kahneman published a major work on simplifying strategies in *Science,* a prestigious journal, and their work has received widespread recognition. Such research and discussion of simplifying strategies stands in sharp contrast to the claims many clinicians make about performing exceedingly complex intellectual operations and integrating all of the data.

REFERENCES

Newell, A., and Simon, H.A. (1972). *Human Problem Solving.* Englewood Cliffs, N.J.: Prentice-Hall.

Simon, H.A. (1981). *The Sciences of the Artificial* (2nd ed.). Cambridge, MA: MIT Press.

Tversky, A., and Kahneman, D. (1974). Judgment under uncertainty: Heuristics and biases. *Science, 183*, 1124-1131.

APPENDIX 5F
PREPARING FOR COMMON COUNTERARGUMENTS TO THE JUDGMENT FINDINGS

The lawyer should be aware of some of the more common responses of expert witnesses to the judgment findings, and be prepared to challenge these arguments. We cannot cover every possibility, but the following are among the most frequent.

IT'S NOT FAIR

Many experts claim, in essence, that the judgment research has been rigged such that psychologists and psychiatrists were handicapped in one or another way and prevented from showing their true abilities. One such argument is that experts were not used in the studies. This argument is simply incorrect. Many of the studies have used experts, and judgment performance has been no better, or even worse. Quite a number of the studies discussed in Chapter 5 included clinicians with extensive experience or training (for additional studies see Chapter 8).

Another refrain is that clinicians were placed at a disadvantage by being denied access to information critical to accurate clinical appraisal. For example, as noted previously, some of the earlier studies on the clinical-actuarial debate were criticized because clinicians did not have interview data with which to work. There may have once been some basis for this objection, but no longer. A number of the studies have allowed clinicians to gather whatever information they wished to gather and to proceed in whatever way they wished to proceed. The results have been the same, if not worse (see Sawyer, 1966; and Wiggins, 1981, for overviews).

Another complaint is that clinicians were forced to make "atypical" judgments that are not actually representative of those made in clinical practice. This assertion is somewhat baffling. The studies commonly involve judgments about diagnosis, or about the prediction of such matters as potential violence or various aspects of everyday functioning, the types of judgments that may be made in the courtroom (see Chapter 7 for further details).

I AM THE EXCEPTION, OR THIS CASE IS THE EXCEPTION

This counterargument comes in various forms, but it almost always comes down to the same contention—the judgment research does not apply to this particular case. One may hear clinicians argue that the particular defendant has a particular type of problem and that the judgment studies did not address this particular set of circumstances. Alternatively, the clinician may try to explain why he was not susceptible to the various erroneous judgment practices, biases, or limits the studies describe.

This approach leaves the expert vulnerable in various ways. For example, if he correctly indicates that the particular judgment task involved in the case under consideration has not been scientifically examined, this obviously means that although there is no negative evidence, there is essentially no positive scientific evidence that the task can be accomplished either. Given such a large body of negative evidence on related judgment tasks, there is, at minimum, considerable doubt that this unstudied judgment can be performed accurately. Alternatively, if the expert argues that he is above all this judgment literature, the lawyer may wish to point out that this may well have been what other experts believed before their judgment accuracy was put to formal test. Additionally, one can point out research showing lack of insight into one's own judgment practices and biases (e.g., hindsight bias and confirmatory bias). Given lack of insight, it may be extremely difficult for experts to form accurate appraisals of their own judgment abilities and accuracy levels. Most of all, the clinician can be asked to prove his assertion, or what formal scientific evidence exists to support his claim.

I AM AN ARTIST

Some experts will admit that their work is as much art as science. As such, they may argue that the judgment research involves science and does not apply to the clinician's artistic abilities. This also places the expert in a vulnerable position. First, clinicians in many of the judgment studies were allowed to proceed in their preferred manner—to perform their "art"—and yet their conclusions were still often wrong. Second, one can ask this artist how much of what he does is science and how much is art. He may respond by stating he cannot say exactly. One might then ask, "Thus, one would not know for sure that it is wrong to assume that what you do is 90% art and 10% science?"

The courts may wish to consider whether psychologist-artists should be serving as expert witnesses. Apparently, even given the same set of facts and the same individual, these artists often "paint" very different pictures. This is shown by the frequency with which the opinions of these artists clash in specific cases. Should we try to decide who is the best artist, and how are we to do this? Should the best painter or storyteller, the one whose picture seems most realistic, be declared the winner? Something seems to be wrong when our courts are reduced to deciding matters of art, rather than fact.

I DEAL WITH SINGLE INDIVIDUALS,
NOT NUMBERS OR GROUPS

A statement like the above one may sound appealing, but it violates rudimentary principles of logic and rationality. The clinician will state something to the effect, "I know that X percent of individuals with this configuration on the MMPI have been shown, by empirical research, to grossly exaggerate their symptoms, but this has nothing to do with this particular individual." The clinician will go on to focus on the absolutely unique features of this individual and disregard any features he may well have in common with those on which this MMPI research was conducted. Thus, the clinician who so readily makes wide leaps in generalization based on research only remotely related to the issue at hand, when the research favors his opinion, becomes super-rigorous about generalization when the tables are turned.

Consider the following. Suppose you are offered a bet on a series of 100 coin tosses with a fair penny. If you can guess the number of heads that turn up, plus or minus 5, you win $5,000. Now everyone knows that every penny is unique. This particular coin may be 23 years old, contain a unique pattern of scratches and scuffs, etc. Would you decide that because of the penny's unique features, you will defy the odds (which would lead you to say 50 heads in 100 tosses) and guess, say, that only 25 heads will turn up? If you do so, you will have greatly decreased your chances of winning. Of course it is conceivable that the result will turn up 25 heads, but the odds are greatly against it. Thus, even though this is a unique and one-of-a-kind penny, you will focus on the features it probably has in common with most pennies (i.e., it comes up heads about 50% of the time) and play the odds.

If you do not play the odds, then you are behaving like the clinician who asserts that numbers or figures derived from groups never apply to individuals. As regards such practices, Meehl (1973) states:

> The vulgar error is the cliché that "We aren't dealing with groups, we are dealing with this individual case." It is doubtful that one can profitably debate this cliché in a case conference, since anyone who puts it quite this way is not educable in ten minutes. He who wishes to reform the thinking in case conferences must constantly reiterate the elementary truth that if you depart in your clinical-decision making from a well-established (or even moderately well-supported) empirical frequency…your departure may save a particular case from being misclassified predictively or therapeutically; but such departures are, prima facie, counterinductive, so that a decision *policy* of this kind is almost certain to have a cost that exceeds its benefits. The research evidence strongly suggests that a policy of making such departures, except very sparingly, will result in the misclassifying of other cases that would have been correctly classified had such nonactuarial departures been forbidden; it also suggests that more of this second kind of misclassification will occur than will be compensated for by the improvement of the first kind. (pp. 234-235)

TRYING TO MAKE A REAL ISSUE A PSEUDO-ISSUE

Finally, some experts may claim that the whole matter of clinical versus actuarial judgment is an artificial creation or a "straw man," and that actually there is no conflict between the two. For example, it may be argued that most clinicians combine clinical and actuarial approaches, or integrate the two. Meehl's (1986) rejoinder clearly explains, however, why this is no pseudo-issue. He states:

> Some critics asked a question...which I confess I am totally unable to understand: Why should Sarbin and Meehl be fomenting this needless controversy? Let me state as loudly and as clearly as I can manage, even if it distresses people who fear disagreement, that Sarbin and I did not artificially concoct a controversy or foment a needless fracas between two methods that complement each other and work together harmoniously. I think this is a ridiculous position when the context is the pragmatic context of decision making. You have two quite different procedures for combining a finite set of information to arrive at a predictive decision. It is obvious from the armchair, even if the data did not show it overwhelmingly, that the results of applying these two different techniques to the same data set do not always agree. On the contrary, they disagree a sizable fraction of the time. Now if a four-variable regression equation or a Glueck actuarial table tells the criminal court judge that this particular delinquent will probably commit another felony in the next 3 years and if a case conference or a social worker says that he will probably not, it is absurd to say that Sarbin and I have "fomented a controversy" about how the judge should proceed. The plain fact is that he cannot act in accordance with both of these incompatible predictions. (p. 372)

REFERENCES

Meehl, P.E. (1973). *Psychodiagnosis: Selected papers.* Minneapolis: University of Minnesota Press.

Meehl, P.E. (1986). Causes and effects of my disturbing little book. *Journal of Personality Assessment, 50,* 370-375.

Sawyer, J. (1966). Measurement *and* prediction, clinical *and* statistical. *Psychological Bulletin, 66,* 178-200.

Wiggins, J.S. (1981). Clinical and statistical prediction: Where are we and where do we go from here? *Clinical Psychology Review, 1,* 3-18.

CHAPTER 6

Challenging Interviews & the Clinical Examination

Psychiatric assessment usually depends partially, if not fully, on interview and history taking, which are often referred to as the clinical method of examination. We will focus on the clinical method in this chapter, deferring discussion of psychological testing, usually representing another form of clinical method, to subsequent chapters. Specifically, we will detail deficiencies in data collection and recording. Deficiencies in interpretation of these data, and/or any other data collected as part of assessment, will be covered in Chapter 7. Although the material in Chapter 7 and the material on clinical judgment in Chapter 5 obviously suggest serious problems in data interpretation, the intent of this chapter is to show that clinicians start out in trouble. This is because the clinical method produces data of such poor quality. Indeed, even were clinical judgment and data interpretation proficient, the data that one must use to form conclusions are so faulty to begin with that the chances for a correct determination are reduced considerably. Of course, given the sorry state of clinical judgment and interpretive processes suggested by the literature, one set of problems (i.e., faulty data) is only likely to compound the other (i.e., faulty judgment), making the total result even worse than the sum of its parts.

There are two major deficiencies in the methods by which data are collected or produced through the use of interviews and the clinical examination method in general. First, due to a host of factors, the data are subject to a great deal of uncontrolled variation. Stated differently, the data that one obtains are not determined solely by the object (person) being examined, but also by such things as who does the examination, where and for what purpose the examination is being conducted, when the examination is conducted, etc. A determination of which data are a product of the individual being examined versus any of these various external factors is not often made, and in fact probably cannot be made in the clinical examination as it is currently employed. Therefore, it cannot be known whether a conclusion drawn from the data reflects some characteristic of the person being examined, or merely reflects one or another of these external factors, such as the clinician conducting the examination. For example, two different examiners may ask widely different questions. One does not know if the results obtained are due to the set of questions asked, and whether a very different result would have been obtained had another set of questions been asked.

Secondly, there is the defect that the examiner—the psychiatrist or psychologist—is far from an adequate recording instrument. The examiner is selective in what he will notice in the clinical situation and what he will remember from the clinical situation. This is extremely important when one bears in mind that all one gets in the psychiatrist's report or in his testimony in the courtroom are those data which he has selectively noted and selectively remembered. The raw data in their entirety are seldom, if ever, available. One would need a videotape of the clinical interview or testing session in order to be aware of everything that went on in that session. Even then, one would have available only those factors which were operating at an overt level and not those which were covert, although research has shown that covert factors, such as the examiner's needs, wishes, attitudes and emotions, conscious or unconscious, also influence the data to be obtained. Also, the "patient" is likely to detect what the clinician is interested in and present that kind of information. Of equal importance is the fact that the clinician has available to him at the time he makes his assessment only that data which he has selectively perceived and selectively remembered.

Because of these deficiencies, the data produced and the conclusions drawn from the clinical method are as much resultant of or characteristic of the situation and the examiner as they are of the subject being examined. Thus, for example, when the psychiatrist says in his report that John Doe is a very hostile individual, based on his observation that John Doe showed a great deal of hostility in the clinical interview, the question arises as to whether John Doe is really a hostile individual or whether there was something about the psychiatrist or the situation which elicited considerable hostile material from John Doe. That is, we have no way of knowing from this approach whether or not it is true that John Doe is a hostile individual. Furthermore, one does not even know that John Doe actually did display a greater than normal amount of hostile behavior in the interview. It is quite possible that for one reason or another, the examiner chose to notice Doe's hostile behaviors and give them more attention than he did to the non-hostile behaviors. It is often observed in hospitals and clinics that some staff members soon become easily identifiable as "health seers" or "sick seers." That is, some staff members display a clear and pronounced tendency to be more alert to the healthy aspects of patients or their strengths and to see them as relatively well-functioning in contrast to some other staff who are exceedingly alert to any possible indication of psychopathology and are prone to interpret data in terms of psychopathology and, thus, frequently come up with diagnoses of much more severe disturbance. It may be worthwhile to ask the expert testifying to psychopathology whether the individual exhibited any normal or healthy behavior, and, if the answer is affirmative, as it must be except in the most florid cases, try to elicit a description of these behaviors. The problem, of course, is that if the labels "neurotic" or "psychotic" or even "normal" *depend upon who is making the assessment,* of what value is such a label or description in determining the mental or emotional status of the person being examined?

We will start by citing material that provides an overview of these problems. Subsequently, we will cover each of these two basic problems in some detail.

In a book which is now somewhat old but continues to be supported by current research, Sarason (1972) provides a thorough description of many of the factors which operate in the clinical situation, and provides ample supporting data for his conclusions from experimental research literature. In his introduction he notes that, "the failure to consider seriously the implications of the interpersonal nature of clinical interaction has not only obscured what different problems have in common but has made evaluation of studies of a particular research problem extremely difficult." There probably are very few clinicians who take seriously the effects of these variables, despite the fact that research has indicated over and over again that they are operating.

Sarason instructs the reader to keep two questions in mind with regard to clinical evaluation. These questions are, "To what extent have these studies explicitly recognized the variables inherent in an interpersonal interaction?" and "To what extent might conflicting findings and opinions be a function of recognized or unrecognized differences in the role of the situational variables?" The pertinence of these questions with the wording slightly modified for use in cross-examination should be apparent.

With regard to the factors in the situation or the examiner which affect the data that is produced, Sarason cites abundant research evidence that the following have an effect: The nature of the instructions given to the subject, the actual purposes of the clinical interaction, the purposes of the interaction as perceived by the subject, the place of the examination, the time of the examination and the race, social class, and sex of the examiner. *No confidence can be placed in data which are subject to variation from so many uncontrolled sources.*

Woody (1972) points out the deficiencies of the clinical examination in terms of the inadequate sampling of behavior, both theoretical and personal biases of the diagnostician, the presence of so many bits of information or types of data within an interview that there is vast latitude for interpreting and weighting data according to a particular diagnostician's theoretical preferences, and that despite protestations that their point of reference is always the individual patient, clinicians in fact may be so committed to a particular school of thought that the patient's diagnosis is largely predetermined.

Kubie (1971) alludes to the general social and political convictions held by the psychiatrist or clinical psychologist which inevitably will bias observation and judgment. He states: "No one is invulnerable to the subtle effects of loyalties especially where quantifiable and objective data are scarce and where the specialist has to depend largely on intuitive judgments and feelings." (p. 486) Diamond (1973b), in his article discussed in Chapter 1, makes a similar assertion.

Aiken (1985) observes that interviewing is not measurement, thus the results of an interview cannot usually be quantified. He notes that interviewing is as much an art as a science and that many extraneous variables in an interview influence what is said and done. He notes that the interview shares with observational methods the problems of low reliability and validity, often being more affected by personality and biases of the interviewer than characteristics of the interviewee in determining the kinds of information that are obtained. He also notes the well-documented tendency of interviewers to give more weight to first impressions and also points out that interviewers are more affected by unfavorable than favorable information about the person being interviewed. He notes that observer errors occur in interviewers' judgments and refers to consistent findings of research that the validity of the interview as an employment selection or clinical diagnostic method is highly overrated.

Robins (1985) describes the lack of consistency in the results obtained across different interviews. He notes that in studies in which individuals are interviewed twice, the symptoms they report are often inconsistent. For example, they may describe certain symptoms in the first interview but not in the second interview. In the studies Robins discusses, these changeable symptom reports cannot be explained by actual changes in individuals' symptoms over time because these different responses were given to questions regarding lifetime prevalence (i.e., during your lifetime, have you ever had symptom X?). Robins also indicates that laypersons who use a structured interview format, or fixed questions, seem to obtain more consistent interview results than psychiatrists who use less structured or less set procedures.

DATA CONTAMINATION AND RELATIVITY, OR, WHAT (DATA) YOU GET DEPENDS ON WHO, WHEN, WHERE, WHY, AND WHATEVER

If ballistics experts had to go through the trials and tribulations of the psychiatrist they too might show a similar rate of professional burn-out. Bullet fragments do not change their nature in the presence of different experts, nor does their structure alter when they are examined in a prison and then a hospital. Bullets do not have something particular to gain should the expert reach one or another conclusion, nor do such interests sometimes lead to deliberate efforts to mislead the expert or carefully screen what they reveal. These, however, are among the types of problems and factors that exert considerable effects on the data obtained through the clinical method, thus making the psychiatrist's task exceedingly difficult.

EXAMINER EFFECTS

The behavior and reactions of the psychiatrist may considerably affect the data that are obtained. As has been shown, even when a psychiatrist or psychologist obtains data under controlled settings, and even in the context of research, *who* does the data collection can make a substantial difference. Rosenthal (1966) produces extensive evidence that even in many laboratory situations the expectancies and characteristics of the experimenter affect the results obtained. In other words, examiners with different attitudes and expectations, or characteristics, will produce different data in the same experimental situation. Rosenthal cites the famous psychologist, Ebbinghaus, who indicated that the experimenter's knowledge of the way his expectations affect the outcome are not sufficient to control the phenomenon. (This is another expression of the point raised in Chapter 5, that is, that even insight into possible biasing influences by no means ensures their correction. This is one reason why the single-blind method we discussed, and other such experimental controls, are often used when conducting research.) Felton (1971) and McCas (1972) report on experiments showing these types of effects. For example, McCas found that nonverbal behaviors that connoted warmth or coldness affected subjects' behaviors.

If examiner effects are evidenced even in controlled laboratory settings, and if researchers must go to great lengths to incorporate procedures that keep these effects in check, imagine what occurs in the clinical context when such controls are lacking, if not entirely absent.

Sarason (1954) cites a number of studies to the effect that it is *examiner* differences which are the most important factor in producing variations in the data produced by the subject. Gill and Brennan (1948) further explicate this influence, observing that even subtle therapist behaviors, such as a shift of visual focus or a questioning glance, can seriously affect the kind of material obtained.

Masling (1966) describes an abundance of research which confirms the fact that in many, if not all, cases the examiner exerts considerable influence on the kind of data that is produced. Even such things as whether or not the examiner has a mustache can affect the data in some situations. Masling cites studies showing that, even where the subjects being examined are small organisms such as rats or planaria, the *expectations* of the examiner or experimenter can influence the outcome.

Storrow (1967) asserts that, unintentionally and without even realizing it, physicians can color what patients say. He notes the accumulation of several journal articles dealing with the subtle ways of influencing what patients and research subjects say. He goes on to state that despite "training" in how not to influence what patients say, there is considerable evidence to show that this process continues even within the psychiatric context. Storrow further points out that even psychoanalysts, despite their assumption of total objectivity, exert an examiner effect.

Pugh (1973) provides observations based on his practice of forensic psychiatry while a medical officer at St. Elizabeth's Hospital in Washington. He points out the problems involved when only a single report is sent to the Court, even though there was frequent disagreement among the clinicians and the report represented nothing more than a compromise or majority rule. He describes the common experience observed by all at the hospital, that new doctors on the service would find virtually every defendant insane, but, after being confronted with the task of trying to manage felons in the hospital, the new doctors would reverse their field and become "very stringent" about finding defendants insane. Referring to writs of habeas corpus alleging confinement was "arbitrary and capricious," he states:

> The phrase stuck in my mind because it described so aptly the process for deciding a defendant's sanity status. When so many doctors had such arbitrary and idiosyncratic standards for determining sanity, the finding for a given defendant depended too greatly upon the specific doctor who was assigned to examine him.

Bachrach (1974) states: "The clinician's observations, perceptions and attitudes toward diagnosis are influenced by his interests, training, experience, identifications, character attitudes, cognitive style, and interpersonal-cultural heritage." Bachrach describes how the information elicited in the clinical examination depends on the stimulus value of the interviewer, including his attitudes and expectations; whether he is reassuring, neutral, confronting; and how the behavior of a patient with one examiner shows you nothing more than how he behaves and reacts with an examiner of that type. Perry's study (1972) demonstrates the effects of some of these factors that Bachrach describes. Perry found that individuals' anxiousness and aggressiveness differed when assessed by an examiner of their own race versus that of another race.

Mann et al. (1992) found that mental health professionals in China, Indonesia, Japan and the U.S. rated the presence and degree of hyperactive-disruptive behaviors in standardized videotapes of eight year old boys significantly differently, with the Chinese and Indonesian giving significantly higher scores than their Japanese and American colleagues.

Fleiss (1970) states that many sources of error in interview data have been identified, concluding that there are individual differences in the way interviewers conduct interviews, which in turn elicits different responses from the interviewee. He also indicates that different interviewers evaluate and interpret responses differently. Along similar lines, Havenburg and Guiter (1976) refer to "the many occasions when the psychoanalyst has 'his own' truth and unconsciously tries to impose it upon his patients."

Angle et al. (1979) recommend use of computer interviewing, stating as one of the benefits "eliminating biases of different interviewers and different interviewing techniques." Derner (1983) also seems to suggest that computers might help to overcome problems evidenced by human interviewers. He notes, for example, that interviews are contaminated by examiner effects and that there are too many concerns or facets of information for the interviewer to keep in mind at any one time.

Leff (1977) notes that the psychiatrist's interviewing technique is strongly determined by his diagnostic scheme and therefore affects his perception of what the patient says and does as well as decisions about the presence of symptoms. As an example of the influence of diagnostic preconceptions on the perception of symptoms, he refers to previous studies showing that American psychiatrists, viewing identical films, find about twice as many symptoms as do British psychiatrists. He also notes that the diagnostic framework from which the psychiatrist works can influence what the psychiatrist will try to elicit from the patient, how he will perceive what has been elicited and how he interprets what has been perceived.

Cooper (1985) notes that the analyst has a wide range of available theories and that the theory will determine how the analyst shapes the patient's material. He points out that theories lead us to collaborate with patients in creating a new personal myth and a life narrative more acceptable to both the analyst and the patient.

He goes on to note that if the Oedipus complex is considered central to a neurosis, then any patient can provide plentiful occasions for exhibiting the existence, vigor and importance of oedipal fantasies. Furthermore, if preoedipal fixations are deemed to be determinants, again, it would be the rare patient who would not provide sufficient opportunity for the clinician to put together a life story in which preoedipal issues would occupy a central position.

Cooper continues, asserting that theories matter crucially but that until there are better ways of testing theories, different theories will coexist and regardless of whether they do it consciously or unconsciously, intentionally or not, clinicians will continue to train their patients to see the world in accordance with the theory they believe represents factual reality.

Combrinck-Graham (1987) states:

> Clearly, one's beliefs and assumptions shape one's diagnosing. Consideration of how data are selected in making an assessment and the attention given to the context and process of assessment could be thought of as assessing the ecology of diagnosing. The diagnostician is never solely that: He or she is also a person with a specific relationship to the system, obligations and responsibilities, and a particular background as well as a defined professional identity. (p. 504)

Combrinck-Graham goes on to note that interviewers who request extensive histories may communicate that history is important and thus encourage that orientation in the patient as an example, thus adding to the literature indicating the potential for suggestion to operate in the clinical interview.

Trull et al. (1987) state, in connection with their attempt to study various kinds of personality disorders, "Lay interviewers were used to minimize the effect of clinical biases on the ratings." (p. 68) Pope (1988) discusses a study which found that the diagnostician's theoretical orientation affected whether labeling an individual a "patient" or a "job applicant" altered the diagnostician's conclusions. He then states, "...Various basic theoretical orientations can lead to very different assessment results. Psychologists conducting assessments and assigning diagnoses need to be continually aware of their own theoretic orientation and the ways in which this orientation is likely to affect the evaluation." (p. 21) As we have noted earlier in Chapter 5, the psychologist's awareness of potential biases does not necessarily neutralize their effects.

Pope (1992), in an article dealing with responsibilities when providing feedback to clients, states that clinicians conducting assessments are vulnerable to a variety of personal, irrational, sometimes unconscious reactions to the person being evaluated. He states, "The clinician who has a strong, perhaps unacknowledged bias toward a particular theoretical orientation or treatment strategy (e.g., behavioral or psychoanalytic) can slant test findings so that they seem to support interventions based on the favored orientation or strategy." (p. 270) He notes that no clinician is invulnerable to such reactions and biases.

Lehman and Salovey (1990) note that although adopting a theoretical orientation may be needed for guiding psychotherapy, this brings with it schemas or sets of expectations that "filter and organize conceptualizations of and interactions with patients." (p. 385)

Mahoney and Craine (1991) found that therapists who identified themselves as having a behavioral orientation rated psychological change as significantly less difficult to accomplish than those who identified themselves as having a psychodynamic, cognitive, humanistic or eclectic orientation. They also found that psychological change was rated as most difficult by those who reported being in therapy themselves for the greatest length of time. This could be an examiner effect which has implications for prognosis in personal injury cases and for sentencing in criminal cases where treatment may be a factor to be considered. The authors note that the sample consisted of therapists who were actively involved in research or transtheoretical integration, and thus the results may not generalize to the full range of mental health professionals.

Sperry et al. (1992) state, "It is axiomatic that one's espoused model of consultation colors perceptions about problem definition and drives the focus and types of interventions." (p. 27)

Lovinger (1992) describes motives that promote attachment to a particular theory (including following the model of an effective supervisor or therapist), defensive responses in the therapist or reluctance to deal with obsolescence and the need for retraining. Whatever the reason, for our purposes it is sufficient that theories are adopted for other than reasons of scientific validity and to some extent the theory-driven evaluation or procedure will vary from clinician to clinician; consequently, the choice of examiner will to some degree determine the approach—i.e., examiner effect.

Treece (1982) notes that while specific criteria as in DSM-III can aid reliability by reducing criterion variance, she also asserts that "Observation variance is related to other types of errors." She notes that training can to some extent reduce observation variance. This type of variance is most heavily dependent on differences in interviewers. She states, "Raters given identical information and criteria, as is the case in formal reliability trials, may nevertheless differ in attending to or giving particular weight to any specific item of information. In normal practice, moreover, differences in the interviewer's qualities and in the subject's reporting ability lead to variations in the quality and quantity of information available to a rater in making a diagnostic judgment."

The manner in which the examiner and examinee relate to each other, or "get along," can apparently have a profound effect on the data that are produced. Applebaum and Roth (1981) describe cases in which a patient would not talk to one psychiatric consultant but would talk to another. They assert, "This kind of difficulty is more likely to arise when patient and physician are of different races or of disparate social classes, but whenever there is reason to believe that interpersonal factors are affecting the patient's ability to formulate a competent decision, the assessment should be performed again with the assistance of someone who is more likely to be found congenial by the patient. The same applies, of course, if the patient displays an antipathy for the psychiatrist who is undertaking the competency assessment and refuses to 'perform' for him or her."

Lewis et al. (1983) describe a case study in which an individual with presumed brain damage behaved, reacted, and performed very differently across time and across examiners. They state: "As illustrated in the case of Mrs. Smith, transient but noticeable reduction in the overt expression of her underlying cortical dysfunction was obtained through the consultant's skillful management of the relationship climate during the interview." (p. 68) When steps were *not* taken to reduce this patient's anxiety, her thinking reportedly became more disorganized and her speech less fluent. Obviously, then, if this patient were assessed by two different psychiatrists, one who was "skillful" in reducing her anxiety and a second who was not, the two could come up with very different data. The second psychiatrist, in turn, might conclude that the individual has serious brain damage. However, had her anxiety been better managed the data might have suggested minor or no brain damage. This case study well illustrates how extraneous factors, or even rapport, may affect the data obtained.

Heilbrun (1987) discusses several problems related to assessments of competency for execution. He raises issues concerning the selection of mental health professionals to perform such evaluations and their competency at the task, and states:

> Further, was there any aspect of the selection process that might result in systematically obtaining examiners with certain kinds of biases? Were 'defense-oriented' professionals excluded? What about those strongly opposed to or favoring capital punishment? (p. 393)

Thus, Heilbrun is acknowledging the problem of examiner effects. Of course, biases that are quite evident should not be a problem in the courtroom context. It is the more subtle biases that may be difficult to determine.

Goldstein (1988) states:

> There is an extreme paucity of research on whether observation and/or recording of psychiatric interviews actually interferes with the process and its outcome. Empirical studies of the effects of recording are sparse and inherently conflicting. The discrepant and inconsistent findings suggest the need for caution in drawing any definitive conclusions at this time. The poor methodology of the clinical studies done so far largely precludes meaningful interpretation of the literature as a whole. (p. 1246)

Goldstein, therefore, argues that in the absence of some definitive research, or at least a strong weight of research on one side of this issue, that the conservative position of dealing with it on a case-by-case basis is probably safest. This would appear to be an issue that needs to be dealt with in view of the substantial body of literature demonstrating the highly significant operation of examiner effects, such that without a clear picture of what went on in the examination (e.g., a videotape of the interview), it is hazardous to draw any conclusions about the absence of such effects.

Apparently, the examiner can even influence the data obtained from a horse! Clever Hans (Pfungst, 1911) was a horse who demonstrated remarkable intellectual ability. This case is particularly important because Hans was not used in a carnival side show, but was purely considered a scientific curiosity. By means of tapping his hoof, the horse was able to spell, read, and solve problems of arithmetic and music harmony. This was a most impressive performance and left many visitors in awe. However, a series of very careful experiments ultimately showed that Hans' questioners unintentionally gave him cues. A forward inclination of the questioner's head served as a signal to Hans to begin his hoof tapping. A slight upward motion of the questioner's head or eyebrow served as a signal for Hans to stop his tapping. Hans' amazing talents, then, may be viewed as an illustration of the power of the self-fulfilling prophecy. Questioners, even skeptical ones, know the correct answers to their queries. Their expectation was reflected in their unintentional signal to Hans that they awaited cessation of his tapping. The signal brought on the expected cessation and Hans was correct again. Pfungst aptly summarized the difficulties in uncovering the nature of Clever Hans' talents by speaking of "looking in the horse for that which should have been sought in the man." It is virtually certain then, given the human nature of examiners, that such unintentional "cuing" takes place commonly in clinical examinations.

Thus, the scientific and professional literature continues to show, overwhelmingly, that examiner effects and biases influence the data produced through clinical examination. Any clinician who denies the effects of such influences is either woefully uninformed or is simply not being candid. The problem of examiner bias is so well established that it is stated as a "given" in much of the scientific and professional literature.

Many psychiatrists will candidly concede that biases do or can play a role in psychiatric diagnostic procedures and that this is true even of them. However, often they will add that they do not believe that in the case at hand they were influenced by biases. Obviously, it can be pointed out to the jury or judge that the clinician cannot possibly be an unbiased judge of the extent to which he has been influenced by his own biases.

A few clinicians will not concede that biases play a role in diagnosis. These clinicians can be asked if it is not true that there is a substantial body of scientific and professional literature to the effect that biases do affect the diagnostic process, and if they either deny it or say they are not aware of it, it will be necessary to produce another expert who will recite the extensive body of literature to this effect, with the result that it becomes clear to the jury that the first clinician is either uninformed or less than truthful.

If the clinician asserts that by reason of personal therapy or personal analysis he has been rendered free of biases and therefore entirely objective, he can be asked to cite scientific studies showing that therapy eliminates clinicians' biases (see Kubie, 1971 and Storrow, 1967, supra). It should be clear that the assumption of objectivity based on personal therapy is not tenable. In the face of so much contrary literature, no such claim by a clinician should be accepted unless he can provide objective proof that he is free of this problem that seems to afflict nearly all of his fellow professionals.

Additionally, there is considerable research showing that clinicians are unaware of their own biases and lack insight into the factors that actually shape their conclusions (see Chapter 5). Although many clinicians maintain that insight into biases and problematic practices offers sufficient safeguards against them, there is little positive evidence in support of this, and a growing body of negative evidence that shows otherwise.

EXAMINEE EFFECTS

Special Populations

A clinician should render a diagnosis based on the examinee's symptoms and problems, and not based on examinee characteristics that seem quite extraneous or secondary to the diagnosis. For example, assuming that the entity of schizophrenia exists, the patient should be diagnosed as such if he or she shows the symptoms of the disorder, and not because of such demographic features as race, age, gender, or social class, etc. There is a considerable body of literature to suggest, however, that such features often impact considerably on the data collection process and the judgments clinicians render. In a sense, these secondary features, or demographic characteristics, most of which often cannot help but be observed and that vary across individuals, create another form of extraneous variation that influences the clinical method. Stated differently, we all bring these data with us because they are us, and they exert uncertain effects on clinical judgments. There is so much material on the influence of these factors that we have devoted all of Chapter 16 to the topic, and thus we will provide just a few examples here.

As pertains to the influence of these factors on the data collected or produced, Carkhuff and Pierce (1957) found that race and social class of both the therapist and the patient were significant sources of effect. The interaction between the patient and therapist variables were also significant: not only did each exert independent effects, but also further effects in combination with each other. Both race and class variables had an effect on patient depth of self-exploration, and these effects were contingent on the therapist variables.

As pertains to the effects of these variables ("data") on interpretation, Gross et al. (1969) found that race and sex of patients made a difference in diagnosis and discharge planning. They found that more non-white women were diagnosed as "schizophrenic" than white women, and thus were more likely to be hospitalized. Watkins et al. (1975) found that black patients admitted to a psychiatric facility were diagnosed as schizophrenic comparatively more often than white patients. The authors conclude that this result was not produced by clinically-relevant features of the patients, but rather from the influence of race on the psychiatric diagnosis.

Abramowitz and Herrera (1981) describe inconsistencies in research, examining whether there is a bias toward rendering more serious or pathological diagnoses for women than men. Some research has supported the presence of this bias and some has not. In their study, Abramowitz and Herrera found small but persistent effects of both examiner and examinee sex. The diagnoses in their study were rendered by psychiatrists in training. However, as previously noted, considerable research suggests that certain biases become more ingrained or extreme as experience increases. In any case, based on this and other studies, it remains uncertain whether this particular form of bias exists, and one surely could not say that it does not nor indicate, specifically, just how it might affect the results of clinical examination.

Reliance on Self-Report

The examinee also exerts considerable effects on the data the clinician can or does obtain. Einstein once stated that nature was subtle but not malicious, meaning that nature's secrets might be difficult to unlock but that the things observed (e.g., atoms and force fields) do not purposely try to mislead the experimenter. This certainly is not true in psychology and psychiatry. It may well be the rare person, indeed, who is completely honest with the psychologist or psychiatrist. For example, many psychologists and psychiatrists discuss the lengthy period of time that might be required, even in the context of a psychotherapeutic relationship, before a patient can really open up and discuss problems freely.

These tendencies to withhold information or to mislead can be considerably greater in the forensic arena, in which the examinee might have a great deal riding on the psychologist's or psychiatrist's opinion. For example, in discussing personal injury suits, Miller (1961) states that "where the patient is engaged in making out a case for proportionate financial redress, some degree of exaggeration of disability might be regarded as no more than an *anticipated human failing.*" (italics added) (p. 995) Of course, these stakes may pale when compared to those involved in a murder charge.

Psychologists and psychiatrists often claim to have special abilities to distinguish truth from falsehood, and to identify malingering. The research conducted on this topic points to the opposite conclusion. We will review this research in detail in Chapter 18.

Not only may patients purposely mislead the examiner, but they may also produce inadvertent falsehoods or simply not know the information the examiner seeks. For example, psychiatrists will often direct detailed inquiry towards early parental relationships. Given the frailty of human memory, how much of this can we really remember, and how much of what we think we "remember" has been shaped and reshaped over time? All psychodynamically oriented clinicians should know that Freud's initial theoretical beliefs were substantially affected by the reports of many of his "neurotic" patients, which indicated that they had been sexually abused as children. Apparently, the patients believed that these incidents had occurred. Freud came to assume that sexual molestation was in fact the cause of many of the miseries his patients evidenced. It was only later that he came to realize, or believe, that these were false memories or reports and that such events had not really occurred. As the example shows, not only can the best clinicians be fooled into accepting faulty memories as fact, but patients can apparently be misleading without intending to be so.

Rogler et al. (1992) contend that the Diagnostic Interview Schedule (DIS) commits itself to dubious assumptions regarding the accuracy of human memory, shared by other history-taking methods, because it relies on retrospective reports of lifetime symptoms and episodic dating of symptom spells and ignores the extensive literature on the fallibility of human memory. Fennig and Bromet (1992), commenting on the Rogler et al. article, state that the problems of memory extend to any life history assessment, not only the DIS. Furthermore, Erdman et al. (1987) found that kappas for the DIS were quite low when used as predictors of chart diagnosis. They conclude that use of the DIS for clinical purposes is questionable, but that it is useful in individual cases for information gathering.

Further, as the judgment research shows, individuals are often not truly aware of the factors that shape their thinking and conclusions. For example, they may think that a factor that actually exerted minimal impact exerted major impact, and vice-versa. Thus, there is good reason to believe that individuals cannot really, or accurately, answer many questions of the type that are common in psychiatric examinations and interviews, e.g., "What factors led you to decide to leave your job?" "What would you say was the single most important factor that finalized your plan to divorce your wife?" "What angered you the most about the treatment you received from Dr. Jones?" Do individuals really know the answers to such questions, even if they think they do? Maybe and maybe not. No one *really* knows, including the psychologist or psychiatrist.

As regards these problems, Klopfer (1984) describes reliance on the self-report of patients as a limitation of interview methods. He notes that an individual can be quite uncommunicative and thus little useful information may be obtained. Further, Klopfer states that, "The subject may provide false information, being untruthful in an effort to anticipate what the interviewer would like to hear."

In a study of structured interview and self-report questionnaires, Perry (1992) finds that sources of error include variance due to discrepancies between self-report and observational data. Slovenko (1984) describes the risks involved in interpreting patient's self-reports. He notes Freud's early blunder in believing that actual sexual trauma had occurred during the childhood of many of his patients, only to realize later that his patients had been "deceiving themselves and him."

As regards the assessment of post-traumatic stress syndrome, Raifman (1983) discusses problems in evaluation. These problems include excessive reliance on inadequate descriptions of the stressor and often exclusive reliance on the patient's self-report about events that may be impossible to verify. In a paper regarding this same disorder, Platt and Husband (1986) also express concerns about reliance on self-report. They state:

> The reliance on the patient's self-report thus can sometimes make it difficult or impossible for the clinician to detect malingering or exaggeration of symptoms. This can be problematic, particularly in cases where the patient is involved in litigation, as it may be difficult for the clinician to obtain concurrent validation of the patient's reported symptoms from other sources while litigation is pending. (pp. 34-35)

Platt and Husband also describe potential problems with role enactment, in which litigants learn what is expected of them and react accordingly. They state:

> By the time the patient/litigant arrives at the clinician's office, he or she often has consulted not only an attorney but a host of medical and allied health professionals as well, depending on the nature and severity of any physical and mental injuries the patient may have sustained. Patients may well pick up cues from their attorneys or treating professionals as to the symptoms they might be expected to have. The questions asked and the messages communicated by these professionals regarding the patient's physical and mental condition can have the effect of covertly or even overtly alerting the patient to additional symptoms he or she had not reported or had not emphasized in previous evaluations, as well as potentially serving to reinforce existing symptoms....The patient feels that, "I am the injured party and a good person; therefore, I deserve compensation for these symptoms I have." Obviously this can make both accurate diagnosis and effective treatment more difficult, at least until the litigation is concluded. (pp. 35-36)

According to the authors, they have observed patients presenting increasing amounts of symptomatology over time and evaluations, but admitting to fewer and fewer socially undesirable behaviors. This increase in reported symptoms can occur even when patients are in treatment for these problems. Platt and Husband state:

> ...paradoxically, reported problems in sexual functioning appear to decrease for some patients and increase for others across evaluations which are fairly close together in time. One might speculate that this occurs because it is more difficult for patients to determine whether it is more appropriate for someone in their situation to have such problems or whether it is "better" (more socially acceptable) to present themselves as sexually "normal." (p. 36)

Some experts will assert that they can or have overcome these limitations in self-report by broadening their data base. Often, this will involve interviewing other individuals, such as a spouse. For example, when a patient complains of problems with memory after a head injury, the clinician might ask the spouse whether they too have observed such problems, have noticed a change in everyday functioning in this area, or whether the reported problems might create practical limitations. Now it should be obvious that such an approach may merely compound the problems involved in self-report, rather than correct them. For example, the spouse might be similarly motivated to create a particular impression on the psychiatrist. In fact, having now heard similar things from both husband and wife, the psychiatrist may feel more confident in his conclusions, whereas he may have just been misled twice. All of the factors that place self-report in doubt in the case of the one being assessed can operate equally when another interested party participates in the assessment process. We might also note that when multiple informants are used in the clinical setting, such as when patient and spouse are interviewed, the clinician may also obtain highly discrepant results. For example, patient reports on intellectual problems following head injury often contrast sharply with reports from family members (see Chapter 15).

Thus, even if the data are consistent, there is often little reason to assume that this makes them more trustworthy. When the data are conflictual, the psychiatrist is left trying to decide which informant to believe, if either, without clear guidelines for making this determination. As Slovenko (1984) states:

> Inferring actual reality from psychic reality, we may say, is more speculative than inferring psychic reality from actual reality....Therapists generally say that they focus on psychic reality, not actual reality, so they do not hire detectives to investigate the actual facts. (p. 458)

Brown et al. (1991) note that while memory complaints are among the most common problems presented to clinical and neuropsychologists, research supporting the accuracy of such complaints is meager. In their study, they found that patients' reports of diminished memory function do not necessarily indicate specific memory function, particularly with younger and better educated subjects. One exception in their study was for subjects who had more than one elevated MMPI/MMPI-2 scale. Also, the discrepancies for older and less educated subjects was less marked, making it less inconsistent with earlier studies which had used those populations.

A series of studies by Lees-Haley and colleagues provide a serious challenge to reliance on self-reports in forensic matters. Such reports, by way of both interview and structured questionnaires or scales, are quite common in forensic practices of psychiatrists, psychologists, and neuropsychologists. There are a number of such instruments (e.g., Symptom Check List, Beck Depression Inventory, etc.) which may be useful in regular clinical practice, but which risk suggesting symptoms to litigants in legal matters. In three recent publications, Lees-Haley et al. provide rather dramatic illustrations of this problem, as well as some badly needed base rate data regarding various symptoms. Because of their potential value to lawyers, we will deal with these in some detail.

Lees-Haley and Brown (1993) report on a study in which prior to psychological evaluation or any discussion with examiner, 170 patients (personal injury claimants) completed a checklist containing 37 common neuropsychological complaints. Patients were excluded if they were filing claims for neuropsychological impairment or if they had any known head injury or other experiences suggestive of neuropsychological impairment. Most of the claims were for emotional or industrial distress (e.g., discrimination, harassment, etc.). Many also reported orthopedic complaints. These constituted the claimants group. A control group of 50 patients was drawn from a group family practice clinic, with a diverse range of common medical complaints (e.g., sore throat, flu, respiratory, fatigue, headaches). Lees-Haley and Brown found that more than 50% of claimants reported symptoms commonly associated with neuropsychological impairment (Table 1).

TABLE 1

NEUROPSYCHOLOGICAL COMPLAINT
BASE RATES[1]

Controls	Claimants	Symptom	x^2	$p <$
54%	93%	Anxiety or nervousness	43.79	0.005
52%	92%	Sleeping problems	42.75	0.005
32%	89%	Depression	68.22	0.005
62%	88%	Headaches	18.23	0.005
48%	80%	Back pain[a]	19.95	0.005
58%	79%	Fatigue (mental or physical)	8.73	0.005
26%	78%	Concentration problems	47.23	0.005
36%	77%	Worried about health[a]	29.80	0.005
38%	77%	Irritability	27.17	0.005
30%	74%	Neck pain[a]	31.64	0.005
36%	65%	Impatience	13.70	0.005
18%	62%	Restlessness	29.64	0.005
24%	61%	Feeling disorganized	21.40	0.005
30%	60%	Loss of interest	14.00	0.005
16%	59%	Confusion	28.35	0.005
16%	56%	Loss of efficiency in carrying out everyday tasks	24.70	0.005
14%	55%	Shoulder pain[a]	26.50	0.005
20%	53%	Memory problems	16.90	0.005
26%	44%	Dizziness	5.28	0.025
6%	41%	Sexual problems	21.60	0.005
12%	39%	Numbness	2.60	0.005
34%	38%	Nausea	0.30	ns
20%	34%	"Word finding problems, not finding the word you want, using the wrong word"	3.61	ns
28%	2%	Diarrhea[a]	0.34	ns
22%	32%	"Visual problems, blurring, or seeing double"	1.77	ns
8%	30%	Trembling or tremors	9.97	0.005
18%	29%	Hearing problems	2.33	ns
16%	29%	Constipation[a]	3.31	ns
22%	24%	Foot pain[a]	0.10	ns
12%	24%	Trouble reading	3.38	ns
20%	21%	Bumping into things	0.03	ns
12%	21%	Elbow pain[a]	1.88	ns
16%	18%	Speech problems	0.13	ns
4%	15%	Impotence	4.44	0.05
12%	11%	Bleeding[a]	0.03	ns
2%	4%	Seizures[b]	0.49	ns
8%	2%	Broken bone or bones[a]	3.52	ns

[a] Indicates items included as distractors.

[b] Several patients self-reported experiencing seizures, but follow-up questioning and medical histories indicated no clinical seizure experience.

---

[1] Reprinted from *Archives of Clinical Neuropsychology*, Vol. 8, Lees-Haley, P.R. and Brown, R.S., Neuropsychological complaint base rates of 170 personal injury claimants, p. 207, © 1993, with kind permission from Elsevier Science Ltd., The Boulevard, Langford Lane, Kidlington 0X5 1GB, UK.

What may be equally or more compelling regarding base rates for these symptoms are the figures reported for the control group. Examples include: 54% nervousness, 58% fatigue, 38% irritability, 36% impatience, 26% concentration problems.

While the claimant data provides an indication of base rates for apparently non-neuropsychologically impaired personal injury claimants, the data for the control group provide some indication of base rates for people not neuropsychologically impaired and not involved in litigation.

The authors also caution regarding the iatrogenic effects of symptom checklists on claimants.

In a follow-up study, Dunn et al. (1993—note that Lees-Haley and Brown are co-authors) report symptom checklist frequencies for three groups—156 claimants similar to those in the study above (the experimental group), 113 patients who were seeking treatment from family physicians and had no reported history of head injury or toxic exposure (control group), and 68 patients who reported a history of head injury or toxic exposure who were seeking treatment from their family physician and were non-litigating (injured/exposed control group). (See Table 2 for results.) These data provide more evidence of the susceptibility of self-report to excessive symptom claims. Also, while the frequencies for some neuropsychological symptoms in this control group are in many cases lower than for the control group above, nevertheless, for many symptoms, the rates indicate that these symptoms occur with considerable frequency in the non-psychoneurological population.

TABLE 2

SYMPTOM FREQUENCIES AND GROUP COMPARISONS FOR EXPERIMENTAL (N=156), CONTROL (N=113) AND INJURED (N=68) GROUPS[2]

Symptom	Exper.	Control	Injured	Chi-Sq.	Sig.	Exper. vs. Injured	Exper. vs. Control	Control vs. Injured
Anxiety	86.50	40.70	55.90	63.59	c	c	c	
Trouble sleeping	81.40	29.50	39.70	80.06	c	c	c	
Headaches	76.90	50.40	57.40	21.65	c	b	c	
Depression	76.30	26.50	41.20	69.39	c	c	c	
Tension	74.40	24.10	39.70	69.91	c	c	c	a
Concentration problems	71.20	21.20	33.80	71.39	c	c	c	
Fatigue	71.20	36.60	55.90	31.68	c	a	c	a
Concentration	69.20	17.70	32.40	75.55	c	c	c	a
Impatience	64.10	32.70	41.20	27.85	c	b	c	
Irritability	62.80	26.50	30.90	41.09	c	c	c	
Restlessness	62.80	16.10	36.80	59.44	c	c	c	b

2 Poster presented at the 13th Annual Conference of the National Academy of Neuropsychology, Phoenix, AZ, October 28-30, 1993.

Table 2 (cont'd)

Symptom	Exper.	Control	Injured	Chi-Sq.	Sig.	Exper. vs. Injured	Exper. vs. Control	Control vs. Injured
Confusion	57.70	5.30	17.60	90.68	c	c	c	a
Feeling disorganized	57.70	19.50	32.40	41.92	c	c	c	
Thinking clearly	57.10	10.60	26.50	64.76	c	c	c	b
Neck pain*	55.80	31.30	39.70	16.62	c	a	c	
Loss of interest	51.30	13.30	14.70	54.88	c	c	c	
Easily distracted	49.40	15.00	23.50	38.31	c	c	c	
Loss of efficiency	49.40	9.70	13.20	60.24	c	c	c	
Loss of temper	48.70	10.60	19.10	50.10	c	c	c	
Attention problems	47.70	9.80	25.00	44.78	c	b	c	a
Memory problems	45.50	12.40	20.60	37.82	c	c	c	
Word finding	45.50	11.60	23.50	37.43	c	b	c	
Feeling partially disabled	44.20	3.50	16.20	61.46	c	c	c	b
Weakness	43.60	6.30	14.70	53.16	c	c	c	
Dizziness	41.00	21.20	27.90	12.41	b		b	
Nausea	39.10	19.50	32.40	11.83	b		c	
Sexual problems	38.50	8.00	17.60	34.93	c	b	c	
Shoulder pain*	37.80	14.30	23.50	18.83	c		c	
Slowed thinking	37.80	5.40	16.20	41.27	c	b	c	a
Blurred vision	37.20	17.70	32.40	12.21	b		c	a
Rapid heartbeat	36.50	15.00	19.10	17.80	c	a	c	
Poor judgment	34.60	3.60	16.20	39.49	c	b	c	b
Recent memory problems	34.60	5.40	17.60	33.87	c	a	c	a
Chest pressure	34.00	13.30	13.20	20.40	c	b	c	
Trouble hearing	34.00	12.40	27.90	16.32	c		c	a
Numbness	34.00	5.40	20.60	31.46	c		c	b
Painful tingling	34.00	5.40	16.20	33.49	c	a	c	a
Visual problems	34.00	7.10	20.60	27.21	c		c	a
Trouble reading	33.30	0.90	5.90	56.13	c	c	c	
Fear of non-cancer illness	32.70	6.20	19.10	27.86	c		c	a
Trouble walking	32.10	3.50	5.90	45.05	c	c	c	
Trembling	30.80	5.40	14.70	28.34	c	a	c	
Feeling totally disabled	30.10	2.70	2.90	48.08	c	c	c	
Bumping into things	29.50	14.20	13.20	12.40	b	a	b	
Diarrhea*	28.20	25.70	47.10	10.23	b	b		b
Perspiring for no reason	25.60	4.50	13.20	22.18	c		c	
Loss of common sense	24.40	3.50	5.90	28.45	c	b	c	
Marital problems	23.70	8.80	11.80	11.90	b		b	
Fine motor coordination	19.90	1.80	4.40	26.01	c	b	c	
Long-term memory problems	17.90	0.00	7.40	24.30	c		c	a
Speech problems	17.30	1.80	5.90	19.22	c	a	c	
Slurred speech	15.40	0.90	5.90	18.17	c		c	
Elbow pain*	13.50	8.00	22.10	7.29	a			a
Impotence	13.50	3.50	1.50	13.72	b	a	a	
Not knowing where I am	11.50	0.00	4.40	15.30	c		c	

Note: * indicates the symptom is a distractor item. The lower case letters indicate the significance level for that particular group comparison: a = significant difference at p < .05; b = significant difference at p < .01; c = significant difference at p < .001

In a third study, Lees-Haley and Dunn (1994) again used self-report questionnaires. This time they asked college students to indicate which symptoms they thought a person would experience if they were suffering from depression, anxiety, effects of a traumatic event or effects of a mild brain injury. They found that 96.9% of the 97 subjects who completed the depression questionnaire were able to satisfy the self-report criteria for Major Depression. For PTSD 98.9% satisfied criterion B, 89.2% satisfied criterion C, 95.7% satisfied criterion D and 86% satisfied all three of the self-report criteria for PTSD. The findings were similar for Generalized Anxiety Disorder. On the brain damage questionnaire, 63.3% of the subjects were able to identify half or more of the mild brain injury symptoms. The authors conclude that this provides a demonstration that naive subjects can accurately endorse enough symptoms to satisfy DSM-III-R criteria for the disorders involved. They cite these results as contrary to the claims of many clinicians that naive subjects could not, without training and familiarity, malinger these disorders.

One would think that these considerations, of which all professionals should be aware, would lead them to adopt safeguards. Most importantly, they might systematically obtain and review all available background records that could provide some means for cross-checking the accuracy of self-reports, particularly when they are conducting forensic assessments. For example, they might carefully check medical records to make certain that the date and complications of an injury were as the person described them. However, even when materials are available, these checks are often disregarded. For example, we were involved in a case in which the plaintiff suffered a minor head injury but provided the psychologist with incorrect facts about the injury. Further, the individual complained of problems in memory, such as forgetting the date of his mother's birthday. The psychologist failed to obtain the background medical records, through which obvious errors in self-report could have easily been detected. Further, he relied on this examinee's self-report about his own memory and his self-report about what his girlfriend had said about his forgetfulness. The psychologist never bothered to speak with this girlfriend nor pursued what arguably would have been less potentially biased sources of information (e.g., the employer).

SITUATIONAL EFFECTS, TRANSIENT EFFECTS, IATROGENIC FACTORS

Situational Effects

Virtually all psychologists acknowledge that one's immediate environment or situation can exert a substantial effect on psychological status and behavior. For example, no matter what their personalities, many people become tense the first time they speak before a large audience. In fact, many psychologists believe, almost all behavioral psychologists included, that situational factors have a greater influence on behavior than an individual's personality. A well-known psychologist, Walter

Mischel (1973), argues (as do some other psychologists) that many of the personality traits we use to describe behavior and personality (e.g., the person is "friendly," "passive," "mean-tempered," etc.) do not even exist as such. As Wilkinson and O'Connor (1982) state, "Controversy still exists as to whether traits within an individual or situations surrounding the individual contribute more to behavior and clinical process." (p. 985)

Vallacher and Wegner (1987) note the continuing controversy and problems with regard to personal versus situational causation of behavior. Rowe (1987) discusses the debate concerning the relative contributions of the individual, or individual traits, versus the situation in determining behavior that can be observed, illustrating that the issue of situation effects is very much alive.

Turner et al. (1986) found that in socially anxious individuals, both thoughts and physiological reactivity were influenced by situational variables. These effects occurred both in cognition and in physiological reactivity as measured by systolic blood pressure. These authors also cite prior research indicating that approximately 30 to 40% of the general population suffers from anxiety. The attorney may wish to keep that bit of base rate data in mind in cases where anxiety is alleged as a post-injury or post-accident symptom.

Heilbrun (1987) states, "The circumstances of the evaluation, including the physical environment and the people present, are an additional consideration." (p. 393) He notes that one is unlikely to have a quiet, uninterrupted and private exchange of information in a maximum security section of a prison. (p. 393)

Perry (1992), studying a number of structured interview and self-report questionnaires for the assessment of personality disorders, concludes that sources of error include variance due to different interview occasions.

May et al. (1993) found that age differences in optimal performance periods between younger and older adults could be identified and that these were important determinants of memory difference. Specifically, substantial differences were found in the late afternoon when younger but not older subjects were at their optimal time. This seems to be a situation effect in which the memory performance of older subjects may be different depending on the time of day it is measured.

Brody et al. (1990) found that scores on a General Self-esteem Subscale decreased and scores on the Beck Depression Inventory increased in relation to the number of prior questionnaires. In their study the questionnaires (from one to five) were administered consecutively on one day. However, we can note that in many cases the MMPI and MCMI and possibly other questionnaires or instruments are administered on the same day. Thus, this may be an important situation effect such that more disturbance may show up on the second questionnaire which, coupled with the tendency to overdiagnose pathology, might result in a diagnosis which is simply the result of overtesting.

Lidz et al. (1989) state, "To put it differently, the judgment of whether someone is committable should be 1) reasonably independent of the situation in which the judgment is made (e.g., who is making the judgment, when they are making it, and what sort of irrelevant situational factors are involved)...." (p. 176)

McConnaughy (1988) argues that therapist personality variables contribute to the outcome of therapy (see Chapter 22).

The relevant point for our purposes is that many professionals believe that situational factors can exert powerful effects on people. Note that DSM-III describes involvement in litigation as a significant stressor, which, therefore, presumably affects psychological condition.

If situations can exert important influences on psychological status and behavior, it naturally follows that one's thinking and behavior can change if one's situation changes. Individuals are reactive creatures—reactive to the events that are going on around them. Herein lies a major problem with the clinical examination. The situation—the time, the place, and the circumstances under which the examination are conducted—can exert powerful influences on the psychological status of the individual. Should these things change, the status of the individual may change accordingly. Hence, the data obtained on the clinical examination will change as well. Thus, situational factors, which themselves may be highly unstable, create a major additional source of uncontrolled variation. This variation, in fact, may well play a critical role in difficulties obtaining consistent or reliable results across clinical examinations. There exist few, if any, reliable means for distinguishing interview data determined by situational factors as opposed to enduring psychological characteristics. Rather, assuming the issue is considered at all, attempts to make the separation is largely a matter of guesswork.

Different authors have discussed these broad-ranging situational effects. Epstein (1980) notes that traditional attempts to obtain a high degree of control, even in the laboratory setting, are "often ineffective because much human behavior is so sensitive to incidental sources of stimulation, that adequate control cannot be achieved." Edelman and Snead (1972) found that the amount of self-disclosure that occurred during a simulated psychiatric interview differed significantly according to the indicated purpose of the interview.

Fossi et al. (1984) state: "The traditional method of evaluation of psychopathology includes the relationship between the physician and the patient at some precise moment which is not necessarily representative of the patient's general behavior." Thus, they point out both examiner and situational effects.

An article in *Marriage and Divorce Today Newsletter* (1986) indicates that seasonal swings and emotions may affect seriously ill psychiatric patients, as well as persons suffering from more mild disorders. In fact, a term used is "Seasonal Affective Disorder (SAD)." First noted by Norman Rosenthal in an article in the *American Journal of Psychiatry,* January, 1986, it was found that patients with depression suffered a worsening of their symptoms in the winter and those suffering from manic-depression experienced a peak of mania during the summer, with substantial increases in depression during the winter. Further research by Dr. Peter A. Bick, M.D., at the Massachusetts Mental Health Center, Boston, found, in his case studies, results that are parallel to those of Rosenthal. He notes that it is important for mental health professionals to ask patients about any seasonal fluctuations in their symptoms and suggests that those showing fluctuation might benefit from light therapy: that is, exposure to greater amounts of light during the season involved. The same newsletter cites research by Dr. Michael Gitlin, UCLA Neuropsychiatric Hospital Institute, indicating that exposure to light is an effective treatment for those who suffer winter depression.

Wehr et al. (1987) report clinical observations of several patients who demonstrated depression in the summer and hypomania in the winter or at other times of the year. They note that many of the patients report their clinical state appears to be influenced by such environmental factors as temperature, humidity, latitude, and light. They also note that some patients who have had severe depressions when in one part of the country had little or no difficulty in another part of the country. It would seem that susceptibility to climatic conditions needs to be taken into account in any assessment of depression or manic or hypomanic states. It is rare in our experience to see this item covered in a clinical report. Nevertheless, this and other work reported in this text indicate that without data to rule out climatic conditions as the "cause" of a diagnosed depressive state or manic state, it would be difficult or impossible to determine that an accident, for example, had been the cause of depression when indeed it may have been climate related. The possibility of seasonal influences makes it important to know when the examination was conducted. That is, if you get a "summer depressive" and examine him in the summer, one might erroneously attribute the depression to an accident rather than the time of year, which might be the true cause. At minimum, inquiry should be made to determine whether the clinician was aware of and investigated this variable.

Jacobsen et al. (1987) describe Seasonal Affective Disorder as, "A cyclic mood disturbance characterized by fall-winter depression and spring-summer hypomania or euthymia." (p. 1301) They note the syndrome occurs predominantly in women. They also note that the winter depressions of SAD can be reversed by treatment with bright artificial light, which, if substantiated, may provide a means of reducing distress, impairment, and damages.

Boyce and Parker (1988) also discuss SAD, as do Garvey et al. (1988). Wehr and Rosenthal (1989) review some of the literature concerning SAD and find that there appear to be two primary opposite seasonal patterns of annual depression, one being winter depression and the other summer depression, and with opposite vegetative symptoms. They also note that SAD is not uncommon. DSM-IV recognizes SAD by including a section on Seasonal Pattern Specifier under Mood Disorders (pp. 389-390).

Transient Effects

A large number of factors can create artifactual and/or transient effects that alter the data obtained in the clinical interview and can produce potentially misleading results and mistaken conclusions. For example, medications given to treat an ailment like hypertension have been reported to create symptoms that mimic psychiatric depressions (see Chapter 12). A psychiatrist who fails to inquire about the use of any such medications, or who is not aware of their full range of potential effects, thus may misdiagnose such an individual as suffering from a depressive illness. In our opinion, psychiatrists often do not take such possible effects seriously enough, or else fail to inquire about them with adequate thoroughness.

Meyer and Fink (1989) note the possibility of iatrogenic effects from various medications prescribed by physicians as well as non-prescription medications. They note that it is not feasible for them to offer a complete and comprehensive reference of this nature, but they do provide a list of some of the more commonly used medications. They properly caution that not all of these medications provide the side effects described and that it is only occasionally that this happens. However, the attorney would obviously want to check this out in any case where it is known what medications were administered. Meyer and Fink do provide a fairly extensive list, in their Appendix, of approximately 100 medications (many of these are duplicated because they are given both by generic name and trade name). We feel this would be a most useful article for attorneys to have available. Of course, the best reference, if an attorney is willing to take the trouble, is the *Physicians' Desk Reference* for the current year. Along the same lines, Lee et al. (1988) provide support for previous studies showing the effects of caffeine on conditions such as anxiety and depression.

Greden (1974) points out the failure of psychiatrists to eliminate caffeine as the source of symptoms. He states that too much caffeine in coffee, tea, cola drinks or aspirin can bring on all the symptoms of an anxiety state, and unrecognized "coffee nerves" could lead one to a psychiatrist and months of useless treatment with tranquilizing drugs. He states that overdoses of caffeine can bring such symptoms as nervousness, irritability, tremulousness, occasional muscle twitching, sensory disturbances, attacks of diarrhea, insomnia, irregular heartbeat, a drop in blood pressure and even circulatory failures. He points out the need for doctors to routinely ask patients about caffeine intake and describes reviewing records of a hundred psychiatric patients, with 42 diagnosed as having anxiety with no question ever having been asked about caffeine consumption. And yet, anxiety is a common element in many psychiatric diagnoses, and the diagnosis of some kind of "anxiety state" is common in so-called "psychic injury" cases. Obviously, the lawyer can probe for this oversight and make a point of it whenever the presence of "anxiety" is listed as a "symptom" supporting some diagnosis, and particularly when some kind of anxiety disorder is the primary diagnosis. Strangely, some clinician's offices provide coffee in the waiting room!

A number of studies support Greden's points and recommendations. Veleber and Templer (1984) found that caffeine increased anxiety, hostility, and depression. They caution about drawing generalizations from their study due to the somewhat large dose of caffeine administered at a single sitting. However, the dosage was at a level that an average coffee drinker usually exceeds in a day. Charney et al. (1985) found that the effects of caffeine were greater for subjects suffering from problems with anxiety, although even healthy subjects showed significant increases in anxiety and nervousness. Boulenger et al. (1984) found that among patients with problems in anxiety or depression, their levels of anxiety and depression correlated with the amount of caffeine they consumed. They also found that patients diagnosed as having "panic disorders" had an increased sensitivity to caffeine, showing reactions to even one cup of coffee. Gilliland and Andress (1981) found that healthy individuals who were moderate and high caffeine consumers showed increases in anxiety and depression when compared to abstainers. These college students also seemed to perform less well in their course work, suggesting the possibility that moderate and high caffeine consumption may hinder clear thinking or some of the intellectual processes potentially tapped in mental status examinations or intellectual tests.

Wells (1984) provides a review of the literature on caffeine in relation to disturbed psychological states. She notes the many sources of caffeine, including soft drinks and over-the-counter medication. She also notes that there may be an interactive effect of caffeine with alcohol and with other drugs. Valium is one of the drugs she mentions, which may be given by a psychiatrist to lessen anxiety or tension. Wells observes that for high level caffeine users, withdrawal from caffeine is related to both psychological and physiological disturbance.

Wells feels that conclusions are still somewhat tentative, due to the difficulty in estimating the amount of caffeine in different substances and differential reactions to caffeine, as well as the difficulty in determining precisely the amount of caffeine intake. She does, however, state quite clearly that diagnostic inquiries of patients should include reference to coffee, tea, chocolate, over-the-counter medications and soft drinks, and that this information should be combined with knowledge of any other drug consumption and the previous medical and psychiatric history.

Apparently, then, caffeine can create "symptoms" in otherwise healthy individuals that can mimic those seen among individuals with so-called anxiety disorders. This could potentially lead to the misdiagnosis of a normal individual as a disordered one. Further, among individuals with assumed disorders, even relatively small amounts of caffeine can exaggerate symptoms. Thus, that cup of coffee offered in the waiting room might well produce a more dramatic symptom presentation that, in turn, could lead the psychiatrist to assume a condition is more serious than is actually the case.

Finally, because reactions to caffeine show substantial overlap with symptoms used to diagnose various disorders, the result could well be diagnostic confusion. The DSM-III notes that effects of caffeine ("caffeine intoxication") may include the following: nervousness, excitement, restlessness, agitation, insomnia, and rambling flow of thought and speech. Further, the manual states that among some individuals, such reactions may occur at levels of caffeine consumption that are equivalent to less than two cups of coffee a day. As regards symptom overlap, the DSM-III states: "Manic episodes, Panic Disorder or Generalized Anxiety Disorder can cause a clinical picture similar to that of Caffeine Intoxication. The temporal relation of the symptoms to caffeine use establishes the diagnosis." (p. 160) These descriptions of caffeine reactions are virtually identical in DSM-III-R and DSM-IV. Additionally, DSM-IV contains a separate diagnosis 292.89, Caffeine Induced Anxiety disorder (p. 443). We might add that these complications will not necessarily be avoided should the psychologist or psychiatrist deny the coffee drinker that cup of coffee. The intent may be to avoid the caffeine reactions that may cloud the picture, but as noted by Wells, withdrawal from caffeine is also associated with psychological and physiological disturbance. Failure to ascertain caffeine consumption means the clinician cannot rule it out as a source of the related problems. Also, it suggests less than a thorough examination.

Agents other than caffeine can also exert effects on an individual's status and clinical presentation. Christensen et al. (1985) found that a dietary change for three subjects consisting of a high protein-low carbohydrate diet void of sucrose and caffeine resulted in a more stable and less distressed individual. They state that their overall results indicate that dietary change can remedy the emotional distress exhibited by some individuals.

The *Los Angeles Times* in June of 1986 carried a story quoting John F. Schlegel, president of the American Pharmaceutical Association, to the effect that smoking cigarettes can interfere with how the body metabolizes drugs. According to the article, Schlegel stated that smokers may need to take greater amounts of the drugs or take them more frequently to get the same effect as non-smokers. Among the drugs that smoking interferes with are anti-anxiety drugs including Diazepam (commonly sold as Valium), painkillers such as Propoxyphene (sold as Darvon), tricyclic antidepressants including Amitriptyline (sold as Elevil, Amitryl and others), anti-blood clotting drugs such as Heparin, Phenothiazines, including Chlorpromazine, sold as Thorazine, anti-asthmatic drugs including Theophylline and the anti-angina drugs known as beta blockers, such as Propranolol.

Iatrogenic and Related Factors

For legal purposes, it is often essential to identify the specific cause of a disorder. For example, in a personal injury suit, an individual may display tension or anxiety, but the implications are very different if this symptom was caused by the injury or "traumatic" event, as opposed to some other factor. For example, it is possible that the repeated questions asked by lawyers and doctors, rather than the accident per se, have led the individual to doubt his own well-being and consequently aroused feelings of distress. The term, "iatrogenic," technically refers to symptoms or reactions caused inadvertently by a physician or his treatment. Iatrogenic factors, or related symptom-producing factors or circumstances, may be the primary or sole cause of disorder, rather than an injury or event in question. For example, if the mismanagement of a patient's therapy case creates symptoms that the patient did not have to begin with, these symptoms can be said to be iatrogenic in nature. If a patient with some physical malady develops feelings of anxiety because he is told to stay home from work and his home life is filled with tension, this anxiety can be accounted for by other factors. It is not the physical malady, but rather the home life or idleness, that may account for the symptoms.

Many psychiatric symptoms can be caused by iatrogenic or other than alleged factors, thus leading to confusion about the actual source or cause of the symptoms or difficulties. For example, is the physical pre-occupation of an individual following a personal injury caused by the injury itself, or by the effects of involvement in litigation, including repeated examinations? Is the tension displayed a result of a trauma or the feelings aroused when an individual may have large sums of money on the line as he tries to bluff his way through the courts with a phony claim? Is the mental confusion an accused murderer displays the result of a longstanding psychiatric disorder or the product of the prison environment? Lacking a technology, or reliable procedures for assessing the role of iatrogenic and related factors, there may often be no way to tell what caused what.

Kubie (1971) states:

> In short, we have shut our eyes to the multiple and powerful iatrogenic influences of our behavior, of the earlier behavior of the patient himself, of the behavior of other patients, and in general the environments in which patients live out their sick lives. These confuse the clinical picture with extraneous contaminants which not only make precise diagnosis difficult but also make it difficult to decide what, when and where to seek correlations. (p. 339)

In Chapters 20 and 15, when discussing post-traumatic stress disorder and mild head injury, respectively, we will cite material which suggests that many, if not all of the symptoms that may be displayed can often be potentially explained by iatrogenic or related factors. Thus, we will provide just a few citations here for purposes of illustration. Simons and Meyer (1986) note that in custody disputes all parties concerned are victims of a collapsing family system and are often at the crisis point in the divorcing process. They state, "The evaluator must keep the perspective that she is viewing these families at their very worst and in the midst of one of the most powerful crises in their lives." (p. 152) One wonders how, under these circumstances, an evaluator could possibly separate out transient effects, or know how these individuals would appear were they not in these circumstances. Halleck (1982) states that the incidence of depression, massive anxiety, psychosis and suicide in jails is very high and is made worse by the dismal, oppressive and unsafe atmosphere of most jails. Thus, Halleck appears to confirm that being incarcerated is likely to alter an individual's mental condition. Further, one cannot determine from an examination of a prisoner what the individual's psychological status may have been prior to his imprisonment.

Suedfeld (1975) describes both laboratory and field research which demonstrates that elimination or reduction of sensory stimulation (often termed "sensory deprivation") may cause or aggravate psychological dysfunction in a wide variety of contexts, citing, among others, prisoners as examples of this situation. He cites examples of depression, loss of concentration, weakened will power, hallucinations, regression, persuasability and mental confusion as examples of the effects of such reduced stimulation. While in some of the cases, the individuals were isolated from all others, the author believes that the deleterious effects of environmental monotony on groups of people strongly resembles the factor of aloneness exhibited by isolates.

Preston (1981) indicates that the extent of iatrogenic disorder is uncertain, but may be significantly under-recognized. He states, "The extent of iatrogenic disease will not be known until we have standards for administering therapies and technologies, and adequate means of measuring results. Until that time, we can only document its existence and estimate its extent." (p. 127) Preston indicates that excessive (medical) testing is the most common source of overdiagnosis. He further notes that excessive testing that leads to a false-positive diagnosis can result in unnecessary treatment that can be harmful, and that leading someone to believe that they are disordered can cause emotional upset or harm. He states, "Diagnosis of dreaded diseases always incapacitates the patient, increases emotional stress, imposes dependency and economic cost, and produces unhealthy fixation on the illness." (p. 131) Thus, for example, raising the possibility of iatrogenic disorder in cases involving mild head injury, one can ask whether the examinee has been told that he has brain damage (even in the absence of neurological findings suggesting such). One can question whether "knowledge" of this supposed diagnosis, which individuals might consider dreadful, may not have a considerably upsetting effect on the examinee.

DEFICIENCIES OF OBSERVATION, RECALL, AND REPORTING OF DATA

The second major deficiency of the clinical method lies in the deficiencies of human beings, including psychiatrists and psychologists, as receivers and storers of information. That people, including psychiatrists and psychologists, tend to perceive and remember selectively according to the way they are "set" is so well known as to require little in the way of statement or citation of experimental literature. As more than adequately documented in research, this set is a function of a number of variables. Sarason (1954) puts it this way:

> If clinicians differ in how much they will note and remember of a patient's overt behavior, then it becomes important to determine the sources of these individual differences. Why is it that individuals differ as to what aspects of a situation will be prepotent for them, in the sense that they become aware of and respond to them? Posing the problem in this way implies that the clinician's response tendencies are not of equal strength or equally evocable by different aspects of the situation. What the clinician is set to see is a function both of his own habit hierarchy and of the nature of the particular situation. (p. 9)

Sarason further indicates that although there is an *assumption* that a clinician's description of a patient's overt behavior is reliable, convincing evidence for such an assumption cannot be found and there are *discouragingly large individual differences in the ability to reliably describe the overt behavior of the patient.* (p. 9) He further states that there is no evidence to suggest that graduate training reduces these differences and that although one hopes that training has such an effect, one does not know that it does.

Sarason states:

> One of the clinician's most revealing experiences is to listen to a recording of his interaction with a patient. He becomes embarrassingly aware how much he forgot or was unconscious of, not only of the patient's behavior but of his own behavior as well....When one remembers that what a clinician concludes about a patient in large part represents inferences based on his description of overt behavior, the importance of the problem is obvious. (p. 9)

In terms of what is perceived and reported of the interview, the following quote is pertinent. Davidman (1964) puts it this way:

> Traditionally, the raw first-hand data of the treatment experience has only been observable by the participant analyst himself. It could only be communicated to others through the therapist's own reports. These accounts written from notes taken during a session are purely from memory, are incomplete, inaccurate and have been subjected to both conscious and unconscious processes of selection and reorganization by the analyst. The auditor of case reports and of studies applying rating scales to interview reports often remains in doubt about whether the approach and the selection does any justice to the actual experience of the therapist and the patient's working together. He often doubts whether the therapeutic changes resemble the forces in actual operation. Many reports, aiming to prove a theoretical point select the data with this end in view and inevitably leave the auditor with a distorted view of the treatment.

Although Davidman refers to treatment, the same statement applies to diagnosis.

Storrow (1967) states:

> The fact that we psychiatrists often influence the "facts" patients tell us seems fairly obvious, but that's only the first problem. The second hurdle comes when we select from the raw data to come up with a description of a patient. Sometimes, indeed, the consultation reports and case conferences are more notable for creative imagination than for sober reflection.

> The trouble is that truly objective psychiatric interviewing is all but impossible. The interview is a damned poor instrument for measuring the subtleties of a human life.

Storrow also points out that out of the hundreds of thousands of experiences, thoughts, feelings and behaviors that constitute a patient's life, the number obtainable by the psychiatrist in his interview represents far too small a sample upon which to predicate an adequate assessment of the individual.

Klein et al. (1970), reporting on a computer-supported procedure for preparing psychiatric case studies, state, "This project was undertaken because of several problems associated with reporting and retrieving case information. The foremost problem is lack of standardization."

Kubie (1971) states:

> At the same time we have also misled ourselves by pretending (to ourselves and to others) that behavior has been more carefully observed, recorded and differentiated than was possible until the recent introduction of audio-visual aids.

The advent of modern devices for audio-visual recording and playback makes a new era possible but only if these devices are used consistently and critically. If we are ever to solve those problems, audio-visual aids must be used on every patient whose record is to be accepted as dependable scientific data. Furthermore, they are needed to provide us with statistically adequate samples of permanent recordings of basic observations which can then be subjected to repeated study by many observers. Until we do this, we will continue to depend on fallible reports of fallible and weighted memories of our skewed perceptions of rapidly changing and emotionally charged moments of behavior in which many things were occurring simultaneously. This is what we have had to work with in the past. It has hardly been a foundation upon which to build an accurate nosological system. (p. 339)

He also states:

> It is on the basis of such defective "histories" and on the basis of fallible reports of fallible observations of current behavior that in the past our so-called diagnoses have had to be based. (p. 339)

Paul Hoch (1972) was a highly respected member of the psychiatric profession, a teacher as well, and an advocate of the clinical approach. However, he does admit that in questioning the patient it is important that the questioning be unbiased in the sense that it covers all the pertinent facts concerning the dynamic, organic and social status of the individual. He notes that many psychiatrists are fascinated by certain schools of thought and by listening to them questioning a patient, one can actually label their school by the way in which they group and interpret facts elicited. He points out it is a bad form of questioning to simply single out one psychodynamic factor in the patient. He gives an example where a patient reveals a very marked attachment to his mother and the examiner immediately concludes that this is the basis of the patient's disorder and from there on directs all questions toward proving the specific type of dynamic or clinical point.

Hoch claims that many case histories are tailored to fit a particular approach or a particular psychiatric trend of thought. He notes that these case histories are valueless because whoever reads them later on will naturally ask questions which have not been asked because the interviewer simply did not get around to them, having been so fascinated by one or another dynamic formulation.

Newmark et al. (1979) express doubts whether unstructured or free form interviews are adequate for either research or clinical purposes. They note that this assessment method increases the risk of disregarding important areas and increases probabilities of bias in both collection and interpretation of information. They note that the unstructured examination may be the primary source of unreliability in psychiatric diagnoses.

Rappeport (1976) observes that it is known that personal prejudices can influence expert witnesses so that they do not look for certain information. Conover (1972) states, "Unreliability in the art of psychiatric diagnosis can be attributed to psychiatrists referring to different bits of information about a patient." Shectman (1983) notes that the data to which the clinician will attend is partially determined by his training and the particular mental health discipline to which he belongs.

A number of authors indicate that clinicians often make serious omissions in data collection. Robins and Helzer (1986) describe literature which shows that *clinicians even omit collecting data on topics that they themselves believe to be essential in making a diagnosis.* Other authors point to failure to inquire into areas that might reveal positive or healthy aspects of personality. Rather, the focus is on eliciting indications of maladjustment. Havens (1981) notes that contemporary psychiatry collects symptoms and signs and groups them into syndromes or disease states. Health is viewed as an absence of these disease states, generally referred to as negative findings. Thus, the foundation of the psychiatric disease concept is, essentially, a negative description of health. Havens continues by asserting that the psychological examination is weakest in those areas where it is most needed by the psychiatrist, namely, in terms of attending to normal affect, sociability, self-image, capacity for self-protection, and coping, among others.

Turk and Salovey (1985) state that: "The theoretical orientation held by the clinician, moreover, provides preconceptions that will guide the nature of the information regarded as relevant and that is sought. The potential bias posed by preconceptions of clinicians is not an especially new idea but one that receives little attention in clinical training and practice." (p. 27) Further, "The clinician's schemata and cognitive processes may confirm hypotheses by guiding perception, information search (e.g., the selection of assessment procedures), and the clinician's behavior vis-à-vis clients." (p. 22) They then state: "Studies illustrate that clinicians' impressions of clients may be guided, to some extent, by what they expect to observe. Moreover, *what they expect to observe is likely to be what they will observe.* In the clinical context, what clinicians expect to observe is pathology. This expectancy may reduce judgmental accuracy, or at least introduce systematic biases in the direction of overestimating psychopathology and underestimating more positive features." (p. 24)

These statements illuminate a deficiency that is not inherent in the clinical examination, as some of the others we have described are, but rather one which is quite common in clinical evaluations, especially those for forensic purposes. In the numerous reports we have reviewed, we find no indication of diligence in searching for non-pathological diagnoses or explanations of behavior to match the zeal with which clinicians search for the most fragmentary and subtle evidence to support their contention of psychopathology. It is our experience that careful scrutiny of a litigant's life data will almost always reveal significant data of which the clinician is either unaware or which he has inadequately explored. We would assert that testifying clinicians are nearly always vulnerable in this regard. As examples, we recall specifically two cases in which we were consulted, involving so-called "psychic injury," and in which one of the indicators of degree of psychopathology, as well as an item of damages, was the "ruination" of plaintiff's marriage. Careful investigation by defense attorneys revealed, in one of these cases, that plaintiff had filed for divorce shortly before the traumatic incident, yet the psychologist in the case asserted confidently that plaintiff's "apparently good marriage had been ruined as a result of her loss of interest in sex caused by the accident." In the other case, similar significance was attached to disruption of the marriage due to the accident. However, in this case, hospital records (which one of the two clinicians had not even bothered to look at) contained a one line statement to the effect that plaintiff had no prior psychiatric contact except that he and his wife had been seeing a marriage counselor. Of course, it is possible for people to have a pretty good marriage with an isolated problem area for which they might consult a marriage counselor. However, absent inquiry establishing this as the case, one is left with only the far more probable assumption, which is that a marriage counselor was consulted because the marriage was in serious difficulty. The fact that one of the major symptoms of the "psychic injury" was a "delusion" that his wife was a "witch," would seem to enhance this probability and certainly ought to have alerted the clinicians to the probability of severe marital problems prior to the accident. Nonetheless, both clinicians asserted that the marital problems they observed some time subsequent to the accident were "caused" by the accident. In any event, the one psychiatrist who read the hospital report either did so carelessly or chose not to deal with this evidence indicating marital problems prior to the accident. We frequently find such carelessness or, even, in some cases deliberate disregard of evidence contrary to the conclusion the clinician is drawing.

A number of studies, comparing the data psychiatrists report or gather to that obtained through more objective or systematic techniques (e.g., videotaping), indicate substantial discrepancies. Muslin et al. (1981) videotaped interviews by medical students in their psychiatric clerkship and compared them with reports of the data made in supervision. They found that fifty-four percent of the themes in the videotaped interviews were not reported in supervision and that some degree of distortion was present in fifty-four percent of the interviews. They also found that there was no significant difference in the degree to which important or unimportant themes were not reported. It should be noted that the study is limited in the sense that the people doing the interviews had not completed their training. However, there are other reports which suggest that the same inaccuracies occur with fully trained professionals and may be more exaggerated among the more experienced. (One is also compelled to wonder how effective the teaching and training of psychiatrists can be when the data on which supervision is based may be so incomplete or potentially misleading and when supervision is perhaps the major teaching tool.)

Xenakis et al. (1983) found that therapists may be poor reporters of their own actions. They found that there was a general lack of inter-rater reliability between therapists and independent judges. They assert that therapists' retrospective accounts, including elaborate process notes, may be subject to various distortions and biases and suggest that caution be exercised when relying on therapists' self-reports as primary descriptions of therapeutic actions or process. This is of some importance because many experts describe their therapeutic successes as evidence of their diagnostic capabilities. This research suggests that they are not reliable reporters of what went on in their own therapy procedures.

Further, research suggests that more knowledgeable or experienced individuals may be more prone to certain errors in recall than less knowledgeable or experienced individuals (see Chapter 19). Studies conducted by Arkes and Harkness (1980), Bransford et al. (1972), Harris et al. (1975), and Johnson et al. (1977) indicate that experts versus non-experts are more prone to believe that a symptom consistent with their diagnostic impression was present when it actually was not present. Further, they are less likely to recall actual symptoms inconsistent with their impressions. As Arkes and Freedman (1984) state, "...experts who infer the presence of stimuli consistent with the diagnosis or judgment would mistakenly believe that there existed more corroborating evidence.

Confidence in their decision would thereby be unduly inflated." (p. 89) Stated differently, the expert shows a tendency to forget actual information that is inconsistent with his impressions and to think he recalls "information" consistent with his impressions, which was actually never present. Arkes and Harkness (1983) state, "...the diagnostician would be well-advised to record not only the diagnosis but also the symptoms actually observed." (p. 574) In a separate article, Arkes (1981) indicates that were clinicians to depend on memory less, they might achieve greater diagnostic accuracy.

It is not only that the clinician may be quite selective in the data noticed and recorded, but also that the means by which the recording is done (e.g., through written notes or sometimes mainly in the clinician's head) creates an additional problem for judge and jury. McGill and Thrasher (1975) point out how difficult it is for a jury to evaluate the examination. They point out that, in contrast to the usual medical testimony, which may be accompanied by photographs, X-rays, laboratory reports, charts, diagrams, and a patient with visible results, psychiatrists deal with intangible, fleeting, varying responses and productions and there are no displays available to depict to the jury what transpired. They state: "As a result the jury is deprived of any real opportunity to observe and evaluate the examination process." They propose an obvious, if somewhat radical, solution which would at least allow the jury to know what went on in the examination, although it would not cure all of the deficiencies. Their proposal is that when psychiatric examinations are being done for the purpose of litigation, they should be videotaped (they refer to one case by name only, *United States vs. Day*, a Coast Guard Court Martial in which this was allowed). Although by no means solving all of the defects of the clinical examination, such a procedure would provide a number of benefits. It would allow the jury to see how and what the psychiatrist explored and, of equal importance, what he did not explore. It would allow the jury to see for themselves whether the psychiatrist influenced or led the responses of the litigant. Perhaps most importantly, it would allow the jury to see for themselves the behavior which is now given to them only in the oral descriptions by the psychiatrist. Thus, for example, in contrast to the present situation, where the jury has no way of assessing the correctness of the psychiatrist's description of the litigant as "lacking affect," they would be able to see for themselves whether he lacked affect. Of course it would also allow opposing counsel and opposing experts to point out deficiencies in the conduct of the examination, an opportunity that is relatively unavailable under present practice.

We would estimate that use of this procedure would apply some appropriate brakes on the unlimited power of the clinician to describe the data of the examination in any way that he wishes. We would further speculate that standard use of this procedure would lead to greater conservatism among forensic psychiatrists and might very well reduce the excessive number of cases in which psychiatric evaluations are utilized (estimated by Dr. Seymour Pollack to be in the neighborhood of a million cases a year in the United States). McGill and Thrasher recognize both legal and clinical problems attached to the implementing of their proposal, but feel that these can be overcome and that, if psychiatric testimony is to be allowed, the need for this kind of check outweighs the possible detriments.

The following example may serve to illustrate how cogent the McGill and Thrasher proposal is. We are sure that it is apparent to all readers of our books, and to all who try cases involving psychiatric evidence, that behavior, demeanor, responsiveness and so on are highly significant elements in forming psychiatric conclusions. We have cited numerous studies and authoritative statements indicating that one cannot rely on the verbal descriptions of the clinician, with regard to these data. This problem was graphically demonstrated in one case in which the author consulted. The case involved a purported traumatic psychosis. Plaintiff was examined by both a psychiatrist and psychologist, each of whom concluded that, as a result of the traumatic incident, he had become chronically schizophrenic and would remain so for the rest of his life, with massive social, personal and economic disabilities, which they attributed to that diagnostic finding. The plaintiff was relatively young, with a skilled occupation that had provided a good income which, aside from social and marital consequences, would alone have been sufficient to support an extremely large award of damages. We might add that liability was fairly clear and, if found, possessed highly aggravating elements. In supporting their diagnostic conclusions both of plaintiff's clinicians relied heavily on descriptions of plaintiff abounding in terms such as "bland affect," "lack of affect," "blunted affect," "incapable of experiencing emotion," "lacks capacity for normal emotional response," and so on. One of the clinicians went so far as to describe plaintiff as "a robot" and a "vegetable." Who is to gainsay these descriptions? As McGill and Thrasher point out, how is the jury to know whether plaintiff did or did not display appropriate affect, other than to accept the descriptions of the clinicians? The lone psychiatrist who examined for the defense also concluded that plaintiff was schizophrenic but not to as severe a degree as did plaintiff's psychiatrists, nor did he find the degree of disability that they found. (Incidentally, despite the dire predictions of plaintiff's clinicians, some time after the accident he had, in fact, gone back to his former occupation and worked for a period of six weeks, very satisfactorily, according to his employer, and quit voluntarily because, as he put it, he "wanted to get his head together.") Particular importance was attached, by plaintiff's clinicians, to the fact that plaintiff displayed no emotion when describing, as part of the examination, a sudden, and understandably from his point of view, unprovoked and unjustified assault by government agents, which resulted in moderately severe physical injuries. Both clinicians asserted that reliving and/or relating such a traumatic event would produce considerable indications of emotion in a normal individual, yet plaintiff, according to them, displayed none.

We must digress here to briefly explain the phenomenon of "habituation," which is well-known and well-established in the psychological literature and amply verified by research demonstration. Habituation refers to the process whereby, upon repeated presentation of the same stimulus the response to it diminishes. In this particular case, prior to his examination by plaintiff's clinicians, plaintiff had related and described the events surrounding and including the traumatic incident to a dozen investigators and/or psychiatrists, as well as having testified as to the matter in considerable detail in a related case involving criminal charges. These facts warranted at least a consideration that plaintiff may have simply become habituated to (bored with) this specific story, particularly as the event had transpired more than two years prior to the clinical examinations in question. If this were so, we felt, it would provide a much more parsimonious explanation of his lack of emotion when relating the events. When consulting with defense counsel, who had taken plaintiff's deposition, they both responded that in their "lay" opinion he did not appear remarkably unemotional. Imminence of the trial, as well as other strategic considerations, precluded any attempt to get any evaluation by yet another clinician. Also, given the well-known predilection of clinicians to interpret behavior pathologically, none of us were optimistic that the defense would be helped by such an additional evaluation. We suggested to the lawyers (there were co-counsel appearing for defense) that if our speculation was correct, there was at least a chance that plaintiff would display some emotion during the course of the trial. We recommended, therefore, that at all times one or the other of counsel should maintain observation of plaintiff and, if he displayed emotion, they should make an immediate note as to where in the proceedings it occurred, so that they might recall it for the jury. Given the immediate concerns in the progress of a trial, counsel were not able to maintain the constant observation we recommended. However, they were able to observe sufficiently to record two clear demonstrations of "affect" in the courtroom by the plaintiff. On one occasion, as frequently happens in trials, a humorous incident occurred, which brought forth laughter from most of the people in the courtroom, including plaintiff. Laughter, of course, is affect, and, as indicated by the general response to the incident, it was "appropriate" affect. On another occasion, when a defense witness, one of the alleged assailants, gave testimony that directly contradicted plaintiff's version, he became visibly angry. That is, he immediately engaged his attorney in conversation that any person of ordinary experience could easily recognize as "heated," speaking rapidly, gesticulating, shaking his head, and so on. Again, this was affect and, again, given the circumstances, it was appropriate. With time to rethink the matter, subsequent to the trial, it has occurred to us that it would have been well for counsel to take some action to call the jury's attention to these emotional displays, even, perhaps, to the point of asking that the record show that plaintiff laughed or displayed anger. It would make little difference whether the request were granted, for it would serve to call the jury's attention to the affect displayed by this individual, determined by two clinicians, with impressive credentials, to be *utterly lacking* in capacity for affect. Counsel were, however, able to remind the jury of these occurrences in argument, with what effect we cannot be sure. No one knows on exactly what element of a trial a jury verdict hinges. All that is known is that the jury verdict was considered highly successful from the defense standpoint and, evidently, highly unsatisfactory from a plaintiff's standpoint, as indicated by a motion for a new trial, despite the fact that an appreciable sum of money had been awarded for actual physical injuries. However, the main point we wish to make is that, had we not hit upon this stratagem, the assertions of plaintiff's experts regarding emotional deficit would have gone uncontested, and the jury would never have known that this individual was capable of affect. It is for problems of this nature that the videotape recommendation seems to have great merit.

It is clear that the clinician who is set in terms of his theoretical orientation to perceive and remember data that is relevant to Freudian approaches will perceive and remember such material, whereas a clinician of a different orientation will be attentive to and remember those aspects of the subject's productions which fit in with his theoretical position. Thus, it is almost inevitable that in forming his conclusions, the clinician has overlooked some of the material produced by the subject. It is then appropriate in cross-examination to ask the clinician, after he has given the bases for his conclusions, if there was not some other material that the patient produced in the diagnostic situation that the clinician may not have noticed or may not have remembered, when he formed his diagnostic conclusion. If he replies that there was no other data, he should be pressed to admit that while there may have been no other data which was relevant to him, there may have been data that would have been relevant to a clinician of a different orientation. (This attack is less appropriate, of course, where a clinician has videotaped the diagnostic interviews.) Thus it seems clear that many of the same factors that operate to influence the data which the examiner obtains from the subject also influence the perception and memory of the examiner.

PROCEDURES THAT COMPOUND PROBLEMS

As if all of these problems with clinical examination were not bad enough, psychologists and psychiatrists often compound these difficulties by the way they go about their work. Stated differently, the material they seek and the means by which they gather it often increases the ambiguity or uncertainty of the data obtained, or makes the already difficult task of interpreting the data more difficult still. A number of the "strategies" discussed in Appendix C of Chapter 5, which are intended to decrease uncertainty but often have the opposite effect, are commonly employed in the clinical examination.

First, psychiatrists and psychologists often search for deep or hidden meanings that they may attempt to infer on the basis of very indirect evidence. For example, a clinician assessing potential for violence, rather than relying primarily on past police records that might be readily available or objective data regarding violent behavior, may try to probe for "internal conflicts" or some such thing in order to formulate opinions. These hypothetical, inferred, psychological states or predispositions are sometimes referred to as "latent entities." Meehl (1979) notes that inferred latent entities, regardless of whether they stem from psychoanalysis, factor analysis, or cluster analysis, have lost much of their value for clinicians as either tools of practice or as objects of theoretical interest. This is because such latent entities are so difficult to assess objectively or reliably, and because they often have very limited predictive power, in particular when compared to more direct and objective data, such as that pertaining to past behavior or history.

Van Praag (1976) points out that there are psychiatrists who prefer symptoms that are difficult to objectify, such as the patient's ability to enter emotional relationships. He points out that the subjectivity of the interpretations concerning these phenomena is one of the reasons different evaluators reach different conclusions. Mischel (1972) notes that the most direct way to explore another individual's characteristics and beliefs is to ask them what they are. He goes on to discuss how psychiatrists and psychologists often fail to do so, however, preferring much less direct and highly inferential approaches. Based on a review of the evidence on direct versus indirect methods of assessment, Mischel observes that assessors may want to pay more attention to what people do and say, regarding them not as indirect indicators of underlying variables but rather as direct specimens of their behavior.

Second, rather than following a set or standardized procedure, examiners often decide what they will do next, or what specific questions they will ask in what order, as they go along. This may be defended as a way of tailoring the examination to the individual, but the obvious result is that two different examiners may ask the same person different questions, the same examiner will ask two different individuals different sets of questions, and even the same examiner assessing the same individual twice may ask very different questions on each occasion. How is one to know if the information obtained, and the conclusions reached, are truly valid or merely a product of the particular questions asked?

For example, in a discussion of the assessment of motor problems (i.e., problems in movement or coordination), Poeck (1986) states, "No standardized battery of tasks is available for *the clinical examination of motor apraxia.* The diagnosis is made mainly on the basis of personal experience and intuition." (p. 130) Poeck also notes that many of the clinical methods that are used to assess this area of functioning were developed at the turn of the century. Other authors discuss the inconsistency that can result when such methods are used. Erdman et al. (1985) note that one of the advantages of having a computer conduct interviews is the high level of consistency that can be achieved.

In another example, Butler et al. (1991) did a survey of neuropsychological test usage covering 116 tests used by neuropsychologists. While there were a number of instances of high agreement in usage (e.g., full WAIS or WAIS-R, 86%) there were numerous tests used only by a small percentage—some as little as less than 5%. They note that there is large variability in choices of instruments and that there is a need to look at issues such as idiosyncratic battery development. To the extent that this is true, it would seem that what is measured and how is a function of the examiner selected, i.e., an examiner effect.

Helzer (1981) notes that among the advantages in using a structured examination in psychiatric research are uniformity and reliability of the data gathered and the reduction of examiner bias in the collection and interpretation of the information. He points out that the same advantages would exist in using structured interviews in non-research situations. He notes that significant oversights have been documented in both psychiatric and non-psychiatric settings when physicians use open-ended methods of examination. Tsujimoto and Berger (1986) note that there is a wealth of research showing that variations in the assessment situation can greatly affect the behavior observed. They also assert their view that variations in the assessment situation can alter the predictive value of the observed behavior.

Saghir (1971) comments that the need for standardization in psychiatry has been underscored by a number of investigators and questions whether a comparison of results from different studies can be regarded as reliable given the wide variability often found between psychiatric researchers. He goes on to note that differences in methodology and in psychiatric training and emphasis account for much of the variation, while additional sources of variation may be attributed to well documented differences in concepts, definitions and diagnostic practices among psychiatrists. He notes that the concept of a diagnostic interview differs from one group of interviewers to another.

It is important to recognize some of the problems created by lack of standardization. First, because the procedures themselves are inconsistent across clinicians and examinees, the likelihood of obtaining consistent results across clinicians and examinations is considerably lessened. As much of the above-cited literature suggests, such inconsistency in method may be one of the more important factors underlying lack of reliability in psychiatric diagnosis. Second, when the examiner, in essence, decides on exactly what procedure to follow or what questions to ask as he goes along, the circumstances are ripe for the operation of the various biases and problematic judgment practices we outlined in Chapter 5. For example, if the clinician varies the order in which he asks questions across two patients, information about certain topics will be collected at different points in these two examinations. As Friedlander and Stockman (1983) indicate in their research and discussion of anchoring effects, however, the same information may be interpreted differently depending on the time at which it is received. For example, information obtained early may have a much greater impact on judgment than the exact same information obtained at a later point in time. Thus, varying the order of questions can lead to different conclusions even if the exact same responses are provided. Studies on confirmatory bias also show that information received early in the assessment process may be given much more weight than it deserves, and that the impressions that result can interfere with the interpretation of subsequent information. Further, such variable examination methods offer little protection against biases that can twist or distort the data collection process. As noted, clinicians tend to ask questions that will confirm impressions and tend to overlook materials or questions (e.g., those pertaining to healthy adjustment) that might disconfirm impressions. A free-form interview offers few, if any, checks against these tendencies. If clinicians adhered instead to a uniform set of questions, such problematic practices as selective questioning based on initial impressions could be partially countered. Faust (1986b) illustrates some of these problems as follows:

> During Judge 1's mental status exam, the patient utters a few highfalutin words. Judge 1 is impressed that the patient has a superior vocabulary and makes no further attempts to assess word knowledge. Judge 2 administers the Vocabulary

subtest of the Wechsler Adult Intelligence Scale-Revised in the standard fashion. Although the patient answers a few difficult items correctly, Judge 2 continues until a ceiling is established. The total score is tallied and compared with established norms, and it is found that the patient obtains an average score. Note that the standardized testing procedure prevents the operation of bad judgment habits that may have hindered Judge 1. The method of data collection and combination protect against overreliance on a few salient cues, such as Judge 1's impression that a few big words reflect the patient's overall vocabulary; and they also protect against failure to evaluate base rates, as in Judge 1's not considering the frequency with which people who use a few big words do not have a superior vocabulary. The testing procedure ensures that one does collect a sufficient sample of responses and does compare performance to a representative sample of individuals, but that one does not overweight a few responses or vary data collection on the basis of subjective impressions. (p. 424)

SUMMARY AND CONCLUSIONS

As one might expect, all of the problems that are created by the deficiencies in the clinical examination method seem to become even more pronounced when assessment is conducted for legal purposes. Zussman and Simon (1983) performed a study in an effort to evaluate the common assertions that mental health professionals are willing to compromise themselves for fees as expert witnesses and that lawyers search for expert witnesses who will agree with a predetermined position. In their study they evaluated the psychiatric evaluations of numerous plaintiffs who were involved in the well-known Buffalo Creek disaster, based on the collapse of a coal slag heap which killed several people and left many more homeless. A number of plaintiffs were psychiatrically evaluated twice: first by experts hired by the plaintiffs, and then by experts hired by the defendant. Also, some of the plaintiffs were evaluated by plaintiffs psychiatric Team A and others by a different group of mental health professionals, plaintiffs Team B. Zussman and Simon found numerous differences in conclusions reached by plaintiffs and defendants teams and also some differences between plaintiffs Team A and Team B. They attribute the differences to three variables. One variable involved differences in the setting in which the examinations took place, as plaintiffs Team A examined the plaintiffs in their homes while plaintiffs Team B and the defendants team performed their examinations in their professional offices. They also note an effect of the examiners' training and orientation (what we have been referring to as examiner effects). They found that plaintiffs Team A were predominantly of a psychoanalytic orientation, where the defense team were primarily of an eclectic approach. There was no information about Team B. Finally, Zussman and Simon note that a process of subtle identification with the side that hired them took place. This was apparently not a conscious or "hired gun" matter, but without intending or even being aware of it, each team tended to emphasize findings and patterns that supported "their side." Zussman and Simon refer to this as an inherent weakness of a system that uses experts in an adversarial system and relies upon subjective measures and evaluations.

The significance of the examiner effect in terms of the legal situation cannot be overstated. It means that there is no way of knowing whether the "anxiety" or "hostility" or "sexual preoccupation" or any other characteristic being attributed to the subject of an examination is in fact an attribute of the subject or whether it is, as the foregoing studies have shown, a reflection of an attribute of the examiner. If, for example, the "anxiety" forms a substantial item of damages subsequent to some traumatic event in the subject's life, before providing compensation to that individual for the anxiety, one ought to make very sure that he really has the anxiety and not award damages for the fortuitous, or perhaps clever, circumstances of his having picked the type of examiner who tends to elicit "anxiety" or who is prone to interpret almost any data as evidence of anxiety. The point can be emphasized that *unless and until adequate methods are provided to control for variation due to examiner and situation effects, the data of the clinical examination are virtually worthless.* It is not necessary to establish that the data are always invalid. It is possible that there may be some cases where data obtained are valid. They are virtually worthless, however, because *there is no way of knowing when one has valid data and when one has data that are the product of situation or examiner influence.*

Clearly, the attorney can ask the psychiatrist or psychologist very bluntly whether he has explicitly taken into account all of the variables inherent in the interpersonal interaction of the clinical situation. If the witness answers that he has, he can be further questioned as to what variables may have been operating, how they operated, how he has taken them into consideration, and what effect they might have had on the data. If he attempts to answer those questions, he can be asked to demonstrate how he knows these variables have or have not operated in the situation in the manner he describes, and how his personality, values, attitudes, and feelings affect the data that will be produced in clinical examinations, and in particular, with patients of the particular sex, character, social class, and race of the individual in question. He can be asked if there are scientifically validated methods for determining the degree of contribution of these variables.

A simple statement by Cattel (1973) perhaps sums things up best: "Anything so important as the evaluation of a human personality should not be left to an interview."

REFERENCES

Abramowitz, S.I., and Herrera, H.R. (1981). On controlling for patient psychopathology in naturalistic studies of sex bias: A methodological demonstration. *Journal of Consulting and Clinical Psychology*, *49*, 597-603.

Aiken, L.R. (1985). *Psychological Testing and Assessment* (5th ed.). Boston: Allyn & Bacon.

American Psychiatric Association (1980). *Diagnostic and Statistical Manual of Mental Disorders* (3rd ed.) Washington, DC: APA.

American Psychiatric Association (1994). *Diagnostic and Statistical Manual of Mental Disorders* (4th ed.). Washington, DC: APA.

Angle, H.V., Johnson, J., Grebenkemper, N.S., and Ellinwood, E.H. (1979). Computer interview support for clinicians. *Professional Psychology*, *10*, 49-57.

Appelbaum, P.S. and Roth, L.H. (1981). Clinical issues in the assessment of competency. *American Journal of Psychiatry*, *138*, 1462-1467.

Arkes, H.R. (1981). Impediments to accurate clinical judgment and possible ways to minimize their impact. *Journal of Consulting and Clinical Psychology*, *49*, 323-330.

Arkes, H.R., and Freedman, M.R. (1984). A demonstration of the costs and benefits of expertise in recognition memory. *Memory & Cognition*, *12(1)*, 84-89.

Arkes, H.R., and Harkness, A.R. (1980). Effect of making a diagnosis on subsequent recognition of symptoms. *Journal of Experimental Psychology*, *6*, 568-575.

Arkes, H.R., and Harkness, A.R. (1983). Estimates of contingency between two dichotomous variables. *Journal of Experimental Psychology: General*, *112*, 117-135.

Bachrach, H. (1974). Diagnosis as strategic understanding. *Bulletin of the Meninger Clinic*, *38*, 390-405.

Boster, J. and Febrega, H., Jr. (1993) Sematic structures and psychiatric diagnosis. *The Journal of Nervous and Mental Disease, 181*, 54-58.

Boulenger, J., Uhde, T.W., Wolff, III, E.A., and Post, R.M. (1984). Increased sensitivity to caffeine in patients with panic disorders. *Archives of General Psychiatry*, *41*, 1067-1071.

Boyce, P., and Parker, G. (1988) Seasonal Affective Disorder in the southern hemisphere. *American Journal of Psychiatry, 145*, 96-99.

Bransford, J.D., Barclay, J.R., and Franks, J.J. (1972). Sentence memory: A constructive versus interpretive approach. *Cognitive Psychology*, *3*, 193-209.

Brody, G.H., Stoneman, Z., Millar, M., and McCoy, J.K. (1990). Assessing individual differences: Effects of responding to prior questionnaires on the substantive and psychometric properties of self-esteem and depression assessments. *Journal of Personality Assessment, 54,* 401-411.

Brown, F.H., Jr., Dodrill, C.B., Clark, T., and Zych, K. (1991). An investigation of the relationship between self-report of memory functioning and memory test performance. *Journal of Clinical Psychology, 47,* 772-777.

Bruce, M.L., and Kim, K.M. (1992). Differences in the effects of divorce on major depression in men and women. *American Journal of Psychiatry, 149,* 914-917.

Butler, M., Retzlaff, P., and Vanderploeg, R. (1991). Neuropsychological test usage. *Professional Psychology: Research and Practice, 22,* 510-512.

Carkhuff, R., and Pierce, R. (1957). Differential effects of therapist's race and social class upon patient depth of self-exploration in the initial clinical interview. *Journal of Consulting Psychology, 31,* 632-634.

Cattell, R.B. (1973). The measurement of the healthy personality and the healthy society. *The Counseling Psychologists, 4,* 13.

Charney, D.S., Heninger, G.R., and Jatlow, P.I. (1985). Increased anxiogenic effects of caffeine in panic disorders. *Archives of General Psychiatry, 42,* 233-243.

Christensen, L., Krietsch, K., White, B., and Stagner, B. (1985). Impact of a dietary change on emotional distress. *Journal of Abnormal Psychology, 94,* 565-579.

Combrinck-Graham, L. (1987). Invitation to a kiss: Diagnosing ecosystemically. *Psychotherapy, 24,* 504-510.

Conover, D. (1972). Psychiatric distinctions: New and old approaches. *Journal of Health and Social Behavior, 13,* 167-180.

Cooper, A.M. (1985). Will neurobiology influence psychoanalyses? *The American Journal of Psychiatry, 142,* 1395-1402.

Davidman, H. (1964). Evaluation of psychoanalysis; a clinician's view. In Hoch, P., and Zubin, J. (Eds.), *The Evaluation of Psychiatric Treatment.* (Proceedings of the 52nd Annual meeting of the American Psychopathological Association.) New York: Grune and Stratton.

Derner, G. (1983, March). Parsimony, meta-psychology and personality assessment. Invited address. Meeting of the Society for Personality Assessment, San Diego, CA.

Diamond, B.L. (1973b). The psychiatrist as advocate. *The Journal of Psychiatry and Law, 1,* 5-21.

Dunn, J.T., Brown, R.S., Lees-Haley, P., and English, L.T. (1993). Neurotoxic and neuropsychologic symptom base rates: A comparison of three groups. Poster, 13th Annual Conference of the National Academy of Neuropsychology, 1993.

Edelman, R.I., and Snead, R. (1972). Self-disclosure in a simulated psychiatric interview. *Journal of Consulting and Clinical Psychology, 38,* 354-358.

Epstein, S. (1980). The stability of behavior. II, Implications for psychological research. *American Psychologist, 35,* 790-806.

Erdman, H.P., Klein, M.H., and Greist, J.H. (1985). Direct patient computer interviewing. *Journal of Consulting and Clinical Psychology, 53,* 760-773.

Erdman, H.P., Klein, M.H., Greist, J.H., Bass, S.M., Bires, J.K., and Machtinger, P.E. (1987). A comparison of the diagnostic interview schedule and clinical diagnosis. *American Journal of Psychiatry, 144,* 1477-1480.

Faust, D. (1986b). Research on human judgment and its application to clinical practice. *Professional Psychology, 17,* 420-430.

Felton, G.S. (1971). The experimenter expectancy effect examined as a function of past ambiguity and internal-external control. *Journal of Experimental Research and Personality, 5,* 286-294.

Fennig, S, and Bromet, E. (1992). Commentary: Issues of memory in the diagnostic interview schedule. *Journal of Nervous and Mental Disease, 180,* 223-226.

Fleiss, J.L. (1970). Estimating the reliability of interview data. *Psychometrika, 35,* 143-162.

Fossi, L., Faravelli, and Paoli, M. (1984). The ethological approach to the assessment of depressive disorders. *The Journal of Nervous and Mental Disease, 172,* 332-341.

Friedlander, M.L., and Stockman, S.J. (1983). Anchoring and publicity effect in clinical judgment. *Journal of Clinical Psychology, 39,* 637-643.

Garvey, M.J., Westner, R., and Godes, M. (1988). Comparison of seasonal and non-seasonal affective disorders. *American Journal of Psychiatry, 145,* 100-102.

Gill, M., and Brennan, M. (1948). Research and psychotherapy, roundtable. *American Journal of Ortho-Psychiatry, 19,* 100-110.

Gilliland, K., and Andress, D. (1981). Ad lib caffeine consumption, symptoms of caffeinism and academic performance. *American Journal of Psychiatry,* 138, 512-514.

Glidewell, J.C., and Livert, D. (1992). Confidence in the practice of clinical psychology. *Professional Psychology: Research and Practice, 5,* 362-368.

Goldstein, R.L. (1988) Consequences of surveillance of the forensic psychiatric examination: An overview. *American Journal of Psychiatry, 145,* 1243-1247.

Greden, J.P. (1974). Anxiety or caffeine: A diagnostic dilemma. *American Journal of Psychiatry, 131,* 1089-1092. (Reported in the *Los Angeles Times,* Wednesday, May 8, 1974.)

Gross, H.S., Herbert, Myra, Knattenial, Genell, and Donner, L. (1969). The effect of race and sex on the variation of diagnosis and disposition in a psychiatric emergency room. *Journal of Nervous and Mental Disease, 148,* 638-642.

Halleck, S.L. (1982). The role of the psychiatrist in the criminal justice system. In *Psychiatry,* (p. 386). 1982 Annual Review, L. Grinspoon (Ed.). Washington, DC: American Psychiatric Press Inc.

Harris, R.J., Teske, R.R., and Ginns, M.J. (1975). Memory for pragmatic implications from courtroom testimony. *Bulletin of the Psychonomic Society, 6,* 494-496.

Hart, S.D., Roesch, R., Corrado, R.R., and Cox, D.N. (1993). The referral decision scale: A validation study. *Law and Human Behavior, 17,* 611-623.

Havenburg and Guiter (1976). The concept of truth in psychoanalysis. *International Journal of Psychoanalysts, 57,* 11.

Havens, L.L. (1981). Twentieth century psychiatry: A view from the sea. *The American Journal of Psychiatry, 138,* 1279-1287.

Heilbrun, K.S. (1987). The assessment of competency for execution: An overview. *Behavioral Sciences and the Law, 5,* 383-396.

Helzer, J.E., (1981). The use of a structured diagnostic interview for routine psychiatric evaluations. *The Journal of Nervous and Mental Disease, 169,* 45-49.

Hoch, P. (1972). M.O. Strahl, and N.D.C. Lewis (Eds.), *Differential Diagnosis in Clinical Psychiatry: The Lectures of Paul H. Hoch.* New York: Liona House.

Hughes, J.R., Oliveto, A.H., Helzer, J.E., Higgins, S.T., and Bickel, W.K. (1992). Should caffeine abuse, dependence, or withdrawal be added to DSM-IV and ICD-10? *American Journal of Psychiatry, 149,* 33-40.

Iacono, W.G. (1991). Psychophysiological assessment of psychopathology. *Psychological Assessment, 3,* 309-320.

Jacobsen, F.M., Wehr, T.A., Skwerer, R.A., Sack, D.A., and Rosenthal, N.E. (1987). Morning versus midday phototherapy of seasonal affective disorder. *American Journal of Psychiatry, 144,* 1301-1305.

Johnson, M.K., Taylor, T.H., and Raye, C. (1977). Fact and fantasy: The effects of internally generated events on the apparent frequency of externally generated events. *Memory & Cognition, 5,* 116-122.

Klein, D.F., et al. (1970). Automating the psychiatric case study. *Comprehensive Psychiatry, 11,* 518-523.

Klopfer, W.G. (1984). The use of the Rorschach in brief clinical evaluation. *Journal of Personality Assessment, 48,* 654-659.

Kubie, L.S. (1971). Multiple fallacies in the concept of schizophrenia. *The Journal of Nervous and Mental Disease, 153,* 331-342.

Lee, M.A., Flegel, P., Greden, J.F., and Cameron, O.G. (1988). Anxiogenic effects of caffeine on panic and depressed patients. *American Journal of Psychiatry, 145,* 632-635.

Lees-Haley, P., and Brown, R.S. (1993). Neuropsychological complaint base rates of 170 personal injury claimants. *Archives of Clinical Neuropsychology, 8,* 203-209.

Lees-Haley, P.R. and Dunn, J.T. (1994). The ability of naive subjects to report symptoms of mild brain injury, post traumatic stress disorder, major depression, and generalized anxiety disorder. *Journal of Clinical Psychology, 50,* 252-256.

Leff, J. (1977). International variations in the diagnosis of psychiatric illness. *British Journal of Psychiatry, 31,* 329-338.

Lehman, A.K., and Salovey, P. (1990). Psychotherapist orientation and expectations for liked and disliked patients. *Professional Psychology: Research and Practice, 21,* 385-391.

Lewis, L., Allen, J.G., and Frieswyk, S. (1983). The assessment of interacting organic and functional factors in a psychiatric population. *Clinical Neuropsychology, 5,* 65-68.

Lidz, C.W., Mulvey, E.P., Applebaum, P.S., and Cleveland, S. (1989). Commitment: The consistency of clinicians in the use of legal standards. *American Journal of Psychiatry, 146,* 176-181.

Los Angeles Times (1986, June). The science and medicine section.

Lovinger, R.J. (1992). Theoretical affiliations in psychotherapy. *Psychotherapy, 29,* 586-590.

Mahoney, M.J., and Craine, M.H. (1991). The changing beliefs of psychotherapy experts. *Journal of Psychotherapy Integration, 1,* 207-221.

Mann, E.M., Ikeda, Y., Mueller, C.W., Takahashi, A., Tao, K.T., Humris, E., Li, B.L., and Chin, D. (1992). Cross-cultural differences in rating hyperactive-disruptive behaviors in children. *American Journal of Psychiatry, 149,* 1539-1542.

Marriage and Divorce Today Newsletter, 3 (February, 1986).

Masling, J. (1966). Role related behavior of the subject and psychologist and its effect upon psychological data. *Nebraska Symposium on Motivation, 14,* 67-104.

May, C.P., Hasher, L., and Stoltzfus, E. (1993). Optimal time of day and the magnitude of age differences in memory. *Psychological Science, 4,* 326-330.

McCas, B.B. (1972). A study of some factors mediating unintended experimenter effects upon subjects in psychological experiments. *Dissertation Abstracts International, 32,* 5A5338.

McConnaughy, E.A. (1988). The person of the therapist in psychotherapeutic practice. *Therapy, 24,* 303-314.

McGill, G.A., and Thrasher, J.W. (1975). Video tapes: The reel thing of the future. *Trial, 11,* 43-49.

Meehl, P.E. (1979). A funny thing happened to us on the way to latent entities. *Journal of Personality Assessment, 43,* 564-581.

Meyer, J.D., and Fink, C.M. (1989). Psychiatric symptoms from prescription medications. *Professional Psychology: Research and Practice, 20,* 90-96.

Miller, H. (1961). Accident neurosis. *British Medical Journal,* 992.

Mischel, W. (1972). Direct versus indirect personality assessment: Evidence and implications. *Journal of Consulting and Clinical Psychology, 38,* 319-324.

Mischel, W. (1973). Toward a cognitive social learning reconceptualization of personality. *Psychological Review, 80,* 252-283.

Muslin, H.L., Thurnblad, R.J., and Meschel, G. (1981). The fate of the clinical interview: An observational study. *American Journal of Psychiatry, 138,* 823-825.

Newmark, C.S., Konanc, J.T., Simpson, M., Boren, R.B., and Prillaman, K. (1979). Predictive validity of the Rorschach prognostic rating scale with schizophrenic patients. *The Journal of Nervous and Mental Disorders, 167,* 135-143.

Olin, J.T., and Zelinski, E.M. (1991). The 112-month reliability of the Mini-Mental State Examination. *Psychological Assessment, 3,* 427-432.

Perry, A.M. (1972). Youthful offenders' aggressive and autonomic reactions to stress as a function of race of examiner and race of subject. *Dissertation Abstracts International, 33,* 2B2353-2B2354.

Perry, J.C. (1992). Problems and considerations in the valid assessment of personality disorders. *American Journal of Psychiatry, 149,* 1645-1653.

Pfungst, O. (1911). C.L. Rahn (Translator), *Clever Hans, the Horse of Mr. Van Osten, A Contribution to Experimental Animal and Human Psychology.* New York: Holt.

Platt, J.J., and Husband, S.O. (1986). Post-traumatic stress disorder in forensic practice. *American Journal of Forensic Psychology,* 29-56.

Poeck, K. (1986). The clinical examination for major apraxia. *Neuropsychologia, 24,* 129-134.

Pope, K.S. (1988). Avoid malpractice in the area of diagnosis assessment and testing. *The Independent Practitioner, Bulletin of the Division (42) of Psychologists in Independent Practice, 8,* 18-24.

Pope, K.S. (1992). Responsibilities in providing psychological test feedback to clients. *Psychological Assessment, 4,* 268-271.

Preston, T.P. (1981). *The Clay Pedestal.* Seattle: Madrona.

Pugh, D. (1973). The insanity defense in operation: A practicing psychiatrist views Durham and Brawner. *Washington University Law Quarterly,* 87-108.

Raifman, L.J. (1983). Problems of diagnosis and legal causation in courtroom use of post-traumatic stress disorder. *Behavioral Sciences and the Law, 1,* 115-130.

Rappeport, J.R. (1976). The psychiatrist as expert witness. *Medical World News* (October, 1976).

Regerstein, Q.R., and Monk, T.H. (1991). Is the poor sleep of shift workers a disorder? *American Journal of Psychiatry, 148,* 1487-1493.

Retzlaff, P., Butler, M., and Vanderploeg, R.D. (1992). Neuropsychological battery choice and theoretical orientation: A multivariate analysis. *Journal of Clinical Psychology, 48,* 666-672.

Robins, L.N. (1985). Epidemiology: Reflections on testing the validity of psychiatric interviews. *Archives General Psychiatry, 42,* 918-924.

Robins, L.N., and Helzer, J.E. (1986). Diagnosis and clinical assessment: The current state of psychiatric diagnosis. *Annual Review of Psychology, 37,* 409-432.

Rogler, L.H., Malgady, R.G., and Tryon, W.W. (1992). Evaluation of mental health: Issues of memory in the diagnostic interview schedule. *Journal of Nervous and Mental Disease, 180,* 215-222.

Rosenthal, R. (1966). *Experimenter Effects on Behavioral Research.* New York: Appleton, Century, Croft.

Rowe, D.C. (1987). Resolving the person-situation debate: Invitation to an interdisciplinary dialogue. *American Psychologist, 42,* 218-227.

Saghir, M.T. (1971). A comparison of some aspects of structured and unstructured psychiatric interviews. *American Journal of Psychiatry, 128,* 180-184.

Sarason, I.G. (1972). *Personality: An Objective Approach* (2nd ed.). New York: John Wiley and Sons.

Sarason, S.B. (1954). *The Clinical Interaction.* New York: Harper & Brothers.

Shectman, F. (1983). Semi-projective questions: Bridging the gap between assessment and interview data. Paper presented at the meeting of the Society for Personality Assessment, San Diego, CA, March, 1983.

Simons, V., and Meyer, K. (1986a). *Behavioral Sciences and the Law, 4,* 1-19.

Slovenko, R. (1984). Commentary: Syndrome evidence in establishing a stressor. *The Journal of Psychiatry and Law, 12,* 443-467.

Sperry, L., Kirschner, S., and Gudeman, J.E. (1992). Executive consultation with an impaired executive and an organization in crisis. *Consulting Psychology Journal, Fall,* 27-30.

Stoll, A.L., Tohen, M., Baldessarini, R.J., Goodwin, D.C., Stein, S., Katz, S., Geenens, D. Swinson, R.P. Goethe, J.W., and McGlashan, T. (1993). Shifts in diagnostic frequencies of schizophrenia and major affective disorders at six North American psychiatric hospitals, 1972-1988. *American Journal of Psychiatry, 150,* 1668-1673.

Storrow, H.A. (1967). *Introduction to Scientific Psychiatry.* Englewood Cliffs, NJ: Prentice-Hall, Inc.

Sturmey, P. (1993). The use of DSM and ICD diagnostic criteria in people with mental retardation. *The Journal of Nervous and Mental Disease, 181,* 38-41.

Suedfeld, P. (1975). The clinical relevance of reduced sensory stimulation. *Canadian Psychological Review, 16,* 88-92.

Treece, C. (1982). DSM-III as a research tool. *American Journal of Psychiatry, 139,* 577-585.

Trull, T.J., Widiger, T.A., and Frances, A. (1987). Covariation of criteria sets for avoidant, schizoid and dependent personality disorders. *American Journal of Psychiatry, 144,* 767-771.

Tsujimoto, R.N., and Berger, D.E. (1986). Situational influences on the predictive value of client behavior: Implication for Bayesian prediction. *Journal of Consulting and Clinical Psychology, 54,* 264-266.

Turk, D.C., and Salovey, P. (1985). Cognitive structures, cognitive processes, and cognitive-behavior modification: II. Judgments and inferences of the clinician. *Cognitive Therapy and Research, 9,* 19-33.

Turner, S.M., Beidel, D.C., and Larkin, K.T. (1986). Situational determinants of social anxiety in clinic and non-clinic samples: Physiological and cognitive correlates. *Journal of Consulting and Clinical Psychology, 54,* 523-527.

Vallacher, R.R., and Wegner, D.M. (1987). What do people think they're doing: Action identification and human behavior. *Psychological Review, 94,* 3-15.

Van Praag, H.M. (1976). About the impossible concept of schizophrenia. *Comprehensive Psychiatry, 17,* 481-497.

Veleber, D.M., and Templer, D.I. (1984). Effects of caffeine on anxiety and depression. *Journal of Abnormal Psychology, 93,* 120-122.

Watkins, B.A., Cowan, M.A., and Davis, W.E. (1975). Differential diagnosis imbalance as a race-related phenomenon. *Journal of Clinical Psychology, 31,* 267-268.

Wehr, T.A., and Rosenthal, N.E. (1989). Seasonality and affective illness. *American Journal of Psychiatry, 146,* 829-839.

Wehr, T.A., Sack, D.A., and Rosenthal, N.E. (1987). Seasonal affective disorder with summer depression and winter hypomania. *American Journal of Psychiatry, 144,* 1602-1603.

Wells, S.J. (1984). Caffeine: Implications of recent research for clinical practice. *American Journal of Ortho-Psychiatry, 54,* 375-389.

Wilkinson, C.B., and O'Connor, W.A. (1982). Human ecology and mental illness. *American Journal of Psychiatry, 139,* 985-990.

Woody, R. (1972). R.H. Woody and J.D. Woody (Eds.). *Clinical Assessment in Counseling and Psychotherapy.* Englewood Cliffs, NJ: Prentice-Hall, Inc.

Xenakis, S.N., Hoyt, M.F., Marmar, C.R., and Horowitz, M.J. (1983). Reliability of self-reports by therapists using the therapists action scale. *Psychotherapy: Theory, Research and Practice, 20,* 314-319.

Zussman, J., and Simon, J. (1983). Differences in repeated psychiatric examination of litigants to a lawsuit. *American Journal of Psychiatry, 140,* 1300-1304.

CHAPTER 7

Challenging the Results & Conclusions of Psychiatric & Psychological Evaluations

In earlier chapters we focused upon the foundations of expert testimony, pointing out the limitations and deficiencies in scientific knowledge and clinical judgment. We next discussed limits in the methods by which evaluations are conducted, including interview and history gathering (problems in the use of psychological tests are discussed in Chapters 10-13, Volume II). In this chapter, we will focus on the "final product" that emerges—the conclusions drawn on the basis of psychological and psychiatric evaluations. (There is considerable repetition of literature reported in other chapters because this literature has application to more than one topic.) Our aim in this chapter is to discuss the reliability and validity of evaluations, no matter the source of the data or the combination of methods used. Further, we will also provide more broad-ranging coverage of commentary and studies on the limits of diagnosis, prediction, or the other types of formulations stemming from the evaluation process.

PROBLEMS IN DATA COLLECTION AND INTERPRETATION

DATA CONTAMINATION

Numerous factors exert uncontrolled or extraneous influences on the data collected in psychiatric and psychological evaluations (see Chapters 6 and 10). For example, dependence on self-report creates substantial problems, because individuals may purposely or inadvertently mislead the examiner. Such examinee characteristics as age, gender, and minority group status can exert substantial, but as yet minimally understood effects on examiner's judgments. (See Chapter 16.)

Examiners also exert considerable effects on the data obtained on clinical exam or psychological testing. Stated somewhat differently, the data obtained can be considerably influenced by the individual who is doing the examining. Sarason (1954) argues that many clinicians have not seriously considered the effects of the many situational and interpersonal variables that operate in the clinical situation. Applebaum and Roth (1981) indicate how differently patients can react when seen by different psychiatrists. They argue that due to this marked variability, assessment should be performed by someone who can establish a positive rapport with the patient. Lewis et al. (1983) discuss a case in which an individual with presumed brain damage performed very differently across examiners. When an examiner did not reduce this patient's level of tension, her performance seemed indicative of much more serious brain damage than was the case when an examiner helped her to achieve a calmer state. Lytton (1971) asserts that distortion of data occurs in all methods of assessing parent-child interactions.

Examiners not only tend to exert different effects on examinees, but their own selectivity may considerably influence, or bias, data collection and recording. Examiners differ in the data to which they attend or remember. Perhaps more importantly, examiners differ in the Tsujimoto questions they ask or the tests they use. Thus, one does not know to what extent the data are a product of the examinee's actual characteristics versus an extraneous product of the clinician's particular selections. These problems are considerably confounded by a lack of uniformity or standardization in methods of data collection.

Saghir (1971) discusses "the need for standardization in psychiatry" and notes that wide variability across observers in research has impeded comparison of results across studies. He concludes, "Differences in methodology and in psychiatric training and emphasis account for a great deal of this variation....Differences in concepts, definitions and diagnostic practices among psychiatrists are well documented and well recognized." (p. 180)

Helzer (1981) notes that more uniform or structured procedures help to reduce the effects of examiner bias in the collection and interpretation of information. He points out that such methods are most frequently used in research but would also be of benefit in nonresearch situations. Tsujimoto and Berger (1986) note that there is a wealth of research showing that variations in the assessment situation can greatly affect the behavior observed. They also assert that variations in the assessment situation can alter the predictive value of the observed behavior.

Although there are more uniform methods available for gathering information, such as structured interviews, these methods are rarely used in forensic assessments, and in any case they generally remain in an experimental stage. The broad exception is the use of standardized psychological tests, although as noted in Chapter 10, examiners may fail to follow standardized test procedures and often differ in the specific tests or combinations of tests used. Further, as we document below, psychological tests are also vulnerable to situation and examiner effects.

EXTRANEOUS FACTORS THAT CAUSE CAUSAL CONFUSION, OR "WHAT CAUSED WHAT?"

Even assuming that description of an examinee's current status is accurate, it often remains critically important to determine the cause of this current status. Misidentification of cause can lead to the wrong diagnosis, the wrong treatment, and errors in forecasting outcome or prognosis. For example, an examinee may show considerable tension, but this tension may be independent of a prior "traumatic" event and may actually be caused by excessive caffeine consumption. Thus, the proper diagnosis might be caffeinism, as opposed to, say, "PTSD" (Post-Traumatic Stress Disorder), and the reduction of caffeine intake might well alleviate the problem, whereas intensive psychotherapy would not.

Various studies outline the manner in which the things we ingest, or physical status, can create symptoms that mimic psychiatric disorders. A mounting body of research and commentary indicates that caffeine, even in relatively small amounts, can aggravate or produce symptoms that mimic a range of psychiatric disorders, especially disorders in which "anxiety" or depression are defined as core components. For example, research by Greden et al. (1978), Gilliland and Andress (1981), Boulenger et al. (1984), Veleber and Templer (1984), and Charney et al. (1985) all indicate that caffeine consumption can exacerbate or create symptoms that are assumed to represent anxiety disorders or depression. In overviews, Greden (1974) and Wells (1984) note that many products, including cola drinks, aspirin, and over-the-counter medications are potential sources of caffeine. Greden describes the wide range of symptoms produced by caffeine, and Wells notes that withdrawal from caffeine is related to both psychological and physiological disturbances (see also Chapter 6). Greden points out that psychiatrists often fail to eliminate caffeine as a source of symptoms.

A host of additional agents have been identified that can mimic or complicate psychiatric symptoms. John F. Schlegel, President of the American Pharmaceutical Association, has been quoted in the *Los Angeles Times* (1986) to the effect that smoking cigarettes can interfere with how the body metabolizes drugs. In particular, nicotine may alter the body chemistry such that larger doses of medications, including those intended to counter psychiatric symptoms, may be necessary to obtain expected effects. Christensen et al. (1985) found that dietary change can remedy the emotional distress exhibited by some individuals. Schuckit (1982) notes that young men reporting symptoms of depression may not actually have depressive disorders but rather transient symptoms related to alcohol or drug abuse.

Physical disorders or problems can also mimic psychiatric disorders. Jacob et al. (1985) report on a study showing that disorders labeled as "panic attacks" or "agoraphobia" may be caused by physiological problems involving the inner ear. Such symptoms, for example, may be unrelated to such common litigation syndromes as "PTSD." They mention that their results should be considered preliminary and that further research is needed. However, it seems reasonable to suggest, in cases in which dizziness is a symptom, that an oto-neurological examination be done, and that for lack of one a clinician cannot state with certainty that the dizziness is not a function of inner ear disorder.

Other authors point out special problems conducting assessments with individuals reportedly suffering from physical pain. Duckro et al. (1985) state that familiar instruments and constructs have not been validated with chronic pain populations. They point out, for example, that anxiety and physical preoccupation may have very different meanings when an individual has chronic pain. In their study, they found that subscales designed to measure anxiety and depression were associated with several measures of pain, but that these measures seemed to offer little specificity. Smith (1986) states that, "chronic-pain is the most widespread, yet least understood symptom confronting the health care delivery professional today." (p. 94) She further notes, "the greatest challenge...is to develop a powerful predictive instrument as a pain index, which of course must contain or at least account for faking and other inconsistencies in order to be a valid and reliable instrument." (p. 95) Thus, when an individual is in pain, overall evaluation may be considerably complicated; and to make matters worse, as Smith points out, the assessment of pain itself is quite difficult and a valid and reliable instrument remains to be developed. Note in this regard that the *Standards for Educational and Psychological Testing* (1985) indicate that distractors present in the testing situation may interfere with the attainment of reliable and valid results, and it would thus seem clear that an individual who is (or purports to be) in pain is being evaluated under less than optimal conditions.

Numerous other authors point out that physical and psychological disorders are frequently confused. For example, both Volume I and Volume II of the popular texts by D. F. Benson and D. Blumer (1975, 1982) are largely devoted to guidelines for distinguishing physical and psychological disorders. Many of the chapters in these volumes are written by prominent authors who indicate that confusion between the two is quite common.

IATROGENIC FACTORS

The author is in receipt of a petition for a division for the study of Iatrogenic Practice and Research to be formed by the American Psychological Association. The petition lists among its various signers a number of distinguished psychologists, including Albert Ellis, George Albee, and Rollo May. The significance of this is that the prevalence of iatrogenic psychopathology or disorder—that is, psychopathology which is caused or aggravated by the helping professions in the process of trying to help—is clearly viewed by the psychological profession as a significant and serious matter.

Yaffe and Mancuso (1977) note that the attitude or behavior of one expert toward the examinee can influence the perception of that individual by other experts and may even be accepted by the individual and become a self-fulfilling prophecy. The lawyer should recognize the importance of such processes, particularly in personal injury situations where a series of experts is often involved. Subsequent experts are typically exposed to the opinion of the first expert and thus view the litigant within the context of the first expert's opinions (see the discussion on confirmatory and hindsight bias in Chapter 5). Additionally, this involvement of helping professionals may exert iatrogenic effects and partially, or even fully account for present symptoms or those that develop over time. Based on the attitudes taken toward him by the experts, the litigant may come to actually believe that he is suffering from some psychological disorder that had not existed independently of the effects of the expert's behavior.

SITUATIONAL FACTORS

Another serious weakness in clinical assessment is the failure or inability of the clinician to adequately evaluate the effects of situational or contextual variables, preferring to explain behavior on the basis of characteristics attributed to the person involved. Yaffe and Mancuso (1977) cite several studies showing that mental illness judgments are influenced by many contextual variables, of which the behavior of the person categorized is but one. Weiner (1983) notes, "today's mainstream psychology views how people act as a complex function of their abiding dispositions to behave in certain ways and the nature of the situations in which they find themselves." (p. 453)

Mischel (1979) states that an extensive analysis of the intuitive psychologist indicates a "pervasive shortcoming, a fundamental attribution error: 'a tendency to underestimate the importance of situational determinants and overestimate the degree to which actions and outcomes reflect the actor's disposition' and defying the dictates of logic the intuitive psychologist is reluctant to deduce the particular from the general but is remarkably ready to infer the general from the particular." He notes that, "Research-based cautions emerging from our scholarly journals may easily be ignored when one meets one 'really' prototypical personality type in clinical practice." (p. 740)

Reppucci and Clingempeel (1978) describe one of the major omissions in the study of criminal behavior as the ignoring of potential effects of situational and environmental factors in precipitating the criminal act. Referring to the trait model of explanations of behavior, they note an abundance of empirical research refuting the cross-situational consistency assumption of the trait models. They note a particular problem in research which ignores the impact of correctional institutions on the behavior of offenders; that is, they assert and cite studies in support of the point that institutionalization has effects on the behavior of the individual being examined and that in order to do adequate research on characteristics of offenders one would have to be able to separate out the effects of institutionalization on the behavior observed.

Monahan (1978) notes that reliance on traits or enduring attributes of a person under study has characterized not only clinicians' predictions of violence but prediction of all types of behavior, with a result that in all cases the correlations between predictor and criterion variables have been low. He also asserts the need to take into account the situational or environmental variables as they interact with personal characteristics.

Bartol (1983) notes the importance of situational variables in personality assessment and states, "failure to consider the context of the behavior is destined to result in sizable inaccuracies and faulty conclusions." (p. 36) He warns readers to expect low accuracy rates in psychological assessment. Wilkinson and O'Connor (1982) note that "person-environment interactions" and environment be "considered as broadly affecting mental health from the biological and physical levels to complex psycho-social levels." They note that there is still considerable disagreement about whether an individual's personality, as opposed to situations, has the greatest impact on behavior. Rierdan et al. (1982) indicate that situational factors and transient emotional states can affect several aspects of subject's productions on human figure drawings, thus indicating the impact of such factors on the results of at least this psychological instrument. Epstein (1980) notes that even in laboratory settings it is hard to gain a high degree of control because individuals are so sensitive to situational factors. Ilfeld (1980) describes previous surveys showing a close connection between symptoms of depression and current marital stressors, such as nonfulfillment of basic role expectations, lack of reciprocity between partners, and nonacceptance by the spouse. This seems to be another illustration of the operation of situational effects in eliciting symptoms of mental disorder. Thus, one might query whether the "mental disorder" observed in an individual subsequent to a personal injury may actually reflect marital discord in cases in which separate evidence has been obtained indicating marital difficulties.

Situational factors may create particular difficulties when assessment is conducted with incarcerated defendants. Suedfeld (1975) notes that reduction of sensory stimulation and such factors as isolation may cause or aggravate psychological dysfunction in a wide variety of contexts, citing prison as an example of such a situation. Halleck (1982) indicates that such symptoms as depression, extreme anxiety, and even suicide and psychosis are very frequent in prison settings. Thus, being incarcerated may well alter an individual's mental condition, which would make it difficult to determine what his mental state might have been prior to his imprisonment.

Obviously, situational factors create numerous problems in psychological and psychiatric assessment. What one observes at one moment or point in time may not be what one would observe at another point in time. Further, behaviors or reactions believed to reflect personality may actually reflect situational factors. Further, because behavior can be strongly influenced by situations, predictions often need to take situational factors into account, as well as the examinee's personality. However, there is often no way to foresee the exact situations in which a person might find himself.

A related, substantial problem is that, although the importance of situational factors is broadly recognized, very few methods have been developed or scientifically validated to aid in their assessment. Levine (1984) discusses problems with cross-situational consistency of personality traits and characteristics. He states, "note, however, that if the interaction hypothesis is valid; unless the examiner can assess how traits viewed in the one situation of clinical examination interact with the circumstances of the examination, predictive validity is highly limited." (p. 154) Levine's basic stance in this paper is that these and numerous other requirements for valid assessment are not satisfied, and thus many of the judgments formulated in forensic evaluations do not achieve standards of reasonable certainty. Lanyon (1984) observes that theorists continue to differ on the issue of dispositions versus situations but that on a practical level, practitioners will likely give situations less than the weight they deserve because methods for measuring them are not readily available.

DEFICIENCIES IN INTERPRETATION OF DATA

The final interpretations that stem from psychiatric and psychological evaluation, with rare exception, are ultimately based on the examiner's judgment. Components of these assessments, such as the interpretation of a specific test or test score, may be based on prespecified rules or procedures (e.g., actuarial methods), but it will be the very exceptional case in which the final conclusions are based solely on methods that are independent of the examiner's judgment. Rather, to a varying extent, the data must be "processed" through the examiner's interpretive, intellectual "machinery" (head). In Chapter 5, we have provided extensive detail on the limits and deficiencies of clinical judgment, and little of that material need be repeated here. Rather, we will focus mainly on what might be considered "contaminants" of clinical interpretations. Extensive literature exists suggesting that clinical interpretations are often based not so much on science, or science alone, but on values, theoretical orientations, and biases.

Thoreson (1973) discussing difficulty in defining terms such as the "healthy personality" states:

> Such terms are based on the complex interpretive judgments of different observers. Hence the data from these judgments are diverse and often noncomparable. Indeed, personality assessment has typically measured the observer's biases more than the characteristics of the person being assessed. Work in personality has suffered from many maladies—an over-reliance on words, an almost exclusive use of paper and pencil assessment, and a sizeable gap between broad concepts and specific behavioral observations.

Ennis (1978) states that most judges are unwilling to limit personal freedom when the basis for the limitation is "a subjective opinion, rather than an objective and verifiable fact." Of course, lawyers are aware of the problem of biases. Shubow and Bergstresser (1977) describe the existence of personal, cultural, class, racial, sexual or economic predilections among psychiatrists, as well as the bias created by the adversary situation, noting that in some instances the same psychiatrist will give contradictory testimony depending upon the interest involved.

Fitzgibbons and Shearn (1972) base their study on the belief that schizophrenia is a function not only of the person being labelled schizophrenic but also of the mental health professional responsible for the labelling. They delineate differences based on variations in training, professional orientation and place of employment as the factors given emphasis in diagnosing schizophrenia. They state:

Surely it makes some sense, for example, that the nature of one's training and professional identification might influence his ideas about the etiology of schizophrenia. These differences in viewpoint associated with professional training seem to us, however, to amount to a bias which tends to hinder rather than facilitate the advancement of knowledge about schizophrenia. Each of the mental health professions in its own way seems to have been locked into a system of beliefs that is relatively impervious to new information whether in the form of reports in the literature or even personal experience with schizophrenic patients.

Graff et al. (1971) state, referring to the typical middle-class background of the psychotherapist and his absorption of the mores and values of the profession:

These inevitably form his ways and prejudices in dealing with patients; he is usually more comfortable with patients who support his own value system. When a patient who is living under a different system presents himself the therapist may view his behavior as evidence of pathology regardless of whether it is really a sign of emotional disorder or simply a manifestation of the subculture. At the same time the lower class patient can view the therapist in the same fashion and have difficulty in dealing with the upper class agency therapist.

Woody (1972) points out the deficiencies of the clinical examination in terms of the inadequate sampling of behavior, biases both theoretical and personal of the diagnostician, and the presence of so many bits of information or types of data within an interview that there is vast latitude for interpreting and weighting data depending upon a particular diagnostician's theoretical preferences. He notes that despite protestations that their point of reference is always the individual patient, clinicians in fact may be so committed to a particular school of thought that the patient's diagnosis is largely predetermined.

Cohen et al. (1975) describe their paper as an attempt to show that psychiatric diagnosis depends to a significant degree, not only on the patient's presenting symptoms, but also on the psychiatrist's psycho-social biases. They describe the extensive agreement that psychiatric diagnoses are loosely defined, possess little predictive value and are negatively influenced by socio-cultural factors. They assert that their findings "definitely confirm that psychiatric diagnoses are changed due to social conditions unrelated to the psychopathological state." They found both gender and socio-economic status to be significant factors.

Kubie (1973) states:

If the expert is a psychiatrist or clinical psychologist he must acknowledge that his personal loyalties and his general social and political convictions inevitably, if unconsciously, will bias both his observations and his judgment. In spite of every effort to correct for such biases, the psychiatrist or psychologist is no more immune to such self-deception than is the layman. No one is invulnerable to the subtle effects of loyalties especially where quantifiable and objective data are scarce and where the specialist has to depend largely on intuitive judgments and feelings. (p. 486)

Braginsky and Braginsky (1973) point out the social class, political, moral, and value judgment biases of clinicians. They describe the "Herculean" dimensions of the diagnostic task and point out that it sounds impossible to sort out relevant symptoms from "infinitely complex" behavior and categorize them while maintaining a detached, objective posture. They assert that it not only sounds impossible but that it *is* impossible. One of the Braginskys' findings was that when a patient expressed negative attitudes toward the psychiatrist or psychologist, he was diagnosed as being more severely disturbed. But when the patient conveyed an attitude that the mental health staff were kind, helpful, competent and, in general, terrific human beings the diagnosis was much less severe. They cited references to the effect that there is as yet no substantial verified body of knowledge in the area of functional mental disorder and that such knowledge as there is is clinical and intuitive and thus not subject to verification by scientific procedures.

Abramowitz et al. (1973) found that experienced, politically non-liberal counselors imputed greater maladjustment to a left-oriented, politically active female than to an identically described male client. They state concerning other research, "But are the expectations and clinical impressions of expert judges readily affected by variation in the attributes of the person being perceived? The available evidence is sparse but generally affirmative. Results from two investigations imply that even experienced clinicians hold differential standards of positive mental health for men and women." The studies they cite are Broverman et al. (1970) and Neulinger (1968). Abramowitz et al. further state: "Furthermore an indirect effect of a trained examiner's and client's sex on the severity of clinical inference has now been demonstrated in two other studies." These studies are Abramowitz and Abramowitz (1973) and Hahn and Livson (1973). They then state, "Such data refute the view that professional status insures immunity to prejudicial judgment and raise the disturbing possibility that such bias may be distributed disproportionately across certain client subpopulations."

Warner (1979) notes previous research indicating that psychiatric diagnoses vary according to biases depending on such differences as the country in which the clinician practices, socio-economic status of the patient, patient's country of origin, patient's political convictions, the extent to which the patient is critical of the psychiatrist, and social stereotypes the clinician may associate with particular illnesses. In his study Warner found that the race of the therapist strongly influenced diagnosis and that non-white therapists differed from white therapists on several diagnostic categories.

Poythress (1977) notes that the psychiatrist's expert opinion may be a function of his personal values or practical judgments and not a function of the defendant's mental illness in any objective sense. Saks (1978), referring to psychiatric testimony before a legislative subcommittee dealing with organ transplants, states, "In the absence of any real evidence, the psychiatrists were saying whatever would advance the interests with which they were associated." He also states, "The readiness of psychiatrists (and other supposed experts on behavior) to offer opinion testimony based on few or no reliable data or empirically confirmed theoretic principles, or to be unduly influenced by their employer's interests is by no means limited to transplant cases. Indeed, the problems created for the courts in this society by such testimony are far better known in other areas."

Cohen and Oyster-Nelson (1981) found that therapists' evaluation of case reports differed in relation to theoretical orientation. They note that those of certain viewpoints tended to view patients as more pathological than those of other theoretical viewpoints. They discuss other research showing similar effects of theoretical orientation on judgments of disorder, and they seem to suggest that clinicians of certain orientations (psychodynamic) tend to diagnose more pathology than do those of other orientations (e.g., behavioral psychologists).

Zussman and Simon (1983) studied the psychiatric evaluations of plaintiffs involved in the Buffalo Creek Disaster, in which several persons were killed and many more left homeless. A number of plaintiffs were evaluated separately by experts hired by the plaintiffs and experts hired by the defendants. The psychiatric conclusions often differed considerably. Zussman and Simon attribute some of these differences to contrasts in the examinations settings and to examiners' training and orientation. They argue that experts, beyond their own awareness, identified with the side that hired them, which influenced their judgment. This interpretation concurs with other research which reveals that factors outside of the examiner's awareness can exert important influences on his judgment.

Cooper (1985) notes that a theory will determine how the analyst shapes a patient's material to produce a result that is likely to conform with the analyst's theoretical orientation. Brody (1985) observes that psychiatry services are interpersonal to a greater extent than other medical fields, and thus can be perceived as more subject to individual and social influences. Mellsop et al.'s (1982) study on psychiatric diagnosis showed considerable rater biases, with different evaluators favoring different DSM-III categories. This study, once again, illustrates that the diagnosis rendered may come down to who is doing the diagnosing.

Derner (1983) notes that interviews are contaminated by examiner effects and that there are too many concerns or facets of information for the interviewer to keep in mind at any one time. Angle et al. (1979) recommend the use of computer interviewing, in part to help counter the biases associated with different interviewers and different methods for conducting interviews. Aiken (1985) notes that many extraneous variables influence interviews, and that the personality and biases of the interviewer often exert greater effects on the information obtained than do the characteristics of the interviewee. He notes the well-documented tendency of interviewers to give more weight to unfavorable, as opposed to favorable information about an individual. He indicates, overall, that interviews are associated with low reliability and validity.

Thorne (1972) states:

> Literally, it is necessary to know what clinician made a judgment in order to evaluate its significance properly. Many institutions and clinicians manifest all kinds of biases and prejudices which must be understood in terms of their local judgment significance. Classification practices vary widely among institutions and areas and involve such specialized purposes and orientations as age, sex, location and socio-economic levels, political affiliations, religions, social class, etc. (p. 78)

As all of the foregoing material shows, the interpretations rendered on psychiatric and psychological evaluation are substantially influenced by the examiner's theoretical orientation and personal biases. It would appear, then, that Freudians make Freudian interpretations of data, Adlerians make Adlerian interpretations of data, and so on. The lawyer can require the expert to acknowledge that the literature indicates a strong probability that experts of another school of thought or orientation would draw different conclusions, even if they did happen to elicit the same data (the probability of this latter condition, of course, being small).

OVERDIAGNOSING ABNORMALITY

As the above literature indicates, various extraneous factors and biases influence both the data obtained in psychiatric and psychological evaluations and the interpretation of these already skewed data. It is important to further specify the nature of these biases, or the *type* of errors they are likely to cause. Perhaps the most pervasive one is to identify pathology where none exists, or to overestimate level of difficulty or dysfunction. The propensity of clinicians to overdiagnose, overpredict, and overemphasize psychopathology and to distort data to fit with this predilection is so well known and so well documented that it must be taken as a fact. Numerous publications provide evidence on this issue. As George W. Albee (1968) states it, "The first and most pervasive myth is that people who exhibit disturbed and disturbing behavior are *sick.*" It appears that the more frequently used psychological tests tend to focus on abnormality or even draw for "deviant" responses (Chapters 10-13). Along these lines, Anastasi (1961) cites research showing that in studies of college students, nearly 40% received abnormal scores on one or more scales of the MMPI. Sharkey and Ritzler (1985) note that the content of the TAT is such that it would tend to elicit unusual or seemingly abnormal responses from almost anyone. Repko and Cooper (1985) indicate that the MCMI may be quite prone to overdiagnosing psychological disturbance. They report that even among a series of medical patients who did not present psychological complaints, almost every one of them obtained scores on the MCMI that, according to suggested interpretive guidelines, indicated some type of psychiatric disorder.

Shah (1969) points out that the general rule in physical medicine—that when in doubt the physician should continue to suspect illness—is appropriate in physical medicine because it is more dangerous for the physician to dismiss the patient as well when he is actually ill than to assume illness when, in fact, the illness may not exist. It is just a matter of being cautious. However, the converse is true in the case of so-called mental illness where far more harm may be done to the patient by judging a well person "sick" than by judging a sick one "well." Yet based on the kind of training they have, the psychiatrist and psychologist, as well as other so-called mental health workers, are far more prone to see psychopathology and maladjustment.

Captain D. Earl Brown, Jr. (1971), then head of the Neuropsychiatry branch of the Navy's Bureau of Medicine and Surgery, made the following statement:

> The area of prediction is certainly not one of psychiatry's strong points; psychiatry has been oversold in this area. Relatively few papers have presented psychiatrists' predictions of patients response to various types of stress and special environment. It surely requires "nerve" for a psychiatrist to reveal what he does in this area. Psychiatrists are taught to detect and assess psychopathology very well. *However, there is little training in the area of measuring assets that will compensate for psychopathology...*(italics ours) intelligence and shrewdness are also compensatory assets. Interpersonal skill and likeable personality serve well in this regard. Even certain pathological traits, such as an appealing dependency, can be assets. (p. 153)

This statement suggests that psychiatrists are poorly trained in assessing strengths. Indeed, so much psychiatric testimony is focused on pathology, it is important to bring out in cross-examination that even if the described pathology exists, there may be assets which enable the person to function within the requirements of the law, at least within minimal limits.

Brown cites earlier studies by Plag and Arthur (1965) and Plag and Goffman (1966), which he states clearly demonstrated that psychiatrists are not good predictors of individual service adjustment in the Navy. Plag et al. studied a subset of 134 patients who had been recommended for separation from service, for various psychiatric disorders following thorough psychiatric evaluation and repeated failures in boot camp. It was found that 72% of the individuals who had been recommended for separation but nevertheless were kept in the service performed effectively at the end of two years of service, compared with 85% of a "normal" control group. At the end of four years, 55% of those recommended for a separation had still performed effectively compared with 72% of the controls. *At each time period studied, the psychiatrists were wrong more often than they were right.*

Schafer (1978) recognizes the need to be hypersensitive to cues indicating psychopathology but notes there is a danger of overshooting the mark and failing to adequately note the patient's concomitant strengths. He stresses the need to take a balanced view of the patient as a whole human being. He notes that one of the major obstructions to the balanced point of view is the abundance of clinical terms that involve implicitly pejorative meanings due to the negative emphasis they put on clinical observation.

Poythress (1977) points out how the psychiatrist's preparatory set (to look for and see psychopathology where it is expected to exist) influences perceptions and interpretations of data about the client. He notes that this set can be exaggerated by some factors such as knowledge of previous hospitalization. Shubow and Bergstresser (1977) observe that psychiatrists tend to overpredict pathological conduct, explaining that this may be because they see so much of it.

Block (1984) notes that clinicians are especially prone to overpathologize members of minority groups, specifically black patients. Block indicates that many behaviors that have actually facilitated adaptation to difficult environmental circumstances may be mistaken for disorder, which may help to explain why a disproportionate number of black patients receive such diagnoses as paranoid schizophrenia. Block further argues that an adequate clinical work-up should include not only assessment of problems but also of strengths. Boyd-Franklin (1984) notes that much of the earlier literature regarding black individuals was biased from a "deficit" viewpoint. Boyd-Franklin observes that black families are often described as disorganized and deprived, but notes that, "a viable and necessary alternative to this view has been the increasing emphasis on the strengths of black families." (p. 54) She argues that one should not begin with the premise that deficit or disorder is present.

In an article from the *Napa Register* (February 25, 1985), Dr. Melvin Sabshin, for the previous ten years Medical Director of the American Psychiatric Association, reportedly indicated that psychiatrists tend to describe all of life's problems as having a psychiatric cause requiring a psychiatric solution. He feels there is optimism for the future if psychiatrists would stop claiming the need for psychiatric intervention in all of life's problems, and he cautions psychiatrists not to "overpathologize."

A series of studies further demonstrates these tendencies to overpathologize. Temerlin and Trousdale (1969) presented a script of an actor who portrays an individual intellectually curious about psychotherapy, relaxed, confident, productive, and free from psychological problems. The script depicts an interview in which this person establishes a positive relationship with the interviewer and describes his inner experience in a coherent and organized fashion, without evasion, defensiveness, withdrawal or guilt. Excluded from the script were any of a broad range of "pathological characteristics." Among the various subjects in the study, a group of psychiatrists were asked to review this script, presumably to aid in a research project. They were told that two psychiatrists had previously done so and agreed "that the man looks neurotic but is actually psychotic," but that two opinions were not sufficient to achieve adequate certainty. Among the 25 psychiatrists who reviewed the script, every single one judged this man to be mentally ill. Note that this study did not involve an individual feigning symptoms in any way but rather portraying an entirely healthy individual. The study shows the massive potential influence of expectancies, especially the expectancy that abnormality will be found. Apparently, this expectancy can "overwhelm" even data which portray a level of psychological well-being that many might envy. Recall that *every* psychiatrist judged the person as mentally disordered. This would suggest, at minimum, that a prior diagnosis of abnormality, whether accurate or not, could exert a profound impact on subsequent opinions. Thus, for example, were an examinee to successfully feign abnormality with a first psychiatrist, a second psychiatrist aware of this first psychiatrist's opinion might be strongly disposed to render a similar diagnosis.

Berry (1973) asked mental health workers, including psychiatrists, to formulate impressions based on case materials, and found that they favored complex labels or explanations of unusual child behavior rather than simpler ones. For example, in evaluating case materials describing a 4-year-old who does not talk, there was a tendency to select a diagnosis of childhood schizophrenia as more probable than explanations unrelated to psychiatric disorder, such as hearing loss. Hsu et al. (1985) found that when observing normal families, raters tended to assume problems in families from different ethnic backgrounds. Sattin (1980) discussed research indicating that professionals' diagnostic decisions usually presume the existence of mental illness. In his study, Sattin found that a condition creating a stronger expectancy of abnormality was indeed associated with judgments of greater disturbance than a low expectancy condition, even though the clinicians (psychiatric residents in this study) were given identical case materials. Schulberg et al. (1985) compared diagnoses rendered by primary care physicians and psychiatrists. They found that the primary care physicians seemed to underdiagnose depression, whereas the psychiatrists seemed to overdiagnose depression.

Apparently, the diagnosis that is rendered can also vary depending on the setting or purposes for which diagnosis is being performed. Within the clinical context, as noted by Shah above, a clinician may tend to err on the side of caution so as to not miss a disorder that is present. A study by Sharfstein et al. (1980) suggests tendencies of the opposite type when psychiatrists render diagnoses on insurance forms. In their study, Sharfstein et al. found a high rate of disagreement between the diagnoses listed on such forms and those rendered separately and confidentially on the same patients by the same practitioners. Sharfstein et al. indicate that these discrepancies were probably due to the therapists' wish to act in their patients' best interests. For example, they may have been concerned about the confidentiality of the information provided to the insurance companies.

Regardless of the reasons, these results suggest that the diagnoses rendered by clinicians may vary depending on purpose or context. In the case of insurance forms, this would likely involve listing a less serious diagnosis than the therapist might actually believe was present. Such fluctuating diagnostic practices lead one to ask whether, and in what direction, some clinicians might vary diagnostic practices with courtroom materials. If some clinicians alter their diagnoses to serve their patients' best interests when filling out insurance forms, might they not act likewise when rendering diagnoses for forensic purposes? For example, perhaps in an ambiguous case, they might render the more serious diagnosis to increase the chances of what they might view as just compensation. It would also seem, based on the report by Zussman and Simon (1983) above, that diagnostic practices can vary due to a process of subtle identification that may occur outside of an expert's awareness.

If it can be established that a clinician alters his diagnosis in some circumstances, what is to say he will not alter his diagnosis to help a client in a forensic evaluation? This is probably best addressed in the context of reports prepared for insurance companies or perhaps client's employees, where the clinician might render a more "benign" diagnosis in order to "protect" his client's interests. Some experts might admit to these matters freely because (1) they may be common practice, and (2) the clinician may view the admission as a minor one and even an opportunity to demonstrate his compassion or concern. However, if such an admission can be obtained, the lawyer is in a potentially formidable position. If the clinician will alter a diagnosis in a certain direction to serve his client's best interests, the clinician has essentially admitted that he is willing to alter, or even falsify information. If he will do this in one instance, how does one know he would not do so in another instance, i.e., that he would not render an abnormal diagnosis in a courtroom setting in order to "serve" the best interests of the individual he has assessed and/or is treating? Through this line of questioning, the lawyer may be able to impeach the expert's credibility.

The judgment habits that foster overpathologizing are apparently pervasive, and ample material for supporting these habits and the errors to which they lead is almost always available, whether a diagnosis of abnormality is warranted or not. In Chapter 5 we discussed "confirmatory bias" at considerable length and pointed out how common this problematic judgment habit seems to be. Given the propensity to begin by assuming the presence of abnormality, confirmatory bias will tend to alter data collection and interpretation such that this initial hypothesis is likely to be "supported," or believed to have been confirmed, regardless of its accuracy. Along these lines, Anastasi (1982) notes that clinicians may be unduly influenced by their early hypotheses, so that they look only for data that support those hypotheses. She notes that this can affect not only interpretation, but even the very behavior or responses of the examinee, such that they tend to conform to the expectancies or hypotheses of the examiner. She describes this process as "soliciting" and contrasts it to less biased ways of obtaining information.

Wolpe (1970) states:

> Psychoanalytic theory which has dominated psychiatric thinking for half a century attributes the symptoms of "functional" psychiatric illness to hidden internal sources. The existence of these hidden processes has never been demonstrated. Nevertheless, the psychoanalytically oriented therapist assumes their presence in every case and then purports to derive a detailed image of them from the patient's verbalizations. This is not difficult to do and, rewarded by the approval of colleagues, *soon becomes a confident habit.* (italics ours)

Miller (1980) notes that the way the human mind works is that it starts with a conclusion, and then searches for evidence to support the conclusion, either directly or indirectly, by cleverly invented arguments. He stresses that the scientific method is supposed to be an antidote to this kind of thinking.

Given what is apparently very considerable overlap in the behavior and thinking of presumably normal and abnormal individuals, these missions to obtain "supportive" data for assumptions of *abnormality* should almost always prove "successful." (For a more extended discussion of the overlapping behavior of those deemed normal and abnormal, see

Chapter 4.) Meehl (1973) points out this overlap and a possible consequence as regards judgment error. Meehl states:

> The second kind of fact about the person is not true of him by virtue of his be-
> ing a "patient," but is true of him simply because he is a human being—namely
> he has conflicts and frustrations; there are areas of life in which he is less than
> optimally satisfied, aspects of reality he tends to distort and performance do-
> mains in which he is less than maximally effective...If you examine the con-
> tents of a mental patient's mind, he will, by and large, have pretty much the
> same things on his mind as the rest of us do. If asked whether there is some-
> thing that bothers him a lot, he will not emphasize his dissatisfaction with the
> weather. The seductive fallacy consists in *assuming,* in the absence of a re-
> spectable showing of causal connection, that this first set of facts, i.e., the
> medical, psychological, or social aberrations that define him as a patient, *flows
> from* the second set, i.e., his conflicts, failures, frustrations, dissatisfactions, and
> other facts which characterize him as a fallible human being, subject like the
> rest of us to the human condition. (pp. 245-246)

Meehl adds:

> Like the preceding statistical mistake, the ad hoc fallacy is one that everybody
> "officially" knows about and recognizes as a source of error, but we find it so
> tempting that we frequently commit it anyway. The ingenuity of the human
> mind in "explaining" things, the looseness of the theoretical network available
> to us in the present state of clinical psychology, and the absence of the quasi-
> definitive criterion (comparable to the pathologist's report in internal medicine)
> of what the truth about the patient really is, all combine to make it easy for us
> to cook up plausible-sounding explanations after the available relevant evi-
> dence is in, of why the patient is the way he is. (p. 261)

Turk and Salovey (1985) note that clinicians often form initial impressions on the basis of insufficient information and then use subsequent data to confirm these beliefs rather than to generate new impressions or appraisals. They review research indicating very considerable
overlap across individuals identified as normal and abnormal, noting that
*histories obtained from normal individuals produced materials
"sufficient to be of etiological significance for the entire range of problems enumerated in the American Psychiatric Association's Diagnostic
and Statistical Manual-I, despite the fact that none of the individuals interviewed reported any current dysfunctional symptoms."* (p. 23) (italics
added) Turk and Salovey further note that clinicians' impressions tend to
be guided by the things they expect to observe, usually abnormality.
They note that this will introduce systematic bias toward overestimating
psychopathology and underestimating positive aspects of adjustment, the
ultimate result being a reduction in judgment accuracy.

McMillan (1984) had normal individuals perform self-ratings of their
memory functioning. Of interest, average self-ratings varied considerably, depending on the specific facet of memory into which inquiry was
made. For example, on average, most individuals reported that they had a

good memory for appointments but a bad memory for jokes. Further, McMillan indicates that individual subjects were not consistent in rating various aspects of their own memory. He notes that "one individual may view himself as having a good memory for jokes and poor one for faces." This type of finding would suggest that if the clinician asks a sufficient number of questions about almost anyone's memory, he would obtain at least some self-reports of inadequate or poor functioning. Hence, for almost any individual, regardless of their actual status, at least some "support" could be obtained for the presence of a "memory disorder."

Although substantial "evidence" for abnormality can apparently be elicited from most anyone, very little may be required before clinicians assume it is present. According to a number of authors, diagnostic conclusions are often formed quite rapidly and on the basis of insufficient information. Leff (1977) states, "It has been shown that psychiatrists confidently reach a conclusion about the diagnosis within the first few minutes of the interview." Klein and Davis (1969) note that:

> Diagnoses are often made and therapy prescribed on the basis of inadequate case study, that is, inadequate even in the light of our limited knowledge. The major reason for this premature closure is the unwarranted belief that an arbitrary stereotyped formulation implies dynamic understanding. Such formulations serve as ritualistic guardians of ignorance for those who cannot stand the anxiety engendered by the ambiguity inherent in our present ignorance. (p. 12)

Yager (1977) notes that psychiatrists frequently form diagnostic impressions in two to three minutes, *and sometimes in as little as 30 seconds.* (For further references regarding these tendencies to reach premature closure, see Chapter 5.)

Clinicians may assert that awareness of their potential biases counters negative effects, but in the section on bias in Chapter 5 we discussed research showing the doubtful nature of these assertions. In that section we cite a number of studies showing that individuals often are not aware of the factors influencing their judgments, including their biases. Further, even if awareness of biases or problematic judgment practices can be achieved, this seemingly does little to alter their impact. Speaking on these matters, Dawes (1986) states: "Making judgments on the basis of experience unexamined for bias in generation or interpretation is likely to lead the judge—clinical or otherwise—astray, in a predictable direction. Precautions must be taken against the pitfalls of such unexamined judgment." (p. 440) Dawes indicates that adequate precautions against bias require more than just awareness but, in addition, active steps or external judgment aids. Dawes notes, for example, that "literally writing down base rates...can prevent us from making irrational judgments." He argues that typical case reports are a substantial obstacle to the use of such external aids because, for example, they are retrospective in nature and can "support" almost any after-the-fact interpretation regardless of validity. Thus, they create the illusion of validity and obscure the need for judgment aids. Dawes describes as an even greater obstacle the difficulty of becoming convinced that one should take precautions against one's self. He notes that "there is even evidence that when such aids are offered, experts attempt to 'improve upon' these aids' predictions—and do worse than they would have had they 'mindlessly' adhered to them."

The use of establishing the influence of biases in clinical situations has been noted already. It would be appropriate to inquire of the expert if it was not true that certain clinicians become known as "plaintiff" experts or "defense" experts, and then to bring out that the particular expert has worked primarily for one side or the other. It will be a rare clinician who has never done any work for what one might call the opposite side. Still, it is worthwhile to establish that the overwhelming majority of his cases are either referred by plaintiff or defense lawyers and that the overwhelming majority of his reports and testifying is on behalf of one side or the other. Many lawyers do this as an effort to show that the expert has been "bought." However, it may also be possible to demonstrate through questioning that, even if forthright, experts are selected by attorneys who are aware of their biases pro-plaintiff or pro-defense, whatever they may be, and that these categorizations by the lawyer have a sound basis in fact as demonstrated by all of the literature on bias. For example, a plaintiff's lawyer in a personal injury case can select from a number of local psychiatrists for whom he can fairly well predict the outcome of his client's evaluation.

Also, because clinical evaluations are so subjective in nature, it is not difficult for the lawyer to influence the clinician's evaluation. Some lawyers refer to this process as "steering" the expert. We do not mean by this that lawyers attempt to induce experts to commit perjury. Rather it is by the manner of referral and in discussion of clinical findings with the expert that the lawyer can influence the outcome. Thus, at the first step of referral the lawyer can in many ways suggest to the expert that the client suffers from a mental disorder. He may make reference to prior psychiatric care or evaluations or he may present minimal facts all slanted in the direction of suggesting psychopathology or may describe a heinous crime or horrendous physical injuries, all toward the end of establishing or encouraging the already existing set in the clinician to find psychopathology. He may do nothing more than say that he has worked with a lot of clients and in his opinion there is just no question but that this client is suffering from a severe psychological disturbance. All of this has the effect of establishing in the mind of the clinician the probability that the person he will see is suffering from a psychiatric disorder, which when coupled with the well established predilection of clinicians to find psychological disturbance virtually insures a finding to that effect. If the clinician has not adequately related the condition to the legal issue, frequently the lawyer can point out to him how it relates and often obtain agreement from the clinician. For these reasons it is very important in deposition or cross-examination to interrogate the clinician in detail as to exactly what information was provided in communication from the referring source.

Some evidence of attempts to reduce some of these deficiencies, through adoption of a standardized psychiatric interview or the use of computerized diagnosis, can be seen in the literature. However, these approaches have not been widely adopted, and, even where adopted, there is, as yet, insufficient evidence to establish with confidence that they do, in fact, sufficiently overcome these deficiencies, or, if they have any effect, whether it is appreciable enough to make a practical difference. No method for determining the influence of situational effects has yet been devised. Nor is there evidence to rebut the conclusion that, because of examiner effects, the clinical examination is inevitably an idiosyncratic process making the data and the conclusions from such examination virtually worthless. In addition, the lack of validated knowledge, principles or specific criteria provides the enormous elasticity and flexibility which allow the clinician completely free rein in his formulations about a particular individual.

PROBLEMS DETERMINING PREMORBID STATUS

In many cases, in particular those involving personal injury claims, it is necessary to determine whether the individual's current status represents a change from his prior, or premorbid status. For example, it may be claimed that a head injury has caused a decline in intellectual functioning. In order to make such a determination, the clinician needs some basis for comparing current functioning with past functioning, except perhaps when severe impairment is evident. (In such cases, of course, one would not need an expert to point out the obvious.) Lacking such a basis for comparison, how could one know how much of a change had occurred, or if current functioning is really any different from past functioning? However, given the considerable difficulties predicting and postdicting mental status or functioning, how can the clinician possibly make a precise determination of the examinee's prior state?

In Chapter 11, for example, we will discuss the deficiencies of procedures for estimating "premorbid" level of intellectual functioning. Klesges et al. (1985) note that even the most promising formulae for estimating prior intellectual functioning "should probably be restricted to research purposes for the present time." (p. 2) Bolter et al. (1982) report that the method they studied for estimating premorbid intellectual functioning with head-injured patients was prone to error and "could exert a negative influence on diagnostic and treatment judgments." (p. 173) Bolter et al. also suggest that these methods be limited to research applications until further improvements are made. Adams and Grant (1985) note that researchers often do not take into account previous risk factors that may adversely affect the functioning of the central nervous system. If such serious deficiencies remain even for one of the most precisely measured and better researched areas—intellectual functioning—then such deficiencies are only likely to be greater in less precisely measured and researched areas. For example, very little research has been devoted to assessing premorbid memory functions, and thus virtually any conclusions in this regard will lack adequate scientific foundation and may be little more than guesswork.

Failure to consider, or to accurately assess premorbid functioning can lead to mistaken opinions about the presence or severity of decline in intellectual or behavioral functioning following a personal injury. Lacking precise methods for determining previous level of functioning, the clinician often does not really know how much of a change, if any, has actually occurred. Thus, even if functioning has remained stable, misappraisal of prior status may lead to the false assumption of loss. In order to make an accurate determination of change, the clinician would have to perform accurate assessment of current status, accurate assessment of prior status, and then devise some means for comparing the two sets of results. Scientifically established procedures for successfully completing any of these needed components is lacking, and rather the clinician is often left to rely on experimental procedures and/or personal judgment. We would also note that many clinicians make little effort to thoroughly investigate prior status and rather tend to assume that what they see, or think they see, represents a change from prior status. Even when systematic attempts are made, as noted above, such determinations of prior functioning must rest primarily on subjective methods or speculation. Thus, the clinician is often vulnerable to questions directed at showing that any methods he may have employed for determining prior status are extremely fallible or imprecise.

One wishes to establish that if the clinician cannot assess prior level of functioning accurately, or has no way to know with certainty whether assumptions in this regard are accurate, he is in no position to make an accurate assessment of change. It can be made evident to the jury that to determine if something has changed, or how much it might have changed, one would first have to know what it was like before. Further, how could a clinician be reasonably certain about the cause of a change when he cannot be certain whether a change has occurred in the first place? Also, the many situational or transient factors described above that can lead to wide alterations in functioning over even relatively brief periods of time further complicate judgments about cause.

PROBLEMS CREATED BY "THE GAP"

An important question to pose, and one for which there is often very little, if any, scientific information, is whether existent methods or knowledge apply to issues of immediate relevance within the courtroom setting. It should be obvious from the discussion up to this point that even the best researched and most familiar tasks may impose considerable difficulties for the clinician. These problems will not disappear, and are only likely to become much worse, when these deficient methods are applied to courtroom questions or issues that require broad inferences and leaps in generalization. We have discussed these and related problems previously under the heading of "the Gap," and here we would mention three facets of this problem. The first involves the practitioner's need to alter, in certain ways, his "modus operandi" and mental "set" when conducting assessments for legal purposes. For example, as noted by Rogers (1984), many psychologists seem to presume that individuals will not purposely try to alter or fabricate scores on psychological tests, but this presumption should not be made when these tests are administered for forensic purposes. Second, diagnostic labels, by themselves, often have little direct relevance to forensic questions and are of minimal help in making the needed determinations. For example, a diagnosis like PTSD, by itself, will not help in determining whether an individual was aware of the nature of his actions, or what his everyday functioning might be. Some individuals diagnosed as such show little difficulty in everyday adaptation, whereas others show what could be considered serious difficulties (see Chapter 20). Third, there is often considerable doubt that any validity which may have been demonstrated for diagnostic or predictive techniques under one set of circumstances generalizes, or applies, to the persons or questions involved in courtroom proceedings.

Adinolfi (1971) discusses some of the limits of diagnosis even when performed for clinical, as opposed to forensic purposes. He states that there is abundant material to suggest that clinical psychologists' "tendencies for ready classification have their origins in other than purely rational or scientific purposiveness."

Note that the problems Adinolfi describes pertain to clinical applications. A statement by Goldstein (1973) indicates how much worse these problems can become in the courtroom setting. Goldstein states:

> Through a combination of historical accidents, social revolution and pragmatic necessity, the infant science of psychiatry has become an inextricable cog in the machinery of the law just as it has become a sometimes embarrassing but firmly entrenched member of the medical-scientific community. A learned and

distinguished body of jurists, legal historians, forensic psychiatrists and other social critics have seriously questioned the wisdom of a growing tendency to attribute to psychiatrists inflated powers of diagnosis and prediction in what is still an uncharted and poorly understood area—the interface of psychiatry, law and society. (p. 1134)

Again, it is important to realize that psychologists and psychiatrists often have considerable difficulties reaching accurate conclusions or predictions even when dealing with the subject matter with which they are most familiar. Luborsky (1954) found that when candidates for psychiatric training were interviewed by experienced psychiatrists, the rate of prediction of success had a validity coefficient of 0.2 to 0.4, which is very low. He also found that individually, the psychiatrists could not predict at all. Only one of nine interviewers exceeded chance prediction.

Kandler et al. (1975) found that senior faculty members at Albert Einstein College of Medicine (certainly no "lightweight" among medical schools) were unable to predict performance of psychiatric residents during their three years of residency. In this study, 17 individuals accepted for psychiatric residencies in 1970 were evaluated, both by 45 minute interviews with three to five senior faculty members, as well as by a Resident Applicant Scale (RAS) consisting of characteristics the faculty members believed were important for successful psychiatric residency. Ratings from each of these methods were tested against a performance scale constructed to measure residents' performance in ten different areas. The interview and RAS measures were tested against performance of the residents at the end of the first, second and third years of residency. The authors of the study found no significant correlation between either RAS or the Global Interview ratings and the Performance Scale ratings for the three years of training. They state that this indicates that: "Neither ratings of applicants based on a number of discrete items nor global ratings were predictive of subsequent performance in the three years of training."

The Kandler study is relevant to forensic psychiatry. It should be noted first of all that it is another instance of psychiatrists being wrong. Their inaccuracy in this study, however, is of particular significance in view of the fact that they may be reasonably expected to have much better understanding, grasp and knowledge relative to the particular performance involved here than they may be reasonably expected to have with regard to forensic psychiatric issues involving predictions such as the ability to appreciate the nature of an act and conform one's conduct or whatever legal issue may be involved. That is, over many years these senior faculty psychiatrists developed a set of characteristics which they believed were important for successful residency. These were the characteristics that went into the 32-item RAS, and the acceptance of the 17 residents out of the 99 applicants was based on the assessment that they possessed these characteristics, including such items as self-awareness, sensitivity to others, creativity, intellectual grasp of psychiatry and type of psychiatric orientation. The results of the study suggest one of two conclusions. Either psychiatric faculty members did not know what characteristics (capacities) were important in successfully accomplishing the task or they were unable to accurately assess the degree to which applicants possessed those characteristics. If psychiatrists either cannot determine what characteristics are related to performance of a task, or are unable to assess accurately the degree to which those characteristics are present in relation to a task with which they ought to have great familiarity, how can it be believed that such determinations are possible with the much less known or familiar issues and "tasks" to which forensic psychiatric evaluations relate?

Thus, regardless of literature an expert might cite, global statements pertaining to validity are of limited use, and the question must always be: "Valid for what?" In each specific case the "bottom line" is the validity a procedure achieves for the particular task at hand, or for which it is being applied. For example, if psychiatric testimony is being introduced on the issue of whether or not a defendant was capable of distinguishing right from wrong at some time in the past, the question of validity then is: "How accurately or with what probability of accuracy, can such diagnoses be made?" If the question is what is the likelihood that a given individual will succeed or fail on parole or probation, the question then becomes: "How valid is psychiatric or psychological evaluation for this purpose?" There are few studies providing a scientific basis for drawing conclusions about the *validity* of diagnoses in general, and virtually none in areas concerning the *validity* of diagnoses for any legally relevant issue, except parole and "dangerousness." When there is no evidence of validity of psychiatric evaluation regarding a particular legal question, it should not be assumed that the evaluations can be made accurately (see discussion of the Tarasoff brief, Chapter 1). Rather, when evidence is lacking, the assumption should be that psychiatrists *cannot* make such evaluations accurately, especially in view of the general findings that validity of diagnosis is usually very low wherever it has been tested. In our opinion, the burden of proof should be on the one who offers expert testimony to show that either the method employed or the individual diagnostician himself has been scientifically demonstrated to have a respectable degree of predictive validity with regard to the question being asked. If this cannot be demonstrated, admission of such evidence is questionable. If it is admitted, cross-examination can be directed to bring out the fact that there is no scientific substantiation for the claim that such a prediction can be made, nor for the claim that this particular diagnostician can do it.

Diamond (1973a) gives as his principal reason for this dismal prediction the inability of psychiatrists to provide accurate diagnosis, as he states is the case in other fields of medicine. Diamond states further:

> Unless the psychiatric expert can testify as to exactly what condition the defendant suffers from and can give a particular description of the manner in which the abnormality affects those mental and emotional processes relevant to the criminal act, he will have no credibility before the jury; however, the psychiatric expert if he is scrupulously honest, can seldom so testify. His evidence should rather sound something like this:

> I think, but I am not certain, that the defendant has a mental disease, or an abnormality, or what merely may be a normal variation, which has substantially affected his mental or emotional processes in ways which I find difficult to understand and explain to you and this has possibly, but maybe not, substantially affected his behavior controls in ways which could be, but are not necessarily, relevant to criminal act of which he is accused and which, as yet, I am not even sure he has committed.

If this is the true expert opinion, it will have little significance to the jury no matter how it is fleshed in with clinical details. (p. 114)

As regards these various facets of the gap, numerous writers have discussed limits in the value of a diagnostic label alone. McMahon (1983) notes that diagnosis of cortical dysfunction, or brain dysfunction, is rarely "a total explanation or sufficient, by itself, for a defense." McMahon indicates that an individual may have severe brain disorder and not meet legal criteria in a number of areas. She notes, "The eventual conclusion is based on considerations in addition to the dysfunction itself." (p. 406) Although addressing a somewhat different matter, Boll (1985) also points out that the diagnosis of a disease or disorder, by itself, is of limited value. Boll states, "any descriptions of the normal treatment process, the normal recovery phase, and the normal morbidity estimates from any disease or disorder will have to factor in all relevant variables, and not attempt to deal with the disease as though it exists in some form of vacuum." (p. 478) Boll is mainly referring to the impact of brain damage, and his statement suggests that diagnosis is of limited value and one must take a wide range of variables into account. Turkington (1986) indicates that symptoms that might be associated with schizophrenic or psychotic disorders are not helpful in determining whether a person acted on his own volition. He notes that volition is not recognized as a meaningful concept in the study of human behavior.

Other writers address the gap between diagnosis and legal issues in reference to involuntary commitment. Suarez (1972) states:

> The role of expert witness has given rise to a great deal of friction and misunderstanding. Most attorneys and judges still have a dim view of psychiatry and

most psychiatrists assiduously avoid legal involvement leaving the job to a
small band of "professional experts"...most legalists are convinced that psychiatry and the other behavioral sciences have little if anything to offer.

Extensive studies have shown that most defendants who have been
labeled incompetent do not really warrant such a determination and
worse, have been committed for indefinite and often lengthy periods to
institutions and then forgotten. (p. 69)

Roesch (1979) asserts that while there may be some evidence to suggest that psychiatric decisions about competency are made with reasonable reliability, the validity of such decisions is highly questionable. He
states there is no evidence that supports the link between psychiatric
symptomatology and incompetency. He found, as did earlier researchers
he cites, that psychiatrists tend to equate psychosis with incompetency to
stand trial. He observes, however that it is not always clear that the diagnosis is made first, then leading to a determination of incompetency. He
describes the possibility that the psychiatrist first made the incompetency
determination, and subsequently attached the diagnostic label consistent
with prevailing views concerning competency. He also notes that psychiatric reports frequently contain statements that appear irrelevant to the
competency question, for example, "his grandmother has been in a psychiatric hospital" or unsubstantiated conclusionary statements, for example, "defendant showed evidence of persecutory delusions," or "he is
hostile and belligerent." He asserts that the reports fail to show how these
behaviors relate to competency to stand trial, observing, for example,
that a hostile and belligerent stance may be an appropriate response to
involuntary hospitalization and examination (see discussion of base rates,
supra).

Others address problems in generalization. Kubie (1973) has described the vast comparative studies necessary before data concerning an
individual can be interpreted with confidence. He notes such studies have
not been conducted and therefore the questions before the court (in the
Jack Ruby case) could not be answered by any expert. Rogers and Seman
(1983) review problems applying psychological tests in forensic assessment. They state that, "there has been little systematic research on the
utilization of psychological tests in the examination of criminal forensic
patients." They review prior work indicating that psychological tests
were not designed to address specific legal questions and that their application for this purpose remains unestablished. They further note that the
clinical utility and validity of test interpretations as pertains to specifically legal questions has been questioned by prominent forensic psychologists. In recent years some tests specifically designed for use in forensic matters, particularly regarding competency to stand trial, child
custody, and malingering have been published. However, these still await

publication of adequate validation studies by others than the test authors or publishers. Wesley (1981) states, "there is no evidence in the history of psychology, or in any of its present systems, that a distinction between free will and determinism can be made." He indicates that "rather than mislead the courts, psychologists should try to persuade the jurist and jurors that nobody can tell whether and to which degree an action was voluntary or involuntary, premeditated or without forethought, willed by the accused or determined by his or her mental disease."

Northwestern University Law Review (1962-1963) contains articles (quotations from these articles are reprinted by special permission from the *Northwestern University Law Review,* Vol. 57, No. 1, 1962-63) dealing with diagnosis contributed by two psychiatrists, whose credentials are at least moderately impressive. While these are old, they are still meaningful as they are not tied to any particular DSM and deal more generally with limitations of psychiatric expertise. Scher (1962-1963) states:

> Neither psychiatrists nor jurors can be mindreaders or antegnosticians. Furthermore, much as I would not wish to state it, I would think that we must face the fact that there are psychiatrists like many others in our society who see their testimony as something to merchandise, rather than something to be expended only with the greatest caution and censure.

> We as psychiatrists are babes in the woods regarding the human mind, human motivation, sanity, insanity, etc. It does us no good professionally, nor in the long run as people and as citizens, to expertise where *we cannot know and do not know* (italics ours). Our profession already suffers under too much of a suggestion of charlatanism. It behooves us greatly not to further demean and cheapen the real contribution we may eventually make as a scientific group. (p. 9)

Referring to the role of the psychiatrist, Scher states:

> He may also be useful in confirming a borderline diagnosis of mental illness, *although one might very often find as many opinions as psychiatrists asked* (italics ours). But the psychiatrists should not go out on a limb. It is patently absurd to attempt to determine the state of mind of an individual at some time in the near or distant past as well as render a reliable judgment in the face of a criminal procedure in which it is the goal of the defending counsel to defend and of the accused perhaps to deny as well as embellish. (p. 11)

Bauer (1962-1963) states:

> Such terms as psychosis, psychoneurosis, and sociopath are essentially indefinable, and if defined the definitions will not be generally accepted for the simple reason they do not exist.

> The danger inherent in descriptive diagnosis is that the same set of symptoms (behavior in this case) may be the result of different causes; also under certain circumstances, behavior may be considered "normal" or "acceptable," and

under other circumstances the same behavior may be considered "abnormal" or "not acceptable." (p. 14)

Bauer also declares:

> The position that psychiatric diagnosing is conceptual and still scientifically inadequate and that the concept of responsibility is indefinable is not meant to imply we should negate efforts toward proper diagnosing in psychiatry or that we should throw out the concept of responsibility. Rather, the thesis is that from an administrative and operational standpoint, in reference to the specific problem of what to do with people who break the law and seem to be suffering from some sort of deviant behavior which may be looked upon as "sick" by society, both psychiatric diagnoses and the concept of responsibility have not helped the situation; rather they have compounded the difficulty. (p. 14)

Meehl (1971) provides broad discussion of the risks involved when the law relies upon, or gives too much credence to knowledge which itself is actually often shaky to being with, and even less certain still when generalization to legally relevant issues is attempted. Meehl states:

> While the sources of error in "common knowledge" about behavior are considerable, the behavior (sic) sciences are plagued with methodological problems which often render their generalized conclusions equally dubious. Legal applications of generalizations from experimental research on humans and animals in laboratory context often involve risky parametric and population extrapolations. Statistical analysis of file data suffers from inherent interpretative ambiguities as to causal inference from correlations. (p. 67)

Meehl states further:

> If we...cannot generalize within the laboratory, moving to the field is presumably risky. How sizable are the relationships? A social scientist who countervails a lawyer's fireside induction by extrapolating from psychological research yielding two correlation coefficients, r .25 or r .40, is just plain silly; but an unsuspecting lawman overly impressed with social science statistical methods might be taken in. (p. 95)

Roth (1986) reports on actions of the Council on Psychiatry and Law. Among the actions taken, he notes, the Council reviewed an informal survey of members of The Academy of Psychiatry and the Law on the issue of psychic harm. He states, "The survey disclosed significant concern over the question of psychic harm and in particular, the ability of psychiatrists to accurately measure the degree of impairment for the purpose of computing damages in litigation. The Council agreed in principle to the establishment of a task force on psychic harm sometime later this year. The council is working on a charge for this task force, to be presented for approval to the APA governance and structure." We would understand this to mean that the Council on Psychiatry and Law, essentially a committee of the American Psychiatric Association, had concluded from its survey that the ability of psychiatrists or the validity of psychiatric conclusions regarding the degree of impairment in psychic harm is questionable.

In connection with discussion of "the gap," recall that the Introduction to DSM-IV describes the imperfect fit between legally relevant issues and the information contained in a clinical diagnosis (p. xxiii) and declares that the considerations involved in categorizing mental disorders may not be wholly relevant to legal judgments that take into account responsibility, disability determination, and competency. (p. xxvii)

A number of authors describe problems created by the change in orientation or set that is required when moving from the clinical to the forensic setting. Halleck (1969) notes that psychiatrists are required to take theoretical positions which contradict the conceptual basis on which they practice outside the courtroom. He also observes that only the psychiatrist is requested to answer questions which go beyond his training and confidence. Robitscher and Williams (1977) note that some expert witnesses are abused under the adversary system, but there are others who are so partisan in their testimony as to cast doubt on their objectivity and that of their profession. They discuss the commitment of psychiatrists to their particular theories about mental disease and the fact that they tend to become loyal to the people they are assisting. They further indicate that lawyers who employ them try to encourage these attachments for their own ends.

Diamond (1973) observes that the principal roles of psychiatrists are those of therapist and physician and thus that their loyalty is to their patients. He indicates that many of those ("some of us") even though doing forensic work have such strong feelings about not having another human suffer because of one's testimony that they will refuse to testify if their testimony would not aid the defendant in a criminal trial. He points out that harming another human being is incompatible with the healing function of the physician. Of course, this "therapist bias" or "therapeutic bias" is something one would expect from people who enter into a profession generally designated as a "helping profession." For most clinicians, the bulk of their practice is involved with treating people and their forensic participation is relatively infrequent. Certainly, a patient going to a psychiatrist would be hoping strongly that the psychiatrist's goals were to be helpful to him, and this kind of orientation may well facilitate treatment. However, given the overwhelming evidence that bias of one kind or another can influence the entire diagnostic process from data gathering to conclusions, it is not an orientation that is helpful in the forensic arena. It would seem clear from Diamond's description that psychiatrists with this kind of orientation could not possibly meet the test of an impartial expert whose sole function is to provide information to the trier of fact. We would note that such individuals as Halleck, Robitscher, and Diamond have been among the most eminent figures in the field of forensic psychiatry.

Coleman (1984) touches on many of the above mentioned topics. He discusses various deficiencies in expert testimony, noting, for example, that a psychiatric interview cannot be equated with a typical medical examination, that the data gathered by examination is "intensely subjective," and that psychiatrists have no means for determining truthfulness. He indicates that despite the extensive utilization of psychiatrists in legal matters, they have no valid scientific tools nor expertise for such a role.

The end product of all of these problems and deficiencies in knowledge and method are "expressed" in studies on diagnostic and predictive accuracy, which will be covered in detail below. For now, we might summarize all of the foregoing material as follows. The literature shows that because of examiner and situational effects which are almost invariably present in forensic matters but are virtually incapable of segregation or measurement, the "data" produced by clinical examination are essentially worthless for legal purposes. Thus, the process commences with contaminated and inadequate data. This problem is further confounded by the incomplete and selective recording and recall of data by the clinician. The clinician "processes" this already seriously flawed information via quite faulty and restricted judgment mechanisms and formulates conclusions which, to a considerable degree, are determined by various, often unknown biases, and the context in which the examination took place. Finally, the methods and knowledge "guiding" such evaluations are often applied to situations, individuals, or questions for which there is little if any direct scientific knowledge and instead require broad leaps in generalization and inference.

CHALLENGING THE RELIABILITY
AND VALIDITY OF DIAGNOSIS

RELIABILITY

Numerous commentaries and studies address deficiencies in the reliability of psychiatric diagnosis. Before reviewing this material, we should note that many of the studies address the reliability with which general psychiatric categories can be identified. Kutchins and Kirk (1986) conclude that, "using major classes of disorders as the categories on which to base judgments of diagnostic agreement, even when there is little or no agreement on specific diagnoses, should be seriously questioned." (p. 11) This point is pertinent to forensic assessment. Even specific diagnostic categories, by themselves, may be of limited utility in addressing forensic issues and questions; the problem is compounded in the case of general diagnostic categories or groupings. For example, the general diagnostic category of "organic brain syndrome" encompasses a broad range of individuals, who may differ greatly as regards their current status or level of functioning, the specific causes or etiologies associated with their conditions, expected response to treatment, suitability of different treatments, and ultimate course or outcome (see Chapter 19). Thus, even could diagnosticians agree on such broad classes or categories it is quite doubtful this accomplishment would be of much practical utility in forensic cases. Of course, to the extent that practitioners cannot agree on even broad diagnostic categories (and they often cannot), agreement on more specific diagnostic categories, at best, would be equally poor and often substantially worse. Such further erosion in reliability when moving from broad to more specific categories is consistently evident, and often substantial, across the studies on DSM-III diagnoses reviewed by Kutchins and Kirk (1986). It will be years before it can be determined whether this problem has been resolved in DSM-IV. Until then, triers of fact should be guided by history.

Commentary & Reviews on Reliability

Spitzer et al. (1975) note as sources of unreliability in the diagnostic system the following: differences in the stage of a condition that patients can be in at different times; different sources of information about patients, such as one clinician getting information only from the patient while another may speak with the patient's family or others, or differences in the areas of functioning and symptoms about which different clinicians regularly inquire; observation variance that occurs when different clinicians presented with the same data differ in what they notice; and criterion variance, meaning there are differences in the formal exclusion and inclusion criteria that are employed by clinicians when categorizing patients. They conclude that criterion variance is the largest source of unreliability. However, they also assert that even if the concepts and criteria were clear, there are no operational rules available to the clinician to determine whether, in a given case, the criteria of a particular diagnostic category have been met. Although problems about criteria variance refer to DSM-II, and may have been reduced somewhat in later versions of DSM, the other sources of unreliability described by Spitzer et al. remain.

Pasamanick et al. (1959) state:

> Psychiatric diagnosis at present is so unreliable as to merit very serious question when classifying, studying, and treating patients' behavior and outcomes. Clinicians may be so committed to a particular school of psychiatric thought that the patient's diagnosis and treatment are largely predetermined. Clinicians may be selectively perceiving and emphasizing only those characteristics and attributes of their patients which are relevant to their own preconceived system of thought. As a consequence, they may be overlooking characteristics which

would be considered crucial by colleagues who are otherwise committed. This makes it possible for one psychiatrist to diagnose nearly all patients as schizophrenic while another equally competent clinician diagnoses a comparable group as psychoneurotic. (p. 127)

Rothman (1962) states: "We still do not know about etiology or how to diagnose or make prognosis. Our treatments are uncertain and our knowledge has but the faintest glimmer or fragment of light." (p. 247)

Prior to the publication of DSM-III in 1980, several commentators described the woeful lack of reliability in psychiatric diagnosis (Loftus, 1960; Halleck, 1967; Halleck, 1969; Bauer, 1962-63; Shepherd, 1971, Pugh, 1973; Baldessarini, 1970; Taylor and Heiser, 1972; Bachrach, 1974; Sletten et al., 1971; Conover, 1972).

Conover (1972) also notes that much of the unreliability can be attributed to psychiatrists paying attention to differing bits of information or differing evaluations of the same bits of information. Several other writers note similar "examiner effects" in handling information as contributing to unreliability (Lowenbach and Shore, 1970; Yager, 1977; Leff, 1977; Strauss et al., 1979; Kubie, 1971; Thorne, 1972).

The above material, which points out longstanding problems in the reliability of psychiatric diagnosis and even disputes about the existence of diagnostic categories, pertains to what may be considered the "pre-DSM-III" era. The publication of DSM-III certainly has not put an end to these arguments. For example, Uebersax (1983) notes that disagreements among diagnosticians are common and argues that more attention should be paid to methods for uncovering sources of disagreement in order to improve reliability. He argues that "techniques for analyzing disagreement data are unfamiliar and virtually unknown in the psychiatric literature." (p. 199)

Shoham-Salomon (1985) notes that the therapist's orientation will make a difference in how the behavior of presumably schizophrenic patients or individuals is perceived. Specifically, Shoham-Salomon notes that there are two major therapeutic models in relation to schizophrenia—the medical model and the psychosocial model. Therapists who follow the medical model attribute less freedom of choice and less purposefulness to the behaviors of such schizophrenic patients than do those who follow the psychosocial model. This is an issue of some importance, particularly in criminal cases where the issue of intent may be crucial. A clinician who uses the medical model may be more likely to conclude that the defendant could not form a necessary intent, whereas a clinician in the psychosocial mode might be less inclined to form that conclusion. Thus, it may well be that ultimate conclusions about the guilt or innocence of the defendant will depend entirely upon the orientation or theoretical model followed by the "expert" who examined him.

Rogers et al. (1988) found that psychiatrists showed marked variability in how often they recommended treatment and how frequently they judged patients to have a poor prognosis. Reviewing earlier research, they state, "In summary, the available research on forensic patients would suggest that treatability is similar to roulette in its de-emphasis of relevant clinical variables, extreme variability of recommendations, and remarkable lack of consensus among the treatment professionals even when MDOs were openly discussed." (p. 488) In their own study, they found extreme variability among psychiatrists' prognoses and treatment recommendations. They note that the most striking implication is that the assignment of a particular psychiatrist, which is largely a matter of chance, may override all other considerations in determining a forensic patient's stated prognosis. They state, "It is likely that *who conducts the evaluation* is at least as important as *who is evaluated* in determining the prognosis and treatment recommendation of MDOs" (p. 494), and they conclude, "At the present time, it would seem that expert opinions on treatability are the obscure product of clinical expertise, unvalidated notions about the treatment response of forensic patients, and a variety of fortuitous factors, which in their cumulative effects, resemble a wheel of fortune." (p. 495) In a later article, Rogers and Webster (1989) note that although clinicians have received strong criticism for their pronouncements on dangerousness and criminal responsibility, they have thus far escaped criticism concerning lack of expertise in addressing assessment of treatability, and they ask whether this apparent incongruity is justified on either empirical or clinical grounds. They conclude, "What is eminently clear from this brief review is (1) the lack of consensual understanding of what constitutes treatability among forensic patients and (2) the absence of empirical research on the relationship of treatment to antisocial behavior and criminal recidivism. Until these two issues can be thoroughly addressed, forensic clinicians will remain in a prognostic quagmire, fraught with clinical and ethical perils." (p. 27)

Wedl et al. (1990) state, "Although reliability does not imply validity, it is a necessary prerequisite. Unfortunately, clinical assessment in psychology is notoriously unreliable." (p. 319) They cite other references to the effect that clinical judgments tend to be unreliable and only minimally related to the degree of experience of the person making the assessment, including some which show an actual decrease in reliability with greater clinical experience. Although some of the studies they refer to are more than 20 years old, we note that they are still being cited as references in the 1990's. Wedl et al. further observe that clinical judgment is subject to context effects and that this problem is not corrected by experience.

Matarazzo (1990), in his presidential address to the American Psychological Association, expresses support and optimism concerning the reliability and validity of mental health evidence. However, with regard to reliability of one- or two-word differential diagnoses (Author's note: We presume that term refers to DSM type diagnoses), he indicates that during the last decade, about half of the studies showed good to very good reliability. We would deduce from this, although Matarazzo does not so state, that the other half of the studies do not show good to very good reliability or, in other words, show "not good" reliability. If, for the sake of argument, one were to concede that this half and half analysis is correct, we feel that puts a judge or jury exactly in the position that we described at the beginning of this book. That is, they are left to decide or resolve an issue or controversy that trained, educated, and experienced scientists and professionals in the field have not been able to resolve. If they are unable to resolve this, we feel that the only reasonable course they can take is to disregard this kind of evidence (but see Matarazzo, 1991, below). Matarazzo also declares that a body of published research is lacking concerning the reliability (and, thus, the potential validity) of the "personal, social, medical and psychological portrait of the individual that is typically contained in the comprehensive 10-20 page psychological or neuropsychological assessment of the patient involved in the increasing number of cases also being adjudicated in our nation's courtroom." (p. 1012) But, of course, it is exactly this "10-20 page assessment" which he says is the typical contribution and which he also says lacks published reliability (and thus potential validity) research. He expresses his hope and belief that this lack will soon be remedied. However, hope and belief cannot substitute for scientific evidence.

Matarazzo (1991) states that high reliability has been established for DSM-III diagnoses, taken in toto, for Axis I and adequate reliability for Axis II. However, he concedes that specific subclassifications of these two axes, as well as the presence or absence of discrete symptoms, show poor levels of agreement. But, often, it is the specific subclass that is relevant in the forensic situation. For example, the diagnosis "Schizophrenic disorder" is too broad to be meaningful in relation to legal issues. It would usually need to be reduced to one of the sub-classes (e.g., Paranoid schizophrenia, etc.).

Stoll et al. (1993) found a significant change in frequency of diagnoses of schizophrenia and major affective disorders at six psychiatric teaching hospitals over the period from 1976 to 1989 for schizophrenia and 1972 to 1990 for major affective disorders. Schizophrenia disorders decreased from 27% in 1976 to 9% in 1989. Major affective disorders increased from 10% in 1972 to 44% in 1990, a threefold decrease and fourfold increase respectively. Although true changes in the frequencies of this disorder may have occurred, it seems highly unlikely that changes of these magnitudes would have occurred in such a short time. The authors suggest various explanations for this phenomenon including narrowing of definitions for schizophrenia in DSM-III and broadening for major affective disorders; treatment-oriented bias due to availability of mood altering drugs such as lithium; economic and social forces such as more favorable third-party reimbursement for affective disorders. Whatever the reasons, it seems clear that substantial numbers of people would have received different diagnoses depending on the time that they were evaluated. This may have implications for both criminal cases and personal injury cases and any other cases where prior psychological conditions can be relevant.

Zimmerman et al. (1993) note that variability exists and that the same diagnostic criteria are interpreted and applied differently at different research centers, which may help to account for discrepant research findings. Note that these last few references are post DSM-III-R. Indeed, recall that DSM-III-R did not provide reliability data for the revision. Of course, it will be years before evaluations by independent researchers of the reliabilities of DSM-IV will appear.

Zimmerman (1994) reviews a number of studies regarding diagnosis of personality disorders, which have utilized a variety of diagnostic methods. The reliabilities reported range from low to high, with more moderately high to high than low by about a 2-to-1 ratio. However, there is little consistency when interactions between type of method and type of personality disorder are considered. Zimmerman notes that one problem of DSM era diagnostic criteria is the differential application of the criteria. He also observes that the validity of Personality disorder measures is an unsettled topic.

Fennig et al. (1994) compared diagnoses at several treating facilities with diagnoses of research psychiatrists using the Structured Clinical Interview for DSM-III-R (SCID). They found that, overall, 38.5% of 65 patients diagnosed with schizophrenic conditions by the facilities received other diagnoses by the research psychiatrists, while 28.6% of 35 patients diagnosed by the facilities with bipolar disorder and 41.7% of 36 patients diagnosed with depression received other research diagnoses. They found that the reasons for disagreement were variability in the information available in 48% of the cases where there was disagreement and variability in clinical judgment in the application of the DSM-III-R criteria in 52% of the cases where there was disagreement. They stress the need for longitudinal follow-up to establish the predictive validity of initial clinical and research diagnoses.

These very recent reports keep conclusions from earlier literature cited above current.

STUDIES ON RELIABILITY

As with commentary on reliability, there is a long history of empirical studies demonstrating inadequacies in diagnostic reliability (Ash, 1949; Norris, 1959; Spitzer et al., 1967; Zubin, 1967; Beck et al., 1962; Black, 1971; Taylor and Abrams, 1975; Weiner, 1983). These studies generally showed agreement in the range of 40% to 60% on diagnoses. It should be noted that these studies pre-dated the DSM-III criteria based format which was designed to produce better reliability. Some studies, however, are not subject to criticism on that basis as they dealt with variables that were not tied to the diagnostic system.

In an impressive earlier study, Stoller and Geertsma (1963) found that psychiatrists could not agree on the application of a large number of descriptive statements concerning a patient viewed on film in a 30-minute psychiatric interview. They found that agreement was low for all groups, but that a group defined as inexperienced by virtue of having less than seven years agreed somewhat better than the "experts" with more than seven years of experience. There was no difference between those with and without psychoanalytic experience. The authors describe their findings as demonstrating that expert psychiatrists were unable to agree as to a patient's diagnosis, prognosis, psychodynamics, the causes of her problems, the feelings she was consciously experiencing, or the feelings that were latent or unconscious. They could not even agree in applying or discarding a number of "nonsense" descriptions that were included in the list of descriptions as items that would be most likely to discriminate between the experienced experts and novices.

A finding of Beck et al. (1962) should be noted. In addition to assessing agreement as to diagnostic category, they attempted to assess the degree of agreement regarding the severity of the particular diagnosis in the case of depression. *In that case the agreement as to severity—mild, moderate, or severe—was only 58.8%.*

Agnew and Bannister (1973) challenge the notion that the diagnostic system in use in psychiatry is a valid specialist language. They state that the notion that psychiatric diagnostic systems are too poorly structured to be looked on as technical or specialist languages has been frequently raised and cite research and literature to the effect that psychiatric diagnosis is a socio-political judgment, that it has frequently been shown to have low interjudge agreements in terms of decisions made about particular patients, and that non-technical factors appear to affect diagnostic judgments to a high degree. They posit that a true specialist language should show greater stability in usage over time and across varying elements than lay language. However, their study shows the opposite to be true; that the language of diagnostic psychiatry is no more stable over time or in terms of interjudge agreement than is the use of lay language by the same professionals.

Presly and Walton (1973) state:

> The present study has attempted to identify some of the sources of disagreement which leads to the low reliability of current category systems for classification of personality disorders which have been demonstrated repeatedly…the chief reasons appear to be the following: (I) A considerable degree of rater bias which results in varying attention to certain facets of the patient's personality and as a result wide variation in the frequency of usage of diagnostic labels. (II) Several meanings are attached to the same term, resulting in the use of diagnostic labels that bear no relation to the ratings made on a basis descriptive of the patient's behavior. (III) Inadequate definition is given to the limits of normal trait variation. These three factors were clearly in evidence, notwithstanding that the psychiatrists were provided with a glossary of the diagnostic terms in use and although a rather constant situation obtained for clinical observation, two factors which should have facilitated agreement between raters. (IV) The use of single category diagnostic labels results in important aspects of variation being obscured; i.e., only similarities between patients are described and the differences between them—which may be far more extensive—are ignored. This type of error is compounded when the label chosen does not describe the constellation of traits on which the patient is most deviant. (V) The system appears to operate differently for men, and women, particularly with respect to the labels "hysterical personality" and "sociopathy."

Tarter et al. (1975) provide an impressive demonstration of the unreliability of psychiatric diagnosis. They note that methodological criticisms have been leveled at some of the earlier research indicating low reliability for failure to consider the level of training of the diagnostician, the type of classification scheme employed, and the interval of time between the first and subsequent diagnosis. They attempt in their study to eliminate the problems presented by these variables. They studied the diagnoses made on 256 consecutive admissions in 1970 who had been referred to a private psychiatric hospital and had been interviewed by any two of five psychiatrists selected for the study. The selection of the psychiatrists whose diagnoses would be evaluated is highly important. Of the 18 full-time practicing psychiatrists on the hospital staff, they selected five of the most experienced. Four of the five were Diplomates in Psychiatry, while three were Fellows of the American Psychiatric Association, and they had an average of 16 years of clinical experience beyond the residency. In addition, the authors describe the psychiatrists as having extensive professional experience, long-standing clinical activity and acknowledgment by their peers of their expertise and professional skills. A patient admitted and assigned a diagnosis by one of these psychiatrists was seen within 24 hours by one of the four other psychiatrists, who also assigned a diagnostic label. The interviews and diagnoses were conducted independently, without any psychiatrist knowing of the other's assessment.

Tarter et al. measured percentage of agreement for the major categories of psychopathology and for specific disorders within each of the major categories. The agreement for major (gross) categories was as follows: organic 72.3%, functional psychosis 54.8%, neurosis 46.4% and personality disorder 47.8%. For specific diagnosis the overall rate of agreement was 48.4%, although it should be mentioned that if, and only if, two psychiatrists had agreed on the major category, their percentage of agreement on the specific condition within that category was higher: 77.8% for organic disorders, 86.3% for neurosis, 69.4% for functional psychosis and 44.4% for personality disorders. These latter, somewhat higher, agreement rates are of little meaning (and 69.4% and 44.4% are not impressive anyway) in view of the fact that for other than organic conditions these experts could only agree approximately 50% of the time on the gross category. As a side finding, lumping together all of the sub-types of schizophrenia as a single nosological entity, there was only 47.6% agreement.

Tarter et al. point out that their investigation clearly indicates that reliability of psychiatric diagnosis is low and that employing diagnoses from DSM-II has not resulted in an appreciable difference from previous investigations where DSM-I had been used. They also point out that the level of competence which must be attributed to the psychiatrists selected for the study negates any argument that the unreliability is a function of different degrees of professional competency. They attribute the difficulty primarily to the inadequacies of DSM-II. They point out that, considering that the classifications in DSM-II were adopted in the more or less arbitrary manner of consensual agreement, one should not be surprised that its reliability has not stood up well in the face of empirical test. This explanation provides little comfort for present reliabilities as DSM-III, III-R and IV were also adopted by consensual agreement. Further, the gross categories of psychotic disorders and personality disorders on which agreement was poor are present in the later DSMs. We view this study as a powerful weapon in the arsenal of an opposing lawyer. It seems unlikely that one would often face a psychiatrist in the courtroom with better indicia of competence than those in this study. Relating this study to validity, it is obvious that, within each pair of thoroughly experienced, competent psychiatrists, at least one psychiatrist was wrong in about 50% of the cases, and this is assuming that when disagreements occurred, one of the two was correct (obviously both could have been wrong). As the pairings of experts were varied, this cannot be attributed to one poor diagnostician among the group, even if it would be possible to assert that one was poor, given their credentials.

Research subsequent to DSM-III leaves the adequacy of diagnostic reliability in doubt.

Drake and Vaillant (1985) found that two independent raters could agree on the presence or absence of some kind of personality disorder at a respectable level of reliability, but that their agreement on the specific personality disorder that was present fell far below any respectable level of reliability. This study illustrates our point above that agreement levels for specific diagnosis are often much lower than those obtained for broad diagnostic categories, and it is these specific categories that are arguably of much greater pertinence in forensic assessment. Houts and Graham (1986) report on a study in which religious and nonreligious clinicians viewed the same videotaped client. The clinicians differed in their views concerning the client and also differed in terms of their views according to the degree of religious conviction expressed by the client (an actor who was working with prepared scripts).

Kutchins and Kirk (1986) provide an overview of the DSM-III field trials and subsequent research on reliability. They note problems and limits in the kappa statistic used in the field trials, including the ambiguities involved in its interpretation. Kutchins and Kirk point out methodological limits of the field trials. For example, agreement was examined for broad diagnostic categories, although the features of subcategories can vary greatly. Agreement figures for broad categories can thus be misleading and of little practical meaning. They note that the majority of reliability figures for the field trials fall below the level (.70) previously suggested as a standard by Spitzer himself, and that problems with reliable diagnosis are particularly evident for child and adolescent disorders and Axis II disorders. Summing up the results of the field trials, they assert that reliability for major classes of disorders was questionable.

Kutchins and Kirk also describe separate studies on DSM-III reliability, which show that agreement levels on the diagnostic categories are often quite low. For example, they describe a study with children and adolescents which suggests that DSM-III reliabilities for Axis I diagnoses may be slightly lower than reliabilities for DSM-II. They observe that, "The same standards that were used to criticize DSM-II would make the claims of reliability for DSM-III even more questionable....One would interpret only a few classes of DSM-III as having high reliability, a few more as only satisfactory, and the rest as no better than fair or poor." (p. 11)

This review of Kutchins and Kirk also illustrates a point we have raised throughout the text. New or innovative systems in psychology and psychiatry typically must be considered experimental, and a number of years may be required before reliability and validity can be assessed adequately. Although DSM-III was assumed by some to have largely "resolved" certain problems in diagnosis, subsequent research has revealed serious deficiencies that were not necessarily apparent at the time DSM-III appeared. DSM-IV is similarly experimental and will require similar testing. We would note that DSM-III at least reported reliability data from field trials. Lack of reported reliability figures in DSM-III-R, particularly for revised or new diagnostic categories, creates even greater ambiguities or uncertainties.

The above cited research raises doubt that clinical diagnosis has demonstrated sufficient reliability, stability, or consistency to allow introduction of such evidence in a court of law. If allowed into evidence, this research represents another point of vulnerability upon cross-examination or rebuttal.

It is also important to bring out the fact that the disagreements in diagnosis do not arise as the result of differences in skill or experience among various clinicians. The evidence does not support such a notion as many of the studies cited involved clinicians of considerable experience or skill (see also Chapter 8). This is important because where there is conflicting testimony, quite often the jury is faced with a decision requiring a choice that one of the experts is "better" than the other (based on whatever criteria the jury uses to reach such a decision: impressive titles, white hair, an honest face), or the jury must choose to disregard the psychiatric or psychological testimony.

VALIDITY OF DIAGNOSES

Many of the above references on diagnostic reliability are actually relevant to the issue of validity. As noted, reliability is generally a precondition for validity, and thus for lack of reliability, diagnoses cannot be valid. Kutchins and Kirk (1986) describe diagnostic reliability as an extremely fundamental concern, and as necessary for validity. Woody (1972) states that, "the overall value of clinical information is dependent upon validity." (p. 26) He indicates, however, that reliability does not ensure validity, but "*you cannot have validity without having reliability.*" (p. 26) He observes that clinicians could achieve consistent results but might do so along criteria that have absolutely no validity. He states: "In appraising research one must not be blinded by high degrees of reliability: validity must also be established." (p. 26)

Fleiss et al. (1972) state, "Perhaps the most telling criticism, and one for which ample data rather than rhetoric are available, has to do with the well-known generally low degree of reliability of current psychiatric diagnostic practice. The validity, i.e., the usefulness of a classification system, is limited by its reliability." (p. 162) Spitzer and Fleiss (1974) state, "There is no guarantee that a reliable system is valid, but assuredly an unreliable system must be invalid." (p. 341)

Commentary and Research Overviews on Diagnostic Validity or Accuracy

Many citations in this section are fairly old. They are included here because there is not an abundance of research on validity, especially as it relates to forensic issues, and because there is an unbroken line of negative comment up to the present.

Reigan (1962) states:

> Such use of diagnostic classifications for a review article would provide a basis for organizing the investigations meaningfully, only to the extent that the diagnoses are valid and subject generally to reliable assessment. Anyone who has worked with patients falling in any of the diagnostic categories which may be associated with psychological deficit, knows the *extreme* (italics ours) difficulties that are associated with general validity and reliability of diagnosis. (p. 416)

Beckett et al. (1967) state, "Psychiatric evaluation is a central procedure in psychiatry, but to quote Grinker, who speaks for many as far as research is concerned, the available records of these evaluations are 'pathetically inadequate.'" The authors further state, "*It is not possible to provide accurate clinical estimates of neurotic or psychotic symptoms in the past* (italics ours) or of central nervous system trauma or physical illness." The authors in this study also find only moderate to poor agreement as to whether a specific stressful situation has precipitated the present "psychiatric illness." This finding would appear relevant in cases of "PTSD."

Little (1967) states:

> One of the most important problems of contemporary clinical psychology is the devising of methods for improving the performance of psychologists in their diagnostic roles. Twenty years of research have produced study after study demonstrating the low validity (as well as reliability) of predictions based upon psychodiagnostic techniques.

Referring to the use and teaching of psychological testing, Little also says, "In view of the mass of negative research results an objective observer might be justified at arriving at a diagnosis of mass hysterical blindness among clinical psychologists."

Livermore et al. (1968) point out the controversy as to whether clinical or actuarial methods give the best assessment and warn against assuming that "intensive clinical psychological understanding of the individual" provides a more trustworthy forecast of behavior than a more behavioral actuarial approach. They point out that this assumption continues to be taken for granted by almost all psychiatrists and, amazingly, by many clinical psychologists despite the overwhelming contradiction of the research evidence. They urge that any psychiatrist or psychologist who opposes the objective actuarial approach in a practical decision-making context should be required to show his familiarity with the research literature and challenged to rebut the theoretical arguments and empirical evidence found therein. They further point out that because of the elasticity of the concept of mental illness, and particularly because of the ambiguity in the diagnostic manual of The American Psychiatric Association, the clinician can "shoehorn" into the mentally diseased class almost any person he wishes. (Note this is prior to DSM-III.)

Klein and Davis (1969) state in their introduction:

...It is still not sufficiently understood that only scientifically controlled studies can generate data that lead to the rational resolution of conflicting clinical opinion. (p. xiv)

Anyone attending the usual diagnostic staff conference cannot but be impressed by the general incoherence of the proceedings. (p. 1)

A major difficulty in outlining the differential indications for psychotropic agreements is the sadly confused state of psychiatric diagnosis. (p. 9)

Throughout the helping professions it is unfortunately true that diagnoses are often made and therapy prescribed on the basis of inadequate case study, that is, inadequate even in the light of our limited knowledge. The major reason for this premature closure is the unwarranted belief that an arbitrary stereotyped formulation implies dynamic understanding. Such formulations serve as ritualistic guardians of ignorance for those who cannot stand the anxiety engendered by the ambiguity inherent in our present ignorance. (p. 12)

Keller (1971) states:

Though the past research does not present an open and closed case against the reliability and validity of clinical interpretation in general, and interpretation of the Rorschach in specific, the trend has been largely negative.

Kubie (1971) points out in his article many fallacies in the concept of schizophrenia, which would make reliability and validity in its assessment virtually impossible. He further declares that the concept of schizophrenia is merely an outstanding example of the deficiencies of the psychiatrist as a naturalist in his own field, and declares that the position he points out in regard to schizophrenia, in fact, applies to varying degree to all psychiatric nosology. Kubie states:

I deplore our bondage to misleading pseudodiagnoses inherited from the past. In fact it is my impression that Szasz has made the mistake of misunderstanding his own position; and what he is really denying is the accuracy of efforts to characterize, identify, and isolate and diagnose discrete processes of mental diseases. This position is sound; and he would have made a useful contribution if he had limited himself to objecting to the pseudonosology which has resulted from the failure of psychiatrists to be better naturalists and if he had also pointed out that in psychiatry much of that to which we have given names which imply that they are separate illnesses are in fact only transient cross sections of long and constantly changing processes, cross sections which are marked by clusters of symptoms. (p. 331)

Koson and Robey (1973) state:

In equivocal cases it is sometimes helpful to employ special diagnostic techniques and an interview under hypnosis or sodium amytal as an aid to uncovering or "lifting" repressed memories. Considerable caution should be used, however, in interpreting the results of such interviews.

In a discussion following the Koson and Robey paper, Maguigad (1973) states:

At this point is it relevant to remind examining psychiatrists that they have a serious responsibility in carefully appraising an amnesic defendant? In my opinion, it is not enough to be aware of the clinical causes and mechanisms of amnesia. Because of the serious implications of our opinions with respect to the amnesic defendant we should try to perfect a high level of diagnostic accuracy. In the forensic setting the matter of malingered amnesia may baffle even the astute clinician. I regret that Drs. Koson and Robey did not elaborate more extensively on this subject. There may be more of an element of malingering in the case of an amnesic defendant than we are willing to accept and are able to recognize.

In our clinical assessment it is also relevant to recognize our subjectivity in our clinical contact with the defendant which was missed in the authors' paper. Our feelings toward the defendant and his alleged defense, our attitudes toward crime in general, our value systems and unconscious motivations are some of the many factors that play a significant role in formulating our opinion about a given defendant, particularly in borderline cases or cases involving unclear diagnostic categories which can create conflict and confusion in forensic psychiatric practice. A diagnostic adjunct such as the sodium amytal interview which was suggested by the authors has questionable value in my opinion. (p. 591)

Fitzgibbons and Hokanson (1973) state, "The issue of psychiatric diagnosis is complex and beset by confusing conceptual difficulties as well as by firmly rooted attitudes and effects that contribute a degree of irrationality to virtually all of the currently popular positions....It is not difficult to justifiably criticize both the reliability and the validity of psychiatric diagnosis." Fitzgibbons and Hokanson cite research indicating that one-third of the variation in psychiatric diagnosis is attributable to inconsistencies within the diagnostician, and which suggests that variations occur at three levels including observation, inference and the employment of the nosological scheme.

Strauss et al. (1973) state:

Clinicians and researchers alike have realized that it is impossible to evaluate methods of treatment, determine aetiology, or measure the course of illness of psychiatric disorders without adequate methods for diagnosis. On the other hand, it has been shown that conventional clinical methods for making psychiatric diagnoses are of distressingly low reliability, except for the broadest categories and have only marginal relationships to such criteria of validity as common aetiology, common response to treatment and common prognosis. (p. 531)

They cite other studies, which, they assert: "…have shown that the usual clinical diagnoses, because of low validity, can actually obscure more important relationships between types of psychopathology and such crucial variables as response to treatment." (p. 531)

The publication of DSM-III did little to quell this continuing controversy and debate, and DSM-III became a matter of dispute even before its official birth. Landers (*APA Monitor,* Feb., 1986) described the rift that has developed across psychologists and psychiatrists as regards diagnosis in general, and DSM-III and DSM-III-R in particular. It was indicated in this and a subsequent issue of the *APA Monitor* (April, 1986) that the American Psychological Association will probably develop its own diagnostic manual due to perceived limitations and criticisms of DSM-III and drafts of its revision (this did not materialize). Landers quotes various prominent psychologists who describe the diagnostic manual as scientifically flawed, prejudiced, and in significant part a product of political self-interest, as opposed to empirical evidence.

Sparr and Atkinson (1986) discuss the problem of lack of validation for DSM-III criteria. Among reports in the literature, some tend to validate the criteria while some do not and still others are equivocal. They note in particular the difficulty of differential diagnosis in the case of PTSD, due to the subjectivity and nonspecificity of the symptoms, which have been well-publicized and are easy to imitate. They state that, while efforts are being made to provide more objective measures and to refine criteria, "reliable applications of these methods in forensic work is not yet possible." We might add that DSM-III-R itself contains many statements about problem areas in DSM-III (see Chapter 4).

We will conclude this section with commentary by some well known scholars. First, a comment made over 20 years ago by Chapman and Chapman (1967) seems equally relevant today. They state:

> One of the most puzzling and distressing problems that confronts clinical psychology today is the persistent report by many psychodiagnosticians of clinical observations which by *objective evidence clearly appear to be erroneous* (italics ours). On the one hand, large numbers of practicing clinical psychologists agree in their observations that each of various symptoms or behavioral characteristics of patients is correlated in its occurrence with certain characteristics of test performance. On the other hand, researchers have, with fair consistency, failed to substantiate many of these observations.

> For example, the clinicians who use the DAP often report observing that those patients who show paranoid behavior clinically show in their drawings more elaboration of the eye. Yet four separate studies have failed to substantiate this observation by a counting of the relevant phenomena….In the light of the

massive negative experimental evidence, how can one account for the consistent agreement between different clinicians as to the clinical correlates of DAP performance? The highly reliable but invalid nature of such observations clearly suggests a systematic error. (p. 193)

In a discussion titled, "Why I Do Not Attend Case Conferences," Professor Meehl (1973) attacks the clinical case conference, discussing a multitude of typical procedures and approaches which render such conferences worthless. It should be borne in mind that Professor Meehl is not merely a critical "academician" but has been a practicing psychotherapist for over thirty years (and a former president of the American Psychological Association). It should also be noted that while many of Professor Meehl's criticisms are directed at the case conference, they are in fact, in many instances at least, equally applicable as criticisms of the clinical method. Among the specific criticisms of Professor Meehl are the practice of treating all evidence as equally good; tolerance of feeble inferences; failure to distinguish between an inclusion test and an exclusion test; failure to distinguish between a mere consistency of a sign and a differential weight of a sign; shift in the evidential standard, depending upon whether one is for or against a particular view; ignorance or repression of statistical logic; forgetting about base rates; forgetting about unreliability when interpreting score changes or difference scores; reliance upon inadequate behavior samples for trait attribution (Professor Meehl points out in this regard that over a period of several hours or days of unsystematic observation practically any human being is likely to emit at least a few behaviors which can be subsumed under almost any trait in the phenotypic or genotypic lexicon); failing to understand probability logic as applied to the single case (which Professor Meehl asserts is a disability apparently endemic to the psychiatric profession and is even found among clinical psychologists, despite their academic training in statistical reasoning).

Another deficiency is inappropriate task specification. Professor Meehl asserts that there are some jobs for which the case conference may not be suitable. He states:

Any psychologist who has practiced long-term, intensive, "uncovering" psychotherapy knows that there are psychodynamic puzzles and paradoxes which remain in his mind after listening to fifty or a hundred hours of the patient's productions. Yet, this same psychotherapist may undergo a strange metamorphosis when he enters the case conference context, finding himself pronouncing (sometimes rather dogmatically) about the psychodynamics of the presented patient, on the basis of ten minutes' exposure to the patient during the conference, plus some shoddy, scanty "material" presented by the resident and social worker...part of the difficulty here lies in American psychiatry's emphasis on psychodynamics at the expense of nosology. A case conference *can* be, under some circumstances, an appropriate place to clarify the nosological or taxonomic issue—provided that the participants have bothered to learn nosology, and that the clinicians mainly concerned with the patient have obtained the relevant clinical data. But since diagnosis is devalued, the prestigious thing to do is contribute psychodynamic ideas to the conference, so we try to do that, whether or not the quality and quantity of the material available to us is adequate to such an enterprise, which it usually isn't.

Meehl discusses a number of common fallacies, stating: "Not all of these fallacies are clearly visible in case conferences and none of them is confined to the case conference, being part of the general collection of sloppy thinking habits with which much American psychiatry is infected." (p. 236) Some of the fallacies described by Professor Meehl are as follows:

(1) The Barnum Effect, i.e., involves attributing significance to minor observations that are true of practically all psychiatric patients and frequently of practically all human beings. Professor Meehl points out that it is of little help to be told that a mental patient has "intrapsychic conflicts, ambivalent object relations, sexual inhibitions or damaged self-image."

(2) The "sick, sick fallacy" or pathological set. Professor Meehl points to the ubiquitous tendency of people in the mental health field to use their personal ideology as to what is healthy or adjusted, even including their religious and political beliefs and values as indicators of freedom from disease or aberration, and their tendency then to find someone who is unlike them as being sick.

Meehl states:

> The psychiatric establishment officially makes a point of never doing this and then proceeds to do it routinely. Thus, for example, many family psychiatrists have a stereotype of what the healthy family ought to be; and if somebody's family life does not meet this criterion, this is taken as a sign of pathology.

Professor Meehl outlines numerous other points which considerations of space do not permit us to reproduce here. The attorney preparing to cross examine a psychiatric or psychological expert would find his time well spent in obtaining a copy of this particular chapter in Meehl's book and digesting it. The potential user of this material should also be aware that Professor Meehl states in his final paragraph that since a highly respected colleague has been directing case conferences, he has been attending and benefiting from them.

In the introduction to the book in which the chapter on case conferences appears, Meehl (1973) states:

> On the other side of the coin how do I preserve my scientific mental habits and values from attrition by the continuing necessity as a helper to think, act and decide on the basis of "scientifically inadequate evidence"—relying willy nilly on clinical experience, hunches, colleagues' anecdotes, intuition, common sense, far out extrapolations from the laboratory, folklore, introspection and sheer "guesswork"?

And further:

> Anybody who doesn't see that there is an important difference to both the patient and taxpayer between a 60% hit rate achieved by 15 high paid clinicians sitting around a table in a smoke filled room engaged in what is called a "case conference" and an 80% hit rate achieved by an actuarial table seems to me to have something wrong with his cerebration. (p. xviii)

Mischel (1979) states with reference to his book, *Personality and Assessment:*

> My intentions in writing that book were not to undo personality but to defend individuality and the uniqueness of each person against what I saw as the then prevalent form of clinical hostility: the tendency to use a few behavioral signs to categorize people enduringly into fixed slots on the assessor's favorite nomothetic trait dimensions and to assume that these slot positions were sufficiently informative to predict specific behavior and to make extensive decisions about a person's whole life. (p. 740)

Mischel also states: "Moreover, the judgments of clinicians—like everyone else's judgments—are subject to certain systematic biases that can produce serious distortions and oversimplifications in inferences and predictions." (p. 740)

Thorne (1972) states: "Many clinicians have been making unreliable and invalid judgments based on invalid premises, illogical assumptions, unproven relationships, inappropriate applications of unproven theories and other types of error." (p. 44) Thorne refers to the "universally repeated research finding that many clinicians are unable to make better than chance judgments," and states further:

> At this time the consensus is that serious gaps, inconsistencies, inadequacies, errors, and misconceptions in the field of psychopathology must be resolved before valid criteria of diagnostic entities can be established and defined exactly enough operationally to permit reliable clinical judgments. Thus the criterion issue becomes the central problem, of psychodiagnosis, clinical inference and clinical assessment. *Nothing should be taken for granted in accepting* clinical judgments as to their validity. (p. 37)

Brown (1990) describes issues in the sociology of diagnosis, including bias and social control in psychiatric diagnosis, diagnosis as part of the extension of the bio-psychiatric medical model, and contemporary diagnostic categorization. He provides some historical material which a judge or a jury might find illuminating regarding the development of psychiatric diagnosis. He notes that Benjamin Rush, considered the founder of American psychiatry, named a diagnosis called "anarchia" right after the American Revolution. This disorder was a form of insanity in people who were unhappy with the new political structure. Rush transformed their negative opinions into mental disease. Brown also notes that in 1843, a Dr. Samuel Cartwright identified a disease "drapetomania" which occurred only in black slaves and resulted in a strange form of pathology—a compulsion to run away. Brown provides other similar examples, some of them as recent as the 1960's, when a well-known psychiatrist informed Congress that student protesters had no serious political agenda but were acting out "an unresolved Oedipal" conflict by attacking the university as a surrogate father.

Brown states, "The psychiatric literature is full of DSM reliability studies on countless numbers of diagnoses on all the axes, yet hardly any research addresses validity. Anyone can achieve inter-rater reliability by teaching all people the 'wrong' material" and getting them to agree on it." (p. 393) Brown also states, "Not only is validation generally lacking, but when researchers study validity, the results are startling—the validity is very low." (p. 394)

Brown cites "Temerlin's (1968) famous experiment" showing clinicians are prone to follow suggestions of experts and the Rosenhan study "...as another case of unwarranted certainty..." which we mention to indicate that these two famous studies continue to be cited in the professional literature.

Mirowsky (1990) states, "The diagnostic categories exist in the subjective and interpretive culture of psychiatry, and not in the objective pattern of correlation among mental, emotional, and behavioral problems." (p. 410) He points out that psychiatry attempted to establish validity by using inter-rater reliability as the measure of validity, noting that inter-rater reliability, which measures the extent of agreement between two judges, is notoriously low in psychiatric diagnoses. However, he points out it can be increased dramatically through the use of standardized interview schedules and rote diagnostic rules. He then states, "The ingenuity of the 'procedural validation' is that it sidesteps any reference to empirical correlation between symptoms, let alone deeper forms of validation. It is only necessary to get the judges to consider the same information and follow the same decision rules." (p. 411) Mirowsky points out that the items of information need not bear any relation to each other, nor do the interpretative rules have to reflect anything other than the ability and willingness of the judges to use them.

To illustrate his point, Mirowsky uses the medieval diagnosis of witchcraft as an example. A number of highly respected inquisitors might agree that witches may be known by three or more of the following signs: talking to animals, foul breath, avoiding churches and men of the cloth, walking on moonlit nights and dancing alone. Then all that is needed to "validate" the diagnostic category and criteria is to demonstrate that any pair of trained inquisitors using these signs and the three-or-more rule will agree on who is or is not a witch more often than expected by chance. The more the guidelines are followed, the greater will be the amount of agreement which will support use of the diagnostic system. He describes the traditional psychiatric categorical diagnostic system as the "poorest possible" means of representing mental problems and enforcing its use as arbitrary, creating an illusion of objectivity and concreteness.

Matarazzo (1990, supra) notes that validation of the typical psychological portrait provided in forensic matters is hoped for but not yet achieved.

DeJong et al. (1992) describe the inability of clinical information to predict violent behavior in criminal or mentally disordered populations, and in particular the unacceptably high rate of false positives. (Note: See Chapter 24 on Dangerousness for literature on reliability and validity of predictions of violent behavior.)

Otto et al. (1993) attempted to evaluate the conclusions of a panel of experts who performed a postmortem reconstruction (i.e., a psychological autopsy) in connection with the House Armed Service Committee investigation of the U.S.S *Iowa* turret explosion in 1989. They aver that the lack of procedural rigor maximizes potential for variation in judgments and conclusions in such reconstructions. They state that clinicians should be cautious in using and making claims regarding the utility of such reconstructions because reliability and validity has not been adequately established.

Turpin (1991) discusses the use of psychophysiological assessment in anxiety disorders, and suggests that, while more research is needed, this is a potentially rich source of assessment information. This may be worth mentioning as a "positive" development which may among other things provide some "objective" indicators of anxiety conditions.

Now, with the new DSM-IV, it will again be many years before a sound body of knowledge concerning validity of conclusions based on diagnosis can be developed.

Studies on Diagnostic Accuracy/Validity

In earlier studies on this topic, Plaut and Cromwell (1955) found that experienced psychologists made errors in more than 40% of the cases when attempting to discriminate the drawings of deteriorated schizophrenics and normal subjects. Goldberg (1959) found that experienced psychologists made frequent errors when attempting to distinguish the Bender-Gestalt records of brain-damaged and non-brain-damaged psychiatric patients. Walker and Lyndon (1967) obtained an error rate of approximately 50% when experienced psychologists attempted to make assessments from sentence completion data. Other studies with high rates of error are Rosenhan (1973), 100% error; Taylor et al. (1974), 94% error; Plag and Arthur, (1965), 72% error. See also Temerlin and Trousdale (1969, supra), 100% error.

Graham (1971) states: "During the past two decades numerous studies have demonstrated the low level of accuracy with which clinical inferences can be made from psychological test data." In his study, Graham asked 21 Ph.D. psychologists to make assessments of either neurosis or psychosis, informing the clinicians that half the profiles were neurotic and half were psychotic, based on other criteria. These experienced clinicians were able to make correct judgments in only 50% of the cases.

Many of the articles cited in Chapter 3 (Challenging the Scientific Status of Psychology and Psychiatry), as well as those in the chapters on psychological testing (Chapters 10-13) assert or demonstrate the low reliability and validity of clinical evaluations and should be considered incorporated by reference in this chapter. For example, Davids (1973), Lewandowski and Saccuzzo (1976), and Cleveland (1976) all refer to the weight of research indicating low reliability and validity for psychological testing in the psychodiagnostic process.

Blum (1978) notes drastic changes in the frequency of various psychiatric diagnoses over a 20-year period from 1954 to 1974, with affective disorders tripling, neuroses going from the largest group to one of the smallest, and schizophrenia increasing significantly. Blum observes that changes in the patient population and symptomatology cannot fully explain these trends, and he suggests that the changes may be correlated with the increasing use of psycho-pharmacological treatments which are available for the classifications which increased. He states: "The threatening ambiguity of mental disorder (Who is mad? Who is sane?) leads us to take our system of perceiving mental illness for granted when it is just that system which should be the object of study since it defines our experience of mental illness."

Farber et al. (1986) had clinical psychologists attempt to identify various types of disorder based on case histories. Error rates were quite high for certain of the categories, including a 28% error rate for major depressive disorders, a 44% error rate for "organic personality syndrome," and a 95% error rate for temporal lobe epilepsy, the latter of which can reportedly produce symptoms that mirror or mimic psychiatric disorders. Wedding (1983) had judges, including Ph.D. psychologists, attempt to separate individuals into diagnostic groups (e.g., brain-damaged individuals, versus schizophrenics, versus neurologically intact subjects) based on their results on neuropsychological tests. Overall error rate was high, and for three of the 30 cases used in the study the error rate was 100%.

The research showing the problems of validity in the prediction of dangerousness will be discussed in a later chapter (Chapter 24).

THE ROSENHAN STUDY

Rosenhan's (1973) study provides evidence that is severely damaging to the belief that psychiatrists can in fact distinguish between "the sane" and "the insane," "the normal" and "the abnormal." It appears to be a piece of research that should be brought to the jury's attention in any case in which there is psychiatric testimony.

A review of the *Annual Social Science Citation Index* (Institute for Scientific Information, Philadelphia, PA), which provides a listing of citations or references to publications in the social science literature, uncovered over 80 citations to Rosenhan's (1973) original report on his study over the 5-year period of 1986 to 1990. These continuing references to the Rosenhan study show that it is still a frequently considered topic in the literature. Further, we are not aware of any studies with contrary results.

Rosenhan basically takes the view that psychiatric diagnoses are in the minds of the observers, that is, the psychiatrists, and are not valid summaries of characteristics displayed by those observed. In this study, eight normal, sane people gained admission to twelve different mental hospitals. These eight are referred to in the article as "pseudo-patients." The eight included a psychology graduate student in his 20's, three psychologists, a pediatrician, a painter and a housewife. Three were women and five were men. None had ever suffered symptoms of serious psychiatric disorders. All were functioning well in their family, interpersonal and occupational lives.

To gain admission, the pseudo-patient arrived at the Admissions Office complaining that he had been hearing voices. When asked what the voices said, he replied that they were often unclear but as far as he could tell they said, "Empty," "Hollow," and "Thud." Rosenhan chose these symptoms by their apparent similarity to existential symptoms, which are believed to arise from painful concerns about the perceived meaninglessness of one's life, a well-known contemporary problem of normal people. The choice was also determined by the absence of any report of existential psychoses in the literature. Rosenhan states:

> Beyond alleging the symptoms and falsifying name, vocation, and employment, no further alteration of person, history or circumstances were made. The significant events of the pseudo-patient's life history were presented as they had actually occurred. Relationships with parents, siblings, spouse and children, with people at work and in school consistent with the aforementioned exceptions were described as they were or had been. Frustrations and upsets were described along with joys and satisfactions. These facts are important to remember. If anything they strongly biased the subsequent results in favor of detecting sanity, since none of their histories or current behaviors were seriously pathological in any way.

Immediately upon admission to the Psychiatric Ward, the pseudo-patient ceased simulating *any* symptoms of abnormality.

The pseudo-patients were diagnosed schizophrenic with one exception (that exception being a diagnosis of manic-depressive in the private hospital). They were never found out and were eventually discharged with the diagnosis of "schizophrenia in remission." The range of stay was from 7 to 52 days with the average being 19 days. In three instances where a record was kept, 35 out of a total of 118 patients on the Admissions Ward felt certain or at least suspected that the pseudo-patient was sane. The report indicates this did not occur at all among the staff.

There are several points to be made in regard to the Rosenhan study. It should be pointed out, of course, that one study involving a relatively small number of people does not provide conclusive proof of the conclusion it suggests. Nevertheless, it should be seen that this was an instance of 100% error occurring in a psychiatric setting where the questions being asked and answered were psychiatric questions, not, as is so often complained of by forensic psychiatrists, questions that the law should not ask of psychiatrists. Note also that the evaluations were of present mental condition, not past or future conditions.

Further, while the number is small, the unanimity of the outcome is striking.

It should be pointed out that the admission of a person who presents himself at a hospital requesting treatment is probably defensible. One can grant that the safest course for the physician in that situation is to place the individual under some kind of protective care even in the absence of clear indicators of need for treatment. Rosenhan, of course, argues that if in fact the normal are distinguishable from the abnormal, the physician should have been able to make such a distinction at the point of admission and suggested some other course of action to the individual. This seems to be a valid point of view in terms of what we know of overcrowded conditions in mental hospitals. It would seem to be a mistake of some seriousness to admit, in fact, to give a hospital place, to one who really does not need it. However, for our purposes, it is not necessary to resolve that particular issue. We could concede that it was appropriate for the physician to admit the "patient" as a precautionary measure without altering the basic conclusions to be derived from Rosenhan's data. To admit the patient is one thing. To diagnose the patient as schizophrenic (a diagnosis with potentially detrimental social and economic consequences) on the basis of a single symptom when such a diagnosis is at complete variance with all the other data presented by the patient is quite another matter. (See Klein and Davis, 1969; Assad and Shapiro, 1986; Bliss et al., 1983; and Stevenson, 1983 to the effect that hallucinations by themselves are not pathonomic of schizophrenia and occur in several other conditions.) Even beyond that, what is devastating in the Rosenhan data is the fact that at no time during the period of observation up to and including discharge of the patient did any of the professional staff perceive that the "patient" was not, and never had been, mentally ill, and certainly not schizophrenic. This is amply demonstrated by the fact that in each case where schizophrenia was the original diagnosis, when the final discharge came it was not noted as a diagnostic error. It was not noted, "disturbance, type unknown." In each case the discharge contained the notation, "*schizophrenia in remission.*"

There is still more in the Rosenhan study. A research and teaching hospital whose staff had heard of the Rosenhan findings reported above, but doubted that such an error could occur at their hospital, participated in a second experiment. The staff was informed that at some time during the next several months one or more pseudo-patients would attempt to be admitted into the psychiatric hospital. The staff members were asked to rate each patient who presented himself at Admissions or on the Ward according to the likelihood that he was a pseudo-patient. Judgments were obtained on 193 patients who were admitted for psychiatric treatment. All staff who had sustained contact with patients, including attendants, nurses, psychiatrists, physicians and psychologists were asked to make judgments. Forty-one out of 193 were alleged, with high confidence, to be pseudo-patients by at least one staff member. Twenty-three were considered suspect by at least one psychiatrist. In fact, no genuine pseudo-patient, at least from Rosenhan's group, presented himself during that period. Thus, 12% of the 193 admitted were actually misclassified by psychiatrists as pseudo-patients. Further, and obviously, the psychiatrists were wrong in 100% of these twenty-three cases they considered possible pseudo-patients.

Rosenhan further deals with the way the patient is perceived once he has been labeled schizophrenic. He states:

> Once a person is designated as abnormal, all of his other behaviors and characteristics are colored by that label. Indeed the label is so powerful that many of the pseudo-patients' normal behaviors were overlooked entirely or profoundly misinterpreted. Some examples may clarify this issue.
>
> Earlier I indicated that there were no changes in the pseudo-patient's personal history and current status beyond those of name, employment and where necessary vocation. Otherwise, a veridical description of personal history and circumstances were offered. Those circumstances were not psychotic. How were they made consonant with the diagnosis of psychosis? Or were those diagnoses modified in such a way as to bring them into accord with the circumstances of the pseudo-patient's life as described by him?
>
> As far as I can determine diagnoses were in no way affected by the relative health of the circumstances of a pseudo-patient's life. Rather, the reverse occurred. The perception of his circumstances was shaped entirely by the diagnosis. A clear example of such translation is found in the case of a pseudo-

patient who had a close relationship with his mother but was rather remote from his father during his early childhood. During adolescence and beyond, however, his father became a close friend while his relationship with his mother cooled. His present relationship with his wife was characteristically close and warm. Apart from occasional angry exchanges, friction was minimal. The children had rarely been spanked. Surely there is nothing especially pathological about such a history. Indeed, many readers may see a similar pattern in their own experience with no markedly deleterious consequences. Observe, however, how such a history was translated in a psycho-pathological context, this from the case summary prepared *after* (italics ours) the patient was discharged:

> This white 39-year-old male...manifests a long history of considerable ambivalence in close relationships which begins in early childhood. A warm relationship with his mother cools during his adolescence. A distant relationship to his father is described as becoming very intense. Affective stability is absent. His attempts to control emotionality with his wife and children are punctuated by angry outbursts and, in the case of the children, spankings. And, while he says that he has several good friends, one senses considerable ambivalence embedded in those relationships also...

The facts of the case were unintentionally distorted by the staff to achieve consistency with a popular theory of the dynamics of a schizophrenic reaction. Nothing of an ambivalent nature had been described in relations with parents, spouse or friends. To the extent that ambivalence could be inferred, it was probably not greater than is found in all human relationships. It is true the pseudo-patient's relationships with his parents changed over time, but in the ordinary context that would hardly be remarkable—indeed it might very well be expected. Clearly the meaning ascribed to his verbalizations (that is, ambivalence, affective instability) was determined by the diagnosis: schizophrenia. An entirely different meaning would have been ascribed if it were known that the man was 'normal.'

Most of the pseudo-patients, once settled into the ward, took notes, and apparently nobody particularly paid any attention to them. Rosenhan then raises the question, how was the writing interpreted in view of the fact that no questions were asked about what they were writing? Records for three patients indicate that writing was seen as an aspect of their pathological behavior. "Patient engages in writing behavior," was the daily nursing comment on one of the pseudo-patients who was never questioned about his writing. As another example, Rosenhan mentions, "One psychiatrist pointed to a group of patients who were sitting outside the cafeteria entrance half an hour before lunchtime. To a group of young residents, he indicated that such behavior was characteristic of the oral acquisitive nature of the syndrome. It seemed not to occur to him that there were very few things to anticipate in a psychiatric hospital besides eating."

Perceiving the Rosenhan study as a "potentially harmful study which might be influential in the psycholegal field" the editors of the *Journal of Psychiatry and Law* published a rebuttal to the Rosenhan article by

David L. Wolitzky, Ph.D. (1973), which the editors introduce by saying it is not a study specifically in the circumscribed area of the *Journal*'s general content but they feel it should be published there because if taken seriously, it (the Rosenhan study) could be quite influential. The principal thrust of Wolitzky's attack seems to be in terms of missing items of information. He states, "Important items of information seemingly available to Rosenhan are unaccountably absent from the report. Even if their addition were to strengthen rather than detract from the findings, his conclusion would remain untenable." (p. 466) While we can understand Wolitzky's complaint that certain additional items of information would have been desirable (as is true of virtually all published articles), we would have to take issue with his use of the term "unaccountably absent" with, what we would take to be, some rather negative implications involved in that terminology. There are many possible ways to "account" for the fact that considerable information which may or may not have been available to Dr. Rosenhan did not appear in the report. The most obvious of these is the consideration of space. As individuals who have served as editors on professional journal articles, we know that articles frequently must be trimmed and tailored to meet space requirements of a particular journal. People who write articles also know that and make an effort to be as brief as they can while still conveying an adequate description of their research. In addition to the need to omit some information in the interests of space, there is the matter of the particular thrust of the article as seen by the author of the article. In Rosenhan's article the major thrust was not the attack on psychiatric diagnosis but concern with what happens to patients who are thus mislabelled. A considerable portion of the article is devoted to that issue. What may have seemed, and perhaps understandably, important to Wolitzky, may have seemed less important to Rosenhan.

Some of the concerns raised by Wolitzky in his article apparently were answered by Rosenhan in reply to an inquiry from Wolitzky. For example, Wolitzky was concerned over the meaning of twelve admissions in terms of what it might mean if there were more than twelve attempts to enter hospitals. In other words, he was concerned that the meaning of the twelve admissions would be considerably less if there had been many attempts and only twelve were successful. However, in a footnote, he concedes that Rosenhan has informed him that the number of attempts was identical with the number of admissions, twelve out of twelve. Wolitzky raised a question which we also have raised in correspondence with Dr. Rosenhan and we both received the same answer. The question had to do with whether or not the diagnoses were being made by experienced or inexperienced psychiatrists and the answer that both of us received was that many of the pseudo-patients were admitted by quite experienced psychiatrists. (Of course, in view of the literature cited in Chapter 8 on Experience, the amount of experience does not appear to be a relevant variable, anyway.) This, of course, misses the whole point. The point is not merely that they were admitted. The point is that they were diagnosed as schizophrenic, and the diagnosis was never changed. Rosenhan reports the only conceivable basis on which the diagnosis could be made is the report of hearing voices and states that in all other respects the patients described the life of a perfectly sane, normal, well-functioning individual. Wolitzky argues that, in the absence of a verbatim report of the admission interview we cannot know what the bases were. We, of course, would be perfectly willing to go along with Wolitzky's argument here if he would be willing to throw out all of the psychiatric literature, upon which most of the psychiatric principles and diagnoses purport to be based, in which verbatim records of the material from which the principles have been formed is not given. We doubt that Dr. Wolitzky would be prepared to do that. We doubt that most psychiatrists would be prepared to do so either. This, of course, is a clear case of what Dr. Meehl (supra) in his objection to clinical case conferences has described as the double evidentiary standard. Sloppy evidence is acceptable to establish your point of view, but if another party wants to argue a contrary point of view that party must meet 110% of the requirements for rigorous scientific investigation.

A third argument advanced by Wolitzky is that, "While the pseudo-patient ceased simulating symptoms after admission how do we know that he behaved 'normally' afterward?" Then Wolitzky points out that there were tensions and stresses associated with being in the hospital and so on. Again, this misses the point, in our opinion. What Wolitzky is saying is there may have been some indications of uneasiness among the pseudo-patients. What Rosenhan is saying is not that there were no indications of uneasiness—he states that there were. What he is saying is, nevertheless, that the psychiatrists were unable to distinguish the fact that individuals involved in the study were not schizophrenic. A great many, if not most, people finding themselves in the unfamiliar position of being patients in a mental hospital, and knowing they were on their own to secure their release, would experience uneasiness or anxiety. One would expect that even a psychiatrist could comprehend that and not, as Wolitzky appears to be doing, use such reactions, which are perfectly normal in the situation, as justification for maintaining a diagnosis of severe psychopathology. Wolitzky simply provides another example of the "base rate" and "Barnum effect" problems.

The fourth point made by Wolitzky has to do with the reasonableness of admitting the patient and the reasonableness of not suspecting that someone has lied to get into a psychiatric ward. One can certainly go along with that notion, as we have already indicated. Wolitzky states, "The pseudo-patients did, after all, feign mental illness.[1] Certain forms of malingering are difficult to detect, especially without sufficient practice, experience or expectation. A medical disease that had a low rate of incidence and no striking signs would likewise be hard to diagnose." One might grant that, and ask what that has to do with schizophrenia, hardly a diagnosis with a low rate of incidence and no striking signs. More importantly, as is well known, some litigants who offer their mental condition as an issue are motivated to, and do, feign mental illness. Thus, the fact that the "pseudo-patients" were feigning in no way reduces the significance of the study so far as its relevance in the legal situation is concerned. Of course, the argument can be made that in the legal situation, the psychiatrist would have more reason to be suspicious and, therefore, more alert to possible feigning.[2]

It is also necessary to keep in mind the well-documented tendency of psychiatrists to see pathology where it does not exist. Further, in the Rosenhan study, the pseudo-patients stopped feigning immediately upon admission, so that at best, Wolitzky's point holds only for the initial diagnosis (and even then we must keep in mind that these were made on inadequate bases and in disregard of the strong counter-indicative data). Wolitzky deals with the cessation of feigning by pointing out that the fact that the pseudo-patient subsequently appeared to be in only a slightly agitated or even normal state is not adequate grounds for doubting the admitting staff's initial impressions, since schizophrenic patients do not constantly hallucinate or act bizarrely and often appear much improved following a few days of hospitalization.

However, if for this reason, as Wolitzky seems to argue, psychiatrists cannot distinguish a normal person from a schizophrenic in the hospital, it simply reemphasizes the importance of the original diagnostic error. His statement also seems to support the literature (see below) to the effect that because of these changes which occur, it is impossible to ascertain from an examination in the present under one set of circumstances, what an individual's mental condition was at another time under different circumstances.

Furthermore, if the pseudo-patients' absence of behavior indicating psychopathology, and particularly schizophrenia, coupled with the

---

[1] Wolitzky's declaration that "mental illness" was feigned can be challenged. The pseudopatients did not give a history indicating psychological disturbance but rather indicating "normality." They did not present a number of symptoms but only one kind of experience which can be, but (as indicated by Klein and Davis, as well as others) is not necessarily a symptom of "mental illness."

[2] See below, Chapter 18, for discussion of lack of evidence that clinicians can detect "faking," even in situations where it might be expected.

normality of their history, would not be adequate grounds for "doubting the initial impressions," we wonder what Wolitzky would consider adequate. If "normal" behavior coupled with a "normal" history is not sufficient to cause a psychiatrist even to doubt that a person suffers from a severe mental disease, how could it ever be established that a normal person is not mentally ill? Of course, as the Rosenhan results show, the people in his study were not able, on these bases, to convince the psychiatrists that they did not have a "mental disease."

In his fifth point, Wolitzky attempts to challenge the significance of the finding that 35 of 118 fellow patients perceived that the pseudo-patients were not mentally ill. He first says that there is no information given as to how these instances were distributed among the three pseudo-patients who recorded them. This does not seem to be a critical omission and one could assume some roughly equivalent distribution over the three patients. Wolitzky seems perfectly willing to make assumptions when such assumptions favor some point he wishes to establish. A more serious criticism would be his contention that we are not given any base rate information concerning the likelihood of patients insisting that fellow patients are sane and do not belong in a hospital. This shows that Dr. Wolitzky is acquainted with the base rate problem. We can only wonder why he did not see fit to raise this issue in connection with other arguments he has presented (for example, the proportion of "normals" who would experience anxiety when incarcerated in a mental hospital or the proportions of people who are not schizophrenic who have experienced a mild hallucination). This is another example of the "double standard" of evidence so prevalent in psychiatry and psychology. He seems to have chosen a poor situation in which to become concerned about base rates. We must apologize to the reader for the following statement, which departs from the principle we have tried to maintain of supplying documentation for what we say, but we find it difficult to just let the point pass. Few, if any, who have worked in or have any knowledge of mental hospitals would seriously contend that any more than a tiny fraction of patients would be likely to assert that a fellow patient is sane and does not belong in a hospital. Certainly, virtually no one would contend that the number, i.e., the base rate, could approach anything even approximating the nearly 1/3 that were reported in the Rosenhan study. Therefore, even if one were to assume that there is some base rate, by the wildest stretch of the imagination reaching to as much as 5% or 10%, still a considerable number above that base rate did perceive the "normality" of the pseudo-patients. Rosenhan's observations concerning the questions that arise when patients could perceive this and professional staff could not, stand. Finally, Wolitzky argues on this point that the pseudo-patients wanted to avoid the embarrassment of being exposed as fraud. "It seems a plausible assumption that the pseudo-patient feared detection by the staff more than he did by the patients and that he let his pose drop somewhat when he was with the other patients and the staff was not present." This is an example of Wolitzky's willingness to make an assumption when it suits his purposes and not Rosenhan's. In fact, the statement he makes is in direct contradiction to the facts as given by Rosenhan who states very clearly that, once in the hospital, the pseudo-patients, particularly in their relations with hospital staff, did everything to establish their sanity so that they could get out and that, further, their posing stopped immediately in all respects upon admission. Then Wolitzky argues that the other patients had more time to observe the pseudo-patients than the staff, and granted that that is true, nevertheless, one might expect the professionals would not need as much time as the patients to be able to recognize a normal from an abnormal state if, indeed, they have the capacity to do so, and while some patients might be able to do it, that still does not explain why the professionals could not do it. There is also research showing that a more extensive database does not necessarily lead to greater clinical judgment accuracy (see Chapter 5). Wolitzky's arguments on this particular point are exceedingly weak.

In his sixth point, Wolitzky questions the basis on which the pseudo-patients were finally discharged and asks whether it was done by the staff member who admitted them[3] and why the range was from 7 to 52 days. It can be conceded that it would be nice to have this information, and perhaps in a future study data of this kind will be built into it. However, while the questions are of interest, the fact that they are not answered in Rosenhan's study does not in any way vitiate his findings.

In the seventh point Wolitzky charges Rosenhan with drawing "almost sinister" implications from the fact that pseudo-patients were not discharged immediately upon announcing that they felt fine. He points out it is poor practice to discharge a patient who one day reports a serious complaint which disappears the next day. He concedes at the same time that an unnecessarily long stay is also bad practice. We find nothing in Rosenhan's report which would justify the pejorative allegation of "almost sinister" implications. Wolitzky questions the meaning of an average of nineteen days stay, asserting that two or three exceptionally long

---

[3] In a personal communication, Dr. Rosenhan has indicated discharge was in some cases made by an individual psychiatrist, in other cases, the discharge and accompanying diagnosis were made by consensus in case conferences attended by several psychiatrists. Whether the admitting psychiatrist was among them seems likely but is in any event irrelevant. Normal procedure for discharge involves a review of the record, so it is difficult to attach great significance to the involvement or non-involvement of the admitting psychiatrist. If the discharge diagnosis was made by other than the admitting psychiatrist, it just shows that still more psychiatrists made the same error.

stays could unduly influence the mean and points out that if there were three very long stays then the other nine could have averaged a little less than two weeks. Query: So what? This difference of a possible four or five days in the average period of stay is relevant to nothing. If two weeks is not enough for the psychiatrist to detect sanity, then neither is nineteen days. Wolitzky seems to be repeatedly seeking out the extreme conditions which would tend to impair Rosenhan's results. For example, he states that a couple of poorly run, understaffed hospitals could easily bias the overall results. One must assume that a scientist of Dr. Rosenhan's stature would report such unique occurrences, if they existed, as is normally expected in reports of this kind. It is not usually considered necessary to state *all* of the ways in which the results were not biased. The absence of statement is normally taken to mean that there was no such biasing apparent in the data. Obviously, there was no such biasing here as shown in Rosenhan's informal communication that the results on initial and discharge diagnosis were the same in all hospitals involved (with the exception of the one diagnosis of "depression").

Similarly, with the second part of the study involving the attempt to detect pseudo-patients when it was known some might appear, Wolitzky makes the same kinds of arguments as to absence of base rates, who was making the mistakes and so on. Again, he makes numerous assumptions as to what might have happened to establish his argument. Also, Wolitzky suggests that the error committed by psychiatrists with regard to 23 of the 193 patients hardly represents a massive error, but of course every identification of a pseudo-patient was wrong and there is no positive demonstration that malingering can be detected. At best, one can say that mistaken identification of actual patients (as far as we know) for pseudo-patients did not occur all too often.

In his ninth point, Wolitzky states that one cannot draw any conclusions concerning diagnostic ability of the psychiatrists in Rosenhan's study to distinguish sane from insane, one can only question their inability to distinguish "insane" from "feigned insane," quite a different matter. As stated before, this is relevant in the legal situation. This argument is, further, applicable only to the finding on the issue at the time of admission, and not at discharge. No "insanity" was feigned for a period of something like two weeks on the average. Thus it is appropriate to conclude that the psychiatrists in the study were unable to distinguish the "sane" from the "insane." If we were to grant all the "unknowns" and "assumptions" posited by Wolitzky, we should still expect a few of the psychiatrists to detect the "sanity" of a few of the pseudo-patients, if in fact such an ability exists among psychiatrists.

Also, in evaluating Wolitzky's comments, most of which appear to be insubstantial upon scrutiny, one must bear in mind that Rosenhan's study was published in *Science*, one of the most prestigious scientific journals in the nation. This does not guarantee its validity, but it seems quite unlikely that if the report was as defective as Wolitzky contends, the editors of that journal would have lacked the sophistication to perceive such defects and deny publication to the study.

Furthermore, Rosenhan's study should be viewed in the context of the extensive literature cited in this book to the effect that psychiatrists are not able to accurately assess mental condition or diagnose "mental illness." Seen in this perspective, Rosenhan's results are startling only in their unanimity. The occurrence of extensive psychiatric error is exactly what the literature would lead one to expect. Therefore, despite any tendentious attempts to refute or minimize this study, its potential impact in the courtroom remains. It is all the more important because it is a validity study in a field where the literature is virtually unanimous to the effect that validity studies are sadly lacking. Not only that, but it is a validity study which overcomes one of the most difficult issues in attempting such studies. That is, the criterion variable—the apparent normality of the subjects being diagnosed—is known, in contrast to other validity studies where the criterion variables, such as diagnoses of other psychiatrists or predictions of specific behavior, are themselves of unknown validity or contingent upon other conditions which may or may not be deemed to have occurred.

If the study has a serious weakness as evidence, it is that it has not been replicated. This weakness can be overcome to some extent by showing that the results are consonant with the general literature. Given the paucity of good research on the subject, Rosenhan's study must be considered one of the best pieces of evidence available to date—a landmark—on the issue of the psychiatrist's ability to accurately assess mental condition *in the present*. Twelve out of twelve wrong is easy for anyone to understand.

One further point. Should the expert, in responding to questions about the Rosenhan study, cite the complaints laid out by Wolitzky or any others, he can then be asked to cite published studies *supporting* the abilities of psychiatrists to make the evaluations in question which do not suffer from similar or equivalent or worse deficiencies. In other words, in such instance, the tactics can be to lead the psychiatrist to admit that he applies one standard of rigor to evidence which is in opposition to his position but applies a much less demanding standard to evidence which supports his position.[4]

---

[4] If a testifying psychiatrist attempts to discredit or diminish the significance of the Rosenhan study, it may be a good tactic to then follow up with questions concerning the vast ignorance of psychiatrists concerning schizophrenia (see Chapter 19). In particular, a psychiatrist who refuses to acknowledge the doubts about psychiatric diagnosis raised by

The continuing furor over the Rosenhan study, and reports we have received from lawyers who have used it extensively, amply justify the extended coverage given to it in this book. While his conclusions have not been without supporters, it is more important for the lawyer who wishes to use this study to attack psychiatric testimony to be aware of the nature of those publications which challenge Rosenhan's conclusions.

Most of the criticisms of the study are represented by a collection of articles published in the 1975 edition of the *Journal of Abnormal Psychology*. The editor of the journal provides the following note (p. 433) explaining this series of articles.

Editor's note. Diagnosis, classification, and labeling, which until recently at least were considered legitimate yet unexciting scientific activities, have come under increasing attack from diverse sources both within and outside psychology. Nondirective therapists, behavior modifiers, humanistic psychologists, minority group spokesmen, and measurement specialists have all inveighed against the unreliability, invalidity, and non-utility of these procedures, as well as against the impediments they place in the way of therapeutic progress and the destructive uses to which they have been put by society. The focus of this criticism has usually been the second edition of the American Psychiatric Association's *Diagnostic and Statistical Manual* (DSM-II) published in 1968. In 1973, David Rosenhan published, in another journal, a report of a field experiment which corroborated in a real-life situation the worst suspicions of the critics of psychiatric diagnosis: It is an unreliable, invalid, anachronistic, and socially destructive procedure. The five articles that follow deal with varied aspects of this research report.

The first article, by Bernard Weiner, was submitted to this Journal as a critique of the Rosenhan study; the other papers were subsequently solicited by the Editor in order to obtain a wider range of response from practicing clinicians and academic psychologists both to the critique by Weiner and the original study by Rosenhan. Robert Spitzer, author of the second paper, is a psychiatrist

---

the Rosenhan study may find himself on the defensive, if confronted with the following study: Taylor, M.A., Gaztanaga, P., and Abrams, R. (1974). Manic-Depressive Illness and Acute Schizophrenia: A Clinical, Family History, and Treatment-Response Study, *American Journal of Psychiatry*, Vol. 131, No. 6, pp. 678-682. Taylor et al. found that out of 26 consecutive patients admitted to an inpatient psychiatric unit with a diagnosis of acute schizophrenia, only one met research criteria for that diagnosis. All 26 were found to be diagnosable in some category of mental disorder (13 manic, 5 reactive psychosis, 3 personality disorder, 3 alcoholic state, 1 organic brain syndrome, and 1 schizophrenic) so the study is not directly comparable to Rosenhan's. If the psychiatrist has acknowledged the *American Journal of Psychiatry* as an authoritative source he relies on (see Chapter 7, Volume III, Cross-Examination), as is likely, but still insists that psychiatrists can diagnose accurately, then this finding of 25 wrong out of 26, following Rosenhan's findings of 12 wrong out of 12, should enable judge or jury to see the light. It should be apparent to them that psychiatric diagnosis is extremely inaccurate and that the particular witness refuses to admit what the literature shows. See also: Plag and Arthur (72% error); Steadman (The Baxstrom Study, 97% error); Egan et al. (82% error); Temerlin and Trousdale (100% error).

who participated in the development of the DSM-II and is currently chairman of the committee working on the development of the third edition, expected to be published in 1978. The third paper is by Sidney Crown, a psychiatrist and psychologist who practices in England. Theodore Millon, a Consulting Editor of this Journal and a consultant to the aforementioned American Psychiatric Association committee, is the author of the fourth paper. In the fifth paper, David Rosenhan is given the opportunity to respond to the four preceding articles. Finally, in the December issue the whole symposium will be summarized and evaluated by I.E. Farber, who is also a Consulting Editor of this Journal.

Leonard D. Eron, Editor

Some of these credentials are noteworthy. In the case of Spitzer and Millon, it seems obvious that they have a participatory interest in the APA *Diagnostic and Statistical Manual.* Obviously, it is appropriate to include individuals from this area in a discussion of this subject. Nevertheless, a question of possible bias can legitimately be raised. Needless to say, the same question would be applicable to Rosenhan's rejoinder.

It should be noted at the outset that none of the critics seriously contend that the psychiatric diagnoses in this study were not 100% wrong. The major thrust of these critiques is that, depending on which critic one is reading, the diagnoses were at the minimum defensible and at the maximum, correct, given the data presented by the pseudo-patients at the time they applied to the various hospitals. If so, it is argued, Rosenhan's conclusions as to the inability to distinguish sane from insane and as to the valuelessness of psychiatric diagnoses are vitiated. A second thrust has to do with the significance of the discharge diagnosis "schizophrenia in remission." It might be pointed out that it is probably unfortunate that Rosenhan chose to use the term "sane" and "insane" as it is well recognized that these are legal and not psychiatric terms. Terms such as "mentally disordered" and "non-mentally disordered" might have been better. It is certainly clear that the term "schizophrenic" and "non-schizophrenic" would provide a narrower base for Rosenhan's more general conclusions without necessarily invalidating them.

In defense of the erroneous original diagnosis of schizophrenia, the critics point to three pieces of data as supporting the diagnosis. These are: (1) the report of hallucinatory experiences, (2) "nervousness" displayed by the pseudo-patients, and (3) the fact of seeking admission to a mental hospital. There appears to be little quarrel with the proposition that the admission of individuals presenting themselves to a mental hospital with declarations of some psychological disturbance was as the only humane, medically proper, and, probably from a malpractice standpoint, safe thing to do. The controversy revolves around the diagnosis of schizophrenia. Therefore, the reader should be aware of at least one alternative diagnosis which the admitting staff could have made. That diagnosis is "DSM-II, 319.0 Diagnosis deferred." Rosenhan asserts this would have been a much preferred classification in this instance and some of the critics indicate that they do not disagree with that point.

Let us now turn our attention to the elements presented in these and other articles in defense of the diagnosis. In order to understand the arguments which follow, the reader needs to have before him the description of schizophrenia as stated in DSM-II (keeping in mind the following statement contained in the foreword to DSM-II with regard to schizophrenia: "Even if it had tried, the committee could not establish agreement about what this disorder is; it could only agree on what to call it.")[5]

DSM-II 295. Schizophrenia

This large category includes a group of disorders manifested by characteristic disturbances of thinking, mood, and behavior. Disturbances in thinking are marked by alterations of concept formation which may lead to misinterpretation of reality and sometimes to delusions and hallucinations which frequently appear psychologically self-protective. Corollary mood changes include ambivalence, constricted and inappropriate emotional responsiveness and loss of empathy with others. Behavior may be withdrawn, regressive and bizarre.

The following will also be relevant to the discussion:

DSM-II 296.2 Manic depressive illness, depressed type. (Manic depressive psychosis, depressed type.)

This disorder consists exclusively of depressive episodes. These episodes are characterized by severely depressed mood and by mental and motor retardation progressing occasionally to stupor. Uneasiness, apprehension, perplexity and agitation may also be present. When illusions, hallucinations and delusions (usually of guilt or hypochondriacal or paranoid ideas) occur they are attributable to the dominant mood disorder....

The critics are in general agreement that the single symptom of hallucinatory experience is not pathonomic of schizophrenia. Therefore, the defense of the diagnosis proceeds on different lines. Spitzer's argument is well organized and, as it appears fairly representative of the others, it is the one that we will focus on here. He points out that the clinical picture not only included the symptom but also the desire to enter a psychiatric hospital, giving the reasonable conclusion that the symptom was a source of significant stress. He also points out that there was knowledge that the auditory hallucinations had occurred over a three-week period which he asserts establishes them as significant symptoms of psychopathology, distinguishing them from so-called "pseudohallucinations" which he describes as hallucinations occurring while falling asleep or awakening from sleep or intense imagination with the voice heard from

---

[5] DSM-II was in use at the time of the Rosenhan study. Should the expert claim that DSM-III resolves the diagnostic problems evident during the time of the Rosenhan study, the discussion of DSM-III in Chapter 4 will provide powerful counterpoints.

inside of one's head. He then points out that such hallucinations can occur in several kinds of mental disorders, proceeding to rule out alcohol, drug abuse, or some other toxin, physical illness and organic psychosis as well as transient situational disturbances of psychotic intensity because there was no recent precipitating stress. He states: "The absence of a profound disturbance in mood rules out an affective psychosis (we are not given the mental status findings for the patient who is diagnosed manic-depressive psychosis)." (p. 446) He then points to the possibility of simulating mental illness but correctly points out in this situation there was no reason to believe the pseudo-patients had anything to gain from hospital admission except relief and therefore no reason to suspect malingering. He then states: "Dear reader: There is only one remaining diagnosis for the presenting symptom of hallucinations under these conditions in the classification of mental disorders used in this country and that is schizophrenia." (p. 446) This appears to be an error, as he has not ruled out "hysteria," another condition in which hallucinations may occur, according to both Klein and Davis, supra, and Bliss et al. (1983). This argument fails on any one of three different bases. To begin with, Rosenhan in his rejoinder points out:

> This is, of course, diagnosis by exclusion and it makes schizophrenia a waste basket diagnosis, a designation to be applied when nothing else fits. One would not have judged as much from the quotation offered above from the DSM-II but perhaps in practice (and with sanction) it is. If that is the case, readers will judge for themselves whether the designation is useful, whether it constitutes a diagnosis in any sense of that term and how likely it is for misdiagnoses to occur under such conditions. (p. 467)

There is a further flaw which lends support to Rosenhan's "waste basket" contention. Spitzer rules out affective psychosis (of which manic-depressive psychosis is one) on the grounds that one of the critical elements, "profound disturbance in mood," is absent. We may note in connection with manic-depressive psychosis, that two of the remaining manifestations—uneasiness, or apprehension (described by the critics as "nervousness") and hallucinations—are present while only one manifestation of schizophrenia—hallucinations—is present. Note that the major manifestation of schizophrenia is described as "characteristic disturbances of thinking, mood and behavior." Further, "disturbances in thinking are marked by alterations of concept formation which may lead to misinterpretation of reality and sometimes to delusions and hallucinations, etc. Corollary mood changes include ambivalence, constricted and inappropriate emotional responsiveness and loss of empathy with others. Behavior may be withdrawn, aggressive and bizarre." Note that everything descriptive of schizophrenia except hallucination is absent in these records. Therefore, applying the same procedure as he did to affective psychosis, Spitzer *must* also rule out schizophrenia. Virtually everything that constitutes this "disease" is absent. For example, using the same process for ruling out alternative explanations for the hallucinations, if Spitzer had first dealt with schizophrenia before considering manic-depressive psychosis, he would have had to rule out schizophrenia and then the only statement he could have made on which to base a diagnosis would have been: "Dear reader: There is only one remaining diagnosis for the presenting symptom of hallucinations under these conditions in the classification of mental disorders used in this country and that is manic-depressive psychosis."

Spitzer admits as much in the paragraph which immediately follows his "dear reader" statement.

> Admittedly, there is a hitch to a definitive diagnosis of schizophrenia: almost invariably there are other signs of the disorder present, such as poor pre-morbid adjustment, affective blunting, delusions or signs of thought disorder. I would hope that if I had been one of the twelve psychiatrists presented with such a patient, I would have been struck by the lack of other signs of the disorder, but I am rather sure that having no reason to doubt the authenticity of the patient's claim of auditory hallucinations, I also would have been fooled into noting schizophrenia as the most likely diagnosis.

In other words, what Spitzer is saying is that he would make a diagnosis of schizophrenia that would be almost totally unrelated to the description of that disease as given in DSM-II. We can think of no greater indictment demonstrating the utter uselessness of this previous system of psychiatric classification, a system only questionably improved upon by DSM-III, than that such a statement should come from a man who is one of its architects.

The "second flaw" in Spitzer's argument is related to the first. Given that the hallucinatory experience is not sufficient to justify the diagnosis of schizophrenia, except on Spitzer's exclusionary argument, one fallacy of which is already shown, there is another fallacy. Goldstein (1976) provides an example of hallucinatory experience occurring in an individual demonstrably within the range of "normality." More importantly, he cites scientific and professional literature to the effect that hallucinatory experiences do occur in "normal" individuals. He cites Holden (1973): "Now mind researchers are discovering that a large number of individuals with healthy non-drugged minds have occasional 'extraordinary' perceptions that were rarely recorded because such perceptions have been regarded as deviant."

Goldstein asserts:

> Even a quick search of the older literature indicates prior support for this recent "discovery." For example, Galton (1907) (Galton, F. *Inquiries into Human Faculty and Its Development*, New York, Dutton, 1907) reports, almost casually, numerous cases of psychiatrically sound individuals who experienced

hallucinations. Other examples could be cited. The point is we have known for a long time that unusual sensory experiences are not symptomatic of psychosis in the same way, for example, increased blood sugar level is indicative of diabetes. A systematic investigation of hallucinatory behavior could provide insights into the issues discussed here.

Asaad and Shapiro (1986) review the literature on hallucinations and indicate that the notion that hallucinations are to be equated with schizophrenia is clearly unfounded and in fact hallucinations, by themselves, can never be considered diagnostic of any disorder. They further observe that a number of studies show that hallucinations occur among people who are not mentally ill or suffering from major mental disorders.

Stevenson (1983) states, "Most people who have hallucinations are not in any way mentally ill. Many members of the general population seem to have had one or several memorable hallucinatory experiences." (p. 1609) Stevenson discusses different studies which show an incident rate of 10% to 27% for hallucinatory experiences among members of the general population, a frequency that is obviously *much* higher than that reported for schizophrenic disorders. Thus, if the one and only reported "symptom" is hallucinations and the diagnostician needs to select between "schizophrenia" versus no mental disorder, the odds are apparently much greater that the correct choice is no mental disorder as opposed to schizophrenia. This point is further strengthened when one considers the guidelines Stevenson provides for separating hallucinations associated with abnormal conditions versus no mental disorder. Stevenson indicates that hallucinations accompanying abnormality are typically associated with other symptoms of abnormality (e.g., decreased awareness of one's surroundings), whereas hallucinations seen among normal individuals usually present in the absence of other psychiatric symptomatology— they are isolated events.

Krier (1989), in a feature article in the *Los Angeles Times* quotes a faculty psychologist and a faculty psychiatrist to the effect that significant numbers of "normal" people have heard voices and that it is not necessarily psychotic.

Bentall (1990), reviewing research on hallucination, much of it in the 1980's, summarized the findings as indicating that approximately 10% of "normals" experience hallucinations.

When considered together, the implication of these different reports seems rather straightforward. Given that the *pseudo-patients in the Rosenhan study reported hallucinations alone and showed no other signs of schizophrenia,* either no diagnosis or assumption of normality were more likely or much more likely possibilities than schizophrenia. At the very minimum, on the basis of the reported symptoms alone, one could not "rule in" schizophrenia by exclusion before first excluding the possibility of normality.

The second and third elements—the fact of seeking admission to a psychiatric hospital and the nervousness displayed in connection therewith—can be disposed of rather briefly. We live in a society which has been highly sensitized to any possible indication of psychological disturbance by both the psychiatric profession and the media. Although we could expect psychiatrists to be reasonably familiar with the literature indicating that hallucinations may occur in the normal population, there is no reason to hold that expectation of laymen. Therefore, the seeking of admission to the mental hospital is simply nothing more than one might reasonably expect from an individual who has cause to suspect that he *might* be suffering from some kind of disorder. If anything, it represents sensible thinking rather than the "disordered thinking" that is supposed to be characteristic of schizophrenia. (If and when questioned as to why they did not consult their personal physicians, the pseudo-patients responded according to plan that they did not have one and came to the hospital because they heard that it was "a good one.") Nervousness upon approaching any kind of hospital, mental or otherwise, with concern over a possible disease or disorder, mental or otherwise, again illustrates the base rate problem. What percentage of the normal population, coming to a hospital under such circumstances, could be expected to display "nervousness"? We do not have a statistical answer to that question and doubt that the profession of psychiatry has the answer to that question either. But we think many of us would share the common observation that many of us and our acquaintances are nervous and apprehensive when we go to a hospital to have an evaluation of some possible disease, be it heart trouble, kidney trouble, pneumonia or psychological disturbance. We imagine that many members of a jury would be nodding their heads in agreement with this proposition if it were presented to them. In fact, a better case for the diagnosis of schizophrenia could have been made had the pseudo-patients exhibited no nervousness whatsoever. Our experience in reading a great number of forensic psychiatric reports supports that, had that been the case, the admitting psychiatrist would have noted this as "lack of affect," "bland affect," "inappropriate affect," "blunting of affect" or some similar term which might then convey the presence of "inappropriate emotional responsiveness" as given in the description of schizophrenia. Based upon the foregoing, it seems blatantly clear that neither the application to the hospital nor its accompanying nervousness in any way whatsoever supported the diagnosis of schizophrenia and, if anything, contraindicated it. With regard to the initial diagnosis of schizophrenia, Rosenhan's assertion that "any diagnostic process that lends itself so readily to massive errors of this sort cannot be a very reliable one" stands. In fact, the point gains even further emphasis from Spitzer's statement:

> Is Rosenhan's point that the psychiatrists should have used "diagnosis deferred" a category that is available but is rarely used? I would have no argument with this conclusion. (p. 447)

This provides another example of the widely recognized and reported propensity of psychiatrists to overdiagnose pathology. With only minimal evidence which nearly all of the critics agree was insufficient, the psychiatrists chose to label the pseudo-patients with a diagnosis of a disease whose definition is vague and tenuous and whose very existence is under serious question, but which nevertheless carries serious stigma and social consequences for an individual so labeled, even though they had the much less severe or serious alternative of classifying the patients as "diagnosis deferred."

A second point made by some of the critics is that if an error was made it was corrected by the discharge diagnosis "schizophrenia in remission."[6] They cite this as a refutation of Rosenhan's assertion that even after a fair period of observation the psychiatrists were not able to discern that the pseudo-patients were in fact "normal" and not suffering from mental illness, particularly schizophrenia. This point is nonsense. All the term "in remission" means is that the person is no longer *displaying* the symptoms of the disease. Schizophrenia, unlike pneumonia or a broken leg, is rarely, if ever, referred to as "cured" by practitioners or in the scientific and professional literature. In answer to Rosenhan's assertion that a broken leg is something one recovers from but mental illness allegedly endures forever, Spitzer declares: "But neither any psychiatric text book nor the American Psychiatric Association's *Diagnostic and Statistical Manual of Mental Disorders* (American Psychiatric Association, 1968) suggests that mental illness endures forever." (p. 447)

Then he accuses Rosenhan of making his statement without any reference to psychiatric literature and raises the question, "Who other than Rosenhan alleges it?" To illustrate his point, he then states: "Thus the *Diagnostic and Statistical Manual* in describing the sub-type, acute schizophrenic episode states that 'in many cases the patient recovers within weeks.'" (p. 447)

Confidence in Spitzer's objectivity is shaken by his partial quote which fails to convey the implications given in DSM-II. The full quote from the manual is as follows: "In many cases the patient recovers within

---

6 Rosenhan states: "Actually eight of the patients were discharged in remission, three as improved and one as asymptomatic. The latter two designations imply less a perception of change than does the phrase 'in remission' but all three descriptors reify the original diagnosis." Rosenhan, op. cit.

weeks but sometimes their disorganization becomes progressive. *More frequently, remission is followed by recurrence.*" (italics added)

By any reasonable interpretation, that statement asserts that the best prediction one can make regarding a person diagnosed schizophrenic is that he will continue to have recurrence of the symptoms of the disease, and that "in remission" does not mean that the disease is cured or gone, it only means that the symptoms have been temporarily controlled. Thus, as one of the architects of the DSM-II, Spitzer ought to know the answer to his question: "Who other than Rosenhan alleges it?"

But all of this begs the real issue. Does anyone really believe the label "schizophrenia" does not carry with it a considerable burden? Applications for employment, insurance applications, and so on frequently require information as to any prior "mental disease," and if the applicant answers honestly, does anyone believe that his declaration that he was discharged "schizophrenia in remission" will allay the fears and concerns of those who have requested the information? It would probably be an unusual employer who would employ one who, according to DSM-II or DSM-III, has a high probability of recurring schizophrenia symptoms. It would seem obvious that the phrase "in remission" does not mean that the psychiatrist was finally able to discern that these individuals were not and had not been schizophrenic. The only way that could be accomplished would be with a diagnostic statement clearly eradicating the original diagnosis and substituting for it some less pejorative label or a classification that would indicate the actual fact which was, to wit: "diagnosis unknown." If the diagnosis does not fit the facts, it simply should not be made. To make the diagnosis in the absence of supporting facts is, in effect, to deny or distort the facts as they are. We would add to the foregoing, for what little value it has, our own experience in consulting in cases of "psychic injury" where the diagnosis was schizophrenia. Invariably, in those cases the psychiatrists have asserted that the individuals would suffer disabilities associated with schizophrenia for the remainder of their lives.

For present purposes it is useful to note that Spitzer and Millon, both of whom are involved in the production of the diagnostic and statistical manual, provide support for some of the findings or implications asserted by Rosenhan. Spitzer states:

> Rosenhan presents one way in which the diagnosis affected the psychiatrist's perception of the patient's circumstances: historical facts of the case were often distorted by the staff to achieve consistency with psycho-dynamic theories. Here for the first time, I believe, Rosenhan has hit the mark. What he described happens all the time and often makes attendance at clinical case conferences extremely painful, especially for those with a logical mind and a research orientation. (p. 448)

He then presents an explanation for this on the basis that the clinicians are "human." For legal purposes, it is obviously the fact that such distortions occur "all the time" and not the reasons for their occurrence, that is significant.[7]

Millon commends Rosenhan for alerting and stirring up "an all too often complacent profession." He then states:

> First there is a slavish adherence to an outmoded psychiatric nomenclature and classificatory system, one devoid of an internal logic, consisting of overlapping and unreliable categories and totally lacking in specific inclusion and exclusion criteria. Second, facile yet immutable diagnostic judgments are made on the basis of flimsy behavioral data, generated largely by transient circumstance, colored by contextual setting and situational expectation, and interpreted in line with preformed theoretical and ideological biases of dubious validity. Third, procedures of semi-arbitrary diagnostic labeling not only contributed significantly to the dehumanizing experiences that debase institutional life, but set the stage for enduring self-fulfilling prophecies.

A final article in this series appeared in the next issue of the *Journal of Abnormal Psychology*. Farber (1975) challenges Rosenhan's conclusion in a number of respects. Much of the article is devoted to what we would describe as a discussion of the philosophy of science. He asserts that the study does not prove the points that Rosenhan makes. We have no dispute with this, having already stated the study does not constitute proof, merely an understandable illustration in a real-life setting to add to the several other studies, more of a laboratory type, which also show "massive" error by mental health professionals. He indicates a number of reasons for the misdiagnoses, mostly dealing with Rosenhan's attack on the diagnostic system, which was then DSM-II. In several instances his arguments are stated either in terms of lack of knowledge of some variables which could be important (i.e., the competence or experience of the mental hospital psychiatrists, but see Tarter et al. wherein the psychiatrists were "the best") or upon assumptions about things that "may" have happened. He does note that large banks of configural information do not

---

[7] Lando, H.A. On Being Sane in Insane Places: A Supplemental Report, *Professional Psychology*, February 1976, pp. 47-52, states (p. 52): "The issue is not that staff failed to overtly detect my simulation but rather they actively misinterpreted behavior that would be viewed as normal in a different context. Thus, virtually all of my interactions with both patients and staff as well as my note taking were interpreted in the light of the admitting diagnosis....Additional evidence was gained concerning the potential harm of psychiatric labeling in leading to misattributions of behavior." (Lando was actually a ninth pseudo-patient whose data were not included in the original report for reasons stated elsewhere.)

exist and that even if they did, "different clinicians, by virtue of variation in ability, training sets, and settings, all those indubitably powerful contextual factors emphasized by Rosenhan, would vary in regard to their apprehension and use of the information, all of which contribute to the possibility of error."

With regard to the failure to use the diagnosis "diagnosis deferred" in the face of an incomplete or ambiguous presenting picture, he offers some explanations (not justifications) but agrees that in general, "people in the clinical business have a tendency to overpathologize." To be consistent with the general polemic tone of this entire set of discussion, we would point out Farber's statement (p. 610) that the use of "diagnosis deferred" would not have been more accurate than the diagnosis of schizophrenia. We find this strange. The diagnosis of schizophrenia was wrong in 100% of the cases so far as anyone knows. If the diagnosis was indeed deferred, to so state would appear to us to have been correct, or at least not incorrect, in 100% of the cases. We would grant that the diagnosis would not convey a lot of information about the patients, except that there was not a clear diagnostic picture, but it would have been sufficient to admit them to the hospitals, which almost everyone agrees was the right thing to do under the circumstances. We find it hard to believe that it is better (or equivalent) to be wrong most of the time than to acknowledge that one does not know. Even if treatment has to be initiated, this has been and can be done on the basis of a tentative opinion or even on an exploratory basis.

After all the polemics and displays of intellectual sharpness, the facts remain as they were. Using what nearly all admit was insufficient evidence, the psychiatrists were wrong in 100% of the cases, a figure they have approached in several other studies.

A few words of advice for the lawyer who would use the Rosenhan study in his challenge to psychiatric testimony. First of all, the study does not "prove" the uselessness of psychiatric diagnoses for legal purposes. No one study could do that. This is particularly true because of the limited generalization that is allowable in view of the "pseudo-patient" aspects of the study, particularly as many of the pseudo-patients were themselves mental health professionals. Its usefulness to the lawyer lies in the remarkable and dramatic illustration of the degree of error involved in psychiatric diagnosis. Therefore, it should be presented not as "the definitive study" but rather as a graphic illustration of the low level of accuracy of psychiatric evaluations as abundantly documented in the literature.

If a testifying psychiatrist attempts to refute the Rosenhan findings by reference to the arguments advanced by Wolitzky, Spitzer, or others, this attempt can be met with questions concerning studies in the literature which show the low reliability and validity of psychiatric evaluations and the deficiencies of the clinical examination. For example, the report of Temerlin and Trousdale (1969) is cogent in this regard. In the Temerlin and Trousdale study, in complete contrast to the Rosenhan study, an individual did not "fake" mental illness nor present any symptoms, but nevertheless, because of a suggestion that other psychiatrists had found him "mentally ill," 100% of the psychiatrists in the study diagnosed mental illness. This and other studies demonstrating frequent error provide additional data in line with Rosenhan's findings. Regarding the argument "there was no reason to suspect faking or malingering," the materials in Chapter 18 (assessing malingering) show that psychopathology can be "faked" successfully, and there is an absence of research evidence showing that psychiatrists can detect "faking" even in situations where there is reason to suspect it. At some point in cross-examination, should a psychiatrist attempt to maintain this defense, it will become clear to a jury that he is irrationally defending an indefensible position.

Some of the critics (Spitzer included) defend the poor quality of psychiatric diagnosis by pointing out that there are a number of instances of medical diagnosis which are equally poor. We do not possess the medical knowledge with which to evaluate that assertion. However, we fail to see where it would have any relevance to the forensic use of psychiatric evaluations. To begin with, we have reported research which shows that laymen can and do assess mental condition as well as psychiatrists but we are not aware of research showing that laymen can or do make medical diagnoses. Also, the argument that psychiatric evidence should be admitted because "it is not any worse" than some medical evidence, can be turned around. That is, on this argument astrologers and tea leaf readers should be allowed to testify as experts on mental condition because their conclusions may be equally poor as those of psychiatrists. Expertise cannot be established by showing that others are equally inexpert.

CHALLENGING DESCRIPTIONS, POSTDICTIONS, AND PREDICTIONS

In addition to specific diagnoses, a psychiatric or psychological evaluation may result in attempts to describe or explain behavior, or to postdict or predict mental status or behavior. Given the limited value of diagnosis by itself in addressing or answering issues or questions of forensic relevance, research on postdiction and prediction is arguably of great relevance. (DSM-III-R and DSM-IV note cautions for forensic application, as described in Chapter 4.) The majority of work on this area has focused on clinical issues, although a body of research is now emerging on predictions or postdictions directly relevant to forensic concerns. We will start by reviewing general commentary on the ability of clinicians to formulate accurate descriptions or predictions, and then briefly mention commentary and research in specific areas, in particular child custody and dangerousness.

As regards the overall capacity of practitioners to describe and predict, Thorne (1972) states:

> A major source of clinical error is in attempting to make clinical judgments for which no logical basis exists. The clinician must know what is and what is not possible in terms of the status of clinical judgment knowledge available at time and place. (p. 33)

And referring to several previous research studies:

> The significance of these studies…is that clinical judges tend to handle information differently and that many are purely idiosyncratic in their decisions as to weighing and assessing cues. The general research finding is that there will be almost as many judgments as there are clinicians. This is a deplorable state of affairs from the standpoint of establishing clinical practice as "being scientific." Until higher reliabilities may be demonstrated on clinical judges interpreting the same data it must be concluded that most clinicians are in a prescientific state of professional competency. (p. 61)

In young sciences such as clinical psychology and psychiatry where there are almost as many theoretical orientations as there are clinicians, it is inevitable that theoretical disagreements must result in great inferential bias and judgmental unreliability. (p. 66)

Goldberg (1968b) states:

> Historically, the earliest research efforts centered on the accuracy of such clinical judgments….Studies of the accuracy of these judgments have yielded rather a discouraging conclusion….Equally disheartening, there is now a host of studies demonstrating that the amount of information available to the judge is not related to the accuracy of his resulting inferences….If one considers the rather typical findings that clinical judgments tend to be a) rather unreliable (in at least two of the three senses of that term), b) only minimally related to the confidence and amount of experience of the judge, c) relatively unaffected by the amount of information available to the judge, and d) rather low in validity on an absolute basis, it should come as no great surprise that judgments are increasingly under attack by those who wish to substitute actuarial prediction systems for the human judge in many applied settings. (p. 485)

Sechrest et al. (1967) state, "the generally low level of accuracy in clinical predictions, whether by experts or novices, is by now so well known as to not need documentation." Stuart (1970) cites many earlier studies showing no meaningful differences in accuracy in the judgments of psychologists and psychiatrists in comparison to laymen. Stuart indicates that research examining the relationship between experience and accuracy is mixed, with some of the studies showing that it may aid judgment under some circumstances and others showing that experience may be associated with decreased judgment accuracy. Liberman et al. (1971) indicate that in their follow-up of men recommended for classification as unfit for military service, the vast majority of them were functioning adequately in civilian life.

Eichman (1972) states:

> Arguments in favor of a more automated, actuarial, or cookbook approach are numerous. Exhaustive, individual assessment has proved to be prohibitive in cost for many clinical installations. Currently many psychologists have become disenchanted with (a) the social purposes to which assessment is put (e.g., psychiatric diagnosis), (b) current personality theory and/or models of psychopathology, and (c) the validity of the techniques themselves.

Hoch and Zubin (1962) state, "If we admit to begin with, that we have no solid basis for making predictions in psychopathology, why do we engage in them?" (p. viii)

Hoch and Zubin then go on to answer their question in terms of the value even of erroneous predictions for the education of the profession. This may be so, but educating psychiatrists does not justify use of such predictions in court.

In the October, 1975, issue of the CASPP/CSPA *Joint Newsletter* (p. 41), Dr. Paul Clement, (then) president of the California State Psychological Association, stated in his presidential message: "Psychologists are involved in marketing a wide range of techniques and programs, most of which have never been empirically validated. The failure to apply even the simplest procedures for evaluating what psychologists do would be both illegal and unethical if it weren't for the fact that other mental health professions and the public at large have been even more irresponsible regarding validation than psychologists have been."

Shaffer (1981) describes some of the complications involved in disability determinations, indicating that many mental health service providers take an overly simplistic view of disability and equate it with such terms as handicap, injury, or impairment. Shaffer also raises concerns about potential bias, and he argues that reliable and valid determinations demand strict neutrality on the part of evaluators (although he does not indicate how this strict neutrality is to be achieved). In a statement pertinent to "the gap," he states, "diagnosis per se is only of secondary or incidental importance, and then only to the extent that it has implications for the primary issues of severity and duration." (p. 5) He describes as "formidable" the problems created when the clinician must attempt to combine information that concerns lesser degrees of impairment in several areas to reach an overall determination of impairment. Shaffer goes on to provide clinical guidelines, but he notes, "although much has been written about psychological factors in disability, comparatively few authors have discussed such factors in the context of disability assessment per se, especially with regard to the reliability and validity of the determinations rendered." (p. 6) He observes that other studies have shown high frequencies of abnormality, or abnormal testing results, even among applicants for disability not claiming an emotional basis. In discussing the use of the MMPI in this context, Shaffer indicates that he purposely uses such descriptors as "potential" and "explored" because "precious little research has been done, either with or without the MMPI, on the subject of disability." (p. 7) He further notes that allegations and work history hold little relationship with impairment severity as objectively assessed, and that studies show that highly motivated individuals who do meet medical criteria for severe impairment may still maintain gainful employment.

Livermore et al. (1968) state:

> Without digressing into the merits of that controversy, we cannot avoid at least uttering two caveats for the benefit of our law trained readers who will in general be unfamiliar with the relevant research literature by now very considerable in scope. First, one should not simply assume as somehow obvious that "individual prediction" is fundamentally different from "actuarial prediction," a quick and easy distinction very commonly presupposed in many quarters. Second, one should not simply assume that intensive psychological understanding of the individual leads generally to more trustworthy forecast of behavior than a more behavioristic actuarial approach to the predictive task. This second assumption seems still to be taken blithely for granted by almost all psychiatrists and—surprisingly, given the research evidence—by many clinical psychologists. The comparative efficacy of different methods of predicting behavior is of course a factual question; and in spite of the armchair plausibility of the above mentioned assumptions (to be skeptical of "understanding the individual" is rather like being against motherhood) there exists a very sizable body of empirical evidence to the contrary.

They state further:

> Probably the most pernicious error is committed by those who classify as "sick" behavior that is *aberrant neither in a statistical sense* nor in terms of any defensible biological or medical criteria but rather on the basis of the clinician's personal ideology of mental health and interpersonal relationships. Examples might be the current psychiatric stereotype of what a good mother or a healthy family must be like or the rejection as "perverse" of forms of sexual behavior that are not biologically harmful, are found in many infra-human animals, in diverse cultures and have a high statistical frequency in our own society. (p. 79)

These continuing problems in reliability and validity would seem to make an earlier statement by Rotter (1967) almost equally relevant today. Rotter argues that clinicians should not so much try to impress individuals, students in particular, with how much they know. Rather, they should point out limits in their knowledge and use the awareness of these limits to launch needed research. Rotter states:

It seems reasonable in the light of the lack of established validity for the particular uses to which most of our clinical instruments are employed, that we need to start training graduate students in clinical psychology by impressing them not with how knowledgeable the experts are, but rather how much everyone has to learn in order to achieve a reasonable prediction. It is an interesting aside that many times when a graduate student arrives at an internship with a reasonable skepticism regarding the validity of the tests in use at that clinic or hospital, this is perceived as a lack of preparation on his part as a result of inadequate training from the university. Often the skeptical attitude is negatively reinforced. The field of clinical psychology has grown and professionalized very rapidly. In many instances, the clinical psychologist is on the defensive because he has been accepted as being able to do more than he actually can do. Our knowledge has not grown as rapidly as our acceptance, both by other professionals and the lay public. Placed therefore in the position where others are expecting us to do more than we are capable of, many clinicians have reacted to their discomfort by trying to prove to themselves that they are far more capable than in fact is the case. The proper motivation for learning from experience is not the approval of teachers and supervisors, or grades, or—in the case of the Ph.D.—promotions and acceptance from colleagues but rather a motivation to continuously acquire data which can be used to improve the basis on which judgments are made. Such a motivation starts with the recognition of the severe limitations of our present state of knowledge and of predictions from objective scoring and rules and recipes for the interpretation of test data.

From the research cited herein, Rotter's statement obviously applies to psychiatrists, as well.

Aldrich (1986) states, "Unfortunately, the results of most predictive studies have been disappointing." This is in reference to predictions by psychiatrists regarding an individual's future adaptation. Aldrich also states, "Prediction in psychiatry, however, may resemble prediction in the stock market, in that too many variables exist for it ever to be accurate in individual cases." He concludes, after indicating the need for future research, "Meanwhile, predictions of future psychiatric incapacity in functioning individuals need to be made and viewed with considerable caution." It should be noted that the predictions in his study were made by psychiatrists in 1946-49 regarding the future of 200 first year medical students. Therefore, it might be suggested that prediction has improved since then. However, research does not support that contention.

Harding et al. (1987a, 1987b), in a long-term follow-up, found that despite poor prognoses, a substantial number of institutionalized and seriously disordered individuals were able to function at anywhere from a moderate to quite adequate level after release from the hospital. Further, the study indicates that while a certain percentage of patients continued to take medications after their release, most of them were in low to medium dose ranges and that in fact only about 25% of the subjects always took their medications, another 25% self-medicated when they had symptoms, and another 34% used none of their medications. There were also 16% who were not currently receiving any prescriptions for psychotropics, so that in total, 50% of the group was not using any medication, yet a number of them functioned reasonably well outside of the hospital setting.

Manderscheid (1987) states with regard to the Harding studies, "Diagnosis was not found to be an accurate predictor. Hence, current diagnostic formulations need to be re-examined and other factors that may influence outcome require investigation" (p. 783). He notes the research demonstrated the feasibility and importance of long-term research on course and states, "To date, very few longitudinal studies have been conducted in the United States" (p. 783) thus suggesting that predictions made by mental health professionals are indeed "fanciful speculation." Such predictions can hardly be well founded in the absence of hard research data.

The literature continues to provide statements which refer to evidence of the inability of psychiatrists and psychologists to predict future dangerousness (Worrell, 1987; McNeil et al., 1988; Applebaum, 1988). On the other hand, we would take notice of a recent study by Klassen and O'Connor (1988), who performed a discriminant analysis using 67 potential predictor variables with violent or non-violent group membership as the criterion measure. The short-term predictions they made (6 months in the community) achieved an overall accuracy rate of 85.3%. A total of 59.3% of those predicted to be violent were actually violent, which also yielded a false-positive rate of 40.7%. Of those predicted to be non-violent, 93.9% were actually non-violent, with a false-negative rate of 6.1%. These results were not cross-validated, and the authors note that caution is warranted in the interpretation of their results. As indicated in Chapter 2, Volume I, statistical analyses of this type need to be cross-validated, and such cross-validation may show lower, or much lower, rates of accuracy. The authors feel that the value of their present analysis "...may lie more in the demonstration of the feasibility of developing an actuarial instrument to assess risk probabilities for violence." (p. 153) Obviously, more research is needed on this, but it is worth noting that there is a potential here for a promising approach. The area continues to be fraught with danger of a high rate of false positives but this topic is discussed much more extensively in Chapter 24, Volume II.

Of course, the most important element of validity is in connection with whatever forensic issue is being addressed. That is, how valid is this method, test, concept in relation to the specific issue (prior mental condition, future impairment, etc.). We use the term "how valid" deliberately. Complete accuracy is very rare. The data the trier of fact needs to possess is the probability that a statement being offered is correct. We think the expert should be required to state this as a number which can be substantiated by relatively unequivocal research literature. If the expert cannot quantify the validity for this purpose in this manner, the trier of fact should be so informed so they can understand that either the expert does not know or is making a guess if he offers an unsubstantiated number. As his opinion is demonstrably a guess, it is then revealed as a guess based upon a guess.

In addition to Chapter 24 indicating problems of validity in assessing dangerousness, Chapter 25 will describe similar problems in evaluations for child custody determinations. Validity of prognoses is discussed in Chapter 22.

We are unaware of research validating opinions regarding prior mental state. Certainly, Matarazzo's statement in 1990 (supra) concerning lack of validation for the types of statements that are "typical" in forensic matters should put the burden on any expert who claims otherwise to prove it.

VALIDITY STUDIES ON OTHER TOPICS

A series of older studies address a range of issues, including prediction, and description of individuals. Luft (1950) found that psychiatrists and psychologists, given a verbatim copy of a one-hour diagnostic interview, were no more successful in evaluating characteristics of the person than were nonprofessionals. In fact, the accuracy of most experts did not surpass chance levels. Kelly and Fiske (1950) report that prediction was poor using all data sources, and that accuracy was better without interview and clinical assessment than with it; that is, objective data alone was better. Soskin (1954) found that experienced users of projective tests did not postdict behavioral characteristics of subjects any better than novices. Professionals showed a significant tendency to postdict predominantly maladjustive behaviors. Cline (1955) reports that clinical psychologists and psychiatrists were somewhat better than laymen, but not better than nursing trainees in predicting real-life social behavior. Gough (1962) reviews research showing that psychiatric prediction of such things as parole outcome and the results of shock therapy are poor, and that higher levels of accuracy were achieved using actuarial methods. Goldsmith and Mandell (1969) found that when experienced psychiatrists attempted to relate psychodynamic information to present mental condition, they were wrong in 75% of the cases. Based on the results of a study and review of previous research, Oskamp (1962) states, "Clinical psychologists are commonly considered to be experts in the area of human behavior and yet many studies have shown them to be subject to major errors in predictions of behavior....the clinician is often inaccurate in his predictions."

Slovenko (1984) overviews an issue highly pertinent to attempts at postdiction. Slovenko indicates that a patient's presenting symptoms are sometimes used to infer whether an event in question actually occurred. He indicates this is founded on the questionable assumption that there are characteristic responses to specific stressors, and thus if certain symptoms are present one can postdict whether a disputed event did or did not occur. In his overview, Slovenko takes a generally negative or dim view of the practice of trying to use presenting syndromes as evidence in establishing the occurrence of a specific stressor or stressful event. He notes, for example, that individuals often react quite differently to the same events, or purported stressors; in fact, some individuals may show no obvious reactions at all. Given this extreme variability in response, reliable means are not available for observing someone's current status and in turn drawing inferences about what may have occurred in the past, or whether a purported incident did or did not take place.

Slovenko indicates that there has been an expansion in subcategories of PTSD, including such things as rape trauma syndrome and battered spouse syndrome. Presumably, there is a common set of symptoms associated with these so-called syndromes, symptoms that when present can supposedly help the clinician to determine whether an event in question has occurred. (This leads one to wonder whether the courts will eventually be inundated with claims for an endless variety of "post-traumatic stress syndromes.") Slovenko notes that attempts to postdict the occurrence of specific events based on current symptoms have met with mixed receptions in the courts. He indicates that one serious potential problem with such practices, aside from their dubious reliability, is that they place the expert in the role of stating opinions (directly or by implication) about ultimate issues. For example, if a clinician testifies that an individual's behavior is consistent with that of someone who has experienced a certain event that is under dispute, by inference this is also testimony that the event has occurred. Slovenko points out how difficult it can be to draw conclusions about how actual events or reality affect an individual's psychological state, or what he calls "psychic reality," and observes that "inferring actual reality from psychiatric reality, we may say, is more speculative than inferring psychic reality from actual reality." (p. 458)

In a chapter in a textbook on clinical diagnosis, Matarazzo (1978) attempts to present a case in favor of the reliability and validity of psychiatric diagnosis. Matarazzo asserts that in this chapter he has shown that psychiatric and behavioral diagnoses have adequate reliability and "beginning" validity; hence, some clinicians may cite Matarazzo (or Wolman, 1978, the edited work in which the article appears), as an authority establishing adequate reliability and some evidence of validity.

The references cited above must at the very least cast serious doubt on such a proposition. The thorough lawyer who wishes to be prepared to meet a citation of Matarazzo as authority for the proposition that psychiatric diagnoses are reliable and valid should be able to make use of the following information indicating that Matarazzo's conclusion is not well supported and in some cases contradicted at least for practical purposes by his data.

Matarazzo acknowledges (page 54) that until a decade prior to his publication the number of studies finding diagnostic judgments based on psychiatric interviews unreliable outnumbered those showing adequate reliability. He advances an argument that in the few negative reliability studies he cites, the agreement in major or global category (organic, psychotic, or character disorder) reached acceptable levels ranging from 70% to 84% in three of these five studies. Agreement on specific diagnosis in these three studies was 54%, 55% and 63%. Inasmuch as global categories, such as organic, psychotic or character disorder are virtually useless for forensic purposes, being so broad in nature as to give little information about the individual, it is the rate of agreement on specific diagnosis that is important. For specific diagnoses, clearly, the reliability is low.

Principally, Matarazzo rests his argument for adequate reliability on two studies which show promising results. Matarazzo himself acknowledges the limitations of this work, including the need to demonstrate generalization and the fact that circumstances in one of these two supportive studies may have produced an artificially inflated level of agreement. When one considers the studies on the reliability of diagnosis cited in this text, in particular the general review by Kutchins and Kirk (1986) that appeared subsequent to Matarazzo's paper, Matarazzo's earlier reservations seem well advised. Indeed, the low reliabilities obtained in subsequent studies obviously suggest that the results of these earlier and more promising studies do not generalize and that agreement may well have been inflated. In any case, positive results from a few studies are certainly not sufficient to overcome the doubts about reliability created by the plethora of negative reports cited in this book.

In something of a back-door approach to supporting his thesis of adequate reliability in psychiatric diagnosis, Matarazzo cites a review (Koran, 1975a, 1975b) showing that reliability in certain branches of medicine is not any better than that in psychiatry, and in several cases is quite low. Koran's review might be of interest to lawyers involved in defense of personal injury claims. However, it seems rather difficult to establish that psychiatric reliability is good by showing that reliability in other branches of medicine is poor. Low reliability is low reliability wherever it occurs. If it is true that reliability is low in some other branches of medicine, then perhaps someone qualified to do so should write a book titled *Coping with Medical Testimony*. The reliability of psychiatric diagnosis is either good or poor on its own. It cannot be made "good" by showing that reliability in other areas of medicine is equally poor or even poorer.

Matarazzo (p. 70) correctly notes that establishing adequate reliability is just the first step and that the critical issue is that of validity. He cites a number of studies performed by the military in support of the validity of psychiatric evaluations. He notes that, as these studies involved predictive validity and were prospective in nature, they are the best such validity studies available. It might be pointed out that all of these studies are the closest analogy to the situation that usually pertains in the legal arena; that is, they all involved psychiatric declarations as to what the servicemen involved were or were not capable of doing, at least on a fairly global basis. Specifically, all of the studies involved questions of whether the individual was suitable or unsuitable for military service for psychiatric reasons. This could easily be translated into a statement that the servicemen involved did or did not have the "capacity" to perform the required military duties. This is at least moderately analogous to the statements that psychiatrists make in court that an individual lacks the capacities necessary for criminal responsibility by whatever tests or lacks the capacity to form a certain intent or, in a personal injury case, is unable to perform the duties of his job, i.e., has been rendered unsuitable for occupational service.

Matarazzo cites a study by Hunt (1959) which he asserts supports the validity of psychiatric evaluations. The study involved rates of discharge of naval recruits during training based on psychiatric screening with different rates occurring at three different bases due to the different attitudes of the commanding officers regarding psychiatric screening. The net effect of the differences was that larger percentages were discharged for psychiatric reasons at the Great Lakes Station where the commander favored psychiatric screening, generally an intermediate percent at Newport Training Station, and a small percentage at Sampson Station where the commander was not favorable to psychiatric screening. Hunt found that the subsequent attrition rates were smallest for Great Lakes where the largest percentage had been discharged for psychiatric reasons during training and largest for Sampson where the smallest percentage had been discharged for psychiatric reasons during training. The percentages are given below in the following order, Great Lakes—first and Sampson—second.

The number of recruits screened in all cases was fairly large, ranging from roughly 1,100 to 1,500 at various times. Dealing only with the data from Great Lakes and Sampson, where the largest differences both in discharge during training and percent subsequently discharged occurred, the following can be noted. For January of 1943, discharging more than six times as many recruits psychiatrically during training resulted in a difference of one-third subsequent discharges. The figures for June, 1943 are even more impressive evidence of low validity. At that time, a ratio of more than eight to one discharged in training by Great Lakes contrasted to Sampson resulted in a ratio of 3.2 to 3.7 savings in subsequent discharges. In actual numbers, these data indicate that Great Lakes psychiatrically discharged 80 of 1,347 recruits during training, while Sampson discharged only 9 out of 1,284. Yet, subsequently, Great Lakes discharged 43 out of the 1,347 while Sampson discharged only 41 out of the 1,284. Thus in effect, the commanding officer at Sampson who disfavored psychiatric screening, saved roughly 70 satisfactory Navy personnel and additionally spared them the stigma of having been psychiatrically discharged from the service. It is difficult to see how this data can be construed as showing good validity for psychiatric evaluations.

Matarazzo also cites the Plag et al. studies (supra) showing that of 134 Navy recruits psychiatrically diagnosed as unsuitable for Navy service, 27.6% were discharged by the end of two years of service and 46.5% total at the end of four years. In contrast for the 134 control-group subjects, matched with the unsuitables on other variables, 14.2% were discharged by two years and 27.6% by four years. Matarazzo interprets the differential rate of success or failure between these two groups as evidence of the validity of psychiatric evaluations. He acknowledges the Plag et al. interpretations of this data which raise questions as to the procedure in view of the fact that 72.4% of those diagnosed unsuitable were still on active duty two years later and 53.5% were still in the service and performing satisfactorily at the end of four years, as contrasted to 85.5% of the suitables and 72.4% of the suitables still performing satisfactorily after two and four years, respectively. (Thus, the base rate of adequate performance, established by the "normal" group, is not 100% but 85.8%, and 72.4%, respectively. The successful performance figures for the "psychiatric" group must be viewed in relation to their base rates and, therefore, are even better than the absolute percent indicates.) The data from this study are crystal clear. The psychiatrists were wrong more often than they were right. It is as simple as that. Continuing in this mode of establishing validity, Matarazzo also cites a study by Egan et al. (1951) in which they follow the Army careers of over 2,000 men who had previously been rejected by the Army for neuropsychiatric reasons but who, for various reasons, were later inducted during 1942 to 1946. A follow-up showed that 18% of these previously rejected inductees were given subsequent neuropsychiatric discharges and 82%—repeat, 82%— performed satisfactorily during their subsequent years of Army service.

This was compared to a rate of 6% neuropsychiatric discharge of enlisted personnel versus 94% who served satisfactorily in the whole United States Army during the same period. Matarazzo, therefore, notes that the former rejectees had a threefold greater discharge rate than did regular inductees, that is, 18% versus 6%. He considers this along with the Plag studies as evidence of predictive validity. In this instance, the psychiatrists were WRONG IN 82% OF THEIR EVALUATIONS. That is a staggering degree of error. Note that the degree of error would have been 94%, only 12% higher, if they had diagnosed the entire United States Army as unfit for military service. Certainly, flipping a coin would have done better.

We would not say that Matarazzo was necessarily wrong in stating that psychiatric evaluations have "some" validity. However, "some" in this case means "not very much." Based on available research, it appears that some psychiatrists and psychologists can formulate some valid predictions, for some of the people, some of the time, regarding some qualities or aspects of behavior. Again, we must reiterate the point that validity is not an omnipresent quality, and rather one must consider whether judgments or predictions are valid for the specific purposes relevant to the case at hand. Further, a considerable body of research shows that diagnostic or predictive conclusions rendered by psychologists and psychiatrists often show absolutely no incremental validity, or even negative incremental validity—that is, higher rates of accuracy could be achieved by eliminating clinicians from the interpretive process entirely and formulating conclusions on base rates, demographic variables, or other factors amenable to actuarial analysis.

It is also of interest to consider some of Matarazzo's more recent statements about the validity of clinical evaluations, and responses to these statements by well-known critics. In one article, Matarazzo (1986a) contends that the "professional psychologist is first and last an artisan." (p. 20) He further states, "clinical psychology today is still an art based on some scientific background and not a mature science." (p. 20) Matarazzo notes that this current situation may well continue for a long period of time. He further argues that, "psychological assessment is currently almost exclusively a still-to-be-well-validated work of a legislatively sanctioned, clinician-artisan." (p. 20) He admits that "our discipline has not yet met the challenge of establishing that the decision-making processes of the clinician are more valid (predictive) than are statistically based, actuarial processes." (p. 18) In the same article, Matarazzo goes on to criticize automated methods of psychological test interpretation, noting that they have not met "even the most primitive scientific tests of validation." (p. 14)

Fowler and Butcher (1986), in response to this paper by Matarazzo, indicate:

> There seems to be general agreement that the task of validation of psychological reports is unusually difficult because there is no established methodology. But the old clinical report, whose validity Matarazzo assumes, has itself rarely been subject to the scrutiny of validation studies, despite the opportunities to do so that have existed for over fifty years. Studies of clinician-generated "interpretations" have yielded unimpressive results. (p. 94)

Responding to Fowler and Butcher, Matarazzo (1986b) states, "*no* evidence has been published indicating that a credentialed clinician's signed test interpretations are any more valid than are the typically unsigned clinical psychological test interpretations being printed by today's computer software." (p. 96) Thus, although Matarazzo does not say this himself, in the first paper he indicates that computerized interpretive programs have not met primitive tests of scientific validation, and in the second paper he indicates that there is *no* evidence indicating that clinicians' interpretations of tests are more valid than computer-based interpretations. Thus, applying fundamental logic, if A (clinicians' test interpretations or reports) has not been demonstrated to be superior to B (computerized interpretations), and if B has not surpassed "primitive" tests of validation, then the obvious conclusion is that A has not passed these "primitive" tests either. It would seem to us that the juxtaposition of comments across these two recent article by Matarazzo could be used to effectively challenge any clinician who asserts that Matarazzo himself makes a strong claim for the validity of clinical interpretations. It is not for us to say whether Dr. Matarazzo's earlier or later statements are inconsistent, whether there is continuity across these works, or whether Dr. Matarazzo's position has evolved over time. But whatever was said in earlier papers as regards validity, the implications from these updated papers are straightforward.

Dahlstrom and Moreland (1983) raise an issue that perhaps best captures the current status of psychological evaluation. They indicate that there has been, and will likely continue to be, considerable dispute over whether psychodiagnosis is performed as much to give the psychologist, rather than the patient, peace of mind. This had led some to argue that "rather than learning to do psychological assessment, psychologists must accept the uncertainty of their profession." (p. 563)

Problems in establishing the validity of psychological testing for legal determinations is discussed by Heilbrun (1992) and will be dealt with in more detail in Chapter 10.

NOT MEDICINE EITHER

The material in this and previous chapters should make it evident that limits and deficiencies in scientific knowledge, in methods of evaluation, and in clinical judgment culminate in a "product" that certainly does not achieve reasonable certainty and that is subject to challenge on a variety of fronts. Nevertheless, given the considerable status and respect accorded to medicine, credibility might be attributed to the psychiatrist due to his standing as a man of medicine. Indeed, some experts might attempt to recapture or establish credibility on this basis. There are two basic approaches for challenging this aura of credibility associated with the field of medicine. First, there is considerable literature to suggest that psychiatry is not primarily a branch of medicine, or to state this differently, there is great doubt and controversy in locating the subject matter of psychiatry within the field of medicine. Second, even if one grants the questionable assumption that psychiatry is a branch of medicine, it should be evident that this, by itself, does not guarantee that criteria for granting expert status will be satisfied. There are obviously branches of medicine that cannot speak to certain issues with reasonable certainty. For example, the causes of many medical illnesses remain unknown, and obviously a person of medicine could not make statements about the etiology of such conditions with a reasonable degree of certainty. Thus, even if dubious claims for status as a branch of medicine are accepted, this does not alleviate psychiatrists from the burden of showing that their particular branch of medicine has achieved the necessary level of certainty.

Our subsequent discussion will focus mainly on the former point, that is, disputes regarding the actual subject matter of psychiatry. The lawyer can benefit from having available some of the literature and statements by authorities as a basis for separating psychiatrists from the aura that laymen, such as judges and jurors, associate with physicians in general. We will cite authorities—some of considerable prestige—to the effect that the mental illness or disease concept is not appropriate. These references are not exhaustive of the literature, but they are exemplary. For the most part, psychiatry lacks reliable or valid laboratory tests for determining the presence of psychiatric disorders. Much of the work in this area of "biological markers" has been devoted to the identification of depression. (We will point out limits in the accuracy of these biological markers or laboratory techniques in Chapter 19.) However, current trends in psychiatry are toward biological or medical bases for many disorders, but convincing evidence is still lacking. The literature is presented for such use as the lawyer wishes to make of it.

During the rise of psychiatry from the position of "stepchild" of medicine to its present status both in the profession and in society, occasional voices have been raised in protest. However, the issue has been most effectively and dramatically presented by Thomas Szasz, a practicing psychiatrist and professor of psychiatry, in the publication of his book, *The Myth of Mental Illness* (1961). In that book, and later in *Law, Liberty and Psychiatry* (1963), Szasz points out that there were historical reasons for the concurrent development of psychiatry and the concept of "mental illness." These origins had to do with the lack of knowledge concerning the behavioral and mental disorders, the need to alter public attitudes and policy concerning people with behavioral disorders, and a variety of other reasons, particularly the long-held belief that mental disorder originated in some form of biological or physiological condition, usually of the brain. As Szasz and others have pointed out, brain disease and mental illness or mental disorder are by no means synonymous, and the term "mental illness" when applied to a condition of brain disease is, in fact, a misnomer. This is because mind and brain are not the same. The brain can be altered without a corresponding alteration of mind and the mind can be altered without any known alteration of the brain. The literature is replete with statements by both psychiatrists and psychologists to the effect that most of the so-called "mental-illnesses" are, in fact, problems of psycho-social adjustment. That is, in almost all cases the reference is made to difficulties the individual is having in making adjustments and learning to cope in relation to himself, to other people, and to his society, without reference to organic pathology.

A distinguished authority, Dr. Philip Q. Roche (1958a, 1958b), author of *The Criminal Mind,* and winner of the Isaac Ray Award of the American Psychiatric Association, has declared that there is no such thing as insanity, nor such a thing as mental disease. In *The Criminal Mind,* Dr. Roche indicates that despite the assumption that the frequently used psychiatric terms "psychosis" and "psychoneurosis" have a commonly understood meaning, such is not the case. Dr. Roche points out that there is theoretical and practical confusion concerning the existence of a pathological process to which either or both terms can be properly applied.

Dr. John R. Cavanagh (1955) has stated that in view of the evidence that exists, the term "disease" as applied to mental conditions should be dropped because it is misleading. D.D. Jackson (1962), a psychiatrist, points out that the public must not be allowed to think of mental disorders as they do such diseases as cancer or heart disease, or they will ultimately turn upon the medical profession with the righteous anger of those who have been misled. Jackson also points out that every year data are collected which provide strong evidence for the fact that various mental disorders arise out of personal relationships, not out of biochemical causes as is annually asserted on the basis of some minimal information. Robert Coles (1967), a Harvard psychiatrist, also states his considerable doubt as to whether the so-called psychiatric disorders should be called disorders or disease and how misleading that language becomes.

H.A. Davidson (1967), a highly eminent psychiatrist who has been the editor of the journal, *Mental Hygiene,* states his fear that eventually by using the "sick" label for all deviations, psychiatry will create a model of conformity and then place a label—sick—on all those who fail to conform. He raises the question of whether the whole field of deviation belongs to psychiatry. For example, is an unhappily married couple "sick"? Davidson (1958) also cautions against the loose and indiscriminate use of the label "mental disease." He points out that the inclusion as mental disorders of such things as learning difficulties, stress reaction, sexual deviation, mental deficiency, and anti-social behavior is going to come back to haunt the medical profession. Davidson points out that categories are so broad that they could easily include such concepts as hostility to an employer, or marital discord over money. Davidson points out that medicine is attempting to practice magic if they think they can make those deviations into sicknesses merely by listing them in their own little book.

Mariner (1967), a psychiatrist, has pointed out that the subject matter of psychiatry is not disease but psycho-social problems of adjustment, that medical education is completely irrelevant to the subject matter of psychiatry, and that the appropriate field of study for those who work with these problems is psychology, or, in a broader sense, behavioral science. Ausubel (1966) makes the same point.

Dr. Edward Stainbrook (1971) states bluntly and specifically that the time has come to establish a non-disease concept in thinking about mental and emotional impairment. Dr. Stainbrook points out that although the mental disease concept has paid off in the past by making it possible to study crime, vice, and impairment in the socializing and humanizing process, and by getting some who had problems to seek help, there are also, now, many negative implications to the illness concept. He implies that it has outlived its usefulness.

Leslie A. Hohman (1960), in his presidential address to the American Psychopathological Association, points out the paradox that if someone points to possible evidence that there is disordered pathophysiology or actual brain disease, or defective constitution, or genetic deficiency which may be the cause of psychopathology or psychiatric disease, most of the members of the dynamic schools would regard this a heresy. In effect, physicians are saying that any evidence that what they have been calling disease is, in fact, disease is to be regarded as a betrayal of the profession.

Jurgen Ruesch (1966b) declares that psychiatry is divided as to whether to declare itself a biological, technical, social, or humanistic discipline. In at least two of the three views according to Ruesch, psychiatry is not seen as properly belonging in the field of medicine. T. Rothman (1962) states, "We have compellingly moved psychiatry far away from medical science, alienating our psychiatrists from the main stream of modern medicine." (p. 247) Glosser (1958) found that psychiatrists lean more strongly toward psychogenic than physiogenic concepts, generally opposing physiological, biological, and biochemical accounts of mental and personality disturbances.

Halleck (1967, 1969), a leading authority on forensic psychiatry, states that more psychiatrists subscribe to the view of "mental illness" as a social role or a "convenient metaphor for describing maladaptive behavior" than as a biological disorder. Cooper (1967) attacks the disease model and states a case for invalidating the doctor, his medical and quasimedical methods, and the institutions and hierarchies which reflect that conception.

Karl Menninger, generally recognized as one of the most outstanding American psychiatrists, states (1968) that the problem of disturbed people is that of making adaptations to the environment. He notes that the adaptation view differs from the notion of diseases that can be identified by name as to form or course.

Sarbin and Mancuso (1970) assert that "mental illness" is simply a term given to describe unwanted behavior. In reply to Sarbin and Mancuso, Crocetti et al. (1972), disagreeing with the Sarbin and Mancuso conclusions, nevertheless concede:

> We use the term "mental illness" advisedly. Mental illness as such is an abstraction...the medical model may be inadequate in some kinds of mental illness...whether the empirical consequences of the sociologic deviance model applied in fields such as delinquency, crime and personality are so startlingly superior to the application of a psychological illness model to disorders like non-process schizophrenia and manic depressive disorder is at least debatable.

Few experienced clinical and consulting psychologists and psychiatrists would argue that the medical illness model is sufficient standing alone. Few would claim that adequate etiological theory exits or that diagnostic obscurity is not demonstrable.

Sarbin and Mancuso (1972) reassert their proposition that the label "mental illness" is employed to refer to unwanted behavior, that is, to conduct that violates social norms. Referring to the Crocetti et al. argument, they state: "They fail to recognize that the conceptual enterprise begins from the observation that one person—a relative, a neighbor, an employer, a physician, a clergyman—places a moral judgment on a set of actions publicly exhibited by another person." (p. 6)

Sarbin and Mancuso cite the famous case of the physician, Thomas Brown, testifying at the witchcraft trial of two women that, in fact, the devil in such cases did work upon the bodies of men and women to stir up and excite such humors in their bodies to a great excess. They note that both these women were subsequently hanged. Sarbin and Mancuso conclude:

> Finally, we reassure our critics that at no time do we attack the illness model per se. We assert its validity and utility for understanding somatic happenings labelled pneumonia, intra-cranial aneurism, measles and tennis elbows. We intend only to declare that the disease paradigm is no longer helpful in understanding persons whose public conduct has violated normative prescriptions.

H.M. van Praag (1971) states:

> Psychiatry is reputed to be the least medical of the medical disciplines....In reality psychiatric pathology deals with factors of three different types. It deals with disturbed intra-individual relations: disturbances in the development of an interaction between the various "components" of the human psyche. It deals with disturbed interindividual relations: disturbances in the relations between man and his fellow man. Finally, it deals with disturbances in the function of the cerebral substratum which "support" the deviant behavior. (p. 1)

Obviously, only the third type is medical.

Robitscher (1972) states:

> Our modern changing and complicated society has thrust psychiatrists into a more public role at the same time they have stimulated the profession to reexamine concepts of health and disease...

> There is also a growing literature in anti-psychiatric thought...which if not overtly anti-psychiatric would like us to redefine many of those we view as patients as merely socially different. These works make many psychiatrists uncomfortable but they also force psychiatrists to redefine our fields and roles.

Stainbrook (1971), discussing several basic scientific and ideological trends within the practice of psychiatry, includes among them the following: the expanding recognition of the social and cultural determinants of deprivation or conflicts which prevent or impair individual gratification, effectiveness or competence; the augmenting countertrend against the social and medical diagnostic labelling of much of individual behavior as illness; and the growing advocacy of a social learning or social response understanding of behavior and the acceptance of the non-disease and non-medical conception of individual adaptational ineffectiveness or impairment.

Salzman (1973), asking the question of what constitutes mental illness, states:

> At the extremes our definitions can at times be precise and unequivocal. This is particularly true when we deal with those disorders which are physiological in origin and have demonstrable and precise symptomatology. However, when we

try to identify the subtleties of disorganization or maladaptation that arise out of our psychological capacities we run into innumerable difficulties. In such instances we begin to deal with cultural definitions that are related to value systems and not the basic physiological functioning of the organism. The differences between adaptive and maladaptive functioning will vary from culture to culture and will be more or less acceptable depending upon one's economic or social status...the concept of disease as it advanced from the primitive magical basis to the ideas of a disturbance of bodily humors, germs and finally a multicausal highly sophisticated bio-chemical basis, required a drastic revision of the prevailing classifications.

This is more notably the case in the psychological disorders since nosology is intimately tied to the state of religious as well as scientific knowledge. Enter the existing socio-cultural prejudices and preconceptions. Because we have no objective standards that can clearly identify or define mental health we use a variety of determinants that grow out of our conceptions of mental health from moral and religious sources...and we tend to label any deviation from the cultural norm as disease processes.

Salzman also states:

The science of nosology which was related to the healer or medical model requires a drastic overhaul when the model gives way to a social cultural or developmental model in which disordered living may or may not be an illness. Such psychological malfunctioning need not follow the medical model but instead could be considered a maladaptation that renders the individual less effective and less adaptive as a functioning animal.

Geertsma (1972) states:

The underlying and compelling factor in the changing scene in mental health is the shift away from the concept of mental "illness." There appears finally to be general acceptance of the principle that abnormal behavior is continuous with normal behavior. There is a growing realization that the "mentally ill" are the persons who present behavior disorders different from the normal population, not in the kind or quality of their basic behavior but in the degree or quantity of particular variety of responses. It is difficult to find any scientific support for the concept that there are discrete, separate and absolute mental illnesses. Rather it is becoming increasingly obvious that behavior which is inefficient, unsatisfactory, bizarre or even downright silly is actually learned as is all other behavior and that there are definite objective explanations for the behavior. (p. 238)

Guiora and Harrison (1973) describe the cyclic rise and fall of three conceptual models—biological, psychological and social—within the mental health professions. They state:

The succession of conceptual models in the mental health field may mean that the essential human needs to which the field has contracted to minister have not yet been precisely identified. We currently conceive of such needs in terms of the familiar disease model. We try to minimize the vague discomfort we feel about its inadequacies by attaching qualifiers. Thus we speak at times of psychological illness or organic illness or social illness. (p. 1275)

There are many who say that we mental health professionals have inherited a legacy that was never meant for us. Though we have never disclaimed the inheritance we are strangely unable to recognize its true nature, let alone use it properly. We have in fact inherited the vacuum in which faith and belief, a priesthood and an all-inclusive value system—the church—once held sway. Although we were unable to extend the same comforts in time of their essential need, we were unsure of our power of absolution and the certainty of salvation and were clearly without a divinity or a divine dogma, we took on the mantle of priesthood. We have recast the existential needs into more familiar and less threatening medical terms, but alas, magic does not work on the non-believer. Renaming the central need has not changed it. We have only fortified an endless cycle of hope and despair. (p. 1275)

Grinker (1972), although arguing for continuation of the medical model, if not exclusively, then at least alongside of others, states, "Psychotherapy is the *least* medical of all therapies as its practitioners are largely non-medical." Albee (1971), responding to Grinker, states:

There is little evidence to support the hypothesis of an underlying organic defect in most functional mental disorders. Therefore, medical training of psychiatrists is not especially relevant to therapeutic activities. Often, when a real organic cause is found to underlie disturbed behavior, the psychiatrist dismisses the case. (p. 130)

Stuart (1970) states:

Beyond arguments about the legitimacy of the metaphor drawn between the medical model and psychotherapy one can also argue that there is voluminous data to support the view that the medical model is not useful and must be purged from our scientific approaches to behavior change. (p. 8)

Garmezy (1971), discussing the "medical model" controversy, states:

Our own scientific efforts are often primitive, our observations too frequently imprecise and unreliable, and even when reliability does exist, our data often allow for a choice of seemingly discrepant, but apparently tenable interpretations. It is not surprising, therefore, that in the study of behavior pathology, contradictory hypotheses readily co-exist. Proof is often the fragile verity and disproof is a rare claimant to our scientific enterprise. To suggest then in the present stage of our scientific development that only one model will suffice or prove to be the one "true" portrait of reality is not at all in keeping with the data base of our discipline.

Sharma (1970) provides discussions by several psychiatrists and psychologists arguing the inappropriateness of a medical model for psychological disturbance.

Tuma et al. (1978) assert that knowledge of the effect of therapist training and experience and the outcome in treatment of schizophrenic patients is scarce, with a large gap in knowledge typically being filled in with a mixture of myth, speculation, anecdote and weak research evidence. They found that among 23 outcome variable studies there was not a single instance in which the effect of therapist experience and general clinical ability was significantly related to outcome.

Guze (1977) observes that American psychiatry is near a watershed period concerning its development as a social science on the one hand, or continued evolution within medicine and neurobiology on the other hand. He notes the debate is intense and the outcome still uncertain. He argues for continuing psychiatry as a branch of medicine. Tarrier (1979), in a reply to Guze, advances arguments favoring the status of psychiatry as a social science rather that a branch of medicine.

Coryell and Wetzell (1978) surveyed 378 third-year residents in various parts of the country and found that, although 59% felt the medical model should be basic to both the practice and research of psychiatry, 25% felt that the medical model had minimal importance in clinical psychiatry. Thus, while a majority favored the view of psychiatry as a medical specialty, a substantial proportion (one-fourth) felt the medical model had little use.

Strupp and Hadley (1977) observe that difficulties in evaluating therapy outcome are influenced by the fact that "problems in living which brings patients to psychotherapists are no longer necessarily viewed as an 'illness' for which psychotherapy is prescribed as a 'treatment.'"

McReynolds (1979) states:

> The medical model is no longer heuristic in social science. What good it brought to our discipline was exhausted long ago. It now entraps our thinking and limits our research and practice. This is true not only for the disease entity conception of behavioral processes but for all categorical representations of behavior, be they mental disorders, personality types or other notions of behavioral discontinuity. In sum, there is little reason to expect a decade of new research on DSM-III to produce findings that substantiate the categorical approach to understanding and modifying unwanted or troublesome behavior. That well is dry. (p. 125)

Shagass (1977), reviewing a book, *Models of Madness, Models of Medicine* by Miriam Siegler and Humphry Osmond, notes that psychiatry's place within medicine is a topic of controversy. (p. 380) He also notes (p. 384) that after going through medical schools psychiatrists afterward often wonder whether their medical training was necessary. Both Shagass and the book he reviewed, however, strongly favor the medical model.

Paris (1975) acknowledges the controversy about the medical model in psychiatry, although he is in favor of retaining it. He states: "Attacks on the medical model in psychiatry have been frequent in recent years and some have gone so far as to question whether psychiatry as a branch of medicine is nothing but an historical accident."

Sarason (1981) discusses a view of the negative consequences for clinical psychology in following the medical model. He states:

> There is a creeping sense of malaise in psychology about psychology. But that malaise is not peculiar to psychology. It is suffusing the atmosphere in all the social sciences. Indeed, in some of the social sciences, like economics, there are those who not only believe that the emperor is naked, but also that he has a terminal disease. But this kind of medical metaphor, however apt it may seem is but another example of how our thinking is imprisoned in an individual psychology.

Goodwin (1984) offers a review of the book, *Disease and Its Control,* by R.B. Hudson. Among his comments, Goodwin indicates that no one has the slightest idea what they mean by "disease." He indicates that no one can define disease, and further observes that psychiatry tends to run about two hundred years behind the rest of medicine.

A study by Lindy et al. (1980) suggests that training in medicine may even have negative effects on critical areas of skill development. The authors note disagreement within the profession regarding the value of the internship year during psychiatry training. Lindy et al. compared two groups of psychiatric residents, one of which had, and one of which had not received a year of internship training. It is during this internship year that psychiatry students usually obtain their most intensive hands-on medical training. Based on faculty evaluation, ratings of performance over a two-year period did not reveal any significant differences across these two groups in areas of "medical psychiatry." However, ratings of psychotherapy skills showed several significant differences in favor of the group of residents that had *not* participated in the year of internship. Lindy et al. note possible limitations of their study, but they nevertheless conclude that, "the superiority of the noninternship residents suggests the disquieting possibility that the internship might even have a negative impact on subsequent education." (p. 79) Thus, this research raises the possibility that this year of focused medical training does not enhance, but may actually impede the development of certain important professional skills.

It can be clearly stated from the foregoing that there is at least considerable dispute and doubt as to whether the conditions with which psychiatry deals involve "illness" or "disease" or fall appropriately within the purview of medicine. Because the premise is false, or at least subject to considerable doubt, the whole structure is vulnerable. Thus it is possible for the attorney to dissolve the myth that the subject matter with which psychiatry deals, to wit, problems of psycho-social adjustment, properly belongs within the field of medicine.

To accomplish this dissolution, the first step is to establish that it is psycho-social adjustment, and not disease, with which the psychiatrist usually or exclusively deals. Although this may be a difficult fact to establish conclusively, some inroads can be made. First, the lack of demonstrable physical disease can be cited. In addition, the statements of authorities in both psychiatry and psychology on the subject can be cited. Obviously, there is not complete agreement among psychiatrists, and even some psychologists hold to the view that the "mental illness" concept is an appropriate one.

Despite all of the foregoing, it is likely that many, perhaps a majority of American psychiatrists will continue to claim priority of a medical model for dealing with psycho-social problems. This may especially be the case with "biological" psychiatrists who insist they deal with medical disorders and may cite the frequency of "medical" interventions (e.g., medication) or studies which suggest there may be a genetic link to certain psychiatric problems. From the objective observation of the material with which psychiatrists most frequently deal, however, especially in the forensic area, it seems clear that the medical model is not appropriate and that the area of knowledge or learning involved is that of psychology, sociology, or in a broader term, behavioral sciences. If this is true, obviously no aura of expertise should be attached to the psychiatrist by virtue of his possession of the M.D. degree; it is superfluous and irrelevant. The attorney can advance this argument in objection to the admissibility of any testimony or bring out in cross-examination the fact that while a majority of psychiatrists may not agree, many psychiatrists of considerable eminence, and many psychologists of considerable eminence strongly dispute the mental illness concept and, at the very minimum, cast serious doubt upon the appropriateness of the medical model. The law simply blinds itself to reality when it allows the physician to testify as to matters in which he has no more competence or appropriate expertise than an economist, a physicist or an accountant. The diligent attorney should have little difficulty capitalizing on this exceedingly ambiguous status of psychiatry.

This controversy will not be settled in the scientific and professional literature. It can only be settled in the socio-political-judicial arena. From an evidentiary standpoint, it is the existence of the controversy that has significance. Although there may be ignorance and error in a few areas of medicine nearly equal to that in psychiatry, as some have argued, virtually no one argues that cancer, heart disease, broken bones, pneumonia, and a host of other organic conditions are not medical matters, or should not be dealt with under a medical model.

Legislation enacted in California and most of the other states reflects legislative recognition of the predominantly non-medical nature of most of the subject matter with which psychiatrists deal. Legislation for the licensing of psychologists, which exists in most states, describes the types of issues and problems with which psychologists may deal, which would clearly encompass nearly all of the subject matter of psychiatry. The methods psychologists are licensed to employ are identical with those that may be employed by psychiatrists, with the exception of drugs and the administration of shock treatment or psychosurgery. Licensing legislation makes clear that medical training is not necessary for dealing with these issues and therefore, by implication at least, declares them non-medical, in contrast to cancer, heart disease, etc., which by law can only be treated by those with medical qualifications. In fact, California and some other states have laws licensing marriage, family and child counselors, as well as psychiatric social workers, which extends the right to deal with these same issues to people with such licenses, all of whom lack medical training or degrees.

In some cases it may be useful to bring to the jury's attention the doubt that exists concerning the legitimacy of psychiatry as a "medical" specialty. Many of the major classifications in the DSMs may be useful in illustrating this issue. In particular, a reading of the descriptive material under the headings of Paranoid and other personality disorders, Anxiety disorders, Adjustment disorders, and Disorders of Impulse Control reveals the non-medical nature of most of the described conditions.

SUMMARY AND CONCLUSIONS

The implications of the research we have cited above on the reliability and validity of psychiatric diagnosis, prediction, and formulations of other types is evident. Examining these results along a series of criteria (to be described more fully in Chapter 10), it appears that the following conclusions are warranted. First, one can ask if results are reliable. The literature suggests that the conclusions drawn from psychiatric evaluations often are of low or doubtful reliability. Second, one can ask whether assumptions are valid, or whether the relationships *assumed* to exist in fact do exist. The research suggests that some assumptions may indeed achieve statistical significance, but that many beliefs and assumptions are actually illusory correlations. Third, are requirements for incremental validity filled, i.e., does the addition of clinical interpretation increase the accuracy of conclusions founded on base rates or known statistical relationships? Virtually without exception, research shows that where available, utilization of statistical or actuarial methods achieve at least equal, and frequently greater overall accuracy than do clinical interpretations, and that overall judgment accuracy would increase if one relied upon these former methods alone and entirely excluded "experts" from the data interpretation process. We would again note that "plugging" data into an actuarial formula does not require the expert's participation and that once given access to the results, laymen should be just as capable of using this information as are mental health professionals. Thus, the participation of the expert in the interpretation of data does not help, and if anything is likely to move the trier of fact further from the truth. Fourth, do demonstrated levels of validity apply or generalize to the questions and persons under consideration? For the most part, we lack data regarding the generalization of clinical method and knowledge to the forensic setting, and in the area that is perhaps best studied—the prediction of violence—the results are overwhelmingly negative. Thus, in the area in which this question has been most thoroughly tested, research indicates that predictions are wrong far more often than they are right. This might lead to the cynical suggestion that experts could be of help to the trier of fact. They offer a backward guide to the conclusions that are most likely correct—the conclusions that are the *opposite* of theirs! For example, in the prediction of violence, if judge and jury would always assume that the correct answer is the opposite of that stated by the expert, they would be right most of the time because the expert is wrong most of the time. Finally, one can ask whether judgments attain reasonable certainty. No detailed analysis is needed here. If not one of the previously stated criteria is satisfied, and each is less stringent than this final one, reasonable certainty will not be achieved either.

Unfortunately, our review of research on the validity of diagnosis and prediction is somewhat "thin," simply because there are not many studies available on these topics. It is commonly pointed out in the literature that it is difficult to do research on validity because objective criteria are usually lacking. Therefore, given the studies that do exist, and which powerfully demonstrate lack of validity—and, in fact, demonstrate the contrary, massive error—no credence should be given to any psychiatrist's assertion, no matter how sincerely felt, to the effect that psychiatric assessments have a reasonably high probability of being correct. Until there is a large body of supportive, contrary research evidence utilizing objective criteria, the only conclusion that can be supported with regard to the accuracy of psychiatric evaluations is that it is extremely clear they are more likely to be wrong than to be right. Of course, this is only what one would expect, given the severe lack of knowledge in this field, the deficiencies of the clinical method of examination and the fact that adequate validity cannot be expected where there is low reliability. Surely, somewhere in this land, there must be a court with the knowledge and courage to finally recognize this reality and refuse to allow waste of the court's time and the taxpayers' money and the muddling of the trial process with evidence that is demonstrably of such poor quality.

REFERENCES

Abramowitz, S.I., and Abramowitz, C. (1973). Should prospective women clients seek out women practitioners? Intimations of a "dingbat" effect in clinical evaluation. *Proceedings of the 81st Annual Convention of the American Psychological Association, 8,* 503.

Abramowitz, S.I., Abramowitz, C., Jackson, C., and Gomes, B. (1973). The politics of clinical judgment: What non-liberal examiners infer about women who do not stifle themselves. *Journal of Consulting and Clinical Psychology, 41,* 385-391.

Adams, K.M., and Grant, I. (1986). Influences of premorbid risk factors on neuropsychological performance in alcoholics. *Journal of Clinical and Experimental Neuropsychology, 8,* 362-370.

Adinolfi, A.A. (1971). Relevance of person perception research to clinical psychology. *Journal of Consulting and Clinical Psychology, 37,* 167-176.

Agnew, J., and Bannister, D. (1973). Psychiatric diagnosis and a pseudo specialist language. *British Journal of Medical Psychology, 46,* 69-73.

Aiken, L.R. (1985). *Psychological Testing and Assessment* (5th ed.). Boston: Allyn and Bacon.

Albee, G.W. (1968). Models, myths, and manpower. *Mental Hygiene,* 168-179.

Albee, G.W. (1971). Response to Grinker. *Professional Psychology, 2.*

Aldrich, C.K. (1986). The clouded crystal ball: A 35-year follow-up of psychiatrists' predictions. *American Journal of Psychiatry, 143,* 45-49.

American Psychological Association (1985). *Standards for Educational and Psychological Testing.* Washington, D.C.

Anastasi, A. (1961). *Psychological Testing* (2nd ed.). New York: The Macmillan Company.

Anastasi, A. (1982). *Psychological Testing* (5th ed.). New York: The Macmillan Company.

Angle, H.V., Johnson, J., Grebenkemper, N.S., and Ellinwood, E.H. (1979). Computer interview support for clinicians. *Professional Psychology, 34,* 49-57.

Annual Social Science Citation Index, Institute for Scientific Information, Philadelphia, PA.

APA Monitor, April, 1986.

Appelbaum, P.S. and Roth, L.H. (1981). Clinical issues in the assessment of competency. *American Journal of Psychiatry, 138,* 1462-1467.

Applebaum, P.S. (1988). The new preventive detention: Psychiatry's problematic responsibility for the control of violence. *American Journal of Psychiatry, 145,* 779-785.

Asaad, G., & Shapiro, B. (1986). Hallucinations: Theoretical and clinical overview. *American Journal of Psychiatry, 143,* 1088-1097.

Ash, P. (1949). The reliability of psychiatric diagnosis. *Journal of Abnormal and Social Psychology, 44,* 272-276.

Ausubel, D. (1966). Relationships between psychology and psychiatry; the hidden issues. In J. Braun (ed.), *Clinical Psychology in Transition.* New York: World Publishing Co.

Bachrach, H. (1974). Diagnosis as strategic understanding. *Bulletin of the Menninger Clinic, 38,* 390-405.

Baldessarini, R.J. (1970). Frequency of diagnosis of schizophrenic versus affective disorders from 1944-1968. *American Journal of Psychiatry, 127,* 759-763.

Bartol, C.R. (1983). *Psychology and American Law.* Belmont, CA: Wadsworth Publishing Company.

Bauer, A.K. (1962-1963). Legal responsibility and mental illness. *Northwestern University Law Review, 57,* 12-18.

Beck, A.T., Wane, E.H., Mendelson, M., Mock, J.E., and Evbaugh, J.H. (1962). Reliability of psychiatric diagnoses: A study of consistency of clinical judgments and ratings. *American Journal of Psychiatry, 119,* 351-356.

Beckett, G.S., Grisell, J., Crandall, R.G., and Gudobba, R.A. (1967). A method of formalizing psychiatric study. *Archives of General Psychiatry, 16,* 407-415.

Benson, D.F. and Blumer, D. (Eds.) (1975). *Psychiatric Aspects of Neurological Disease.* New York: Grune and Stratton.

Benson, D.F. and Blumer, D. (Eds.) (1982). *Psychiatric Aspects of Neurological Disease.* New York: Grune and Stratton.

Bentall, R.P. (1990). The Illusion of reality: A review and integration of psychological research on hallucinations. *Psychological Bulletin, 107,* 82-95.

Berry, K.B. (1973). Parsimony and complexity as related to the diagnostic process with children. *Journal of Clinical Psychology, 29,* 39-41.

Black, S. (1971). Labeling and psychiatry: A comment. *Social Science and Medicine, 5,* 391-392.

Bliss, E.L., Larson, E.M., & Nakashima, S.R. (1983). Auditory hallucinations and schizophrenia. *The Journal of Nervous and Mental Disease, 171,* 30-33.

Block, C.B. (1984). Diagnostic and treatment issues for black patients. *The Clinical Psychologist, 37,* 51-54.

Blum, J.D. (1978). On changes in psychiatric diagnosis over time. *American Psychologist,* 1017-1030.

Boll, T.J. (1985). Developing issues in clinical neuropsychology. *Journal of Clinical and Experimental Neuropsychology, 7,* 473-485.

Bolter, J., Gouvier, W., Veneklasen, J., and Long, C.J. (1982). Using demographic information to predict premorbid IQ: A test of clinical validity with head trauma patients. *Clinical Neuropsychology, 4,* 171-174.

Boulenger, J., Uhde, T.W., Wolff, III, E.A., and Post, R.M. (1984). Increased sensitivity to caffeine in patients with panic disorders. *Archives of General Psychiatry, 41,* 1067-1071.

Boyd-Franklin, H. (1984). Issues in family therapy with black families. *The Clinical Psychologist, 37,* 54-58.

Braginsky, D.D., and Braginsky, B.M. (1973). Psychologists: High priests of the middle class. *Psychology Today, 7,* 138.

Brody, N. (1985). The validity of tests of intelligence. In B.B. Wolman (Ed.), *Handbook of Intelligence* (pp. 353-389). New York: John Wiley and Sons.

Broverman, Clarkson, Rosenkrantz, and Vogel (1970). Sex role stereotypes and clinical judgments of mental health. *Journal of Consulting and Clinical Psychology, 34,* 1-7.

Brown, D.E., Jr. (1971). *American Journal of Psychiatry, 128,* 153.

Brown, P. (1990) The name game: Toward a sociology of diagnosis. *Journal of Mind and Behavior, 11,* 385-406.

Cavanagh, J.R. (1955). A psychiatrist looks at the Durham decision. *Catholic University Law Review,* 25-30.

Chapman, L.J., and Chapman, J.P. (1967). Genesis of popular but erroneous psychodiagnostic observations. *Journal of Abnormal Psychology, 72,* 193-204.

Charney, D.S., Heninger, G.R., and Jatlow, P.I. (1985). Increased anxiogenic effects of caffeine in panic disorders. *Archives of General Psychiatry, 42,* 233-243.

Christensen, L., Krietsch, K., White, B., and Stagner, B. (1985). Impact of a dietary change on emotional distress. *Journal of Abnormal Psychology, 94,* 565-579.

Clement, P. (1975). CASPP/CSPA *Joint Newsletter, October 1975, 41.*

Cleveland, S.E. (1976). Reflections on the rise and fall of psychodiagnosis. *Professional Psychology, 7,* 309-318.

Cline, V. (1955). Ability to judge personality assessed with a stress interview and sound film technique. *Journal of Abnormal and Social Psychology, 50,* 183-187.

Cohen, E.S., Harbin, H.T., and Wright, M.J. (1975). Some considerations in the formulation of psychiatric diagnosis. *The Journal of Nervous and Mental Disease, 160,* 422-427.

Cohen, L.H., and Oyster-Nelson, C.K. (1981). Clinicians evaluations of psychodynamic psychotherapy: Experimental data on psychological peer review. *Journal of Consulting and Clinical Psychology, 49,* 583-589.

Coleman, L. (1984). *The Reign of Error.* Boston: Beacon Press.

Coles, R. (1967). *The Progressive, 31,* 32.

Conover, D. (1972). Psychiatric distinctions: New and old approaches. *Journal of Health and Social Behavior, 13*, 167-180.

Cooper, A.M. (1985). Will neurobiology influence psychoanalyses? *The American Journal of Psychiatry, 142*, 1395-1402.

Cooper, D. (1967). *Psychiatry and Anti-Psychiatry.* London: Tavistock.

Coryell, W., and Wetzel, R.D. (1978). Attitudes toward issues in psychiatry among third-year residents: A brief survey. *American Journal of Psychiatry, 135*, 732-735.

Crocetti, G., Spiro, H., Herzi, R., Lebrau, P., and Siassi, T. (1972). Multiple models and mental illness. *Journal of Consulting and Clinical Psychology, 39*, 1-5.

Dahlstrom, W.G., and Moreland, K.L. (1983). Teaching the MMPI: APA-approved clinical internships. *Professional Psychology: Research and Practice, 14*, 563-569.

Davids, A. (1973). Projective testing: Some issues facing academicians and practitioners. *Professional Psychology, 4*, 445-453.

Davidson, H.A. (1958). *American Journal of Psychiatry, 115,* 411.

Davidson, H.A. (1967). *Mental Hygienist, 51,* 5.

Dawes, R.M. (1986). Representative thinking in clinical judgment. *Clinical Psychology Review, 6*, 425-441.

DeJong, J., Virkkunen, M., and Linnoila, M. (1992). Factors associated with recidivism in a criminal population. *The Journal of Nervous and Mental Disease, 180,* 543-550.

Derner, G. (1983, March). Parsimony, meta-psychology and personality assessment. Invited address. Meeting of the Society for Personality Assessment, San Diego, CA.

Diamond, B.L. (1973). From Durham to Brawner, a futile journey. *Washington University Law Quarterly*, 109-125.

Drake, R.E., and Vaillant, G.E. (1985). A validity study of Axis II of DSM-III. *American Journal of Psychiatry, 142*, 553-558.

Duckro, P.N., Margolis, R.B., and Tait, R.C. (1985). Psychological assessment in chronic pain. *Journal of Clinical Psychology, 40*, 499-504.

Egan, J.R., Jackson, L., and Eaves, R.J. (1951). Study of neuropsychiatric rejectees. *Journal of the American Medical Association, 145*, 466-469.

Eichman, W.J. (1972). Review in O.K. Buros (Ed.), *The Seventh Mental Measurements Yearbook,* Highland Park, NJ: Gryphon Press.

Ennis, B.J. (1978). Traditional involvement in the public practice of psychiatry. In Barton, W.E., and Sanborn, C.J. (Eds.), *Law and the Mental Health Professions*. New York: International University's Press.

Epstein, S. (1980). The stability of behavior. II, Implications for psychological research. *American Psychologist, 35*, 790-806.

Farber, L.G., Schmaltz, L.W., Volle, F.O., and Hecht, P. (1986). Temporal lobe epilepsy: Diagnostic accuracy. *The International Journal of Clinical Neuropsychology, 8*, 76-79.

Fennig, S., Craig, T.J., Tanenberg-Karant, M., and Bromet, E.J. (1994). Comparison of facility and research diagnoses in first-admission psychotic patients. *American Journal of Psychiatry, 151*, 1423-1429.

Fitzgibbons, D.J., and Shearn, C.R. (1972). Concepts of schizophrenic among mental health professionals: A factor analytic study. *Journal of Consulting and Clinical Psychology, 38*, 228-295.

Fitzgibbons, J.J., and Hokanson, D.T. (1973). The diagnostic decision making process: Factors influencing diagnosis and changes in diagnosis. *American Journal of Psychiatry, 130*, 972-975.

Fleiss, J.L., Spitzer, R.L., Endicott, J., and Cohen, J. (1972). Quantification of agreement and multiple psychiatric diagnosis. *Archives of General Psychiatry, 26*, 168-171.

Fowler, R.D., and Butcher, J.N. (1986). Critique of Matarazzo's views on computerized testing: All sigma and no meaning. *American Psychologist, 41*, 94-96.

Galton, F. (1907). *Inquiries into Human Faculty and Its Development.* New York: Dutton.

Garmezy, N. (1971). Comment. *Professional Psychology, 2*, 135-139.

Geertsma, R.H. (1972). Clinical assessment. In R.H. Woody, and J.D. Woody (Eds.), *Counseling and Psychotherapy.* Englewood Cliffs, NJ: Prentice-Hall.

Gilliland, K., and Andress, D. (1981). Ad lib caffeine consumption, symptoms of caffeinism and academic performance. *American Journal of Psychiatry, 138*, 512-514.

Glosser, H.J. (1958). Psychiatric v. psychological opinion regarding personality disturbances. *American Psychologist, 13*, 477-281.

Goldberg, L.R. (1959). The effectiveness of clinicians' judgments: The diagnosis of organic brain damage from the Bender-Gestalt Test. *Journal of Consulting Psychology, 23*, 25-33.

Goldberg, L.R. (1968b). Simple models or simple processes? Some research on clinical judgments. *American Psychologist, 23*, 483-496.

Goldsmith, S.R., and Mandell, A.J. (1969). The psychodynamic formulation: A critique of a psychiatric ritual. *American Journal of Psychiatry, 125*, 1738-1743.

Goldstein, A.G. (1976). Case report: Hallucinatory experience: A personal account. *Journal of Abnormal Psychology, 85*, 423-429.

Goldstein, R.O. (1973). The fitness factory, part 1: The psychiatrists role in determining competency. *American Journal of Psychiatry, 130,* 1134-1147.

Goodwin, D.W. (1984) Review of the book, *Disease and Its Control* by R.B. Hudson. *American Journal of Psychiatry, 142,* 235-237.

Gough, H. (1962). Clinical versus statistical prediction. In L. Postman (Ed.), *Psychology In The Making.* New York: Alfred A. Knopf.

Graff, H., Kenig, L., and Roadoff, G. (1971). Prejudice of upper class therapists against lower class patients. *Psychiatry Quarterly, 45,* 475-489.

Graham, J.R. (1971). Feedback and accuracy of clinical judgments from the MMPI. *Journal of Consulting and Clinical Psychology, 36,* 286-291.

Greden, J.P. (1974). Anxiety or caffeine: A diagnostic dilemma. *American Journal of Psychiatry, 131,* 1089-1092. (Reported in the *Los Angeles Times,* Wednesday, May 8, 1974.)

Greden, J.P., Fontaine, E.P., Lubetsky, M., and Chamberlin, K. (1978). Anxiety and depression associated with caffeinism among psychiatric inpatients. *American Journal of Psychiatry, 135,* 963-966.

Grinker, R.R. (1972). Emerging conceptions of mental illness and models of treatment: The medical point of view. *Professional Psychology, 2,* 129-130.

Guiora, A.Z., and Harrison, F.I. (1973). What is psychiatry? A new model of service and education. *American Journal of Psychiatry, 130,* 1275-1277.

Guze, S.B. (1977). The future of psychiatry: Medicine or social science? An Editorial, *The Journal of Nervous and Mental Disease, 165,* 225-230.

Hahn, N., and Livson, N. (1973). Sex differences in the eyes of expert personality assessors: Blind spots? *Journal of Personality Assessment.*

Halleck, S.L. (1967). *Psychiatry and The Dilemma of Crime.* New York: Harper and Row.

Halleck, S.L. (1969). The psychiatrist and the legal process. *Psychology Today, 2.*

Halleck, S.L. (1982). The role of the psychiatrist in the criminal justice system. In *Psychiatry,* (p. 386). 1982 Annual Review, L. Grinspoon (Ed.). Washington, DC: American Psychiatric Press Inc.

Harding, C.M., Brooks, G.W., Ashikaga, T., Strauss, J.S., and Brier, A. (1987a). The Vermont longitudinal study of persons with severe mental illness, I: Methodology, study sample and overall status 32 years later. *American Journal of Psychiatry, 144,* 718-726,

Harding, C.M., Brooks, G.W., Ashikaga, T., Strauss, J.S., and Brier, A. (1987b). The Vermont longitudinal study of persons with severe mental illness, II: Long-term outcome of subjects who retrospectively met DSM-III criteria for schizophrenia. *American Journal of Psychiatry, 144,* 726-735.

Heilbrun, K. (1992). The role of psychological testing in forensic assessment. *Law and Human Behavior, 16,* 257-272.

Helzer, J.E., (1981). The use of a structured diagnostic interview for routine psychiatric evaluations. *The Journal of Nervous and Mental Disease, 169,* 45-49.

Hoch, P., and Zubin, J. (Eds.) (1962). *The Future of Psychiatry.* New York: Grune and Stratton.

Hohman, L.A. (1960). Hoch and Zubin (Eds.), *Current Approaches to Psychoanalysis.* New York: Grune and Stratton.

Holden, C. (1973). Altered states of consciousness: Mind researchers meet to discuss exploration and mapping of inner space. *Science, 179,* 982-983.

Houts, A.C., and Graham, K. (1986). Can religion make you crazy? Impact of client and therapist religious values on clinical judgments. *Journal of Consulting and Clinical Psychology, 54,* 267-271.

Hsu, J., Tseng, W.S., Ashton, G., McDermott, J.F., Jr., and Char, W. (1985). Family interaction patterns among Japanese-American and Caucasian families in Hawaii. *American Journal of Psychiatry, 142,* 577-581.

Hunt, W.A. (1959). An investigation of naval neuropsychiatric screening procedures. In H. Guetzkow (Ed.), *Groups, Leadership and Men* (pp. 245-256). Pittsburgh: Carnegie Press.

Ilfeld, F.W., Jr. (1980). Understanding marital stressors: The importance of coping style. *The Journal of Nervous and Mental Disease, 168,* 375-381.

Jackson, D.D. (1962). *Stanford Medical Bulletin, 20,* 202.

Jacob, R.G., Mler, M.B., Turner, S.M., and Wall, III, C. (1985). Otoneurological examination in panic disorder and agoraphobia with panic attacks: A pilot study. *American Journal of Psychiatry, 142,* 715-720.

Journal of Abnormal Psychology (1975).

Kandler, H., Plutchik, R., Cone, H., and Siegel, B. (1975). Prediction of performance of psychiatric residents: A three year follow-up study. *American Journal of Psychiatry, 132,* 1286-1290.

Keller, C.W. (1971). Characteristics of Rorschach interpretive types: An exploratory study. *Dissertation Abstracts International, 32,* 2400.

Kelly, E.L., and Fiske, D.W. (1950). Prediction of success in veterans administration program in clinical psychology. *American Psychologist, 5,* 365-406.

Klassen, D. and O'Connor, W.A. (1988). A prospective study of predictions of violence in adult male mental health admissions. (1988). *Law and Human Behavior, 12,* 143-157.

Klein, D.F., and Davis, M.M. (1969). *Diagnosis and Drug Treatment of Psychiatric Disorders*. Baltimore: The Williams and Wilkins Company.

Klesges, R.C., Fisher, L., Vasey, M., and Pheley, A. (1985). Predicting adult premorbid functioning levels: Another look. *The International Journal of Clinical Neuropsychology*, *7*, 1-3.

Koran, L.M. (1975a). The reliability of clinical methods data and judgments: Part I. *New England Journal of Medicine*, *293*, 642-646.

Koran, L.M. (1975b). The reliability of clinical methods data and judgments: Part II. *New England Journal of Medicine*, *293*, 695-701.

Koson, M.D., and Robey, A. (1973). Amnesia and competency to stand trial. *American Journal of Psychiatry*, *130*, 588-592.

Krier, B.A., (1989). Hearing voices; a call more common than believed. *Los Angeles, Times* June 29, 1989. Part V.

Kubie, L.S. (1971). Multiple fallacies in the concept of schizophrenia. *The Journal of Nervous and Mental Disease*, *153*, 331-342.

Kubie, L.S. (1973). The Ruby case, who or what was on trial. *Journal of Psychiatry and Law*, *1*, 475-491.

Kutchins, H., and Kirk, S.A. (1986). The reliability of DSM-III: A critical review. *Social Work Research and Abstracts*, Winter, 3-12.

Landers, S. (1986). *APA Monitor* (February, 1986), *17*, 7.

Lando, H.A. (1976). On being sane in insane places: A supplemental report. *Professional Psychology*, *5*, 47-52.

Lanyon, R.I. (1984). Personality assessment. *Annual Review of Psychology*, *35*, 667-701.

Leff, J. (1977). International variations in the diagnosis of psychiatric illness. *British Journal of Psychiatry*, *31*, 329-338.

Levine, M. (1984). The adversary process and social science in the courts: Barefoot v. Estelle. *The Journal of Psychiatry & Law*, *12*, 147-181.

Lewandowski, D., and Saccuzzo, D.P. (1976). The decline of psychological testing. *Professional Psychology*, *7*, 177-184.

Lewis, L., Allen, J.G., and Frieswyk, S. (1983). The assessment of interacting organic and functional factors in a psychiatric population. *Clinical Neuropsychology*, *5*, 65-68.

Liberman, R.P., Sonnenberg, S.M., and Stern, M.S. (1971). Psychiatric evaluations for young men facing the draft: A report of 147 cases. *American Journal of Psychiatry*, *128*, 147-152.

Lindy, J.D., Green, B.L., and Patrick, M. (1980). The internship: Some disquieting findings. *American Journal of Psychiatry*, *137*, 76-79.

Little, K.B. (1967). Research etiquette and the study of clinician's behavior. *Journal of Consulting Psychology*, *31*, 16-18.

Livermore, J.M., Malmquist, C.P., and Meehl, P.E. (1968). On the justification for civil commitment. *University of Pennsylvania Law Review, 117.*

Loftus, T. (1960). *Meaning and Methods of Diagnosis in Clinical Psychiatry.* Philadelphia: Lea and Feiberger.

Lowenbach, H., and Shore, J.H. (1970). Clinical psychiatry. In E.A. Spiegel (Ed.), *Progress in Neurology and Psychiatry*, Vol. 25. New York: Grune and Stratton.

Luborsky, L. (1954). Selecting psychiatric residents, survey of the Topeka research. *Bulletin of the Menninger Clinic, 18*, 252-259.

Luft, J.B. (1950). Implicit hypotheses and clinical prediction. *Journal of Abnormal and Social Psychology, 45*, 756-759.

Lytton, H. (1971). Observation studies of parent child interaction: A methodological review. *Child Developments, 17*, 651-684.

Maguigad, L.C. (1973). Discussion of Koson and Robey, Amnesia and competency to stand trial. *American Journal of Psychiatry, 130*, 593.

Manderscheid, R.W. (1987). Long-term perspectives on persons with chronic mental disorder. *American Journal of Psychiatry, 144*, 783-784.

Mariner, E.S. (1967). A critical look at professional education in the mental health field. *American Psychologist, 22*, 271-281.

Matarazzo, J.D. (1978). The interview: Its reliability and validity in psychiatric diagnosis. In B.B. Wolman (Ed.), *Clinical Diagnosis of Mental Disorders: A Handbook.* New York: Plenum Press.

Matarazzo, J.D. (1986a). Computerized clinical psychological test interpretations: Unvalidated plus all mean and no sigma. *American Psychologist, 41*, 14-24.

Matarazzo, J.D. (1986b). Response to Fowler and Butcher on Matarazzo. *American Psychologist, 41*, 96.

Matarazzo, J.D. (1990). Psychological assessment versus psychological testing. Validation from Binet to the school, clinic, and courtroom. *American Psychologist, 45*, 999-1017.

Matarazzo, J.D. (1991). Psychological assessment is reliable and valid: Reply to Ziskin and Faust. *American Psychologist,* August, 882-884.

McMahon, E.A. (1983). Forensic issues in clinical neuropsychology. In Golden, C.J., and Vicente, P.J. (Eds.). *Foundations of Clinical Neuropsychology,* NY: Plenum Press.

McMillan, T.M. (1984). Investigation of everyday memory in normal subjects using the Subjective Memory Questionnaire (SMQ). *Cortex, 20*, 333-347.

McNeil, D.E., Binder, R.L., and Greenfield, T.K. (1988). Predictors of violence in civilly committed acute psychiatric patients. *American Journal of Psychiatry, 145*, 965-970.

McReynolds, W. (1979). DSM-III and the future of applied social science. *Professional Psychology*, 123-132.

Meehl, P.E. (1971). Law and the fireside inductions: Some reflections of a clinical psychologist. *Journal of Social Issues*, Vol. 27.

Meehl, P.E. (1973). *Psychodiagnosis: Selected papers*. Minneapolis: University of Minnesota Press.

Mellsop, G., Varghese, F., Joshua S., and Hicks, A. (1982). The reliability of Axis II of DSM-III. *American Journal of Psychiatry*, *139*, 1360-61.

Menninger, K. (1968). *The Crime of Punishment*. New York: The Viking Press.

Miller, G.A. (1980). (Interviewed by Elizabeth Hall). Giving away psychology in the 80's. *Psychology Today*, *13*, 38.

Mirowsky, J. (1990). Subjective boundaries and combinations in psychiatric diagnoses. *The Journal of Mind and Behavior, 11,* 407-424.

Mischel, W. (1979). On the interface of cognition and personality. *American Psychologist, 34*, 740-754.

Monahan, J. (1978). *The prediction of violent criminal behavior: A methodological critique and prospectus in deterrence and incapacitation: Estimating the effects of criminal sanctions on crime rates.* National Academy of Sciences, Washington, DC, pp. 244-269.

Napa Register, February 25, 1985.

Neulinger, J. (1968). Perceptions of the optimally integrated person: A redefinement of mental health. *Proceedings of the 76th Annual Convention of the American Psychological Association, 3*, 553-554.

Norris, V. (1959). *Mental illness in London.* Maudsley Monograph 6. London: Chapman and Hall.

Northwestern University Law Review (1962-63). Copyright by the Northwestern School of Law, *57*, entire issue.

Oskamp, S. (1962). Clinical experience and training and clinical prediction. *Psychological Monographs*, 76.

Otto, R.K., Poythress, N., Starr, L. and Darkes, J. (1993). An empirical study of the reports of APA's peer review panel in the Congressional review of the U.S.S. Iowa incident. *Journal of Personality Assessment, 61,* 425-442.

Paris, J. (1975). Diagnosis before treatment. *Canadian Psychiatric Journal, 20,* 305-307.

Pasamanick, B., Divity, S., and Lefton, M. (1959). Psychiatric orientation and its relation to diagnosis and treatment in a mental hospital. *American Journal of Psychiatry, 116.*

Plag, J.A., and Arthur, R.J. (1965). Psychiatric re-examination of unsuitable naval recruits. *American Journal of Psychiatry, 131,* 534-541.

Plag, J.A. and Goffman, J.M. (1966). The prediction of four-year military effectivenesss. *Military Medicine, 131,* 729-735.

Plaut, E., and Cromwell, B. (1955). The ability of the clinical psychologist to discriminate between drawings by deteriorated schizophrenics and normal subjects. *Psychological Reports, 1,* 153-158.

Poythress, N.G., Jr. (1977). Mental health expert testimony: Current problems. *Journal of Psychiatry and Law, 5,* 201-227.

Presly, A.S., and Walton, H.J. (1973). Dimensions of abnormal personality. *British Journal of Psychiatry, 122,* 269-276.

Pugh, D. (1973). The insanity defense in operation: A practicing psychiatrist views Durham and Brawner. *Washington University Law Quarterly,* 87-108.

Reigan, R.M. (1962). Psychological deficit. *Annual Review of Psychology, 13.*

Repko, G.R., and Cooper, R. (1985). The diagnosis of personality disorder: A comparison of MMPI profile, Millon inventory, and clinical judgment in a workers' compensation population. *Journal of Clinical Psychology, 41,* 867-881.

Reppucci, N.D., and Clingempeel, W.G. (1978). Methodological issues in research with correctional populations. *Journal of Consulting and Clinical Psychology, 46,* 727-746.

Rierdan, J., Koff, E., and Heller, H. (1982). Gender, anxiety, and human figure drawings. *Journal of Personality Assessment, 46,* 594-596.

Robitscher, J. (1972). The new face of legal psychiatry. *American Journal of Psychiatry, 129,* 91-97.

Robitscher, J., and Williams, R. (1977). Should psychiatrists get out of the courtroom? *Psychology Today, 11,* 85.

Roche, P.Q. (1958a). Symposium on Criminal Responsibility and Mental Disease. 19th Annual Law Institute, University of Tennessee (1958), and 26 *Law Review* (1959), 221, 240-241.

Roche, P.Q. (1958b). *The Criminal Mind.* New York: Farrar, Straus, & Cudahy.

Roesch, R. (1979). Determining competency to stand trial: An examination of evaluation procedures in an institutional setting. *Journal of Consulting and Clinical Psychology, 47,* 542-550.

Rogers, R. (1984). Towards an empirical model of malingering and deception. *Behavioral Sciences and The Law, 2, No. 1,* 93-111.

Rogers, R., and Seman, W. (1983). Murder and criminal responsibility: An examination of MMPI profiles. *Behavioral Sciences and The Law, 1, No. 2,* 89-95.

Rogers, R., and Webster, C.D. (1989). Assessing treatability in mentally disordered offenders. *Law and Human Behavior, 13,* 19-29.

Rogers, R., Gillis, J.R., Dickens, S.E., and Webster, C.D. (1988). Treatment recommendations for mentally disordered offenders: More than roulette? *Behavioral Sciences & the Law, 6,* 487-495.

Rosenhan, D.L. (1973). On being sane in insane places. *Science, 179,* 250-258.

Roth, L.H. (1986). The council on psychiatry and law. *American Journal of Psychiatry, 143,* 412-413.

Rothman, T. (1962) In Hoch, P., and Zubin, J. (Eds.) (1962). *The Future of Psychiatry.* New York: Grune and Stratton.

Rotter, J.B. (1967). Can the clinician learn from experience? *Journal of Consulting Psychology, 13,* 12-15.

Ruesch, J. (1966b) The future of psychoanalytically oriented psychiatry. In J. Masserman (Ed.) *Science and Psychoanalysis, 10.* New York: Grune and Stratton.

Saghir, M.T. (1971). A comparison of some aspects of structured and unstructured psychiatric interviews. *American Journal of Psychiatry, 128,* 180-184.

Saks, M.J. (1978). (Boston College) social psychological contribution to a legislative subcommittee on organ and tissue transplant. *American Psychologist,* 68-689.

Salzman, L. (1973). Changing styles in psychiatric syndromes: Historical overview. *American Journal of Psychiatry, 130,* 147-149.

Sarason, S.B. (1954). *The Clinical Interaction.* New York: Harper and Brothers.

Sarason, S.B. (1981). An asocial psychology and a misdirected clinical psychology. *American Psychologist, 36,* 827-836.

Sarbin, T.R., and Mancuso, J.C. (1970). Failure of a moral enterprise: Attitude of the public toward mental illness. *Journal of Consulting and Clinical Psychology, 35,* 159-173.

Sarbin, T.R., and Mancuso, J.C. (1972). Paradigms and moral judgments: Improper conduct is not disease. *Journal of Consulting and Clinical Psychology, 39,* 6-8.

Sattin, D.B. (1980). Possible sources of error in the evaluation of psychopathology. *Journal of Clinical Psychology, 36,* 99-105.

Schafer, R. (1978). Psychological test responses manifesting the struggle against decompensation. *Journal of Personality Assessment, 42,* 563-571.

Scher, J.M. (1962-63). Expertise and the post hoc judgment of insanity, or the antegnostician and the law. *Northwestern University Law Review, 57.*

Schlegel, J.F. (1986). *Los Angeles Times* (June). The science and medicine section.

Schopp, R.F., and Quattrocchi, M.R. (1984). Tarasoff, the doctrine of special relationships, and the psychotherapist's duty to warn. *The Journal of Psychiatry and Law, 12,* 13-37.

Schuckit, M.A. (1982). Prevalence of affective disorder in a sample of young men. *American Journal of Psychiatry, 139,* 1431-1436.

Schulberg, H.C., Saul, M., McClelland, M., Ganguli, M., Christy, W., and Frank, R. (1985). Assessing depression in primary medical and psychiatric practices. *Archives of General Psychology, 42,* 1164-1170.

Sechrest, L., Gallimore, R., and Harsch, P.D. (1967). Feedback and accuracy of clinical predictions. *Journal of Consulting Psychology, 31,* 1-11.

Shaffer, J.W. (1981). Using the MMPI to evaluate mental impairment in disability determination. In J. Butcher, G. Dahlstrom, M. Gynther, and W. Schofield (Eds.), *Clinical Notes on the MMPI.* Nutley, NJ: Roche Psychiatric Service Institute.

Shagass, C. (1977). Book review. *The Journal of Nervous and Mental Disease, 164,* 380-384.

Shah, S. (1969). Crime and mental illness, problems in defining and labeling deviant behavior. *Mental Hygiene, 53,* 21-33.

Sharfstein, S.S., Towery, O.B., and Milowe, I.D. (1980). Accuracy of diagnostic information submitted to an insurance company. *American Journal of Psychiatry, 137,* 70-75.

Sharkey, K.J., Ritzler, B.A. (1985). Comparing diagnostic validity of the TAT and a new picture projective test. *Journal of Personality Assessment, 49,* 406-412.

Sharma, S.L. (Ed.). (1970). *The Medical Model of Mental Illness.* Woodland Hills, CA: Logistic Publishing Company, Inc.

Shepherd, M. (1971). A critical appraisal of contemporary psychiatry. *Comprehensive Psychiatry, 12,* 302-321.

Shoham-Salomon, D.V. (1985). Are schizophrenics' behaviors schizophrenic? What medically versus psycho-socially oriented therapists attribute to schizophrenic persons. *Journal of Abnormal Psychology, 94,* 443-453.

Shubow, L.D., and Bergstresser, C.D. (1977). Handling the psychiatric witness. *Trial, 13,* 32-35.

Sletten, I.W., Altman, H., and Ulett, G.A. (1971). Routine diagnosis by computer. *American Journal of Psychiatry, 127,* 1147-1152.

Slovenko, R. (1984). Commentary: Syndrome evidence in establishing a stressor. *The Journal of Psychiatry & Law, 12,* 443-467.

Smith, W.L. (1986). The thirteenth nerve diagnosing the chronic pain patient: New role for the neuropsychologist. *The International Journal of Clinical Neuropsychology, 8,* 94-96.

Soskin, W.F. (1954). Bias in post-diction from projective tests. *Journal of Abnormal and Social Psychology, 49,* 69-74.

Sparr, L.F., and Atkinson, R.M. (1986). Posttraumatic Stress Disorder as an insanity defense: Medicolegal quicksand. *American Journal of Psychiatry, 143,* 608-613.

Spitzer, R.L., and Fleiss, J.L. (1974). A re-analysis of the reliability of psychiatric diagnosis. *British Journal of Psychiatry, 125,* 341-347.

Spitzer, R.L., Cohen, J., Fleiss, J., and Endecott, J. (1967). Quantification of agreement in psychiatry diagnosis. *Archives of General Psychiatry, 17,* 83-87.

Spitzer, R.L., Endicott, J., and Robins, E. (1975). Clinical criteria for psychiatric diagnosis and DSM-III. *American Journal of Psychiatry, 132,* 1187-1192.

Stainbrook. E. (1971). Psychiatry. E.A. Spiegel (Ed.), *Progress in Neurology and Psychiatry* (Chapter 19). New York and London: Grune and Stratton.

Steadman, H.J. (1973a). Follow up on Baxstrom patients returned to hospitals for the criminally insane. *American Journal of Psychiatry, 130,* 317.

Stevenson, I. (1983). Do we need a new word to supplement "hallucination"? *American Journal of Psychiatry, 140,* 1609-1611.

Stoll, A.L., Tohen, M., Baldessarini, R.J., Goodwin, D.C., Stein, S., Katz., S., Geenens, D., Swinson, R.P., Goethe, J.W., and McGlashan, T. (1993). Shifts in diagnostic frequencies of schizophrenia and major affective disorders at six North American psychiatric hospitals, 1972-1988. *American Journal of Psychiatry, 150,* 1668-1673.

Stoller, R.J., and Geertsma, H. (1963). The consistency of psychiatrists' clinical judgments. *Journal of Nervous and Mental Disease, 151,* 58-66.

Strauss, J.S., Bartko, J.J., and Carpenter, W.T. (1973). The use of clustering techniques for the classification of psychiatric patients. *British Journal of Psychiatry, 122,* 531-540.

Strauss, J.S., Gabriel, K.R., Kokes, R.F., Tizler, B.A., Van Ord, A., and Tarana, E. (1979). Do psychiatric patients fit their diagnoses? *The Journal of Nervous and Mental Disease, 167,* 105-113.

Strupp, H.H., and Hadley, S.W. (1977). A tri-partite model of mental health and therapeutic outcomes. *American Psychologist, 32,* 187-196.

Stuart, R.B. (1970). *Trick or Treatment.* Champagne, IL: Research Press.

Suarez, J.M. (1972). Psychiatry and the criminal law system. *American Journal of Psychiatry, 129,* 69-73.

Suedfeld, P. (1975). The clinical relevance of reduced sensory stimulation. *Canadian Psychological Review, 16,* 88-92.

Szasz, T.S. (1961). *The Myth of Mental Illness, Formulation of a Theory of Normal Conduct.* New York: Hoerber-Harper.

Szasz, T.S. (1963). *Law, Liberty & Psychiatry.* New York: The Macmillan Co.

Tarrier, N. (1979). The future of the medical model. A reply to Guze, an editorial. *The Journal of Nervous and Mental Disease, 167*, 71-73.

Tarter, R.E., Templer, D.I., and Hardy, C. (1975). The psychiatric diagnosis. *Diseases of the Nervous System, 36*, 30-31.

Taylor, M.A., and Abrams, R.A. (1975). A critique of the St. Louis psychiatric research criteria for schizophrenia. *American Journal of Psychiatry, 132*, 1275-1280.

Taylor, M.A., and Heiser, J.F. (1972). Phenomenology: An alternative approach to diagnosis of mental disease. *Comprehensive Psychiatry*, 12.

Taylor, M.A., Gaztanaga, P., and Abrams, R. (1974). Manic-depressive illness and acute schizophrenia: A clinical, family history, and treatment-response study. *American Journal of Psychiatry*, Vol. 131, No. 6, pp. 678-682.

Temerlin, M.K., and Trousdale, W.W. (1969). The social psychology of clinical diagnosis. *Psychotherapy: Theory, Research and Practice, 6*, 24-29.

Thoreson, C.E. (1973). The healthy personality as a sick trait. *The Counseling Psychologist, 4*, 51.

Thorne, F.C. (1972). Clinical judgment. In R.H. Woody and J.D. Woody (Eds.), *Clinical Assessment in Counseling and Psychotherapy*. Englewood Cliffs, NJ: Prentice-Hall.

Tsujimoto, R.N., and Berger, D.E. (1986). Situational influences on the predictive value of client behavior: Implication for Bayesian prediction. *Journal of Consulting and Clinical Psychology, 54*, 264-266.

Tuma, A.H., May, F., P.R.A., Yale, C., and Forsythe, A.B. (1978). Therapist experience general clinical ability and treatment outcome in schizophrenia. *Journal of Consulting and Clinical Psychology, 46*, 1120-1126.

Turk, D.C., and Salovey, P. (1985). Cognitive structures, cognitive processes, and cognitive-behavior modification: II. Judgments and inferences of the clinician. *Cognitive Therapy and Research, 9*, 19-33.

Turkington, C. (1986). Brief examines volition. *The American Psychological Association Monitor, 17*, 22.

Turpin, G. (1991). The psychophysiological assessment of anxiety disorders: Three-systems measurement and beyond. *Psychological Assessment: A Journal of Consulting and Clinical Psychology, 3*, 366-375.

Uebersax, J.S. (1983). Structural analysis of diagnostic disagreements. *The Journal of Nervous and Mental Disease, 171*, 199-206.

van Praag, H.M. (1971). The position of biological psychiatry among the psychiatric disciplines. *Comprehensive Psychiatry, 12*, 1-7.

Veleber, D.M., and Templer, D.I. (1984). Effects of caffeine on anxiety and depression. *Journal of Abnormal Psychology, 93,* 120-122.

Walker, R.C., and Lyndon, J. (1967). Varying degrees of psychological sophistication in the interpretation of sentence completion data. *Journal of Clinical Psychology, 23,* 229-231.

Warner, R. (1979). Race and sexual bias in psychiatric diagnosis. *The Journal of Nervous and Mental Disease, 167,* 303-310.

Wedding, D. (1983). Clinical and statistical prediction in neuropsychology. *Clinical Neuropsychology, 5,* 49-55.

Wedl, D.H., Parducci, A., and Lane, M. (1990). Reducing the dependence of clinical judgment on the immediate context: Effects of number of categories and types of anchors. *Journal of Personality and Social Psychology, 58,* 319-329.

Weiner, A.S. (1983). Emotional problems of adolescence: A review of affective disorders and schizophrenia. In C.E. Walker and M.C. Robert (Eds.), *Handbook of Clinical Child Psychology.* New York: John Wiley and Sons.

Weiner, I.B. (1983). The future of psychodiagnosis revisited. *Journal of Personality Assessment, 47,* 451-459.

Wells, S.J. (1984). Caffeine: Implications of recent research for clinical practice. *American Journal of Ortho-Psychiatry, 54,* 375-389.

Wesley, F. (1981). Burger's Challenge. *APA Monitor,* 3.

Wilkinson, C.B., and O'Connor, W.A. (1982). Human ecology and mental illness. *American Journal of Psychiatry, 139,* 985-990.

Wolitzky, D.L. (1973). Insane versus feigned insane: A reply to Dr. D.L. Rosenhan. *The Journal of Psychiatry and Law, 1,* 463-473.

Wolman, B.B. (Ed.) (1978). *Clinical diagnosis of mental disorders: A handbook.* New York: Plenum Press.

Wolpe, J. (1970). In R.B. Stuart, *Trick or Treatment.* Champaign, IL: Research Press.

Woody, R. (1972). In R.H. Woody and J.D. Woody (Eds.). *Clinical Assessment in Counseling and Psychotherapy.* Englewood Cliffs, NJ: Prentice-Hall.

Worrell, C.M. (1987). Psychiatric prediction of dangerousness in capital sentencing: The quest for innocent authority. *Behavioral Sciences and the Law, 5,* 443-446.

Yaffe, P.E., and Mancuso, J.C. (1977). Effects of therapist's behavior on people's mental illness judgments. *Journal of Consulting and Clinical Psychology, 45,* 84-91.

Yager, J. (1977). Psychiatric eclecticism: A cognitive view. *American Journal of Psychiatry, 134,* 736-741.

Zimmerman, M. (1994). Diagnosing personality disorders: A review of issues and research methods. *Archives of General Psychiatry, 51,* 225-245.

Zimmerman, M., Coryell, W., and Black, D.W. (1993). A method to detect intercenter differences in the application of contemporary diagnostic criteria. *The Journal of Nervous and Mental Disease, 181,* 130-134.

Zubin, J. (1967). Classification of the behavior disorders. *Annual Review of Psychology, 18,* 373-407.

Zussman, J., and Simon, J. (1983). Differences in repeated psychiatric examination of litigants to a lawsuit. *American Journal of Psychiatry, 140,* 1300-1304.

CHAPTER 8

Challenging the Experts' Experience

Despite the innumerable problems we have documented in psychiatric and psychological evaluation, the attorney will nevertheless encounter clinicians who insist they are capable of reaching sound opinions on the basis of their "experience." The attorney must be prepared to demonstrate that research provides little support for belief that a particular expert's experience has given him a degree of skill enabling him to make better evaluations than are made by his colleagues or, in fact, that experience has contributed much to his diagnostic or predictive skills.

There is an abundance of literature consisting of both authoritative statements and research findings, many in the late 1970s, the 1980s, and the 1990s, which clearly support the position that psychiatric and psychological assessment skills do not improve as a result of experience or training. This chapter contains more than 150 references. While some are old, more than 50 of them are from the 1980s and 1990s, providing continuity to this line of evidence. The material we will report in this chapter, however, can be most difficult for laymen, and even professionals, to accept. Most of us are imbued with the conviction that experience does teach, and that one improves with practice. It is therefore difficult to believe that a psychiatrist who has made a thousand evaluations will not be better at the task than one who has made fifty, or than someone who is completely lacking in formal training and clinical experience. Thus, after reviewing studies on experience and accuracy, we will examine factors (and research) that may explain the limited benefits of experience and provide examples that may make the findings comprehensible and believable to the trier of fact.

As regards research on experience and accuracy, many of the studies cited previously which show low validity of diagnosis and prediction included highly trained and experienced psychologists and psychiatrists. Thus, in a general way, the argument can be presented that if after many years of experience, these experts still have low validity in assessment, it is reasonable to conclude that experience has not made them accurate assessors. Even more startling are studies which indicate that experienced clinicians are not, in any practical sense, better in diagnosis or prediction than inexperienced clinicians or even untrained laypersons and may, in fact, show greater problems in judgment bias. Evidence revealing this "state of the art" can be presented to the court to challenge the testimony of the psychiatrist or psychologist on the grounds that it has not been adequately demonstrated that he has any expertise or can contribute anything other than what laymen could contribute. (See Leifer, R., The Competence of the Psychiatrist to Assist in the Determination of Incompetency: A Skeptical Inquiry into the Courtroom Functions of Psychiatrists, 14 *Syracuse Law Review,* 1962-63, pp. 564-575. Dr. Leifer illustrates the point that the psychiatrist has neither knowledge nor methods that make him in any way superior to laymen in determining the existence of "competency." He then generalizes to the use of psychiatrists in court generally, pointing out that psychiatry is a pseudo-science and fails to meet several scientific standards.) The evidence to be cited below can certainly be presented to the judge or jury if for no other purpose than to help them feel self-assured in rejecting the opinions of the expert and using their own judgment instead. The material can be introduced through cross-examination on the scientific and professional literature or by calling a consultant expert.

To the expert who still refuses to concede what this literature shows, it is appropriate to ask that expert if he has established, scientifically, what his reliability and validity figures are. There will be extremely few, if any, psychiatrists who could honestly say that they have followed up all of their diagnostic evaluations. (If a psychiatrist claims he has done such follow-up, it will then be necessary to question him carefully concerning the follow-up methodology. The objective should be to see if he employed the scientific method in his follow-up. If not, of course, the follow-up means very little. For example, what criteria of accuracy were employed? Were independent evaluators used?) If they have not, they cannot possibly know what their validity is. The expert may also be considerably shaken by having someone ask him to produce some kind of quantitative evidence that he knows what he is talking about. He can be pressed to admit that he does not "know" what he claims to know, but only "hopes" or "thinks" he knows. Paradoxically, many of the same psychiatrists who do not know what their own reliability or validity is will attempt to discredit psychological tests (especially when they disagree with the conclusions) on the grounds that the reliability and validity of these tests are insufficient. If this attitude towards tests can be elicited on cross-examination, such psychiatrists can be embarrassed by asking them how their diagnostic decisions have been demonstrated to be any better. Proceeding thusly, one should be able to show that the psychiatrist is exhibiting a "double standard" of evidence in evaluating the accuracy of his own judgment versus that of any other techniques he is trying to discredit.

RESEARCH AND COMMENTARY ON EXPERIENCE AND ACCURACY

A number of earlier studies have been conducted on experience and accuracy. Soskin (1954) found that experienced users of projective tests did not postdict behavioral characteristics of subjects any better than novices. Cline (1955) found that a series of professionals, including clinical psychologists and psychiatrists, demonstrated a statistically significant advantage in assessment over laymen but not over nursing trainees. Cline also found that greater experience was related to slightly better accuracy in predicting verbal behavior and significantly lower accuracy in predicting real-life social behavior. It would seem obvious that prediction of "real-life" behavior as opposed to verbal behavior is much more pertinent to typical issues addressed in forensic assessments. Plaut and Cromwell (1955) found that experienced psychologists were no better in discriminating drawings of deteriorated "schizophrenics" versus normal subjects than were non-clinical faculty members and college students. No one did particularly well at this task. The experts' accuracy ranged from 44% to 69%, and that of the college students, for example, ranged from 50% to 63%. Luft (1950) found that a group of professionals, including clinical psychologists and psychiatrists, were not superior to physical scientists in evaluating the characteristics of a person based on a verbatim copy of a one-hour diagnostic interview. Further analyses showed that about four-fifths of the experts did not even exceed chance levels of accuracy. Luborsky (1954) studied prediction of success in psychiatric training. He found that accuracy of prediction was not related to the age or experience of the interviewers, psychiatrists in this case. Based on a review of literature available at that time, Taft (1955) concluded that non-psychologists, at least physical scientists and personnel workers, appear more capable of appraising others accurately than are clinical psychologists. Taft also expressed doubt that professional psychologists are better judges of individuals than graduate students.

A study by Pasamanick et al. (1959) indicates that as a result of experience, clinicians may become overcommitted to a particular school of thought, leading to evaluations that are largely predetermined. Ullmann and Bergman (1959) found that social workers experienced in a particular program or setting were no more accurate in predicting outcome of homecare placement of patients than were four students just starting work in this setting. Mendel and Rapport (1963) found that experienced psychiatrists were slightly less effective in treatment than were untrained psychiatric aides. Walker and Lyndon (1967) found no practical difference between experienced psychologists, undergraduate psychology students, and undergraduate engineering students in making assessments from sentence completion data. Two of the four engineering students did better than four of the five experienced psychologists, although none of these groups achieved greater than 50% accuracy. Goldsmith and Mandell (1969) found that highly experienced psychiatrists performed no better than laypersons in matching explanatory descriptions of patients' disorders to these patients' actual current symptoms or status.

Lewis Goldberg has published a number of articles in prestigious psychology journals on the topic of experience and accuracy. In an earlier study, Goldberg (1959) found that experienced psychologists were no more accurate than hospital secretaries when using the Bender-Gestalt to distinguish brain-damaged and non-brain-damaged individuals. In another study, Goldberg (1965) examined the effects of experience on the accuracy achieved with the MMPI. In this study, Goldberg created extremely favorable conditions for experiential learning by providing clinicians with very extensive practice, as well as immediate and explicit feedback about their judgment accuracy. The clinicians' initial level of accuracy was relatively low and improved little, if at all, even after this exhaustive practice or experience under near optimal conditions. (See below for further details of this important study.) In a subsequent article, Goldberg (1968b) indicates that the same finding appears across a number of studies: that "the amount of professional training and experience of the judge does not relate to his judgmental accuracy..." Goldberg cites ten studies supporting his point.

Oskamp (1962) found no statistically significant difference between staff psychologists and psychology trainees in prediction in a simple discrimination task. Although the staff psychologists were superior to untrained evaluators, on a basis of statistical significance, the actual difference in rating ability was quite small, a matter of 4 percentage points, 69.6% accuracy for the untrained and 73% accuracy for the staff psychologists. Also, Oskamp found that the difference shriveled to 1 percentage point when the undergraduates, the untrained, were given a very brief training period.

In a subsequent study, Oskamp (1965) found that psychologists did no better than non-professionals in formulating predictions on the basis of a detailed case history. The predictive accuracy of both groups did not exceed chance levels.

Beckett et al. (1967) found that agreement across staff psychiatrists and first-year residents was about equal to that of staff psychiatrists alone, thus suggesting that the more experienced staff members did not achieve greater consensus (reliability) in their judgments than did these beginning students. Stuart (1970) cites many of the earlier studies showing no meaningful difference in the judgment accuracy of psychologists and psychiatrists as compared to laymen. He asserts that although most studies in this area demonstrate that experience does not enhance reliability, other studies show that it may aid judgment accuracy in some circumstances but actually decrease accuracy in other circumstances. Wiggins (1973) states, "surprisingly, there is little empirical evidence that justifies the granting of 'expert' status to the clinician on the basis of his training, experience, or information-processing ability." (p. 131)

In an impressive earlier study, Stoller and Geertsma (1963) found that highly experienced psychiatrists could not agree on the application of a large number of descriptive statements concerning a patient viewed on film in a 30-minute psychiatric interview. They found that, while agreement was low for all groups, a group defined as "inexperienced" by virtue of having less than seven years, agreed somewhat better than the experts with more than seven years of experience. There was no difference between those with psychoanalytic and those without psychoanalytic experience. The authors describe their findings as demonstrating that expert psychiatrists were unable to agree as to a patient's diagnosis, prognosis, psychodynamics, the causes of her problems, the feelings she was consciously experiencing, or the feelings that were latent or unconscious. They could not even agree in applying or discarding a number of "nonsense" descriptions that were included in the list of descriptions as items that would be most likely to discriminate between the more and less experienced psychiatrists. They assert that their study, without being so intended, may have demonstrated the weakest link in the psychiatrist's chain of inferential judgment, namely the jump from his observations to his concepts. They point out that psychiatrists draw confidence in the consensual validation deriving from what they assume to be shared expert opinion, saying for example, "The people who are expert in my field would agree with my judgment." They assert that their findings *categorically contradict such a belief.* The study is of particular importance because one often hears clinicians say, "Well, we may not agree on diagnosis but we agree very well on description of psychodynamics." This study contradicts such an assertion.

Wanderer (1969) found that experts in human figure drawing interpretation could not distinguish the DAP productions of such groups as "schizophrenics" and normals at greater than chance levels. The experts in this study were selected by peer ranking, or ratings of expertise provided by their professional colleagues. Experts were contacted in order of rank and, from among fifty, the twenty highest ranking cooperating experts participated in the study. Among these participants, a negative correlation was obtained between their ranking and their actual judgment accuracy. This -.36 correlation did not achieve statistical significance, perhaps due to the relatively small sample size, but the trend was obviously towards a negative relation between colleagues' ratings of expertise and accuracy. Wanderer goes on to describe a variant of confirmatory bias as a possible explanation for the continuing popularity of the DAP despite its deficient validity.

Woody (1972) quotes Thorne:

> Most parsimoniously, *clinical judgment* properly refers simply to the correctness of *the problem solving thinking of a special class of persons,* namely clinically trained persons with special levels of training, experience and competence. Judgments concerning clinical matters can be made by anyone. Such *lay opinions* have only the weight of the level of intelligence, education and experience of the person making them. It always remains to be demonstrated whether specialty training and experience make possible judgments of higher validity than lay opinions. (p. 9)

Thorne (1972) takes a somewhat varying position on experience and accuracy, at times stating that experience does help and at other times that it does not help. He notes, however, that "many clinical judgment studies indicate that the intelligent layman is able to make clinical judgments with practically as high reliability as trained professionals and even better than professionals with large areas of judgmental bias." Thorne further cites studies by Hiler and Nesvig and by Stricker indicating that given a predictor formula objectifying pertinent cues and eliminating inappropriate cues (in the Hiler and Nesvig study), students using the predictor formula achieved significantly greater accuracy than experienced clinicians without the formula. (p. 65) In the Stricker study, first and third year graduate students in a clinical training program made significantly more accurate judgments than experienced clinicians when all were provided with predictor formulas. According to Thorne, the findings might be interpreted as support for the theory that the experienced clinicians apparently were more influenced by invalid, theoretical orientations which they were unable to supersede even when provided with more valid predictors on which to base judgments. Thorne refers to repeated findings that highly trained professionals often cannot perform as well as intelligent laymen, confirming that invalid theories and nonpertinent experience may be more detrimental to clinical judgment than no training or experience at all. He asserts that each clinician should systematically evaluate his judgments repeatedly to determine if he is doing better than chance, and how much better she is doing than an intelligent layperson.

Abramowitz and Abramowitz (1973) assert that results from two studies indicate that even experienced clinicians hold differential standards of positive mental health for men and women.

Fitzgibbons and Shearn (1972), analyzing the results of their factor analytic study, state:

> Of the four subject variables for which data were collected it would seem logical to expect that length of experience would be among the ones most likely to show some kind of systematic relationship to beliefs about schizophrenia if the latter were actually a meaningful and reliable diagnostic category. That is, as one accumulates experience in observing schizophrenic patients, his ideas about this disorder should come closer and closer to those held by other professionals with similar amounts of experience if all of them are observing the same phenomenon, even though the observations might be made in different settings and the observers might vary in their educational backgrounds. The data presented in this paper fail to confirm this expectation, however. Length of experience is the 'one' variable which shows no relationship to any of the factors (correlations range from 0.01 to 0.15 and are statistically insignificant). (p. 292)

One strong demonstration of the inefficacy of experience in producing valid clinical assessment because objective physical evidence was the criterion of accuracy is the study of Goldstein et al. (1973), and will be dealt with at length here. These authors state:

> Even more disconcerting for the clinician have been the data which suggests that neither amount of clinical experience...nor amount of information available to the clinician...appear to be reflected in incremental predictive accuracy. These latter findings have been particularly disheartening in the face of renewed attempts to highlight specific strengths of the clinical method used singly...or when used in combination with various actuarial approaches to measurement and prediction....Hence the clinician neither achieves success as great as statistical prediction, nor does he appear to be able to lay claim to any special skills by virtue of his clinical training and sophistication. (p. 30)

The authors point out that in spite of these findings many clinicians continue to rely on their own clinical acumen in interpreting test data and making predictive statements, and they point out that such methods are still the most widely used and are being transmitted to future generations of psychologists.

In the Goldstein et al. study, two groups of patients were examined. The first group of ten were those who were demonstrably impaired in adaptive abilities dependent upon organic brain function—that is, by "demonstrably impaired," the authors mean that physical evidence of this organic impairment existed. In other words they were dealing with clearly, independently confirmable conditions, not with constructs. In the article, they cite the nature of the demonstrable evidence. The other ten patients, constituting a control group, had been referred for psychological examination. There was no reason based on their histories to suspect impairment of adaptive abilities dependent on organic brain function. Two groups of raters were constituted and asked to specify whether they judged the patient's performance as reflected in the protocols of tests to be organically impaired or not organically impaired. The first group consisted of five experienced clinicians. Their postdoctoral clinical experience ranged from 9-18 years with a mean of 14-1/2 years. Four of the five held the ABPP diploma (board certification). Further, all of these were employed in clinical settings where the question that they were being asked to make a judgment about was not at all an uncommon occurrence, so that the results of this study are not subject to the argument advanced against many of the actuarial versus clinical judgment studies, that in such studies the questions posed were frequently not of the type that a clinician is accustomed to answering. The second group of raters were inexperienced. Three were fulfilling their internship requirement for the doctoral degree and two had just completed their doctoral degrees and were taking a postdoctoral year of training. Available to the raters were a battery of what we will call "traditional" tests, these being the WAIS, the MMPI and the Bender-Gestalt. Also available was the Halstead-Reitan battery, with three of the five experienced psychologists stating that they could not utilize the latter, since they would not understand it—this from possessors of the ABPP diploma—despite the fact that at the time the study was conducted 15 years had passed since the development and extensive validation of this battery. The inexperienced clinicians were asked first to make the rating on the basis of the traditional battery and then subsequently to make ratings utilizing the Halstead battery. And finally, ratings were made purely on the basis of the Halstead battery, setting a cutoff point where suggested by Reitan, that is, prediction was made or classification was made purely on the basis of the test, without any clinical judgment involved. It should be pointed out that 6 months earlier the inexperienced clinicians had taken part in a 15 hour seminar on the use of the Halstead-Reitan battery.

Both groups of clinicians indicated that a clear determination was impossible for them to make with some of the patients' protocols when only the standard battery was available, and chose to exercise an option of declaring these "indeterminate." (This option is important in countering any argument that perhaps the battery of tests was not adequate. Apparently, the experts were satisfied with the battery in most cases as they exercised the option in only one-fourth of the cases.) A rule for final classification was established, and was relatively stringent. Any four of the five judges had to agree on classification in order that a patient be so declared.

Independent, objective criteria were available, and thus the results of this study present a powerful challenge to the notion commonly held that clinical experience leads to a high or a higher degree of accuracy in clinical judgment on a commonplace clinical task. First of all, on an absolute basis, the experienced clinicians correctly classified three of the impaired patients as impaired but erroneously classified four of the impaired as non-impaired. They erroneously classified three of the non-impaired as impaired and correctly classified five of the non-impaired as non-impaired. They exercised the "indeterminate" option with regard to three of the impaired and two of the non-impaired. Thus they were able to make only eight correct classifications out of the 20 cases. Taking out the cases which they held indeterminate, the results show that they were right approximately 53% of the time and wrong approximately 47% of the time in those classifications they felt they could make. Flipping a coin would have produced equivalent accuracy. Granting that the number of raters and the number of patients was small, this result provides about as clearcut a demonstration as is possible that extensive clinical experience fails to produce a high degree of judgmental accuracy or in fact a degree of accuracy that exceeds what could be accomplished by flipping coins. The results also seem to dissolve the reassurance one might hope to feel when dealing with a clinician who possesses the ABPP diploma. (See below, Chapter 9.)

Even more distressing to the notion of the contribution of experience to accuracy is the finding in the Goldstein et al. study that using the same traditional battery as the experienced clinicians, the inexperienced correctly identified five impaired subjects as impaired and only three as non-impaired and correctly identified six non-impaired as non-impaired and incorrectly identified only two non-impaired as impaired, and in each category found two indeterminate, thus performing better than the experienced in all categories. The Halstead impairment index without any kind of clinical interpretation correctly identified eight impaired and misidentified two impaired as not impaired while correctly identifying seven non-impaired and incorrectly classifying three non-impaired as impaired. And finally, the inexperienced clinicians utilizing the Halstead battery along with the traditional battery made 19 out of 20 correct identifications. The differences between experienced and inexperienced with the traditional battery were not statistically significant, although they were contrary to the direction one would expect if one believes that experience contributes to superior performance in clinical assessment. The Halstead battery alone and the inexperienced clinicians using the Halstead battery showed a statistically significant advantage over the experienced clinicians using the traditional battery.

Graham (1971) states:

> During the past two decades numerous studies have demonstrated the low level of accuracy with which clinical inferences can be made from psychological test

data...more discouraging are those studies which have suggested that level of accuracy is not related to amount of training or clinical experience...or to amount of information available to judges.

Several studies have indicated that predictive accuracy is not enhanced following feedback when feedback is defined as increased training, for example, a course in projective techniques...or as additional general clinical experience...Likewise, it appears that feedback after large numbers of trials...does not increase the accuracy of inferences by professional judges. (p. 286)

In his study Graham provided three groups of clinicians—High Experience, Medium Experience and Low Experience (21 in each group) with sets of MMPI profiles for each of which an independent psychiatric diagnosis of neurosis or psychosis was available. The clinicians were simply asked to indicate whether or not the given MMPI profile indicated a neurosis or a psychosis and were given the additional information that half of the profiles were neurotic and half were psychotic. The High Experience group was made up of 21 clinicians, 10 of whom held clinical positions (three in academic settings, seven combined clinical/academic responsibilities and one an administrator). Most of the clinicians reported using the MMPI occasionally, five never used it and seven used it frequently or routinely. About half had used it for more than 10 years and only three reported using the instrument for less than a year. The Medium Experience group was made up of 21 graduate students in Clinical Psychology who had completed at least one course in which the MMPI was considered, but none had more than very limited clinical experience with the instrument. The Low Experience group was made up of 21 undergraduate students who knew little or nothing about the MMPI and who participated in the study as part of the requirements for an introductory psychology course.

Each judge evaluated 90 MMPI protocols in blocks of 30. In the first 30 cases, there was no feedback of any kind. In the second and third blocks of 30, judges were given either random feedback or correct feedback. In the first block of 30, with no direct feedback involved, any difference which occurred among the three groups would be attributable to the greater experience of the experienced group. The results showed that in this first block of 30 judgments, for the very gross distinction between "neurotic" and "psychotic," with the knowledge that each protocol represented one or the other, the mean correct judgments for the Low Experience group was 12.71, for the Medium Experience group it was 15.71 and for the High Experience group it was 14.14 (less than 50% correct). None of these differences was statistically significant but if, in fact, clinical experience is an indicator of greater diagnostic acumen, it is astonishing that there was no difference of any practical meaning between the High Experience clinicians and the undergraduate students with no experience. Additionally, although not statistically significant, the "Medium Experience group," which was made up of graduate students, actually did slightly better than the High Experience group. In fairness, it should be noted that the Graham study showed that with immediate feedback—in the second and third blocks of trials, the judges could simply turn over and find the correct diagnosis on the back of the profile sheet—the experienced clinicians did show greater improvement than either the Low Experience or the Medium Experience groups. However, even under this condition of immediate feedback of results, a condition which rarely occurs in actual practice, the experienced judges were not able to achieve a hit rate beyond slightly better than two out of three. Graham states:

> More discouraging is the reaffirmation of the conclusion of other investigators...that learning over trials is at best minimal although the trials' effect was statistically significant indicating an improvement in accuracy across blocks of trials. The differences among the means of the three blocks were quite small with significant change in accuracy occurring only during the latter trials of the study. The best performance for any treatment group was for the High Experience judges in the correct feedback condition for trials 61-90 (X equals 21.71). Although this level of accuracy represents a significant increase over beginning trials and is statistically greater than a chance level of accuracy (15.30) it does not encourage one concerning the clinician's ability to learn the judgmental task even under what have been defined in this study as "ideal" conditions. (p. 289)

He also states:

> Even under "ideal" conditions, however, the absolute level of accuracy was quite low and improvement was not great. Further studies must determine if this low level of accuracy is due to methodological problems or to actual limitations in the clinician's ability to make accurate clinical inferences. (p. 290)

Livermore et al. (1968) state, in reference to assessments of dangerousness or need for care, custody or treatment: "There is a ready inclination to believe that *experts* in the behavioral sciences will be able to identify those members of society who will kill, rape, or burn. The fact is, however, that such identification cannot presently be accomplished." (p. 84) (italics added)

Kubie (1971), referring to the use of the term schizophrenia in spite of the fact that it is vague and there are other alternatives, states:

> Therefore, it is especially unfortunate that psychiatrists, young and old, have actually become afraid not to use the term lest some colleague point a scornful finger and say, "He does not even recognize schizophrenia." This has resulted in a timid conformity which has blunted our clinical perceptions and paralyzed our clinical thinking by freezing it into rigid molds rendering our clinical language so stereotyped as to be almost meaningless. Assumptions which are dominated by overriding preconceptions lead to pseudoperceptions. These in turn lead to the recording of stereotyped clinical histories and examinations and

506   Coping with Psychiatric & Psychological Testimony

to descriptions which are shaped to fit our preconceptions. Therefore, if we continue to accept the concept of schizophrenia uncritically our clinical discriminations will remain dulled and our clinical histories and our reports of mental status examinations will be cliche ridden. It is especially unfortunate that our *senior* (italics ours) psychiatrists and clinical psychologists have been blunted by this stereotype; because the effects of this have trickled down to impede the growth of our residents. (p. 333)

Kubie's use of the words "old" and "senior psychiatrists" indicate the relevance of his statement to the failure to learn from experience.

Sattler and Ryan (1973) found that examiners differ in their scoring of Stanford-Binet responses and that the scoring accuracy of Ph.D. psychologists with a mean of 9.37 years of postdoctoral experience was similar to that of a minimally trained group of graduate students and an untrained group of graduate students. They state: "These findings are congruent with those of a number of other investigations that have reported that experience is not a critical variable in the scoring of test responses." (p. 37)

Adinolfi (1971) indicates that clinicians are often unaware of the nature of their impressions, reflected, for example, by "reliance on 'Barnum' statements in their conceptualizations of clinical cases." He discusses the problem of illusory correlation and cites the work of the Chapmans in this regard. He summarizes the Chapmans' 1969 study as demonstrating how an observer's maintaining a high associative value between two behaviors can lead to his reporting a correlation between occurrence of those behaviors even though they occur together only by chance. Of course, maintaining illusory correlations is the opposite of learning from experience.

In their study of interpretation of Rorschach responses as a function of ascribed social class, Koscherak and Masling (1972) found that experienced clinicians (psychology faculty of the State University of New York at Buffalo) showed a greater social class bias in attributing pathology to case history and Rorschach protocols than did those with less experience (students in the Clinical Psychology program at the State University of New York at Buffalo who were in their internship).

Moxley (1973) found no difference in accuracy on a clinical judgment type task between a group of four Ph.D. professional clinical psychologists and four clinical psychology graduate students trained in applications of statistical decision theory, although both of these groups did somewhat better than four unsophisticated clinical graduate students who were not trained in statistical decision theory. With increasing amounts of information, the two former groups both improved approximately the same amount from an accuracy level of around 60% to one of close to 70%, but the years of experience made no difference.

Melges (1972) states:

Despite considerable advances in psychiatric research in the last three decades, many research reports that deal with complicated measurements and average differences between groups of subjects are difficult for the clinician to apply to his individual patients. On the other hand, the clinical psychiatrist who commonly focuses on subjective changes that occur over time within his individual patients lacks systematic methods for evaluating his influence on the process of change for a given patient. (p. 206)

And thus, we might add, he is likely to learn little, if anything, from experience.

Meehl (1971) states:

As a clinical practitioner...I sense a deep analogy between the problems faced by judge or legislator in balancing the fireside inductions again purportedly scientific or sociological findings and the perennial problem of how far we clinicians are entitled to rely upon clinical experience lacking (or apparently contradicting) experimental or quantitative research. For myself, as clinician, I have not been able to resolve this dilemma in an intellectually responsible way, although I have been steadily conscious of it and engaged in theoretical and empirical research on it for over a quarter century. As I have argued elsewhere it may be that a naive judge will (over the long run) make better decisions than one who knows just enough psychology or psychiatry to rely on medical or social science experts making an intensive study of the offender. The efficiency of actuarial prediction is almost always at least equal to or usually better than prediction based upon (purported) clinical understanding of the individual subject's personality...second, behavior science research itself shows that by and large the best way to predict anybody's behavior is his behavior in the past (known among my colleagues as Meehl's Malignant Maxim). Hence the naive judge's reliance on the fireside inductions may yield better results than the intermediate level sophistication which knows enough to ask the psychologist's or psychiatrist's opinion but does not know enough to take what he said *cum grano salis,* especially when clinical opinion conflicts with extrapolation from the offender's record.

Chapman and Chapman (1969) report, in their study demonstrating the operation of illusory correlation with regard to certain DAP signs, that of the 44 clinicians who responded most had Ph.D.'s and they averaged 8.4 years of experience in psycho-diagnostics. According to the Chapmans' report, the experienced clinicians used the signs involved in the same way as observers with no clinical experience at all. In a later study, the Chapmans (1971) demonstrated that expert psycho-diagnosticians on the basis of their clinical experience and naive judges on the basis of their observation of random materials reported the same Rorschach signs as being valid indicators of homosexuality despite the fact that the signs had no valid relations with homosexuality either empirically or in the experimental task. Further, both the experts and the naive judges tended not to report other Rorschach signs of potentially greater validity. Thus, of 32 clinicians who responded, they most often mentioned five signs which have not been supported by research. On the other hand, only two of the 32 mentioned a sign which has been validated. Obviously, despite many years of experience, they continue to make the same errors.

Kandler et al. (1975) demonstrated that the predictions of performance of psychiatric residents by senior psychiatric faculty showed no relationship to actual performance.

Tarter et al. (1975) showed only 50% agreement between psychiatrists with an average of 16 years of clinical experience, who were acknowledged experts, when they attempted to diagnose patients into the very gross categories of functional psychosis, neurosis and personality disorder. Obviously, under these circumstances, at least 50% of the diagnoses were wrong despite the extensive experience and status of the psychiatrists making the evaluations.

Andreasen et al. (1974), showing that clinicians could not accurately diagnose "thought disorder," found no differences between faculty psychiatrists, psychologists and social workers and residents and, therefore, pooled all of their results. Obviously, if there was no difference between faculty psychiatrists and residents, the considerably greater experience of the faculty psychiatrists did not enable them to draw more accurate conclusions than the much less experienced residents.

Blankenhorn and Cerbus (1975) found no difference in accuracy between nine psychologists and nine other judges, with degrees in some other field, in distinguishing between the test results of brain damaged and non-brain damaged patients. They also found no difference in terms of the level of training among the psychologists, of whom three had Ph.D.'s with a mean of nine and one-half years of experience, three had Master's degrees with three years of experience, and the remaining judges had Bachelor's degrees with virtually no experience. No differences as a result of training or experience were found.

Schinka and Sines (1974) state: "There is an impressive literature…that has failed to demonstrate any relationship between amount of clinical training and experience and the level of accuracy in clinical judgments." (p. 374) In their study they similarly found no difference based on experience and training, and state in conclusion: "These data constitute a constructive replication of the other findings in that they fail to demonstrate a positive relationship between amount of training and judgmental accuracy." (p. 377)

Andreasen et al. (1982) conducted a study seeking to evaluate sources of variance in the reliability of psychiatric ratings and diagnoses. They found no significant differences based on training or background, and no significant differences between physicians and non-physicians or between clinicians with many year of clinical experience and clinicians with less experience. In their study, they established three levels of experience, those with less than four years, those with five to 10 years, and those with more than 10 years of experience. It should be noted that, although their study does not show experience to make any difference so far as reliability is concerned, for most of the items studied, the reliability coefficients reported are higher than have been reported earlier.

Poythress (1977) charges that psychiatrists have been allowed to "get considerable mileage" by utilizing years of experience as the basis for conclusions. He notes that this vague "clinical experience," while not enlightening to judge or jury, is less vulnerable to cross-examination. (We disagree. Based on literature available in this book, we feel it is quite possible to attack experience on cross-examination.) Poythress further notes that this evasiveness may be an intentional tactic employed by a witness, and further notes that it has been recognized and recommended as a maneuver to avoid some kinds of questions on cross-examination.

Warner (1979) found different racial biases among therapists of different races, noting that the length of therapist experience was not a significant factor in eliminating bias. Warner also found that therapists may tend to choose diagnoses with which they are familiar and comfortable and diagnoses which lend themselves to the clinicians' usual therapeutic approach. Half of the clinicians in their study had more than five years of experience.

Coryell et al. (1978) found that using a structured psychiatric interview, non-physician interviewers made ratings comparable to those of physicians even for items thought to require the most clinical and medical judgment. They compared the degree of agreement for pairs of non-physicians with pairs consisting of a physician and a non-physician and found that neither practice nor prior medical training appeared to influence reliability. They assert that non-physician interviewers are often superior as interviewers to physicians because they rely less on subjective "clinical impression" and tend to be more thorough and consistent. Thus, their findings support the contention that data gathered and conclusions formed are likely to be little different after many years of experience than they would be with little or no experience when a structured interview format is employed. This is of some importance because there is considerable current literature recommending the use of the structured interview as a means of attempting to standardize interviewing and potentially to reduce some of the extreme variability due to differences in examiner procedures.

Heaton et al. (1978a), in their article demonstrating fakability of neuropsychological testing (see Chapter 18), utilized 10 neuropsychologists as judges in their study. The 10 differed greatly with respect to previous experience in interpreting the neuropsychological battery involved, with a range of from eight weeks to 18 years. Five of the judges had four or more years of experience and a range of experience was deliberately used in order to assess a possible role of experience in increasing diagnostic accuracy. They found no statistically significant relationship between correct classification rates and amount of previous experience in neuropsychology. Incidentally, they also found no significant relationship between the confidence with which the ratings were made and the accuracy of diagnosis. Similarly, in the study of Albert et al. (1980), experienced psychologists (Fellows of the Society for Personality Assessment) were unable to distinguish between faked and genuine Rorschach records, although they were forewarned that some of the records were faked.

Along related lines, Resnick (1984) notes that "no research has demonstrated the ability of mental health professionals to accurately detect malingering." (p. 26) He indicates, however, that psychiatric patients may be skillful in detecting malingerers. The majority of psychiatric patients, of course, lack formal professional training. Resnick notes that in Rosenhan's study (see Chapter 7) and in another study, malingerers were recognized by a number of psychiatric patients. Thus, although Resnick does not state matters in this way, if research is lacking which demonstrates the ability of mental health professionals to detect malingering and some research suggests psychiatric patients may be skillful in this regard, the obvious implication is that psychiatric patients may be better at this task than professionals.

Leli and Filskov (1981) compared the success with which experienced clinical psychologists and graduate students distinguished brain-damaged and non-brain-damaged individuals on the basis of IQ testing. The performance of the experienced and inexperienced judges did not differ, and accuracy was low across both groups. An actuarial formula achieved better overall results than either group of judges. These results suggest that the "expert" was not the inexperienced clinician, nor the experienced clinician, but the actuarial formula. Wedding (1983) found that accuracy in identifying presence or type of brain damage on the basis of neuropsychological testing was not related to experience. Neither level of training, nor years of experience with the battery used in the study was positively correlated with accuracy. As was the case in the study by Leli and Filskov, a statistical procedure achieved a higher overall level of accuracy than did the judges, once again suggesting that the "expert" (if one is to make this identification on the basis of accuracy) was not the experienced judge but the statistical procedure. Wedding indicates that statistical procedures are superior in general but that "few neuropsychologists incorporate statistical models in their practice." (p. 50) As we have noted before, actuarial procedures for data interpretation do not require the expert's participation, and indeed by eliminating experts from the interpretive process entirely and instead relying on actuarial methods where available, equal or higher overall levels of accuracy can be achieved. Along these lines, Wedding states, "the neuropsychologist's most appropriate role in the decision making process is deciding which variables are germane and beginning a database. It is a beginning long overdue." (p. 54)

Wittmann (1985) discusses the role of mental health experts in child custody cases. Wittmann states:

> Statements derived solely from "intuition," clearly limited clinical contact, speculation, a lack of converging indicators, or those representing strong personal bias unsupported by research or clinical data should be evaluated as "unscientific."...Mental health professionals often make less extreme, yet "unscientific" statements during testimony. We are often questioned regarding matters about which there is little consensus within our disciplines. *Our field is famous for supporting conclusions during testimony simply on the basis of "accumulated clinical experience", a phrase which may mean nothing more than accumulated personal bias.* (italics added) (p. 77)

Robins (1985), in a general critique of studies on the prevalence of DSM-III disorders, compares the interview results of psychiatrists and laymen, the latter of whom used a structured diagnostic interview (the DIS). Robins observes that results obtained by the laymen were, if anything, more reliable and perhaps more valid than those obtained by the psychiatrists. He notes, for example, that across different research centers the lay interviewers (using the DIS) produced more consistent prevalence rates than did the psychiatrists. There was no obvious reason to assume different rates of disorder across the centers, and thus problems in reliability may well explain the less consistent results obtained by the psychiatrists. Robins also notes that "the lay interviewers' interviews were as useful as the psychiatrists' for predicting treatment seeking within the following year." (p. 924) This amounts to saying that for this important clinical prediction, the lay interviewers had the same validity as the psychiatrists.

Schulberg et al. (1985) compared the diagnostic impressions of primary care physicians and psychiatrists to results obtained on objective measures. The primary care physicians seemed to underdiagnose depression, whereas the psychiatrists seemed to overdiagnose depression. Overall, the former group demonstrated a higher level of agreement with the objective measures than the latter group, with the primary care physicians achieving a kappa of .43, and the psychiatrists a kappa of .10. Although the difference in kappa may have been accounted for by varying prevalence rates in the populations seen by the two groups, the study, at best, provides no evidence that the psychiatrists performed better than the primary care physicians. In a statement suggesting that greater experience may exert negative effects on judgment accuracy, Schulberg et al. note:

> Clinicians confronted with a patient's ambiguous symptoms are likely to interpret them with diagnostic paradigms most familiar to their specialty and theoretical orientation; as a consequence, physical or psychiatric illnesses with similar manifestations often are treated inappropriately. (p. 1165)

Other authors also indicate that the involvement of professionals, even experienced ones, in the data interpretation process does not improve upon the accuracy that laymen could achieve given access to statistical or factual information. This point has repeatedly been made in articles addressing the prediction of violence. Levine (1984) observes that the "only" basis for predicting violence is a history of repeated violence in the past. He observes that laymen can draw the same inferences as experts when given such information, and thus the expert has nothing special to contribute in this regard. In discussing the prediction of violence, Menzies et al. (1985) state, "the present study indicates that nonclinicians, with minimal exposure to forensic patients, can achieve levels of accuracy at least equal to those of psychiatrists demonstrated in earlier work." (p. 67) Morse (1983) indicates that certain demographic or factual information, such as past behavior and socio-economic status, has some value in predicting violent behavior. He observes that given access to this type of information, laypersons are as capable of formulating predictions of violence as are mental health professionals and may do so in a less prejudicial manner. He argues that if laymen formulate judgments on the basis of this relevant information, experts should be prevented from offering alternative predictions.

A number of studies suggest that experience may breed increased error and bias. Arkes (1981) describes preconceived notions as a major impediment to accurate clinical judgment. Obviously, one would expect the expert to start with more initial ideas or preconceptions, such as assumptions about the relationship between specific behaviors and abnormality, than naive individuals. As Arkes states, "Prior associations...impede the accurate processing of the individual datum." (p. 324) Arkes discusses various studies, or re-analyses of prior studies, such as those by Shweder (1977) and Lord et al. (1979) that provide evidence for his statement. Arkes also mentions another possible contributing factor—that the most confident judges tend to be the least accurate ones. One might expect experts to generally show greater confidence on clinical judgment tasks than less expert ones, or novices.

A study by Arkes and Harkness (1980) with nonclinicians demonstrates that knowledgeable individuals are more prone to certain errors in the retention of previously presented material than less knowledgeable ones. Arkes and Harkness point out that experts are more prone to believe that a symptom consistent with the diagnostic impression they have formed, but that actually was not present, was indeed present. As a possible illustration of this point raised by Arkes and Harkness, if an expert assumes that schizophrenia is present, he may think he remembers observing certain symptoms consistent with the diagnosis, when the symptoms were actually never present. In contrast, experts are less likely to recall symptoms that were actually present but that were inconsistent with their diagnostic impressions. For example, this presumably schizophrenic individual may exhibit certain behavior inconsistent with the diagnosis, but these behaviors are more likely to be forgotten by experts than non-experts.

Studies by Bransford et al. (1972), Harris and Monaco (1978), Harris et al. (1975), and Keenan and Kintsch (1974) also provide demonstrations of this tendency to falsely recall non-existent "information" that is consistent with one's impressions and to forget actual information inconsistent with one's impression. As stated by Arkes and Freedman (1984), "...experts know more potentially interfering facts than non-experts do..." (p. 84) In discussing the implications of this possible disadvantage of expertise, Arkes and Freedman cite the work of Johnson et al. (1977), which they indicate shows that: "...experts who infer the presence of stimuli consistent with the diagnosis or judgment would mistakenly believe that there existed more corroborating evidence. Confidence in their decision would thereby be unduly inflated." (p. 89) Based on such research showing experts' particular disadvantages in recall, Arkes and Harkness (1980) indicate that, "...the diagnostician would be well-advised to record not only the diagnosis but also the symptoms actually observed." (p. 574) As their research, and research by Lingle and Ostrom (1979) shows, the judgments that one makes may be better recalled than the actual data on which these judgments are based. Thus, "This will tend to impede revision of an erroneous diagnosis unless the original symptoms are carefully recorded..." (p. 574)

Although much of the above research on the disadvantages of expertise has been conducted with college students, it relates closely to the mental processes performed by psychologists and psychiatrists when forming diagnostic impressions and predictions, and the research is consistent with various studies conducted with professionals. For example, Friedlander and Stockman (1983) found that psychologists and psychiatrists evidenced "anchoring bias" in review of case materials—they were unduly influenced by earlier information and did not adjust their views sufficiently on the basis of subsequent information. In a replication of this experiment, Friedlander and Phillips (1984) found that college students reviewing the same material did not show anchoring bias. In discussing why this bias was only shown by the professionals, Friedlander and Phillips state, "...experienced, confident judges may integrate new information immediately to fit the existing clinical impression or prototype....When new facts become available, the judge expands the existing representation rather than weighing the new evidence against the old." (p. 370)

Thorne (1972) also discusses the greater biases that experts may show. He states:

> These findings also indicate that "advanced" knowledge often may be more of a handicap than a help if it introduces inapplicable considerations or otherwise distracts the clinician from weighting priorities properly. The finding that many students show more efficient clinical judgment processes than their professors creates a challenge to academicians to demonstrate the actual validity of their theoretical and applied teachings. (p. 66)

Other studies with professionals, such as those on confidence and accuracy, and on illusory correlation (see Chapter 5) provide further evidence consistent with the above described work of Arkes and the other researchers.

Separate research by Arkes et al. (1986) shows another possible disadvantage of expertise. Their work suggests that more knowledgeable or experienced individuals are more likely to disregard, or to abandon potentially helpful decision rules (e.g., actuarial aids). This research was also conducted with college students, but it is obviously consistent with a number of other reports which show the resistance of clinicians to decision aids (e.g., Goldberg, 1965), and to surveys showing that many, if not the majority of clinicians tend to rely on idiosyncratic versus standard procedures for scoring and interpreting psychological tests (e.g., Wade and Baker, 1977). Along similar lines, a number of studies and reviews suggest that feedback or outcome information may actually lead to a decrease in judgment accuracy. Apparently, when clinicians find that their decision-making strategies lead to errors, as invariably occurs given the state of the "art," they often do not reach the seemingly rational conclusion—that although the best available methods are far from perfect, one should nonetheless stick with them because the alternatives are worse. Instead, they tend to abandon these rules and, in an effort to do better, come to rely more and more on what are actually idiosyncratic, as opposed to better researched, interpretive procedures. A considerable body of literature suggests that when clinicians abandon prespecified or actuarial decision rules, the end result is a decrease in overall diagnostic accuracy (see Chapter 5). For further discussion of the potential detrimental effects of feedback, the reader can consult a number of sources (Brehmer, 1980; Einhorn and Hogarth, 1978, 1981). In summing up these matters, Arkes et al. (1986) state:

The factors we examined in our two studies are present in a large number of important decision-making contexts....due to their long period of training clinical psychologists are presumed to have considerable expertise. They receive substantial monetary incentives. And finally, creative or innovative use of diagnostic signs is apparently not at all discouraged...Therefore, decision aids are rather unlikely to be used. (p. 108)

Apparently, then, clinicians who are highly motivated to achieve accurate results or that feel particularly experienced or knowledgeable come to believe that they should try to beat "the odds" by deviating from empirically established practices and instead relying on their own judgment. As noted above, a large body of research suggests that increased reliance on such personally-developed approaches, and decreased reliance on established procedures and decision aids, decreases overall accuracy. Thus, it may be useful for the lawyer to elicit from the expert statements to the effect that due to his experience, he is "qualified" to "go beyond" straightforward or actuarial interpretations of data and incorporate his experiential learning into the interpretive process. Many clinicians may indeed report proudly that because of their experience, they need not be restricted to limited or rudimentary decision-making strategies or actuarial procedures. One can then ask such a clinician whether he is aware that virtually all evidence on this topic shows that increased reliance on experientially-based "learning" and decreased regard for actuarial decision rules or established procedures produces lower, and not higher, overall accuracy.

Faust (1986a) has described this matter from a different angle in a satirical paper covering a series of common judgment practices that are intended to increase, but that actually decrease judgment accuracy. Supposedly speaking in the voice of PATHOS (or Psychologists Against Tough-Hearted and Offensive Scientists, an imaginary group formed to *protect* common judgment practices that *decrease* judgment accuracy), the author outlines "Rule 3":

Assume that your experience and knowledge are more valuable than everyone else's combined. PATHOS wishes to call Rule 3 to the attention of novices and beginners, especially, who violate it without alarming regularity. Lacking confidence and experience on which to draw, they often rely on previously established methods. Novices collect and compile data in a systematic manner and compare them to established norms and interpretive guidelines. For example, they score the Rorschach! They use MMPI cookbooks! They administer all of the Wechsler subtests! Such naivete is likely to increase, not decrease, accuracy. These beginners overlook both the painstaking efforts necessary to develop predictors of even modest validity and the innumerable errors littering the road to predictive accuracy.

A feature distinguishing the wise and experienced practitioner, according to PATHOS, is the awareness that disregarding well-validated decision rules or methods, formulating personal judgment rules at will, and never subjecting these rules to systematic evaluation are extremely effective in decreasing accuracy. These practitioners know that one or a few predictive failures are sufficient to abandon well-validated procedures and are a call for developing their own. They know enough to ignore that virtually all prediction contains an element of chance, that all predictors thus fail at times, and that the great majority of attempts to improve upon established predictors do not succeed. (p. 593)

Further:

Studies consistently indicate that experience and expertise have minimal beneficial effects, and not infrequently detrimental effects, on judgment accuracy. The underlying reasons are uncertain, but it may well be that experience encourages clinicians to rely less on systematic and well-founded methods of data collection and interpretation and more on personally constructed strategies. Thus, treating one's own experience and knowledge as superior to all others, particularly when the evidentiary bases are subjective impressions and hunches, will almost certainly prove productive for decreasing judgment accuracy. (p. 594)

Lanyon (1986) discusses problems in psychologists' participation in legal matters, offering some suggestions and some hopes for improvements in some areas. However, he opens his article by stating, "It is by now no secret that widespread dissatisfaction exists with the use of traditional psychological evaluation procedures in court-related settings (e.g., Poythress, 1981). Such procedures have often been justified on the basis of the psychologist's 'experience,' a justification that nowadays has diminishing credibility in the absence of empirical back-up." (p. 260)

A number of recent reviews have appeared on the relation (or lack thereof) between experience and diagnostic or predictive accuracy. Dawes (1989), in an article titled, "Experience and Validity of Clinical Judgment: The Illusory Correlation," states, "Mental health experts often justify diagnostic and predictive judgments on the basis of 'years of experience' with a particular type of person....However, research shows that the validity of clinical judgment and amount of clinical experience are *unrelated*." (p. 457) Dawes further reports that an American Psychological Association task force, which was convened in the early 1980s, noted the lack of evidence demonstrating a relationship between professional competence and experience. Dawes observes that it was not as if there were a lack of evidence available on the issue, but rather that the evidence up to that time showed, and since that time continues to show, a lack of relation between clinical experience and the accuracy of clinical judgment. He discusses the persisting belief in the value of experience in the mental health field and states that it is necessary to "shatter the illusion of 'learning from experience'." (p. 467)

Garb (1989), while noting that research provides limited support for the benefits of clinical training, indicates that studies "generally fail to support the value of on-the-job experience in mental health fields."

(p. 387) He describes the results of studies examining the relation between judgment accuracy and experience as "disappointing." Wedding and Faust (1989) state, "Dozens of studies have failed to demonstrate any significant relationship between experience and judgmental accuracy." (p. 249) They note that studies on this topic in neuropsychology "align with the more general literature." (p. 249)

Walters et al. (1988) found that MMPI experts were no more accurate than graduate students (and that both were less accurate than the actuarial approach) in identifying malingering on the basis of the MMPI (see Chapter 5 for further details about this study).

Faust et al. (1988a) examined relations between neuropsychologists' training, experience, and judgmental accuracy. Ten cases were selected to represent a cross-section of presentations seen in common practice settings, such as general hospitals. Each clinician evaluated one case and rendered a series of judgments. The materials provided to the practitioners included basic demographic variables and the results from an expanded version of the Halstead-Reitan Battery. The clinicians attempted to determine the presence, location, and cause of brain damage, and to distinguish between stable versus progressive neurological condition. The clinicians who returned cases showed an overall range and level of training and experience similar to that demonstrated in a national survey of practitioners who offer neuropsychological services. The researchers calculated correlations between eight variables relating to training and experience and six categories relating to judgmental accuracy. These correlations ranged from .21 to -.22 (negative correlations indicating an inverse relation between higher standing on the background variables and level of accuracy). The majority of correlations fell below.10. As the authors note, the set of correlations between the background variables and judgmental accuracy was "about what one would expect if the data consisted of randomly selected numbers. The results clearly suggest that for the overall sample, standing on the background variables and judgment accuracy are unrelated." (p. 157)

Faust et al. also conducted a separate analysis of extreme groups, or practitioners who fell at about the top versus the bottom 20% on these background variables. This approach created highly contrasting groups, for example, those with a median level of clinical experience in neuropsychology of 500 versus 12,000 hours. (The median is the middle point in a distribution of numbers, or is equivalent to the 50th percentile.) Even for these highly contrasting groups, judgmental accuracy was similar, with no consistent performance advantage demonstrated by either group. The only trend uncovered in relation to the background variables was a greater tendency on the part of more experienced versus less experienced practitioners to misdiagnose normal cases as abnormal.

Lambert and Wertheimer (1988) state that prior research has consistently reported only a modest, if any, relationship between the amount of experience of clinical psychologists and the accuracy of their diagnoses of psychopathology. They also note that it is because it seems so obvious that diagnostic ability "is" improved by relevant training and experience as to require no empirical demonstration that the findings from the few studies on the issue are so disturbing. They note that it makes no sense to require extensive experience for licensure if there is no evidence that diagnostic accuracy is related to training and experience. They advance the potential argument that the failure of experienced clinicians to be superior in accuracy to advanced graduate students may simply mean that the training has been so effective that by the time the students complete, or are near completing, their training, they have been brought up to a level of skill that is equivalent to that of practicing clinicians. Thus, the failure to show benefits of experience is due to a restricted range. This argument makes the expert's years of experience completely meaningless as an indication of accuracy as it contends that maximum accuracy is achieved upon the completion of training. In their study, they found that there were distinguishable differences between students who had zero or at most an introductory course in psychology (a no education group), undergraduate students who had completed between two and six courses relevant to clinical psychology (a low education group), and ten individuals who were either enrolled in the graduate program in clinical psychology or were functioning in a paraprofessional clinical capacity (a moderate education group). They presented these subjects with 14 fictional case histories constructed so as to illustrate a variety of disorders characterized in DSM-III. The subjects performed by placing a check mark in front of the most appropriate diagnostic category for the individual described in that case history. They found that there were differences between the groups based on education, with the groups going from none through low to moderate showing increasing levels of accuracy in mean number of cases diagnosed "correctly," with 2.3 for the no education group, 5.2 for the low education group, and 7.3 for the moderate education group. With regard to experience, they found little difference in accuracy between none and low (3.2 and 3.8, correct diagnoses, respectively), but with moderate doing better, with 6.4 correct diagnoses, according to the criteria that they used. It seems obvious that the study does nothing more than suggest that those with more education, as education and experience are inevitably mixed together in this study, are better able to select from a checklist the label that is given in DSM-III when the task is to match symptoms to label. Let it also be noted that the highest accuracy achieved was based on education and was at just about 50%, while the highest based on experience was slightly less than 50%.

In any event, the authors of the study recognize that what is needed is a comparable study with genuine cases and participants who have a broader range of training and experience, including seasoned practitioners. We have mentioned this study only in the event some witness cites it as evidence that experience does make a difference.

Helzer et al. (1987) attempted to examine the relative predictive power of lay Diagnostic Interview Schedule (DIS)-derived psychiatric diagnoses versus that of standard psychiatric diagnoses. The DIS is a highly structured examination based on DSM-III and two other sets of criteria. The interview provides a set of questions to be read verbatim for each criterion item for about 40 diagnoses. They found that within the limits of available data, lay and psychiatric diagnoses appear to be essentially equal in terms of the number of outcomes that are predicted, and few of the differences in predictive power approach statistical significance. However, they are quite candid in discussing many of the limitations and methodological problems of their study, which considerably dilutes its evidentiary value, although it is consistent with some earlier studies that we had reported in indicating that a professional's diagnoses are not appreciably more accurate than evaluations performed by laypersons.

Carson (1990) discusses the issue of the clinician versus the computer and states his view that it is really not a question of where the ultimate responsibility for decisions rests; it is with the clinician. (We are not necessarily agreeing with this point of view, but are simply stating it as a context for what follows.) He goes on to point out that perhaps the wrong questions have been asked about the validity of tests and the question needs to be changed to an interaction approach: What is the validity of a particular assessment instrument, such as the Rorschach, for example, with a particular clinician? He cites a remarkable judgment made by Samuel J. Beck (producer of one of the older Rorschach systems), diagnosing precisely not only that a patient had brain damage, but exactly where the lesion would be. One hears of these remarkable performances from time to time. Of course, we may not know how often the same clinician is wrong, how memorable (or recognizable) everyday errors might be, or how successful the testifying clinician might be with the same instrument. Carson expresses his belief that some individuals working with particular assessment instruments in which they have acquired vast experience are capable of assessments that far exceed the standard for the particular instrument and acknowledges that such skills may be difficult to articulate in a form that makes them readily teachable to others or reducible to explicit variables in an actuarial table. Of course, one could argue that if skills are not teachable or capable of actuarial expression, they do not belong in the realm of science, but that of art. In any event, what we are most interested in is the following statement by Carson, "In other words, the validity of an assessment instrument is not and should not be estimated in terms of an independent main effect—although that has been the standard route. What we should have been looking at all along, it seems to me, is the interaction term—the interaction of instrument with assessor, where at least some of the subject-assessors have a proven track record, not merely 'experience'...with the assessment instrument being evaluated." (p. 439) If we are interpreting Carson correctly, he appears to be saying what we have argued for many years, that given the research findings showing validity to be relatively low, or given the lack of research findings establishing validity, the only way one could find validity in instruments being used for psychological assessment is through the establishment of a "proven track record." We have argued for this in terms that when a clinician claims the ability to be able to accurately evaluate an individual along certain parameters, his opinion on his "virtuosity" should not be accepted in the absence of independently-conducted research which shows what the level of accuracy is for this assessor. It does seem fairly clear that Carson is indicating that experience alone is not a sufficient indicator of accuracy.

Rickles et al. (1988) state, "Uncontrolled case reports, essential as they are in clinical pharmacology, will always be double-edge swords." (p. 52) They suggest that because such uncontrolled reports are often misleading, they should be used circumspectly to generate leads but never to make firm conclusions. They note that, "The causal reality of the events 'observed' may seem very persuasive but prove illusory." (p. 52) It might be noted that what experts refer to as their experience is largely a collection of their own uncontrolled case reports. Even though they are not necessarily formal reports, experience consists of material retained in the expert's mind from his uncontrolled cases.

Lanyon (1986) declares that psychological evaluation procedures in court-related settings have often been justified on the basis of the psychologists's "experience" but that at present, this justification has diminishing credibility because of the absence of empirical back-up.

Bolocofsky (1989) states that the present system of relying on training or experience, among other criteria, has not been found to have any significant relationship to competence in forensic mental health services. Bedard and Chi (1992) discuss expertise generally. They state, "The studies have shown that a large body of domain knowledge is a prerequisite to expertise." (p. 135) We think it follows that in those areas in which such a domain has not been shown to exist, expertise is doubtful. We refer the reader to Chapters 1 and 3, supra, for evidence that the existence of such a large knowledge base in psychiatry and psychology is in doubt.

Ford and Widiger (1989) studied sex bias in diagnosis of histrionic and antisocial personality disorders. Subjects were 354 psychologists randomly selected from the National Register of Health Service Providers in Psychology who reported an average of 15 years of experience. They found that among these highly experienced psychologists there was a clear tendency to diagnose women with histrionic personality disorder and not with antisocial personality disorder even when the cases were more antisocial than histrionic. They state that their results cannot be readily explained by a rational consideration of base rate differences. Although they do not specifically discuss experience as a variable in their study, it does provide an illustration of the failure of experience to overcome a diagnostic bias.

Rubenzer (1991) states that highly experienced clinicians are not more accurate or likely to agree among themselves than are novices, that psychologists are no better than graduate students, and that experienced psychologists are no better than new graduates.

Garb (1992) declares that Rubenzer's statements about the findings in empirical studies comparing judgments by psychologists vs. graduate students and more experienced vs. less experienced clinicians are correct.

Borum et al. (1993) discuss suggestions for improving clinical decision making in forensic evaluations. In discussing illusory correlations they note that this type of error occurs when clinicians form intuitive connections for events that "seem to go together" or "seem to make sense." They state, "Thus, the appropriate measure to correct for this difficulty is to rely on empirically established relationships and treat relationships that have been 'established' in any other way (e.g., 'in my extensive clinical experience') *very* skeptically." (p. 52)

Bersoff (1992), in discussing reliability and validity of clinician's decision making, observes that in many cases experience is more of a hindrance than a help.

Dawes (1994) devotes a whole chapter to experience with the subtitle "The Myth of Expanding Expertise." He points out that the empirical data indicate that mental health professionals' accuracy of judgment does not increase with increasing clinical experience.

These last dozen or so citations are important because many other citations in this chapter are somewhat old. What is revealed is that over a period of some 30 years, there has been a consistent stream of literature which stands in contradiction to claims of mental health professionals to credibility based on their experience. The thrust of this impressive quantity of literature is that experience is unrelated to accuracy.

Some witnesses may attempt to counter this literature with references to a popular book by Brodsky (1991), which gives advice on how to testify in court (this book is discussed more extensively in Volume III,

Chapter 6). In a chapter dealing with challenges to experience, Brodsky suggests, among others, the following response: "While a series of pro and con articles have appeared, my reading of the literature is that the commonsense notion that experience is important has been supported." (p. 25) Upon being challenged to produce such a body of supporting literature, Brodsky has not done so. In an exchange of letters with David Faust (co-author of the Fourth Edition of this book) on this subject, Brodsky wrote in a letter (which he has graciously permitted us to quote) dated January 31, 1994, "Since we spoke, I have reviewed more of the literature on experience. If I were writing *Testifying in Court* now, I would definitely rewrite pages 24-26 (Chapter 8) in the book. The statement about responding to queries about experience call for a change. When I revise the book, I plan to make those corrections." Any witness who cites Brodsky regarding experience, can be confronted with this statement by Brodsky.

We think lawyers should be aware, also, of a study by Rock and Bransford (1992). While most of the findings in this study are consistent with the above (i.e., no association between judgmental accuracy and clinical training and experience), one finding may encourage clinicians to attempt to discount this body of literature. In their study, Rock and Bransford had 16 graduate students in psychology diagnose two outpatients using DSM-III diagnoses. Eight of the students made their diagnoses on the basis of a transcript of an initial assessment interview and the third therapy session for each individual. The other eight made their diagnoses from audiotapes of the initial assessment interviews and video tapes of the therapy sessions. The criterion of accuracy was the degree of agreement with the diagnoses of four clinicians designated as experts. A perfect agreement (exact match on all five digits of the diagnostic code) was given 2 points; agreement within the same diagnostic category (i.e., if the criterion diagnosis was generalized anxiety disorder and the subject gave a diagnosis of panic disorder), the diagnosis would receive a score of 1; and 0 points were given if the diagnosis was not in the same category. Rock and Bransford found that while there was no relationship between DSM-III experience and accuracy in the transcript diagnoses, there was a relationship of both prior and present experience with DSM-III and accuracy in the tape diagnoses, with correlations of .6372 and .6647 respectively which were statistically significant. The authors conclude, "Findings from these analyses indicate that level of judgmental accuracy on diagnostic tasks is positively associated with the amount of specific training and experience associated with that task." (p. 564)

We have some concern that some MHEs will use that conclusion in an overbroad way. We find a number of problems with this conclusion. First, the results obtained have nothing to do with accuracy of diagnosis.

They only demonstrate that people with more experience in applying DSM-III labels apply them more consistently with other people who have still more experience than people with less experience in applying those labels. This only demonstrates that there is more RELIABILITY among people with more experience in using DSM-III labels. One can only call this accuracy if one confuses reliability with VALIDITY. A demonstration of the validity of DSM-IV diagnoses is a matter for future research (see Chapter 4). As we have noted elsewhere, clinicians can agree with higher degrees of correlation than found in this study, even 100% agreement, and can all be wrong. Secondly, absent research on the ACCURACY of the four criterion experts, we do not know how accurate they are. It may be worth noting that in the introductory paragraph to their article, the authors seem to indicate that their study is to some extent in response to our citations in earlier editions of this book and in our *Science* article (Faust and Ziskin, 1988), but the citations they point out involved comparisons of clinical judgments against OBJECTIVE CRITERIA (e.g., Stoller and Geertsma, 1963). Third, the number of subjects in each group (8) is small, as is the number of evaluations. Finally, Rock and Bransford quite responsibly state that they do not argue that their data show that previous studies of problems in clinical diagnosis are not useful, only that more attention needs to be paid to the complexity of clinical judgment and research assumptions in assessing clinical competence. The bottom line remains that there is a substantial body of scientific and professional literature indicating a lack of relationship between experience and accuracy of psychological assessment.

UNDERSTANDING THE LIMITED BENEFITS OF EXPERIENCE

Difficulties in uncovering expert or outstanding judges are most likely rooted, in large part, in the limited benefits accrued through practice and experience. That the judgment accuracy of psychologists and psychiatrists frequently fails to improve with experience, and in fact may get worse, is counterintuitive. Thus, it is important to explain why this lack of benefit may occur. Unless the findings are plausible and comprehensible to the lawyer, the lawyer might have a hard time making them plausible and comprehensible to a jury. Belief in the benefits of experience are so ingrained in people that merely citing the research findings in the absence of a rationale can have limited persuasive power.

RESTRICTED FEEDBACK

How does one learn through experience? One of the more important ways is to obtain information about the accuracy of one's efforts, or what mental health workers refer to as feedback. For example, imagine you were attempting to learn archery blindfolded and could not observe the success of your efforts, or could not receive this critical feedback. Obviously, it would be pretty difficult, if not impossible, to become an accurate marksman or improve your aim. Likewise, in theory, a psychiatrist might learn to improve his diagnostic or predictive accuracy by obtaining follow-up data on the patients he assesses and then determining whether his conclusions or predictions were correct. If one found he had missed the mark, one might learn from these mistakes and correct them the next time.

Psychiatrists and psychologists, however, often do not obtain feedback. Dershowitz (1969) deplores the paucity of follow-up studies, for example, in the prediction of antisocial behavior. In a survey of the literature, he found that among the many studies conducted on the topic of antisocial behavior, less than a dozen provided data which assessed the accuracy of predictions. Saunders (1975) states that many clinical settings foster a professional vacuum in which the psychologist rarely receives feedback about the accuracy or relative importance of his diagnostic efforts. In a broad-based discussion, Schmideberg (1962-1963) notes:

> The hard fact remains that unlike other medical specialties, psychiatry lacks adequate statistics and follow-ups because psychiatrists have not seriously attempted to check on their methods and results in the way other doctors regard as their scientific duty. (p. 21)

Thus, as these authors indicate, it is quite common, especially when a psychologist or psychiatrist sees a patient on one or a few occasions, to conduct a diagnostic workup and leave any treatment to someone else, so that little or no feedback is obtained about the conclusion reached. Under these circumstances, how could one correct systematic error? Some psychologists and psychiatrists will assert that they do obtain such feedback about the results of their assessments, or at least that they obtain extensive feedback in the context of the treatment they perform. However, as we will describe, due to the method by which this feedback is obtained and other complications, there is substantial doubt that it is of much use. For example, feedback about the accuracy of evaluations is rarely gathered in a systematic fashion or in a way that controls, scientifically, for the potential biases of the one giving or receiving the feedback.

THE CAPACITY TO UTILIZE FEEDBACK

How Well Is Informative Feedback Utilized?

Clinicians appear to evidence minimal benefits, even when given access to potentially useful information or feedback. In a study on this topic, Goldberg (1965) created very favorable conditions for the proper utilization of feedback. Clinicians were given a large series of MMPI profiles and tried to distinguish those of patients who on discharge were diagnosed as "neurotic" versus "psychotic." Immediately following each judgment, the clinicians were told whether their judgments were or were not correct. Thus, the feedback that the clinicians received was rapid, accurate, and explicit. Further, they were given feedback on well over a thousand MMPI profiles, or perhaps more cases than are seen over the entire careers of some practitioners. Compare these conditions to those more typical of everyday clinical practice. If feedback is received at all, it may be received weeks or months after judgments are made, and such feedback is rarely explicit or unambiguous. Thus, in almost every conceivable way, Goldberg created conditions optimal for learning through feedback.

Starting from a typical level of performance that was not particularly good at the onset, this extensive and near optimal feedback produced little, if any increase in judgment accuracy across the clinicians. Of interest, Goldberg had also developed a simple actuarial formula for sorting the MMPI profiles, which achieved a higher level of accuracy in predicting discharge diagnosis. Even when Goldberg provided the actuarial formula to the judges and they were allowed to use it at their discretion and compare, on a case-by-case basis, the accuracy of their judgments to that achieved with the formula, they persisted in relying on their own, inferior judgment. Thus, even when given a helpful decision rule and continual feedback indicating that this decision rule produced a higher level of overall judgment accuracy, nonoptimal practices still persisted. This says something about the faith, or overconfidence, that clinicians can hold in their own judgment methods, and their marked resistance to counterevidence or to utilizing available methods for improving accuracy. Graham's (1971) previously described, related study showed what Graham described as "discouraging" improvement with practice and feedback.

The "moral" of these studies is obvious. Even when informative and unquestionably useful feedback is received, which is the rare occurrence in psychology and psychiatry, it still may have little beneficial effect. If clinicians stubbornly adhere to their current judgment practices and refuse to change them even when the feedback shows that these procedures are flawed, there is little hope that feedback can be beneficial. Obviously, even informative feedback is not necessarily utilized properly, in large part because clinicians misinterpret what the feedback might teach them, for reasons we will discuss below.

Typical Feedback: What One Sees
Is Not Necessarily What Is There

If clinicians seem to have so much difficulty utilizing clear or useful feedback, imagine the situation or results when very questionable, or distorted feedback is received. Much of the feedback that clinicians actually do obtain is potentially quite misleading, ambiguous, and prone to misinterpretation.

Patients' statements provide one potential source of feedback. For example, after conducting an evaluation, the psychologist or psychiatrist may discuss the results with the patient. Patients may indicate that the results do not seem accurate, or that the results are "right on the mark." We have seen many experts claim that such feedback about the results of their evaluations, in particular feedback of the latter type, not only helps them to refine their skills but "proves" that their clinical judgments or impressions are accurate. Should we accept such claims at face value?

Before describing the research on this topic, we must introduce the phrase, "Barnum statement." Paul Meehl used this term to refer to statements about people that are usually true merely because they apply to almost everybody. Thus, the fortune teller who says that one is sensitive and has experienced hurts in the past is almost sure to be correct because almost everyone believes this about themselves. One creates a "Barnum effect" through the use of such statements, that is, one impresses others with "insight" into their personal characteristics through statements that have a good chance of being accepted as correct regardless of to whom one says them.

Carnivals often have a handwriting analyst who, for a fee, will describe your character from a sample of your handwriting, often as minimal as just writing your name. It may go something like this, "You like people generally but are discriminating in your choice of friends. You tend to work too hard." (Who does not believe that?) "Sometimes you get angry about things you realize afterward were unimportant." And so on for a dozen or so statements all of which have a high probability of being true for almost anyone. One may leave the analyst impressed with the accuracy of the method or of his insights although adding something like, "He had me pretty well figured out although he was wrong about a couple of things." The analyst knows that the frequency of the behaviors or feelings he describes are high and he knows therefore that he will much more often be right than wrong in attributing them to any given individual, thus creating a "Barnum" impression of having really assessed the individual's personality from a cursory glance (although a real showman may make it look much harder) at a totally inadequate sample of behavior.

Common sense would suggest that people seeking help from a clinician might have a strong need for the clinician to be correct and thus prone to confirm the clinician's judgments. However, it is not necessary to rely on common sense, as there has been considerable research in this area. Snyder et al. (1977) provide an extensive review of nearly 50 studies in this area. Based on the literature reviewed, they conclude, "Situational factors that elicit acceptance are examined, with the conclusion that clientele acceptance cannot be construed as validation of either the clinician or his assessment procedures." They state: "On the basis of the present review, clients may be expected to readily accept such personality feedback. Not surprisingly, then, clinicians are likely to be praised by their clientele. In no sense, however, can such praise be interpreted as 'validation' of either the clinician's skill or assessment procedures." (p. 111)

Snyder et al. (1978) state that previous Barnum Effect literature does not support the notion that a client can be a source of valuable feedback to the clinician honing his or her clinical skills.

Snyder (1974) provides an interesting demonstration of the Barnum effect. The purpose of Snyder's study was to investigate the degree of agreement among individuals with a description of their personality purportedly based upon their horoscope. He used three groups. The first group was given horoscope descriptions described as "generally true of people." The second group was given a description purportedly based on the year and month in which the subject was born. The third group was given a description based on the year, month and day in which the subject was born. In all three groups, each subject actually received the identical handwritten horoscope which follows:

> You have a very practical bent and enjoy earning money but sometimes your deep desire to be a creative person triumphs over your practicality. You lead other people with your innovative ideas or could do this if you felt more sure of yourself. Insecurity is your greatest weakness and you would be wise to try to overcome this. Your deep sense of humor and warm understanding nature wins you true friends and although they may not be numerous you share a rather intense loyalty to each other. With your innovative mind you rebel against authority either inwardly or openly. Even though you could make a very stable businessman you would be a very idealistic one, finding it hard not to defend the underdog or try to settle arguments that arise. You like to think of yourself as unprejudiced but periodically examine yourself to make sure you're not overlooking some harmful judgments. You will live a long full life if you take care of yourself. You love to have freedom in whatever you're doing, and this makes you dislike monotonous tasks and being in large crowds where you can't seem to move freely. If someone pays you a well deserved compliment, you enjoy hearing it, but you may not show that you do. Sometimes you find that the actions you take do not accomplish as much as you would like them to, especially in dealing with people. You have a real grasp on how people are feeling or what they are thinking without their necessarily telling you.

Subjects in the first group found the horoscope personality interpretation fairly accurate for people in general, while the subjects in the second and third groups, apparently as a function of the aura of a specificity that was conveyed, found the statements to be highly accurate descriptions of their individual personalities. The study indicates how easy it is to convince people that an accurate evaluation according to workable principles has been done.

The problem with depending on patient feedback goes beyond Barnum effects or the possibility that clinicians can elicit support for their statements, whether the support is justified or not. In addition, regardless of what the patient does say, there are always the things that he does not say. It is very widely recognized that patients may withhold information or opinions. This is one reason why the MMPI contains scales that measure how honest individuals were in responding to items, or how open they were in reporting symptoms (see Chapters 12 and 18). In fact, it is assumed that individuals will not or should not be completely honest or open, and that some level of defensiveness is the more normal attitude. Further, any lawyer who has dealt with psychologists and psychiatrists almost surely has been exposed to a decided propensity on the part of some to look beyond surface level appearance or behavior and to try to uncover hidden meanings, or what people "really" think or mean.

There is indeed evidence that patients hold information back from psychologists and psychiatrists, and that this information may well involve beliefs or attitudes that individuals feel would not please the professional. This makes a good deal of sense, after all, because individuals will naturally be cautious about displeasing those upon whom they may depend. In this context, Klopfer (1984) states that subjects may provide false information, being untruthful in an effort to anticipate what the interviewer would like to hear. Kaschak (1978) performed a study which showed that patients and their therapists often attributed positive change in psychotherapy to different factors. Although the therapist attributed gains to their therapeutic skill and technique, the clients mainly attributed it to "just having someone to talk to." Perhaps they did not wish to tell their therapist that they may have done just as well had it been another professional they were doing the talking to. A study by Kass et al. (1980) found that patients may have withheld critical information from their therapists because they were concerned about the reactions they might elicit.

Could it be that the psychiatrist or psychologists tends to believe the things that patients say when what they say is consistent with what the professional believes, and to not believe what they say when it is inconsistent with what they believe? The value of feedback is to alter erroneous beliefs, and would not such practices bias the situation such that the professional is more likely than not to find his beliefs "supported," regardless of their accuracy? Would this not seriously impede the capacity to abstract from feedback the things that could be learned? The research certainly suggests that the answers to these three respective questions may commonly be yes, yes and yes.

(MIS)UTILIZATION AND (MIS)USE
OF TREATMENT OUTCOME AS FEEDBACK

An expert may claim that treatment outcome provides information that has helped to sharpen his judgment skills. Along related lines, an expert will cite his "success" in psychotherapy as evidence that his experience has made him competent or that the theory he uses is valid. Thus, the clinician's reported observations of treatment outcome can become a linchpin for claims of major importance.

However, treatment data, or observations or research pertaining to patients' responses to specific therapeutic actions or therapeutic approaches, are perhaps even more shaky than a patient's verbal feedback about the accuracy of professionals' judgments. Given the current state of knowledge, such data rarely, if ever, provide clear evidence in support of the validity or accuracy of professionals' beliefs or judgments, no matter how the data seem to turn out. There are at least four reasons for this (see also Chapter 22, Treatment).

1. Lack of Specificity

First, treatment responses often lack specificity, or fail to show clear relationships with the form of treatment that is provided. For example, suppose a patient is given an antidepressant medication because he is believed to be depressed, and subsequently gets better in relatively short order. Would this not seem to "prove" that the initial diagnosis of depression was correct? No! This same medication may be useful in the treatment of "panic attacks" (i.e., episodes of extreme anxiety), and perhaps it took care of the panic attacks such that the patient was no longer complaining about symptoms. Alternatively, perhaps the patient was not really depressed in the first place but was trying to elicit a sympathetic reaction. The point is that although the patient indicated he was better, this could have occurred for any of a number of reasons, only one of these being that the patient had been depressed and that the medication helped the depression. As another example, the medication, Ritalin, is often used to treat children who have problems sustaining attention. However, individuals who seem to have similar symptoms but are actually depressed may also have a beneficial response to this medication, and indeed even normal individuals may show improvements in sustained attention when they take the medication. Thus, if the medication is given and attention improves, this hardly provides clear evidence that an initial diagnosis of problems in sustained attention was correct.

Contrast this nonspecificity in treatment response to a hypothetical situation. One has a disorder that never gets better on its own. The disorder can be treated with one medication that works for only this disorder and for no other. In this situation, if an individual did indeed get better with the medication, one could reason backwards from the treatment response and infer the correct diagnosis, or claim that the initial diagnosis was confirmed by the treatment response. The actual situation in psychiatry, however, is far removed from these hypothetical circumstances. Rather, there are few or no treatments that impact on only one form of disorder (this is assuming we even have clearly identified disorders in the first place), and there are few disorders that never get better on their own without a specific form of treatment. As such, it is almost always hazardous to reason backwards from treatment response to diagnosis, and thus it is difficult to use treatment response as a test of the initial diagnostic impression. If this initial diagnosis was correct, then indeed the treatment response may have been consistent with it, but this response, by itself, will not tell you whether the specific diagnosis was correct. The validity of the diagnosis, therefore, almost never can be established or proven by the treatment response and must be evaluated in some other way. Note that we are also discussing here rather "clean" forms of treatment, such as specific medications. As difficult as the problem is under these circumstances, it is far more problematic still when the treatment is some form of psychotherapy. As we will see, various types of psychotherapies may not actually differ much from one another in certain respects and contain a largely unspecified and complex mixture of treatment components and the factors or active agents that might account for any positive results are largely unknown. Stated differently, when one provides psychotherapy one does not really know, precisely, what specific treatment has been provided, so how could one possibly learn about specific relationships between responses to treatment and the validity of initial diagnostic impressions?

Aside from the fact that even a positive treatment outcome does not establish the validity of judgment, an additional consideration is that individuals do not respond uniformly to "specific" treatments. Some may get much better, some may get a little better, and some may show no response or even a negative response. Thus, in the study by Stewart et al. (1985), among patients with the same diagnosis, a certain percentage improved with antidepressant medication but a fairly large percentage did not. Further, among those not given this treatment, a majority did not get better, but a fairly large percentage did get better. A related problem is that individuals who should show specific responses to treatment do not necessarily do so. Tamminga and Carpenter (1982) report on research which indicates a lack of expected differences in response to medication among individuals diagnosed as having different subtypes of schizophrenia. If a practitioner claims that treatment response is an adequate way to gauge validity, then he should maintain a consistent standard and not simply use this argument when treatment outcome is positive. Presumably, then, these failures to respond as expected, which are very common, provide evidence for diagnostic error. Of course, if one takes this argument to its logical extension, the whole position becomes ridiculous. If positive responses support accurate judgments or diagnostic validity and negative responses disconfirm them, should we then assume that in every case of an untreatable condition a misdiagnosis has been made? In this way, the patient with cancer that does not respond to radiation treatment must have been mistakenly diagnosed. The point is that one cannot have it both ways. Either one can accept that as things currently stand in psychiatry, treatment response, whether positive or negative, is a very poor test of validity or diagnostic accuracy, or one is stuck in the position of accepting that the good treatment responses support diagnoses and the bad treatment responses do not, creating the types of untenable conclusions shown above.

2. Uncertainty Regarding "Curative" Factors

A second basic problem with using treatment outcome, even successful outcome, as support for one's knowledge or therapeutic technique, is that we often have little more than the foggiest idea of what leads to good treatment outcome in the case of psychotherapy. This problem has been discussed in various ways, but the bottom line is that we do not know, specifically, what works and does not work for what. Parloff (1982) points out that there is lack of evidence as to what kinds of psychotherapy are most effective for specific types of problems. Stiles (1983) states:

> For the major approaches, such as psychoanalytic therapy, client centered therapy, behavior therapy and rational-emotive therapy, there is now strong objective evidence that therapists behave systematically differently depending on their theoretical orientation....That is, there really are different ingredients in the different psychotherapies. Furthermore, these differences are so large and so systematically related to theory that it seems unreasonable to attribute any common success to overlap in therapists' techniques. (p. 183)

He states further:

> The combination of technical diversity and no differential overall effectiveness has evoked dismay and attempts to challenge or deny one or the other of these findings. It is not hard to see where this resistance comes from. If every school of therapy does something different and none are demonstrably better than any other, then perhaps it doesn't matter what you do! (p. 183)

The literature seems to have changed little over the years. A recent issue of the *Journal of Consulting and Clinical Psychology* (Volume 54, No. 1, February, 1986) was devoted entirely to research on psychotherapy outcome. One general theme across a number of articles was that substantial additional research of improved quality has been conducted but that work in this area is very difficult. Thus, it remains quite uncertain what form of therapy is best for whom and what factors, specifically, account for therapy responses. Kazdin (1986), the journal editor and the author of one of the articles in this issue, states, "Individual comparative outcome studies and evaluations of the literature have produced ambiguous conclusions and have continued to stir controversy about the relative effectiveness of alternative techniques for specific clinical problems." (p. 95) Further, "Both individual outcome studies and large-scale evaluations of the literature have generated relatively consistent conclusions that alternate treatments produce few differences in treatment outcome." (p. 102)

Dumont (1991) states that the widely entrenched conviction that experts in the behavioral sciences do significantly better than novices in accurately representing problems and making decisions has yet to be substantiated. He notes there is much evidence to the contrary. He notes the existence of generally recognized principles constitutes the common knowledge base of experts in any domain, but that in the field of psychotherapy there is relatively little that could be termed "common knowledge base" because virtually every principle of one system is contradicted by one or more of the other systems. He questions whether it is possible to have experts where such a knowledge base does not exist, and holds that one therefore cannot be certain that experts working in one paradigm will be any more effective than novices working in another paradigm. Dumont does state that he did not intend to sap the confidence of veteran colleagues and that there are many skills common to most theoretical approaches that are honed to a fine edge only after many years of experience.

Given this state of affairs, how can treatment outcome or response to one or another variant of psychotherapy teach us anything about diagnosis or anything about how to refine our treatment or judgment skills? If, within very wide latitude and freedom to vary approach and technique, one gets pretty much the same overall result, how can we learn anything much about what we should or should not do with patients, or about the accuracy or validity of our judgments, based on patients' treatment responses? Even if you do something very different, you still might well get the same response. How does one know what would have happened if one had done something different from what one did do? In addition to showing the limited value of treatment outcome in gauging validity or accuracy, this research can be used to create considerable difficulties for any professional who claims that his particular type of psychotherapy approach is the preferred one. This research shows that virtually no particular approach has a distinct advantage over any other. Therefore, an expert who makes such a claim not only is likely unjustified in doing so, but can be shown to exhibit a lack of objectivity, or blatant disregard for what is now a very large body of research that shows otherwise.

3. Biased Interpretation of Outcome Data

A third problem with the use of treatment outcome to determine or demonstrate validity or judgment accuracy is that interpretation of such data are subject to considerable bias on the part of the clinician doing the interpreting. Put simply, the evaluation is subject to considerable variability in interpretation, and the conclusion reached may be as much, or more, a product of the one doing the interpreting than a product of the "objective" facts. One therapist's good outcome may be another therapist's poor one. For example, for a behavioral therapist, a change in behavior may be an indication of good outcome, whereas for a Freudian therapist, who is more interested in internal psychic processes, such a change may be viewed neutrally or even negatively. One additional problem here is that the one doing the evaluating, or the expert who declares in court that his good treatment outcome proves the validity of the theory or diagnosis, is possibly in the worst position of all to provide an objective assessment. After all, a therapist can have a great deal of personal investment in his own skills, and this certainly can lead to a less than objective appraisal of his own treatment outcomes.

This last problem can be raised any time an expert makes claims about his own treatment powers. The lawyer should inquire as regards the source of this judgment. In the great majority of cases, the expert will say that it is based on his own observations, or perhaps on the compliments or acknowledgements of colleagues and patients. One can then ask the expert about the use of what are called single-blind techniques in research, and particularly research on treatment outcome. What is typically meant by a single-blind technique in this context is that the one evaluating the effectiveness of a treatment is not told what type of treatment was administered, or is "blinded" to the treatment method. The reason for doing this is avoid biases and maintain objectivity. For example, the researchers might be trying out a new technique they invented, and naturally they might have an investment in a positive outcome. Thus, they might have someone, say, interview the patients and inquire about the effectiveness of the treatment. The individual doing the interviewing will not be told which patient received which treatment. This single-blind method is not used to keep researchers from "cheating," but because even the most scrupulous attempts to remain neutral and objective when one has a personal investment in a certain outcome often fail and biases creep in one way or another.

If the expert has any sophistication whatever in research design, he should be able to outline the various reasons why a single-blind technique is used in evaluating treatment outcome, and in many related forms of research, as well. One might wish to draw him out on these points, and have him elaborate on the many difficulties that can occur when the technique is not used and how untrustworthy results are if produced in its absence. It may even be the case that the expert has conducted some of his own research in which a single-blind technique was used, and the lawyer might ask the expert to explain why this method was preferred. All of this, of course, leads up to a question like the following, "Given what you have told us about the need for single-blind techniques in order to obtain reliable information about treatment effectiveness, aren't the impressions you have formed about your treatment effectiveness in the absence of this technique open to considerable doubt?"

A good deal of work points out these problems of bias in treatment evaluation and the variability of impressions in relation to the professional's theoretical orientation. London and Klerman (1982) discuss problems involved when a therapist with one theoretical orientation attempts to evaluate the work conducted by a therapist with another theoretical orientation. They indicate that the diversity in theoretical viewpoints makes it difficult to achieve any "collectively authoritative" evaluations, or evaluations that cut across the different orientations. Xenakis et al. (1983) discuss the problem of bias on the part of individual therapists. They found that even therapists' reports on their own behavior in therapy often show poor correspondence with observations made by independent judges. The authors assert that therapists' accounts of their own work may be subject to various distortions and biases, and they suggest that caution should be exercised before relying on therapists' self-reports as accurate descriptions of their actual behaviors in therapy. Greenwald et al. (1986) discuss a body of research which indicates that individuals selectively attend to information that confirms their initial beliefs, opinions, and self-concepts. As applied to professionals, these results imply that a therapist with a belief in his treatment effectiveness will selectively attend to data that support this belief and disregard data that do not, an obvious form of bias.

Mora (1985) provides an historical overview which shows how often judgments about treatment effectiveness can be mistaken. He discusses skull trepanation (drilling holes in the skull), swinging the "disordered" from wicker baskets, and infecting patients with malaria. He notes that

Benjamin Rush, often considered the father of American psychiatry, relied extensively on bloodletting.

Campbell (1985), who reviews various treatment approaches thought promising but shown ineffective by subsequent scientific research, states:

> Although patients may improve despite medical interventions, rather than because of them, those interventions are quickly credited with an improvement in the patient's condition, whereas failure to improve is blamed on something else. Often, this failure reflects errors in logic that can be excused only because they spring from physicians' hopes that sometime, somehow, they will hit on the right treatment for patients whose anguish they share. Nonetheless, past errors should at least alert one to the dangers of jumping too quickly to indefensible conclusions...(p. 1569)

Although Campbell does not use the term, he seemingly is referring to confirmatory bias.

A study by Cohen and Oyster-Nelson (1981) provides a dramatic illustration of the effects that theoretical orientation can have on the evaluation of treatment effectiveness. Psychologists who served as reviewers for health services for military personnel were asked to provide various ratings for a series of treatment cases based on detailed case reports. These reviewers believed that their evaluations would be used to help make practical decisions about reimbursement, such as the number of additional sessions for which a patient's costs would be covered. Of the reviewers, one-third had a psychodynamic orientation, one-third a behavioral orientation, and one-third an eclectic orientation. For every dimension the therapists rated, there was a significant relationship between the ratings and the theoretical orientation of the reviewers. For example, the reviewers with a psychodynamic orientation were more positive in their evaluations of the therapy than were the behavioral or eclectic reviewers. The results show that clinicians of differing theoretical orientations differ in their evaluation of treatment quality. The authors state: "These data do seem to point to a tendency on the part of psychodynamic clinicians, relative to behavioral clinicians, to overstate pathology (or, conversely, a tendency on the part of the behaviorists to understate pathology)." (p. 588) The same could be said for rating of treatment effectiveness. One should note from the above that one cannot state which groups of practitioners was right or wrong, or what the direction of the error might be, pointing to the problems encountered distinguishing subjective elements and actual objective features in the evaluation of treatment.

Mash and Hunsley (1993) state with regard to reluctance to study treatment failures, "Concomitantly, though, therapists may overlook true errors in practice to maintain a sense of professional worth and competence (Hayes and Nelson, 1986). Failures in therapy may also not be readily noted because they are sometimes hidden by the client, perhaps out of deference to authority, a desire to please the therapist, or the anticipation of therapist disapproval." (p. 292) Such a statement illustrates why so little credibility can be attached to a therapist's opinion about how good his opinions are based on his perception that he has been successful in treatment.

4. Lack of Relationship Between Experience and Outcome

Although the three reasons we have discussed above regarding problems using treatment effectiveness to establish validity should provide more than enough fuel for the lawyer, there is one more.

Perhaps most important is research which examines the relationship between experience and treatment outcome. Among the 23 therapy outcome variables studied by Tuma et al. (1978), not a single one was related to therapist experience. Gomes-Schwartz and Schwartz (1978) found that patients were as satisfied with non-professional therapists (male professors identified by university personnel as teachers frequently approached by students for personal counseling) as they were with highly experienced professional therapists. This study is important because, as noted, client satisfaction or statement of improvement is frequently one of the subjective "measures" used to "validate" psychotherapy. McLean and Hakstian (1979) also found that therapist experience was unrelated to treatment outcome. Hynan (1981), briefly reviewing the literature on therapy outcome, concludes that outcome is unrelated to therapist training or experience.

Smith and Glass (1977) performed an extensive analysis of outcome research, and found essentially no relationship between years of therapist experience and treatment outcome.

Although it can be argued that work of Smith and Glass provides evidence for treatment effectiveness, it does not establish that in order for therapy to be effective, treatment need be provided by a professional. Indeed, dozens of studies have compared the treatment effectiveness of professionals versus paraprofessionals (those lacking in professional training). Berman and Norton (1985) performed a systematic and comprehensive review of studies on this topic. They note that a previous review suggested that nonprofessionals achieve better overall outcome, although in their review no clear differences emerged between the professionals and nonprofessionals. These results remained the same even when studies were excluded that involved less experienced professionals or more thoroughly prepared paraprofessionals. Thus, even when a sharp boundary was drawn between professionals and nonprofessionals, no systematic differences in treatment effectiveness were uncovered. For any therapist who stakes his claim to validity or judgment accuracy mainly on the basis of treatment effectiveness, the obvious implication of these studies is that such claims are not good enough and would equally qualify nonexperts, or even nonprofessionals, as expert witnesses.

Eysenck (1984), as quoted in the *APA Monitor*, sums up these matters as follows:

> The analysis also found no correlation…between the extent of a therapist's training and successful treatment. In other words, somebody who has just been told how to treat patients is just as successful as a psychoanalyst with twenty years of practice. This I do not doubt.

Preston (1981), discussing medical practice in general, touches on many of the points we have raised in this section. He indicates that physicians often attribute positive results to treatment, but that:

> Physicians do not have a systematic method for classifying facts of illnesses and treatment so as to be able to say that a particular treatment was definitively responsible for a particular recovery. As a rule, they believe the benefits of medical practices are self-evident, and therefore do not require testing. (p. 99)

Preston further observes that many physicians allow biases to affect case appraisals, and that their conclusions commonly rest on "unsubstantiated assumptions. They rely not on science but on intuition and clinical experience." (p. 100) Although he does not refer to it as such, Preston implies that confirmation bias is one factor that underlies such errors. He states:

> Scientific evidence bearing on a case becomes subordinated to the physician's interpretation of that evidence. He regards scientific evidence as too general to apply to individual patients—as incomplete if not incompatible with his own evaluation—and he disregards it if it does not confirm his own experience. He will even reject statements and policies of medical societies and institutions if they do not conform to his personal experience. (p. 100)

Preston is particularly critical of testimonials, noting that physicians often rely on testimonials in the same way that "quacks do." He states:

> The real problem with testimonials is that they are a source of error in medical practices when they are used selectively to promote a favorite therapy. In this way, they are like testimonials in television advertisements and faith healer meetings. The natural tendency of physicians is to select and to believe those testimonials supportive of their opinions. (p. 102)

Preston further notes:

> In no aspect of clinical medicine is the use of scientific method more needed or less in evidence than in the assessment of therapies. Historically, doctors have enthusiastically embraced therapies which ultimately turned out to be of no benefit to their patients, and there is evidence of the same today. (p. 105)

Further:

...we can judge the new therapy only by comparison to what would have happened without it. Always a comparison is necessary for a scientific conclusion.
And comparisons in medicine are very difficult and complicated. (p. 107)

Preston states:

...most of the "knowledge" on which therapy has been based has been incorrect, but, at every stage in the history of medicine, the knowledge of contemporary doctors was considered authoritative....Current practices always have been
believed to be true and accurate. (p. 158)

Further:

A second type of deception is systematic and grows out of the notion of the
special powers of healers. This is the belief that the physician's own clinical
judgment is superior to scientific knowledge derived from carefully controlled
studies and investigations. This deception is perpetuated by accepted methods
of assessing medical practices.

The assessment of therapy by those who provide it is one of the most astonishing inconsistencies in Western society. In no other sphere of public life is the
producer of the service or product pronounced the sole evaluator and protected
as such by law, with no real attempt by those who receive the service to make a
comprehensive assessment of it. This is comparable to politicians being the sole
judges of their actions, or automobile dealers being the sole appraisers of the
vehicles they sell. (p. 159)

Christensen and Jacobson (1994) describe seven meta-analyses of
treatment studies (Durlak, 1979; Nietzel and Fisher, 1981; Berman and
Norton, 1985; Stein and Lambert, 1984; Smith and Glass, 1980; Shapiro
and Shapiro, 1982; and Weisz et al., 1987). While they point out methodological problems and/or limitations of these analyses, they also point
out that as of the time of writing their article (we would assume sometime in 1992 or 1993) the evidence "strongly suggests that under many,
if not most, conditions paraprofessionals or professionals with limited
experience perform as well or better than professionally trained psychotherapists."

Clement (1994) in a report of his unusual and remarkable self-study
(quantifying and counting, not "impression") found that contrary to his
expectation, there was absolutely no improvement in his effectiveness
over 25 years of professional experience. Although this is obviously limited by the fact that Clement did his own ratings of success, rather than it
being done by an independent evaluator, this is an impressive anecdotal
illustration of lack of relationship between experience and therapy outcome. It also suggests that, when an expert cites success in treatment, the
lawyer could ask her if she has conducted the kind of study that Clement
did or is merely stating an impression.

THE LACK OF RELATION BETWEEN EXPERIENCE
AND ACCURACY: SUMMARY AND ILLUSTRATIONS

These factors described above may well explain something about the limited benefits of experience. First, clinicians often do not receive feedback. Second, in most cases, any feedback they do receive is quite ambiguous and open to considerable biases and misinterpretation. Third, even when clear, precise, and immediate feedback is offered, and even when this feedback clearly points out the superiority of available methods, it is still often disregarded. In fact, as noted, a number of studies (Arkes et al., 1986; Hammond et al., 1973; Schmitt et al., 1976) show that feedback can actually decrease judgment performance. Apparently what happens is that one may start by placing full, or at least partial reliance on previously demonstrated decision rules, such a "canned" programs for MMPI interpretation. If one obtains no feedback, these habits may well be maintained. However, if feedback is obtained, one uncovers errors because all decision rules are faulty, or by no means perfect, and thereby lead to a certain percentage of mistakes. Upon discovering these errors, the clinician may feel that he must try to do better and gives in to the temptation to violate or supersede these rules at his own choosing. The result, of course, is a lower level of accuracy than would be attained by sticking to the initial decision rules more closely.

Rotter (1967) summarizes some of these factors that limit the value of feedback:

> Finally, we come back to the issue of the kind of use that should be made of feed-back or knowledge or criterion. If the clinician bases his interpretations on holistic impressions and "gut" reactions and is told only that he is correct or incorrect, he is not likely to obtain clear-cut indication of the nature of the necessary changes in his interpretive methodology. If feed-back is to be useful, then the first requirement is that a basis for predictions be made as explicit as possible. Even where the basis for the predictions is explicit and the nature of the feed-back is behavioral or objective data, it may still take a great many instances of studying concomitant variations before the errors or the correct bases for prediction can be identified. In fact, where so many variables are involved (tests, personal, cultural, and situational) the problem of learning from individual experience may be close to hopeless (italics ours). (p. 14)

Note that Rotter does not even address the problems with bias in the interpretation of feedback, an additional complication that may make matters even worse. Faust (1986b) provides a summary statement that includes this and additional factors:

> Failure to benefit from clinical experience is often attributed to insufficient feedback. However, clinicians seem to evidence minimal gains, even when potentially useful feedback is obtained. The problem cuts more deeply, and the essential question may be this: When provided with informative feedback, to what extent do (and can) clinicians learn from it? The judgment literature

suggests that bad judgment habits and cognitive limitations restrict the ability to use feedback productively, and that this is the primary factor hindering experiential learning.

The interpretation of feedback is hardly a straightforward process. First, in attempts to form impressions about such things as specific therapeutic actions and client responses, the available information is exceedingly complicated. There occur behavior and thinking that are complex and subtle, that can be analyzed on various levels, that may have multiple causal agents (some immediate and some temporally remote), and that, in small or large part, take place outside of conscious awareness. These complexities apply to both the therapist and the client and are increased manifold by the need to consider the two in interaction.

...There is little doubt that the interpretation of feedback is open to numerous bad judgment habits and that the available information outstrips one's "processing" abilities. Thus, discerning such things as the links between specific therapist actions and outcome is arduous at best. Feedback may often be of little use because one does not know how to decipher (judge) what it could tell one. (p. 426)

For the interested reader, Brehmer (1980), and Einhorn and Hogarth (1978, 1981) provide more detailed discussion of the factors that impede the productive use of feedback.

Although the lawyer may now have a good handle on the limited value of experience and on problems using treatment outcome to gauge validity or judgment accuracy, it is another thing to convey these findings to the jury. Let us suggest a few analogies and metaphors that one might use to illustrate, or concretize, the notion that the judgment accuracy of psychologists and psychiatrists does not necessarily improve no matter their level of practice or experience.

The essential point to bring home to jurors is that experience and practice do not necessarily, or always, lead to improvement, or that experience and practice can actually make individuals worse at what they do, rather than better. As one example, take the individual who has married and divorced multiple times. They have indeed experienced more marriages than individuals with a single, stable marriage, but we would not assume they are better at the enterprise. Rather, they keep on repeating the same, or similar mistakes. Would one claim that Elizabeth Taylor is better at marriage because she has been married so many times?

Examples that illustrate problems in the "processing" of feedback can also serve a useful purpose. We are reminded of one of our friends, who is the ultimate stereo buff, but who has a "tin ear." This friend initially relied on published material when selecting stereo equipment, and in fact made some excellent selections (although he really couldn't tell). As he became a more experienced collector, he began to rely on his own ear more and more, and his collection deteriorated more and more. The problem, of course, was that he was unable to make adequate discriminations by ear, or to correctly "process" the information or feed-back, so that as he came to rely on himself increasingly and published reports less, his choices become worse and worse. This situation seems quite close to that of the novice, who starts out relying heavily on published materials and standardized assessment methods, and who scores tests very carefully and makes detailed records. Over time, however, as his experience grows, he starts relying on his own judgment increasingly and becomes less scrupulous in his habits. Stated differently, he comes to rely less on prespecified procedures and established decision aids, and more on what is, essentially, his own idiosyncratic way of drawing conclusions. As shown by research on the actuarial judgment method versus the clinical method, decreased reliance on the former and increased reliance on the latter, which seems to be encouraged by experience, is much more likely to have negative, rather than positive effects on judgment accuracy.

As a further set of parallels, suppose a golfer has a tendency to slice because of some defect in his swing. The more experience he has swinging in that particular manner the more he will harden and entrench his tendency to slice. Similarly, to the extent that a psychiatrist continually bases his conclusions on defective theory, unvalidated principles or knowledge, or unreliable methods, the validity of his conclusions will not be improved. If the golfer blames the ball for his slice, or the psychiatrist blames the patient for not producing the data the psychiatrist expects, or distorts the data to fit his expectations, neither will improve the effectiveness of his performance. If the golfer hits many golf balls but always in a dense fog so that he does not know how the shots really turn out, and therefore, he has no opportunity for making such corrections as might be necessary, it is unlikely that the fact that he has hit numerous golf balls, under such circumstances, will result in improving his game. Similarly, when a psychiatrist makes many diagnostic evaluations but lacks the opportunity or fails to follow up his diagnostic conclusions to determine by objective indices whether or not they were correct, his diagnostic accuracy is not likely to improve. In fact, neither he nor anyone else will know what his diagnostic accuracy is. If the golfer does observe where his shots go and finds that some slice and some go straight, unless he keeps a count of the straight shots and the slices he may overemphasize the good shots and conclude that his swing is really all right and that there are only occasional slices when, in fact, he may be slicing as often or more often as hitting straight. Similarly, if some rare psychiatrist does follow up his cases and finds that he is sometimes right and sometimes wrong, unless he has kept an accurate count of each type of outcome, based on independent, objective criteria, he may fool himself into feeling that he is generally accurate when, in fact, this may not be the case (see

Chapter 5, supra, re: "Illusory Correlation"). In any event, short of making an actual count, there is no way of knowing what his percentage of accuracy is. He may be right more often than wrong, but still may have something like a 60% success rate, for example.

One last illustration perhaps comes closest to the circumstances that restrict the benefits of experience. Psychologists are fond of referring to the human mind as the "black box." It is called black because it is impenetrable, or because one cannot observe its workings directly and its actual operations remain largely uncertain. This suggests the following analogy. Almost anyone who has received a gift, at one time or another, has tried to guess what the contents might be before opening it. One might determine how much it weighs or try to shake it, or whatever. Obviously, before opening the package, one cannot look directly inside to see what it might be, so that this is much like our black box, in which one cannot observe the object of interest directly but must try to infer the contents through indirect evidence.

Now suppose an individual, or group of individuals, set out to become professionals or experts at identifying the content of packages before opening them. However, they labor under a particular disadvantage—they never get to open the packages, much as the psychologist or psychiatrist never gets to open the "black box." They could practice all they wanted, but they would probably never get better at the task, because they would never be sure if their guesses or inferences were correct or not. However, they very well could come to believe that they are getting better, because individuals get better with practice, do they not? Further, they might be able to hold conferences or committee meetings, and decide upon standard means for assessing the inner contents of boxes, and agree upon methods for classifying the results of their assessments that could lead to a high level of consensus or shared views among different practitioners of the art. They could teach these practices to newcomers, who after considerable experience and training might be able to reach judgments that aligned with that of the "experts." They might even testify in court, if they could convince the court of their worth, and claim that their extensive experience and training helped them to make more accurate judgments. And because no one else could see into the packages either, these practitioners could continue to make these assertions, regardless of their validity, without fear of definitive counterevidence. In many respects, the psychologist and psychiatrist are in much the same position, for their attempts to learn through experience are frequently impeded by a lack of feedback or by feedback that is so indirect, or unclear, or open to theoretical biases that the lessons it could potentially teach are often indecipherable.

EXPERIENCE AND INNOVATION

The frequent changes or "innovations" in psychiatry and psychology can quickly make the experienced inexperienced. For example, significant modifications in the use or composition of a psychological test, such as the introduction of the Exner system for the Rorschach, may lead even highly experienced professionals to take up entirely new techniques. Thus, the lawyer may wish to question the expert's experience with specific methods or systems, particularly new ones.

An important example is provided by the frequent changes in diagnostic systems. The publication of DSM-III in 1980 rendered nearly all psychiatrists and psychologists, at that time, inexperienced in using the contemporary diagnostic manual and the specific diagnoses described therein. At the time of this writing, clinicians may have accumulated 6 or 7 years of experience using the DSM-III and the 7 years with partially different DSM-III-R, but little or no experience with the new DSM-IV. This point may be relevant with experts who have been in practice for longer periods of time, and who state that they have 15, or 25, or some such number of years of experience with diagnosis. This may be true, but a substantial proportion of this time may have involved the use of prior, now outdated diagnostic manuals. Thus, they do not have such extensive experience using the DSM-IV. Along these lines, with the appearance of any new DSM most clinicians will have had little, if any experience with any of the revised, or new diagnostic categories within this system. Thus, in cases involving certain diagnostic categories within the new manuals, they will be no more experienced than the most fledgling clinicians or students.

SUMMARY

Summing up the available research, it seems clear that there is virtually no basis to support the claim of superior ability in psychiatric or psychological assessment as a result of experience. If anything, the research suggests the contrary. Of course, the previous chapter citing studies on low validity would indicate that even if experience helped, apparently it does not help enough to make good diagnosticians. Indeed, what the research does suggest is that the expert, if one is to use accuracy as the means for identification, is to be found in actuarial or statistical methods of data interpretation where available, and not among clinicians with many years of experience. Laymen, with minimal help, are equally able to draw conclusions from such methods and one could eliminate the clinician from the data interpretation process entirely.

On cross-examination it may well be advisable for the attorney to doggedly pursue the above points with the psychiatrist or psychologist who places the basis for his predictive ability on his "experience." He can be asked if he is aware of a number of studies showing that experience does not improve diagnostic ability. He can be asked if he has had controlled studies done by independent evaluators, counting his percentage of correct and incorrect diagnoses or predictions under controlled conditions, so as to be able to derive a validity coefficient or at the very least be able to state precisely the percentage of errors that he makes. Not only should he be required to do this for his evaluations, in general, but he should be required to do it for the specific psychological traits or characteristics to which he is testifying. That is, if he is testifying that at a point in the past a certain defendant was not capable of distinguishing right from wrong, he should be required to testify in how many cases he has made an evaluation of this particular characteristic and in exactly what percentage of cases he was proved right and in exactly what percentage of cases he was proved wrong based on independent and objective criteria. It is doubtful that any clinician has actually made such a study of his own diagnostic predictions. Almost always, the most he will be able to state is that it is his impression that he is right in X percent of the cases. In other words, he can only "guess" how valid he is. As indicated by many of the studies previously cited, both his perception and memory of his hits and misses are almost certain to be inaccurate and distorted. Certainly, it cannot be taken as a reliable or valid demonstration of his diagnostic accuracy. Further, because for many judgments there is ultimately no objective or definitive method for determining whether the clinician was correct (e.g., when he postdicts "insanity"), the clinician cannot possibly know, really, what his accuracy level might be. In each case, it can be shown that there is no way of knowing how valid the particular clinician is. In the absence of such a showing of validity of the individual clinician, the best evidence as to how good he is and the effect of experience on his skill must then be derived from the general research in these areas, which strongly indicates that the clinician has a low validity rate and that his experience has not made him superior to others without such experience.

As noted, the findings reported in this chapter are the most difficult for laymen and most professionals to accept. Yet, the testimony of the experts themselves will often provide a courtroom demonstration on this issue. Almost always, the experts called by each side have considerable experience—enough so that any difference between them is meaningless. There is little difference for practical purposes between an expert with 10 years of experience and one with 15, or one who has done 1,100 diagnoses and one who has done 2,000. If learning was taking place, it would long since have leveled off for each. Therefore, in addition to the presenting of an expert who will inform the jury as to the inefficacy of experience in this field, their attention can be directed to what they have seen themselves. In the usual case, two or more experts, each with considerable experience, will have drawn disparate conclusions. As both cannot be right, one must be wrong, and perhaps both are, and certainly the amount of their experience provides no guide. Thus, the jury can see for themselves, that hard as it may be to believe, one cannot put much faith in expertise or conclusions based on experience, at least in the fields of psychiatry and clinical psychology. However, if one looks to the material cited in this book, one may be able to comprehend this exception to the rule.

The materials in this book provide a base for understanding why experience may not be helpful in psychological assessment. These materials make it clear that the tools and techniques of assessment currently in use are inadequate to the task, or at the very least, have not been demonstrated to be adequate. More serious is the fact that we simply do not know enough about human psychological functioning to perform the task. We have not yet established or accurately defined the basic variables or dimensions upon which human behavior rests, much less the combination of these variables which would allow us to determine with any reasonable degree of accuracy the relationship of behavior to these states or processes.

Each practitioner either follows the teachings of others or develops his own private set of theories and principles. If the latter course resulted in publicly verifiable and demonstrably valid propositions or conclusions, there could be no objection. But as we have seen, this is not the case. What we have seen is that despite years of experience, the problems of the deficiencies of the clinical examination have not been solved, and tools and techniques which are demonstrably ineffective continue to be used. Theories, principles, and beliefs which, according to the literature, are at least in serious doubt continue to form the basis of assessment. Until correct and valid methods and principles emerge, the psychiatrist can learn little, if anything, from his experience, except that if he is a critical thinker he may learn that he knows, and can do, very little. The experience of such critical thinkers may contribute to the emergence of valid tools and principles eventually, but this will not be accomplished by an individual practitioner. Validation can only be accomplished by the efforts of many, continually checking and challenging the conclusions of others by the scientific method, and it is only through validation that experience becomes meaningful.

We believe that given the large body of research showing that experience is unrelated to accuracy, more direct and valid means for assessing credibility are needed. Obviously, level of experience is one criterion that has been used to gauge an expert's credibility, based on the reasonable presumption that skills improve with practice. This presumption, however, has been soundly discredited in the fields of psychology and psychiatry. Experience does not provide a helpful index of accuracy, but rather a potentially misleading one, and by allowing this presumption to stand the courts potentially introduce a factor that can only lead the trier of fact further from, and not closer to the truth. A serious injustice may be done when jurors are swayed by an expert's experience when, unrecognized by them, this experience may well do nothing to enhance the accuracy of this expert's opinions. We would hope that the courts would not encourage, and in fact would disallow such biasing information from exerting any influence whatsoever.

There is a simple solution to this problem. An expert's credibility, if not his qualifications as an expert witness, can be tested directly by conducting a controlled study of the accuracy of his judgments on cases and questions pertinent to those under consideration. Such study might be conducted, for example, by professional boards. Thus, if a neuropsychologist is to testify in cases involving, say, the presence of brain damage subsequent to head injury, he would first be required to demonstrate his abilities on a series of 100 cases. Whether his demonstrated level of accuracy qualifies him as an expert is a matter for the courts to decide. But it would seem infinitely more useful to the trier of fact to be informed of this expert's level of accuracy on comparable cases rather than having to depend on essentially useless, and potentially quite prejudicial indices or self-assertions about the "benefits" of training or experience. EXPERTS DO NOT KNOW THEIR LEVELS OF ACCURACY. EXPERTS DO NOT REALLY KNOW WHETHER THEIR TRAINING OR EXPERIENCE HAS BEEN OF ANY USE IN IMPROVING JUDGMENT ACCURACY. YET EXPERTS OFTEN THINK THEY KNOW SUCH THINGS AND THUS FOOL NOT ONLY THEMSELVES BUT OFTEN THE TRIER OF FACT AS WELL. HOW CAN THE COURTS ALLOW THIS TRAVESTY TO CONTINUE WHEN THERE IS A MEANS FOR SUBSTANTIAL IMPROVEMENT? BAR SUCH UNFOUNDED SELF-ASSERTIONS AS UNPROVEN AND POTENTIALLY PREJUDICIAL; DO NOT RELY ON AN EXPERT'S ASSERTIONS ABOUT HIS ACCURACY—TEST IT!

REFERENCES

Abramowitz, S.I., and Abramowitz, C. (1973). Should prospective women clients seek out women practitioners? Intimations of a "dingbat" effect in clinical evaluation. *Proceedings of the 81st Annual Convention of the American Psychological Association, 8*, 503.

Adinolfi, A.A. (1971). Relevance of person perception research to clinical psychology. *Journal of Consulting and Clinical Psychology, 37*, 167-176.

Albert, S., Fox, H.M., and Kahn, M.W. (1980). Faking psychosis on the Rorschach: Can expert judges detect malingering? *Journal of Personality Assessment, 44*, 115-119.

Andreasen, N.C., McDonald-Scott, P., Grove, W.M., Keller, M.B., Shapiro, R.W., and Hershfeld, R.M.A. (1982). Assessment of reliability in multicenter collaborative research with a video tape approach. *American Journal of Psychiatry, 139*, 876-882.

Andreasen, N.J.C., Tsuang, N.T., and Caner, A. (1974). The significance of thought disorder in diagnostic evaluation. *Comprehensive Psychiatry, 15*, 27-34.

Arkes, H.R. (1981). Impediments to accurate clinical judgment and possible ways to minimize their impact. *Journal of Consulting and Clinical Psychology, 49*, 323-330.

Arkes, H.E., Dawes, R.M., and Christensen, C. (1986). Factors influencing the use of a decision rule in a probabilistic task. *Behavior and Human Decision Processes, 37*, 93-110.

Arkes, H.R., and Freedman, M.R. (1984). A demonstration of the costs and benefits of expertise in recognition memory. *Memory and Cognition, 12*, 84-89.

Arkes, H.R., and Harkness, A.R. (1980). Effect of making a diagnosis on subsequent recognition of symptoms. *Journal of Experimental Psychology, 6*, 568-575.

Beckett, G.S., Grisell, J., Crandall, R.G., and Gudobba, R.A. (1967). A method of formalizing psychiatric study. *Archives of General Psychiatry, 16*, 407-415.

Bedard, J., and Chi, M.T.H. (1992). Expertise. *Current Directions in Psychological Science, 1*, 135-139.

Berman, J.S., and Norton, N.C. (1985). Does professional training make a therapist more effective? *Psychological Bulletin, 98*, 401-407.

Bersof, D.N. (1992). Judicial deference to nonlegal decisionmakers: Imposing simplistic solutions on problems of cognitive complexity in mental disability law. *SMU Law Review, 46*, 329-372.

Blankenhorn, A., and Cerbus, G. (1975). Clinical and actuarial evaluation of organic brain damage by psychologists and non-psychologists using the memory for designs. *Perceptual and Motor Skills, 40,* 99-102.

Bolocofsky, D.N. (1989). Use and abuse of mental health experts in child custody determinations. *Behavioral Sciences & the Law, 7,* 197-213.

Borum, R., Otto, R., and Golding, S. (1993). Improving clinical judgment and decision making in forensic evaluation. *Journal of Psychiatry and Law, 21,* 35-76.

Bransford, J.D., Barclay, J.R., and Franks, J.J. (1972). Sentence memory: A constructive versus interpretive approach. *Cognitive Psychology, 3,* 193-209.

Brehmer, B. (1980). In one word: Not from experience. *Acta Psychologica, 45,* 223-241.

Brodsky, S.L. (1991). *Testifying in Court.* Washington, DC: American Psychological Association.

Campbell, R.J. (1985). Miscellaneous organic therapies. In H.I. Kaplan and B.J. Sadock (Eds.), *Comprehensive Handbook of Psychiatry* (4th ed.). Baltimore: Williams and Wilkins.

Carson, R.C. (1990). Assessment: What role the assessor? *Journal of Personality Assessment, 54,* 435-445.

Chapman, L.J., and Chapman, J.P. (1969). Illusory correlation as an obstacle to the use of valid psychodiagnostic signs. *Journal of Abnormal Psychology, 74,* 271-280.

Chapman, L.J., and Chapman, J.P. (1971). Test results are what you think they are. *Psychology Today, 5.*

Christensen, A., and Jacobson, N.S. (1994). Who (or what?) can do psychotherapy: The status and challenge of nonprofessional therapies. *Psychological Science, 5,* 8-13.

Clement, P.W. (1994). Quantitative evaluation of 26 years of private practice. *Professional Psychology: Research and Practice, 25,* 173-176.

Cline, V. (1955). Ability to judge personality assessed with a stress interview and sound film technique. *Journal of Abnormal and Social Psychology, 50,* 183-187.

Cohen, L.H., and Oyster-Nelson, C.K. (1981). Clinicians evaluations of psychodynamic psychotherapy: Experimental data on psychological peer review. *Journal of Consulting and Clinical Psychology, 49,* 583-589.

Coryell, W., Cloninger, C.R., and Reich, T. (1978). Clinical assessment: Use of non-physician interviewers. *The Journal of Nervous and Mental Disease, 166,* 599-606.

Dawes, R.M. (1989a). Experience and validity of clinical judgment: The illusory correlation. *Behavioral Sciences & the Law, 7,* 457-467.

Dawes, R.M. (1994). *House of Cards.* New York: The Free Press.

Dershowitz, A.M. (1969). The psychiatrist's power in civil commitment. *Psychology Today, 2.*

Dumont, F. (1991). Expertise in psychotherapy: Inherent liabilities of becoming experienced. *Psychotherapy, 28,* 422-428.

Einhorn, H.J., and Hogarth, R.M. (1978). Confidence in judgment: Persistence of the illusion of validity. *Psychological Review, 85,* 395-416.

Einhorn, H.J., and Hogarth, R.M. (1981). Behavioral decision theory: Processes of judgment and choice. *Annual Review of Psychology, 32,* 53-88.

Eysenck, H. (1984). The American Psychological Association *Monitor.*

Faust, D. (1986a). Learning and maintaining rules for decreasing judgment accuracy. *Journal of Personality Assessment, 50,* 585-600.

Faust, D. (1986b). Research on human judgment and its application to clinical practice. *Professional Psychology, 17,* 420-430.

Faust, D., Hart, K., Guilmette, T.J., and Arkes, H.R. (1988b). Neuropsychologists' capacity to detect adolescent malingerers. *Professional Psychology: Research and Practice, 19,* 508-515.

Faust, D., and Ziskin, J. (1988). The expert witness in psychology and psychiatry. *Science, 241,* 31-35.

Fitzgibbons, D.J., and Shearn, C.R. (1972). Concepts of schizophrenic among mental health professionals: A factor analytic study. *Journal of Consulting and Clinical Psychology, 38,* 228-295.

Ford, M.R., and Widiger, T.A. (1989). Sex bias and the diagnosis of histrionic and anti-social personality disorders. *Journal of Consulting and Clinical Psychology, 2,* 301-305.

Freidlander, M.L., and Phillips, S.D. (1984). Preventing anchoring errors in clinical judgment. *Journal of Consulting and Clinical Psychology, 52,* 366-371.

Friedlander, M.L., and Stockman, S.J. (1983). Anchoring and publicity effect in clinical judgment. *Journal of Clinical Psychology, 39,* 637-643.

Garb, H.N. (1989). Comment on "The study of clinical judgment: An ecological approach." *Clinical Psychology Review, 8,* 441-444.

Garb, H.N. (1992). The debate over the use of computer-based test reports. *The Clinical Psychologist, 45,* 95-100.

Goldberg, L.R. (1959). The effectiveness of clinicians' judgments: The diagnosis of organic brain damage from the Bender-Gestalt Test. *Journal of Consulting Psychology, 23,* 25-33.

Goldberg, L.R. (1965). Diagnosticians vs. diagnostic signs: The diagnosis of psychosis vs. neurosis from the MMPI. *Psychological Monographs, 79,* 28.

Goldberg, L.R. (1968b). Simple models or simple processes? Some research on clinical judgments. *American Psychologist, 23*, 483-496.

Goldsmith, S.R., and Mandell, A.J. (1969). The psychodynamic formulation: A critique of a psychiatric ritual. *American Journal of Psychiatry, 125*, 1738-1743.

Goldstein, S.G., Deysach, R.E., and Kleinknecht, R.A. (1973). Effect of experience and amount of information on identification of cerebral impairment. *Journal of Consulting and Clinical Psychology, 41*, 30-34.

Gomes-Schwartz, B., and Schwartz, J.M. (1978). Psychotherapy process variables distinguishing the "inherently healthful" person from the professional psychotherapist. *Journal of Consulting and Clinical Psychology, 46*, 196-197.

Graham, J.R. (1971). Feedback and accuracy of clinical judgments, from the MMPI. *Journal of Consulting and Clinical Psychology, 36*, 286-291.

Greenwald, A.G., Pratkanis, A.R., Leippe, M.R., and Baumgardner, M.H. (1986). Under what conditions does theory obstruct research progress? *Psychological Review, 93*, 216-229.

Hammond, K.R., Summers, D.A., and Deane, D.H. (1973). Negative effects of outcome feedback in multiple cue probability learning experiments. *Organizational Behavior and Human Performance, 9*, 30-34.

Harris, R.J., and Monaco, G.E. (1978). The psychology of pragmatic implication: Information processing between the lines. *Journal of Experimental Psychology: General, 107*, 1-22.

Harris, R.J., Teske, R.R., and Ginns, M.J. (1975). Memory for pragmatic implications from courtroom testimony. *Bulletin of the Psychonomic Society, 6*, 494-496.

Heaton, R.K., Smith, H.H., Lehman, R.A., and Vogt, A.T. (1978a). Prospects for faking believable deficits on neuropsychological testing. *Journal of Consulting and Clinical Psychology, 46*, 892-900.

Helzer, J.E., Spitznagel, E.L., and McEvoy, L. (1987). The predictive validity of lay diagnostic interview schedule diagnoses in the general population. *Archives of General Psychiatry, 44*, 1069-1077.

Hynan, M.T. (1981). On the advantages of assuming that the techniques of psychotherapy are ineffective. *Psychotherapy: Theory, Research and Practice, 18*, 11-13.

Johnson, M.K., Taylor, T.H., and Raye, C. (1977). Fact and fantasy: The effects of internally generated events on the apparent frequency of externally generated events. *Memory & Cognition, 5*, 116-122.

Journal of Consulting and Clinical Psychology, 54, February, 1986.

Kandler, H., Plutchik, R., Cone, H., and Siegel, B. (1975). Prediction of performance of psychiatric residents: A three year follow-up study. *American Journal of Psychiatry, 132*, 1286-1290.

Kaschak, E. (1978). Therapist and client: Two views of the process and outcome of psychotherapy. *Professional Psychology, 33*, 271-277.

Kass, F., Skodol, A., Buckley, P., and Charles, E. (1980). Therapists' recognition of psychopathology: A model for quality review of psychotherapy. *American Journal of Psychiatry, 137*, 87-90.

Kazdin, A.E. (1986). Comparative outcome studies of psychotherapy: Methodological issues and strategies. *Journal of Consulting and Clinical Psychology, 54*, 95-105.

Keenan, J.M., and Kintsch, W. (1974). The identification of explicitly and implicitly presented information. In W. Kintsch (Ed.), *The Representation of Meaning In Memory.* Hillsdale, N.J.: Erlbaum.

Klopfer, W.G. (1984). The use of the Rorschach in brief clinical evaluation. *Journal of Personality Assessment, 48*, 654-659.

Koscherak, S., and Masling, J. (1972). Noblesse oblige effect: An interpretation of Rorschach responses as a function of ascribed social class. *Journal of Consulting and Clinical Psychology, 39*, 415-419.

Kubie, L.S. (1971). Multiple fallacies in the concept of schizophrenia. *The Journal of Nervous and Mental Disease, 153*, 331-342.

Lambert, L.E., and Wertheimer, M. (1988). Is diagnostic ability related to relevant training and experience? *Professional Psychology: Research and Practice, 144*, 133-143.

Lanyon, R.I. (1986). Psychological assessment procedures in court-related settings. *Professional Psychology: Research and Practice, 17*, 260-268.

Leifer, R. (1962-63). The competence of the psychiatrist to assist in the determination of incompetency: A skeptical inquiry into the courtroom functions of psychiatrists. *Syracuse Law Review, 14*, 564-575.

Leli, D.A., and Filskov, S.B. (1981). Clinical-actuarial detection and description of brain impairment with the W-B form 1. *Journal of Clinical Psychology, 37*, 623-629.

Levine, M. (1984). The adversary process and social science in the courts: Barefoot v. Estelle. *The Journal of Psychiatry & Law, 12*, 147-181.

Lingle, J.H., and Ostrom, T.M. (1979). Retrieval and selectivity in memory-based impression judgments. *Journal of Personality and Social Psychology, 37*, 180-194.

Livermore, J.M., Malmquist, C.P., and Meehl, P.E. (1968). On the justification for civil commitment. *University of Pennsylvania Law Review, 117*.

London, P., and Klerman, G.L. (1982). Evaluating psychotherapy. *The American Journal of Psychiatry, 139*, 709-717.

Lord, C., Lepper, M.R., and Ross, L. (1979). Biased assimilation and attitude polarization: The effects of prior theories on subsequently considered evidence. *Journal of Personality and Social Psychology, 37*, 2098-2110.

Luborsky, L. (1954). Selecting psychiatric residents, survey of the Topeka research. *Bulletin of the Menninger Clinic, 18*, 252-259.

Luft, J.B. (1950). Implicit hypotheses and clinical prediction. *Journal of Abnormal and Social Psychology, 45*, 756-759.

Mash, E.J., and Hunsley, J. (1993). Assessment considerations in the identification of failing psychotherapy: Bringing the negatives out of the darkroom. *Psychological Assessment, 5,* 292-301.

McLean, P.D., and Hakstian, A.R. (1979). Clinical depression: Comparative efficacy of out-patient treatments. *Journal of Consulting and Clinical Psychology, 47*, 818-836.

Meehl, P.E. (1971). Law and the fireside inductions: Some reflections of a clinical psychologist. *Journal of Social Issues, 27.*

Melges, F.P. (1972). Integrating psychiatric research with clinical training: N = 1. *Journal of Nervous and Mental Disease, 154*, 206-212.

Mendel, W., and Rapport, S. (1963). Outpatient treatment for chronic schizophrenic patients. *Archives of General Psychiatry, 8*, 190-196.

Menzies, R.J., Webster, C.D., and Sepejak, D.S. (1985). The dimensions of dangerousness: Evaluating the accuracy of psychometric predictions of violence among forensic patients. *Law and Human Behavior, 9*, 49-70.

Mora, G. (1985). Historical and theoretical trends in psychiatry. In H.I. Kaplan and B.J. Sadock (Eds.), *Comprehensive Handbook of Psychiatry* (4th ed.). Baltimore: Williams and Wilkins.

Morse, S.J. (1983). Predicting future dangerousness. *California Lawyer*, 16-18.

Moxley, A.W. (1973). Clinical judgment: The effects of statistical information. *Journal of Personality Assessment, 37*, 86-91.

Oskamp, S. (1962). Clinical experience and training and clinical prediction. *Psychological Monographs, 76.*

Oskamp. S. (1965). Overconfidence in case-study judgments. *Journal of Consulting Psychology, 29*, 261-265.

Parloff, M.B. (1982). Psychotherapy research evidence and reimbursement decisions; Bambi meets Godzilla. *American Journal of Psychiatry, 139*, 718-727.

Pasamanick, B., Divity, S., and Lefton, M. (1959). Psychiatric orientation and its relation to diagnosis and treatment in a mental hospital. *American Journal of Psychiatry, 116.*

Plaut, E., and Cromwell, B. (1955). The ability of the clinical psychologist to discriminate between drawings by deteriorated schizophrenics and normal subjects. *Psychological Reports, 1,* 153-158.

Poythress, N.G., Jr. (1977). Mental health expert testimony: Current problems. *Journal of Psychiatry and Law, 5,* 201-227.

Preston, T.P. (1981). *The Clay Pedestal.* Seattle: Madrona.

Resnick, P.J. (1984). The detection of malingered mental illness. *Behavioral Sciences & The Law, 2,* 21-38.

Rickles, K., Schweizer, E., and Case, W. (1988). The uncontrolled case report: A double-edge sword. *The Journal of Nervous and Mental Disease, 176,* 50-52.

Robins, L.N. (1985). Epidemiology: Reflections on testing the validity of psychiatric interviews. *Archives of General Psychiatry, 42,* 918-924.

Rock, D.L., and Bransford, J.D. (1992). An empirical evaluation of three components of the tetrahedron model of clinical judgment. *The Journal of Nervous and Mental Disease, 180,* 560-565.

Rotter, J.B. (1967). Can the clinician learn from experience? *Journal of Consulting Psychology, 13,* 12-15.

Rubenzer, S. (1991). Computerized testing and clinical judgment: Cause for concern. *The Clinical Psychologist, 44,* 63-66.

Sattler, J.M., and Ryan, J.J. (1973). Scoring agreement on the Stanford-Binet. *Journal of Clinical Psychology, 29,* 35-38.

Saunders, R.T., Jr. (1975). Toward a distinctive role for the psychologist in neurodiagnostic decision making. *Professional Psychology, 6,* 161-166.

Schinka, J.A., and Sines, J.O. (1974). Correlates of accuracy in personality assessment. *Journal of Clinical Psychology, 30,* 374-377.

Schmideberg, M. (1962-1963). The promise of psychiatry: Hopes and disillusionment. *Northwestern University Law Review, 57.*

Schmitt, N., Coyle, B.W., and King, L. (1976). Feedback and task predictability as determinants of performance in multiple cue probability learning tasks. *Organizational Behavior and Human Performance, 16,* 388-402.

Schulberg, H.C., Saul, M., McClelland, M., Ganguli, M., Christy, W., and Frank, R. (1985). Assessing depression in primary medical and psychiatric practices. *Archives of General Psychiatry, 42,* 1164-1170.

Shweder, R.A. (1977). Illusory correlation and the MMPI controversy. *Journal of Consulting and Clinical Psychology, 45,* 917-924.

Smith, M.L., and Glass, G.V. (1977). Meta-analysis of psychotherapy outcome studies. *American Psychologist, 32,* 752-760.

Snyder, C.R. (1974). Why horoscopes are true: The effect of specificity on acceptance of astrological interpretation. *Journal of Clinical Psychology, 30,* 577-580.

Snyder, C.R., Handelsman, M.M., and Endelman, J.R. (1978). Can clients provide valuable feedback to clinicians about their personality interpretations? A reply to Greene. *Journal of Consulting and Clinical Psychology, 46,* 1493-1495.

Snyder, C.R., Shenkel, Jr., and Lowery, C.R. (1977). Acceptance of personality interpretations: The Barnum effect and beyond. *Journal of Consulting and Clinical Psychology, 45,* 104-114.

Soskin, W.F. (1954). Bias in post-diction from projective tests. *Journal of Abnormal and Social Psychology, 49,* 69-74.

Stewart, J.W., McGrath, P.J., Liebowitz, M.R., Harrison, W., Quitkin, F., and Rankin, J.G. (1985). Treatment outcome validation of DSM-III depressive subtypes: Clinical usefulness in outpatients with mild to moderate depression. *Archives of General Psychiatry, 42,* 1148-1152.

Stiles, W.B. (1983). Normality diversity and psychotherapy. *Psychotherapy: Theory, Research and Practice, 20,* 183-189.

Stoller, R.J., and Geertsma, H. (1963). The consistency of psychiatrists' clinical judgments. *Journal of Nervous and Mental Diseases, 151,* 58-66.

Stuart, R.B. (1970). *Trick or Treatment.* Champagne, IL: Research Press.

Taft, R. (1955). The ability to judge people. *Psychological Bulletin, 52,* 1-23.

Tamminga, C.A., and Carpenter, W.T., Jr. (1982). The DSM-III diagnosis of schizophrenic like illness and the clinical pharmacology of psychosis. *The Journal of Nervous and Mental Disease, 170,* 744-751.

Tarter, R.E., Templer, D.I., and Hardy, C. (1975). The psychiatric diagnosis. *Diseases of the Nervous System, 36,* 30-31.

Thorne, F.C. (1972). Clinical judgment. In R.H. Woody and J.D. Woody (Eds.), *Clinical Assessment in Counseling and Psychotherapy.* Englewood Cliffs, NJ: Prentice-Hall.

Tuma, A.H., May, F., P.R.A., Yale, C., and Forsythe, A.B. (1978). Therapist experience general clinical ability and treatment outcome in schizophrenia. *Journal of Consulting and Clinical Psychology, 46,* 1120-1126.

Ullman, L., and Bergman, V. (1959). Judgments of outcome of homecare placement from psychological material. *Journal of Clinical Psychology, 15,* 28-31.

Wade, T.C., and Baker, T.B. (1977). Opinions and use of psychological tests: A survey of clinical psychologists. *American Psychologist, 32,* 874-882.

Walker, R.C., and Lyndon, J. (1967). Varying degrees of psychological sophistication in the interpretation of sentence completion data. *Journal of Clinical Psychology, 23,* 229-231.

Walters, G.D., White, T.W., and Greene, R.L. (1988). Use of the MMPI to identify malingering and exaggeration of psychiatric symptomatology in male prison inmates. *Journal of Personality Assessment, 56,* 321-333.

Wanderer, Z.W. (1969). Validity of clinical judgments based on human figure drawings. *Journal of Consulting and Clinical Psychology, 33,* 143-150.

Warner, R. (1979). Race and sexual bias in psychiatric diagnosis. *The Journal of Nervous and Mental Disease, 167,* 303-310.

Wedding, D. (1983). Clinical and statistical prediction in neuropsychology. *Clinical Neuropsychology, 5,* 49-55.

Wedding, D. and Faust, D. (1989). Clinical judgment and decision making in neuropsychology. *Archives of Clinical Neuropsychology, 4,* 233-265.

Wiggins, J.S. (1973). *Personality and prediction: Principles of personality assessment.* Reading, MA: Addison-Wesley.

Wittmann, J.J. (1985). Child advocacy and the scientific model and family court: A theory for pretrial self-assessment. *The Journal of Psychiatry and Law,* 61-82.

Woody, R. (1972). In R.H. Woody and J.D. Woody (Eds.). *Clinical Assessment in Counseling and Psychotherapy.* Englewood Cliffs, NJ: Prentice-Hall, Inc.

Xenakis, S.N., Hoyt, M.F., Marmar, C.R., and Horowitz, M.J. (1983). Reliability of self-reports by therapists using the therapists action scale. *Psychotherapy: Theory, Research and Practice, 20,* 314-319.

CHAPTER 9

Challenging Credentials & Qualifications

PART I

CHALLENGING EDUCATION & TRAINING OF PSYCHOLOGISTS & PSYCHIATRISTS

Among the most important supports for the credibility of the expert are his credentials including education and training, licensing, Board Certification, memberships, positions held, awards, and publications. At one seminar, the speaker advised the experts to "go heavy on credentials, light on facts." For this reason it is useful to have some information with which to let some, if not all, of the air out of these balloons. We will deal first with education and training. We note that many clinicians received their education and training 30 or more years ago, and therefore literature of that vintage applies to them, if not to more recent graduates.

The chapters on education and training, scientific status, clinical method, clinical judgment, and reliability and validity of evaluations are in reality interdependent. That is, the effectiveness and sufficiency of education and training in psychiatry and psychology is, to a large degree, dependent upon the state of knowledge that exists in each of the disciplines, the effectiveness of the methods that are being taught, and so on. Rotter (1973) observes that the uncertainty of training programs as to what they should be teaching is related to the state of knowledge in the field or to current emphasis and practice.

The subject matter of psychology is approximately as broad in scope as the entire spectrum of human behavior, attitudes, propensities, capacities, feelings, habits, norms, and deviations. Thus, for example, an introductory survey course in psychology will usually include such titles as motivation, emotion, learning, memory, sensation, perception, vision, audition, abnormal psychology, personality, physiological psychology, and social psychology. In terms of what psychologists actually do, the area is broken down into four major classifications—clinical, counseling, industrial and experimental or theoretical psychology.

The clinical psychologist is the one with whom the attorney is most likely to have contact, for his specialty is mainly concerned with the diagnosis or assessment and treatment or modification of problems of personal, inter-personal, or social adjustment. He is frequently employed in or associated with a hospital, clinic, or counseling agency, as well as being engaged in private practice. He may also be on a university faculty. Some clinical psychologists also engage in research.

The counseling or consulting psychologist is somewhat similar to the clinical psychologist. He also engages in the evaluation and modification of personal or interpersonal problems. If a valid distinction can be drawn, it would be that the counseling psychologist may more often be concerned with problems having to do with educational, vocational, marital, or social concerns, whereas the clinical psychologist may more often be concerned with problems analogous to the problems of "psychopathology" or "intra-psychic" conflicts with which the psychiatrist presumably deals. However, it is not highly uncommon to find the individual with his Ph.D. in counseling psychology, working in a hospital or clinic or engaging in the private practice of psychotherapy the same as the clinical psychologist. His work may also overlap with that of the industrial psychologist in the area of personnel psychology. However, if a case involves a clinical issue, one can question why a counseling psychologist rather than a clinical psychologist was retained. In many programs, there are differences in training that can be brought out.

The field of industrial psychology includes such areas as personnel selection, time and motion study, human factors, sensitivity training, executive development, and consumer research. Psychologists are thus often found employed either in industry, government, the military, or by one of several consulting industrial psychology firms. They are most likely to be involved with the law in areas of human factors or consumer research.

Experimental or theoretical psychologists are usually engaged in teaching and/or research. They are generally employed by a college or university, although some find employment with private research firms, with government agencies, or in research departments of various large industries such as the telephone company. Their work tends to be oriented toward the "pure" research aims of expanding the boundaries of psychological knowledge, although at times their work will be oriented toward applications of such knowledge. Their area of research interest may range over the entire spectrum of psychology. Thus, while they may deal with the same subject matter as the clinical psychologist, their task is often the development and testing of hypotheses, more or less in the abstract, whereas the clinician is engaged in diagnosis and treatment. We should note that some neuropsychologists who perform clinical assessment of brain damage (see Chapter 15) hold experimental and not clinical degrees. Although many of them have received training and supervision in clinical work, for some the amount is minimal and few will have received clinical training comparable to that of clinical psychologists. Further, many of these experimental psychologists will have received narrowly based training and may have had minimal supervised clinical education in a range of pertinent psychiatric "disorders," e.g., depression.

Psychiatry, by definition a branch of medicine, by and large, in its function and its subject matter, overlaps with the field of clinical psychology—that is, the psychiatrist is engaged primarily in the diagnosis and treatment of so-called "mental illness" or "emotional illness." At the present time there is essentially no meaningful distinction or differentiation between the meaning of terms such as "mental" or "emotional" "illness" and terms such as personal or interpersonal or social maladjustment. Both the psychologist and the psychiatrist may use any one of a variety of psychotherapy techniques. The main difference between the two is that the psychiatrist is permitted to prescribe drugs and shock treatment in his work while the psychologist is not (a movement for prescription privileges for psychologists is currently under way). On the other hand, the psychologist differs particularly in the assessment area in that he may employ psychological tests which ordinarily would not be used by the psychiatrist, as the latter lacks training in their use, although he is not prohibited by law from using tests. Even these distinctions may become blurred because the psychologist can indirectly make use of drugs in his treatment by soliciting the cooperation of the "patient's" physician and the psychiatrist may have the benefit of psychological testing by employing a psychologist for that purpose. Generally, the same treatment techniques may be employed by both psychiatrists and psychologists. Many psychologists use the term "clients" rather than "patients" as a means of avoiding a medical connotation to the problems with which they work.

There is an unresolved dispute as to whether the evaluation and treatment of "disturbed" people properly falls within the province of psychiatry or psychology, because each of the two professions works with essentially the same kind of problems. The dispute boils down to the question as to whose training and education is the most relevant and appropriate. Psychologists may claim that because their training and education encompasses a great deal more of the subject matter of psychology, they are at least as qualified, and perhaps more so, than psychiatrists in their area. The psychiatrists, on the other hand, may assert that they have greater clinical experience and, in any event, that only medical doctors should treat mental "illness." The argument that the psychiatrist has more clinical experience often can be questioned—in many cases the clinical psychologist has equal experience. The second part of the argument concerning the treatment of illness is of dubious force in view of the fact that the whole concept of "mental illness" is in dispute. Kingsbury (1987) brings an unusual perspective to questions concerning differences between psychiatrists and clinical psychologists, many of which relate to education and training issues. Kingsbury has been through an American Psychological Association approved clinical psychology program and internship and has taught in another such program and has also been through an American Medical Association approved medical school and, at the time of this article, was in an American Psychiatric Association approved psychiatric residency. His article is neither a research study nor a review of literature, but represents his attempt to bring an insider's perspective to a discussion of differences in viewpoint. It is not feasible to do justice to his article here, including his cautionary statements and the care he takes to favor neither profession over the other. We would therefore recommend to the reader who wishes to fully and accurately experience the viewpoint he brings to read the article. Bearing in mind then that the article contains numerous caveats, we would summarize his descriptions as indicating, not surprisingly, that clinical psychologists receive more training and more emphasis on science as a method of inquiry rather than a set of facts, with a concomitant tendency to avoid jumping to conclusions and to read literature with a sharp eye to attending to the references involved. In contrast, in medical school, science was presented as a set of facts, a body of knowledge, and procedures shared by those educated in the science without the emphasis on checking the sources of conclusions and data. He states, "The ramifications of viewing science as an approach versus as a body of fact appear to be several. First, many psychiatrists may act more certain of their information than they should be, whereas psychologists are more tentative about their information than they need to be...." (p. 153) He notes different perspectives of the two professions as to the importance of differential diagnosis. He notes differences in the kind of experience provided in the psychologist's internship in contrast to the much more extensive experience of the psychiatric residency. He states in conclusion, "At no time have I meant to imply that one type of training is better preparation than the other for assuming patient care." (p. 156)

EDUCATION & TRAINING OF PSYCHOLOGISTS

To earn a bachelor's degree in psychology an individual would take somewhere between 30-36 semester units of undergraduate psychology courses. The educational qualifications of a person with only a bachelor's degree are subject to attack on the grounds that all of these courses are at the undergraduate level and are generally considered to be something of beginning courses. There is usually no practicum or training in psychological assessment. Thus, although the individual has touched upon most of the areas in psychology, cross-examination could point out that such an individual has not taken the trouble to educate himself in their field in depth as would be the case with the master's or doctoral person. The situation may be roughly compared to that of an individual who starts out to practice medicine having completed nothing more than his premedical training. Even long experience working in the field may be relatively meaningless, lacking a sufficient base of formal knowledge.

Graduate study may lead to one of four degrees: master of arts, master of science, Doctor of Philosophy in Psychology (Ph.D.) or Doctor of Psychology (Psy.D.). A master's degree ordinarily requires completion of 30 semester units at the graduate level, approximately one-half of the total required for a doctoral degree. The exact course requirements will vary from institution to institution. It may be a good risk to inquire on cross-examination as to the exact courses taken by the individual as, at least in some cases, it will turn out that he has had no formal graduate course work in the area in which he claims to have expertise. The reader should also be aware that these degrees are constantly undergoing refinement and expansion. Thus, an individual whose degree is 20 years old probably obtained his degree under requirements considerably different than an individual who received his degree within a relatively recent period. It may be of some value in attacking the weight of the individual's testimony to have available the current catalogue from the institution which granted his degree to show that, in fact, under the current requirements for such a degree, his education would not qualify. In general, the work required to obtain a master's degree does not fully qualify the individual as a specialist in any specific area of psychology.

Some people with bachelor's or master's degrees will be certified or licensed by virtue of grandfather clauses. It can be shown, then, that they did not receive their license by meeting present educational requirements or by passing an examination, as the license implies.

The Doctor of Philosophy degree is often considered the mark of the fully trained person in psychology, although there is increasing emphasis on postdoctoral training for psychologists who wish to concentrate in certain specialty areas (e.g., neuropsychology or forensic psychology). However, formal standards for post-doctoral programs had not been adopted prior to 1993 (see *APA Monitor*, January, 1993). The Ph.D. degree usually requires the completion of 60 semester units of graduate level course work. These programs often include advanced courses in general psychology, statistics and psychological research, research design, physiological psychology, sensation and perception, learning and memory, motivation and emotion, several courses in psychological assessment, several courses in theories of personality or behavior, psychotherapy, and a course in neuropsychiatric information for psychologists. The courses taken will vary to some degree in relation to the area of specialization of the doctoral candidate, whether his specialty is clinical, industrial, experimental, or whatever. Courses may also vary somewhat from institution to institution. In a survey (112 of 180 clinical psychology training programs responding) Steinpreis et al. (1992) found considerable variation of course area requirements. They found that only 38% required a course in individual differences, *6% in motivation*, and 59% in cognition. Paradoxically, they found that 85% required a course in personality assessment but only 58% required a course in personality. The American Psychological Association provides accreditation to clinical and counseling programs that meet their standards. It is useful to determine if the Ph.D. is from an APA accredited institution, as "diploma mills" do exist and may indeed be expanding (see below). The APA publishes a list of accredited doctoral programs as well as accredited internship programs annually in the *American Psychologist.*

In general, the Ph.D. programs train the individual to be questioning and skeptical in his field. Course content usually attempts to cover a wide variety of recognized theories and to implement this with constant reference to the research literature. As with the master's degree, the requirements for the doctoral degree have changed considerably over the years. It is pertinent to inquire as to the requirements met where the individual's doctorate is of advanced age. For example, an individual receiving his doctorate in the 1940's, and perhaps in the 1950's, is likely to have had considerable emphasis in his course work on psychoanalytic psychology, whereas those with a doctorate in the 1960's and later are likely to have much greater breadth of educational exposure.

In the field of clinical psychology, the individual is required to complete at least one full year of internship as a prerequisite to obtaining his degree. This internship ordinarily will involve experience with both children and adults and severely disturbed and less disturbed individuals. Generally, the internship will have its greatest emphasis in the individual's area of special interest. The formal education of the Ph.D. psychologist *in psychology* is typically far superior to that of the psychiatrist. However, the psychologist's internship is usually considerably shorter than that of the residency. Given the lack of relationship between experience and judgment accuracy, it would be hard to say, however, that this greater length of experiential training is of any particular benefit as regards diagnostic or predictive skills. Some psychologists compensate for this by taking post-doctoral training. Also, because psychology has traditionally been more associated with assessment, the psychology intern may spend a larger portion of his shorter training doing assessment which is usually the function most relevant in forensic matters.

The Psy.D. is a relative newcomer. It was originally believed to have more of an applied or practice approach compared to the Ph.D., which has been primarily an academic degree, and in clinical psychology the concept of the scientist-practitioner has been prevalent. This difference still seems to be the case, but the difference has shrunk as Psy.D. programs have increased research emphasis and many clinical Ph.D. programs have increased practice emphasis. However, as noted above, there is considerable variation in both degree programs and one would need to look at the specific requirements of any particular program.

With regard to education and training of psychologists, the following references are pertinent. Garfield and Kurtz (1973) state: "Over the years the importance of studies on diagnostic testing as a function of the clinical psychologist has appeared to decrease with resulting modifications in university training programs." Garfield and Kurtz also cite evidence to the effect that the majority of approved internship centers believe that university training is inadequate and instills an overly critical attitude.

Hedberg et al. (1973) discuss the inefficiency of traditional Ph.D. training programs, with their emphasis on research skills, in the development of clinical skills and suggest a Doctor of Psychology (Psy.D.) degree program (a number of which have emerged) as the solution.

In this regard, we would note that although the curriculum in a psychology doctoral program is less subject to the criticisms of irrelevant subject matter than is psychiatry, the clinical psychologist does spend a good deal of time studying statistics and experimental methods, and doing research. This is not necessarily wasted, as it should help him to evaluate research reports and assess the state of knowledge—what is known and what is not known in the field. Unfortunately, as references in this and other chapters show, all too often the clinician puts this scientific aspect of his training aside and functions in ignorance or disregard of the research literature.

Thorne (1972) states that evidence has accumulated indicating that curriculum as of that time appears invalid and obsolete at the moment it is taught.

Neuropsychologists seem to be appearing in the courts with sharply increasing frequency, particularly in cases involving personal injury in which the presence or impact of brain damage is in issue. Currently, there are no formal restrictions on who can call himself a neuropsychologist, and some clinicians use this label themselves when, according to various authors, they have not received the education or training necessary to acquire professional competence. Qualifications for neuropsychologists will be dealt with in Chapter 15.

Blakey et al. (1985) note that background education and training may not even ensure competence in as fundamental a task as intelligence testing. They state, "no procedure to verify WAIS-R administration competency was found in any of the APA-approved training sites except for global subjective evaluations submitted by supervisors to the director of training on the trainee's overall assessment skills." Speaking more broadly, they note that a three-year study by an APA task force indicated a lack of evidence documenting relationships between existing educational and training requirements and professional competence, as well as the need to develop competency based training and evaluation systems "which ensure in a verifiable manner minimal competency for practice."

Mittelstaedt and Tasca (1988) discuss contradictions in the training of clinical psychologists due to reliance on a general scientist-practitioner model. They state, "Students are taught the virtues of rigorous experimental research and they are also trained as highly skilled practitioners. However, the research and clinical objectives idealized by the Boulder model are often experienced as working against each other; that is, on the one hand, the research focus of training tends to sensitize trainees to the limitations of the accumulated body of knowledge pertaining to human behavior, but at the same time, the clinical focus of training requires confidence in this knowledge for effective service delivery." (p. 353) They go on to note that while such contradictions can be seen as detrimental, an alternative perspective holds that they may provide an impetus for the development of the discipline.

Schippmann et al. (1988) state, "The issues surrounding the education and training of psychologists are the focus of much controversy." (p. 141) They note that there has been controversy concerning the linkage between education and training and professional competence, noting problems in education and training due to a great diversity of settings in which psychologists are trained. They state that "the second component in the linkage, professional competence, is perhaps an even larger source of controversy, as is clearly reflected in licensing and certification activities." (p. 141) They further state, "Thus, it may no longer be feasible to consider the competence of a psychologist in the generic sense; rather, specific competence for a subdiscipline might also be assessed." (p. 141) O'Donohue et al. (1989) also note that there is considerable variation in the specifics of curricula in doctoral training programs in clinical psychology, although there are some general trends that can be perceived.

Newman et al. (1988) note that there are few specific and direct evaluation procedures for assessing effectiveness and quality of supervision in connection with trainee performance and skill acquisition or in the trainee's own evaluation. They note from a survey that accredited clinical doctoral programs indicated that personal impressions and informal and qualitative evaluation measures were used most frequently. They state:

> However, investigations that have specifically measured the effects of training have reached disappointing conclusions. First, there has been little evidence that the amount of training or experience affects treatment effectiveness....Second, evidence that training changes therapists' behavior either in vivo or in response to analogue situations has been mixed....Even the most comprehensive study...which examined over three years of training, found that the only statistically significant effects revealed the trainees asked fewer questions over time and provided more encouraging utterances. (p. 660)

Tori (1989) notes that it is estimated that more than 50% of all doctoral students pursuing clinical degrees now enroll in professional schools. He notes that this has troubled many in the profession, some of whom argue that free-standing professional schools are "not an appropriate setting for the education of psychologists," citing a number of concerns including inadequate faculty leadership and poor quality control practices. He states, "The most recent National Conference on Graduate Education in Psychology concluded that 'there is good reason to presume that doctoral programs achieve their highest potential as academic units affiliated with universities. University settings are more likely than free-standing schools to provide high quality education in psychology' (American Psychological Association [APA], 1987, p. 1074)." (p. 203) Tori notes, however, that empirical findings were not offered in support of these opinions, but that nevertheless, free-standing training programs must undertake and make public responsible quality control research. Tori then provides reliability and validity data obtained from some objective measures used at the nation's largest autonomous professional school. (Author's note: Tori is on the faculty of the California School of Professional Psychology, Berkeley-Alameda, a free-standing professional school.) Tori notes some severe limitations of his research and states, "These are very broad evaluative questions that must await the development of valid and ubiquitous outcome measures. It is hoped that the present instruments are a contribution to this end," (p. 207) thus indicating that his study does not establish the equivalence of programs of free-standing professional schools with those at more traditional universities. This is of importance in the growing number of cases in which expert testimony is provided by graduates of free-standing professional schools.

Bootzin and Ruggill (1988), discussing training issues in behavior therapy, note the necessity for evaluating the appropriateness and effectiveness of the conceptualization or formulation of individual cases, but that the little research that exists indicates there is a lack of consensus on such formulation. They note that one of the difficulties is that human judgment research shows that decision-making processes are vulnerable to numerous biases, and that therapists' case conceptualizations may be affected more strongly by prior expectations and heuristics than by the client's information. They state:

> There has been much public hand wringing about the paucity of research related to the empirical evaluation of training methods used in behavioral clinical training....This lack of data on training is by no means unique to behavioral training programs. The American Psychological Association (1982) Task Force on the Evaluation of Education, Training, and Service in Psychology stated that, 'There is no evidence that any specific educational or training program or experience is related to professional competence' (p. 2). Incentives to evaluate clinical training methods are virtually non-existent...and few contingencies encourage their systematic review.

They do go on to suggest that published research may underestimate the extent of the evaluation activity that does take place. Unfortunately, research that is not published does little good beyond the researchers and the limited circle with whom they may communicate.

Slate and Jones (1989) note that there are significant problems in scoring ambiguous verbal responses to items on the Wechsler Intelligence Scale for Children-Revised; that is, clerical and mathematical errors are not unusual, even when the scoring is done by professional psychologists. They note that a major cause of scoring errors is poor instruction in intelligence testing courses, and, as a result, a critical lack of assessment skills has been found among both graduate students and interns in clinical psychology. These statements underscore our admonition to lawyers that in all cases where there are psychological tests that can be scored, it is imperative to obtain the raw test data and, among other things, to have that data checked for errors of scoring and administration. Any errors impact on the credibility of the psychologist and substantial numbers of errors may vitiate the test altogether.

Tipton (1983) surveyed clinical and counseling psychologists. Counseling psychologists rated themselves as more involved with less "pathological" groups than did clinical psychologists. Clinical psychologists indicated that they worked less with normal or slightly disturbed groups and more with individuals with significant problems. This survey thus suggests the possibility that counseling psychologists will have had limited or minimal exposure to "pathological" groups, and clinical psychologists minimal exposure to normal groups. Exposure to skewed samples is one factor that seems to foster the development of illusory correlations (see Chapter 5).

A number of authors note deficiencies in training for work with minority groups. Ridley (1985) states, "graduate programs in psychology have failed to prepare trainees for effective practice with clientele from culturally diverse populations." (p. 611) He further indicates, "the time has arrived when a focus on ethnic and cross-cultural issues is not only desirable, but mandatory." (p. 611) Speaking more specifically, Everett et al. (1983) observe that psychologists typically do not receive sufficient preparation for effective work with Indian patients. They note that psychologists often lack sufficient awareness of cultural values and behavioral patterns within this subgroup. They indicate that this lack of awareness, "typically results in conflicts and frustrations for both the psychologist and his or her Indian clientele; ultimately American-Indian children and families may not receive appropriate mental health services." (p. 588)

Bernal and Padilla (1982) surveyed accredited clinical psychology programs and found that 31 of 76 programs responding offered minority related courses. They note that program directors acknowledge the variability of opinion among their faculty on the importance of minority training. Jones and Block (1984) describe a series of potentially pertinent differences in behavioral patterns and manners of adaptation across black and white patients. They indicate that training programs in psychology have done a poor job in providing students with the knowledge necessary to understand these different characteristics among black patients.

Norcross and Stevenson (1984), discussing a related topic, indicate that guidelines for evaluating students appear to be primarily subjective and highly variable across training sites. Again, lacking more rigorous assessment or evaluation procedures for monitoring student progress, one must wonder how proper guidance or correction could be provided. In their study, Norcross and Stevenson surveyed the directors of clinical psychology doctoral programs in order to determine the methods used to evaluate students. Norcross and Stevenson report that clinical training programs are "pursuing radically different methods and strategies of training and evaluation and, furthermore, that many clinical programs are relying primarily on informal, qualitative measures." (p. 504) Norcross and Stevenson argue that lack of appropriate training evaluation technology and evaluation standards are significant problems, and that a "pervasive problem is lack of clarity about training objectives." (p. 507)

Much in the way some experts attempt to "prove" the value of their experience by citing their "success" as therapists, the same argument may be presented in order to support the value of education and training. In other cases, an expert may attempt to denigrate the credibility of a competing expert's opinion by arguing that this expert was trained in some type of psychotherapy orientation inferior to the type in which he was trained. As regards the claim that treatment effectiveness establishes the value of education, we would once more reiterate that there is now a considerable body of literature, as reviewed recently by Berman and Norton (1985), which strongly suggests that lay therapists achieve treatment outcomes comparable or equal to professional therapists (see Chapter 8 for further discussion in this regard). As regards arguments that one psychotherapy approach is better than another, Stiles (1983) notes:

> For the major approaches, such as psychoanalytic therapy, client centered therapy, behavioral therapy and rational-emotive therapy, there is now strong objective evidence that therapists behave systematically differently depending on their theoretical orientation....That is, there really are different ingredients in the different psychotherapies. Furthermore, these differences are so large and so systematically related to theory that it seems unreasonable to attribute any common success to overlap in therapists' techniques....The combination of technical diversity and *no differential overall effectiveness* has evoked dismay and attempts to challenge or deny one or the other of these findings.

More recent reviews on the effectiveness of different therapy approaches produce virtually the same conclusions as those noted by Stiles in 1983 (e.g., Kazdin, 1986). It is not hard to see where the resistance described by Stiles might arise. If approaches to therapy differ substantially but research shows that outcome is similar across the approaches, it may matter little what one does or what approach is used. Aside from indicating that claims regarding the superiority of one method over another are unwarranted, these findings also suggest that the content of professional training is irrelevant to conducting successful (or unsuccessful) therapy. Whatever technique you happen to use, you end up with about the same result.

London and Klerman (1982) also discuss some of the difficulties of evaluating the effectiveness of different psychotherapy approaches. They note that one such problem in evaluation is that examiners do not feel qualified to treat their views of a particular technique or school as relevant to their judgments regarding the expertise of the professional adhering to that technique. They further state, "the granting of degrees, licenses and diplomas is an entry barrier to independent professional practice, not an evaluation of the efficacy or safety of its practices." (See also Chapter 22, for references indicating that relatively untrained therapists are as effective as those professionally trained.)

Sechrest (1985), in his Presidential Address to the Clinical Division of the American Psychological Association, described clinical training as chaotic and as neither standardized nor rationally constructed. He observed that there is no list specifying competencies or methods for acquiring or teaching these competencies, and that if clinical practice is an art, we do not know how to train for art.

Some of the work on licensing is relevant in the context of the education and training of psychologists. Howard (1983) points out that the paper-and-pencil test used for national licensing measures background knowledge rather than competence to practice psychology. Kane (1982) notes that there are essentially no studies on the predictive validity of licensing exams. He indicates that deriving proper criterion-based measures creates potentially insurmountable barriers for research on this topic. Stated differently, according to Kane, the field currently lacks objective standards against which competency can be evaluated. In another article, Kane (1983) states: "The development and validation of a criterion measure of professional performance presents fundamental conceptual problems as well as great practical difficulties. *The distinction between good practice and poor practice is not clear-cut in most cases.*" (italics added) (p. 20)

If Kane is correct, that is, if it is often difficult to distinguish good and bad practice, this would seem to create serious problems for education and training. If one does not really know what good practices are, how does one formulate training goals, decide on directions for education, or correct students when they go "astray"? For how would one even know that they have gone astray, if one cannot be sure what astray is—what the difference is between good and bad practices?

Fox et al. (1985) present a series of proposals for overhauling professional training, licensure, and certification for specialty practice. They note that their proposals are controversial and even revolutionary, but state that "it is only through such a comprehensive change that the profession will be able to achieve maturity as an independent discipline worthy of the support and sanction of society." (p. 1042) They criticize the current licensing exam, noting that it not only fails to measure actual clinical competence but that it could be passed by "a capable undergraduate psychology major...with a little extra study." (p. 1043) They state:

> The current system for inducting individuals into the profession of psychology, preparing them for the roles they will serve, licensing them in order to protect the consumers of their services, and encouraging the recognition of appropriate specialties within professional psychology is in great disarray. (p. 1042)

They further state:

> Persons currently functioning as licensed psychologists are from such diverse educational backgrounds and experience that it is all but impossible to define common elements in their preparation for practice. Individuals currently functioning as licensed psychologists have received training in almost two dozen

kinds of academic programs and carry eighteen distinguishable degrees. (p. 1042)

Fox et al. additionally warn:

> Another development of concern to both practitioners and academicians is the explosive expansion over the past decade in the number and size of professional schools designed to produce practitioners. The expansion has stirred angry debate within psychology about the proper training model for practitioners...the appropriate degree to be granted in recognition of such education (Ph.D. vs Psy.D.), and the best kind of institutional base for professional education (university versus freestanding), etc. (p. 1042)

One of Fox et al.'s various recommendations is that freestanding professional schools, proprietary professional schools, and professional schools "without walls" should be rejected as providing tenable training. This article by Fox et al., and this recommendation in particular, may be worthwhile to bring to the attention of judge and jury when a psychologist has been trained in one of these types of settings.

EDUCATION & TRAINING OF PSYCHIATRISTS

Some question may exist as to the utility of extensive inquiry into the psychiatrist's education and training. However, because of general publicity, and movie and television portrayals of the "wise and knowing" psychiatrist, the trier of fact may have accepted the illusion of knowledge and assume the psychiatrist has had education adequate to his task. It is likely that some jurors, and even judges, may tend to react with disbelief to the evidence that psychiatric evaluation is quite inaccurate and unreliable, and that there is very little solid knowledge in the field. Many people tend to respond to substantial evidence in this regard with an attitude that "with all of that education psychiatrists must know a great deal." Therefore, exposition of the deficiencies and controversies in psychiatric education is valuable in order to provide a base upon which such people can critically evaluate and more easily accept the high degree of psychiatric fallibility.

The psychiatrist holds an M.D. degree. One of the most obvious and serious defects of psychiatric formal education lies in the fact that a large proportion of time is devoted to the study of general medical subjects, much of which is irrelevant to the subject matter of much of the work he will perform. More serious is the lack of training in psychology, the basic science with which the psychiatrist works.

While not taking the position that medical training is irrelevant for psychiatry, a report of a conference conducted by the American Psychiatric Association (1962) states,

It was generally agreed that the process of professional growth involves a certain amount of "unlearning" of some of the aspects of traditional medical practice during the first year of residency. (p. 35)

The suggestion was made that present deficiencies in the residency program could to a large extent be offset by the development within the medical school of a widely based department of behavioral science with the same status as departments of biochemistry, pharmacology and anatomy. Such a department would represent all of the sciences which deal with behavior including the biological part of the spectrum as well as the psychological and social. (p. 64)

E. S. Mariner (1967), a psychiatrist, describes the nature of these defects extensively, pointing out the fallacies of many of the arguments advanced for medical training for psychiatrists, concluding that nearly all of his own premedical and medical education was irrelevant to the work that he does and possibly even antithetical to it, and concluding that the proper course of study would be psychology. Mariner states:

From a theoretical point of view, to an observer unhampered by institutional concerns, it would seem apparent that a knowledge of human behavior, thought and emotion, would be the logical and necessary foundation on which a professional practice dealing with disturbance of behavior, thought and emotion would have to rest. Thus psychology—or more generally "behavioral science"—would seem unquestionably to be the basic academic discipline of choice (That this should be considered a heretical statement when made by a psychiatrist is evidence of the almost incredible irrationality of the medical profession in this area; a psychological background for dealing with psychological problems would seem as obvious a choice as a biological background for dealing with biological problems). (p. 278)

Given that much prestige is attached to the physician in our society, and because in most of the fields of medicine one is not accustomed to questioning the education and training of the physician, it is important to cross-examine the psychiatrist in regard to these deficiencies. The attempt can be made to draw from the psychiatrist the admission that much of his medical education does not deal with problems of human behavior, thought, emotion or social adaptation. Similarly he can be asked if he has taken the traditional courses in such subjects as learning, perception, memory and so on. Attendance at brief seminars and lectures on these topics cannot substitute for the formal academic courses such as those taken for the Ph.D. in Psychology, which are not only more extensive but require preparation for examinations, etc. If he has not taken such courses, as is probably the case, he can be asked if these processes are not relevant to understanding human behavior, thought, and emotion. It should thus be possible to obtain, at least, an admission that there is controversy regarding the relevance of medical education for psychiatrists, as well as criticism of psychiatric training for its failure to provide sufficient education in basic psychology.

Additional relevant quotations on these points may be found in a report of a conference organized and conducted by the American Psychiatric Association with the co-sponsorship of the Canadian Psychiatric Association (1962). While this report obviously does not take the position that medical training is irrelevant for psychiatry, nevertheless, this authoritative body does illuminate some of the points mentioned above.

Reference is made to the findings of surveys of state hospitals with approved residency training programs concerning subjects taught in the area of behavioral science:

> In the 37 state hospitals replying, psychology headed the list of subjects taught with 26 hospitals providing an average of more than 10 hours each. Sociology came next with 17 hospitals providing an average of 8 hours, followed by anthropology with 11 hospitals with an average of 5 hours. (p. 88)

(Authors' Note: At the time of the survey, only three-fourths of the hospitals provided training in psychology, and then only a minimal amount.)

> Most of the superintendents spoke optimistically and with considerable enthusiasm of the value of teaching these subjects. Some plan to increase the amount of time to them. (p. 89)

> Participants discussed at some length their personal reactions to collaborative contacts with scientists from the behavioral disciplines and to the introduction of behavioral subject matter in the residency program. Many admitted having a certain resistance to incorporating a new discipline. There is fear of "identity-diffusion" and some antagonism against the newcomers, against new approaches in a domain that formerly belonged exclusively to the physician and psychiatrist. Such reactions were considered sufficiently typical to serve as clues to the problem of developing and integrating a curriculum dealing with the behavioral sciences. (p. 90)

Chessick (1971), referring to the problem of professional identity formation as an identity crisis of the beginning psychiatric resident, states:

> This problem is familiar to all psychiatrists. Not only is there a need for a beginning resident to move away from the medical model but he must mourn his systemized and controlling medical styles painstakingly developed over recent years, must suffer tension and depression, and must struggle to comprehend the unknown inside himself as well as what is around him and his patients.

Chessick points out the irrelevance for the psychiatrist of much of what he learned in medical school and also the fact that, because of the limited time period, the resident rarely has the opportunity for long-term treatment in his training program. Chessick points out that because he rarely sees cases through completely, the resident is in the embarrassing position of having to take the convictions of the supervisor on faith. Chessick points out that these problems create several dangers.

According to him, these are the development of a psychiatrist who is mediocre or worse, or one who reaches premature closure in his point of view and becomes rigid, or develops an uncritical eclecticism. Chessick states: "Thus, the shift toward eclecticism and the disappointment in psychodynamics and psychotherapy are *symptoms that the training program is defective.*" (p. 275)

Chessick also points out the conflicting views as to the function of the supervisor with the resident, one view being that the supervisor should focus on the resident and his problems, essentially a "psychotherapy for the resident" approach, and the other view being that supervision should be purely educational and dictated by the needs and problems of the patient. In this view the supervisor is a teacher, not a psychotherapist. There are, of course, gradations of viewpoint between these extremes. Chessick also points out that frequently without actually understanding the case at hand the residents go along with the supervisor's suggestions in order to save face, thus getting through but learning nothing. Chessick also points out that residents constantly complain about supervisors who have overloaded schedules, lack time for the resident, or are poorly prepared.

Brody (1971) states:

> Within medical schools, in spite of extensive curricular changes, the student of psychiatry is still at a disadvantage. On the one hand he does not acquire the knowledge base of the behavioral, social or neurobiological scientist. On the other, he does not learn enough of the community relevant knowledge available to the student of psychiatric social work or clinical psychology....In contrast to residents in medicine, surgery and pediatrics, who begin with a solid core of relevant, basic, scientific knowledge as well as supervised clinical work, the psychiatric house officer must start again almost as if he were beginning a totally new career. This wasteful and discouraging circumstance can be altered only by educational changes beginning in the undergraduate medical curriculum that can then become integrated with the residency years. (p. 55)

Taylor and Torrey (1972) state:

> A second educational deficiency stemming from the board's strict time-place training requirements is the general over-training of psychiatrists. By supporting the necessity for a complete medical education plus an additional five years of training and experience, board members have played their part in guaranteeing that psychiatrists are trained for a fantasy profession.

> Looking over the educational background of a psychiatrist, a Martian newly arrived on this planet might reasonably predict that this professional's practice would consist of performing tonsillectomies, delivering babies and treating heart failure and epilepsy while engaging in psychotherapy on the side and organizing the community in the evenings. (p. 659)

Greenblatt et al. (1977) found that of 200 candidates taking the 1972 Board Certification examination for the first time, nearly one-third did not pass the written portion of this test which claims only to assess "minimal competency." That is, after four years of medical school and completion of their residency, 32% did not display minimal competence. Surely this raises doubt about the effectiveness of their education and training.

Borus and Yager (1986) discuss concerns about quality control in psychiatric training. They note that these concerns have been heightened due both to lack of standardized assessment within residencies to ensure that graduates reach a level of competence appropriate for the independent practice, and the high failure rate on the American Board of Psychiatry and Neurology (ABPN) examination. They note that about 25% of American and foreign graduates never even apply to take the examinations of the ABPN for certification and of those who do take them, approximately 36% of United States graduates and 58% of foreign medical graduates do not pass the entire certification process on their first attempt. They state, "Board examiners are frequently shocked at and mystified by the lack of clinical skills and basic diagnostic, formulative, and therapeutic knowledge displayed by candidates during the part II (oral) examinations." (p. 1415) They wonder how these young psychiatrists get so far and why these deficiencies are not caught earlier by their teachers, and if caught, why they are not remedied, and if they cannot be remedied, why the candidates are allowed to complete training and then practice independently on unknowing patients.

The 1992-1993 Annual Report of the American Board of Psychiatry and Neurology, Inc. shows that 44% of 2,982 psychiatrists taking the written examination in March, 1992 failed. The Report also shows that on the part II examination in 1992, 36% taking it for the first time failed *(American Journal of Psychiatry,* 1993, p. 1289).

Leibenluft et al. (1989) note that inpatient units are predominantly utilizing junior faculty members as their directors, the consequence being that it is an entry level position afforded low status and poor pay. Frequently it is a burn-out job with overwhelming clinical, administrative and teaching responsibilities, and junior faculty members soon attempt to move on to another position or may abandon the idea of an academic career altogether. They point out that because of this, inpatient directors are frequently inexperienced and have short tenures, the result being considerable adverse effects on training and clinical care. They state, "Resident and medical education is compromised by the inpatient director's inexperience and multiple commitments." (p. 73) All of this despite the critical role the inpatient unit plays in academic departments of psychiatry.

Strupp et al. (1988) state, "Psychotherapy practice in our time is a potpourri and the same may be said about training....Although state licensing laws have provided a first step toward regulating the practice of clinical psychology (including psychotherapy), more must be done to upgrade the quality of training." (p. 689) McDermott et al. (1974) note that clinical competence is an elusive entity and that studies have begun in an attempt to define basic clinical competence. They assert that if competence can be defined and broken down into various components, it may then be more easily assessed, and this also will promote better feedback to training programs throughout the country. In other words, at some time in the future when they have discovered the components of clinical competence, they will then for the first time be in a position to teach them.

Morgenstern (1970) also points out that competence has not been adequately defined, nor have the body of knowledge and skills been adequately defined, for board certification candidates. He cites research showing that performance in formal education as measured by grade point averages bears no relationship at all to the factors having to do with performance as a physician.

Karasu et al. (1979) note the lack of a universally accepted definition of thought disorder and little consensus on how to measure or describe thought disorder. They indicate that such developments would help in resident training.

Shagass (1977) notes that after going through medical school, psychiatrists afterward often wonder whether their medical training was necessary. Shagass, however, strongly favors the medical model.

Aside from these disputes about the relevance of medical training, a study by Lindy et al. (1980) suggests that this training may even exert negative effects on therapeutic skills. Lindy et al. compared the performance of two groups of psychiatric residents after two years of training, one group that had received a year of medical internship training and another group that had not. Ratings of psychotherapy skills across the two groups showed several differences in favor of the non-internship group. The authors mention possible limitations of their study but note that their results suggest "the disquieting possibility that the internship might even have a negative impact on subsequent education." (p. 79) Lindy et al. also mention the considerable controversy within the profession as regards the relevance of medical training, and the mere fact that their study raises the possibility that this training diminishes the benefits accrued from subsequent education is noteworthy.

Zonana et al. (1990) provide a fairly current description of typical four-year medical school programs. In the first two years, students take courses in basic medical sciences such as anatomy, biochemistry, physiology, cell biology, human genetics, microbiology, pathology, and pharmacology. They may also get introductory training in clinical medicine, such as history-taking, clinical examination, laboratory medicine and mechanisms of disease. This concludes their formal course work. In the next two years they receive instruction in clinical medicine which includes four to 12 week rotating clerkships in areas such as medicine, surgery, pediatrics, psychiatry, and obstetrics and gynecology. There is not a great deal in these four years which seems directly related to psychology or psycho-diagnostic evaluation. Most of their training in psychiatry comes during their residency, which is pretty much on-the-job training, although seminars of various kinds are included.

Much as is the case within psychology, it is argued that the psychiatrist's education and training provide insufficient preparation for work with individuals from different cultures or backgrounds. Wong (1978) notes lack of adequate training regarding psychiatric involvement with Asian-Americans. Bradshaw (1978) points out that psychiatrists are lacking in critical knowledge of black people. The tenor of Bradshaw's article indicates that the training and experience needed to offer proper services to black patients is rarely, if ever, provided during residency training. Bradshaw notes that given existing biases, there is "an inevitable tendency" to label prematurely or to mislabel as psychopathological some phenomena which may be normal in black patients. LaDue (1983a) states, "the standard methods of assessment and diagnosis have been devised by a group of practitioners who generally have not had exposure to and/or training in the multitude of cross-cultural views of pathology or health." LaDue notes that training programs are deficient in this regard and that major changes may be needed. Lee-Dukes (1983) discusses research consistent with Bradshaw's concerns about overpathologizing minority group members. This research demonstrates that more serious diagnoses, such as "schizophrenia," are assigned with greater relative frequency to blacks and minority group members than to members of the dominant culture. Lee-Dukes notes that findings demonstrating such problems have actually created little change in the profession, and that training programs do not adequately sensitize their students to racial biases in the diagnostic process that can produce misdiagnosis. We should note that the work of LaDue and Lee-Dukes was presented at the Annual Convention of the American Psychological Association, but that the subject matter of their presentations pertains to both psychiatrists and psychologists. Recent years have seen some improvement in this area, but for those receiving their training more than a few years ago, this remains as a deficiency in their formal training.

Another serious deficiency in the education and training of psychiatrists is the lack of a genuinely acceptable and reasonably validated theory or body of scientific knowledge upon which to base training. Thus, Woodmansey (1967) states: "There can be no more urgent or conspicuous problem in psychiatry as a scientific discipline than that it lacks a generally agreed theoretical framework on which to base practice and teaching." (p. 1035) Woodmansey goes on to state there are many theories but they are, in fact,

> ....a glut of conjectural systems of psychopathology but generally without much root in factual evidence. This state of affairs has led to an emphasis in psychiatric education and training on psychoanalytic theory and concepts, an emphasis which is based upon a premature and uncritical acceptance of that theory. (p. 1036)

For a considerable period of time, many psychiatry training programs placed primary, or even nearly exclusive, emphasis on psychoanalytic training. Many psychiatrists educated in the 1940's to 1970's will have been trained in such programs and, although there may be a general shift away from the emphasis on psychoanalytic training, a considerable percentage of relative "newcomers" to the field continue to receive such training. It appears that the teaching of psychoanalytic theory has been based more on personal preferences or biases rather than on any foundation of good scientific investigation, as illustrated in the following quotes from the above mentioned Report on Training. Although the material is now well over forty years old, it retains much of its relevance given the general lack of scientific advance in the area of psychoanalytic theory (see Chapter 3) and the continuing dependence of many psychiatrists on such theory.

> The place of psychoanalysis in the core curriculum was discussed in length by the conference. At the outset a distinction was made between psychoanalytic theory and psychoanalysis as a form of therapy practiced as a sub-specialty. "Psychoanalytic theory" a participant said "has significantly influenced American psychiatry for good and should continue to be taught in proper proportions to psychiatric residents along with other theories coming from the biological and social sciences. If a comprehensive theory is an essential of a science, then psychoanalysis is properly called a science, however difficult to validate its hypotheses." Exception was taken to this statement. Giving expression to the dissenting view, a participant said, "Psychoanalysis, while initially a liberating influence in freeing psychiatry from a purely phenomenological orientation has in turn had a stultifying effect on further continuation of psychiatric thinking. Its simulation of comprehensiveness has led to premature closure in some circles. Too many residents are satisfied with so-called explanations of behavior that are philosophic exercises rather than scientific theories subject to tests. This satisfaction deadens their curiosity to further critical study. It can be argued that major advances in psychiatric research and practice will have to be based on critical questioning and perhaps even rejection of psychoanalytic theory." These opposing views were not resolved. Indeed no attempt was made to do so. The conference held that psychoanalytic theory as one of psychiatry's basic frames of reference, should be taught in a residency program.

> Introduction of this subject, however, raises complex problems. The various hypotheses, theories and concepts of psychoanalysis do not remain as neutral elements. When they are presented to a resident as part of the basic knowledge

of psychiatry, they often engender reverberations which tend to make it difficult for the resident to see other basic aspects of psychiatry and thus, may lead him to substitute psychoanalysis for everything else in the field.

Van Buren O. Hammet (1965) has contributed an extensive appraisal of this problem. In addition to providing a number of statements which would be valuable to the attorney in terms of the highly disputed state of psychoanalytic theory within psychiatry, Hammet describes the emotional factors leading to the uncritical acceptance of psychoanalytic theory by the psychiatric resident. He points out that in the early stages of training many residents are discouraged by their chosen specialty's apparent inadequacy in the treatment of mental and emotional illness. They are troubled by feelings of futility. Then psychoanalytic theory and therapy enters the picture and new light dawns. Discouragement and frustration are replaced by hope and enthusiasm as the resident engages in psychoanalytic training, which supplements, and frequently engulfs, his general psychiatric residency. Thus, psychoanalysis provides an intellectual and emotional lift at the time it is needed. Hammet states:

> The emphasis upon psychoanalytic theory which has prevailed in psychiatry residency and post-residency training during the past twenty years is largely due to two factors: the resident's great need—born of the urgent emotional determinants described above—for an orderly method of approach to the problem of therapy in psychiatry and the absence of any other reasonably complete body of knowledge or convincing theory about the psyche in health and in disease. The unvarnished truth is that we are beset by great ignorance regarding the factors which determine human behavior. Psychodynamics has attempted to remedy this uncomfortable situation by elaborating on explanatory theory. In so doing it has responded to the emotional needs of psychiatrists in training and hereby has won much favor with them.

Hammet also points out the emphasis on psychoanalytic training works to the detriment of the resident's effectively learning about other systems of understanding human nature because the demands on his time in learning psychoanalysis are so enormous. Thus, says Hammet, the biological disciplines and the socio-psychological disciplines are neglected. The Report on Training states it thusly:

> One result of the present uneven emphasis in training, it was said, is that residents are prone to use the process of history taking as a means of reinforcing preconceived hypotheses regarding behavior rather than as a basis for constructing a working hypothesis most appropriate for the individual case. (p. 70)

Where appropriate, the attorney can bring out in cross-examination the fact that the psychiatrist's education has been considerably a matter of training in psychoanalytic theory and technique. Thus, the stage is set for attacking his training as being deficient when it is shown that psychoanalytic theory itself is an unvalidated, conjectural, and highly disputed approach (see Chapter 3).

Other deficiencies in psychiatric education exist. Among these deficiencies are the lack of a scientific basis and approach in teaching psychiatry. It has been noted in the literature that the approach has been one of dogmatism, particularly in the past where failure of the psychiatric trainee to accept psychoanalytic concepts was interpreted as a "resistance" on his part and jeopardized his future. In general, the psychiatrist is trained to accept what is taught, in contrast to the psychologist, who is trained to critically evaluate theory and concepts before accepting them. Another charge made against psychiatric training is that not only does it fail to provide sufficient background in psychology and the social sciences but there is also a neglect of or minimal experience in neurology and biological sciences. There is also the charge that there is a lack of uniformity in psychiatric education to the point that the mere possession of a degree is not convincing evidence that one individual has had the same kind of training as another. Such inconsistency points up the considerable disagreement among psychiatric faculties as to what is important.

Preston (1981) points out that the scientific training of physicians in general is often deficient. He notes:

> Students are not taught techniques of information gathering and problem solving, the rules of evidence and inference from data, the need for controlled studies and epidemiological studies for assessing the real effects of therapies, or the fundamental fact that human responses to therapies can be predicted at best only as probabilities.

> No one tells the student of the uncertainties of clinical medicine, of the absence of sufficient knowledge to make well-informed decisions in many cases, of the ease with which observations may deceive if they are not properly checked, of how the physician's own interest may conflict with those of patients. (p. 95)

Giller and Strauss (1984) argue that adequate exposure to research might help to counter certain problematic clinical judgment practices, including the tendency to mistake hypotheses or conjectures for validated facts. They state:

> An active involvement in research provides clinicians with the experience of evaluating the validity of clinical impressions and learning to test the truth of clinical hypotheses. Such experiences are not usually possible otherwise in psychiatry or in general medicine. The learning experience provided by being clinically involved in such situations can rarely be found in other settings, since whatever happens in other settings might be rationalized retrospectively. (p. 1077)

Furthermore, the whole training system is contaminated by its reliance, indeed its insistence, upon the use of the clinical method. The deficiencies and undesirable by-products of this method were discussed in Chapter 6, but it may be said here that, at the minimum, this method leads to distortion, misinterpretation, and forcing data into preconceived models so that true learning is seriously restricted or precluded.

Klein et al. (1970) point out the deficiencies of current case materials and further point out that proper clinical training demands adequate case materials. An article by Goldberg (1983) suggests that residents may be deprived of another potentially important source of educational material, this being the opportunity to witness the work of their supervisors. Goldberg discusses the advantages of using videotape technology in psychiatric training and resistance to this technological advantage. He notes that not only are students resistant to and anxious about having their work scrutinized by peers and supervisors as presented on videotape, but that teachers of psychotherapy are also reluctant to demonstrate their work through videotape, one reason for this resistance being fear of exposure and criticism.

Storrow (1967) states in his preface:

> Prefaces usually present florid tributes to "the teachers who made me what I am today." I've never been able to decide whether these are compliments or efforts to share the blame. In any event, after careful introspection—including heroic attempts to probe the depths of my unconscious mind—I am unable to blame my present intellectual position on any of my flesh and blood mentors.
>
> I had a brand of psychiatric training that is still much too common. All of my earliest teachers were either psychoanalysts or strongly influenced by Freud's ideas (one of them later rebelled and became a neuro-physiologist). My required readings lists repeated Freud's name so often that a ditto mark was used to save typewriter ink. These documents were also stuffed with names like Abraham, Ferenczi, and Sullivan. I wasn't taught that psychoanalysis was the *best* theory of human behavior; I was taught that it was the *only* one.
>
> I didn't rebel immediately. How was a psychiatric resident with almost no previous background to question the opinion of men who have devoted their lives to the field? I meekly followed the professional folkways and interpreted my occasional questioning behavior as "resistance."

Storrow then describes his difficulties in accepting the "historical-geological-hydraulic model of the mind" and how he eventually learned he was not the only rebel. He points out that the teachers who influenced him most were the ones who were authors of papers and books "conspicuously absent from my residency reading lists." He then states: "By this time I was fully 'trained' in psychiatry and had a certificate to prove it but I was still in search of a frame of reference."

Lesse (1977) asserts that psychiatric education is grossly inadequate. He notes that psychiatric education is geared to train medical students and residents for the 19th century and that psychiatric concepts and teachers are not preparing trainees for either the present or the future. He notes that for the previous 17 years (relative to the appearance of his article), the *American Journal of Psychotherapy* had carried numerous editorials describing frailties, inadequacies and anachronistic concepts which dominated traditional schools of psychotherapy. He notes particularly the failure to appreciate the influence of socio-economic, socio-political and socio-technologic forces that demand changes in theory and technique if patients are to be adequately helped. He notes that psychiatry is taught primarily by persons who are employed on a full-time basis by large institutions who have little comprehension of the outside world and do not adequately understand the stresses and compensations to which a high percentage of patients are exposed. He asserts that the educational framework in health sciences generally must be totally redesigned because it fails to reflect current realities and future probabilities. He feels the development and teaching of appropriate concepts will require a new breed of clinician and teacher and suggests that the present crop of psychiatric instructors should be phased out.

Several articles appear in the *American Journal of Psychiatry,* Volume 139, August 1982, that are concerned with the decline in the number of medical students specializing in psychiatry. Among the factors reported relevant to this decline are the views of medical students that in comparison to other medical specialties, psychiatry is low in status and both unscientific and imprecise. Another factor referred to was "a boomerang of psychiatry's over-promises in the 1950's and 60's." A further factor given was diminished regard for psychiatry by other academic departments.

Pierce et al. (1968) found that a college underclassman, without training in formal psychology, given 17 hours of programmed study, could get a better grade on an examination in psychiatry than medical students who had a minimum of 250 hours of classroom instruction in psychiatry, under conditions where the medical students clearly should have been expected to perform better. Even more stunning, however, was their finding that out of 19 college freshmen, unconnected with medical careers, several could, with only very limited programmed study (as little as three or four hours in some cases) "perform in a respectable manner" on the 1966 version of the Psychiatry National Board Examination. Several with less than twenty hours of instruction got scores above 60 out of a possible 100, and one with twelve hours of study got the remarkable score of 77. These results are still more remarkable in light of the fact that 15 out of 100 possible points involved questions on psychology, neurology, neuropathology, EEG, or child psychiatry, subjects which were not included in the brief instruction. If, taking this total absence of information into account, these 15 questions were eliminated, then a score of 60 out of the total of 85 would be slightly better than 70%: thus nine of the 19, with less than 20 hours of instruction, would have obtained what could be considered equivalent to a passing score on the written part of the Board examination!

In terms of passing the written portion of the Board examination, apparently, the equivalent of the psychiatrist's twelve years of education and training could be accomplished in a few hours of instruction by non-medically and non-psychiatrically educated college freshmen. It seems obvious that either all of those years of education are completely unnecessary and accomplish little, or the requirements for passing the psychiatric Boards are so inadequate that passing them, and receiving certification, is virtually meaningless, or possibly both statements are correct. But of course that is what the Taylor and Torrey article tells us. The Pierce study is merely an objective demonstration.

Along similar lines, Weinstein and Russell (1976) state:

> To date [1975], psychiatry has not clearly defined the skills, knowledge and attitudes that the psychiatrist in training must demonstrate in order to be certified as competent. It is our belief that the profession can no longer avoid beginning the difficult, often emotional, task of specifying what a psychiatrist should know and be able to do. (p. 935)

If the skills, knowledge and attitudes are unclear and the task of specifying what a psychiatrist should know and be able to do has not even begun, as these authors assert, what is it that Board Certification can attest to? There would seem to be almost no way of knowing. It would thus be difficult to find in such credentialing a basis for expertise.

Hoffmann (1986) raises concerns about the preparation of psychiatrists for forensic work. He notes, "Increasingly, specialized training is recommended before general psychiatrists perform forensic assessment and give expert court testimony, especially in criminal cases." (p. 164) This quote might be useful if a testifying psychiatrist lacks such training.

Greenblatt et al. (1977) provide data for candidates for ABPN certification in 1972. Their data show that of 200 candidates at that time, 68% passed the written examination on the first try. As the stated purpose of the board certification examinations was to establish "minimal competence necessary for the practice of psychiatry," it is of interest that nearly one-third of psychiatrists having completed all of their education and training and with the five years of experience needed to be eligible for the examination, could not demonstrate this minimal level on the written portion of the board examination. It may be noted that the third author of this study, C.M. Pierce, is the senior author of the study (supra) showing that undergraduate students not involved with medical training at all could perform at a near passing level on the written part of the board examination with as little as 12 hours of programmed instruction. Combining the data from these two studies leads to the conclusion that at least one-third of psychiatrists applying for board certification could perform no better on a similar examination than some of the group of non-medical undergraduates with as little as 12 hours of instruction. The reader is again reminded that the programmed instruction was not designed specifically for the purpose of taking the board's written exam. The years spent in medical school education, psychiatric residence and other psychiatric experience, then, appear to have approximately the same value as could be achieved in roughly a week or less of programmed instruction. These facts allow one to be considerably less impressed than one might otherwise be with the many years of education and training that the psychiatrist has.

The foregoing references strongly indicate that imputation of expertise to psychiatrists is not warranted by virtue of their education and training. Much of what they study is irrelevant (medicine), and they lack adequate education and training in fields which are vitally important to understanding human beings—psychology, sociology, and anthropology.

This point may be worth a moment's reflection. The literature cited in previous chapters often elicits reactions of shock and disbelief in readers who have accepted the facade of knowledge presented by psychiatrists. Others feel that certainly with all that education and training, psychiatrists must know a great deal and that somehow the literature must be wrong—certainly psychiatrists may feel that way. The references cited in this chapter, indicating the sorry state of psychiatric education and certification, may help the reader, as well as judge or jury, to accept the plethora of negative literature that has been presented in other chapters.

The foregoing might be less damaging if there was a sufficiency of data showing that in spite of these deficiencies of training, psychiatrists still are quite skillful in diagnosis and prediction. However, the thrust of available research indicates the contrary; that, in fact, the reliability and validity of psychiatric diagnosis and prediction are highly problematic (see Chapter 7 on Reliability and Validity, Chapter 8 on Experience). Illuminating these deficiencies of training helps to dispel the illusion of expertise imputed to the psychiatrist by virtue of his education and training.

Some psychiatrists, when challenged on the issue of their training and education, may indicate that their expertise is not based so much on the latter as on their actual experience. Chapter 8, on Experience, deals with the potent challenge that can be made to a claim for expertise based largely on experience.

DEFICIENCIES IN CONTINUING EDUCATION

Given the frequent "innovations" or changes in psychology and psychiatry, unless a practitioner keeps up with developments in the field, a good deal of what he learned during his training will be rendered obsolete. This point is evident in the case of the diagnostic manual(s). In fact, most psychiatrists and psychologists in practice today received little or no formal training or supervision in the use of DSM-III-R or DSM-IV but instead were trained in the use of the earlier DSMs. Thus, if such a clinician asserts that his formal training and education were important or helpful in learning to identify different categories of disorder, the lawyer may counter by pointing out, where appropriate, that the clinician has received none of this "helpful" formal training in the use of the current diagnostic manual, or in the identification of the specific category of disorder rendered by the clinician in the case under consideration. A similar approach can be used with the DSM-III-R or DSM-IV. To the extent that a new DSM adds, omits, or alters prior DSM diagnostic criteria or categories, then initially almost no psychologist or psychiatrist will have been formally trained in the use of these brand-new, "innovative" categories or disorders.

As regards "educational" activities subsequent to the completion of formal training, we will draw the somewhat artificial distinction between "experiential" learning—direct, hands-on clinical activity—and more didactically based activities, such as reading or interaction with professional colleagues. As discussed extensively in Chapter 8, experiential "learning" may be virtually useless as regards diagnostic or predictive accuracy. We will focus on more didactically based activities here.

Cohen (1979b) performed a mail survey of clinical psychologists in various work settings to determine the extent to which they read research articles and/or relied on other sources of information for their professional work activities. He found that academic clinicians and medical school psychologists read slightly more than four research articles per month, whereas other psychologists read slightly more than two articles per month. Discussions with colleagues appeared to be the most important source of information, receiving the highest rankings overall. The reader should be aware that even though the reading of research literature by clinicians may be viewed as inadequate (see below), it does indicate that most clinicians do rely to some extent on the literature in the conduct of their practice and on this basis (and others discussed in Volume III, especially Chapter 2) should be open to questioning regarding the state of the literature. In discussing results from the survey, Cohen states, "it is unclear what the long range consequences might be of psychologists relying on each other for information, when seemingly few of them read the research literature on a frequent basis." We would note that one of these likely consequences is the dissemination and perpetuation of illusory correlations, as originally described by the Chapmans.

The reader may recall that the term, illusory correlation, refers to belief in relationships that *appear* to exist but actually do not exist. Thus, these beliefs represent illusions. Chapman and Chapman (1967) state:

> It also seems likely that in clinical practice the observer is reinforced in his observation of illusory correlates by the reports of his fellow clinicians, who themselves are subject to the same illusions. Such consensual validation, especially among experts, is usually regarded as evidence of the validity of observation. (p. 203)

This and other work by Chapman and Chapman (1971) help us to understand why reliance on colleagues' observations or input, particularly if this is the primary source of "continuing education," may do little more than strengthen erroneous beliefs. Chapman and Chapman point out the likelihood that in actual practice the illusory correlations that a clinician "observes" become reinforced by the reports of fellow clinicians who are subject to the same illusions themselves. This consensus strengthens everyone's illusions, and the "gospel" is also spread to aspiring students. Eventually, the illusion ceases to be questioned. The lack of adequate proof, and even the presence of negative evidence, are ignored, and the illusion becomes "fact" because it has "withstood the test of time" (see the discussion of confirmatory bias, Chapter 5). Hence the origin of much clinical lore.

The clinical case conference is one context in which illusory correlations may be disseminated or strengthened. These conferences, in which students and staff get together to discuss cases, are often viewed as an important teaching tool for students. In the case of professional staff, case conferences may be the main format in which views are exchanged and opportunities exist to "learn" from colleagues. Thus, these case conferences may be the major form of "continuing education" for many professional psychologists and psychiatrists.

Paul Meehl (1973) indicates, however, that case conferences may be virtually worthless teaching tools for reasons that extend well beyond illusory correlations alone. As regards the general quality of case conferences, he states:

> I am deeply offended by the intellectual mediocrity of what transpires in most case conferences; but this personal reaction is of only autobiographical interest. The ignorance, errors, scientific fallacies, clinical carelessness, and slovenly mental habits which I have discussed are not merely offensive "academically." They have—sometimes dramatically—an adverse impact upon human lives....I freely admit that a major component of my attack is a claim that the case conferences I have attended have been unrewarding to me largely because of the low level of competence—*both scientific and clinical*—of most participants. (p. 298)

In discussing some of these "slovenly mental habits," Meehl makes general reference to what he describes as "tolerance of feeble inferences (e.g., irrelevances)." He states:

> The ordinary rules of scientific inference, and reliance upon general principles of human development, which everyone takes for granted in a neurology staff conference, are somehow forgotten in a psychiatric case conference. This is perhaps due to the fact that the psychiatrist has had to learn to live with the sorry state of his specialty after having had training in the more scientific branches of medicine, with the result that once having learned to live this way, he assumes that the whole set of rules about how to think straight have to be junked, so that logic, statistics, experiments, scientific evidence, and so on don't apply. (p. 229)

Dr. Meehl points out that a major reason why case conferences are lacking in value is that typically, given the state of scientific knowledge in the field, participants rarely know what the "right answers" might be. As a result, practitioners can say almost anything, no matter how implausible, and get away with it because they cannot be proven wrong. Of course, at the same time, if one cannot tell if an answer is right or wrong, one must wonder how anyone could learn from such an exercise. Along these lines, Meehl states:

> A clinicopathological conference in neurology or medicine is an educational experience for students and staff largely because there is a *right answer*. And one desirable fringe benefit of the existence of this quasi-criterial "right answer" is the non-reinforcement of foolish conversation. If you say something grossly stupid, you are almost certain to be found out when the pathologist enters the fracas at the end of the conference. (p. 285)

However, in contrast, as regards case conferences in psychiatry, Meehl states:

> The rules of the game are so loose in psychiatry that it is interesting to speculate how far out, either in terms of conceptual vagueness or evidentiary weakness, one would have to go before his brethren called him on it. My teacher Dr. Starke Hathaway once mentioned that he was having so much trouble in one of his seminars in getting the psychiatry residents to adopt a critical posture, toward either the received doctrine or his own iconoclastic verbal productions, that he was about to go in and propound some absolute nonsense about the influence of sunspots in schizophrenia, just to see whether they would rise to debate him or would dutifully note it down. (pp. 289-290)

And further regarding case conferences, Meehl notes:

> I cannot emphasize too strongly that part of the social and intellectual tradition of American psychiatry and clinical psychology tending to perpetuate the counterproductive mental habits described above is precisely this "buddy-buddy" syndrome which forbids anyone to call attention to instances of scientific or clinical incompetence, no matter how severe....There are too many psychoclinicians who implicitly equate the (valid) Popperian thesis that "every informed, experienced, and intelligent professional is free to indulge his

preferences among competing unrefuted conjectures" with the (preposterous) thesis that "every professional or student is morally and intellectually entitled to persist in egregious mistakes, and it is wickedly authoritarian or snobbish to point them out." I take it that no one who values the life of the intellect would subscribe to the latter thesis. (p. 299)

Yager et al. (1988) declare, "There are no minimum standards for the clinical training of psychiatrists with regard to the type and number of patients evaluated or treated. Interest in such standards derives from a need for greater accountability, a high fail rate on the clinical portion of the American Board of Psychiatry and Neurology examinations, and an increasing demand for precise documentation of competence in specific areas by hospital privileging committees." (p. 1409)

Tasman (1993) states, "Unfortunately, because so little information is available about adequacy of psychotherapy training, discussions usually reflect individual points of view about the place of psychotherapy training in residency." (p. 94)

PART II

CHALLENGING BOARD CERTIFICATIONS

Typically, before the expert presents any substantive testimony, he is introduced to the trier of fact by the recitation of a very impressive set of credentials and other qualifying material. He describes his education and training and indicates in one way or another the extent of his experience. The bases for challenging expertise based on such material have been presented in this and preceding chapters. In addition to education and experience, most experts also describe other material which is designed to impress the listener with his expertise. Such materials include administrative positions, offices held in professional associations, teaching, and board certification, such as certification by the American Board of Psychiatry and Neurology, possession of the Diploma of the American Board of Professional Psychology and two relatively new certifications, the Certification of the American Board of Forensic Psychiatry and the Diploma of the American Board of Forensic Psychology. The former came into existence in 1977 and the latter in 1979. Frequently this recitation of qualifications is the most important part of the expert's testimony. Lawyers and experts alike are aware of this and the problem is illustrated by the recommendation by one expert to other experts quoted in Chapter 1, "In short, go long on qualifications, short on facts." Therefore, it is essential to take the air out of this balloon. It is possible to demonstrate that the other "decorations" can either be shown to have little relationship to the accuracy of evaluations or that a relationship between such credentials and accuracy has not been demonstrated.

In our experience clinicians rarely understate their qualifications. Therefore, if they do not mention teaching, publications, association offices, board certification or the like, it is fairly safe to assume that they lack such credentials. The absence of such credentials can be brought out on cross-examination.

Approaches to dealing with credentials such as teaching, administrative positions, association offices and the like are dealt with at the end of this chapter and in another chapter (see Chapter 8, Volume III), as they are based on common sense and ordinary experience rather than on the scientific and professional literature. The present section will focus on the literature diminishing or casting doubt upon the significance of board certification. Likely, where the expert lacks board certification, cross-examining counsel will focus on the lack of such a credential rather than attacking the credential, particularly if his own expert possesses board certification.

The critical open questions concerning the certifying examination are: What does it measure? How reliably and how validly does it measure what it purports to measure? A brief description of the examinations may be useful for the lawyer. The descriptions that follow pertain to the older and more traditional certifications by the American Board of Psychiatry and Neurology (ABPN) and the American Board of Professional Psychology (ABPP). The new certifications in forensic psychiatry and forensic psychology are discussed later in the chapter.

BOARD CERTIFICATION IN PSYCHIATRY

The ABPN examination consists of two parts, one a written examination, the other an oral examination consisting of a 30-minute live interview with a patient followed by a 30-minute discussion with two examiners who observed the interview, and a viewing of a 20-25 minute videotaped psychiatric interview followed by a 30-minute discussion with two different examiners. Some deficiencies of this procedure seem clear. It is generally recognized that a 30-minute clinical interview is not an adequate amount of time for accomplishing its purposes. Therefore, the evaluation is based on an atypical or nonrepresentative clinical situation. Finally, the examination relates only to the manner in which the candidate conducts his evaluation and not to the accuracy of the evaluation.

There is sufficient negative literature to cast serious doubt that psychiatric board certification attests to even adequate, let alone superior, professional competence. The recurrent themes in this literature are uncertainties regarding what skills and competencies should be measured and doubts as to the adequacies of the measures employed. Of course, board certification deals only with competence in psychiatry generally.

Even if it were valid for that purpose, it would not provide evidence of competence in forensic evaluations (see below, American Board of Forensic Psychiatry).

Pierce et al. (1968, supra) found that out of 19 college freshmen, unconnected with medical careers, several with only a few hours of programmed study (as little as three or four in some cases) could "perform in a respectable manner" on the 1966 version of the psychiatry national board examination. Several with less than 20 hours of instruction got scores above 60 out of a possible 100 and one, with 12 hours of study, got the remarkable score of 77. These results are still more remarkable in light of the fact that 15 out of the 100 possible points involved questions on psychology, neurology, neuropathology, EEG or child psychology, subjects which were not even included in the brief instruction. Taking this total absence of information into account, 9 of the 19 who had less than 20 hours of instruction obtained what would be at or near a passing score on the written part of the board examination!

In terms of passing the written portion of the board examination, apparently the equivalent or near equivalent of the psychiatrist's 12 years of education and training could be accomplished in a few hours of instruction for nonmedically and non-psychiatrically educated college freshmen. It seems obvious that either all those years of education are completely unnecessary and accomplish little or the requirements for passing the Board examination and receiving certification are virtually meaningless. Possibly both statements are correct. That is what the literature generally indicates. The Pierce study provides an objective demonstration. It should be pointed out that the programmed instruction given the students was not designed specifically for the purpose of their taking the board examination but rather was an experiment to see if the content of psychiatry could be taught via programmed methods in less time than is normally taken.

Morgenstern (1970) describes his skepticism that a single day of testing can achieve the aim to "identify safe professional competency." He asserts that the value of the board examinations cannot be known until they have been studied and statistically analyzed. He notes that while the certification process is taken seriously, there has been no information as to the validity of the tests. He also notes that the body of knowledge and skills required of the candidates has never been adequately defined. He states there is no evidence that the board's examiners can measure behaviors basic to the practice of psychiatry and that many of these behaviors remain undefined. Morgenstern asserts that despite the obvious dedication of the examiners there is no assurance that they can achieve discriminative judgments that would make certification meaningful. He notes many studies indicating the opposite, that comprehensive oral examinations provide little validity and a low level of inter-examiner reliability. (It might be noted at this point that Dr. Morgenstern is board certified, so these are not the ravings of a jealous outsider.) He cites research by Pokorny and Frazier (1966) to the effect that no significant correlation could be found between overall competence ratings of supervisors of residents and their performance on a set of examinations modeled closely after the psychiatry examination of the ABPN. He notes that Pokorny and Frazier made reference to the lack of a "universally accepted standard of excellence" in psychiatry. Morgenstern raises questions as to whether the oral examination is worth the effort involved in it when weighed against the records of its reliability and validity as a measure of professional competence.

Taylor and Torrey (1972) state, regarding the two part certifying examination, that performance on it has never been correlated with psychiatric effectiveness and thus it is essentially meaningless. They state it has never been established that the examination measures the "ingredients" that are necessary for psychiatric practice.

Morgenstern (1972) observes that because of limitations of time and manpower, the board examinations allow observation of only a small fragment of the examinee's competence. He recommends at the minimum that the two patients examined should present quite different problems of interviewing technique and therapy.

Small and Regan (1974) discuss board certifications in medicine generally and assert that the tests are best equipped to test fundamental universally required knowledge and are at their weakest in testing clinical knowledge and skill. They note that a difficulty arises from the fact that test reliability and validity diminish as the test moves from general knowledge toward clinical competence and that this is compounded by the artificiality of the testing situation. They note there is currently no proof that the results are predictive of a subject's real clinical competence in the stresses and ambiguities of real life clinical practice. They also note the potential influence of "testmanship." They assert that the closer one comes to dealing with questions of clinical management and treatment, the less secure the findings of examinations are. They assert that the relationship between testing and a subject's actual clinical ability is tenuous at every level of validity and reliability. In the same journal in a discussion following the Small and Regan article, Eaton (1974) notes the inability of present evaluation mechanisms to accurately measure the process of clinical judgment, skills and habit patterns. He expresses doubt that there is a commonly agreed upon set of standards for the clinical practice of psychiatry and that therefore it is hard to examine for clinical competence when there is no agreement on what clinical competence is.

McDermott et al. (1974) note that there has been criticism within psychiatry of the way in which the board functions are carried out. They note problems concerning the limited nature of professional competence that the examinations sample and often that the information chosen for examination may be arbitrary and frequently highly variable from one candidate to another. They note that clinical competence is elusive and is a many faceted entity.

Greenblatt et al. (1977) provide some data that is relevant to the discussion of Napoliello's article below. They studied the success rates for the 200 psychiatrists who took the board examination in 1972 and followed them through the January 1976 oral examinations to determine success rates. They found that a total of 64% of the psychiatrists in their sample obtained certification in the four-year period. Forty-eight percent of these candidates passed both examinations (the written and the oral) on their first attempt. Of the candidates who passed Part I on their first try (68% of the total sample), 88.2% eventually obtained certification, although 17.6% had to repeat Part II (the oral examination). They conclude their article with the observation that while many colleagues are critical to varying degrees concerning the examination process, almost all of them nevertheless believe that oral examination is essential, particularly in psychiatry. They then note that the obvious problem is to ensure that the oral examination is valid and reliable or, stated differently, they express doubts concerning the reliability and validity of the oral examination. It is worth noting that after completing all medical education and psychiatric residency, plus two years of experience, one-third of the applicants were found lacking competence necessary to practice, although legally qualified to do so.

Napoliello (1977), based on his examination of 16 candidates, describes the quality of interviews as "varied" with a few excellent, a few poor and the majority marginal to satisfactory. The reader should bear in mind that these candidates had five years of experience in psychiatry and had passed the written portion of the board examination. Thus, with at least five years of experience and apparently adequate knowledge of psychiatry generally on the written examination, indicating substantial knowledge of psychiatry and enough experience to be considered "experienced," the overwhelming majority of these candidates did not perform with a high level of proficiency. Napoliello found the most common interview errors included a mechanical approach, with failure to allow the patient to "tell the story"; an abrupt closure of the interview; inability of the candidate to control his or her own anxiety level; and awkwardness and inconsistency of the interview structure. He found the errors most commonly seen in the question and answer period included inability to summarize; difficulty in coming to the point; weakness in differential diagnosis; and use of technical terms without being able to define them, which he views as inexcusable. Thus, with all of their education, training and experience the majority, or at least substantial numbers (no numerical breakdown is given), could not conduct an interview properly, were inadequate in making differential diagnoses and were prone to use jargon which they could not define. This provides another line of evidence that neither education and training nor experience can be taken as indicia of a high level of competence in psychiatry.

A look at Napoliello's report and the data of Greenblatt et al. together reveals that board certification does not assure quality. Greenblatt's data indicates that the written examination is the major stumbling block to certification, with only 10% of those who pass the written part ultimately failing the oral examination. Thus an overwhelming majority, nearly all, of the candidates who pass the written examination and become eligible to take the oral examination eventually pass it and become certified. Yet Napoliello states that in his admittedly somewhat small sample, weakness in differential diagnosis was apparent in the majority of candidates. If weakness in differential diagnosis is characteristic of a majority of candidates but a majority of candidates are passed, it seems clear that one can be board certified although weak in differential diagnosis. In light of these combined findings, the assertion that board certification represents even minimal competence in diagnosis, let alone superior ability in diagnosis, is simply not tenable. This conclusion might be challenged on the ground that Napoliello's sample was small and conceivably could have been grossly less competent than the Greenblatt sample. However, there is nothing in the data to indicate that was the case. Napoliello does not suggest that the candidates he examined were in any way different from the general run of candidates. In any event, the findings are not particularly surprising in view of the other criticisms of the examination procedures that have been cited above. If nothing else, the Greenblatt and Napoliello data combined at least represent a rather graphic illustration of the relative meaninglessness of board certification in psychiatry. It might be noted that these data reflect the situation in the early to mid 1970's, a time at which, presumably, the certifying procedure had been greatly improved over previous years so that even greater doubt would exist with regard to those certified earlier.

Naftulin et al. (1977) point to lack of standardization of the testing situation and unreliability of examiner's ratings as weaknesses in current board examination procedures. In their study, 28 psychiatrists who were preparing for the ABPN examination each interviewed a patient and observed a videotaped interview as part of a review course. Each examination was reviewed by two examiners, all of whom had served as examiners on the ABPN examination. They found that while overall mean performance scores for the live interview and the videotaped interview did not differ significantly, there was no relationship between the score an examinee earned on one examination and the score on another. Even when the scores were categorized simply as pass, condition or fail there was no relationship between the scores on the two examinations. They also found no significant relationship between performance on the written and live interview examination nor with the written and videotaped interview examination. On the scoring of the real patient interviews by the examiners they found no significant difference among examiners' ratings of ability to obtain history and ability to relate well to the patient. (Scoring was on an 8-point scale with 1 being inadequate and 8 equalling outstanding.) It might be noted that the range of mean ratings, however, was 4.63 for the lowest examiner on ability to obtain a history and 5.86 for the highest. These might not be statistically significant but they do represent considerable difference of opinion, that is a difference of 1.23 points on an 8-point rating scale seems substantial. In rating ability to apply factual information in a clinical setting, there were significant differences among the examiners with the four examiners giving mean ratings of 3.75, 4.13, 4.83 and 5.57. Similarly, there were differences on the overall rating which, however, probably would relate to difference on the previous item. The authors suggest that the significant difference was because of the low ratings given by examiner No. 1 in large part. However, there is no reason to believe that examiner No. 1 was particularly harsh, as his ratings were third highest out of four on ability to obtain a history and second highest out of four on ability to relate well to the patient. In any event, the authors are satisfied to state that their data show significant differences among examiners in their assessment of candidates in real patient interview examinations. They also note that apparently the examiner's experience in ABPN examinations did not successfully establish standardized criteria for evaluating psychiatric performance. They also note that the ABPN procedure of using real patients means that some examinees will interview easy patients, while others will have difficult patients to interview, which may lead to a major source of error in assessing the performance of psychiatrists expected to show a minimal level of competence. They suggest this error could be corrected by utilizing videotaped interviews for standardizing the clinical test situation. They conclude by stating that the means by which certification and recertification are to be achieved continue to be a persistent challenge for psychiatry.

It may be worth noting that in the Tarter et al. (1975) study (see Chapter 7), in which pairs of psychiatrists were unable to agree with each other at better than a 50% rate on the very gross classification of patients as psychotic, neurotic, or personality disorder, four of the five psychiatrists comprising the sample were board certified. These findings would be further evidence of the relative meaninglessness of board certification in psychiatry as in the 50% of cases in which they disagreed, one (or both) of the board certified psychiatrists had to be wrong.

Weinstein and Russell (1976) assert that psychiatry has not clearly defined the skills, knowledge and attitudes that psychiatrists in training must demonstrate in order to be certified as competent. They state their belief that the profession can no longer avoid starting the difficult task of specifying what a psychiatrist should know and be able to do. If the skills, knowledge and attitudes are unclear and the task of specifying what a psychiatrist should know and be able to do has not even begun, as these authors assert, one has to wonder what it is that board certification can attest to.

Langsley (1981) points out that methods of specialty certification are undergoing changes in English speaking countries. He points out that until recently, only about 1/3 of psychiatrists in the United States were board certified, although this percentage has increased markedly in recent years. The certification process has been criticized. In 1976, a referendum of APA members showed 80% of the voting members expressing concern about the certification process. Among the concerns raised were: 1) reliability—the exam was nonstandardized and seemed to lack reliability; 2) there was no demonstrated validity, and it was questioned whether a brief exam could provide a valid measure of competence; and 3) lack of examiner training and established criteria seemed to be "serious" hindrances to the guarantee of competence and safety. It was not until the late 1970's that the United States began informal training for new examiners. At the time of the article there were still no specific criteria for use by examiners who make ratings.

Talbott (1983) reviews concerns about board certification procedures in psychiatry, including questions about reliability and validity. Questions about validity include the concern that the exam does not measure a sample of behavior representative of actual clinical practice or skill in treating versus simply interacting with patients. The operation of chance in the selection of examiners and the patient for the oral interview is also raised as a concern. The author studied examiner agreement in evaluating applicants' performance on the oral section of the exam and the videotaped section. Sixty-one percent of the applicants received concordant scores on their audio-visual and "live patient" examination hours and 52% received identical grades. Agreement about pass-fail decisions was 80%. When scores were not identical, roughly 2 out of 3 candidates performed higher on the audio-visual section. The author concludes that the two examination formats may test somewhat different skills or carry different weights in the judgment of the examiners. Although the author claims that the above reported rates of agreement are high, given the base rates (that the majority of applicants received passing grades) these figures do not necessarily represent an improvement over the base rates. The author ends by stating that the study addresses only the reliability of the examination process, and not the validity of its content or its relevance to clinical competence. The latter are considered "open questions."

McDermott et al. (1993) analyzed agreement on grades between two examiners on both the live interview and videotape sections. They found (across different sites and times) perfect agreement (pass, fail, or condition) between the two examiners ranged from 56% to 64% for the live interview and 69% to 72% for the videotape section. The grades given were pass, condition, or fail, with condition being assigned to candidates who were neither clearly passing nor clearly failing. McDermott et al. describe this level of agreement as fair-to-good or moderate and a matter of concern. They describe the disagreement in 26% of the cases as "minor"—pass versus condition or condition versus fail—and easily resolved to a consensus through discussion. In the 7% of cases where disagreement was "major" it was usually a disagreement about how important an act of omission or commission was, and this too was resolved through discussion. While disagreements were resolved, it is clear that there was a considerable amount of disagreement on initial evaluation. Of course, this study deals only with reliability, not validity.

Wettstein et al. (1991) found considerable variation among four Board Certified psychiatrists in the application of various legal standards (ALI, M'Naughton, etc.) in arriving at opinions in insanity defense cases.

Effective October 1, 1994, only 10 year time-limited certificates will be issued, according to the 1995 *Information for Applicants*. This means that for those certified on or after that date, recertification will be required every 10 years, clearly a move in the right direction. However, this apparently will not be required of those certified prior to that date. Questions as to the reasons for this new requirement might be addressed to those who have been "grandfathered."

The *Information* also states that beginning in 1995, DSM-IV will be the primary authority on psychiatric nomenclature for its written examinations, with DSM-III-R or IV acceptable on oral examination until 1996 when DSM-IV will be the primary authority. Thus, anyone certified before 1995 will not have been examined with the same requirements as will be required of future applicants.

Board certification in psychiatry can be summed up as an indicator that the psychiatrist has not been found to be grossly incompetent by his peers and nothing else. There is no evidence of superior competence and, in particular, regarding diagnostic accuracy on the part of board certified psychiatrists, what evidence is available appears to strongly indicate that the certifying examinations fail to provide support for such superior ability (see examples below). At the minimum, a psychiatrist who asserts from the witness stand that board certification signifies a superior level of competence is simply uninformed or less than candid.

One more point requires mention. Some psychiatrists, when asked if they are board certified, reply that they are not, but that they are "board eligible." As far as we can determine, to be board eligible simply means that the individual has five years of experience in psychiatry, including his residency. Indeed, the 1995 *Information for Applicants* of the American Board of Psychiatry and Neurology states that they do not recognize or use the term "board eligible." Therefore, we think this declaration can be shown to be an attempt to mislead a judge or jury as to the individual's qualifications. It seems like an attempt to acquire some sort of "credit by association" with the terminology of "board certification." A competent cross-examiner should be able to demonstrate that being eligible to take the boards has no similarity whatsoever to actually being board certified.

DIPLOMATE IN CLINICAL PSYCHOLOGY

The diploma awarded by the American Board of Professional Psychology (ABPP) is approximately the psychological equivalent of board certification in psychiatry and purports to indicate that the psychologist has demonstrated proficiency in the areas of industrial, counselling, clinical psychology, or clinical neuropsychology, the latter two being the ones most likely to be encountered by lawyers. The diploma of the American Board of Forensic Psychology has recently been incorporated into the ABPP and will be discussed separately. The assessment procedure involves letters of recommendation from ABPP diplomates who are familiar with the candidate's work, submission of a work sample, a field demonstration which may be either a diagnostic or therapy session and an oral examination by five diplomates. Thus, as with the psychiatric boards, the procedure lacks standardization and deals with only a small sample of the candidate's clinical performance. Therefore, as with the psychiatric boards, issues of reliability and validity remain unresolved. We have not and could not, even with a computer search, find published studies indicating a high level of competence among diplomates nor a higher level of competence among diplomates than among non-diplomates (nor could we find such studies for board certification in psychiatry). At least one study, conducted by Goldstein and Deysach (1973), showed that ABPP psychologists were wrong in 50% of the cases in determining presence or absence of organic impairment and were inferior to novices in this study. We find no evidence that the diploma reflects a capability that overcomes all of the deficiencies of assessment, whether by psychiatrists or psychologists, that are described in this book (see below examples of work of diplomates which make it clear that one cannot rely on that status as evidence of even competent, let alone superior, evaluation).

Schoon (1978), discussing current pressures on licensing and certification agencies to assess competency, asserts that competency is very difficult to measure because it is a complex combination of knowledge, skills, abilities and personal characteristics. He notes that no profession has yet produced a definitive set of criteria that precisely pinpoints what competency is in that profession. He also notes that while competency is composed of many measurable components, there are many other attributes of competency that are difficult, if not impossible, to measure. He asserts that before developing more measures the critical issue is development of a clear definition of what it is that should be measured.

Koocher (1979) states, "There are no empirical data in print which demonstrate that extant licensing or specialty board certification examinations correlate with the successful treatment or diagnosis of clients. There are, on the other hand, a number of studies which purport to show that novice diagnosticians or paraprofessional therapists can be correct or effective at least as often as are senior clinicians." He notes that the ABPP has no requirement for continuing education of diploma holders and that it is virtually impossible to revoke an ABPP diploma once it is granted. He states, "In the final analysis it seems that whatever existing credentials in psychology do measure, they are clearly not highly valid measures of professional competence…given the current difficulty in refining the construct of competence as it applies to the practice of psychology, it is unlikely that the credentials' validity will soon improve on this score…current credentials in psychology may provide some helpful information to the consuming public, but two Latin words may be inappropriately absent from most of these diplomas: *caveat emptor.*"

Howard (1983) claims that the evaluation of professional competence in psychology by state licensing boards and the American Board of Professional Psychology has not fully utilized expertise in psychological measurement in the profession. The author points out that the paper-and-pencil tests used for national licensing measure background knowledge rather than competence to practice psychology. Oral exams used by some licensing boards lack standardization. The ABPP examination relies on work samples, but also lacks standardization, and reliability and validity remain unproven. The author discusses the possible use of work samples and simulations that might be useful in providing more valid measures of performance competency, but as yet such approaches remain largely unapplied. She points out that a number of other professional boards do use performance samples, and have more fully utilized measurement technology developed within psychology than have psychology boards.

State licensure attempts to evaluate minimal competency, usually in the generic field of psychology. This screens out those without proper knowledge but does not determine competency in actual practice. ABPPs do not use standardized measures of background knowledge. Further, ABPP examinations rely on non-standardized, prepared-in-advanced work samples to evaluate competence.

Kane (1982) notes that there are essentially no studies on the predictive validity of licensing exams. He further argues that the hope of obtaining exams with predictive validity is unrealistic for a series of reasons, including extreme difficulty deriving proper criterion-based measures and because of the variability of performance over time. Rather he suggests that exams should measure critical skills that are required (prerequisites) for competent practice or for safeguarding public welfare. He outlines requirements of this approach, including the need to establish empirically-based relationships between knowledge or abilities and client outcome. Although not directly stated, clearly the author feels that current licensing exams do not begin to meet his preference for the assessment of critical abilities.

In a separate article, Kane (1986) states:

> *The Problem.* The usefulness of predictive validity for licensure and certification examinations is limited greatly by the fact that criteria of proven validity are not available for licensure examinations. The development and validation of a criterion measure of professional performance presents fundamental conceptual problems as well as great practical difficulties, in part because practice requires a high level of professional judgment for effective performance. The distinction between good practice and poor practice is not clear-cut in most cases (e.g., see Strupp, Hadley, & Gomes-Schwartz, 1977), and the development of general measures of the quality of practice that are reliable, valid, and complete is probably not possible for most professions. Assumptions about the validity of the criterion are likely to be questionable at best, and to the extent that the validity of the criterion is questionable, any conclusions drawn from a predictive validity study would be questionable. (p. 155)

In the material above, we have been discussing only those certifications or diplomas issued by boards under the jurisdiction of or associated with the American Psychiatric or Psychological Associations or other well-established and recognized professional organizations. The reader should be aware that in recent years there has been a proliferation of "organizations" issuing certificates or diplomas requiring little if anything more than an application, some letters of reference, and a check. No examination is required. While we do not say that all or any of these are not legitimate, we do recommend in all cases that the attorney inquire whether or not a given credential was obtained through examinations of reasonable rigor, and that the attorney maintain an attitude of reasonable skepticism.

Sechrest (1985) (at the time President of the Clinical Division of the American Psychological Association) describes his amazement at receiving an application for academic employment from an individual whose Ph.D. was only four years old but who claimed specialty diplomas from four "board" or "academy" organizations, "one 'international,' no less." He notes that none of the diplomas was from ABPP and asks, "What the hell is going on?" He asks how a psychologist with less than fifteen years total experience and a four-year-old Ph.D. which presumably took up some of the fifteen years could have acquired so much expertise. He might be even more surprised if he knew a psychologist one of the present authors knows, who at a relatively young professional age had FIVE diplomas. Sechrest states, "I have been in and around the field of clinical psychology for nearly 30 years, and I would not want a diploma based on any test I could pass."

ABPP does not recognize the term "Board Eligible" and does not allow applicants or candidates to represent themselves as such outside of communications within ABPP. This applies to ABFP also.

As with board certification in psychiatry, there is a lack of research evidence to support any claim for superior performance by Diplomates in Clinical Psychology of ABPP. The only published evidence we have found is in the examples discussed below which are opposite to claims of adequate, let alone superior, performance.

BOARD CERTIFICATION IN FORENSIC PSYCHIATRY

The American Board of Forensic Psychiatry was established in 1976 and its purposes and functions are best described by the following contents of its brochure issued in July of 1977 and current at least as of mid-1979. In 1992 this board ceased to function and its functions were taken over by a Committee on Certification of Added Qualifications in Forensic Psychiatry (the Committee) under ABPN. Some changes in requirements were made, but as most forensic psychiatrists will have been certified under the old requirements at least through the end of the Twentieth Century, we will continue to present those requirements, and then describe the changes.

BACKGROUND, FUNCTIONS, and PURPOSES
OF THE
AMERICAN BOARD OF FORENSIC PSYCHIATRY, INC.

The need unequivocally to identify forensic scientists qualified to provide essential professional services for the nation's judicial and executive branches of government has long been recognized. In response to this professional mandate, the American Board of Forensic Psychiatry was organized in 1976 to provide, in the interest of the public and the advancement of the science, a program of Certification in forensic psychiatry. In purpose, function and organization, the ABFP is thus analogous to the certifying boards in various medical specialties and scientific fields.

The object of the Board is to establish, and enhance, and revise as necessary, standards of qualification for those who practice forensic psychiatry and to Certify as qualified specialists those voluntary applicants who comply with the requirements of the Board. In this way, the Board aims to make available to the judicial system, and other interested parties a practical and equitable system readily identifying those persons professing to be specialists in forensic psychiatry who possess the requisite qualifications and competence.

Excerpts from the Board's Standards for Certification in Forensic Psychiatry are contained in the statement on "Qualifications and Requirements for Certification in Forensic Psychiatry" which follows.

QUALIFICATIONS and REQUIREMENTS for
CERTIFICATION in FORENSIC PSYCHIATRY:

1. General Qualifications.

    A. Applicants must be persons of good moral character, scientific integrity, with high ethical and professional standing.

    B. Certification is limited to permanent residents of the United States of America, its territories and possessions, or of Canada.

2. Professional Education and Licensure.

    A. Applicants must possess an M.D., D.O., or a recognized equivalent medical degree.

    B. Applicants must have a valid license to practice medicine in a state, territory, or province of the United States or Canada.

    C. Applicants must be Certified in Psychiatry by the American Board of Psychiatry and Neurology or by the Canadian equivalent.

3. Professional Experience and Training.

    A. Applicants must have a minimum of five years of post-residency exprience in clinical psychiatry with substantial experience in forensic psychiatry, including but not limited to, contributions in research, teaching and the administrative aspects of forensic psychiatry.

    B. One year of accredited full time training in forensic psychiatry shall be two years of equivalent credit.

    C. The applicant must provide evidence of all training in forensic psy chiatry. Credit will be considered for forensic psychiatric training within an approved psychiatric residency training program.

    D. On approval by the Committee on Credentials the applicant may apply for examination to be conducted by the Committee on Examination at an appointed time and place.

4.   Examination.

    A. Applicants who meet the requirements and qualifications set forth in Sections 1, 2, and 3 above shall be accepted for written examination. Upon successful completion they shall be eligible for an oral examination.

    B. Applicants remain eligible to undergo examination within two years after admission to the examination.

    C. Applicants who fail in either written or oral examination may apply within one year for one re-examination without payment of additional fee. Before a third examination, an applicant must file a new application and pay an additional fee.

The ABPN 1995 *Information for Applicants for Added Qualification*, Section V Forensic Psychiatry, has a requirement that the applicant must have satisfactorily completed training in a forensic psychiatry program consisting of as minimum of a one-year fellowship in forensic psychiatry beginning no sooner than PGY-5 level. Until 1999 this requirement can be met through a clinical pathway consisting of spending 25% of an applicant's practice time in forensic psychiatry. It seems clear that this board does not view experience in forensic psychiatry as important as formal training. In fact there is no experience requirement as in the prior requirements. This forensic program requirement cannot be met by the exposure to forensic psychiatry given to most general psychiatry residents. Starting in 1995, the Board will use DSM-IV as its primary authority in psychiatric diagnostic nomenclature.

As of the date of this writing, we are aware of no published research providing data with which to assess issues of reliability and validity in relation to Diplomates of the American Board of Forensic Psychiatry (ABFP). Therefore, considering the long time period required for generating and publishing research, it is likely to be many years before any appreciable body of research evidence on these issues has been accumulated, assuming that diligent efforts will be made to produce such data. Of course, there is no assurance that when such data appears, its results will be any more favorable to the ABFP certification than it has been to the more traditional board certification. In the absence of a considerable body of evidence to the contrary, the best assumption one could make is that if and when such research appears, its results are likely to be similar to the results found in the traditional board certification, that is, lack of demonstrated reliability and validity. We note the board repeatedly refers to forensic psychiatry as a science and refers to "scientific integrity." Therefore, we assert it should be judged by scientific standards. These assertions can also be used to confront psychiatrists who attempt to denigrate scientific research.

The original board was established by several psychiatrists who had achieved some distinction in forensic psychiatry by virtue of research, publication, teaching or administrative contributions. It should be noted that distinctions of this kind may have no relation to the validity of conclusions offered by such individuals as expert testimony. These board members then became the first to be certified as Diplomates in Forensic Psychiatry *by examining each other.* In a display of seeming integrity the original board refused to allow anyone to acquire diplomate status by a "grandfathering" procedure, so that they were all required to take the examination themselves. In sworn testimony, one of these original diplomates stated in reference to the three-part examination as to who put the examination together that he "was involved in one part entirely and partially in another part and none in the third part." An examination procedure in which the examinee has written somewhere between 40 and 60% of the examination is somewhat less than confidence inspiring. Although one can readily acknowledge the logistical problems of getting a project of this kind off the ground and the need to start someplace, nevertheless it would seem that some procedure could have been devised whereby an examiner would not have been examining himself in effect. It seems most likely that some of the other original diplomates would have attained that status also by virtue of taking examinations to which they had contributed some considerable portion. It does seem to us on this basis that the noble intention of avoiding "grandfathering" was not achieved in a practical sense by this procedure.

Given the present lack of evidence concerning a high correlation between forensic psychiatry certification and accuracy of forensic evaluations, this diploma fails to provide any significant information as to the validity of assessments in forensic matters by such individuals. Like the more traditional psychiatry certification, the absence of such certification may be significant while its presence is not. That is, the brochure published by the Board (consisting of many of the most distinguished names in American forensic psychiatry) states very clearly that even possession of the traditional psychiatric board certification is not sufficient to identify a psychiatrist as qualified in forensic psychiatry. Thus, a witness who is board certified in psychiatry but not board certified in forensic psychiatry would in the view of these authorities be lacking in the appropriate credential to attest to his qualification in forensic matters. Two of these board members, Dr. Bernard Diamond and Dr. Seymour Pollack, should be recognized by any such expert as authorities in forensic psychiatry.

Robitscher and Williams (1977) doubt that certification in forensic psychiatry is a sensible solution to the criticisms of psychiatric testimony that have appeared. They also note that such certification would confer on those obtaining the certification a presumption of credibility that would not necessarily be justified. They also disagree with the idea of using "super experts" who are trained in both law and psychiatry as they feel this would increase the danger that psychiatrists would tailor their investigations and testimony to fit the requirements of the law. Some examples of ABFP diplomate holders are provided below which do not support claims of superior performance.

BOARD CERTIFICATION IN FORENSIC PSYCHOLOGY

Board certification in forensic psychology is analogous to board certification in forensic psychiatry. The American Board of Forensic Psychology (ABFP2)[1] was established in 1978 and, as was the case with forensic psychiatry, the board members examined and certified each other. While the differences between the two forensic certifications appear to be minor at present, some are noted below.

As many diplomates will have been certified under its provisions, we will first discuss portions of the 1978 brochure of this board and then indicate material changes in the 1994 brochure.

The brochure of the American Board of Forensic Psychology (ABFP2) describes their certification as of 1978 as follows:

WHAT IS A FORENSIC PSYCHOLOGIST?

The word *forensic* comes from the Latin word *forensis*, meaning literally, "of the forum." The Forum was where the law courts of ancient Rome were held. Other important issues of the day were also debated there.

Forensics in our modern society refers to the application of scientific principles and practices to the adversary process, where the specially knowledgeable scientist plays an advisory role. [Author's note: Once again, note the reference is to "scientific" principles.] The forensic psychologist is one who has made a study of the adversary process, and is aware of such factors as relevant case law, legislation, and legal theory, and who incorporates these factors into his/her psychological determinations. Thus, forensic psychology is the application of psychology to legal concerns.

CAN ANY PSYCHOLOGIST BE A FORENSIC PSYCHOLOGIST?

Any psychologist is entitled to provide professional services at the interface between law and psychology as long as the psychologist does not go beyond his/her area of expertise. Traditionally, however, the training of the psychologist has not included familiarization with the adversary process, or the civil and criminal justice systems and the issues they confront. Psychologists without

---

[1]To avoid confusion, the forensic psychology board will be designated as ABFP2. However, since 1986, ABFP2 has merged with ABPP and the diploma is issued by ABPP in Forensic Psychology. The name of ABFP also appears in the diploma. Otherwise there is little change from the description below. We have in this instance relied on information obtained by a telephone call to a current ABFP2 board member.

such training, who may be called upon to provide forensic services, may find themselves at a disadvantage, especially in such areas as rules of evidence or issues involved in establishing legal competency and responsibility.

WHAT IS THE PURPOSE OF THE BOARD?

Consumer advocates are bringing increasing pressure on virtually all professional groups to clearly define and identify those persons who are qualified to provide various services. One of the mechanisms for attesting to competence is professional certification at the diplomate level. Several specialties in forensic science have responded to this public demand by creating boards of diplomate examiners, including a board of examiners in forensic psychiatry. In recognition of a need to provide a similar service for psychologists, the American Board of Forensic Psychology (ABFP) was established in 1978. Its purposes are to provide a service to the public by identifying qualified practitioners of forensic psychology, and to promote forensic psychology as a recognized discipline within professional psychology. By certifying Diplomates in Forensic Psychology, the ABFP is thus analogous in purpose and function to other certifying boards in various distinguished specialties of professional and scientific practice.

WHAT DOES THE BOARD DO?

The function of the American Board of Forensic Psychology is to establish, promote, and revise as necessary, standards of certification for those who practice forensic psychology, and to certify as diplomates those voluntary applicants who qualify under the standards established by the Board. By this procedure, the Board intends to make available to the consumer a practical system for identifying forensic psychologists who possess the requisite credentials and competencies.

WHAT IS THE FORMAL EXAMINATION?

After the applicant submits his/her credentials, and the Board determines that the requirements for education and experience have been met, the applicant is requested to submit a work sample. If this is deemed acceptable, the applicant is declared a *Candidate for the Diploma*. An examination is then set with a three-member examining committee comprised of Diplomates in Forensic Psychology. Candidates should expect the examination to cover core forensic content as well as their own area of specialty. It may also include hypothetical situations from which the Candidate will be asked to draw psychologically sound conclusions, and to justify the conclusions on both legal and ethical grounds. The examination will take several hours.

GENERAL PROVISIONS CONCERNING THE DIPLOMA

* * * *

4. *General Qualifications.* Applicant must be a psychologist of good moral character and scientific integrity, with high professional standing. Applicant must conduct self in accordance with the prevailing ethical standards of the American Psychological Association or the Canadian Psychological Association, as appropriate to the location of the practice.

5. *Professional Education and Licensure.*

   a. Applicant shall have an earned doctoral degree in psychology. All doctoral degrees must be earned from an institution appropriately regionally accredited. Under exceptional circumstances the Board may accept doctoral degrees in closely related fields as substantially equivalent to a doctorate in psychology.

b. Applicant must be a licensed psychologist, meaning any psychologist licensed, certified or otherwise registered to practice psychology in any state, territory or province of the United States of America or of Canada. Psychologists practicing in a jurisdiction where licensing appropriate to the practice is not available shall present evidence that (save for residence requirements) they qualify for licensure in the nearest jurisdiction where such licensing is available.

c. Applicant must be a member in good standing of the American Psychology-Law Society, the American Psychological Association, or the Canadian Psychological Association.

d. The Board, at its discretion, may exempt an applicant who has made a distinguished contribution to the field of forensic psychology, and whose primary function is research or teaching in an academic setting, from meeting a particular qualification. A two-thirds affirmative vote of the Board is required for each such exemption.

6. *Professional Experience and Training.*

a. Applicant must have accumulated at least one thousand (1,000) hours of experience over a minimal five (5) year period in forensic psychology. At least four of those years must be post-doctoral. Holders of an earned LL.B. or J.D. degree may substitute that degree for two of the five years of experience.

b. During the five qualifying years of practice, applicants must have received at least two hundred (200) hours of appropriate professional individual and/or group supervision and/or consultation in their field(s) of forensic specialization.

7. *Limited Period for Special Qualifications and Requirements.* Up to and including the last day of 1980, the Board may, on its own motion and upon request by an applicant, modify the qualifications and requirements regarding:

a. Education and experience. A masters degree in psychology may be substituted for the doctorate, provided that the experience required be extended to two thousand (2,000) hours over a minimal ten (10) year period. Holders of an earned LL.B. or J.D. degree may substitute that training for two of the ten years of experience.

b. Supervision and/or consultation may be waived.

c. An applicant of national repute who has made significant contributions to the field of forensic psychology.

There are a number of changes in the 1994 brochure that are worth noting.

The 1994 brochure describes the diploma as attesting to the fact that an established organization of peers has examined and accepted the recipient as being *at the highest level of excellence* (italics added) in his or her field of forensic competence. This is somewhat more grand than the previous statement. It requires that those substituting an LL.B. or J.D. for two years of experience must still have 1000 hours of experience. It reduces the 200 hours of specialized training to 100 hours.

There are some differences between the ABFP and the ABFP2. It is noted that the ABFP2 diploma does not require that the applicant possess the diploma of the ABPP in clinical psychology, so it may be somewhat weaker than the ABFP certification in that area. However, it requires considerably more experience. It does not have a written examination as does ABFP, but does require real-life work samples which ABFP does not. Also, the oral examination appears more extensive and is of considerably greater duration.

The Forensic Psychology certification requires not only a minimum number of years (5) in forensic psychology, but at least 1,000 hours of experience during that time. However, it allows two years of credit for holding of the LL.B. or J.D. degree, presumably on the assumption that knowledge of the law is one of the requirements for expertise in this area. One might question the wisdom of this substitution. For example, in the case of an attorney who graduated from law school in 1958 and has practiced corporation law for 20 years and then switched to psychology, one might legitimately question the relevance of his training and experience for certification in the 1990's with all the changes in laws that have occurred.

As the first diplomates of this specialty were certified in 1979, several years have now passed without, to our knowledge, publication of research on issues of reliability and validity of the certifying process and demonstration of superior competence in forensic evaluation by diplomates. Pending development of such a body of data, there is no reason to believe that evaluations by certified forensic psychologists will be any better than those delivered by any other psychologist, including those with the ABPP diploma. As there is a dearth of evidence concerning superior evaluation and accuracy by ABPP diploma holders, and some negative research concerning such individuals and a plethora of negative research concerning evaluations by psychologists generally, until the appearance of such validating research evidence, board certified forensic psychologists should not be considered any more accurate in their evaluations than are psychologists in general.

Otto et al. (1990) state, "The actual value of national forensic board credentialing has not been empirically demonstrated. Although efforts are underway, the ABFP has not yet completed empirical studies to verify the reliability of its credentialing procedures, or the degree to which its diplomates' practices maintain the standards supported by the board. Until this is done, the value of a national forensic board remains unsubstantiated." (p. 229) (By telephone calls the present author determined that people who should know did not know of any such empirical studies done or being done as of 1994. The "efforts" apparently consisted of talking about it.) The above statement takes on added significance as two of its authors have been, and are, advocates of the diploma, and recognized leaders in the field of forensic psychology. We welcome their apparent concurrence in the point we have been making in somewhat blunter language, to wit—until the value has been demonstrated, no value should be attributed to it.

At the Annual Convention of the American Psychological Association in Boston, August 1990, the author attended a session put on by the American Board of Forensic Psychology. He put two questions to the representatives of the Board who were on the platform. Has any research been done to determine the validity of its Diplomates? If not, does the Board have any plans to do this? The answer to both questions was "no." We did not have a similar opportunity regarding the American Board of Forensic Psychiatry, but are not aware of any such research plans on their part. Absent such research, and in view of the negative literature and case evidence we have provided, such credentials are essentially meaningless, no matter how impressive they sound. The sum and substance of the Board certifications in forensic psychiatry and psychology at the present time is that no greater expertise should be imputed to these people until they have demonstrated such superiority or competence, not to each other, but in a form that is amenable to research evaluation. Having so stated, it is appropriate to acknowledge that holders of these certifications are likely to be more knowledgeable in regard to the nature of forensic issues than people lacking such a credential. This, however, provides no assurance that they have properly conducted their examinations, that they have drawn proper conclusions, have appropriately related data to the legal issues or that their assessments are of a high degree of accuracy or that they will properly acknowledge limitations of knowledge or methods in their field.

Lacking research data demonstrating greater expertise, clinical acumen, freedom from the deficiencies of clinical evaluation, and so on, on the part of holders of any of the diplomas or certifications described above, our review of the work of several holders of these credentials in actual cases constitutes evidence of probative value equal to any other evidence presently existing. The case material which follows obviously does not constitute scientific research and the number of cases is too small to warrant generalization. However, this material clearly demonstrates that board certified clinicians disagree in their conclusions, thus indicating at least in this minimal material that reliability may be low and that one cannot assume accuracy of evaluation or conclusions based on board certification, because where two board certified clinicians disagree with each other, at least one must be wrong. The material will also show that some board certified clinicians perform inadequate examinations in forensic matters. As this book is part of the professional literature in forensic psychology and psychiatry, it will at least make it possible to ask questions such as, "Doesn't the scientific and professional literature provide illustrations of cases where diplomates in forensic psychiatry disagree in their conclusions?" therefore raising questions as to the validity of conclusions reached by such individuals, or, "Doesn't the scientific and professional literature show instances in which psychologists certified in forensic psychology have performed inadequate examinations?" thereby showing that such certifications are indeed no assurance of adequate, much less excellent procedure in the particular case.

The material below should be read with the following admonition in mind. The facts that we report are facts. For example, when we say a psychologist made four scoring errors on the WAIS, that means that he made four clear-cut, unarguable scoring errors. When we say that the psychiatrist failed to obtain or at least to note certain data from a litigant's history, that is a fact. In addition to such facts, however, we will also make some comments about the material which may be subject to some disagreement. We hope the distinction between the two kinds of material will be apparent.

As we do not intend any of the material as an attack on any of the clinicians involved, we have done the best we can to avoid identifying information. In some instances the nature of the material is such that some will feel that they recognize the individual involved. We regret that this may be so and would urge readers to focus on the substance of the material and not to waste their time on the insignificant question as to the identity of the clinician involved. We are not suggesting that these clinicians are less competent or perform less adequate evaluations than their colleagues. On the contrary, we are suggesting only that the validity or adequacy of their examinations or conclusions, as represented in the cases covered, is not superior to that of non-board certified clinicians.

BOARD CERTIFIED PSYCHIATRISTS: ILLUSTRATIVE EXAMPLES

CASE 1

This case involved two psychiatrists who are certified both in psychiatry and in forensic psychiatry—Psychiatrist 1 appearing for the defense and Psychiatrist 2 appearing for the prosecution. The case was a criminal matter involving violation of a government regulation. The critical issues were whether the defendant's state of mind allowed him to be cognizant of the act he was performing and to form the intent necessary to constitute the crime. The essence of the crime was failure to list or declare several valuable items upon a return flight from overseas. Psychiatrist 1 examined defendant approximately six weeks after the crime, interviewed his family physician and wife and had affidavits of several companions on the trip available. Psychiatrist 2 examined defendant approximately six months after the crime, and had available the report of Psychiatrist 1 as well as the various other materials that had been furnished to Psychiatrist 1. Psychiatrist 2 also administered an MMPI which he sent to one of the automated interpretation services. At the time of the consultation in this case, the MMPI had not as yet been returned and therefore plays no role in the discussion which follows. Facts which were apparently not in dispute were that defendant for many years had family problems, particularly with his wife and teen-age child, and that the marriage was in a tenuous state. Also he had become ill on this business trip, and was taking various medications and drinking a considerable amount of alcohol; on the return flight of several hours, he consumed both antibiotics and a considerable quantity of alcohol, although the precise amount is in dispute.

There are discrepancies in significant information obtained by each psychiatrist, suggesting either that defendant was not being completely honest with one or both, or that one cannot rely on diplomates in forensic psychiatry to obtain the same information from a litigant.

The two doubly certified psychiatrists render diametrically opposed diagnoses and conclusions. Psychiatrist 1 diagnosed "acute organic brain syndrome (toxic) superimposed on acute depressive reaction." Neither of these conditions were found to exist at the time of his examination. He made these diagnoses as of the time of the offense on the basis of historical data. He concluded that defendant's mental state was such that he was incapable of properly judging the accuracy and completeness of the customs declaratory statements nor did he have the capacity to intend to defraud the United States "knowingly and willfully." His conclusions were based to a considerable extent upon side effects that can occur from some of the medications and the consumption of alcohol. Psychiatrist 2, having Psychiatrist 1's report available, disagrees with the diagnosis and conclusion stating, "At the time of the commission of the purported offenses, defendant suffered from no mental disease or defect that impaired his substantial capacity to appreciate the wrongfulness of his conduct or to conform his conduct to the requirements of the law. It is my opinion, based on my interview and the sources that I have read, that no mental disorder, disease or defect prevented defendant from forming the necessary intent to commit the act for which he is charged or from acting willfully and knowingly at the time of the purported offenses." He disagrees with the diagnosis of depression, stating, "Examining the stresses from the information available from defendant and other sources, there is little evidence for even a neurotic degree of depression. He describes himself as being too busy, too obviously enjoying his food and drink and other activities, too proud of his commercial and administrative accomplishments....These are not the activities or moods of a depressed person. He reported no characteristic sleep disturbances. His repeated awakening with cold symptoms or sweating is not the insomnia of depression. His appetite was not disturbed, he had no agitation or psychomotor slowing. And the reported activities that filled his last two days on the trip did not indicate any decreased energy. Any person with a neurotic depression would have several of the above pathological characteristics in addition to the reported feelings of guilt and alteration of mental functions that he claims...defendant did not even describe the elements of a clinically diagnosable neurotic depression and certainly not the more severe psychotic depression." It appears that one or the other of these two doubly certified psychiatrists does not know how to diagnose depression. Note they were using the same data for the most part, with some differences.

Psychiatrist 2 also disputes Psychiatrist 1's contention of impaired mental functioning due to the combination of a cold, medications and alcohol, and provides thirteen references to current medical literature negating any serious impairment of mental functioning as a result of any of these factors individually or in combination. (A defense pharmacologist supported Psychiatrist 1's contention.)

It should be noted that neither of these psychiatrists viewed the case as a marginal or borderline diagnosis. Neither granted any validity to the conclusions of the other. Psychiatrist 1 on cross-examination states his belief that his opinion is very much the correct one and that he advocates it very strongly. Dr. 2's report very clearly states that there is no basis on which 1's diagnosis could have been made. Therefore we are not dealing with a close case of subtle distinction or fine discrimination but rather an out-and-out disagreement in which each expert is strongly convinced that he is correct and that the other is wrong. Therefore, in this instance, one of these two diplomates in both psychiatry and forensic psychiatry has to be wrong. While it is only one example, it does stand as a warning that one should not place a great deal of faith in accuracy of evaluation by virtue of experts' board certifications. The following exchange from the transcript of the testimony may be illustrative:

Q. Well, you're also aware that a diplomate of your forensic psychiatry board disagrees with your opinion, are you not?

A. Yes, I'm quite aware of that.

Q. Now, can you give us an explanation of that, doctor. I mean, how would two equally trained psychiatrists come to exactly opposite conclusions in a case.

A. Well, I believe that 2's opinion is incorrect and improper.

Q. He based his opinion on exactly the same criteria that you did, did he not?

A. Well, I prefer not to say what he based his opinion on because it seems to me in reading his reports that his own conclusions do not justify his opinion and that in his report itself and the information he provides, it seems to me it supports my opinion rather than his own.

Thus, Psychiatrist 1 is saying that given the same facts two certified psychiatrists reach different conclusions. Also, in stating that 2's opinion is incorrect and improper, one is compelled to wonder if 2 would have been board certified had 1 been one of his examiners (which the testimony indicated he was not). In other words, each of these two is saying that the other certified psychiatrist's diagnosis and conclusion are not justifiable.

Under questioning, regarding Psychiatrist 2's use of a computerized MMPI, Psychiatrist 1 asserts that that particular psychological test has problems of reliability. In our opinion, it takes considerable gall for a psychiatrist to charge psychological tests with problems of reliability in the face of an overwhelming quantity of research evidence that psychiatric diagnoses are unreliable. He compounds the situation in response to questions as to which psychological tests would have reliability and that he would rely on, by stating, "Well, I think a properly administered Minnesota Multi-phasic can be reliable, a Rorschach test is reliable, a Wechsler-Bellevue, a Bender Gestalt—all of those tests." As noted in the chapter on psychological tests (see Chapter 13, Volume II), the Rorschach shows serious problems with reliability and certainly has not been established such as to justify a statement "a Rorschach test is reliable." So, on this score also, this doubly certified psychiatrist is simply wrong. Incidentally, the Wechsler-Bellevue had been obsolete for more than 20 years. Apparently, he was not aware that it had been replaced by the WAIS, at the time of his testimony.

CASE 2

This case provides a rare opportunity to observe four board-certified psychiatrists in action on the same case. For purposes of this discussion, they will be designated Psychiatrists 1, 2, 3 and 4. In addition to the traditional ABPN certification, Psychiatrist 1 is also a Diplomate in Forensic Psychiatry. In addition to these four, the case also involved two uncertified psychiatrists who will be designated X and Y. The case also involved a psychologist who is an ABPP and ABFP2 diplomate. His participation will be discussed separately under psychologist cases. Briefly stated, the facts of the case were that defendant, following a not uncommon kind of domestic quarrel over money, which included the usual kind of recitation of past grievances, asked his wife if she was prepared to take the consequences of her most recent act. She responded that there was nothing he could do about it and he responded that he was "not going to have to put up with this shit anymore," went upstairs and got his rifle, came back downstairs and killed his wife with one shot and then went back upstairs and stating, "I'm sorry," shot and killed his son and niece, and fired at his daughter but missed her. He then went back downstairs, placed a long distance call to his sister and had the surviving daughter talk to her, following which he went back upstairs to get a checkbook to give to the daughter and then he called the police and sat on the sofa waiting for them to arrive.

Defendant is a black man who was married to a white woman. He claimed that some years prior to the homicide, while residing in a community that could be described as "red neck," he had been harassed on his job, partly on the basis of the inter-racial marriage. He also claimed teasing and insults from co-workers about his wife being unfaithful. He also claimed his wife had been unfaithful. Some of the psychiatrists concluded that these beliefs were delusions. The examinations were spread out over a period of about six months and during that period the prosecutor was able to develop evidence from a psychiatrist who had seen the couple in marriage counseling a few years prior to the crime that at some point the wife, in fact, did admit to him, and later to defendant, that she had had affairs with the minister of their church and one other individual. He also developed evidence that, in fact, defendant had been teased and harassed by co-workers on his job. Thus defendant's beliefs on these matters were not delusions—they were true. After moving to a new location, defendant had a series of difficulties with employment and apparently developed the idea that there was some kind of plot against him—a belief in which the wife concurred. He held several jobs, but none of them for an extended period of time. However, the prosecution developed evidence from co-workers during the period that he was friendly, although a little on the quiet side, easy to get along with, with a sense of humor and strong interest in sports which he frequently discussed with co-workers. They observed nothing to indicate that he was in any way unusual or that he suffered from any kind of mental disorder.

It should be noted that between the time of the initial examinations and reports and the matter coming to trial, the state changed its insanity test from M'Naughton to ALI. Thus, the clinicians in the case rendered opinions under both tests.

Psychiatrist 1, examining defendant on February 13 and March 23, found that defendant was not psychotic at the time of examination although there was a "paranoid flair" to his thinking. He found defendant psychotic at the time of the crime with the diagnosis of paranoid state at that time. He found that defendant was M'Naughton insane, although he may have known the nature and quality of his acts, and also found that he was insane under the ALI test. Psychiatrist 2, examining on April 15 and April 30, and May 12, found he was psychotic (paranoia) at the time of the examination and "assumes" that he was psychotic (paranoid) at the time of the crime. He found that he was sane under both M'Naughton and ALI. Psychiatrist 3 examining on March 9, April 1, June 9 and June 23 found that he was psychotic at the time of examination, suffering from paranoia but "without symptoms"! He also found that he was actively psychotic at the time of the crime for a period of approximately five minutes during which he committed the homicides. He found him insane under both M'Naughton and ALI.

Psychiatrist 4, examining on August 15 and August 28, found that he was not psychotic and essentially normal at the time of the examination, was not psychotic at the time of the crime and was sane under both M'Naughton and ALI.

Just to round out the picture, Psychiatrist X (apparently not ABPN), examining on September 13 and September 14, found that he was not psychotic at the time of the examination and there were no psychotic symptoms. Regarding the time of the crime, X comes up with the opinion that defendant was not psychotic when he shot his wife but the act of so doing plunged him into a psychotic state (paranoia) so he was psychotic when he shot his son and niece. He found that he was M'Naughton sane regarding all three killings and that he was ALI sane regarding the shooting of the wife but ALI insane regarding the shooting of the son and niece. Psychiatrist Y (apparently not ABPN), examining on August 18 and 29, and September 8, found he was psychotic and paranoid at both the time of examination and the time of the crime and was both M'Naughton and ALI insane.

The psychologist examined defendant on March 2 of the same year and May 6 of the following year. His report of March was available to the psychiatrists at the time they rendered their reports. He rendered no opinion as to psychosis at the time of the crime or sanity under either of the tests and did not render a clear opinion regarding psychosis at the time of examination but notes that diagnoses of paranoid and depressive psychoses are the most common diagnoses associated with defendant's test performance.

Thus, of the four board certified psychiatrists, two found defendant psychotic at the time of the examination and two found him not psychotic; three found him psychotic at the time of the crime, and one found him not psychotic at that time; two found him M'Naughton and ALI sane and two found him M'Naughton and ALI insane.

Thus, in this instance, the board certified psychiatrists demonstrated approximately the same degree of low reliability as is found in 20 to 30 years of research that is cited in Volume I, Chapter 7, at least insofar as the diagnosis at the time of the examination. Three of the four agree he was psychotic at the time of the crime, although one of these states that diagnosis as an "assumption," differing in that manner from the other two who clearly state he was psychotic at the time. One of the others who finds him psychotic at the time of the crime defines the period of psychosis as approximately five minutes as a result of a dissociative re-action, thus also differing to some extent from the others. Regarding the application of their diagnostic findings to the legal tests, Psychiatrists 1 and 3 find him psychotic at the time of the crime and insane under both tests, 2 finds him psychotic at the time of the crime by assumption but nevertheless finds that he was sane under both tests, and 4, finding him not psychotic at any time, finds him sane under both tests. Thus, 50% of the board certified psychiatrists have to be wrong in their diagnosis of defendant at the time of the examination, either 25% or 75% had to be wrong in their diagnosis of his condition at the time of the crime although this reduces to 1/3 or 2/3 wrong if one eliminates Psychiatrist 2, who does not state his opinion firmly. With regard to sanity or insanity under either test, again 50% of the board certified psychiatrists have to be wrong.

During the trial, a set of notes prepared by Psychiatrist 3 for the use of defense counsel came to light. In these notes, 3 advises defense counsel on strategies to be employed, not only with regard to his testimony but that of other experts, including a specific statement as to how to "coach" (his words) one of the other defense experts to deal with certain material. He is also severely critical in these notes of the work of 1; that is, the psychiatrist who is both ABPN and ABFP. He states that 1's examination and report represent an "extreme departure from the standard of practice both in psychiatry and forensic standards." That is, according to this board certified psychiatrist, this other psychiatrist, both board certified and forensic certified, did not even perform an adequate examination. Psychiatrist 4 was quite critical of the work of 3. It might be noted that following defendant's testimony in the trial, 1 and 2 both withdrew from the case apparently on the grounds that defendant's statements at the trial were discrepant with statements he had made to them. Evidently, these two certified psychiatrists, one doubly certified, could not determine as of the time they wrote their reports that they were being misled by defendant. Ergo, they were not able to judge the credibility of his statements. On this issue, defendant's testimony at the trial is most revealing. Defendant was asked about his statements to the psychiatrist about his thoughts before the killings. His responses were as follows:

> Q. Did you tell...the psychiatrist who spoke to you why you did the things that you did?
>
> A. They asked me for an explanation and I gave them one.
>
> Q. Was that explanation your memory of what was going on at the time you acted or an interpretation you were offering as an inference after the fact?
>
> A. It was my interpretation.

Defendant testified that when he spoke to the psychiatrist he had no actual memory of his thoughts before and at the time of commission. The explanations he offered to the psychiatrists were merely his theories about why he would have done such things. The certified psychiatrists were either unaware of or unable to discern this distinction. Defendant was also examined about his thoughts concerning his killing of the two children.

> Q. Before you entered the bedroom had you decided to kill the children?
>
> A. I didn't think of it that way.
>
> Q. Didn't you decide that you would kill the children to spare them from a difficult unpleasant life. Did you think that before you killed them? [Author's note: One psychiatrist had asserted this.]
>
> A. No, I didn't.

At his request, a statement was prepared for the prosecutor detailing deficiencies of data gathering, data consideration, and formation of conclusions of these board certified psychiatrists. That report, too lengthy to reproduce here, ran to over 50 pages. Incidentally, after the trial, the jury described the psychiatric testimony as "worthless."

CASE 3

This is a Workers Compensation case. Claimant, a teacher, was assaulted by some female students who struck her several times. Physical injuries were minor, consisting of a couple of broken fingernails in the scuffle and some bruises. She lost no time from work as a result of this episode but claims that she became more anxious about the school situation, particularly where students of the same group as the assaulters were concerned. She was examined a month after the incident by an internist who found no physical, medical problems but made a diagnosis of anxiety reaction, chronic, mild. She was examined seven months later by Psychiatrist 1 and eleven months later by Psychiatrist 2, both diplomates of the American Board of Psychiatry and Neurology.

Psychiatrist 1 found no evidence of anxiety, tension, agitation or depression. Based on the history obtained, he felt that she had a temporary period of anxiety and feelings of loss of confidence in the administration. However, he states that these symptoms have now completely subsided and at the time of his examination, there were no psychiatric residual symptoms. She stated that she felt no need for psychiatric assistance and had suffered no interruption of her work.

Psychiatrist 2 diagnosed "depressive neurosis with anxiety secondary to assault in the course of her employment and the sequelae in terms of work stress and strain manifested by anxiety, depression, gastrointestinal distress, headaches, sleep disturbances and possible hormonal imbalance." He states that she had become depressed, apathetic and that her self-esteem is greatly impaired. He states that it is clear that her symptoms are in the range of moderate for work disability which seems strange in view of the fact that she lost no time from work.

Once again, the board certified psychiatrists disagree in their diagnosis and conclusions. Therefore, one of them must be wrong. It might be noted that in this instance the evaluations concerned present condition, not a prior mental state, as in the criminal cases (although in Case 2 we may note that there was disagreement as to mental status at the time of the examination also). It should also be noted that this does not appear to be disagreement on a close or ambiguous case. Psychiatrist 2 describes several symptoms. Psychiatrist 1 says there are none of these.

CASE 4

This case involves a series of bank robberies. Defendant was examined by board-certified Psychiatrist 1 and by Psychiatrist 2 who is board certified and also a diplomate in forensic psychiatry. Psychiatrist 1 states, "[defendant] in my opinion shows many manifestations of a chronic schizophrenic illness. He has some disturbance. His affect is flat. His associations are loose. His thinking is concrete. His approach to these instant offenses are manifestations of concrete thinking and his judgment is impaired. He is preoccupied with inner experience. I think that he has a rather elaborate grandiose paranoid delusional system in which he perceives himself as being justified in returning to his wife, and the bank offenses have no real importance to him except as a means of returning to his wife. He has low tolerance to stress. He has been isolated and depressed. He has a great deal of ambivalent feelings towards almost everything including his wife and marriage, and his behavior and thinking is somewhat unpredictable.

"It is my opinion that he has a mental illness, the diagnosis of which is schizophrenia paranoid type."

Psychiatrist 2, however, states, "I found no evidence during my interview with [defendant] nor from the available file of reports and current descriptions of his past history or recent behavior for the diagnosis of a mental disorder."

Both of these certified psychiatrists performed their examinations in a single session, allowing no opportunity to observe differences that might be evident at another time.

CASE 5

This is a case of a man who was injured as a result of the explosion and burning of a truck. When the truck exploded, he was in a shack owned by the construction company he worked for and as a result of the explosion apparently was thrown against a wall. There is no clear evidence that he was rendered unconscious although his statements at times suggested that he may have been unconscious. He was given emergency treatment at a nearby hospital for injuries described as relatively minor, consisting principally of cuts and bruises. None of the three physicians who treated him during the two weeks following the explosion notes any kind of indication of psychiatric problems. However, after these two weeks of treatment, plaintiff's attorney referred him to Psychiatrist 1. The case file contains reports of a large number of physicians, psychiatrists and psychologists. For the purpose of the present discussion, only the reports of four board certified psychiatrists are discussed.

The diagnosis of Psychiatrist 1 is: "1) Anxiety neurosis, posttraumatic manifested by anxiety, depression, phobic fears, disorders of sleep, disorientation, confusion, impaired concentration, forgetfulness and irritability. 2) Rule out psycho-physiologic musculo-skeletal disorder." Psychiatrist 1 initiated treatment for this alleged condition which was continued for a period of two and a half years until the conclusion of the case. While he does not in his report (which is undated) expressly make the diagnosis of post-concussion syndrome or organic brain damage, this diagnosis later became relevant to the case and in his deposition he testifies that he "presumptively" made such a diagnosis even though he had not stated it specifically. More than two years after the accident, he referred plaintiff to a neurologist for performance of an EEG or other tests to ascertain the possibility of brain damage. Thus, according to his own testimony, he continued conventional psychotherapy for treatment of an anxiety neurosis with an individual in whom he had presumptively diagnosed brain damage years earlier. It is difficult to view this as demonstrating in this particular instance a high level of proficiency of psychiatric practice.

Board certified Psychiatrist 2 examined plaintiff about six weeks after Psychiatrist 1. He does not make a formal diagnosis but states that on the basis of his examination he is unable to make a diagnosis of traumatic or post-traumatic neurosis. He has reviewed records of some of the other physicians and notes that one of those who had treated plaintiff on several occasions immediately following the injury indicated that he did not see any psychiatric illness or injury and that he was surprised to find the plaintiff's attorney had referred him to a psychiatrist. He also notes that plaintiff appeared histrionic but did not appear at all depressed or in any particular emotional distress. He states, "His performance on some of the psychological tests could not be considered reliable and could only be explained on the basis of a purposeful attempt to make errors."

Board certified Psychiatrist 3 was an agreed-upon medical examiner who states that he conducted no physical examination nor made use of psychometric tests. He did review reports that were in the file at that time which was approximately fifteen months after the date of the explosion. His diagnosis is "psycho-neurosis, post-traumatic consistent with industrial injury." He does not in any way suggest the possibility of an organic brain syndrome. He indicates that plaintiff showed no major impairment of memory.

Board certified Psychiatrist 4 examined plaintiff two and a half years after the accident. At the time he had available all of the medical and psychiatric records as well as the reports and test results of four different psychologists. He discussed and ruled out all of the various diagnoses that had been made, giving as his final diagnosis "malingering at this time in a person with underlying hysterical personality (of minimal clinical significance) with socio-pathic traits." Past history of hysterical neurosis with transient dissociative or psychotic episodes was possible but not likely. He also states, "If the patient were truly having as much dysfunction in mentation, with unconsciousness, as he said he had, his physicians are required to report him to the local health officer with ultimate review by the department of motor vehicles to determine the patient's eligibility to operate a motor vehicle."

Here again, we see at least two differing opinions among four board certified psychiatrists and more accurately, based on the deposition of Psychiatrist 1, there are really three different opinions. While not using identical terminology, both Psychiatrists 1 and 3 render diagnoses of posttraumatic anxiety neurosis and Psychiatrists 2 and 4 render diagnoses of malingering and no genuine psychiatric disturbance. In addition, Psychiatrist 1 according to his testimony made an additional diagnosis, a presumptive diagnosis of post-concussion syndrome or brain damage which Psychiatrist 3 does not even mention or appear to consider. Which board certified psychiatrists' (or pair of psychiatrists') certification attests to a high degree of accuracy in diagnosis?

In addition, what level of proficiency is indicated in a situation where a psychiatrist has made a presumptive diagnosis of brain damage and initiates treatment and and yet lets more than two years go by without seeing to it that the brain damage diagnosis is subjected to appropriate examination to rule it in or rule it out?

CASE 6

In this case, the plaintiff, a 50-year-old white male, ruptured a muscle in his left arm at work. The incident occurred on March 3rd, and plaintiff committed suicide on March 28th. The claimant in the case is the widow.

A Board certified psychiatrist who had never seen the deceased or the widow testified that this accident triggered what he classified as "involutional depression" and that the suicide was a result of this accident-caused disorder. This diagnosis and conclusion was made more than three years after the publication of DSM-III. The psychiatrist acknowledged that there was no diagnosis "involutional melancholia" or "involutional depression" in DSM-III, but that there was in DSM-II. He conceded that under DSM-III the diagnosis would probably be a "major depression."

However, throughout his testimony, he continues to refer to the diagnosis as "involutional melancholia." He based his diagnosis primarily on reports of the decedent's on-the-job performance which showed him to be rather compulsive and extremely conscientious. He states there is no information indicating any emotional or mental difficulty prior to the injury. However, other data obtained from co-workers report him as being "white as a ghost," "sweating," "having dizziness" several months prior to the accident and that he was extremely socially withdrawn at work, for example, never having lunch with co-workers and always eating by himself. In addition, there is data that, although he did not engage in hunting, he owned a large number of guns. There being no evidence that he collected guns as a hobby, this would seem to indicate at least potential mental disorder. Also, it was reported that in the recent past, he bought a new car and when a minor piece of equipment would not work, he immediately sold it. Again, none of these things is conclusive about mental disorder, but they certainly provide information which would suggest the possibility.

However, the overriding criticism in this instance is attributing the suicide to the accident via the development of the "involutional melancholia." Involutional melancholia in DSM-II (296.0) is described as "a disorder occurring in the involutional period and characterized by worry, anxiety, agitation and severe insomnia." And further "it is distinguished from psychotic depressive reaction (q.v.) in that the depression is not due to some life experience." A similar statement is made with regard to the major heading under which involutional melancholia is listed, which is 296 Major Affective Disorders (Affective Psychosis) where it stated, "The onset of the mood does not seem to be related directly to a precipitating life experience and therefore is distinguishable from Psychotic Depressive Reaction and Depressive Neurosis." Therefore, if the diagnosis is correct, attribution to the accident seems clearly unattainable. This, of course, is in addition to the very questionable act of rendering an opinion on a matter such as this without speaking to the widow who obviously would be a critical source of information, if not the most important source of information concerning the decedent's behavior in the few weeks prior to his suicide, as well as his behavior prior to the accident.

CASE 7

This is a special circumstance, multiple homicide, death penalty case. Defendant went to the home of one of the victims, apparently in regard to a dispute over some property. Defendant shot and killed the victim, with some evidence it may have been in self-defense, the victim having made a threatening gesture. The defendant then kidnapped the victim's wife and one-year-old baby daughter, drove out to the country, parked, took the woman and baby into a wooded area, shot the woman in the head three times, killing her and leaving the baby unharmed next to the mother where both were found the next day by a laborer. Prior to these events, defendant had been charged with sexual molestation of a young boy and was out on bail at the time of these killings. In connection with the sexual misconduct incidents, he was examined by two psychiatrists, one of whom found him suffering from acute depression; the other found no evidence of depression, but diagnosed an anxiety reaction. He was also given an MMPI by a psychologist at that time. This testing will be discussed in connection with a diplomate in forensic psychology whose participation will be discussed below.

In connection with the homicide case, defendant was examined by three psychiatrists and two psychologists. Of the three psychiatrists, one was Board certified and the other two were not. The Board certified psychiatrist made a diagnosis of "clearly chronic paranoid schizophrenia" and concluded that defendant had the capacity to understand his actions and to understand its wrongfulness, but that the actions were the product of his mental illness and were automatic reactions triggered by paranoid perceptions. None of the other four mental health professionals agreed with this diagnosis. Psychiatrist 2 diagnosed a mixed personality disorder with schizoid and paranoid features which he asserted were not disabling. He stated that the psychologist who did the testing for him concurred in this evaluation. Psychiatrist 3 also diagnosed a mixed personality disorder with paranoid, schizoid and borderline features. This psychiatrist described the case as a complex diagnostic problem and indicated that it was debatable that it met the criteria for chronic schizophrenia. While not Board certified, this psychiatrist is a professor of psychiatry at a major university medical school. This psychiatrist also has more than thirty years of experience in the field, has been awarded a research prize by the American Psychiatric Association and has been elected to fellow status in the American Psychiatric Association and also has numerous publications, although none of them are of particular relevance to the diagnosis in the case.

It should also have been noted that Psychiatrist 2, in addition to the personality disorder, gave as the first diagnosis "atypical psychosis with delusions and hallucinations." The significance of this is that, obviously, if there was atypical psychosis then it was not "clearly paranoid schizophrenia" or conversely if it was "clearly paranoid schizophrenia" then a diagnosis of atypical definitely would not apply.

Psychiatrist 3 states that at the time of the shootings, defendant was under personal stress and in that state was acting planlessly, almost randomly or reflexively and was incapable of the mental processes necessary to think over, reflect on, deliberate and weigh the consequences of his actions. Psychiatrist 4 also makes a diagnosis of atypical psychosis stating that the defendant's capacity to premeditate and to form intent to commit a criminal act was substantially diminished. He suggests that for the first shooting, the defendant was fearful for his life and became irrationally concerned that the first victim was plotting to kill him. The first shooting then caused further confusion, so that he was further handicapped at the time of the second murder.

Presumably, then, in order for his capacities to become more diminished, there must have been some capacities available at the time of the first shooting. Psychologist 1, while not making a formal diagnosis, essentially states, "In summary, this patient suffers from a severely disabling, borderline personality disorder of chronic, longstanding duration," so that he apparently is diagnosing a personality disorder. Psychologist 2, who is a diplomate of the American Board of Forensic Psychology, gives the following diagnoses: "Axis I: 302.00 Ego Dystonic Sexual Disorder, 302.20 Pedophilia, 298.90 Intermittent Atypical Psychosis. Axis II: 301.89 Mixed Personality Disorder with Borderline, Schizoid, Paranoid and Dependent Features." He asserts that based on a history of intermittent psychotic episodes, there is sufficient reason to "question" his capability to premeditate first degree murder and indicates that he would be limited in his ability to reason properly about his actions, or to deliberate, and that his capacities were diminished.

Thus, out of a total of six mental health professionals examining the defendant, no one agrees with the Board certified psychiatrist's diagnosis. In general, they make diagnoses that are contradictory in that, for example, one cannot make the diagnosis of atypical psychosis if there is a specific diagnosis that would apply, such as paranoid schizophrenia. Of course, this does not mean that the Board certified psychiatrist was wrong and all the rest were right, inasmuch as they disagreed a good deal among themselves. However, it is notable that at least one of those disagreeing holds an equivalent status to the Board certification in forensic psychology. (This psychologist's work will be discussed at more length, along with other Board certified psychologists below).

CASE 8

This is a personal injury case, in which a Board certified psychiatrist diagnoses plaintiff with "adjustment disorder with mixed emotional features." The psychologist, who is a Diplomate in clinical psychology, does not directly state a diagnosis but states that "the data is most commonly associated with paranoid schizophrenia and related psychotic diagnoses." While this is a comparison of a psychiatrist with a psychologist, both hold the certification or diploma and their diagnoses are about as far apart as one can get. Parenthetically, a third mental health professional, a psychologist who does not possess the diplomate, diagnoses a generalized anxiety disorder and hysterical neurosis, conversion type. While he is not Board certified, he is known to one of the authors to have a considerable amount of experience. All three examinations were conducted within a period of 10 days. Both the psychiatrist and the psychologist saw plaintiff on only one occasion, which generally is not considered good practice in forensic evaluations.

On deposition, the psychiatrist indicates that he has destroyed all notes of his interview, which he states is his customary practice. This seems irresponsible, in view of the fact that this psychiatrist has an extensive forensic practice and therefore must be aware that these notes constitute part of the basis from which his conclusions are drawn, and that both opposing counsel and other experts would be entitled to review this material.

CASE 9

This is a personal injury case, and the psychiatrist is Board certified.

He states that "pertinent to this evaluation is the fact that this man, who has functioned at a high and responsible level all of his adult life, has been unable to work since the accident." However, the records seem to clearly contradict this statement, showing that plaintiff's military history reveals considerable difficulty with authorities, including going

AWOL during the period of his service. This does not seem to indicate a high degree of responsibility "all" of his life. Also, his occupations, other than the military, have been either as a butcher or as a truck driver, which, while certainly respectable occupations, generally do not conform to what most people would think of from the adjective "high level." Therefore, the psychiatrist's statements seem to be misleading in this regard, also.

In his report, the psychiatrist makes repeated references to lowered or impaired self-esteem as a result of the accident. In this regard, it is noted that plaintiff divorced his first wife after one year of marriage after discovering her infidelity—an event that many people would view as impairing a man's self-esteem. He remarried and his second wife requested a separation and divorce shortly before the time of this accident. One would think this second rejection by a wife would also be a cause of lowered self-esteem. We do not believe there is any method by which the psychiatrist could ascertain that any impairment of self-esteem resulted from the accident rather than from these two events. There is virtually no body of knowledge that provides a basis for doing so. Additionally, there is an indication that the plaintiff may have failed in his one attempt to operate his own business—another factor other than the accident which could have caused any supposed loss of self-esteem. However, generally the test material counterindicates low self-esteem. That is, on a questionnaire, plaintiff answers "TRUE" to each of the following statements: "I do not feel like a failure;" "I don't feel particularly guilty;" "I don't feel disappointed in myself;" "I don't feel I am any worse than anybody else." These statements seem to be flatly contradictory of an evaluation of low or impaired self-esteem.

The psychiatrist saw plaintiff on only one occasion which, as previously noted, is not good practice, particularly in a forensic situation, since the particular day the person was seen may not be a representative one.

The psychiatrist notes that plaintiff has gone into social withdrawal, but on the MMPI, his score on the social introversion scale is low, meaning that he is not suffering from social withdrawal, assuming that the test scores have any meaning. Certainly, a low score is the opposite of what one would expect from someone who is socially withdrawn.

DISCUSSION

Unfortunately, only five of the cases cited above are ones in which we have participated in which two or more board certified psychiatrists were involved. Therefore, they are in the nature of case reports or case studies which do not constitute scientific research. In any event the sample is much too small to allow for generalization (although it is as large as or larger than several of the samples of various diagnostic categories reported in the preliminary field studies reported in support of reliability in DSM-III). With this caveat in mind, the following statements are justified. In 100% of the cases with which we have had contact, there was serious disagreement between or among the board certified psychiatrists. No cases were encountered in which there was not disagreement. These results are entirely consistent with the research encompassing several decades showing low reliability among psychiatric diagnoses (see Chapter 7, Volume I) concerning psychiatrists generally, board certified or not. These results are also consistent with the findings of Tarter et al. (see Chapter 8, Volume I) wherein five psychiatrists, four of whom were board certified, working in pairs, disagreed on major diagnostic category—psychosis, neurosis or personality disorder—50% of the time. As the cases we have described took place in the late 1970's and early 1980's, they can be taken as further evidence along with the previous years of research that reliability of psychiatric diagnosis is low even when performed by board certified psychiatrists. Low reliability connotes low validity. As can be seen from the cases above, half of the 14 board certified psychiatrists (actually there were only 13 individuals as one of the psychiatrists took part in two of the cases) have to be wrong in their opinion regarding the legal issues involved, and with regard to diagnosis, at least half had to be wrong, although it is possible that all were wrong.

It is still more unfortunate that only one of the cases involved two diplomates in forensic psychiatry. However, this is only to be expected in view of the fact that this is a relatively new diploma. There are only a small number of psychiatrists so certified and they are scattered throughout the country. It is likely that it will be years before a body of actual case data will develop involving two or more such diplomates. In the absence of such data, the case we have reported represents, so far as we know, the only publication of material of any kind on this issue and, while it is certainly far too meager to draw any firm conclusions, at least it can be said that this one case indicates that reliability and validity as between diplomates in forensic psychiatry does not at first blush appear to be any better than that for other board-certified psychiatrists, which does not appear to be better than that for psychiatrists in general, which has over the past several decades been found to be low. We might add that although there were no other cases of two forensic psychiatry diplomates reported here, two of the other cases involve at least one forensic psychiatry diplomate with other traditionally board-certified psychiatrists, and disagreement continues to be high. Thus, looking at Case 4, it can be seen that the disagreement between the forensic diplomate and the traditional diplomate were not on the application of diagnostic findings to a legal issue but went to the heart of the matter, which was complete disagreement as to the presence or absence of any mental disorder, let alone one of the seriousness described by the first psychiatrist. This is a clinical and not a forensic disagreement.

Based on the foregoing, there is no justification for according to traditional or forensic certified psychiatrists a high degree of accuracy in their evaluations, nor is there any justification for according to them a higher degree of proficiency than that found among the non-certified psychiatrists.

We have seen, in addition to the above cases, some other cases in which we consulted in which there was at least one board-certified psychiatrist and we found numerous deficiencies of examination and/or conclusion drawing. These deficiencies appeared generally equal in quality and quantity to errors and deficiencies found in the work of non-certified psychiatrists in cases on which we have consulted.

BOARD CERTIFIED PSYCHOLOGISTS:
ILLUSTRATIVE EXAMPLES

As with certified psychiatrists, the number of cases on which we have consulted that involved ABPP diplomates or ABFP diplomates has been very small. None of the cases we have consulted on involved more than one diplomate in psychology so we lack opportunity to illustrate possible low reliability or disagreement among board certified psychologists. However, in each of the cases, in our opinion, the quality of the performance is such as to raise serious doubts as to the level of proficiency required to obtain ABPP and ABFP diplomate status or at least doubts that such credentials ensure adequate performance in actual cases. None of the psychologists is in any material way distinguishable from other diplomates.

CASE 1

This case is an application for change of custody of one child from the mother to the father following the father's remarriage. The psychologist involved in the case is a diplomate of the American Board of Professional Psychology (ABPP) and a diplomate of the American Board of Forensic Psychology (ABFP) and, in addition, has an impressive set of other credentials.

Several features of the psychologist's report point to bias in favor of the father. The influence of examiner biases in psychological assessment is well known and well documented and this portion of the material is presented to illustrate that diplomates are not immune from it. Such biases may arise out of identification with or shared value systems with one litigant as contrasted to another litigant. In this case there appeared to be shared value systems between the psychologist and the father, as indicated by the fact that both have earned Ph.D.'s (in different fields), both are very much achievement oriented, as indicated by their accomplishments, and as indicated by the similarity of their choices as to areas of residence (Eastern, metropolitan) in contrast to the mother's choice of area of residence (Western, small city). The following objective material indicating bias appears in the report.

(1) Throughout the report when using the proper names of the litigants, psychologist refers to the father as "Mr." but refers to the mother by her first name, indicating a considerable difference in the status he accorded to each.

(2) He saw the father first (there is nothing wrong with that) but then saw the father a second time before seeing the mother at all, thus obtaining a great deal of negative information about the mother before ever having seen her. He spent a total of five hours with the father and less than two hours with the mother, again resulting in obtaining considerably more information from the father than the mother. For example, while his report shows considerable information concerning business successes accomplished by the father, there is nothing in his report or notes to indicate that he obtained similar information concerning the lesser, but still considerable business successes of the mother.

(3) His report contains no mention of possible disturbance for the child resulting from a change of residence and consequent upheaval in his life. It is well known that a change of residence can be upsetting to normal children even in a stable and intact family situation. Thus an unbiased and fair report attempting to illuminate positive and negative aspects of the change of custody would at least require some attention and discussion of this issue.

(4) The psychologist states that it is difficult to evaluate the mother's statements because she is motivated to explain away or counteract data which might be favorable to the father or negative to her. He does not, however, attribute any such motivations to the father in regard to his many negative statements concerning the mother or positive statements concerning himself, although almost anyone with ordinary life experience, even without training as a psychologist, would be aware of the existence of such motives in both parties in a custody action.

(5) In his report, the psychologist gives weight to the advantages of the two-parent home of the father but does not deal with some of the risks and serious questions that exist about that home in this specific case. He does not deal with the fact that this is a very new marriage and thus one cannot know how well it is going to work out with the possibility that there may be yet another broken marriage and broken home with which the child might have to cope. This possibility is heightened by the

fact that the father has already been involved in two previous unsuccessful marriages, and it is striking that having spent nearly five hours with
the father the psychologist mentions no exploration whatsoever of the
reasons behind the previous marital failures. This omission is highlighted
because the report does deal with the stepmother's previous, unsuccessful marriages by offering several reasonable explanations for the failure
of her marriages. Even without that information it is widely believed that
in the early period of a marriage there may be stresses and strains of adaptation which might create problems for a new child coming into that
situation and might even be aggravated by the presence of the child. The
report does not deal with this issue. Further, the psychologist's report
does not indicate in any way that he made any inquiry into possible
problems in regard to privacy in sleeping arrangements in the father's
home, which has only three bedrooms for the parents, the stepmother's
daughters, (one a teenager who likely would want a private bedroom),
and the boy. If this is not a result of bias, it at least seems to overlook this
question.

(6) In his report, the psychologist engages in speculations which tend
to diminish factors favorable to retention of custody by the mother. In
particular, he states that the child's obvious affectional behavior with the
mother may stem from the fact that she had been absent for a period of
time or he suggests that this may have been a response to a "fleeting
nonverbal cue" on her part which seems to diminish the significance of
this affectional behavior which might favor the mother and is clearly
speculative.

While each of the above factors by itself may not be sufficient to establish bias, together they present a strong case that the psychologist was
biased in favor of the father and either was not aware of his bias or chose
to ignore it.

In addition to the problem of bias, there are a number of technical errors of procedure, scoring and interpretation in the testing by this doubly
certified psychologist. There are at least four errors in the scoring of the
Wechsler Intelligence Scale for Children-Revised (WISC-R). These are
clear cut errors according to instructions and examples given in the manual for the test. They are not arguably matters of judgment as is sometimes the case where the manual is not clear or where the responses do
not fit any of the examples given. On the Comprehension subtest of the
WISC-R, the manual and proper procedure call for an examiner, in case
the child has given one idea to a question which requires two ideas for a
two-point score, to question the child to see if he can give a second idea,
which would then warrant the two-point score instead of a one-point
score. Normal convention in recording the test is that when a question is
asked, it is indicated by the letter (Q) with a subsequent recording of the

response to the question. The absence of any such indication on the test form suggests that this procedure was not followed and thus the test was incorrectly administered. Based on the erroneous scoring, the psychologist derives an IQ of 118 for the boy which he describes as "near the superior range," which he then interprets as a factor favorable to placing the boy with his father, an individual of obviously high IQ. Correct scoring would place the IQ at 114 which, if one is going to indulge in such verbal stretching as "near" the superior range, one could then argue is closer to the average range (90-109) than the superior range (120-129). One could thus argue this would be a factor in favor of placement with the mother rather than the father whose highly discrepant intelligence might create a problem for the boy (we are not advancing that argument, we are stating it simply because it would follow from the kind of logic that this psychologist seemingly used).

In addition, this doubly-certified psychologist is wrong about the significance of several subtest scores. Thus, he describes scale scores of 9 on some subtests as being lower than normal and a scale score of 11 on another subtest as being higher than normal. This is not congruent with the psychometric properties of this test. The arithmetic mean for each subtest scaled score is 10; however, it is well known that "normal" is a range rather than a point. Thus, most authorities view scores falling between 8 to 12 as being within the normal range. In addition, it is well known that some fluctuation of scores is expected in all children attributable to chance alone and there is a statistic for measuring the operation of chance which is called the standard error of measurement. In the case of the WISC-R subtests, the standard error of measurement is greater than 1 for each of the subtests, therefore a deviation of one point from the arithmetic mean—10—cannot be considered anything other than within the normal range and no significance can be attributed to scores of 9 or 11; that is, such scores are not considered higher or lower than normal. The psychologist cites research to the effect that the below-normal scores such as those he described, and above normal scores such as those he described, are characteristic of children with reading disability and, partly on this basis, concludes that the boy in the case was a child with a reading disability. Correct interpretation of the scores would have required him to describe the boy's performance on the WISC-R as not similar to that of disabled readers. (Another test the psychologist gave did indicate a reading problem. However, the point here is that correctly interpreted, the WISC-R scores do not support the findings on the other test.)

This doubly certified psychologist administered no psychological tests to the father, the mother or the stepmother. While the method of assessment is a matter of the professional judgment of the psychologist, the principal technique of assessment in which psychologists are trained is that of psychological testing. The merit of such testing is obviously open to question, but it is quite unusual in our experience in custody matters for a psychologist's opinion to be offered without any tests administered to the parental figures. More importantly, there is no indication in the notes or the report that any independent evaluation of the stepmother was performed; that is, there is no indication that she was seen individually, although she would obviously be a person of considerable importance in the event that the child came to live in the father's home. She was seen briefly with the child. However, one must be aware that some different information or attitudes might become apparent in a private, individual session with the stepmother.

What can one say about diplomate status from this case? It is of course true that it is only one case. Still, there is such a variety and such a number of errors and deficiencies that if this was a graduate student in psychology or one doing his internship, it is quite possible that he would be sent back to redo the whole thing. We have lectured or taught courses in testing and in psychological assessment and we would not give a passing grade to a student who performed in this manner. Unless this psychologist is markedly deviant from other diplomates (and there is no reason to believe so), one is compelled to wonder what the requirements for attaining the diploma are or what degree of skill is measured by the examinations. Possibly, when being examined for the diploma, psychologists exert a great deal of care in their work but abandon this level of care in their everyday practice. (For various reasons, a highly unusual approach was taken in this case. The decision was made to inform the psychologist prior to trial of the various deficiencies described above. To his credit, he took the critique with very good grace, acknowledged several of the deficiencies and agreed to perform a re-evaluation of the material. Based on this re-evaluation and additional information about the father, he changed his conclusions and recommendations.)

CASE 2

This is the same case as Psychiatrist Case 2, in which the black man slew his wife, one child and a niece, firing at, and missing, his daughter. It should be pointed out that several of the psychiatrists who found psychopathology relied in part on this psychologist's testing and findings. The psychologist holds both the ABPP and ABFP diplomas. It should also be noted that this is a case in which, following the verdict, the jury indicated that the expert evidence had been worthless. The reader should be aware that in connection with a motion all of the experts had available to them the author's written statement in support of the motion and his testimony in court in support of the motion. The psychologist acknowledged reading the statements in connection with the motion but denied that he had read any portions dealing specifically with his report, although in fact the statement did in part deal specifically with his report. In addition, he acknowledged that, while he was not present when the author testified, his psychological assistant was present and reported on the testimony to him, thus he was forearmed as to the nature of cross-examination—a situation relatively unusual in criminal cases. This psychologist examined defendant twice, once about a month after the killings and again over a year later, shortly before the commencement of trial. He wrote a report after the first examination and submitted a set of handwritten notes after the second. The psychologist was not a forensic novice, having testified in several cases prior to this one.

The author had available not only the report of the first examination, the notes on the second examination and all test data, but the transcript of the psychologist's testimony in trial as well. It is necessary to go into an extended discussion and considerable detail in order to demonstrate the quality of the performance by this double diplomate.

The psychologist's report of the first examination indicates that the examination was conducted over several hours in one session. He indicates the procedures administered as a clinical interview, MMPI, Rorschach Ink Blot Test, Thematic Apperception Test (TAT), Wechsler Adult Intelligence Scale (WAIS) (brief form), Wechsler Memory Scale and Bender Visual Motor Gestalt test. His report indicates that he had received no information concerning the instant offense. In his testimony, he indicates that the interview was fairly brief. In his report, information obtained from the interview is contained in a brief paragraph consisting of five sentences and includes nothing about the severe marital problems that are described by every other expert that was involved in this case. Either the psychologist failed to obtain this highly significant information or did not feel it was important enough to include in his report. The latter possibility seems most unlikely as it would be obvious to almost anyone in performing a psychological evaluation that severe marital problems would be more important to report than the fact that defendant has some sisters and brothers. This information takes up one of the five sentences. Thus, it seems that this diplomate psychologist failed in the interview to obtain significant information.

Regarding the WAIS, he administered only five of the 11 subtests that comprise the WAIS—Information, Comprehension, Similarities, Digit Symbol and Picture Arrangement. Appropriately, because of this incomplete administration, he did not compute a verbal, performance, or full-scale IQ. On the second testing, a year later and shortly before the trial, he administered the full WAIS. When confronted on cross-examination with the partial administration on the first testing and the contrast between the partial administration in the first test and the full administration of the WAIS on the second testing, he offered the explanation that his understanding of the assignment in the first testing was merely to assess defendant in terms of mental retardation or brain damage. We now quote from his report of the first examination:

> My specific role was to administer psychological tests for a *comprehensive evaluation* of (defendant's) *psychological and intellectual functioning.* (italics ours)

Testimony showed that the referral letter from the attorney stated, "Please perform the following testing, one, complete psychological battery, two, personality assessment." The psychologist testified that as a result of a telephone conversation with lawyer, he felt the battery was adequate. However, at another point he testified his role included assessment of defendant's personality. This testimony seems to contradict his assertion that the task on the first testing was merely to rule out intellectual deficiency or brain damage. In addition, in the report roughly half a page is devoted to discussion of intellectual functioning, concluding that defendant's intellect and memory are adequate and indicating no evidence of brain damage or neuropsychological impairment. Thus, if his understanding of his role was as he testified, that would have completed the report. However, he then goes on to devote a full page to personality functioning, thus indicating that he in fact did more than assess brain damage or mental deficiency. Also he did not give a neuropsychological battery as one would expect in an assessment for brain damage. To give the TAT, a test hardly regarded as a means for assessing brain damage, and not a neuropsychological battery does not make sense to us. Thus, we find his explanation on cross-examination to justify the incomplete administration of the WAIS difficult to accept.

In response to a question as to why he did a more complete administration of the WAIS on the second testing, his first response is, "I had the time." As this is in response to a request to distinguish the two situations, the only conclusion we can come to is that he did not have the time on the first administration. Arguably, if there was not time to do a proper administration of the test, he should have declined the assignment rather than to do an incomplete testing. Also, there were discrepancies of as much as six scaled scores between the two administrations on some of the subtests he had administered. When questioned as to whether this raises a question of the test's reliability, he states it would not cause him to question it because he knows the reliability of the test is quite high. Actually, the reliability of the full scale and the verbal and performance IQ's are quite high, but for some of the subtests of the WAIS they are relatively low. In particular, two of the subtests he administered had reliability coefficients of 0.74 and 0.64, meaning they are below even the more liberal standard for test reliability. Thus, his statement seems to convey an incorrect impression relative to the subtests he had administered in the first testing.

His administration of the Rorschach was incomplete. He administered only that portion of the procedure called the "free association" or "performance proper." This is the part of the test where the subject states what the ink blots look like to him. However, nearly all Rorschach systems and authorities indicate this should be followed by a second part called "the inquiry." In this part, the psychologist determines from the subject what parts of the blot he was using for his percept and what features of the blot, called "determinants," such as color or shading or shape, played a role in the percept. This is essential for scoring of the Rorschach to be accomplished. It should be understood that the Rorschach is used both qualitatively (content of responses, sequence of responses, quality of verbalization) and quantitatively (numbers and proportions of various locations and determinants used, for example), and that nearly all systems require scoring and computing of relationships between different quantitative aspects of the subject's performance. In this case, the psychologist attempts to justify incomplete procedure by citing one authority with regard to simply using the test qualitatively. This would be in direct contrast to the system of Klopfer which at the time was one of the most widely used by psychologists and in direct contrast to the statements of Exner whose system the psychologist says he uses. The Exner system requires inquiry and Exner states in quite strong language (see Chapter 10, Psychological Tests) that the Rorschach administrator or interpreter who ignores all of the components of the test including the scoring and scoring structure, is negligent in his work, offers a less than complete service to the client, and abuses the process of Rorschach assessment.

To compound his error, after he had properly administered the second Rorschach, he went back and scored the first Rorschach. This is inappropriate because you cannot accurately score a Rorschach without having performed the inquiry, for there is no way of knowing for sure what characteristics of the blot the subject was using, all of which enter into the scoring procedure. However, even with this questionable scoring of the first Rorschach, it was quite clear that approximately half of the defendant's responses were different from the first testing to the second, changing the quantitative proportions and requiring different interpretations. Nonetheless, this double diplomate testified that the differences from one testing to another were not material.

With regard to the MMPI, which he administered only on the first testing but not the second, he asserted that race was not an issue in utilization of the MMPI and cited four studies to the effect that when education level is controlled, there are no racial differences. This assertion ignores the substantial number of studies which found differences both in MMPI scores and in behavioral correlates of the scores in a number of other studies based on racial differences, even when education level was controlled. One of the references he cites is the *Annual Review of Psychology* referring to the study of Davis indicating that racial differences disappear when education is controlled, but omits the concluding line of the discussant's paragraph which states this is an issue which requires more research. Thus, the literature establishes that this issue is in doubt (see Chapter 16, above, on Challenging the Assessment of Special Groups, in which we cite more than forty studies establishing that there is a definite issue on this matter.)

In his report of the first testing, in the section titled Personality Functioning, he uses, virtually verbatim, a report he had received from one of the computerized MMPI interpretation services. However, he does this without attribution; that is, he does not indicate in his report that these are the statements of the computer service rather than statements that he wrote himself. This may seem minor, but a user of the report is entitled to know where the material of the report came from, that is, to know if the psychologist did not do the interpretation himself. The user is entitled to know which of the many computerized services did the evaluation, as some are more reputable than others. The psychologist knew that his report was going to be used by one or more psychiatrists who were also involved in this matter. If, for example, one of them had been the psychiatrist in Case 1, the psychiatrist above who made negative statements concerning computerized MMPI's, it would seem likely that such a psychiatrist being so informed might have discarded those findings rather than using them. He is at least entitled to know the source of the interpretation.

However, in view of the nearly verbatim use of the computerized report, this double diplomate psychologist made one highly significant deletion. The psychologist at the conclusion of his report states, "diagnostic impression: diagnosis of depressive and paranoid psychosis are the most common with this pattern of personality characteristics." That is word for word the diagnostic impression stated in the computerized report. However, the computerized report contains an additional sentence: "HOWEVER THIS PROFILE IS MORE AMBIGUOUS THAN MOST" (capitals ours). It would be difficult to find a clearer statement of doubt concerning the diagnosis, yet this double diplomate psychologist saw fit to include nearly everything else from the computerized report (except the portion devoted to treatment considerations) but to delete this extremely important qualifying statement. It should be noted that he testified that he sent a copy of the computerized report along with his.

However, one wonders if the psychiatrist seeing the almost verbatim duplication would read the Program report to the point where the statement of ambiguity is made. This would seem highly questionable, standing by itself. However, it takes on added significance because in his testimony this diplomate psychologist states that none of the other tests indicated a psychosis; therefore, the diagnostic impression he rendered had to come only from the MMPI which, according to the computerized report, is ambiguous. It would seem inappropriate to base a diagnosis of psychosis on a test that is "ambiguous" in the face of several other tests which do not reveal a psychosis, particularly when some of the tests, such as the Rorschach, are often viewed by clinicians as being sensitive in revealing psychosis.

The psychologist testified under oath that he scored the MMPI. The profile shows after "Scorer's Initials" the initials of his psychological assistant, not his. We do not know the assistant's qualifications but the jury would seem entitled to know if the scoring was done by someone who was not a licensed Ph.D. psychologist, if that is actually the case.

We do not view this double diplomate psychologist's performance in this matter as showing a particularly high or a very superior degree of proficiency.

CASE 3

In this case the psychologist is an ABPP Diplomate in clinical psychology. He enjoys an excellent reputation among his colleagues, has been on the faculty at major universities, has an active involvement in forensic work and not infrequently receives referrals for psychological evaluations from the courts. His particular area of expertise is with children and adolescents.

The case at hand involves an eighteen-year-old male charged with a felony.

The psychologist saw the defendant on only one occasion. His report states that he examined the defendant by means of an interview, Wechsler Adult Intelligence Scale, Draw-A-Person technique, Rorschach Inkblot technique, and the Minnesota Multiphasic Personality Inventory (MMPI).

As this examination was conducted in late 1983, it is noted first of all that in employing the WAIS instead of the revised version, the WAIS-R, which was published in 1980, he was using an obsolete version of the test. Obviously, the publishers of this test published the revision as a means of remedying deficiencies known to exist in the original WAIS. Therefore, this Board certified psychologist was using an obsolete testing instrument when a current one was available. Even then, he did not administer the test correctly. One error was discontinuing the Information subtest after four consecutive errors, although the manual is very clear that the test should not be discontinued until there are five consecutive errors. This is of some importance because in his report the psychologist makes a point of the fact that this young man's fund of information was below his general level of intelligence, as indicated on other subtests. Thus, because of the error of administration, that statement is unjustifiable, because had he gone on with the items there is no way of knowing whether the young man might have obtained a higher score, had he been given the required opportunity to do so. The psychologist also commits a serious violation of guidelines in the manual by giving only four of the six Verbal subtests and four of the five Performance subtests and then going on to compute a Verbal I.Q., a Performance I.Q., and a Full Scale I.Q., although the manual is very clear on this point, stating (p. 31), "Full Scale Scores should always be based on at least five Verbal tests and four Performance tests." A graduate student in psychology who did not follow this instruction might well fail the course in testing.

On the MMPI, he appears to have administered a short form as there are only four hundred and thirty-five items completed. While these may have represented omissions by the subject, because most of the omissions occur in the last half of the test, it is more typical of a short form. However, in his test report, he does not indicate that a short form was used. Nor did he in the case of the WAIS, above, indicate that it was a short or incomplete version of the WAIS that was employed. To compound this problem, he incorrectly transfers scores from the MMPI answer sheet to the profile sheet on Scale 6 (Paranoia). On the answer sheet he indicates that the raw score on Paranoia is 11, but when he records it on the profile sheet, he records it as 17. This makes the Paranoia Scale one of the two scales for this young man which are above the T-score of 70 required to be in the pathological range, which almost undoubtedly played a role in the ultimate diagnosis of Schizophrenia with Paranoid features. The score of 11, which was the true score, actually leaves the young man in the average range on this scale.

He makes a diagnosis of Schizophrenia, Simple Type, with Paranoid features. Note that DSM-III appeared in January of 1980 and that this examination was conducted 3-1/2 years later and there is no such diagnosis as Schizophrenia, Simple Type in DSM-III. This diagnosis does appear in DSM-II which, of course, was obsolete and outdated at the time this report was written. Furthermore, even if DSM-II had still been in effect, the young man does not meet the criteria for this disorder as defined in DSM-II 2.295.0 Schizophrenia, Simple Type: "This psychosis is characterized chiefly by a slow and insidious reduction of external attachments and interests and by apathy and indifference leading to impoverishment of interpersonal relations, mental deterioration and adjustment on a lower level of functioning." In point of fact, the boy got in trouble, at least partially, because of his very close attachment to an older man and because of a great deal of interest in sexual activity with minors. Whatever problems he may have had, they were not manifested by "reduction of external attachments and interests" or by "apathy and indifference." He might well have avoided the serious trouble he wound up in had he been so afflicted. In any event, without going further into the facts of the case, it is clear that he does not meet the requirements of this disorder which, according to DSM-III, no longer existed at the time the diagnosis was made.

To his credit, this diplomate did state in response to a question, "There is absolutely no way to divine the state of mind of anyone at the time of the crime. To do so is pure mind reading."

CASE 4

This is the same case discussed previously involving a multiple homicide with a trial for the death penalty under special circumstances, the case in which the defendant shot and killed a man and then took the wife and small baby out in the country and shot the wife three times in the head. This discussion involves the psychologist, who is a diplomate of the American Board of Forensic Psychology. His report asserts that he extensively interviewed defendant, as well as administering a "variety of clinical and forensic tests." In the attachment to his report there are MMPI answer sheets and profile, the Shipley Institute of Living Scale (vocabulary tests and abstraction tests), and an apparent verbatim recording of defendant's responses to eight TAT cards, and nothing else. Unless there are some other tests which this psychologist administered which were not included with his materials (which itself would raise questions about his ethics), there is nothing here that could be called a forensic test nor have we ever heard anyone either in print or otherwise refer to any of these three tests as forensic tests. Based upon this data that we see, it seems to indicate that there was a misrepresentation of what had been done by mislabelling one or more of these tests as a "forensic" test. The entire assessment was performed on one date, which then would have included the extensive interviewing as well as the three tests administered. This, in general, violates the understanding that any person should be evaluated on more than one occasion simply to determine whether or not something was operating on a given day which may have affected the way he responded. He states that defendant has "never" been able to adjust socially, educationally or vocationally. This is patently wrong based on recorded historical data concerning the defendant, which shows that he served in the military service for four years and also held another job for three years. These were some years prior to the crime at hand; however, it is simply patently wrong to use the word "never" in connection with his vocational adjustment. He states in his report, quite clearly, that the defendant has a severe borderline or mixed personality disorder with occasional psychotic breaks which, however, quickly clear and that such patients "do not present with long-term psychotic symptomatology as seen in schizophrenic disorder," thus placing himself in direct contradiction to Psychiatrist 1, the Board certified psychiatrist in the case.

He gives a diagnosis on Axis I of 302.00 "Ego-Dystonic Sexual Disorder" which either states a diagnosis which does not exist in DSM-III or fails to use the language of DSM-III in giving the diagnosis. In DSM-III, 302.00 is "Egodystonic Homosexuality." However, it should be understood that this is a report intended to be used by other people and that the connotation of a sexual disorder is quite different from the connotation of a homosexual disorder, so the reader would be misled. This report runs only slightly over a page in length, and one would think that a "diplomate" would be able to read it carefully enough to see that the correct label was used. Also, of the other five mental health professionals (plus an additional two who examined the defendant with regard to the child molesting incident) none came up with the diagnosis of any kind of homosexual disorder, including Psychiatrist 1, the Board certified psychiatrist. The psychologist gives no basis for his conclusion of a homosexual disorder.

On the MMPI profile sheet, he erroneously writes a code number, 78-245, which indicates that the highest score was on Scale 7, the next highest on Scale 8, with the grouping of the next higher scores being on Scales 2, 4 and 5. Actually, the defendant's scores show a T-score of approximately 90 on Scale 7, so that one is correctly stated. But, the next highest score is a T-score of 77 on Scale 2 followed by T-scores of 76 for Scales 4 and 5, and then a T-score of 74 for Scale 8, so that the code should have read 7-2458 rather than 78-245. Aside from any differences in interpretation which might flow from different codes, the fact of making an error of this kind hardly suggests a high level of performance.

It is also noted that he is the only one of the mental health professionals who makes a diagnosis of "Pedophilia" although it is noted that according to Psychiatrist 1, defendant has vehemently denied the child molestation charge and has not come to trial or been convicted on that charge. Thus, it is once again difficult to see where the psychologist gets this diagnosis unless he has, on his own, tried and convicted the defendant of that charge, or the defendant has admitted it to him (which would be in considerable contrast to what he apparently did with Psychiatrist 1). Also, according to the criteria in DSM-III, it is doubtful that one incident of this kind would qualify anyone for a diagnosis of Pedophilia even if it actually occurred.

CASE 5

In this case, the psychologist is an ABPP Diplomate in clinical psychology. He does not hold the Diplomate in either forensic psychology or clinical neuropsychology. Plaintiff is a young woman who alleges negligence in the administration of anesthesia during the delivery of her baby daughter, which required severe emergency measures and apparently resulted in clearly severe impairment of the baby, both mental and physical. Approximately two years after this event, she is seen by a Board certified psychiatrist who diagnoses her as having (1), Major Affective Disorder, Chronic and Severe and also (2), Organic Affective Syndrome. It might be noted that according to DSM-III, these are incompatible diagnoses, as the manual states at page 212, "Only by excluding organic etiology can one make the diagnosis of a major depressive episode." On page 206, the manual states, "These major affective episodes are not diagnosed if the affective episode is due to an organic mental disorder or if it is superimposed on schizophrenia." And on page 117, regarding Organic Affective Syndrome, the manual states, "The clinical phenomenology of this syndrome is the same as that of a manic or major depressive episode." Under Differential Diagnosis, again on page 117, the manual distinctly states, "in affective disorders, no specific organic factor can be demonstrated."

Thus, this Board certified psychiatrist appears to be unfamiliar with the requirements of the diagnoses as stated in DSM-III, and sees the plaintiff in treatment involving both psychotherapy and medication for seven months before referring her for psychological testing.

The psychologist in his report shows that he is aware of the psychiatrist's diagnoses of depression and organic affective disorder by making specific reference to them. In view of this fact, it seems highly questionable that he elected to interview the plaintiff and perform an extensive series of neuropsychological tests all in one day, since people with depressive disorders tend to tire readily. This is in addition to the usual problems associated with drawing conclusions about an individual after having seen them on one occasion only. He gives no tests, such as the MMPI, to evaluate the nature and extent of any possible psychopathology or personality disorder that would not be organically based. Although this evaluation was done several years after the publication of the WAIS-R, he administers the WAIS which could be viewed as obsolete at that time. Plaintiff obtains a Full Scale I.Q. of 93, which he describes as in the "low average range," although the WAIS manual very specifically states that 90-109 is average and does not make a distinction between a

93 and a 106. His language, however, would suggest that he is really placing her in the "dull normal" category, although she does not belong there. For example, in the manual for the WAIS-R the term "low average" applies to I.Q's of 80-89, clearly below the plaintiff's level, and the manual similarly states that "low average" corresponds to the term "dull normal" in the WAIS manual. So, on this ground he has misclassified her descriptively.

Her Verbal I.Q. is 95 and her Performance I.Q. is 91, which he notes are not significantly different. He also states that her "WAIS subtests were performed fairly consistently, although some variability was observed within many of the verbally based subtests, which may well have been related to problems in verbal retrieval and expression." Inspection of the WAIS shows that there is less inter-subtest variability on the verbal subtests than on the performance subtests, and that the intra-test variability is about the same for the verbal as for the performance, so that he seems here to be stretching the data to justify a conclusion of some brain dysfunction. Even his statement "may well have been related" indicates that he is speculating in the direction favorable to the side that hired him. He refers to mild difficulties in arithmetic calculations revealed in one test, thus leaving the reader with the impression that this woman has some impairment performing calculations. Perusal of all the data indicates only one possible source from which this statement could be drawn: she miscalculated one out of six arithmetic items on the Aphasia Screening Test, on which she was asked to compute 17 X 3, which she answered as 52. Otherwise, she completed the other five problems, some of which are considerably easier and some of which are of comparable difficulty, but more significantly, she obtained a scale score of 9 on the Arithmetic subtest of the WAIS. This score places her very clearly in the average and not impaired range, and clearly not impaired inasmuch as the scale score of 9 is her average scaled score on the verbal subtests of the WAIS, and is entirely consistent with her I.Q. level as measured by that test. It would thus seem clearly erroneous to leave any statement in the report indicating or suggesting impairment of arithmetic calculation unless one simply wants to note the fact that she did make this one mistake, but to rectify any impression by indicating that in all other respects her performance of arithmetic calculations was at the expected level and, therefore, there is no impairment indicated in that function.

It is also noted that the psychologist did not administer the tests himself, but had them administered by someone who is not listed in the Directory of Psychologists and presumably would be either a secretary or a psychological assistant, but in any event, not someone fully qualified for this task.

CASE 6

The psychologist in this case is a Diplomate of the American Board of Forensic Psychology. Although he lists his main field as Clinical Psychology in the Directory of the American Psychological Association, his Ph.D. is actually in Counseling Psychology. (The differences in these two fields are described in the Part 1 of this Chapter). He lists his specialties as Psychotherapy and Psychodiagnosis. Inasmuch as the case at hand involves a neuropsychological assessment, it is noted that the Directory does not list neuropsychology as one of his specialties.

The facts of the case are that the plaintiff, a 35-year-old married male electronics technician, sustained injuries to his head in two separate motorcycle accidents approximately seven months apart. The cases had been consolidated for trial and the psychologist examined the plaintiff after each of the accidents, although the first examination was about five months after the first accident. On both occasions most of the tests, including the neuropsychological battery, were administered not by the psychologist but by a psychological assistant allegedly "under the supervision" of the psychologist. There is nothing to indicate that the psychologist was present during any of this testing, so that he would not have had an opportunity to observe plaintiff's behavior while being tested.

One of plaintiff's complaints is headaches, but the psychologist acknowledges that he did not pinpoint this or even ask him how many days a week he has the headache, and he admits on deposition that it would have been a good idea if he had tried to ascertain the frequency. He accepts plaintiff's declaration that his memory problems were worsened by the second accident, although nearly all of the tests given after the second accident showed an improvement in memory. In fact, after having indicated memory problems in his report, under intense questioning on deposition, he finally acknowledges that the safest conclusion would be that the testing does not pick up any exacerbation in memory impairment. He also asserts in his deposition that plaintiff's school records are consistent with information given by plaintiff regarding his grades, and then after being taken through a series of questions in which he reviews the school records, he acknowledges that the record is not consistent with the history that was given. He also gives an opinion about plaintiff's intellectual level based solely on his conversation and indicates that plaintiff has a high average I.Q., somewhere between 100 and 110, "So we are looking at something around maybe an I.Q. of 105 or 108, that's what I had in mind and that was based just on the nature of his conversation and the level of his vocabulary." In the first place, this is just flatly wrong. An I.Q. between 100 and 110 is not high average. According to the Wechsler manual, it would just be average. Also, we wonder if any substantial number of psychologists would believe that there is a psychologist who can estimate an individual's I.Q. within a range of four points just by listening to his conversation.

He states that the psychological testing after the second accident was the same as after the first accident, with the exception of two tests not administered the second time. A review of the test records show that there were six tests administered on the first occasion which were not administered on the second occasion, unless the psychologist has violated the subpoena by withholding four tests. It is noteworthy that among the tests not administered on the second testing were some tests which produced results which did not support the psychologists's conclusions.

In this particular case, plaintiff's school records show a gap for two grades. That is, there is nothing recorded for the second and third grades. However, the psychologist says he does not know whether it means the plaintiff missed school those two years or whether the records are not available. It is almost incredible that a psychologist would not make a determination on something of as much potential significance as this, for example, determining whether plaintiff may have suffered some severe illness which might have affected his brain functioning, or whatever reason. Obviously, in making a determination of plaintiff's condition prior to these two accidents, the fact that he missed two years of schooling would be an absolutely vital piece of information, and the reasons for missing the two years would be essential. Did the plaintiff, for example, have a disease which might have affected his brain? A Rorschach test is administered on the first testing, but while there is a location chart supplied, there are no locations marked and there is no scoring or quantitative analysis of this test.

In his report he states that plaintiff was "apparently married," but when confronted on deposition with the proposition that one either is married or not, he indicates that he was distracted thinking about something else and this was just a dictational error. We note, of course, that he signed the report with that statement in it.

CASE 7

The psychologist in this case is a Diplomate of the American Board of Forensic Psychology. The case is a personal injury case involving as plaintiff a 30-year-old woman who is a refugee from Southeast Asia, married to an American man whom she met when he was in the service in Vietnam. She has been in the United States for about twelve years. She states that she would much prefer to live in her own country and that she finds the United States scary.

The psychologist administers part of the WAIS, omitting the entire verbal section and omitting the Picture Arrangement subtest on the performance section. His report states no reason for doing this. Appropriately, he does not give an I.Q., but nonetheless, estimates an I.Q. from the four performance subtests that he did give, suggesting that his estimated I.Q. of 80 is very likely to be low and that her I.Q. is likely to be higher because it is his opinion that she is depressed, which reduced her performance on the test. He indicates that, in part, she was quite slow (which is one of his bases for concluding that she is depressed). First of all, it should be noted that it is not likely that there is any substantial amount of research data indicating what the norms might be for people from her culture and how their performance might vary in terms of being faster or slower than one would expect from an American born subject.

However, in addition, his statement does not accurately reflect the way she performed. She may have been slow on some tasks, but she clearly was not slow on many other tasks. For example, on the Block Design subtest on the WAIS, she successfully completed the first six items in anywhere from one-sixth to one-half of the time allowed for completion of the tasks. For example, on an item where the individual is allowed 60 seconds, she correctly completed the design in 21 seconds, and on another item, where 60 seconds are allowed, she successfully completed it in 22 seconds. Clearly, there is no way these performances could be considered slow. Also, on the Object Assembly subtest, which is another timed test, she completed the first item, for which 120 seconds are allowed, in 41 seconds, and the fourth item for which 180 seconds are allowed in 55 seconds, which is very close to the time for which she would have been given a time bonus. That is, completion in from 31 to 50 seconds gives a two-point bonus in the score for speed. So, once again, it cannot be said that she was consistently slow due to depression or that her slowness was a sign of depression—because for the most part, she simply was not that slow, at least not on these timed tests.

The psychologist also states that on the Bender-Gestalt her design reproductions were done in a very sketchy manner, which is true only of the first of the designs, but not of the remainder of the designs, all of which on the copy in our possession are done in a heavy, firm hand.

The psychologist administered a Rorschach and five of the TAT cards. It is hard to understand why he would administer those tests which require a reasonable amount of verbal facility, if his reasons for not administering the verbal portions of the WAIS were that plaintiff had some difficulty with the English language which he does describe in his report. One might ask what one can determine from these tests, if one knows at the outset that the person taking them has difficulty expressing herself in the English language. For example, how can one know what kind of stories she would have told in response to the TAT cards if she had been asked to tell the stories in her native language? They might have been much more full and rich and revealing, if in fact this procedure reveals anything. Similarly, with the Rorschach, how can one know what she may have seen in the inkblots for which she did not know the English word and therefore did not give that response?

In addition, the psychologist did not perform any inquiry on the Rorschach, nor was there any scoring or quantitative analysis (as of course there could not be for lack of inquiry). As Exner has pointed out, this is an abuse of the test.

The psychologist also miscounted the scores on two of the four subtests of the WAIS that he gave.

It might also be noted, in connection with the administration of the Rorschach and TAT but omission of the verbal part of the WAIS, that if his reason was that the verbal part has a certain amount of cultural influence, this would also be true of the Picture Completion subtest on the performance part, which he did give. (For example, one of the items involved snow and one has to wonder how familiar with snow someone would be who grew up in Vietnam and moved from there to Southern California.)

CASE 8

This case involves a claim for alleged brain damage due to toxic inhalation. One of the psychologists involved is a Diplomate of ABPP in Clinical Psychology and is also a Diplomate in Clinical Neuropsychology. In appreciation of the irony involved, this psychologist will be referred to throughout this section as the Double Diplomate. This case and its companion cases will be reported on in detail in Appendix A of Volume III. For the purposes of the present chapter we will only touch upon a few of the items.

Prior to being examined by this Double Diplomate, the plaintiff had been examined and tested by another psychologist and also by a psychology intern under the alleged supervision of one of the Double Diplomate's colleagues at the institution where both had been employed. Subsequently, the plaintiff was also examined and tested by a technician under the alleged supervision of a Ph.D. psychologist at the same general institution, but in another department. With regard to the latter, the Double Diplomate stated that the test results, in particular the WAIS-R, could not be used because some errors were found on re-scoring and also because there was a question in the psychologist's mind as to the degree of rapport between the technician and the plaintiff.

Under questioning as to the propriety of having neuropsychological examinations done by interns or technicians, the psychologist states, "It depends upon the situation, the reasons for the examination, the degree of skill and sensitivity required and the maturity and skill of a technician or intern. So that I cannot make a blanket statement." The psychologist was then asked if any attempt was made to ascertain whether the tests performed by the intern, under the supervision of the psychologist's colleague, were properly administered and accurately scored. The reply was that the psychologist didn't remember, but would take a look at the test then and there; and upon so doing, pointed out, "There were two errors on the Comprehension subtest, two scoring errors, and one scoring error on the Information subtest, both on the Wechsler Adult Intelligence Scale."

Q: Were there any consequences to you of the scoring errors?

A: Yes there were. The Information subtest score should be seven instead of six.

Q: Is that all?

A: That was the major consequence, it wasn't a big one, but it was there.

Q: Are there any other scoring errors that you are aware of?

A: No, not that I'm aware of.

Counsel proceeds to interrogate the Double Diplomate in terms of how one ascertains the so-called "premorbid" intellectual functioning and ability, and extracts information that history, school records, family, information from work place and so on, are all of use in directly establishing the level of functioning. Further, counsel brings out that the testimony is based on the other way of doing things: that is, it is based on current testing, utilizing what the psychologist refers to as the "best performance method." This consists of estimating the intellectual level from the highest or best scores on the subtests of the WAIS or whatever measure is being used. In this instance, the Double Diplomate concludes that plaintiff had premorbid, high average intelligence based on the fact that he obtained scale scores of 12 on the Arithmetic subtest, 12 on the Comprehension subtest and 14 on the Similarities Subtest, all of these on the WAIS-R administered by the psychological intern. In this regard, the following exchange took place:

Q: My note says to your direct examination with regard to plaintiff, indicates that one of the bases for your arriving at an opinion that he was of high average original intelligence was that he had a high average arithmetic score.

A: That's right.

Q: Are you referring to a scaled score on one of the WAIS-R which you have reviewed?

A: Yes, the psychological intern's. He did not use age graded scores. When I converted plaintiff's raw score to an age graded score so that I was comparing him to men of his age, that is, men of 35 rather than to an age group in the range of 21 to 34, his score was high average. His scaled score technically became 12.

Q: Did you have some sort of normative table that you referred to?

A: Yes, I used the normative table in the Wechsler manual.

Q: Then his arithmetic score became what?

A: Twelve.

Q: Instead of 11?

A: That's right, when comparing him to people his own age. I do not believe in comparing a person of one age to another age group, when possible.

Q: That is what I thought you had done. Now, I want to discuss that.

A: Sure.

Q: So on the basis that he had a twelve on the scaled score on the WAIS-R Arithmetic subtest—

A: Right.

Q: —you concluded that he is of high average intelligence.

A: No. On the basis of a scaled score of 12, on Comprehension—now both of those scores are seventy-fifth percentile—and a scale score of 13 on the Similarities—and Similarities is about the eighty-second percentile, eighty-fourth percentile, something like that—it was on the basis of these three tests, not one indicator, but on—because one is much more likely to be due to chance—but on three, it was hard for me not to conclude that plaintiff had at least a high average original endowment.

Q: Perhaps you misspoke yourself, but you said that he had 11 on the Comprehensive subtest.

A: No, no, 12.

Q: You said he had 12 on the Comprehension subtest?

A: That's right, oh yeah I see what your problem is, there were interns misscoring. You are looking there.

Q: He has a 7, doesn't he?

A: I know. That is a really gross piece of misscoring.

Q: You didn't tell us about that before.

A: No, I forgot about that. I'll show that to you if you want to see. If you want to just compare him to even a younger group, you will see that a scaled score, that a raw score of 25 gives him a scaled score of 12, even for the younger group; and it's true for his age group, as well. The intern misscored.

Q: That is all well and good. Are there any other errors of this magnitude that you haven't told us about?

A: No, there weren't. I was only looking at my own scores and I forgot about (intern's) and I hadn't noted that. I can see now why you were so puzzled about my saying so definitely that he had these scores and why you didn't see where I was coming from.

Q: Because 7 definitely isn't 12?

A: Because 7, that is not very good. But no, he didn't have a 7 here and he didn't have a 7 when tested on the WAIS at any other time either. He had a raw score of 25 which translates for people both in the 21 to 34 age range and 35 to 44 age range—it doesn't change in those two age ranges—it translates into a scaled score of 12 and there is no problem with that piece of data.

Q: What is the average, 10?

A: Ten. Well, you have to think of it as a range and it's the range, the middle 50% which is 8, 9, 10 and 11, are within the average range.

Q: And 12 isn't within the average range?

A: No, 12 is high average, seventy-fifth percentile. 12 and 13 are high average.

Q: So, you go two down from 10 and it is still average and you go two up from 10 and it is high average?

A: Yes, because the average range covers the middle 50% of all the population and therefore is the largest range of all.

Q: Isn't one of the things which people in your business worry about that unsophisticated people will take these scaled scores and make more out of them than they are, actually?

A: That is why I report out in terms of ranges, rather than numbers, whenever possible.

Q: As a matter of fact, there really isn't any difference at all between a 9 and an 11 is there?

A: Statistically, no, no. What a 9 means is that it's a range, it represents a range of scores the range of scores represented by a score of 12 is higher than the range of scores represented by a 7.

Q: In fact a score difference of two is more likely than not a chance variation, isn't it?

A: That's right.

One scaled score relied upon by the psychologist for this estimate is the scaled score of 12 on the Arithmetic subtest, based upon the psychologist rescoring according to the age norms appropriate for plaintiff, rather than the standard norms for the test.

However, plaintiff did not earn a scaled score of 12 on the Arithmetic subtest, even when applying the norms for his age group, because the intern made another error of scoring which the Double Diplomate did not pick up, although apparently this Double Diplomate did check the scoring. On the Arithmetic subtest, the intern had scored a total raw score of 14, which would translate to a scaled score of 12 for plaintiff's age group. However, the raw score of 14 is incorrect, because on one item on which the plaintiff obtained a correct answer, the time recorded is 11 seconds and the scoring rule given on the answer sheet is that there is a time bonus if the answer is given within 1 to 10 seconds (i.e., it is scored as two), but, for 11 to 60 seconds, there is just the standard credit of one point. As there is no possibility of an error on what is recorded as the time (it is clearly 11 seconds), there is a scoring error in giving the bonus. Therefore, plaintiff's raw score is not 14, but rather is 13 which, going to the manual for the plaintiff's age group, shows that for a raw score of 13 on the Arithmetic subtest the scaled score is 11. Therefore, by no stretch of the imagination could this be considered anything other than very average—clearly not high average. Inasmuch as the psychologist is, at best, going to make a "guess," one would hope that a psychologist would at least be making the "guess" from an accurate data base. What level of skill or expertise should one deduce from the possession, in this case by the psychologist, of the Diploma of the American Board of Examiners in Professional Psychology, in Clinical Psychology and possession of the Diplomate in Clinical Neuropsychology, as well?

In addition, of course, there is the rather paradoxical approach taken by the Double Diplomate in discarding the test data of the technician from another department, while accepting the test data of the intern, as was done, despite the number of scoring errors that were discovered, as well as some errors that were not discovered, plus the really "gross" error on the scaled score of the Comprehension subtest, which far exceeds any error made by the technician, so far as we could determine.

We also note that this Double Diplomate did not obtain school records at the time the conclusion was reached and the report written, which would have revealed that plaintiff had all his life performed at a rather poor level, getting mostly D's in his school work, while on a crude measure of intelligence administered while a student, he scored at the fifty-seventh percentile, which certainly does not support any notion of premorbid high average intelligence. This information might have been useful to this Double Diplomate in assessing premorbid intelligence had this Double Diplomate taken the trouble to obtain this available "objective" information.

Similarly, the Double Diplomate relies to some extent on plaintiff's position of shop steward, yet admits under cross-examination that this was done without any knowledge of what the job actually entails other than a layman's knowledge, and without any knowledge of how long the plaintiff had performed in this position or how well he was performing the position, which therefore renders it without meaning other than signifying the fact that the plaintiff was popular enough to get elected by his fellow workers.

Similarly, this Double Diplomate did not obtain, or at least does not remember requesting or obtaining military records, which would have revealed that plaintiff had both suffered some physical injuries which might affect his functioning and displayed emotional or psycho-pathological problems connected with the service, which also might have an impairing effect on his functioning. If this case had been the one presented to the certifying Board as a work sample, we wonder if certification would have been granted. If it would have been granted, we then wonder what significance should be attached to possession of the Diplomate, if its possessor may do work of this quality.

CASE 9

This case involves the same psychologist as the previous case, who has the Diplomate in both Clinical Psychology and Clinical Neuropsychology, and is a companion case to the previous case, again involving brain damage due to toxic inhalation.

As in the previous case, there was testing by a technician under the same supervision and testing by a different intern under the same supervision, whom we will call Intern 2. As in the previous case, the Double Diplomate discarded the test data produced by the technician on the grounds that there were scoring errors and indeed, in this case, there appeared to have been seven or eight scoring errors. Of course, we have no objection to discarding test data this deficient. However, on being questioned regarding the testing done by Intern 2, the Double Diplomate first did not recall any problems and then looking at the data again, noted that there was one test where the intern counted one point too high; this would have lowered one subtest score from a 12 to an 11. That was all the Double Diplomate noted. However, we counted additional, clear-cut errors of administration and scoring by Intern 2. We note that on the Vocabulary subtest, which calls for the test to be discontinued after five consecutive failures, it is indicated that Intern 2 discontinued the test after the plaintiff had three consecutive failures. Thus, plaintiff was not given an opportunity to achieve a higher score as were the people in the normative population. Also, on the Vocabulary subtest there was one item for which the answer, according to the manual, calls for the examiner to ask for another answer. This was not done, so this is another error of administration. Additionally, there is a clear-cut scoring error on the Vocabulary subtest. On the Block Design subtest which requires the test to be discontinued after three consecutive failures, the answer sheet indicates only two consecutive failures before discontinuance of the test. This would be another case of premature termination of the test, again depriving plaintiff of the opportunity to obtain additional credit. On the Comprehension subtest there is another answer for which the manual calls for questioning by the examiner. The questioning was not done, so this is another error of administration, and no scoring is justified under those circumstances, because the answer is too ambiguous without clarification by the required questioning. There are several other instances of probable scoring errors in Intern 2's testing, but there is some degree of ambiguity so we are not going to assert those. The clear-cut errors of administration and scoring alone are sufficient to vitiate Intern 2's testing at least to the same extent as that of the technician, and we would argue that no conclusions should be based on testing done by someone who makes so many errors.

In brief, the psychologist's report states that this plaintiff had a premorbid intellectual level that was average. The psychologist acknowledges that this was determined on the basis of the plaintiff's self-report and the test results without having seen school records or military records. The inutility of the test data has been described above, so that this would appear to be an inadequate or a very thin reed on which to predicate such conclusions.

As to plaintiff's self-report, he informed the psychologist who recorded same, that he graduated from high school with a "C-average." We do not know whether the dash represents a C minus or just represents a dash which would indicate that he was representing a C average. It really does not matter because either one would be false: he had a D average, and not a C or C minus average, obtaining two B's (one of which was in physical education), six C's, twelve D's and five F's. This would calculate out to a gradepoint average of roughly 1.2, which would be a D. One would assume that the minimum required for a C minus would be a 1.6, closer to a 2.0 than a 1.0. His grades also show a great deal of what psychologists refer to as "scatter," such that if one was using the best performance measure to determine his ability, then based on his two B's, one would have to conclude that he would be a B student, which he quite obviously was not. Looked at in another way, one could say his most typical level of performance was below average, as indicated by the fact that his overwhelmingly predominant grade was "D." It is also noted in his records that of the courses he took that involved the use of numbers, he got an F in general math, and an F in bookkeeping. In another course that seems to involve some sort of math (the word is illegible but might be "review," which was probably a review course taken in a summer session to get a passing grade), he did get a D. Thus, his level of functioning in high school courses dealing with numerical operations was even below his general average of D. For this reason, his low score on the Arithmetic subtest on the WAIS-R, or any test using numbers, cannot be given any meaning as a diagnostic indicator of an impairment. In any event, it is clear that this Double Diplomate was at best less than adequately thorough in not obtaining information about plaintiff's previous performances from other and more objective sources than the plaintiff.

In addition, plaintiff's military records flatly contradict the Double Diplomate's conclusions. The records also contained an I.Q. measure, apparently the California Test of Mental Maturity on which he obtained an I.Q. of 87, which would be below the "average" range and fairly consistent with his school performance, although it should be noted that on a test shown as the Iowa Composite he obtained a placement at the 37th percentile, which would put him in the average range, albeit in the lower quarter of that range. In I.Q. terms as indicated in the WAIS-R manual, an I.Q. of 95 would be equivalent to the 37th percentile in the population. One problem here is that percentiles or I.Q.s are not directly comparable from one test to another as none of them correlate perfectly. Also, the Iowa Composite is not a test of I.Q. but is more of an academic achievement test.

Military records, which the Double Diplomate had not bothered to obtain, show that plaintiff enlisted in the service in early September and was discharged in late November, surviving no more than eight weeks in the service. He was given an honorable discharge by reason of "unsuitability." The report showed the presence of a number of emotional problems, his overall aptitude for training was noted as poor, and the report is topped off with the statement from the Company Commander, "He is unable to perform the simplest of maneuvers." Thus, the objective data of the level at which this person performed places him at a clearly below average level, against the psychologist's "guess" from the test data and plaintiff's misleading self-reports that his school performance level was average. Actually, on the WAIS-R administered by Intern 2, plaintiff comes out with an I.Q. of 89, which is similar to the I.Q. achieved on the California Test of Mental Maturity while he was in school. Therefore, he does not appear to have suffered any loss of measurable I.Q. as a result of the alleged brain injury. We might also note that the I.Q. obtained by Intern 2, for whatever it is worth, is not so far below the 37th percentile I.Q. of 95 as to indicate any significant loss. This may be particularly true in view of the fact that Full Scale I.Q.'s on the WAIS-R are known to be an average of about eight points lower than they would have been on the WAIS; this means that had he been given the WAIS (which would have been the test used if he was tested two years earlier), the best prediction is that he would have come out with an I.Q. of 96 or 97.

Thus, while our files contain only a few cases involving psychologists of diplomate status, in each of the cases, their performance was subject to considerable criticism. One obviously cannot generalize from a few cases to make the statement that all or most diplomate psychologists show this level of proficiency or perform evaluations in such a manner. However, one can state clearly that a psychologist's possession of the ABPP or ABFP diplomas provides no assurance that one is dealing with a psychologist who performs at a high level of proficiency. If these diplomates performed in such a manner as this, one has simply no assurance that there are not others with the diplomas who do not perform in the same manner at times, also. Therefore, from a forensic point of view, the credentials should carry no weight whatsoever. (Suggestions for voir dire and/or cross-examination dealing with board certification, as well as other types of credentials, are presented in Volume III.)

One further issue needs to be addressed. Upon being confronted with this body of negative case material, some credential holders are likely to counter with something to the effect that there are always a "few rotten apples in the barrel." We can provide two answers to that response.

Out of this small number of cases, and without identifying anyone, it can be stated that at least four of the professionals discussed (both psychiatrists and psychologists) are well known, and would be described by their colleagues as "outstanding," "distinguished," "leaders in the field," "leading authorities," and other such adjectives. All four have held many offices in professional organizations and have anywhere from adequate to very impressive publication records. They simply do not seem to fit the general notion of "bad apples."

Also, while our sample is small, these 25 or so represent nearly all of the certified or diplomate professionals whose work we had an opportunity to observe at the time they were published in 1988. We cannot rule out the possibility that, for some unknown reason, all the cases were coming from the bottom of the barrel (except as counterindicated by the preceding paragraph). However, in the absence of some evidence that that was the case, the most probable assumption is that they were not a highly skewed sample, but a group that is representative of the population of certificate or diploma holders involved in forensic assessment.

We can add at this point (1994) that since our publication of these cases in 1988 we have seen many more cases illustrating similar problems in the work or results of evaluations by similarly credentialed clinicians. However, we do not see much value in simply increasing the amount of such anecdotal evidence. We feel that what we have presented is sufficient to cast doubt on any special credibility to be given by virtue of these credentials. We feel we have presented enough to place on those who promote them, or claim they represent anything regarding quality of performance, the burden of demonstrating their value through research.

OTHER INDICES OF QUALIFICATION

Several states have laws providing for certification or licensing of psychologists. Certification Acts generally prohibit only the use of the term "psychologist" or "psychological services," by persons other than those who received the State certification, but do not restrict the services offered.

Licensing Acts ordinarily refer not only to the offering of psychological services or the use of the label "psychologist," but define the practice of psychology and limit such practice to those who possess a license. The cross-examining attorney can attempt to determine whether or not the testifying psychologist is certified or licensed in those states where such laws exist. If he is not certified or licensed the point can be made that he has not established possession of the minimal legal requirements for the expertise he claims to have and he is probably violating the law.

One comment needs to be made concerning a special category of people who will possess a license or certificate without having had to demonstrate their qualifications by examination. Most certification or licensing acts contain a "grandfather" clause which provides that the certificate or license shall be granted to persons who have been engaged in the profession for a given number of years prior to the enactment of the certification or licensing act. As most certification or licensing acts came about in the late 1950's and through the 1960's, and some are still to come in other states, there will be a period of some years during which time there will be people possessing certification or licensing simply by virtue of their having been engaged in the profession and not by virtue of having passed an examination and met other requirements. Where such is the case, the cross-examining attorney may find it advisable to bring this point to the attention of judge or jury.

On the other hand, possession of the license does not indicate anything about accuracy of evaluations, as such a demonstration is not part of licensing examinations (see supra, Schoon, 1978, Koocher, 1979, Howard, 1983, and Kane, 1982 and 1986).

Lack of membership in professional associations may provide a clue worth following in some cases. In addition to the American Psychological Association, to which nearly all reputable psychologists belong, there are state associations, and in most populous areas, county or other types of local psychological associations. Non-membership may indicate the psychologist is not eligible for membership, or has been "kicked out" of the association. Removal from an association would ordinarily indicate either that he has not paid his dues, or that he has been found guilty of engaging in unethical conduct or practices. Local memberships can be quickly determined by a telephone call to the local associations. The

APA publishes a directory, which would be available in any nearby university library. Current information can be obtained by contacting APA in Washington, D.C. A further implication to non-membership, even in the cases where it is based on legitimate grounds, such as "rugged individualism," is that such a person is not likely to receive association newsletters and other publications and probably does not attend association meetings. Therefore, he is probably less well informed and less up to date than his colleagues who do hold such memberships. On the other hand, membership in many associations tells virtually nothing about the clinician's diagnostic skills or accuracy as demonstration of such skill is not required for membership.

Some other credentials are often presented to bolster the expert's stature.

Administrative positions (e.g., director of a hospital) attest to just that—administrative ability, not necessarily clinical ability.

Academic positions, if they are truly academic, such as professorships, probably indicate knowledge in the area. However, such positions do not necessarily indicate accuracy of evaluations. The lawyer should be aware of certain titles such as "clinical professor" or "adjunct professor." These usually do not have the same connotation as the title "professor." Typically, people in these positions do not teach courses but provide some service such as supervision or an occasional lecture.

Obviously publications in the area at issue lend credibility, although they also do not attest to accuracy of evaluations. The lawyer should look to see if the publications are relevant to the testimony. Also, if most publications are in some other area, that would indicate this is not the main area of interest or expertise for this expert.

Offices in professional organizations do not reflect clinical accuracy, but popularity or, in many cases, reward for contributions of time and effort to the organization.

REFERENCES

American Journal of Psychiatry (1982). 139.

American Journal of Psychiatry (1993), xx, 1289.

American Psychological Association (1963). *Monitor, 24.*

Berman, J.S., and Norton, N.C. (1985). Does professional training make a therapist more effective? *Psychological Bulletin, 98, 401-407.*

Bernal, M.E., and Padilla, A.M. (1982). Status of minority curricula and training in clinical psychology. *The American Psychologist, 37, 780-787.*

Blakey, W.A., Fantuzzo, J.W., and Moon, G.W. (1985). An automated competency based model for teaching skills in the administration of the WAIS-R. *Professional Psychology: Research and Practice, 16, 641-647.*

Bootzin, R.R., and Ruggill, J.S. (1988). Training issues in behavior therapy. *Journal of Consulting and Clinical Psychology, 56,* 703-709.

Borus, J.F., and Yager, J. (1986). Ongoing evaluation in psychiatry: The first step toward quality. *American Journal of Psychiatry, 143,* 1415-1419.

Bradshaw, W.H. (1978). Training psychiatrists for working with blacks in basic residency programs. *American Journal of Psychiatry, 135,* 1520-1524.

Brody, E.B. (1971). Psychiatric education in the Americas. *American Journal of Psychiatry, 127,* 55-60.

Chapman, L.J., and Chapman, J.P. (1967). Genesis of popular but erroneous psychodiagnostic observations. *Journal of Abnormal Psychology, 72,* 193-204.

Chapman, L.J., and Chapman, J.P. (1971). Test results are what you think they are. *Psychology Today, 5.*

Chessick, R.D. (1971). How the residents and the supervisor disappoint each other. *American Journal of Psychotherapy, 25,* 272-283.

Cohen, L.H. (1979b). The research readership and information source reliance of clinical psychologists. *Professional Psychology, 10,* 780-785.

Eaton. (1974). An evaluation of evaluations. *American Journal of Psychiatry, 131,* 56-57.

Everett, F., Proctor, N., and Cartmell, B. (1983). Providing psychological services to American Indian children and families. *Professional Psychology: Research and Practice, 14,* 588-603.

Fox, R.E., Kovacs, A.L., and Graham, S.R. (1985). Proposals for a revolution in the preparation and regulation of professional psychologists. *American Psychologist, 40,* 1042-1050.

Garfield, S.L., and Kurtz, R.A. (1973). Attitudes toward training and diagnostic testing. *Journal of Consulting and Clinical Psychology, 40,* 350-355.

Giller, E., and Strauss, J. (1984). Clinical research: A key to clinical training. *American Journal of Psychiatry, 141,* 1075-1077.

Goldberg, D.A. (1983). Resistance to the use of video in individual psychotherapy training. *American Journal of Psychiatry, 140,* 1172-1175.

Goldstein, S.G., and Deysach, R.E. (1973). Effect of experience and amount of information on identification of cerebral impairment. *Journal of Consulting and Clinical Psychology, 41,* 30-34.

Greenblatt, M., Carew, J., and Pierce, C.M. (1977). Success rates in psychiatry and neurology certification examinations. *American Journal of Psychiatry, 134,* 1259-1264.

Hammet, V.O. (1965). A consideration of psychoanalysis in relation to psychiatry generally, circa 1965. *American Journal of Psychiatry, 122,* 42-54.

Hedberg, A.G., Meredith, R., and Fitts, M. (1973). The doctor of psychology degree, an alternative model for relevant clinical training. *Journal of Behavior Therapy and Experimental Psychiatry, 4,* 191-193.

Hoffman, B.F. (1986). How to write a psychiatric report for litigation following a personal injury. *American Journal of Psychiatry, 143,* 164-169.

Howard, A. (1983). Work samples and simulations in competency evaluation. *Professional Psychology: Research and Practice, 14,* 780-796.

Jones, J.M., and Block, C.B. (1984). Black cultural perspectives. *The Clinical Psychologist, 37,* 58-62.

Kane, M.T. (1982). The validity of licensure examinations. *American Psychologist, 37,* 911-918.

Kane, M.T. (1983). *The Future of Testing for Licensure and Certification Examinations.* The American College Testing Program, Iowa City, Iowa.

Kane, M.T. (1986). The future of testing for licensure and certification examination. In B.S. Plake and J.C. Witt (Eds.), *The Future of Testing.* Buros-Nebraska Symposium on Measurement and Testing, Vol. 2. Hillsdale, NJ: Erlbaum.

Karasu, T.B., Plutshik, R., Nemetz, P., and Conte, H.R. (1979). Measurement of thinking dysfunction—an empirical study. *The Journal of Nervous and Mental Disease, 167,* 696-703.

Kazdin, A.E. (1986). Comparative outcome studies of psychotherapy: Methodological issues and strategies. *Journal of Consulting and Clinical Psychology, 54,* 95-105.

Kingsbury, S.J. (1987). Cognitive differences between clinical psychologists and psychiatrists. *American Psychologist, 42,* 152-156.

Klein, D.F., Honigfeld, G., Burnett, L.L., Steckler, M., Leader, M., and Forman, M. (1970). Automating the psychiatric case study. *Comprehensive Psychiatry, 11,* 518-523.

Koocher, G.P. (1979). Credentialing in psychology: Close encounters with competence? *American Psychologist, 34,* 696-702.

LaDue, R.A. (1983a). Racial and gender disproportionalities in psychotic diagnosis: Professional implications. Presented at Annual Convention of the American Psychological Association, Anaheim, California, August, 1983.

Langsley, D.G. (1981). Changing patterns of psychiatry specialty certification in the English-speaking countries. *American Journal of Psychiatry, 138,* 493-497.

Lee-Dukes, G. (1983). Differences in psychiatric diagnoses related to race & gender: Causes. Symposium conducted at the Annual Convention of the American Psychological Association, Anaheim, California, August, 1983.

Leibenluft, E., Sumergrad, P., and Tasman, A. (1989). The academic dilemma of the inpatient unit director. *American Journal of Psychiatry, 146,* 73-76.

Lesse, S. (1977). Editorial: What price confusion—the status of psychiatric education. *American Journal of Psychotherapy, 3,* 181-184.

Lindy, J.D., Green, B.L., and Patrick, M. (1980). The internship: Some disquieting findings. *American Journal of Psychiatry, 137,* 76-79.

London, P., and Klerman, G.L. (1982). Evaluating psychotherapy. *The American Journal of Psychiatry, 139,* 709-717.

Mariner, E.S. (1967). A critical look at professional education in the mental health field. *American Psychologist, 22,* 271-281.

McDermott, J.F., Mcguire, C., and Flinch, S. (1974). Board certification in child psychiatry: Recent developments. *American Journal of Psychiatry, 131,* 463-465.

McDermott, J.F., Tanguay, P.E., Scheiber, S.C., Juul, D., Shore, J.H., Tucker, G.J., McCurdy, L., and Terr, L. (1993). Reliability of the part II board certification examination in psychiatry: Examination stability. *American Journal of Psychiatry, 150,* 1077-1080.

Meehl, P.E. (1973). *Psychodiagnosis: Selected papers.* Minneapolis: University of Minnesota Press.

Mittelstaedt, W., and Tasca, C. (1988). Contradictions in clinical psychology training: A trainee's perspective of the Boulder Model. *Professional Psychology: Research and Practice, 19,* 353-355.

Morgenstern, A.L. (1970). A criticism of psychiatry's board examinations. *American Journal of Psychiatry, 127,* 33-39.

Morgenstern, A.L. (1972). A systematic approach for oral board examinations in psychiatry. *American Journal of Psychiatry, 129,* 54-57.

Naftulin, D.H., Wolkon, G.H., Donnelly, F.A., Burgoyne, R.W., Kline, F.M., and Hansen, H.E. (1977). A comparison of videotape and live patient interview examinations and written examinations in psychiatry. *American Journal of Psychiatry, 134,* 1093-1097.

Napoliello, M.J. (1977). From board candidate to rookie examiner. *American Journal of Psychiatry, 134,* 1264-1266.

Newman, F.L., Kopta, S.M., McGovern, M.P., Howard, K.I., and McNeilly, C.L. (1988). Evaluating trainees relative to their supervisors during the psychology internship. *Journal of Consulting and Clinical Psychology, 56,* 659-665.

Norcross, J.C., and Stevenson, J.F. (1984). How shall we judge ourselves? Training evaluation in clinical psychology programs. *Professional Psychology: Research and Practice, 15,* 497-508.

O'Donohue, W., Plaud, J.J., Mowatt, A.M., and Fearon, J.R. (1989). Current status of curricula of doctoral training programs in clinical psychology. *Professional Psychology: Research and Practice, 20,* 196-197.

Otto, R.K., Heilbrun, K., and Grisso, T. (1990). Training and credentialing in forensic psychology. *Behavioral Sciences and the Law, 8,* 217-231.

Pierce, C.M., Mathis, J.L., and Pishkin, V. (1968). Basic psychiatry in twelve hours: An experiment in programmed learning. *Diseases of the Nervous System, 29,* 533-535.

Pokorny, K.D., and Frazier, S.H. (1966). An evaluation of oral examinations. *Journal of Medical Education, 41,* 28-40.

Preston, T.P. (1981). *The Clay Pedestal.* Seattle: Madrona.

Ridley, C.R. (1985). Imperatives for ethnic and cultural relevance in psychology training programs. *Professional Psychology: Research and Practice, 16,* 611-622.

Robitscher, J., and Williams, R. (1977). Should psychiatrists get out of the courtroom? *Psychology Today, 11,* 85.

Rotter, J.B. (1973). The future of clinical psychology. *Journal of Consulting and Clinical Psychology, 40,* 313-321.

Schippmann, J.S., Smalley, M.D., Vinchur, A.J., and Prien, E.P. (1988). Using structured multi-domain job analysis to develop training and evaluation specifications for clinical psychologists. *Professional Psychology: Research and Practice, 19,* 141-147.

Schoon, C.G. (1978). Measuring competency. *The California State Psychologist, 6.*

Sechrest, L.B. (1985b). President's message: Specialization? Who needs it? *The Clinical Psychologist, 38,* 1-3.

Shagass, C. (1977). Book review. *The Journal of Nervous and Mental Disease, 164,* 380-384.

Slate, J.R., and Jones, C.H. (1989). Can teaching of the WISC-R be improved? Quasi-experimental exploration. *Professional Psychology: Research and Practice, 20,* 409-414.

Small, S.M., and Regan, P.F. (1974). An evaluation of evaluations. *American Journal of Psychiatry, 131,* 51-55.

Steinpreis, R., Queen, L., and Tennen, H. (1992). The education of clinical psychologists: A survey of training directors. *The Clinical Psychologist, 45,* 87-94.

Stiles, W.B. (1983). Normality diversity and psychotherapy. *Psychotherapy: Theory, Research and Practice, 20,* 183-189.

Storrow, H.A. (1967). *Introduction to Scientific Psychiatry.* Englewood Cliffs, NJ: Prentice-Hall.

Strupp, H.H., and Hadley, S.W. (1977). A tri-partite model of mental health and therapeutic outcomes. *American Psychologist, 32,* 187-196.

Strupp, H.H., Butler, S.F., and Rosser, C.L. (1988). Training in psychodynamic therapy. *Journal of Consulting and Clinical Psychology, 56,* 689-695.

Talbott, J.A. (1983). Is the "live patient" interview on the boards necessary? *American Journal of Psychiatry, 140,* 890-893.

Tarter, R.E., Templer, D.I., and Hardy, C. (1975). The psychiatric diagnosis. *Diseases of the Nervous System, 36,* 30-31.

Tasman, A. (1993). Setting standards for psychotherapy training: It's time to do our homework. *Journal of Psychotherapy Practice and Research, 2,* 93-96.

Taylor, R.L., and Torrey, E.F. (1972). The pseudo-regulation of American psychiatry. *American Journal of Psychiatry, 129,* 658-664.

Thorne, F.C. (1972). Clinical judgment. In R.H. Woody and J.D. Woody (Eds.), *Clinical Assessment in Counseling and Psychotherapy.* Englewood Cliffs, NJ: Prentice-Hall.

Tipton, R.M. (1983). Clinical and counseling psychology: A study of roles and functions. *Professional Psychology: Research and Practice, 14,* 837-846.

Tori, C.D. (1989). Quality assurance standards in the education of psychologists: Reliability and validity of objective comprehensive examinations developed at a free-standing professional school. *Professional Psychology: Research and Practice, 20,* 203-208.

Weinstein, H.M., and Russell, L. (1976). Competency based psychiatric education. *American Journal of Psychiatry, 133,* 935.

Wettstein, R.M., Mulvey, E.P., and Rogers, R. (1991). A prospective comparison of four insanity defense standards. *American Journal of Psychiatry, 148,* 21-27.

Wong, N. (1978). Psychiatric education and training of Asian and Asian-American Psychiatrists. *American Journal of Psychiatry, 135,* 1525-1529.

Woodmansey, A.C. (1967). Science and the training of psychiatrists. British *Journal of Psychiatry, 113,* 1035-1037.

Yager, J., Borus, J.F., Robinowitz, C.B., and Shore, J.H. (1988). Developing minimal national standards for clinical experience in psychiatric training. *American Journal of Psychiatry, 145,* 1409-1413.

Zonana, H.V., Crane, L.E., and Getz., M.A. (1990). Training and credentialing in forensic psychiatry. *Behavioral Sciences and the Law, 8,* 233-247.

INDEX OF TOPICS

Note: This index covers topics found in Volume I *only*. A complete index of topics for Volumes I and II will be found at the end of Volume II.

INDEX OF AUTHORS

Note: This index covers authors found in Volume I *only*. A complete index of authors for Volumes I and II will be found at the end of Volume II.

Los Angeles Times (1986), 354, 382
Los Angeles Times (1988), 3
Lovinger (1992), 335
Lowenbach and Shore (1970), 412
Luborsky (1954), 403, 497
Luchins (1942), 233
Luft (1950), 459, 497
Luger and Petzel (1979), 220
Lytton (1971), 381
MacKay (1988), 95
Maguigad (1973), 423
Mahoney (1977), 92, 233, 236
Mahoney and Crane (1991), 335
Manderscheid (1987), 458
Mann et al. (1992), 333
Margulies and Havens (1981), 234
Mariner (1967), 468, 570
Marmor (1966), 115
Marriage and Divorce Today Newsletter (1986), 350
Marx and Hillix (1973), 321
Mash and Hunsley (1993), 535
Masling (1966), 332
Matarazzo (1978), 460
Matarazzo (1986a), 99, 253, 464
Matarazzo (1986b), 253, 465
Matarazzo (1990), 29, 414, 429, 459
Matarazzo (1991), 414
May et al. (1993), 348
McCas (1972), 331
McConnaughy (1988), 349
McDermott et al. (1974), 574, 590
McDermott et al. (1993), 594
McFall (1991), 101
McGill and Thrasher (1975), 362
McHugh (1987), 26
McLean and Hakstian (1979), 536
McLemore and Benjamin (1979), 159
McMahon (1983), 405
McMillan (1984), 397
McNeal (1972), 11, 29
McNeil et al. (1988), 458
McReynolds (1979), 157, 159, 473
Mechanic (1967), 146
Mechanic (1978), 11, 29, 30
Meehl (1954), 205, 274, 275, 294
Meehl (1960), 237
Meehl (1971), 11, 32, 408, 506
Meehl (1973), 100, 225, 235, 274, 312, 317, 325, 397, 425, 584
Meehl (1978), 92, 151
Meehl (1979), 100, 111, 366

Meehl (1984), 205, 299, 302
Meehl (1986), 257, 274, 326
Meehl (1989), 196
Meehl and Rosen (1955), 266
Melges (1972), 506
Mellinger et al. (1985), 144
Mellsop et al. (1982), 161, 390
Melton (1990), 28, 37
Melton and Wilcox (1989), 39
Mendel and Rapport (1963), 498
Mendelsohn et al. (1978), 225
Menninger (1968), 151, 469
Menzies et al. (1985), 512
Meyer and Fink (1989), 351
Miller (1961), 314, 340
Miller (1980), 396
Miller and Alexander (1972), 116
Millet (1966), 115
Millon (1984), 160
Mirowsky (1990), 428
Mischel (1972), 313, 366
Mischel (1973), 348
Mischel (1979), 306, 385, 427
Mischel et al. (1976), 233
Mitchell and Kalb (1981), 230
Mittelstaedt and Tasca (1988), 563
Monahan (1978), 29, 385
Monahan (1981), 29
Montandon and Harding (1984), 212
Mora (1985), 54, 534
Morey (1988), 178
Morgenstern (1970), 574, 588
Morgenstern (1972), 589
Morse (1978), 19
Morse (1982), 8, 9
Morse (1983), 134, 512
Mosher and Feinsilver (1973), 151
Moxley (1973), 506
Mullen and Reinehr (1982), 29
Muslin et al. (1981), 361
Mynart et al. (1977), 233
Naftulin et al. (1977), 591
Napoliello (1977), 590
Natale (1979), 117
Neulinger (1968), 389
Newell and Simon (1972), 322
Newman et al. (1988), 564
Newmark et al. (1979), 359
Nisbett and Ross (1980), 233, 247, 305
Nisbett and Wilson (1977a), 249
Nisbett and Wilson (1977b), 249
Nisbett et al. (1976), 226, 305